Lecture Notes in Computer Science 16129

The series Lecture Notes in Computer Science (LNCS), including its subseries Lecture Notes in Artificial Intelligence (LNAI) and Lecture Notes in Bioinformatics (LNBI), has established itself as a medium for the publication of new developments in computer science and information technology research, teaching, and education.

LNCS enjoys close cooperation with the computer science R & D community, the series counts many renowned academics among its volume editors and paper authors, and collaborates with prestigious societies. Its mission is to serve this international community by providing an invaluable service, mainly focused on the publication of conference and workshop proceedings and postproceedings. LNCS commenced publication in 1973.

Daniel Escudero · Ivan Damgård
Editors

Progress in Cryptology – LATINCRYPT 2025

9th International Conference on Cryptology and Information Security in Latin America
Medellín, Colombia, October 1–3, 2025
Proceedings

Springer

Editors
Daniel Escudero
JP Morgan AI Research and JP Morgan AlgoCRYPT CoE
New York, NY, USA

Ivan Damgård
Aarhus University
Aarhus, Denmark

ISSN 0302-9743 ISSN 1611-3349 (electronic)
Lecture Notes in Computer Science
ISBN 978-3-032-06753-1 ISBN 978-3-032-06754-8 (eBook)
https://doi.org/10.1007/978-3-032-06754-8

This Springer imprint is published by the registered company Springer Nature Switzerland AG
The registered company address is: Gewerbestrasse 11, 6330 Cham, Switzerland

Preface

This book contains the proceedings of the 9th International Conference on Cryptology and Information Security in Latin America, LATINCRYPT 2025. The conference was held in Medellín on October 1–3, 2025. This event was organized in cooperation with the International Association for Cryptologic Research.

The 17 accepted papers collected in this volume and presented at the conference were carefully selected by the Program Committee (PC) after a rigorous double-blind peer review process, from a total of 41 submissions by researchers from around the world. The PC co-chairs were supported by a Program Committee consisting of 88 experts in various areas of cryptologic research. As in previous editions, submissions received approximately four reviews each, with five reviews assigned to papers co-authored by PC members. Strong conflict-of-interest policies were enforced to ensure the integrity and fairness of the selection process. The program chairs did not submit any papers to the conference.

In addition to the contributed talks, the LATINCRYPT 2025 program featured three invited talks by distinguished researchers in the field. Preceding the main conference, the ASCrypto school in cryptography took place over two days and offered a series of expository lectures aligned with topics in the conference program. This edition of ASCrypto was chaired by Arantxa Zapico and Javier Verbel.

The present volume contains the revised versions of the 17 papers selected for presentation. These versions were not reviewed again after revision, and the responsibility for their content lies with the authors.

We are grateful to all those who contributed to the success of LATINCRYPT 2025. We sincerely thank the authors for submitting their work, the PC members for their dedication and careful reviewing, and the external reviewers for their valuable insights. We also thank Daniel Cabarcas, the General Chair of LATINCRYPT 2025, for his leadership and tireless efforts in organizing the event. Our appreciation extends to the Local Organizing Committee, the Steering Committee for their guidance, and Springer for managing the publication process. Finally, we would like to express our heartfelt thanks to Sofía Celi and Francisco Rodríguez-Henríquez for their unwavering support and direction throughout the organization of the conference.

October 2025

Daniel Escudero
Ivan Damgård

Organization

General Chairs

Daniel Cabarcas Jaramillo	Universidad Nacional de Colombia, Colombia
Juan Guillermo Lalinde	Universidad EAFIT, Colombia

Local Organizing Committee

John B. Baena	Universidad Nacional de Colombia, Colombia
Carolina Arbelaez Montoya	Universidad EAFIT, Colombia

Program Committee Chairs

Daniel Escudero	JP Morgan AI Research & JP Morgan AlgoCRYPT CoE, USA
Ivan Damgård	Aarhus University, Denmark

Steering Committee

Sofia Celi	Brave Software, Portugal
Michel Abdalla	CNRS and DI/ENS, Université PSL, France
Diego Aranha	Aarhus University, Denmark
Paulo Barreto	University of Washington, Tacoma, USA
Ricardo Dahab	Universidade Estadual de Campinas, Brazil
Alejandro Hevia	Universidad de Chile, Chile
Kristin Lauter	Meta, USA
Julio López	Universidade Estadual de Campinas, Brazil
Daniel Panario	Carleton University, Canada
Francisco Rodríguez-Henríquez	CRC-TII, UAE
Nicolas Thériault	Universidad de Santiago de Chile, Chile
Alfredo Viola	Universidad de la República, Uruguay

Program Committee

Abdelrahaman Aly	Technology Innovation Institute, UAE
Miguel Ambrona	IOHK, Spain
Sebastian Angel	University of Pennsylvania, USA
Marshall Ball	New York University, USA
Gustavo Banegas	Inriaand École Polytechnique, France
Zhenzhen Bao	Tsinghua University, China
Magali Bardet	University of Rouen Normandie, France
Thais Bardini Idalino	Universidade Federal de Santa Catarina, Brazil
Paulo Barreto	University of Washington – Tacoma, USA
Lejla Batina	Radboud University, The Netherlands
Alexander Bienstock	JP Morgan AI Research & JP Morgan AlgoCRYPT CoE, USA
Allison Bishop	Proof Trading, USA
Katharina Boudgoust	CNRS, University of Montpellier, LIRMM, France
Dung Bui	IRIF, CNRS, Université Paris Cité, France
Fabio Campos	Bonn-Rhein-Sieg University of Applied Sciences, Germany
Nishanth Chandran	Microsoft, India
Anamaria Costache	Norwegian University of Science and Technology, Norway
Anders Dalskov	Aarhus University, Denmark
Bernardo David	IT University of Copenhagen, Denmark
Luca De Feo	IBM Research Europe, Switzerland
Andre Esser	Technology Innovation Institute, UAE
Diego F. Aranha	Aarhus University, Denmark
Antonio Florez-Gutierrez	NTT Social Informatics Laboratories, Japan
Chaya Ganesh	Aarhus University, Denmark
Juan Garay	Texas A&M University, USA
Adria Gascon	Google, USA
Valérie Gauthier-Umaña	Universidad de los Andes, Colombia
Maria Isabel Gonzalez Vasco	Universidad Carlos III de Madrid, Spain
Elisa Gorla	University of Neuchâtel, Switzerland
Ziyi Guan	EPFL, Switzerland
Lucjan Hanzlik	CISPA Helmholtz Center for Information Security, Germany
Andreas Hülsing	Eindhoven University of Technology, The Netherlands & Sandbox AQ, USA
Elena Kirshanova	Technology Innovation Institute, UAE
Lisa Kohl	CWI Amsterdam, The Netherlands

Markulf Kohlweiss	University of Edinburgh, UK
Yashvanth Kondi	Silence Laboratories (Deel), USA
Hilder Vitor Lima Pereira	Universidade Estadual de Campinas, Brazil
Chen-Da Liu Zhang	Lucerne University of Applied Sciences and Arts & Web3 Foundation, Switzerland
Patrick Longa	Microsoft, USA
Cuauhtemoc Mancillas-Lopez	Cinvestav, Mexico
Elisaweta Masserova	Carnegie Mellon University, USA
Kelsey Melissaris	Aarhus University, Denmark
Nicky Mouha	FedWriters, USA
Pratyay Mukherjee	Supra, USA
Leah Namisa Rosenbloom	Northeastern University, USA
Ngoc Khanh Nguyen	King's College London, UK
Anca Nitulescu	ENS Paris, France
Ariel Nof	Technion, Israel
Miyako Ohkubo	NICT, Japan
Claudio Orlandi	Aarhus University, Denmark
Elena Pagnin	Chalmers University of Technology, Sweden
Daniel Panario	Carleton University, Canada
Alberto Pedrouzo-Ulloa	atlanTTic, Universidade de Vigo, Spain
Octavio Perez Kempner	NTT Social Informatics Laboratories, USA
Ray Perlner	NIST, USA
Ludovic Perret	EPITA and Sorbonne University, France
Bart Preneel	University of Leuven, Belgium
Divya Ravi	University of Amsterdam, The Netherlands
Mariana Raykova	Google, USA
Francisco Rodríguez-Henríquez	Technology Innovation Institute, USA
Carla Ràfols	Universitat Pompeu Fabra, Spain
Thomas Schneider	TU Darmstadt, Germany
Peter Scholl	Aarhus University, Denmark
Phillipp Schoppmann	Google, USA
Sruthi Sekar	Indian Institute of Technology, Bombay, India
Luisa Siniscalchi	Technical University of Denmark, Denmark
Daniel Slamanig	Universität der Bundeswehr München, Germany
Daniel Smith-Tone	NIST, USA
Yifan Song	Tsinghua University and Shanghai Qi Zhi Institute, China
Eduardo Soria-Vazquez	Technology Innovation Institute, UAE
Katerina Sotiraki	Yale University, USA
Nick Spooner	Cornell University, USA
Ajith Suresh	Technology Innovation Institute, UAE

Akira Takahashi	JP Morgan AI Research & JP Morgan AlgoCRYPT CoE, USA
Mehdi Tibouchi	NTT Social Informatics Laboratories, Japan
Ida Tucker	Zondax AG, Switzerland
Muthuramakrishnan Venkitasubramaniam	Georgetown University, USA
Javier Verbel	Technology Innovation Institute, UAE
Frederik Vercauteren	KU Leuven, Belgium
Alfredo Viola	Universidad de la República, Uruguay
Fernando Virdia	King's College London, UK
Sophia Yakoubov	Aarhus University, Denmark
Arantxa Zapico	Ethereum Foundation, USA

Additional Reviewers

Marzio Mula	University of the Bundeswehr Munich, Germany
Vicente Muñoz	Universidad Complutense de Madrid, Spain
Sihem Mesnager	University of Paris VIII, France
Deepak Kumar Dalai	National Institute of Science Education and Research, India
Barak Nehoran	Princeton University, India
Eric Culf	University of Waterloo, Canada
Dustin Moody	National Institute of Standards and Technology, USA
Robert Schädlich	École normale supérieure, PSL University, CNRS, Inria, France
Filip Trenkic	King's College London, UK
Calvin Abou Haidar	NTT Social Informatics Laboratories, Japan
Lorenz Panny	Technical University of Munich, Germany
Nicholas Carlini	Google DeepMind, USA
Tzu-Shen Wang	Texas A&M University, USA
Rutvik Patel	Texas A&M University, USA
Luke Parker	Serai DEX, USA

Contents

Symmetric-Key Cryptography and Attacks

Machine Learning and Cryptanalysis

Implementation and Efficiency

Position Paper

Cryptography and Collective Power

Leah Namisa Rosenbloom(✉)

Northeastern University, Boston, USA
l.rosenbloom@northeastern.edu

Abstract. This paper continues the conversation of *What Happened to the Crypto Dream?* (Narayanan, 2013), *The Moral Character of Cryptographic Work* (Rogaway, 2015), and *Crypto for the People* (Kamara, 2020) by examining the relationship between cryptography and *collective* power. In particular, it considers cryptography in the context of *grassroots organizing*—a process by which marginalized people build collective power toward effecting systemic change—and illustrates the ways in which cryptography has both helped and hindered organizing efforts. Based on the synthesis of dozens of qualitative studies, scholarly critiques, and historical artifacts, this work introduces a *paradigm shift* for cryptographic protocol design—general principles and recommendations for building cryptography to address the lived needs and experiences of marginalized people. Finally, it calls for *abolition cryptography*: cryptographic theories and practices which dismantle harmful systems and replace them with systems that sustain human lives and livelihoods.

1 Introduction

Cryptographers make sense of the field of in different ways, segmenting work into categories such as "applied" vs. "theoretical" cryptography, or "crypto-for-security" vs. "crypto-for-privacy" [104]. In his 2013 article *What Happened to the Crypto Dream?* Arvind Narayanan argues that while crypto-for-security has thrived due to its role in protecting e-commerce and capitalist interests, crypto-for-privacy—motivated by social and political goals—has largely failed to materialize, citing human factors such as the broad inaccessibility of cryptography knowledge and misaligned incentives [104,105]. Narayanan further distinguishes "'*Cypherpunk Crypto*'—the dream of wielding crypto as a weapon for social and political change" from "'*Pragmatic Crypto*'—a more down-to-earth view that seeks to engineer modest privacy enhancements in specific applications." Drawing on the visionary work of Chaum, Narayanan traces the legacy of the cypherpunks, including their proximity to "crypto-anarchism," which "recognizes no laws except those that can be described by math and enforced by code," and also to "an overly technologically determinist view in which crypto has its own logic that's powerful enough to reshape society against the collective will." He argues that the cypherpunk vision has largely failed to produce more widespread crypto-for-privacy due to being too radical and counter-democratic, and that the status quo of technology exists "with the consent of the governed."

D. Escudero and I. Damgård (Eds.): LATINCRYPT 2025, LNCS 16129, pp. 3–39, 2026.
https://doi.org/10.1007/978-3-032-06754-8_1

Rogaway unpacks a more favorable view of the cypherpunks in his 2015 paper *The Moral Character of Cryptographic Work*, calling them "the strongest advocates for cryptography" and noting that they address the threat of power by imagining a world with "privacy for the individual, and transparency for the government and corporate elites" [120]. He contends that cryptography can be developed in ways that "benefit the weak *or* the powerful," including in ways that "benefit nobody but the cryptographer." Rogaway names the latter phenomenon "crypto-for-crypto"—the increasing tendency of cryptography research to be "self-referential" and "inward-looking" in ways that do not have any material impact on the worlds of security or privacy. The paper begins with two core historical events: the Snowden disclosures of 2013 and the Russell-Einstein manifesto of post-war 1955, which affirmed the state of science—and especially nuclear science—as deeply political, and inherently tied up with the fate of humanity. Rogaway emphasizes an "ethic of responsibility" for cryptographers in the context of mass surveillance, and, drawing on the history of academic cryptography, decries its decline in favor of "crypto-for-crypto."

Cryptographers and privacy advocates such as Diffie and Hellman, Chaum, Rogaway, and the cypherpunks have contributed vital insights to the relationships between mass surveillance, cryptography, and power. However, their analyses of power in the context of mass surveillance fall short of addressing the systemic harms and critical insights of power structures as they apply to *marginalized people*. Cypherpunks in particular focus explicitly on *individual* rights and freedoms, which implicitly center privileged intersections of identity and afford legitimacy to the same criminal legal systems and power structures which impose mass surveillance on people with marginalized intersections of identity [132].

Narayanan's point about the "consent of the governed" similarly ignores that many marginalized people who stand to benefit most from cryptography and privacy technologies have never consented to the violent abuses of power enacted by governments—including democratic governments—especially in the name of "scientific advancement," such as eugenics research, the forced sterilization of Black and Indigenous women, or the U.S. Public Health Service, Centers for Disease Control and Prevention, and Tuskegee University's infamous syphilis study [12]. The pursuit of "crypto-for-crypto" based on the same institutional funding systems that oppress marginalized people not only "starves crypto-for-privacy" [120], it does so in a way that perpetuates harmful systems, prevents the pursuit of research which explicitly addresses the needs of marginalized people, and excludes researchers from diverse demographic and intellectual backgrounds [76] from participating in cryptography and privacy knowledge production. Furthermore, the exclusion of "crypto-for-privacy" based on diverse perspectives and methodologies discounts the expertise of those who are most intimately familiar with—and therefore best positioned to advise on—the weaponization of and resistance to mass surveillance, thereby preventing cryptography and privacy as a field from realizing its potential to combat mass surveillance in general.

In his 2020 talk "Crypto for the People," Seny Kamara centers the histories and perspectives of marginalized people such as anti-apartheid activists in South

Africa, asking "Who benefits from cryptography?" and "Who's going to make crypto for the marginalized?" [76]. He critiques the "pipeline approach" which falsely assumes cryptography and privacy technologies will trickle down from corporations and governments to marginalized people, and positions crypto-for-people as distinct from both academic cryptography (which he likens to a free corporate research lab) and the libertarian perspective of cypherpunks. Instead, Kamara defines crypto for the people as "concerned with fighting *oppression and violence*," focusing on adversaries such as law enforcement agencies, systems of social domination, neo Nazis, White supremacists, and beyond. Both Rogaway and Kamara propose design directions for more socially relevant cryptographic protocols, Rogaway with a focus on more general counter-surveillance protocols and Kamara with a focus on protocols which serve the needs of marginalized people specifically.

This work further develops the call to action of making "crypto-for-people," deepening and expanding the historical case studies and dialogue between cryptography, privacy, and the collective power-building of marginalized people. In particular, it uniquely frames this conversation around grassroots organizing, which approaches power from the collective practices of marginalized people who work toward effecting systemic change. Where relevant, it draws on the insights and recommendations of Rogaway and Kamara in conversation with a vast array of transdisciplinary scholarship and expertise. It presents new paradigm shifts as *actionable frameworks* that scaffold new ways of thinking about, critiquing, and developing cryptography and privacy technologies.

Grassroots Organizing. *Grassroots organizing* is a process by which people work from within marginalized communities to build collective power and effect systemic change. The result of grassroots organizing is a grassroots movement, during which people leverage their collective bodies, voices, and resources. Because participants in grassroots movements, also called activists, use their collective power to dismantle and replace dominant power structures and hierarchies [52], they are disproportionately subject to suppression tactics such as police brutality, incarceration, disenfranchisement, assassination, prosecution, stalking, harassment, employment deprivation, surveillance, deception, and censorship [16,20,33,75,103,106,110,133].

Organizing, Technology, and Cryptography. Many scholars have studied the fraught relationship between activists and digital technologies (see Sect. 3), and suggest that digital technologies both facilitate grassroots movements and create additional risk for movement participants. More specifically, digital technologies increase the "speed, scope, and scale" [123] of vital processes like direct action planning and community-building [37,91,103,107,136,137,141]. They also expose activists to additional surveillance systems of state and local adversaries [16,63,101,103,110,145], putting them at greater risk of harm.

While cryptographic tools might afford grassroots movements some protection from surveillance, scholars and activists have critiqued cryptographers and privacy advocates for developing technological solutions to the problems of marginalized people that unintentionally reinforce dominant power structures and hierarchies, and which ignore the important historical and contemporary context of activists' lived experiences [8,52,56,76,120,146]. In other words, while cryptography has *the potential* to *help* rearrange power [120], rearranging power in practice requires a deep commitment to understanding and confronting power, and to designing powerful tools in such a way that they can be easily accessed and leveraged by *the people* who do the rearranging.

This work synthesizes and applies insights from studies at the intersection of grassroots organizing and digital technologies toward developing ways of studying, designing, and deploying cryptographic tools that facilitate collective power-building. It establishes a tangible relationship between cryptography and collective power as the theory and practice, or praxis, of *cryptography for grassroots organizing*: a new field with roots in both organizing and cryptography spaces. More broadly, it continues the conversation between Rogaway [120], Kamara [76], and many other scholars [53,74,116,139,144] who consider fundamental questions of technology production—*"Why? For whom? And to what ends?"*

Main Contributions and Organization. This work solidifies a *paradigm shift* in cryptography and privacy technology research, design, implementation, education, and culture that focuses on the lived experiences of activists and marginalized people. In this paper, lived experiences are represented by an extensive years-long review of both academic literature and alternate sources of expertise, the process of which is unpacked in Sect. 2. To ground aspects of the paradigm shifts in the concrete lived realities of activists, Sect. 3 contains an in-depth analysis of several the role of cryptography, privacy, and surveillance technologies in shaping various grassroots movements. Section 4 expands upon a "crypto-for-people" paradigm shift, while Sect. 5 foments the shift into a call toward *abolition cryptography*—cryptography with a liberatory ethos [11] designed explicitly to help grassroots movements dismantle harmful systems and replace them with systems that sustain human lives and livelihoods.

2 Methods

The approach of this work is transdisciplinary: it considers the role of both digital and non-digital technologies in the context of many different disciplines, from the more traditional cryptography and digital privacy literature, to science and technology studies, to human-computer interaction (HCI) and human-centered computing (HCC), social science research, Black intersectional feminism, critical theory, abolitionist praxis, and beyond. The core of the work, which is the two paradigm shifts proposed in Sects. 4 and 5, are informed by an extensive literature review and a four-year process of synthesis and refinement that took place iteratively over the course of several projects [123–127] and talks [77–79,122]. Some of the projects were published in cryptography and computer science spaces, while others—of equal weight and importance to the production of this paper—were unpublished community-facing projects. This section considers the methods and sources of expertise which inform the paper, the paper's intended audience and outcome, and limitations and future work.

2.1 Literature Review

The literature review for this paper began in 2020 while preparing a study of 50 informal conversations with Black Lives Matter activists about digital security practices (discussed in Sect. 3.9) [124], and continued in 2021 for a computer science (CS) ethics paper entitled *Toward Secure Social Networks for Activists* [123]. These two reviews proceeded with an initial search at the intersection of activism and digital technologies, followed by snowball sampling from the initial papers' references. Concurrently, starting in 2020 as part of participating in a racial justice committee, a similar snowball-style literature review stemming from Bettina L. Love's *We Want to Do More Than Survive: Abolitionist Teaching and the Pursuit of Educational Freedom* began, and continued through the 2023 publication of a CS education paper entitled *A Living Framework for Abolitionist Teaching in Computer Science* [126]. The literature review was concluded in 2024 as part of a PhD thesis on *Cryptography for Grassroots Organizing* [127].

2.2 Other Sources of Expertise

Many of the insights in this paper came from reflection on interpersonal conversations and organizing toward collective liberation between 2020 and 2024. As conversations and organizing are inherently personal, this work has autoethnographic elements. Various academic disciplines (including human-centered computing [3] and CS education [74]), affirm author positionality and autoethnography as rigorous methods for knowledge production.

During this period, I had many conversations with cryptographers and privacy researchers, for instance surrounding the talks *Cryptography for Grassroots Organizing* [77,79] and *Cryptography from Roots to Fruits* [78], which gave me the opportunity to reflect through critical dialogue [50] on the state of cryptography and privacy research in relation to collective power. I had similar conversations about the relationship between math and systemic injustice with fellow high school teachers while participating in the aforementioned racial justice committee and surrounding the talk *Confronting Eurocentrism in Math History Education* [122]. Conversations with students and mentors were also vital to forming my understanding of the role of STEM in perpetuating various systems of harm and oppression, as well as mechanisms of resistance to harm.

My experience of being clandestinely surveilled by administrators through the webcam of my school-issued laptop as a 16-year-old also had a substantial impact on my understanding of cryptography and computer security, making my approach to cryptography research inherently trauma-informed [125]. There are aspects of my identity (being trans, disabled, and Jewish) which make me better positioned to understand the harmful impact of technologies on minoritized communities, while other aspects of my identity (being White, from the

Global North, and middle class) privilege my experience in ways that obscure impact, especially at the critically important intersection of race and class. For illumination at this intersection, I have turned extensively to the scholarship of abolitionist, critical Black and intersectional feminist scholars, Indigenous scholars, and scholars from the Global South, as well as to the lived personal expertise and spoken testimonies of colleagues, comrades, friends, and loved ones. Finally, I have over twenty years' experience organizing in various capacities.

2.3 Synthesis and Refinement

The analysis of ideas in this paper happened as an iterative, non-systematic process of synthesis and refinement over the course of four years, mostly as a lived cycle of personal reflection, close reading, and critical dialogue. Some of the aforementioned projects included deductive and inductive coding processes which then informed a final round of axial coding. The codes elicited from this iterative process represent the overarching themes and takeaways from the review of literature and alternate sources of expertise. The closest formal methodology to this process is grounded theory [27,143], with the results of each project informing the direction of the literature review and analysis in the next. The final overarching axial codes (resp. subcodes) from this process are presented as section headers (resp. subheaders) of both paradigm shifts.

2.4 Intended Audience and Outcome

While the literature review, topics, and insights in this work are relevant to technologists in many disciplines, the target audience of this work is people who are—or are interested in becoming—cryptography and privacy researchers, with a focus on academic research. Even though most of the citations in this paper are not cryptography and privacy citations, the insights and conclusions of the work very much reflect the critical dialogue happening in the margins of cryptography and privacy spaces—dialogue that is not centered in mainstream cryptography and privacy culture, community processes, formal proceedings, or publications.

One intended outcome of this work is to bring those conversations from margin to center [65], and to make room for human-centered cryptography which is currently not well-resourced enough (in terms of time, space, money, and respect) to thrive [78]. Another intended outcome is to help the cryptography and privacy community work toward changing not only our research processes, but the surrounding ecosystem of our field. The first goal is centered in the "Cryptography for the People" paradigm shift (Sect. 4) while the second goal is centered in the "Abolition Cryptography" paradigm shift (Sect. 5).

2.5 Limitations and Future Work

This paper is more a roadmap of critique and imagination than a set of concrete technical accomplishments or recommendations. It goes as far as to explicitly discourage technical advancements which are not grounded deeply in the specific lived needs and experiences of marginalized people. Such deep grounding and technical development is not possible in the limited span of this paper, but is ripe for future work. Furthermore, the method of reviewing expertise across multiple disciplines and synthesizing insights from not only literature but interpersonal conversations without a more systematic or quantitative system of evaluation is unorthodox. Some readers, especially those who are more familiar with the traditional cryptography and privacy literature, might consider this a limitation.

While Sects. 4 and 5 offer some guidance about how to implement the aspects of the paradigm shifts, the bulk of the contribution is in the frameworks' ability to scaffold new ways to think about the role of cryptography and privacy research and technology in society, and to approach problems at the intersection of cryptography, privacy, and collective power. This process would always benefit from a more extensive and comprehensive review of existing literature and alternate sources of expertise, including more focused and systematic critiques of particular framework aspects. Extensive future work is needed to evaluate the lived process, feasibility, and impact of the proposed shifts in practice.

3 Background

To contextualize and motivate aspects of the paradigm shifts in the subsequent sections, this section presents important historical background as well as several formative case studies of activists' relationships with surveillance, cryptography, and digital technologies. There are many examples included in the full version of the paper which are not mentioned due to space constraints, but which played a role in the analysis and creation of the paradigm shifts.

The paradigm shift is also strengthened by expert analyses of the historical modes of suppression of grassroots movements [16,20,110,133] that have been reproduced, reinforced, and expanded in the digital age. In addition to the case study on COINTELPRO below, Edward Snowden revealed in 2013 that military and intelligence agencies, with support from U.S. technology corporations, had widely adapted and deployed these techniques in digital spaces—and have since wielded them disproportionately against marginalized people [8,63,103,106,110]. Simone Browne [21], Ruha Benjamin [11], Antony Loewenstein [93], and many others have discussed the systematic ways in which surveillance technologies disproportionately impact People of Color and people with intersections of multiply-marginalized identities, for instance Black women [22,108], Palestinians [69,93], working-class people [48], and trans and queer people [84,85]. The same is true of state powers' "scientific" data collection in collaboration with academic and industry research partners, for instance in the case of eugenics and racial statistics [149] or IBM's lucrative partnership with Nazi authorities [13].

3.1 Synco, or Project Cybersyn

While not directly related to cryptography and privacy, the Popular Unity government of Chile's *Proyecto Synco*, or Project Cybersyn, was a powerful conception of an early internet which illustrates the potential of a technological paradigm shift and *grassroots optimization* (Sect. 4.4). In the vision of *Synco* set forth by the Popular Unity government from 1971–1973, each site of material and later societal production (such as factories and homes) would be equipped with a computer and networked in such a way that workers could provide direct feedback to the government about problems, resources, and working conditions. Rather than facilitating a corporatized and increasingly monopolized, ad-driven economy like the internet of today, *Synco* imagined an internet which bolstered a grassroots economy, where each individual could participate in distributing the wealth they helped to generate, and in making sure their environments were livable and sustainable. While the technical reality of *Synco* differed substantially from the vision [47]—with Operational Director Raul Espejo reflecting later that "Cybersyn emphasized technology at the expense of a significant involvement of those transforming the Chilean economy on the ground" and that time pressure did not allow them to "reflect enough upon critical relationship"—it is nevertheless a fascinating case study at the intersection of technology and collective power-building. *Synco* was destroyed in the military coup of 1973.

3.2 COINTELPRO

From 1956–1971, the United States' Federal Bureau of Investigation (FBI) illegally and extensively surveilled and intimidated civil rights activists as part of the COINTELPRO operation [33]. Though the COINTELPRO operation took place in the pre-digital era, it is an important illustration of many standard grassroots movement suppression tactics [16,20] which have been bolstered by digital technologies or adapted into digital spaces. COINTELPRO operations began with extensive "intelligence gathering," demonstrating the short, malleable distance between state surveillance and state violence, even against citizens in a democratic republic. Digital surveillance and other digitally-facilitated movement suppression tactics have become a regular part of the U.S. law enforcement playbook, as evidenced by the Snowden revelations, police responses to numerous grassroots movements in the U.S., including the Black Lives Matter movement (Sect. 3.9) and Dakota Access Pipeline protests (Sect. 3.6) discussed below. The FBI's diversity of surveillance tactics and the ways in which they went hand-in-hand with violence during the COINTELPRO operation emphasizes the importance of *big-picture security* (Sect. 4.3).

3.3 Operation Vula

The first documented use of modern cryptography for grassroots organizing was the African National Congress' (ANC) Operation Vula cryptosystem, which anti-apartheid activists used to send secure communications between local and exiled ANC members in South Africa, England, Zambia, and the Netherlands from 1986–1990 [71,76]. Activists needed the system be *asynchronous* (since parties were not guaranteed to be online at the same time), *covert* (since use of encryption and computers was suspicious at the time), *correct over long distances* (since lots of errors were introduced from Lusaka to London), and *public* (since not all activists had phone lines at home). The details of this cryptosystem are available in the full version of the paper.

In building out Operation Vula, activist Tim Jenkin reported, "I went to find out about secure encryption algorithms...All I discovered was that cryptology was an arcane science for bored mathematicians, not for underground activists. However I learned a few tricks and used these to develop a system to meet our security needs" [71]. Many of the most challenging aspects of the security modeling in Operation Vula were considerations, both technical and non-technical, that had nothing to do with the encryption algorithm. Rogaway notes that cryptography literature rarely explores even technical problems that are outside the scope of what cryptographers can model with traditional complexity theoretic techniques, even when the problems are highly relevant to the intended use-case [120]. Jenkin's testimony and the technical considerations and constraints of Operation Vula emphasize the importance of *one size fits one* (Sect. 4.1), *big-picture security* (Sect. 4.3), and *grassroots optimization* (Sect. 4.4).

3.4 Arab Spring

Formal extensive study of digital technologies in the context of grassroots organizing largely began in 2010 as a result of the Arab Spring, which was a series of widespread anti-establishment protests in Tunisia, Libya, Egypt, Yemen, Syria, Bahrain, Morocco, Iraq, Algeria, Lebanon, Jordan, Kuwait, and many other places [7,66,67,140]. In particular, activists who participated in the Arab Spring used blogs and social media to increase the speed of information sharing among other participants and global supporters, the scope of the information they were able to share (such as personal opinions and visual evidence of authoritarian brutality), and the scale of the movement in general [123]. Contemporary studies of other grassroots movements such as the YoSoy132 movement in Mexico also commented on social media's ability to facilitate both "frontstage" and "backstage" tasks such as protest organizing and community building, respectively [136]. The word *facilitate* is important: scholars who study the role of social media in grassroots movements are careful to position it as a tool that grassroots organizers wield to their ends, rather than a direct or independent cause of change [66,141]. Arab Spring activists' tactics and especially their fluent use of social media to galvanize a strong grassroots base inspired activists in countless movements across the world. Activists' widespread adoption of human profile- and interaction-centered *social* media for organizing is a powerful reminder that *digital trust is human trust* (Sect. 4.2).

3.5 Euromaidan Uprising

The interplay between physical and digital spaces formed a vital part of the Euromaidan uprising in Ukraine, which ultimately led to the ousting of Russian-backed Ukranian President Viktor Yanukovych in 2014. Kyiv's *Maidan Nezalezhnosti*, or Independence Square, was taken over and held by an encampment of thousands of protesters who created a sustainable crowd-sourced ecosystem within it. According to Tetyana Bohdanova, protesters' occupation of Independence Square started with Ukranian journalist Mustafa Nayyem's Facebook post: "'We are meeting at 22:30 under the Monument of Independence. Dress warm, bring umbrellas, tea, coffee, good mood and friends. Reposts are highly encouraged!"' [15]. Social media was later used to coordinate vital support for demonstrators: to track those who were detained or missing, provide legal advice, conduct sousveillance on police brutality, organize medical brigades, financial resources, and media campaigns, visualize protesters' needs using crowdmapping technology, collaborate on movement art, and coordinate the motivational "online/offline information centre Don't Ditch Maidan" to keep the movement going. Bohdanova writes, "it was the use of social media and other ICT tools for crowdsourcing physical and creative resources that was the most crucial for sustaining Euromaidan over a long period of time."

One crowdsourced resource in the Euromaidan uprising that provides important insight into the potential role of cryptographers and privacy technologists in grassroots organizing spaces is that of the information technology (IT) tent: a physical space initially offering "free Internet access and computer equipment for protesters, which later evolved into a space where technology specialists met and collaborated with professional activists on a number of ICT-enabled social projects" [15]. Bohdanova warns, however, that it was "not social media but offline social ties" that formed the bedrock of the movement, and that the "loose, decentralised" nature of social media networks hindered the ability of the Euromaidan movement to form "a clear vision and a strategy" after a critical mass of people had been mobilized to participate [54]. Developing a balance between physical and digital, centralization and decentralization, visioning and mobilization that is tuned to activists' strategies is a problem of *grassroots optimization* (Sect. 4.4). Finally, the vital importance of "offline social ties" again reaffirms that *digital trust is human trust* (Sect. 4.2).

3.6 Dakota Access Pipeline Protests

The Dakota Access Pipeline resistance (NoDAPL) protests were part of a Standing Rock Sioux- and Native American youth-led movement against the U.S. government's ongoing theft and environmental degradation of native land, sacred sites, and water sources—in this case, to accommodate Energy Transfer Partners' multi-billion dollar pipeline. Similar to the important role of intersecting physical and digital spaces in the Euromaidan uprising discussed above, NoDAPL protesters, also known as water protectors, organized heavily using Facebook, and their digital organizing was intimately tied to the land they were occupying.

To overcome the hurdle of spotty service in the Standing Rock reservation, water protectors established "Facebook Hill"— the closest place to their encampment with enough service to spread news in the form of first-person accounts, images, and videos to the world about what was happening at Standing Rock [72]. When water protectors put out a call for help after hypothesizing that the Morton County Sheriff's Department was surveilling them using Facebook, over 1.5 million people all over the world used Facebook's "check-in" feature to claim that they were at Standing Rock in an attempt to stymie surveillance efforts [83]. While the Sheriff's Department was likely not using check-in data to determine water protectors' locations or movements—making the digital action largely symbolic—it showed supporters' awareness and receptiveness to aiding in counter-surveillance of grassroots movements, and that the movement was supported by people all over the world. All of the water protectors' workarounds highlight the ways in which technologies must be made *one size fits one* to accommodate users' environments (Sect. 4.1), while their mass-leveraging of would-be surveillance technology (the Facebook check-in feature) for cover is an excellent example of the ways in which *big-picture security* considerations can subvert normative understandings of security and privacy (Sect. 4.3).

3.7 Anti-Corruption Foundation

In "Be Safe or Be Seen? How Russian Activists Negotiate Visibility and Security in Online Resistance Practices," Tetyana Lokot discusses the ways in which Russian opposition activists organizing with the Anti-Corruption Foundation use a non-mutually-exclusive mixture of conspicuous security and strategic visibility practices [94]. For example, Lokot documents activists' use of digital privacy tools like Tor and end-to-end encrypted messaging alongside their use of YouTube to educate their supporters and spread awareness about these tools, as well as to foster a sense of organizational transparency and community. The model of encouraging radical transparency and digital security education in larger, public-facing organizational ecosystems while using digital privacy tools like end-to-end encryption among smaller collections of trusted individuals such as leaders and organizers is echoed throughout modern grassroots movements, for instance during the anti-ELAB protests in Hong Kong (Sect. 3.8). Context-dependent information sharing and safety-visibility tradeoffs are also a fundamental part of activists' collective security culture considerations [4,16,94], and should therefore be incorporated into analyses of *big-picture security* (Sect. 4.3) and *grassroots optimization* (Sect. 4.4).

3.8 Anti-ELAB Movement

Finally, the anti-Extradition Law Amendment Bill (anti-ELAB) movement, also known as the Water Movement or the 2019–2020 Hong Kong protests, was a series of widespread demonstrations against a bill which would have expanded the Chinese government's ability to extradite and arrest political dissidents in Hong Kong. The movement also sought justice for brutalized and incarcerated protesters. Albrecht, Blasco, Jensen, and Mareková conducted qualitative interviews with 11 movement participants, and found that protesters had developed intricate collective digital security culture [16] and decision-making practices which informed their choices and use of privacy-preserving technologies [4].

As discussed in Sect. 4.3 on threat modeling mismatches, protesters had one key requirement that no existing end-to-end encrypted technology could meet:

they wanted a way to determine whether someone had been arrested and, if so, remotely wipe the contents of their device. This requirement led protesters to adopt Life360—software with fine-grained remote mobile device-monitoring capabilities. Cryptographers and privacy technologists largely consider applications like Life360 to be "stalkerware" that exploits those with the application installed and fails to preserve their privacy. However, anti-ELAB activists needed to engage in a form of consensual stalking in order to keep track of one another in high-risk situations, and keep the entire group safe in the event that one person was arrested and their mobile device compromised. Similarly, activists adopted the messaging application Telegram, whose group messages are not end-to-end encrypted, because of Telegram's support for 200,000-member groups (as opposed to Signal's 1,000 and WhatsApp's 512), remote deletion of messages, polls, and live location sharing. Albrecht et al. also found that activists perceived Telegram as the "most secure," with one participant significantly misunderstanding the end-to-end encryption security guarantees (claiming that end-to-end encrypted group messaging can be enabled, which is not true) [4].

Like the practices of Anti-Corruption Foundation activists discussed in Sect. 3.7, anti-ELAB protesters also formed larger public groups and smaller private groups on digital messaging platforms for more fine-grained control over information sharing and action planning. And, similar to the inundation of content that activists experienced during the fast-paced organizing of Black Lives Matter protests in 2020 (Sect. 3.9), anti-ELAB protesters also faced "a sense of information overload" on their digital communication channels which "often made it difficult for them to keep up with evolving protest tactics" [4]. This led to participants making ad hoc "tactical decisions within seconds" about which information channels to close off and which to keep open in an effort to receive information on a need-to-know basis. They also relied on face-to-face meetings preceding digital interactions, with one participant explaining that "seeing each other and standing on the front line together is very important for trust" [4]. This again affirms that *digital trust is human trust* (Sect. 4.2), while activists' lack of options for privacy-preserving technologies again demonstrates a pressing need for *one size fits one* (Sect. 4.1), *big-picture security* (Sect. 4.3), and *grassroots optimization* (Sect. 4.4).

3.9 Black Lives Matter

Following Derek Chauvin and the Minneapolis Police Department's murder of George Floyd in 2020, Black Lives Matter (BLM) activists across the U.S. and around the world organized widespread protests. The protests were planned quickly, and BLM organizers relied heavily on social media to spread the word about them. I synthesized 50 conversations with Black Lives Matter activists in Philadelphia into an informal study [124] and found that the speed of organizing coupled with the ease of manufacturing identities, malicious content, and misinformation on social media led to higher-risk situations. For example, a group of activists reported encountering an event on Facebook that appeared to be a BLM event, but was actually organized by members of the neo-fascist

White nationalist group Proud Boys posing as BLM organizers [124]. It was later revealed that Russian state actors had also attempted to destabilize BLM organizing efforts and further stratify U.S. voters across racial lines via race-baiting, misinformation, and paid advertising on social media [111,114]. To vet the trustworthiness of digital information during the risky period of organizing in 2020, BLM activists turned to discussing the trustworthiness of digital artifacts from within established personal networks. Daffalla, Simko, Kohno, and Bardas observed similar practices in their study of the Sudanese revolution, reporting that activists used a form of "crowd-sourced content moderation" and reliance on "first hand sources" to verify the authenticity of digital information [37].

The speed of organizing coupled with anti-BLM algorithmic bias [121] led to simultaneous content inundation [100,107] and content suppression, both of which made information about protests difficult to find consistently and reliably online. While an overwhelming majority of people in the informal study ($84\%, N = 50$) used social media to find information on actions in general, only 48% reported that they heard of that day's action through social media. By contrast, while only 40% of participants reported tapping personal networks to find information in general, 42% heard about that day's action through personal networks. I concluded that while the majority of participants used social media to find information about actions, intimate and physically-grounded discovery methods such as word of mouth had a more consistent yield of in-person participation. These results further confirm that *digital trust is human trust* (Sect. 4.2), and emphasize the importance of *big-picture security* (Sect. 4.3).

3.10 Human-Centered Cryptography and Privacy Research

Several recent works have demonstrated the capacity of the cryptography and privacy research community to work with institutional community partners such as non-profits to address the lived needs and realities of marginalized people. The Callisto project is one example of a system that leverages multi-party computation to help survivors of sexual assault privately identify repeat perpetrators. A recent paper by Little, Qin, and Varia demonstrates a trauma-informed approach to the necessary but cryptographically-complex task of account recovery for Callisto, detailing the ways in which the team worked closely with Callisto project engineers to ensure design goals grounded in survivors' needs were satisfied [92]. Similarly, recent work by Luvison, Chatel, Sukaitis, Narbel, Troncoso, and Lueks describes a partnership between researchers and the International Committee of the Red Cross, where researchers defined their design constraints according to the privacy needs of humanitarian aid recipients [99]. Other works in multi-party computation, one of which was a collaboration between Kaptchuk, Benoit-Bryan, Dak Albab, Locks, Varia, and Museums Moving Forward [80], and another of which was a collaboration between Qin, Lapets, Jansen, Dak Albab, Flockhart, Issa, Varia, Bestavros and the Boston Women's Workforce Council [117], allowed workers in Boston to provide feedback to employers and the government about working conditions and pay equity in a privacy-preserving way.

4 Paradigm Shift Part 1: Cryptography for the People

This section solidifies a "cryptography for the people" [76]-inspired paradigm shift in cryptographic protocol design which foregrounds the lived needs and experiences of marginalized people. The first aspect of the shift is the design justice principle of *one size fits one* [36]: that protocol design should begin with the unique needs of the population the protocol is meant to serve. Second, *digital trust is human trust*—that digital trust is an extension of, and inextricably entangled with, complex human identities, collective trust relationships, and physicality. Third, the shift aims toward a notion of *big-picture security*—security that considers comprehensive threat models, not just technical components. And finally, a new evaluation metric for cryptographic protocols called *grassroots optimization*, which asks cryptographers to consider whether protocols are useful on the scale of communities, as opposed to corporations and governments.

4.1 One Size Fits One

It is standard practice in computer science and in research to design protocols with the greatest generalization possible. Using a fully abstract model and leaving the target population otherwise unspecified implies a "normal" user who conforms to normative standards of race (White), class (wealthy), gender (cisgendered male), ability (able-bodied), etc. [36]. In cryptography, "Alice and Bob" often serve as stand-ins for marginalized end-users of cryptographic systems such as activists and journalists, without any details about who Alice and Bob might be or what specific privacy needs might be surfaced by their lived circumstances.

Counter to the universalist standard, the *one size fits one* approach grounds technology design in the specific needs of the population(s) the technology is meant to serve [36]. It demands generalization from the roots up rather from the top down—in the spirit of Fannie Lou Hamer and Black intersectional feminism, it is the "nobody's free until everybody's free" [58] approach to technology design, which positions universal accessibility in relation to all of the rich particulars [26] of diverse userbases, rather than implicitly in relation to a privileged minority [36]. This work considers one size fits one approach more broadly, not only as a design principle but as a general way of knowing, being, and relating in research, education, and community spaces.

There are several important nuances that arise in applying the one size fits one approach to cryptography for grassroots organizing, especially when cryptography designers and deployers are not members of the population(s) with whom they are designing. As Ghoshal, Mendhekar, and Bruckman note, the disproportionate concentration of technological skills among young, cisgender White men leads to their inequitable control of technology adoption and use in grassroots organizations [52]. Power dynamics in the process of technology production not only impact manifestations of technology—explicit designs, artifacts, and processes—but ways of knowing and being, producing technoculture [112].

In order to counteract this technocultural power dynamic in grassroots organizing spaces, Ghoshal, Mendekar, and Bruckman propose a *grassroots culture of technology practice*—technology practices which are aligned with the existing cultures in grassroots organizing spaces. The following subsections highlight and discuss different aspects of *one size fits one* toward developing a grassroots culture of cryptography and privacy technology practice.

Marginalized People Are Not a Monolith. Activists—like any other people who form a marginalized group—are not a monolith. This is a recognition that while activists come together to form communities and coalitions, they are individuals with diverse backgrounds, needs, and opinions. Human collectives according to Aimé Césaire form "a universal rich with all that is particular, rich with all the particulars there are, the deepening of each particular, the coexistence of them all" [19,26]. Césaire's formulation stands in opposition to neoliberal cosmopolitan universalism, which homogenizes human beings into identity categories when convenient for the maintenance of racialized capitalism and other dominant systems [6,11,132,147,149]. Similarly, flattening or abstracting marginalized people's privacy needs neatly into definitions and theorems without considering the rich particulars of their lived experiences—especially for the sake of expedient publication or implementation—reinforces existing norms.

Historically and systemically, people with dominant intersections of identity have classified people with marginalized intersections of identity into groups for the purpose of preserving hierarchies that benefit the dominant group [147,149]. The same power dynamic renders dominant intersections of identity normative or invisible, and therefore impervious to identity-based discrimination [11,12,147]. The "double-bind" of being folded into a homogeneous, stereotyped identity and simultaneously hypertargeted by oppressive power structures manifests widely in the design and deployment of digital technologies [11,22,69,93,108] and also in academic settings [12]. As observed by Aouragh, Gürses, Rocha, and Snelting, this trend continues into popular cryptography and digital privacy resources, which offer broad, static solutions to activists' privacy problems without meaningful engagement with the granularity, fluidity, collective values, labor structures, and cultures of grassroots movements [8].

In order to design cryptography and privacy technologies that counteract the double-bind, *one size fits one* practitioners can start by recognizing the context of widespread "research injustice" [62]—a scientific research culture which has historically exploited and tokenized individuals with marginalized intersections of identity. They can facilitate many one-on-one and group conversations, documenting with consent the self-chosen narratives [62] of each individual member of a group, slowly working with them to draw connections and synthesize communal aspirations and design goals. Simultaneously, practitioners must cultivate an awareness of the opposite effect of the double-bind—what Ruha Benjamin calls the *overserving* of people with privileged intersections of identity [12]—that often come with the terrain of technology "expertise." In practice, the rejection of overserving requires people in positions of power and with normative forms of expertise to step back, listen, recognize, and uplift forms of expertise that have been historically devalued in cryptography, computer science, and beyond.

Finally, activists' differentiation between platforms and group sizes for digital communications based on context and function, for instance as discussed in Sects. 3.7 and 3.8, suggests that *one size fits one* must go beyond addressing the generalized needs of activists to addressing their needs with respect to a particular task or moment in time. This does not necessarily mean that one digital technology would or should cover all of the contexts, but rather that designers should take *specific* use cases into account when designing technologies. For example, incorporating end-to-end encryption into a platform designed to spread awareness of a grassroots movement may make the platform less accessible while providing no benefit with respect to confidentiality (since the information communicated on the platform is supposed to be public anyway). On the other hand, integrating anonymous communication channels into such a platform might be of great benefit, and a worthwhile tradeoff for accessibility if the activists in question are at high risk of state violence for simply accessing the platform.

Collaborative Development. Typical technology research, design, and development practices do not support "non-expert" collaboration or co-creation—they leave knowledge production processes to a privileged minority. Notable exceptions include work from organizations like the Algorithmic Justice League [90], Callisto [92,119], Data for Black Lives [49], the Detroit Digital Justice Coalition [34], the IDA B. WELLS Just Data Lab [88], the Distributed AI Research Institute (DAIR) [68], Our Data Bodies [14], the Technology, Race, Equity, and Ethics in Education (TREE) Lab [1], and more. Kotturi, Hui, Johnson, Sanifu, and Dillahunt summarize the recommendations of human-computer interaction (HCI) researchers for building successful academic-community partnerships: "academic teams can volunteer in the community, familiarize themselves with local histories, reflect on their own identities and standpoints, and set expectations and mutually beneficial goals" [87].

There are many challenges to subverting existing practices and establishing more community-centered ones in academic research, for instance financial and reputational incentive structures that encourage exploitation of community partners and rigid standards about what kind of research deserves funding. Participants in the Community Driven Approaches to Research in Technology & Society Workshop raised suggestions for how to resist "the field of computing's myopic and extractive tendencies" [87] and dismantle barriers to collaborative technology development, including establishing common language and values, respecting each community partner as an individual rather than a member of a monolithic group, offering community partners forms of currency that are valuable to them, clarifying researchers' roles and positionalities, and creating recourse for any potential harms [142].

Overall, the research methods offered by community-collaborative approaches [62], participatory design [9], participatory action research [9,24], community-based participatory research [128], and citizen science [12,134] have much to offer cryptographers and privacy technologists looking to engage in collaborative technology development with activists and beyond. These methods are, however, not without issue: Harrington, Erete, and Piper unpack participatory design workshops as "an affluent and privileged activity that often neglects the challenges associated with envisioning equitable design solutions among underserved populations" [62]. Framing their critique around the harm and historical injustice that researchers have perpetuated against marginalized communities [12,149], Harrington et al. call on researchers to consider the history and context of participating communities especially with respect to "research injustice," to encourage participants to "engage on their own terms and share narratives that they deem important" rather than looking to extract complete personal narratives, and to challenge corporate and overly-technical design mechanisms which may "devalue existing assets or environments" and create distance between marginalized communities and the participatory design process [62].

Collaborative Trainings and Teach-Ins. Borradaile, Kretschmer, Gretes, and LeClerc found that hands-on training workshops can produce sustained use of cryptographic tools for grassroots organizing, even when the tool (PGP) is notoriously difficult to navigate [17]. In general, collective co-education practices such as collaborative trainings, teach-ins, and skills shares have the potential to expand and sustain activists' use of digital privacy and security tools. As noted by Aouragh, Gürses, Rocha, and Snelting [8] and Ghoshal, Mendhekar, and Bruckman [52], the process of researching available tools, determining the extent to which they are useful, and deploying them in a way that is accessible to the entire grassroots community requires an immense amount of labor [8,52]. While activists are the best people to determine the relevance and accessibility of tools for their work, they are also often already overburdened with roles and tasks, and feel as though the bar of entry to acquiring and synthesizing technical knowledge is too high [8]. This leads to stratifications that Aouragh et al. and Ghoshal et al. identify as harmful and inequitable: the control of critical technological processes by privileged minorities [52], and the systematic separation of sites of technological production from the technologies' material use [8].

Education as a practice of freedom [50,51,64] and *abolitionist teaching* [97] are two educational lenses which are pre-aligned with grassroots culture and values—and when instantiated with technological material, could create what Ghoshal, Mendhekar, and Bruckman might call a grassroots culture of technology education [52]. As part of formulating a grassroots culture of technology education, this work highlights two types of education that are common in grassroots movement spaces—trainings and teach-ins—and what they might look like when instantiated on the subject of cryptography and digital privacy.

Trainings are closest to traditional conceptions of education in that they typically involve a transfer of knowledge or skill from people with expertise and/or experience to people without expertise and/or experience. While perhaps due to this top-down structure trainings leave the most room for hegemonic structures of technical knowledge to remain active in grassroots spaces [52], they also place the least preparatory burden on participants, and at least provide space for a synchronous gathering in which collective participation, question-answering, and discussion can take place [8]. “Collaborative” trainings imply there is a higher degree of interaction and participation from everyone involved, and serve to bring the traditional notion of a training more squarely into the fabric of inclusive and democratic grassroots practices [52]. In the context of cryptography and digital privacy, collaborative trainings could help all participants (including the trainer) map the landscape of threats that digital technologies pose to grassroots movements, provide an accessible and qualitative review of possible digital interventions, and begin to solidify the ways in which the landscape and interventions might take shape in particular contexts and communities. Rather than the directive approach taken by many digital privacy initiatives, which instruct activists to use particular technologies that may or may not apply to their specific priorities [8], collaborative trainings can help all participants build context toward one-size-fits-one digital privacy practices.

Teach-ins are also typically a knowledge transfer, though they are rooted in community spaces and are a form of direct action. In particular, teach-ins call on community members to occupy a space and to hold that space while engaging in teaching and learning as a form of political resistance. Teach-ins could be a very effective way to explore cryptography and digital privacy from the contexts of the specific issues that grassroots movements are looking to address. They also require a high degree of community contact and solidarity, as anyone participating in the teach-in is inherently participating in the grassroots movement itself. Therefore, teach-ins afford opportunities not only to democratize technical knowledge, but also to bridge the categorical gap between “tech activists” and “social justice activists” [8] toward a coalition which is demonstrably aligned in both values and practice. Free public workshops in hackerspaces and makerspaces can also serve as political resistance by rendering spaces and knowledge typically reserved for university settings more actionable and accessible.

4.2 Digital Trust is Human Trust

Aside from “crypto parties” and PGP’s web of trust, which saw niche adoption primarily among technologists in the 1990s, digital trust mechanisms flatten the richness of human trust relationships into binary individualized values held on devices—a singular digitized entity that is either trusted or not trusted—for the purpose of protecting digitized property. Unlike computers, humans do not operate on binary: they may or may not trust people or information within particular contexts or with respect to particular risk-related tasks, and sometimes they are simultaneously trustful and distrustful of the same person or piece of information in ways they cannot explain or quantify. Human trust can change over time, sometimes drastically from one moment to the next, and is inextricably shared between people collectively and interdependently.

Despite its murkiness and variability, trust is an essential part of the ways in which human beings relate to one another. It is also the (ill-specified) foundation of cryptographic systems for digital security and privacy in practice. As stated by Lu, Sannon, Moy, Brewer, Green, Jackson, Reeder, Wafer, Ackerman, and Dillahunt in "Shifting from Surveillance-as-Safety to Safety-through-Noticing: A Photovoice Study with Eastside Detroit Residents," "one's everyday navigation and negotiation of safety is always conditioned by inseparable relationships with other humans, including family, friends, neighbors, acquaintances, and unknown others" [98]. Rather than attempt to simplify or extrapolate the complexities of human trust into a digital medium with rigid constraints, this work proposes that cryptographers and digital privacy technologists who are interested in securing people over property ground their design thinking in the recognition that *digital trust is human trust.* Acknowledging that trust is inherently a human experience and cannot be fully digitized calls on us to work with, rather than around or by flattening, human-centered definitions of trust. This section discusses human-centered approaches to incorporating and evaluating trust in digital systems.

Fine-Grained, Collective Authentication. Privacy scholars and cryptographers have criticized the corporatist and individualist conceptions of trust in cryptographic knowledge systems and protocol design [8,76,120,146]. In short, conceptualizing trust and authentication procedures for digital tools as being tied to a single identity is not reflective of the ways in which human beings share tools generally, and the distinction is even more pronounced in the setting of collaborative work like grassroots organizing. Single-party authentication is instead reflective of capitalism and, more specifically, property ownership: cryptographers imagine end-users of digital tools as people who are looking to secure their individual identities and digital property from forgers and thieves, or else they imagine end-users as corporations who want to restrict people's use of hardware, software, cloud, and streaming services to one-user-per-purchase.

As part of the paradigm shift, *digital trust is human trust* asks cryptographers and digital privacy technologists to consider collective authentication, or trust mechanisms that allow for multi-party ownership, authorization, and access to digital systems. In a client-server system with collective authentication, clients may not exist to the server as individual entities; the server might not even be aware of how many entities own a particular digital artifact. To coordinate different levels of access among collective owners without relying on the server, it will be necessary to make the collective authentication process as fine-grained as possible. That way, a collective may decide amongst themselves who has access to what, and when. While cryptographic tools like anonymous credentials [23,30], group signatures [31], and threshold cryptosystems [39,40] can afford versions of fine-grained, collective authentication and relative anonymity, constructions still rely on individualized identity management and enforcement at the root.

Access restriction in the setting of grassroots organizing may be for the security culture principle of sharing information on a need-to-know basis. That is, access restriction might not be tied to ownership or even trust; mutually trusted parties might intentionally restrict one another from accessing sensitive information that could unnecessarily incriminate them [4,16]. It should be up to all of the occupants of a digital "safe house" to collectively decide who gets access to what, when—it is not up to the service providers, for instance the lock-makers (i.e. cryptographers), the architects (i.e. protocol designers), or the bank who provides a loan on the mortgage (i.e. a cloud hosting service). Cryptography and privacy designers might work on both the decision-making mechanisms *and* ways to make the mechanisms clear and accessible to participants.

Digital Trust and Physicality. Research on activists' use of digital technologies to facilitate organizing has surfaced an intimate connection between activists' digital trust relationships and physical collective presence, or co-presence, in offline organizing [4,35,44,57,60,130,141]. In general, digital human trust relationships rely, for better or for worse, on perceptions of how people exist in the world physically, and physical properties can be used to authorize individuals' presence in digital spaces such as online forums and support groups [61]. In digital spaces such as public group pages, state actors and counter-protesters have been known to use fake profiles to look like credible members of grassroots organizations while spreading misinformation, inciting arguments, and attempting to destabilize grassroots movements [103,111,114,124]. To combat this, activists rely on in-person trust networks and, where in-person access is not possible, first-hand authentication of digital artifacts from people who are physically connected to the creator(s) of the artifact in question, and can vouch for them [4,37,124].

In other words, rooting digital trust and authentication procedures in perceptions of physicality is already something that people (and especially activists) do on an everyday basis. As part of acknowledging that *digital trust is human trust*, cryptographers and digital privacy researchers might actively work to accommodate people's physical-to-digital trust conversion process, making it easier for people to discern whether the owner of a particular digital artifact is someone that the viewer knows in person, either directly or through a trusted third party.

Trust in Technology. Finally, people's perception of the trustworthiness of technologies factors greatly into their decisions about when and how to use those technologies. In a study of the usability of and motivation behind people's adoption of secure communication tools, Abu-Salma, Sasse, Bonneau, Danilova, Naiakshina, and Smith found that human factors such as social pressures, misunderstanding or mistrust of a particular technology's security and privacy guarantees, and misconceptualizations of security and privacy guarantees in general were more substantial obstacles to adoption than the technology's usability [2]. Ermoshina, Halpin, and Musiani likewise found that even among populations of "high-risk" users such as activists, "the properties of protocols are not understood by users" [45]. One study participant, a privacy technology designer, dreams that in the future, the "trust relationships that we are imagining match the actual trust relationship[s] that actually exist" [45].

While understanding does not necessarily imply trust, it can motivate trust in a way that combats users' privacy-nihilistic perceptions that secure communications are "futile" [2], especially against powerful adversaries like state governments [124]. As discussed in Sect. 4.1, hands-on initiatives that encourage participants to reflect on and actively co-create technology practices can create a sustainable trust relationship between high-risk populations like activists and privacy-preserving technologies, even when the technologies may not be the most user-friendly [17]. However, as Aouragh, Gürses, Rocha, and Snelting propose in their critique of online digital privacy education websites and as Abu-Salma et al. confirm in their reporting of study participants' misunderstanding of the EFF Secure Messaging Scorecard, more flattened, top-down digital initiatives organized by "tech activists" [8] and "knowledge brokers" [2] do not substantially increasing activists' understanding of and trust in technology. In order to foster trust and appropriate use of digital privacy technologies, cryptographers and technology designers might consider applying *digital trust as human trust* not only as part of the protocol design process, but also as core part of presenting the technology to its intended user-base in a hands-on and accessible way.

4.3 Big-Picture Security

Like the admission that trust is inherently human, *big-picture security* asks cryptographers and digital privacy technologists to situate security considerations within the context of human lives, rather than within the easy-to-model yet reductive landscape of digital technologies. In many cases, cryptographers and privacy technologists' unfounded expectations that human conceptions of security will conform to their modeling-friendly conceptions lead to what Qin, Shrishak, and I call "threat modeling mismatches"—misalignments between proposed privacy technologies and lived privacy needs [104,105,118]. This section expands upon the ways in which mismatched security models can end up making people less secure in digital environments.

Big-picture security aims to retain the realistic (non-digitizable) complexities of human conceptions of security, and is therefore impossible to realize through digital technologies alone. While cryptographers and digital privacy designers will by definition not be able to account for every dimension of big-picture security in their protocol designs and implementations, keeping big-picture security in mind throughout the design process will help them create technologies that are compatible with, and therefore useful in sustaining, human lives.

Deniability and Deletion. Cryptographic threat modeling practices, security definitions, and design goals often miss the mark of capturing the lived uses and impact of the tools they produce [8,76,118]. While developers at every stage from ideation to formal security proofs to implementation and adoption might claim their tools are privacy-preserving, several factors can prevent the tools from preserving privacy in practice. Similar to how the trust relationship between people and technology discussed in the previous subsection can impact the lived functionality of digital privacy tools, developers' misunderstanding, dismissal, or deprioritization of the "big-picture" landscape of a digital tool's application can lead to a worse outcome for vulnerable populations than if they had avoided the tool altogether. To capture the ways in which researchers' priorities and mental models of desirable security and privacy properties can misalign with lived use to the detriment of marginalized populations, Qin, Shrishak, and I developed the concept of *threat modeling mismatches* [118].

We cite forward secrecy [55] and deniability [25] as examples of cryptographic security properties which have received widespread attention from researchers for their usefulness in protecting marginalized populations from specific adversaries, and that have been proven insufficient for those purposes in practice. In the case of forward secrecy—which states that even if an adversary compromises a key at a particular time (for instance by issuing an "adaptive corruption" like an arrest), it cannot decrypt any messages sent before that time—anti-ELAB activists in Hong Kong found that a more pressing threat was the compromise of contacts and plaintext messages that appeared on activists' devices in a search incident to arrest [4]. Rather than using tools like Signal with ubiquitous end-to-end encryption and forward secrecy, anti-ELAB activists chose what cryptographers would undoubtedly characterize as less-secure technologies like Telegram (whose group messages are not end-to-end encrypted) and Life360 (a stalkerware application) because those technologies allowed them more fine-grained control over determining whether someone had been arrested and, if so, remotely wiping the contents of their mobile devices [4].

Similarly, deniable encryption affords people who have produced ciphertexts as part of end-to-end encrypted communications the ability to decrypt the ciphertexts to reveal two or more plaintexts. Cryptographers purport that this process allows vulnerable people—for instance activists or whistleblowers under prosecution—to "deny" that they wrote a particular plaintext, since each of the alternative plaintexts are equally mathematically likely to have produced the ciphertext. In the practical context of compelled decryption and legal discovery, however, judges often already know some information about the underlying plaintexts. Therefore, providing decryption keys that produce completely unrelated plaintexts could lead to deeper legal trouble [118]. Yadav, Gosain, and Seamons point out that deniability "requires social and legal acceptance to be effective" as a security property, and that acceptance is far from reality. They further identify specific harms that can result if an application supports deniability without the grounding of social or legal acceptance, such as attackers forging messages that might be trusted from social and legal perspectives, or defendants falsely assuming they can deny messages in court [148]. Carefully examining these and many other kinds of threat modeling mismatches can help researchers and activists identify blind spots in the ways that digital tools are developed and presented to users.

Technology and Movement Suppression. An important part of big-picture security is acknowledging the role of digital technologies in the landscape of movement suppression tactics deployed by powerful state actors, often with the help of technology corporations and academic institutions [16,20,69,93]. What Aouragh, Gürses, Rocha, and Snelting describe as the "sneaky moment" in which grassroots organizers turned to a corporatized ecosystem of digital privacy technologies in the fallout of the Snowden revelations has underscored the cognitive dissonance of trying to use hegemonically-aligned technologies to counteract those same hegemonies and shift power toward dismantling interlocking systems of oppression [8]. For example, the process of "threat modeling" invokes the name of military procedure [8]; it has also helped grassroots organizers and marginalized populations identify priorities and decide when and how to collectively adopt digital privacy tools.

In order to create technology with what Ruha Benjamin calls a "liberatory ethos" [12], it is necessary to identify the aspects of technology which are leveraged to suppress movements, and contrast them with aspects of technology which, if wielded from within the "big-picture" context of grassroots movements, might align with and facilitate those movements. The same technologies used to suppress movements can sometimes be wielded in counter-hegemonic ways, for instance sousveillance is the process of wielding would-be surveillance technologies like publicly-uploaded footage from smartphone cameras against the people who typically exploit surveillance technologies against marginalized people, such as police officers [18]. Citizen journalist practices like filming police officers in the context of high-risk direct action and arrest can help enforce transparency and accountability of the criminal justice system where non-violent democratic processes exist, and help non-local populations understand the extent of authoritarian violence where they do not.

As Audre Lorde warns, however, "the master's tools will never dismantle the master's house" [95]—only a collective of people, in the strength and spark of our diversity, can do that. Reclaiming technologies that have been wielded to oppress marginalized people—including cryptography, which has roots in global military history—is a subtle art. Section 5 presents the lens of *abolition cryptography*, which can help cryptographers and privacy technologists re-imagine the processes of technical knowledge and production in a way that aligns with grassroots values. In short, it is not enough to build, wield, and popularize technologies of any kind, cryptography or otherwise—they must be systematically evaluated and re-evaluated in the context of shifting power dynamics.

Accessibility and Usability. Another "big-picture" consideration is that the technological systems which are the most secure in practice have large and diverse user bases that motivate a high standard of technical maintenance and greater overall attention to accessibility and usability, as opposed to smaller niche tools, which are typically built for technically-fluent users [41]. On the surface this fact could pose a challenge to sustaining the design principle of one size fits one, because it is tempting to position generalized accessibility and usability in direct opposition to the specific accessibility and usability needs of marginalized users. However, by paying attention to diverse needs within marginalized populations, cryptographers and privacy technologists can develop tools that do indeed generalize to wider populations.

Take for example a collection of grassroots organizers, who, despite having a wide array of values and practices in common, are incredibly diverse with respect to race, ethnicity, gender, sexuality, religion, age, language, ability, geographic location, and more. Recognizing activists as composed by these rich particulars [26] opens up the possibility of widening the user base of digital technologies for organizing to populations with each overlapping intersection of identity. With each protocol design aspect that is meant to increase accessibility and usability for specific intersections of the diverse identities of organizers, organizing tools become more useful for general diverse populations. Technology design and development which starts by addressing some specific need of a marginalized population and works to include more and more intersections of identity will produce technologies whose universal accessibility is comprised of rich particulars, rather than a purported universal accessibility that invisibly caters to a privileged minority [12,19,26,59].

4.4 Grassroots Optimization

It is standard practice in cryptography to pay strict attention to the problem of optimization, or making a protocol as efficient as possible. Echoing many other computer science critical scholars [53,74,76,116,120,139,144], this work asks: Optimal for whom? To what end? The material answer to these questions is typically: for corporations and governments, and to the end of protecting property—capital, intellectual, etc.—and government systems, data, and power, respectively. (Cryptographers might tell you it's because they find optimizing things fun, but materially, fun doesn't keep the lab lights on.)

In contrast to optimizing for corporations and governments, *grassroots optimization* is the act of optimizing for the unique needs of grassroots organizers. Cryptographically, grassroots optimization puts a new frame around constraints and possibilities—some grassroots organizations may not have sufficient computational power to run cryptographic algorithms that activists with the latest smartphones can run easily, while some of those activists might be willing to use more of their device battery to perform intensive computations over small datasets that, on a corporate scale, are prohibitively consumptive. This section considers some of the nuances of grassroots-optimized cryptography, including cases in which access to technology is limited, non-existent, or undesirable.

Devices, Computation, and Communication Complexity. Three important efficiency metrics in benchmarking new technologies are to identify the devices for which the technology is relevant, the technology's computation complexity (corresponding to how much electricity is consumed), and its communication complexity (corresponding to how much information is transmitted), both asymptotically and heuristically with respect to the relevant devices. Activists and marginalized populations all over the world use a diverse range of devices which are severely underrepresented in the cryptography and digital privacy literature. Even researchers who work directly with implementations of cryptographic protocols tend to leverage cloud providers like Amazon Web Services, cutting-edge central and graphics processors, and up-to-date operating systems, ignoring the fact that the vast majority of the world uses years-old technology. Backwards compatibility and device interoperability are seldom if ever discussed in cryptography research, and even companies and organizations who produce technologies and technology advice for practical everyday use do not generally consider the timeliness or relevance of their protocols and recommendations with respect to older devices [8]. *Grassroots optimization* asks technologists to reframe technology design and benchmarking around the realistic availability of devices, energy, and network connectivity for activists and their communities.

Censorship Circumvention. State actors intentionally create internet "blackouts" to cut off activists' internet access, forcing them to use alternate communication technologies. For example, activists participating in the Arab Spring used a combination of satellite phones and dial-up to circumvent widespread internet outages [7,66,67,140]. Authoritarian regimes in particular censor citizens' access to particular content and platforms, leaving internet connectivity intact but preventing activists from using well-known digital channels for communicating and disseminating state-critical content and information. Several information and communication technologies such as Tor [41], Bridgefy [5], Firechat [38,102], Session [45], and Briar [45] attempt to get around state censorship using peer-to-peer network connectivity, though of the privacy-preserving technologies only Tor (which is only semi-decentralized) has been consistently used and maintained over a substantial period of time, likely due to its focus on modeling security as usability [41]. Tor developers still struggle to circumvent new censorship techniques, continuously finding work-arounds to keep connectivity up for activists and other vulnerable populations facing more aggressive forms of suppression.

In places where encryption itself is illegal or suspicious, steganography—the process of concealing sensitive information by disguising it as innocuous information—can provide a form of censorship circumvention that maintains strong cryptographic security guarantees [73,81]. While steganography has been largely discounted by the cryptography and privacy technology community as being "security through obscurity," the renewed attention and rigorous treatment of steganography by Kaptchuk, Jois, Green, and Rubin [81] and Jois, Beck, and Kaptchuk [73] has the potential to offer activists cryptographically-secure communications that circumvent encryption-based censors.

Non-Digital Development. One important takeaway from the Community-Driven Approaches to Research in Technology and Society Workshop (discussed in Sect. 4.1) was participants' support of the *right not to be digital* [142]—that providing non-digital alternatives to digital services is an important and necessary part of ensuring equitable access. This is especially for older participants in grassroots movements living in rural localities [52].

As implied by the previous subsections on physicality (Sect. 4.2) and censorship circumvention (Sect. 4.4), non-digital considerations are of vital importance to activists, both in solidifying interpersonal trust and, as demonstrated by the Euromaidan uprising (Sect. 3.5) and the Dakota Access Pipeline Protests (Sect. 3.6), in providing the contextual shared ground upon which digital organizing becomes meaningful and effective. Even though cryptographers and privacy technologists are not experts in non-digital security, they should be aware of how the technologies they design and create fit into and work alongside physical infrastructures. When developed in parallel and for mutual benefit, digital and physical technologies have the potential to enhance one another. For example in the case of the Euromaidan uprising, activists' organization of physical IT tents for supporting protesters' digital activities led to the development of new, activist-centered technologies [15].

5 Paradigm Shift Part 2: Abolition Cryptography

Phillip Rogaway states and expands upon the idea that "cryptography rearranges power" [120]. Given activists' use of cryptography and privacy-preserving technologies from Operation Vula through the present day, this work suggests cryptography has *the potential* to *help* rearrange power, though, as Rogaway and other critics point out, cryptography as a field often reproduces norms which serve to keep hegemonic systems of power firmly in place [8,76]. While cryptography for grassroots organizing is one idea for cryptography with an ethos of rearranging power, it is not enough: there are many ways in which cryptography as a field perpetuates a status quo that elevates the security of property over people, fuels technologies such as cryptocurrencies and privacy-preserving AI (whose need for energy and precious metals poison the environment especially in the Global South [82]), and opens opportunities disproportionately to privileged minorities. None of the issues mentioned in this section are unique to cryptography. As it says in *Pirke Avot*, we aren't required to finish the job, nor are we free to desist from it: we can use our positions to prioritize systems of knowledge production that center human well-being.

This section applies the *Living Framework for Abolitionist Teaching in Computer Science* [126], inspired by the work of abolitionist scholars Bettina L. Love [97], Jones and melo [74], and more [10,11,42,43,50,53,64,89,96,115,135,138], to propose the idea of *abolition cryptography*. Abolition cryptography aims to create a theory and practice (praxis) of cryptography which is values-aligned with the collective power of grassroots movements—and with marginalized people—by suggesting ways in which we might replace harmful technological systems with ones that sustain human lives and livelihoods. The following aspects, which mirror the aspects of the framework [126], are a first try: like grassroots organizing, abolition cryptography is a collective, ongoing, and iterative process. This first iteration drawn on the work of not only abolitionist teachers, but on the work and perspectives of fellow cryptographers and privacy technologists who offer invaluable insight into the hidden interlocking forces that undergird the field.

5.1 Becoming Organizers

The work of cryptography is intimately connected with systems of power whether cryptographers recognize it or not [120], and choosing not to recognize it means tacitly supporting the status quo. In order to work ethically on systems which are enmeshed in the fabric of power, we need a better understanding of the fabric of power and of the impact our work might have on it. One of the best ways to understand the boundaries and intricacies of power is by trying to shift or rearrange power ourselves, by organizing toward material change in our field. This process can take many different forms, some of which are discussed below.

5.2 Reframing Cryptography History and Resistance

If you ask a cryptographer about the history of cryptography, they will likely cite some combination of the following phenomena: Caesar cipher, Shannon cipher, Enigma, public-key crypto, clipper chips, export controls, Snowden, cypherpunks, and a myriad of more modern cryptographic research areas. While these are all valid components of cryptography history, they are not the only components, and taken together they tell a story that is decidedly rooted in White, male, Global Northern ways of knowing that ignore the stories of marginalized people—even when those stories document the application and development of landmark cryptography and privacy technology. For example, Seny Kamara was (to my knowledge) the first cryptographer to talk publicly about the Operation Vula cryptosystem (Sect. 3.3) in 2020 [76], 34 years after the project began and 30 years after it had played a significant role in ending apartheid in South Africa. How many more groundbreaking uses of cryptography to rearrange power have been ignored by cryptographers over the last 34 years? It is up to us to find out, and to learn from those stories the ways in which cryptography can help people resist systems of oppression beyond the individualist cypherpunk approach, beyond a citizen-centered "right to privacy," and toward a cryptography resistance framework which works for the liberation of all people, collectively.

5.3 Equitable Access to Conferences, Funding, and Publication

Advances in cryptography research are primarily disseminated through conferences and their proceedings, which are organized, for example, by the International Association for Cryptologic Research (IACR). Crypto, the de facto flagship IACR conference, takes place every year in Santa Barbara, CA, U.S.—a country with some of the strictest and most exclusionary visa requirements in the world. The only other IACR conference with an A^* ranking from the International Computing Research and Education (ICORE) Conference Ranking Portal is EuroCrypt, which is always held in Europe. Several other conferences in the field such as Asiacrypt, Latincrypt, and AfricaCrypt, are also explicitly segregated by geographic location. While having conferences in different regions of the world with accompanying schools able to serve students in diverse languages is vital to the broad accessibility of the field, by and large the most widely-published and well-resourced cryptographers do not consider conferences outside of the U.S. and Europe to be "separate but equal."

Access to funding is similarly gate-kept by multinational corporations such as the biggest sponsors of Crypto 2023: Google, Amazon Web Services, and the Technology Innovation Institute. One of the most important requirements for publication is the ability to understand and produce cryptography knowledge in English, which already severely limits access and participation in cryptography to a privileged minority. Again, these problems are not at all unique to cryptography: they appear in almost all CS disciplines and in many other scientific and academic fields in general. Taken together, it is clear that more equitable access to conferences, funding, and publication in cryptography is sorely needed.

At the rump session of Crypto 2022, Daniel Escudero called cryptographers' attention to Criptolatino, an organization that centers Latin American cryptographers' work and experiences in cryptography [46]. As part of the talk, Escudero explained that many people with accepted papers who wanted to attend Crypto could not be there because of visas and cost, that only a tiny number of countries have visa-free access to the U.S., and that people from Colombia, for example, might have to wait 696 calendar days (almost two years) for a visa. As a collective, Criptolatino offers strategies for addressing these issues: increasing visibility of Latin American students and researchers, hosting events like workshops that raise awareness and offer opportunities for students in Latin America and beyond, building networks between different regions, and creating resources in Spanish and Portuguese for better accessibility of cryptography content.

Pagnin, Celi, and Takahashi released a set of recommendations for the IACR, "On Creating a More Inclusive and Supporting Community," which call attention to the need for more visa support, online accommodation, and financial assistance, pointing out that even the IACR's registration cost of 25 U.S. dollars alone corresponds to a month's worth of food in certain places in the Global South [113]. Supporting Criptolatino and initiatives like Pagnin, Celi, and Takahashi's—first by listening, talking about, and financially backing them, and then by taking organizational roles to overhaul exclusionary practices—is one way to start working toward equitable access and accountability.

5.4 Against Surveillance Techno-Solutionism and Centering Property

The techno-complexes identified in the abolitionist teaching framework [126] manifest in cryptography in many ways, for instance in surveillance techno-solutionism, which positions cryptography as the one-size-fits-all solution to surveillance, or in the techno-colonialist tendency of cryptography research to consider the security of property and devices over people. As indicated in Sect. 4, the idea of a one-size-fits-all, top-down solution does not adequately address the needs of the marginalized populations who may need cryptography the most [8]. Furthermore, centering cryptography in conversations about mass surveillance and focusing on individual privacy rights ignores the historical context of why and how state powers have wielded mass surveillance disproportionately against marginalized people.

Cryptographic "solutions" to mass surveillance which obscure systemic issues and omit marginalized perspectives from the problem-solving conversation create a seemingly progressive "stumbling block" [86]—an incomplete or ineffective solution which masquerades as progress while failing to fix the problem, simultaneously slowing down and drawing attention away from more comprehensive, but perhaps less shiny or technically novel, initiatives. Finally, as discussed in Sect. 4.2, many cryptographic protocol designs prioritize the security of property over people by defining trust and ownership on an individual basis, reducing human beings to their devices for technical convenience, and optimizing applications and algorithms for the benefit of corporations seeking to protect capital and intellectual property. Centering the design principles outlined in Sect. 4 and continuing to learn from the people, organizations, and work that inspired them are just one way to go about resisting the techno-complexes in cryptography.

5.5 Cryptography and Creative Expression

Cryptography and privacy have deep and under-explored psychological, emotional, and spiritual dimensions. Non-technical ways of knowing and being like visual art, song, dance, creative writing, prayer, and storytelling [43,70,74,129, 131] [19,32,109] therefore have a lot to offer cryptographers in the process of getting to the bottom of our relationship with surveillance, and toward a more radical understanding of privacy and security. For example, Lu, Sannon, Moy, Brewer, Green, Jackson, Reeder, Wafer, Ackerman, and Dillahunt used photovoice, a participatory technique where participants offer "photographic narratives," to discuss the "lived experiences of navigating personal and community safety" of 11 older Black members of a Detroit-area community organization [98]. The study offers "an epistemological shift from *surveillance-as-safety* to *safety-through-noticing*," radically re-imagining safety as driven by mutual community noticing which, like surveillance, involves watching and observing but, unlike surveillance, does not involve institutional power and the threat of violence. Opening up our definitions of technology to include mechanisms of creative expression can help cryptographers understand, process, and confront surveillance and systems of marginalization on a deeper level.

5.6 The ReCAP Workshop

Chator, Kamara, Qin, and I offer a new space and vision for cryptography and privacy scholarship in the "Re-Imagining Cryptography and Privacy" (ReCAP) Workshop. The focus of the ReCAP Workshop is Re-Imagination: "identifying the aspects of cryptography and privacy technology production that contribute to marginalization, and solidifying approaches, ideas, and designs that center marginalized voices, resist toxic aspects of technology production, and leverage cryptography and privacy tools toward dismantling systems of oppression" [29]. Like the Community-Driven Cryptography Project [28], the ReCAP Workshop "seeks to build and sustain an interdisciplinary community" and "contribute to the broadening of access to the field." We can each "start where we are" [126] in this moment to create more designated spaces for re-imagining, thinking, discussing, and building in our own communities toward a cryptography praxis that supports collective power for marginalized people.

6 Conclusion

This work belongs in theoretical cryptography spaces because it speaks to the moral and ethical obligation of all cryptographers to understand the lived impact of their work on systems of power [76, 120]. While to date there have been few if any transdisciplinary papers published at theoretical cryptography conferences, this work argues and demands space for considerations of the real-world impact of cryptography at all levels of the cryptography production pipeline, starting with theoretical foundations. Applied cryptographers, privacy technology developers, and even activists (in the case of Tim Jenkins of Operation Vula) look to the work of theoretical cryptographers to determine what is possible—to form a basis for their ideation and implementation of cryptographic tools in the real world. Therefore, theoretical cryptographers hold a great deal of power: the ability to set the stage for future work on privacy-preserving technologies. In order to wield this power in a way that helps to break cycles of systemic harm and works toward building collective power for marginalized people, cryptographers must be literate in the language of power. By drawing closer together the worlds of cryptography and transdisciplinary scholars—who have developed rigorous theory at the intersection of technology and collective power—and by shifting our mindsets and priorities toward the self-articulated perspectives of marginalized communities, we can begin to create cryptography praxis with a lived positive impact on all human lives and livelihoods.

Acknowledgments. Thank you to Seny Kamara and Anna Lysyanskaya for affirming this work as part of my PhD in cryptography, thereby creating space for this work to exist and thrive. Thank you to Seny for ongoing reflection on and discussion of the ideas in this paper and beyond. Thank you to Lucy, Alishah, and all the participants in the Community-Driven Cryptography Seminar and the Re-Imagining Cryptography and Privacy Workshop for your insights and camaraderie. Thank you to Yash, Sofi, Daniel, the cryptographers of Criptolatino, and all those working to shift power in cryptography toward inclusion and collective well-being. Thank you to the Latincrypt 2025 Program Committee and Program Chairs, and especially to the reviewers of this paper, for engaging with the ideas in a way that sought to improve them, for making space for the work to be heard and discussed, and for helping to legitimize the work within our institutions. Thank you to all of the people whose work I cite, formally or in spirit, for inspiring me in a big way. And thank you to all my comrades, near and far, for the same reason. Finally, thank you to my family and my ancestors, for the value of questioning:

Why? For Whom? And To What Ends?

References

1. The TREE Lab: Examining technology, race, equity, and ethics in education (2024). https://tree.northwestern.edu/
2. Abu-Salma, R., Sasse, M.A., Bonneau, J., Danilova, A., Naiakshina, A., Smith, M.: Obstacles to the adoption of secure communication tools. In: 2017 IEEE Symposium on Security and Privacy (SP), pp. 137–153. IEEE (2017)
3. Ajmani, L.H., Bhatt, T., Devito, M.A.: Moving towards epistemic autonomy: a paradigm shift for centering participant knowledge. In: Proceedings of the 2025 CHI Conference on Human Factors in Computing Systems, pp. 1–17 (2025)
4. Albrecht, M.R., Blasco, J., Jensen, R.B., Mareková, L.: Collective information security in large-scale urban protests: the case of Hong Kong. arXiv preprint arXiv:2105.14869 (2021)
5. Albrecht, M.R., Blasco, J., Jensen, R.B., Mareková, L.: Mesh messaging in large-scale protests: breaking bridgefy. In: Paterson, K.G. (ed.) CT-RSA 2021. LNCS, vol. 12704, pp. 375–398. Springer, Cham (2021). https://doi.org/10.1007/978-3-030-75539-3_16
6. Alexander, M.: The New Jim Crow. The New Press (2011)
7. AlSayyad, N., Guvenc, M.: Virtual uprisings: on the interaction of new social media, traditional media coverage and urban space during the 'Arab Spring'. Urban Stud. **52**(11), 2018–2034 (2015)
8. Aouragh, M., Gürses, S., Rocha, J., Snelting, F.: Fcj-196 let's first get things done! on division of labour and techno-political practices of delegation in times of crisis. Fibrecult. J. (26 2015: Entanglements–Activism and Technology) (2015)
9. Bang, M., Vossoughi, S.: Participatory design research and educational justice: studying learning and relations within social change making. Cogn. Instr. **34**(3), 173–193 (2016)
10. Bell, D.A.: Who's afraid of critical race theory. Univ. Illinois Law Rev. **4**(3), 823–846 (1995)
11. Benjamin, R.: Race After Technology: Abolitionist Tools for the New Jim Code. Polity Press (2019)
12. Benjamin, R.: Viral Justice: How We Grow the World We Want. Princeton University Press, Princeton (2022)
13. Black, E.: IBM and the Holocaust: The Strategic Alliance Between Nazi Germany and America's Most Powerful Corporation. Dialog Press (2012)
14. Our Data Bodies. About (2024). https://www.odbproject.org/about-us-2/
15. Bohdanova, T.: Unexpected revolution: the role of social media in Ukraine's euromaidan uprising. Eur. View **13**(1), 133–142 (2014)
16. Borradaile, G.: Defend Dissent. Oregon State University Corvallis (2021)
17. Borradaile, G., Kretschmer, K., Gretes, M., LeClerc, A.: The motivated can encrypt (even with PGP). In: Proceedings on Privacy Enhancing Technologies (2021)
18. Borradaile, G., Reeves, J.: Sousveillance capitalism. Surveill. Soc. **18**(2), 272–275 (2020)
19. Boyarin, D.: The No-State Solution: A Jewish Manifesto. Yale University Press (2023)
20. Boykoff, J.: Limiting dissent: the mechanisms of state repression in the USA. Soc. Mov. Stud. **6**(3), 281–310 (2007)
21. Browne, S.: Dark Matters: On the Surveillance of Blackness. Duke University Press (2015)

22. Buolamwini, J., Gebru, T.: Gender shades: Intersectional accuracy disparities in commercial gender classification. In: Conference on Fairness, Accountability and Transparency, pp. 77–91. PMLR (2018)
23. Camenisch, J., Lysyanskaya, A.: An efficient system for non-transferable anonymous credentials with optional anonymity revocation. In: Pfitzmann, B. (ed.) EUROCRYPT 2001. LNCS, vol. 2045, pp. 93–118. Springer, Heidelberg (2001). https://doi.org/10.1007/3-540-44987-6_7
24. Cammarota, J., Fine, M.: Revolutionizing education. Youth Participatory (2008)
25. Canetti, R., Dwork, C., Naor, M., Ostrovsky, R.: Deniable encryption. In: Kaliski, B.S. (ed.) CRYPTO 1997. LNCS, vol. 1294, pp. 90–104. Springer, Heidelberg (1997). https://doi.org/10.1007/BFb0052229
26. Césaire, A.: Discourse on colonialism. In: Postcolonlsm, pp. 310–339. Routledge (2023)
27. Charmaz, K.: Constructing Grounded Theory: A Practical Guide Through Qualitative Analysis. Sage (2006)
28. Chator, A., Kamara, S., Qin, L., Rosenbloom, L.N.: Community-Driven Cryptography Seminar (2021–2023)
29. Chator, A., Kamara, S., Qin, L., Rosenbloom, L.N.: Re-Imagining Cryptography and Privacy (ReCAP) Workshop (2024–2025)
30. Chaum, D.: Blind signatures for untraceable payments. In: Chaum, D., Rivest, R.L., Sherman, A.T. (eds.) Advances in Cryptology, pp. 199–203. Springer, Boston, MA (1983). https://doi.org/10.1007/978-1-4757-0602-4_18
31. Chaum, D., Heyst, E.: Group signatures. In: Davies, D.W. (ed.) EUROCRYPT 1991. LNCS, vol. 547, pp. 257–265. Springer, Heidelberg (1991). https://doi.org/10.1007/3-540-46416-6_22
32. Christian, B.: The race for theory. Feminist Stud. **14**(1), 67–79 (1988)
33. Churchill, W., Wall, J.V.: The COINTELPRO papers. South End Press (1990)
34. Detroit Digital Justice Coalition. About (2024). https://www.detroitdjc.org/about-1
35. Coopman, T.M.: Networks of dissent: emergent forms in media based collective action. Crit. Stud. Media Commun. **28**(2), 153–172 (2011)
36. Costanza-Chock, S.: Design Justice: Community-Led Practices to Build the Worlds We Need. The MIT Press (2020)
37. Daffalla, A., Simko, L., Kohno, T., Bardas, A.G.: Defensive technology use by political activists during the Sudanese revolution. In: 2021 IEEE Symposium on Security and Privacy (SP), pp. 372–390. IEEE (2021)
38. Dalek, J., Winter, P., Dranka, A., Crete-Nishihata, M., Senft, A.: Asia chats: update on line, Kakaotalk, and FireChat in China. The Citizen Lab (2014)
39. Desmedt, Y.: Society and group oriented cryptography: a new concept. In: Pomerance, C. (ed.) CRYPTO 1987. LNCS, vol. 293, pp. 120–127. Springer, Heidelberg (1988). https://doi.org/10.1007/3-540-48184-2_8
40. Desmedt, Y.: Threshold cryptosystems. In: Seberry, J., Zheng, Y. (eds.) AUSCRYPT 1992. LNCS, vol. 718, pp. 1–14. Springer, Heidelberg (1993). https://doi.org/10.1007/3-540-57220-1_47
41. Dingledine, R., Mathewson, N.: Anonymity loves company: usability and the network effect. In: WEIS. Citeseer (2006)
42. Web, D.B.: Black Reconstruction in America, 1860–1880. In: Racism Essential Readings, pp. 27–34 (2001)
43. Dumas, M.J., Ross, K.M.: "Be Real Black for Me:" imagining BlackCrit in education. Urban Educ. **51**(4), 415–442 (2016)

44. Earl, J., Kimport, K.: Digitally Enabled Social Change: Activism in the Internet Age. MIT Press (2011)
45. Ermoshina, K., Halpin, H., Musiani, F.: Can johnny build a protocol? Coordinating developer and user intentions for privacy-enhanced secure messaging protocols. In: European Workshop on Usable Security, pp. 1–13 (2017)
46. Escudero, D.: Criptolatino: a group that advocates for cryptography research made by/for Latin-Americans (2022). https://youtu.be/_qSja6VpPbQ?t=588
47. Espejo, R.: Cybernetics of governance: the cybersyn project 1971–1973. In: Social Systems and Design, pp. 71–90 (2014)
48. Eubanks, V.: Automating Inequality: How High-Tech Tools Profile, Police, and Punish the Poor. St. Martin's Press (2018)
49. Data for Black Lives. Index (2024). https://d4bl.org/
50. Freire, P.: Pedagogy of the oppressed 30th anniversary edition. The Continuum International Publishing Group, 1970 (2005)
51. Freire, P.: Education: The Practice of Freedom (1976)
52. Ghoshal, S., Mendhekar, R., Bruckman, A.: Toward a grassroots culture of technology practice. Proc. ACM Hum.-Comput. Interact. **4**(CSCW1), 1–28 (2020)
53. Gilmore, R.W.: Abolition Geography: Essays Towards Liberation. Verso Books (2022)
54. Gladwell, M.: Small change. New Yorker **4** (2010)
55. Günther, C.G.: An identity-based key-exchange protocol. In: Quisquater, J.-J., Vandewalle, J. (eds.) EUROCRYPT 1989. LNCS, vol. 434, pp. 29–37. Springer, Heidelberg (1990). https://doi.org/10.1007/3-540-46885-4_5
56. Gürses, S., Kundnani, A., Hoboken, J.: Crypto and empire: the contradictions of counter-surveillance advocacy. Media Cult. Soc. **38**(4), 576–590 (2016)
57. Haciyakupoglu, G., Zhang, W.: Social media and trust during the Gezi protests in Turkey. J. Comput.-Mediat. Commun. **20**(4), 450–466 (2015)
58. Hamer, F.L.: Speech Delivered at the Founding of the National Women's Political Caucus (1971)
59. Hampton, L.M.: Black feminist musings on algorithmic oppression. In: Proceedings of the 2021 ACM Conference on Fairness, Accountability, and Transparency (2021)
60. Harlow, S.: Social media and social movements: facebook and an online guatemalan justice movement that moved offline. New Media Soc. **14**(2), 225–243 (2012)
61. Harmon, A.: Discussing Blackness on reddit? Photograph your forearm first. New York Times (2019)
62. Harrington, C., Erete, S., Piper, A.M.: Deconstructing community-based collaborative design: towards more equitable participatory design engagements. Proc. ACM Hum.-Comput. Interact. **3**(CSCW), 1–25 (2019)
63. Heh, E., Wainwright, J.: No privacy, no peace: urban surveillance and the movement for Black lives. J. Race Ethn. City **3**(2), 121–141 (2022)
64. Hooks, B.: Teaching to Transgress: Education as the Practice of Freedom. Routledge (1994)
65. Hooks, B.: Feminist Theory: From Margin to Center. Pluto Press (2000)
66. Howard, P.N., Duffy, A., Freelon, D., Hussain, M.M., Mari, W., Maziad, M.: Opening closed regimes: what was the role of social media during the Arab Spring? SSRN 2595096 (2011)
67. Howard, P.N., Hussain, M.M.: Democracy's Fourth Wave?: Digital Media and the Arab Spring. Oxford University Press (2013)

68. Distributed AI Resesarch Institute (2024). https://www.dair-institute.org/about/
69. Amnesty International. Automated apartheid: How facial recognition fragments, segregates and controls palestinians in the OPT (2023)
70. Iseke, J.: Indigenous storytelling as research. Int. Rev. Qual. Res. **6**(4), 559–577 (2013)
71. Jenkin, T.: Talking with Vula. Mayibuye (1995)
72. Johnson, H.: # nodapl: Social media, empowerment, and civic participation at Standing Rock. Libr. Trends **66**(2), 155–175 (2017)
73. Jois, T.M., Beck, G., Kaptchuk, G.: Pulsar: Secure steganography through diffusion models. Cryptol. ePrint Arch. (2023)
74. Jones, S.T., Melo, N.A.: We tell these stories to survive: towards abolition in computer science education. Can. J. Sci. Math. Technol. Educ. **21**(2), 290–308 (2021)
75. Kamara, S.: COINTELPRO. Algorithms for the People (2020)
76. Kamara, S.: Crypto for the people (2020). https://www.youtube.com/watch?v=_qSja6VpPbQ
77. Kamara, S., Rosenbloom, L.N.: Cryptography for grassroots organizing. Real World Cryptography (2023). https://namisa.art/files/Cryptography_Grassroots_Organizing_RWC_2023_condensed_slides.pdf
78. Kamara, S., Rosenbloom, L.N.: Cryptography from roots to fruits. Advanced Cryptography School at Latincrypt 2023 (2023). https://namisa.art/files/Cryptography_Roots_Fruits_ASCrypto_2023_condensed_slides.pdf
79. Kamara, S., Rosenbloom, L.N.: Cryptography, the internet, and grassroots organizing. Internet Engineering Task Force 116 (2023). https://namisa.art/files/Cryptography_Internet_Grassroots_Organizing_IETF_116_condensed_slides.pdf
80. Kaptchuk, G., Benoit-Bryan, J., Albab, K.D., Locks, M., Varia, M.: The good, the bad, and the ugly—lessons from an MPC for social good deployment. Talk given at RWC 2024 (2024). https://www.youtube.com/watch?v=l-HrnrnB6dU
81. Kaptchuk, G., Jois, T.M., Green, M., Rubin, A.D.: Meteor: cryptographically secure steganography for realistic distributions. In: Proceedings of the 2021 ACM SIGSAC Conference on Computer and Communications Security, pp. 1529–1548 (2021)
82. Kara, S.: Cobalt red: How the blood of the Congo powers our lives. St. Martin's Press (2023)
83. Kennedy, M.: More than 1 million "check in" on Facebook to support the Standing Rock Sioux. NPR. org (2016)
84. Keyes, O.: The misgendering machines: trans/HCI implications of automatic gender recognition. Proc. ACM Hum.-Comput. Interact. **2**(CSCW), 1–22 (2018)
85. Keyes, O.: Counting the countless: why data science is a profound threat for queer people. Real Life **2** (2019)
86. King, M.L.: Letter from Birmingham City Jail (1963)
87. Kotturi, Y., Hui, J., Johnson, T.J., Dillahant, T.: Sustaining community-based research in computing: Lessons from two tech capacity building initiatives for local businesses (2024)
88. Wells, I.B.: Just Data Lab (2024). https://www.thejustdatalab.com/about
89. Laura, C.T.: Being Bad: My Baby Brother and the School-to-Prison Pipeline. Teachers College Press (2014)
90. Algorithmic Justice League (2024). https://www.ajl.org/about

91. Lee, F.L.F., Chan, M., Chen, H.T.: Social media and protest attitudes during movement abeyance: a study of Hong Kong university students. Int. J. Commun. **14**, 20 (2020)
92. Little, R., Qin, L., Varia, M.: Secure account recovery for a privacy-preserving web service. Cryptology ePrint Archive (2024)
93. Loewenstein, A.: The Palestine Laboratory: How Israel Exports the Technology of Occupation Around the World. Verso Books (2023)
94. Lokot, T.: Be safe or be seen? How Russian activists negotiate visibility and security in online resistance practices. Surveill. Soc. **16**(3), 332–346 (2018)
95. Lorde, A.: The master's tools will never dismantle the master's house. The Personal and the Political Panel (1979)
96. Lorde, A.: Sister Outsider: Essays and Speeches. Crossing Press (1984)
97. Love, B.L.: We Want to Do More than Survive: Abolitionist Teaching and the Pursuit of Educational Freedom. Beacon Press (2019)
98. Lu, A.J., et al.: Shifting from surveillance-as-safety to safety-through-noticing: a photovoice study with eastside Detroit residents. In: Proceedings of the 2023 CHI Conference on Human Factors in Computing Systems, pp. 1–19 (2023)
99. Luvison, E., Chatel, S., Sukaitis, J., Narbel, V.G., Troncoso, C., Lucks, W.: A low-cost privacy-preserving digital wallet for humanitarian aid distribution. In: 2025 IEEE Symposium on Security and Privacy (SP), pp. 1234–1250. IEEE (2025)
100. Marwick, A.E., Boyd, D.: I tweet honestly, I tweet passionately: twitter users, context collapse, and the imagined audience. New Media Soc. **13**(1), 114–133 (2011)
101. Mateescu, A., Brunton, D., Rosenblat, A., Patton, D., Gold, Z., Boyd, D.: Social media surveillance and law enforcement. Data Civ. Rights **27**, 2015–2027 (2015)
102. Morrison, L.P., Team, B., Nguyen, B., Kannan, S., Ray, N., Lewin, G.C.: Airchat: ad hoc network monitoring with drones. In: 2017 Systems and Information Engineering Design Symposium (SIEDS), pp. 38–43. IEEE (2017)
103. Mundt, M., Ross, K., Burnett, C.M.: Scaling social movements through social media: the case of black lives matter. Social Media+ Soc. **4**(4), 2056305118807911 (2018)
104. Narayanan, A.: What happened to the crypto dream?, part 1. IEEE Secur. Priv. **11**(2), 75–76 (2013)
105. Narayanan, A.: What happened to the crypto dream?, part 2. IEEE Secur. Priv. **11**(3), 68–71 (2013)
106. Neef, A.: Infrared aerial surveillance used at Standing Rock to monitor and track protesters (2019)
107. Nielsen, R.K.: Mundane internet tools, mobilizing practices, and the coproduction of citizenship in political campaigns. New Media Soc. **13**(5), 755–771 (2011)
108. Noble, S.U.: Algorithms of Oppression. New York University Press (2018)
109. Nxumalo, F., Ross, K.M.: Envisioning Black space in environmental education for young children. Race Ethn. Educ. **22**(4), 502–524 (2019)
110. Owen, S.: Monitoring social media and protest movements: ensuring political order through surveillance and surveillance discourse. Social Ident. **23**(6), 688–700 (2017)
111. O'Sullivan, D., Byers, D.: Exclusive: fake black activist accounts linked to Russian government. CNN Bus. **28** (2017)
112. Pacey, A.: The Culture of Technology. MIT press (1985)
113. Pagnin, E., Celi, S., Takahashi, A.: On Creating a More Inclusive and Supporting Community (2023)

114. Parham, J.: Russians posing as Black activists on Facebook is more than fake news. Retr. August **22**, 2018 (2017)
115. Peña, L.G.: Community as Rebellion: A Syllabus for Surviving Academia as a Woman of Color. Haymarket Books (2022)
116. Philip, T.M., Bang, M., Jackson, K.: Articulating the "how," the "for what," the "for whom," and the "with whom" in concert: a call to broaden the benchmarks of our scholarship. Cogn. Instr. **36**(2), 83–88 (2018)
117. Qin, L., et al.: Deploying MPC for social good. Talk given at RWC 2019 (2019). https://www.acsu.buffalo.edu/~mblanton/cse410/rwc2019-lucy-qin.pdf
118. Qin, L., Rosenbloom, L.N., Shrishak, K.: Where do threat models come from? Challenging implicit assumptions (2023). https://namisa.art/Threat_Modeling_Mismatches_condensed_slides.pdf
119. Rajan, A., Qin, L., Archer, D.W., Boneh, D., Lepoint, T., Varia, M.: Callisto: a cryptographic approach to detecting serial perpetrators of sexual misconduct. In: Proceedings of the 1st ACM SIGCAS Conference on Computing and Sustainable Societies, pp. 1–4 (2018)
120. Rogaway, P.: The moral character of cryptographic work. Cryptology ePrint Archive (2015)
121. Roose, K.: Social media giants support racial justice: their products undermine it. The New York Times (2020)
122. Rosenbloom, L.N.: Confronting Eurocentrism in math history education. In: UTeach STEM Educators Conference (2021). https://namisa.art/files/Confronting_Eurocentrism_in_Math_History_Education_slides.pdf
123. Rosenbloom, L.N.: Toward secure social networks for activists. In: Moving Technology Ethics at the Forefront of Society, Organisations and Governments, pp. 491–502. Universidad de La Rioja (2021)
124. Rosenbloom, L.N.: Activists Want Better, Safer Technology. arXiv preprint arXiv:2209.01273 (2022)
125. Rosenbloom, L.N.: Stickers on webcams (2022). https://namisa.art/stickers_on_webcams.html
126. Rosenbloom, L.N.: A living framework for abolitionist teaching in computer science. In: Proceedings of the ACM Conference on Global Computing Education, vol. 1, pp. 133–139 (2023)
127. Rosenbloom, L.N.: Cryptography for grassroots organizing. Brown University (2024)
128. Saksono, H., Parker, A.G.: Socio-cognitive framework for personal informatics: a preliminary framework for socially-enabled health technologies. ACM Trans. Comput.-Hum. Interact. **31**(3), 1–41 (2024)
129. Sium, A., Ritskes, E.: Speaking truth to power: Indigenous storytelling as an act of living resistance. Decolonizat. Indigeneity Educ. Soc. **2**(1), 1–10 (2013)
130. Skoric, M.M., Poor, N.D., Liao, Y., Tang, S.W.H.: Online organization of an offline protest: from social to traditional media and back. In: 2011 44th Hawaii International Conference on System Sciences, pp. 1–8. IEEE (2011)
131. Solórzano, D.G., Yosso, T.J.: Critical race methodology: counter-storytelling as an analytical framework for education research. Qual. Inquiry **8**(1), 23–44 (2002)
132. Spade, D.: Normal Life: Administrative Violence, Critical Trans Politics, and the Limits of Law. Duke University Press (2015)
133. Starr, A., Fernandez, L.A., Amster, R., Wood, L.J., Caro, M.J.: The impacts of state surveillance on political assembly and association: a socio-legal analysis. Qual. Sociol. **31**, 251–270 (2008)

134. Strong, L., Das, A., Morales-Doyle, D.: Abolition science praxis (part 1) (2018). https://www.abolitionscience.org/home/2018/11/27/abolition-science-praxis-pt-2-dr-danny-morales-doyle
135. Strong, L., Das, A., Robinson, R.P.: The history of abolition (2018). https://www.abolitionscience.org/home/2018/9/4/historically-grounding-abolition
136. Treré, E.: Reclaiming, proclaiming, and maintaining collective identity in the #yosoy132 movement in Mexico: an examination of digital frontstage and backstage activism through social media and instant messaging platforms. Inf. Commun. Soc. **18**(8), 901–915 (2015)
137. Treré, E.: The banality of whatsapp: on the everyday politics of backstage activism in Mexico and Spain. First Monday **25** (2020)
138. Truth, S.: Ain't I a Woman? (1851)
139. Tuck, E., Yang, K.W.: Toward what justice. In: Describing Diverse Dreams of Justice in Education. Routledge, Abingdon (2018)
140. Tufekci, Z., Wilson, C.: Social media and the decision to participate in political protest: observations from Tahrir Square. J. Commun. **62**(2), 363–379 (2012)
141. Valenzuela, S.: Unpacking the use of social media for protest behavior: the roles of information, opinion expression, and activism. Am. Behav. Sci. **57**(7), 920–942 (2013)
142. Venkatasubramanian, S., Gebru, T., Topcu, U., Griffin, H., Rosenbloom, L.N., Sonboli, N.: Community driven approaches to research in technology & society. In: CCC Workshop Report (2024)
143. Vollstedt, M., Rezat, S.: An introduction to grounded theory with a special focus on axial coding and the coding paradigm. Compend. Early Career Res. Math. Educ. **13**(1), 81–100 (2019)
144. Vossoughi, S., Vakil, S.: Toward what ends? A critical analysis of militarism, equity, and STEM education. In: Education at War, pp. 117–140. Fordham University Press (2018)
145. Wade, K., Brubaker, J.R., Fiesler, C.: Protest privacy recommendations: an analysis of digital surveillance circumvention advice during Black Lives Matter protests. In: Extended Abstracts of the 2021 CHI Conference on Human Factors in Computing Systems, pp. 1–6 (2021)
146. Watson, H., Moju-Igbene, E., Kumari, A., Das, S.: "We hold each other accountable": unpacking how social groups approach cybersecurity and privacy together. In: Proceedings of the 2020 CHI Conference on Human Factors in Computing Systems, pp. 1–12 (2020)
147. Wilkerson, I.: Caste: The Origins of Our Discontents. Random House (2020)
148. Yadav, T.K., Gosain, D., Seamons, K.: Cryptographic deniability: a multi-perspective study of user perceptions and expectations. In: 32nd USENIX Security Symposium (USENIX Security 23), pp. 3637–3654 (2023)
149. Zuberi, T.: Thicker Than Blood: How Racial Statistics Lie. University of Minnesota Press (2001)

Zero-Knowledge Proofs and Distributed Computation

Post-Quantum Zero-Knowledge with Space-Bounded Simulation

Prabhanjan Ananth[1] and Alex B. Grilo[2(✉)]

[1] UCSB, Santa Barbara, USA
prabhanjan@cs.ucsb.edu
[2] Sorbonne Université, CNRS, LIP6, Paris, France
alex.bredariol-grilo@lip6.fr

Abstract. The traditional definition of quantum zero-knowledge stipulates that the knowledge gained by any quantum polynomial-time verifier in an interactive protocol can be simulated by a quantum polynomial-time algorithm. One drawback of this definition is that it allows the simulator to consume significantly more computational resources than the verifier. We argue that this drawback renders the existing notion of quantum zero-knowledge not viable for certain settings, especially when dealing with near-term quantum devices.

In this work, we initiate a fine-grained notion of post-quantum zero-knowledge that is more compatible with near-term quantum devices. We introduce the notion of (s, f) space-bounded quantum zero-knowledge. In this new notion, we require that an s-qubit malicious verifier can be simulated by a quantum polynomial-time algorithm that uses at most $f(s)$-qubits, for some function $f(\cdot)$, and no restriction on the amount of the classical memory consumed by either the verifier or the simulator.

We explore this notion and establish both positive and negative results:

- For verifiers with logarithmic quantum space s and (arbitrary) polynomial classical space, we show that (s, f)-space-bounded QZK, for $f(s) = 2s$, can be achieved based on the existence of post-quantum one-way functions. Moreover, our protocol runs in constant rounds.
- For verifiers with super-logarithmic quantum space s, assuming the existence of post-quantum secure one-way functions, we show that for all polynomials f, (s, f)-space-bounded QZK protocols, with channel black-box simulation (a quantum analogue of black-box simulation) can only be achieved for languages in BQP.

1 Introduction

Zero-knowledge is a foundational notion in cryptography. Invented in the 80 s by Goldwasser, Micali and Rackoff [28], this notion has slowly transitioned from being a purely theoretical notion to having applications in practice. Some notable applications of zero-knowledge include secure computation [26] and cryptocurrencies [38].

D. Escudero and I. Damgård (Eds.): LATINCRYPT 2025, LNCS 16129, pp. 43–75, 2026.
https://doi.org/10.1007/978-3-032-06754-8_2

A zero-knowledge proof (or argument) system for a language in NP is an interactive protocol between a prover, who receives as input an instance-witness pair (x, w) and a verifier, who receives as input x. The zero-knowledge property states that the verifier, after interacting with the prover, should not gain any information about the witness beyond what is leaked by the statement. That is, in the words of the inventors of zero-knowledge [28], "*... what the verifier sees in the protocol (even if he cheats) should be something which the verifier could have computed himself...*". Formally, we define the notion of a simulator and we require that the view of the verifier after interacting with the prover should be computationally indistinguishable from the output of the simulator.

When we consider poly-time verifiers we typically require the simulator to run in polynomial time. In particular, the storage and the computational power used by the simulator can be an arbitrary polynomial, respectively, in the storage and computational power of the verifier. One might worry that this definition is not strong enough: the verifier might gain knowledge from a protocol that would need far more computational resources in order for it to have computed by itself.[1] Nonetheless, this is a reasonable assumption to make in the present day as getting access to more computational resources is cheaper than ever before.

Quantum Zero-Knowledge. The advancement in quantum technology forces us to re-think the design of cryptographic protocols. But even before we build protocols that are secure against quantum adversaries, we need to first focus on formal definitions and appropriately define post-quantum security for existing cryptographic primitives. We focus on the notion of zero-knowledge against malicious quantum verifiers, also referred to as quantum zero-knowledge.[2] One approach to formalize this definition is to modify the definition of classical zero-knowledge as follows: instead of considering probabilistic polynomial-time adversaries in the traditional zero-knowledge definition, we instead consider quantum polynomial-time (QPT) adversaries. And instead of modeling the auxiliary input to the verifier as a classical string, we model it as a quantum state. Almost all the works [2,3,5,9,10,17,33,43] take this approach of defining quantum zero-knowledge. While this is the most general definition one can think of, it does not accommodate the subtleties on the computational power of the quantum verifier, as we show in the example below.

Definitional Issues. Let us consider the following language based on factoring:

$$\mathcal{L}_{\mathsf{FACT}} = \{\langle N, L, U\rangle : \exists \text{ prime } p \text{ that divides } N, \text{ s.t.} L \leq p \leq U\}.$$

Consider the following protocol for $\mathcal{L}_{\mathsf{FACT}}$ between a prover P and a verifier V:

[1] See the discussion on precise zero-knowledge in Sect. 1.3.

[2] In this work, we say that a protocol is *post-quantum zero-knowledge* when we want to stress that the protocol is classical but safe against quantum adversaries. If instead, we are only interested in the simulation of quantum malicious verifiers, we simplify and use the term *quantum zero-knowledge*.

1. P sends the smallest prime p that divides N and moreover, $L \leq p \leq U$
2. V checks if: *a*) p is prime; *b*) p divides N; and *c*) $L \leq p \leq U$. If all the checks pass, then V accepts. Otherwise, V rejects.

It is not hard to see that this protocol is complete and sound. Interestingly, according to the existing definition, this protocol satisfies the quantum zero-knowledge property. The simulator works as follows:

1. Using the Shor's algorithm for factoring [39], find all the prime factors $p_1, ..., p_\ell$ of N.
2. Send p_i to the verifier, such that p_i is the smallest prime that divides N and $L \leq p_i \leq U$.

Notice that when describing the simulator, we did not take into consideration the computational power of the verifier. In particular, let us consider a malicious verifier V' which is a hybrid computer, consisting of a quantum device available today and a classical machine.[3] Therefore, if V' participates in the protocol described above then V' could be gaining knowledge, i.e., a non-trivial factor of N, that it could not have been able to compute by itself; despite the protocol being quantum zero-knowledge!

This discrepancy appears because the definition of quantum zero-knowledge allows the simulator to be an arbitrary quantum polynomial-time algorithm, regardless of the computational power of the verifier. For instance, even if the malicious verifier is a classical polynomial-time algorithm, the simulator is still a quantum polynomial-time algorithm.

A more realistic definition should instead consider the resources used by the verifier and require the simulator to run under (roughly) the same constraints. There are many resources we can take into consideration when formulating this definition. In this work, we focus on the resource of quantum memory. More specifically, we focus on the number of qubits utilized by the simulator in relation to the number of qubits used by the verifier.

Constructions of QZK: Prior Work. We first observe that the existing works on post-quantum zero-knowledge propose simulators whose space complexity is a large polynomial overhead in the space complexity of the verifier. One main reason behind this is the fact that all the existing black-box simulation techniques [16–18,33,40,43] first purify the verifier;[4] that is, they convert the next message function of the verifier into a unitary[5] by delaying the measurements.

[3] Notice that none of currently available quantum devices (such as the implementations of low-depth Random Circuit Sampling devices [6], Boson sampling [47], etc.) have the capability to factor large numbers, even with classical post-processing. Moreover, we do not expect to implement Shor's algorithm at any time in the near future since full-scalable quantum computers is a daunting challenge in experimental physics and engineering.

[4] For this reason, we call such notion as purified black-box to distinguish it from other notions of black-box. See a discussion on Sect. 2.1.

[5] Technically, it is converted into a unitary followed by measurement, where the measurement outcome will be the message communicated to the prover.

The purification process increases the space complexity, proportional to the number of intermediate measurements. In fact, [46] shows that any black-box compiler that maps an arbitrary quantum circuit with intermediate measurements into an unitary followed by one layer of measurements leads to a polynomial overhead in space or exponential overhead in time.

Even if we ignore the above issue and consider verifiers where the next message functions are implemented as unitaries, the existing simulators still have large polynomial overheads in the space complexity of the verifier. In [43], the reason for this is the fact that the space complexity of the simulator depends on the communication complexity of the protocol which in turn is some function of the security parameter. In [16,17,33], the simulator runs the verifier coherently multiple times and thus, the space complexity additionally depends on the number of iterations.

Definitional Challenges. In order to conduct a systematic study of this subject, we first observe some challenges in defining the space complexity of the simulator. For instance, should we count the memory usage of the verifier towards the space complexity of the simulator? Furthermore, we also need to carefully define how the simulator has access to the verifier. For instance, if the verifier is purified and the simulator is given access to the purified verifier (along with its inverse) then, should we also count the additional qubits incurred as a result of purification? With these questions in mind, we propose new notions of post-quantum zero-knowledge.

1.1 Our Contributions

We propose a new definition of quantum zero-knowledge, where the amount of quantum memory used by the simulator is closely related to the quantum memory used by the verifier. We also investigate the feasibility of the new notion.

1. New Definition: Space-Bounded QZK. We formulate a new definition of post-quantum zero-knowledge, that we call (s, f)-*space-bounded* QZK, where $s \in \mathbb{N}$ and $f(\cdot)$ is some function. Suppose the malicious quantum polynomial-time (QPT) verifier is a quantum algorithm that uses at most s qubits of quantum memory. We require a polynomial-time simulator that uses at most $f(s)$ of qubits in the simulation. For example, if f is defined to be $f(x) = 2x$ then (s, f)-space bounded QZK states that the simulator should take up at most twice the number of qubits as the verifier. On the other hand, we don't place any restriction on the classical memory of the simulator. The amount of classical storage of the simulator could be an arbitrary polynomial in the amount of classical storage of the verifier. Since classical storage is much cheaper than quantum storage, we need to be more precise about modeling the latter.

We consider three different notions of (s, f)-space-bounded QZK:

- *Channel Black-Box*: In this notion, the simulator gets oracle access to the verifier. More precisely, the verifier is modeled as a sequence of channels (one per round) and the simulator can make polynomially many queries to each of these channels. The output of the channel consists of the (quantum and classical) memory of the verifier and its message to the prover. This notion of quantum zero-knowledge is a direct analogue of classical zero-knowledge. In terms of space complexity, the space undertaken by the simulator would also take into account the space needed to store the private state of the verifier in-between the executions of every two consecutive rounds.

In this work, we mainly focus on understanding the feasibility of (s, f)-space-bounded QZK for different $s(\cdot)$ functions.

- *Purified Black-Box*:[6] In this notion, the simulator gets oracle access to the purification of the verifier and its inverse. More precisely, suppose the verifier is represented as a sequence of channels and let $U_1, \dots, U_k$ be their *canonical* purifications[7]. Then, the simulator gets oracle access to U_i and also oracle access to $U_i^\dagger$, for every $i \in [k]$. Although, in this model, the verifier's code is modified before giving access to the simulator, we still call it black box in order to be consistent with most of the previous works on black box quantum zero-knowledge who adopt this model.

  Note that here, we model the quantum space complexity of the simulator as a function of the quantum space complexity of the original verifier (and not the one obtained after purification). A (canonically) purified verifier can take significantly more space than the underlying non-purified verifier. For example, purifying an s-qubit verifier with ℓ measurements will result in a unitary that consumes at least $s + \ell$ qubits. Thus, (s, f) space-bounded purified black-box QZK, for any polynomial $f(\cdot)$, is impossible to achieve. On the other hand, prior works [3,16,17,33,43] are (s, f)-space-bounded black box QZK for super-polynomial $f(s) = 2^{\omega(\log(s))}$[8].
- *Non Black Box*: Finally, one can consider non black box quantum zero knowledge, where the simulator is allowed to arbitrarily depend on the verifier and in particular, could make use of the code of the verifier. This definition resembles the counterpart definition of (classical) non-black box zero-knowledge. Prior works [9,10] satisfy (s, f)-space-bounded non black box QZK for super-polynomial $f(s) = 2^{\omega(\log(s))}$. We leave the investigation on the feasibility of (s, f)-space-bounded non black box QZK, when $f(\cdot)$ is a *polynomial*, as an interesting open problem.

We notice that our definition of channel black-box QZK is not an exact analog of classical black-box ZK: in the classical setting, we do not give the simulator access to the internal state of the verifier. Instead, the simulator only submits the transcript to the *stateless* verifier oracle, and the verifier using the transcript and the initial randomness, can recompute its internal state. This lets the simulator

[6] This notion was called simply "Black-box" in previous results.

[7] This means that the purification is computed in a specific manner: that is, by delaying the measurements of the channel.

[8] Notice that in these previous results, the number of qubits used by the simulator is polynomial but it might scale with the *time-complexity* of the verifier and that is why we can only achieve a super-polynomial upper-bound on the number of qubits.

execute any given round more than once. However, we argue that a quantum analog of this definition is not useful. Unlike the classical setting, the verification oracle must be stateful: due to the no-cloning theorem, we cannot expect the verifier to be able to create a second copy of its internal state given the transcript, and therefore its internal state must be stored. Then, if the simulator does not have access to the internal state of the verifier, the only admissible operations it can do is to query the verifier in a straightline manner. Such a simulator could be used to violate soundness, unless the language is in BQP. Thus, we believe that our definition of channel black-box QZK is closer to a quantum analog of classical black-box zero-knowledge.[9]

2. Space-Bounded QZK Against Logarithmic Space Verifiers. We first focus on a restricted case when the malicious QPT verifiers only have access to logarithmically many qubits. In this case, we demonstrate a feasibility result.

Suppose $s = O(\log(\lambda))$. We show that there exist, even constant-round, (s, f)-space-bounded quantum zero-knowledge protocols for NP, where $f(x) = 2x$, based on the assumption of post-quantum one-way functions. In fact, our protocol even achieves channel black-box quantum zero-knowledge.

3. Space-Bounded QZK Against Super-Logarithmic Space Verifiers. We then investigate the case when the malicious verifiers have access to super-logarithmically many qubits. In this case, we present a negative result.

Suppose $s = \omega(\log(\lambda))$. Assuming the existence of post-quantum one-way functions, we show that there do not exist channel black-box (s, f)-space-bounded quantum zero-knowledge protocols for languages outside BQP, for all polynomials f.

Our negative result only applies to channel black-box quantum zero-knowledge and it is an interesting open problem to either prove a negative result or circumvent our negative result using non black box techniques (Fig. 1).

Definitions	**Feasibility**	**Impossibility**
Channel BB	$s(\lambda) = O(\log(\lambda))$ $f(x) = 2x$ (Section 3)	$s(\lambda) = \omega(\log(\lambda))$ $f(x) = O(\mathsf{poly}(x))$ (Section 4)
Purified BB	$s(\lambda) = O(\mathsf{poly}(\lambda))$ $f(x) = \omega(\mathsf{poly}(x))$ [43,3,17,33]	$s(\lambda) = O(\mathsf{poly}(\lambda))$ $f(x) = O(\mathsf{poly}(x))$ (Section 2.3)
Non-BB	$s(\lambda) = O(\mathsf{poly}(\lambda)), f(x) = \omega(\mathsf{poly}(x))$ [10,9]	OPEN

Fig. 1. Feasibility and Impossibility of (s, f)-space-bounded QZK.

[9] As we discuss in Sect. 2.1, a direct analog of classical black-box is not possible in the quantum setting, and therefore we need to consider more relaxed models.

1.2 Technical Overview

In this section, we present an overview of the techniques employed in the results.

Zero-Knowledge Against Logarithmic Quantum Space Verifiers. Rewinding has been the quintessential technique employed in proving purified black-box simulation security of cryptographic protocols against probabilistic polynomial-time classical adversaries. A rewinding-based simulator has to store copies of the intermediate states of the verifier so that it can use these copies whenever it rewinds the execution of the verifier to an earlier round. However, adopting rewinding to prove post-quantum security has not been easy; this was first identified by [42]. At a high level, the reason for the difficulty arises since rewinding implicitly requires the ability to store copies of the intermediate states, which is not allowed in general by the no-cloning theorem [20,44]. Thus, most of the recent works on post-quantum zero-knowledge [3,15,17,18,33,41,43] have proposed various rewinding techniques to perform simulation without having the need to store intermediate copies of the verifier's state.

State Recovery. To rewind the verifier to an earlier round, the most commonly adopted strategy is to invert the operations performed by the verifier in the hope that we can completely recover the earlier states. There are two issues with it:

1. Firstly, this means that the verifier has to be a unitary and thus needs to be *purified*; that is, all the intermediate measurements of the verifier needs to be pushed to the end of each round. As a consequence of the purification process, the simulator could take much larger quantum space than the verifier.
2. Secondly, each round could disturb the verifier's intermediate state in an irreversible way. Thus, we might not be able to recover the earlier states.

All the recent works on black-box quantum zero-knowledge give up on the first issue (leading to what we call purified black-box in this work). Regarding the second issue, they provide a workaround by showing a simulator that still retains some useful properties about the original intermediate state, even if the recovered state is quite different from the original intermediate state. For example, the probability that the verifier does not abort on the recovered state could be at least as much as the probability that the verifier does not abort on the original intermediate state. We will not go into the details of how state recovery is performed in each of the recent works [16–18,33,43] since it is not relevant to our approach.

An Observation. Consider an M-qubit quantum state ρ, where $M = O(\log(\lambda))$. Our observation is that a maximally mixed state $\frac{I}{2^M}$ is a good approximation of ρ. That is, suppose there exists a binary positive operator valued measure (POVM) Λ such that $p = \mathrm{Tr}(\Lambda(\rho))$ then it holds that $\mathrm{Tr}(\Lambda(\frac{I}{2^M})) \geq \frac{p}{2^M}$. This suggests a new approach to perform rewinding: to rewind the verifier to an earlier round, say i, simply execute the ith round of the verifier on input $\frac{I}{2^M}$.

The advantage of this approach is two-fold. Firstly, there is no need to purify the verifier! Secondly, we only need M additional qubits of quantum storage to initialize the maximally mixed state.

Case Study: Four Messages Protocol due to Goldreich-Kahan [24]. Let us try to use this idea to prove post-quantum security of a zero-knowledge protocol. We will start with the four-round protocol due to Goldreich and Kahan [24]. Denote the four rounds in the protocol to be $(\alpha, \beta, \gamma, \delta)$.

Simulating Classical Verifiers: We first recall the strategy to simulate classical adversaries. The classical simulator, running in expected polynomial time, receives as input α, which is nothing but the commitment of verifier's challenges. Let the verifier's state at this point be st.

- *First Step. Execution of Main Thread*: The simulator then sends β, which is nothing but the commitment of 0. There are two things that can happen. Either the verifier aborts, in which case, even the simulator aborts. Or it could happen that the verifier does not abort. In this case, the simulator moves on to the second step.
- *Second Step. Execution of Lookahead Threads*: At this point, the simulator has the opening of α, denoted by γ. The simulator then rewinds the verifier to st, i.e., the state where it just sent α. It uses the information from the opening γ, to compute the commitment β^*. It sends β^* to the verifier. If the verifier sends γ^* then the simulator completes the transcript $(\alpha, \beta^*, \gamma^*, \delta^*)$, and additionally outputs the verifier's final state. If the verifier aborts then the simulator keeps repeating the rewinding process until it wins.

The important thing to remember is that the simulator first runs the main thread to decide whether to continue or not. If it continues, it outputs one of the lookahead threads that did not abort.

Simulating Quantum Verifiers: Suppose we need to simulate quantum verifiers. We extend the above approach to the quantum setting as follows. The quantum simulator receives as input α, which is nothing but the commitment of verifier's challenges. Let the verifier's state at this point be (ρ, st), where ρ is a M-qubit quantum state and st is a classical string.

- The first step is the same as above. The simulator executes the verifier on input the state (ρ, st). Let the resulting state of the verifier be (σ, st').
- If the verifier has not aborted at this point, it moves to the second step. At this point, if the simulator has to rewind, it no longer has a copy of ρ since it was computed upon in the first round. Thus, the simulator uses the maximally mixed state $\frac{I}{2^M}$ in place of ρ whenever it rewinds.

As per our observation earlier, $\frac{I}{2^M}$ serves as a good approximation of ρ. In particular, if p is the probability that the verifier on input ρ outputs a valid third message then the verifier on input $\frac{I}{2^M}$ outputs a valid third message with probability at least $\frac{p}{2^M}$. It can be argued that, as long as M is logarithmic, the simulator in expected polynomial time can recover a valid transcript $(\alpha, \beta^*, \gamma^*, \delta^*)$

from one of the lookahead threads just like the classical simulator. However, this is not sufficient. The quantum simulator should not also output the residual state of the verifier along with the transcript $(\alpha, \beta^*, \gamma^*, \delta^*)$. But note that the residual state of the verifier obtained in the lookahead thread is useless: it is the state obtained by replacing the intermediate state ρ with a maximally mixed state. One option is to output (σ, st'), which is the state obtained in the main thread, along with $(\alpha, \beta^*, \gamma^*, \delta^*)$. However, the state (σ, st') is obtained in the main thread and hence, is inconsistent with the lookahead thread transcript $(\alpha, \beta^*, \gamma^*, \delta^*)$. Thus, we need a different approach where we can simulate in such a way that the joint distribution of the transcript and the verifier's state is computationally indistinguishable from the real world.

Protocol Template. We propose a different protocol and prove their post-quantum security using our key observation. As a starting point, we consider a commitment scheme. For the current discussion, we will consider commitments that are non-interactive and satisfy perfect binding and computationally hiding property. In the technical sections, we relax the requirement to allow the commitment to be interactive and moreover, we only require statistical binding.

We present a simplified version of the protocol template first. Let $\mathcal{L}$ be the NP language associated with the protocol. We denote the prover to be P and the verifier to be V. The prover receives as input instance-witness pair (x, w) and the verifier receives as input x.

1. V sends two commitments of random bits α_0 and α_1.
2. P sends a bit b.
3. V sends the opening of commitment of α_b.
4. P uses a witness-indistinguishable protocol to prove to V that either $x \in \mathcal{L}$ or it knows $\alpha_0 \oplus \alpha_1$.

The above protocol is sound since a malicious prover can only receive one of the two decommitments and thus, will not know $\alpha_0 \oplus \alpha_1$ in order to complete the WI phase. To prove that the above template satisfies post-quantum zero-knowledge, we first need to demonstrate a simulator.

- The simulator receives as input commitments of α_0 and α_1 from the malicious verifier. Let (ρ, st) be the state of the verifier at this point, where ρ is the M-qubit state and st is the classical state.
- *First Step. Execution of Main Thread*: The simulator sends a random bit b. It receives an opening of the commitment of α_b from the verifier. Let the state of the verifier at this point to be (σ, st').
- *Second Step. Execution of Lookahead Threads*: The simulator then rewinds the verifier to just after the first round. This means that the simulator restarts the verifier on the state $\left(\frac{I}{2^M}, \mathsf{st}\right)$. The simulators sends a random bit b' to the verifier and it hopes that $b' \neq b$ and the verifier does not abort. The simulator keeps repeating this process until it succeeds.

Once the simulator succeeds, it has both α_0, α_1. It discards all the lookahead transcripts and only retains the main thread transcript. Continue the execution of the protocol with the verifier, where the state of the verifier is (σ, st'). The simulator then convinces the verifier in the WI phase using $\alpha_0 \oplus \alpha_1$.

Note that unlike Goldreich-Kahan, the simulator retains the main thread transcript along with the verifier's residual state, just after the rewinding process, whose joint distribution is computationally indistinguishable from the real world.

While the main approach is sound, implementing the above approach encounters some issues. We mention the issues and how we fix them. The first issue is that it could happen that the verifier doesn't abort with non-negligible probability and also, that the simulator never succeeds when the verifier does not abort. Indeed, the verifier could decide that it will not abort if and only if the bit b sent by the prover is 0. In this case, the simulator will never be able to recover two valid transcripts if the verifier does not abort. We fix this by increasing the challenge space. Instead of requiring the verifier to send two commitments, it sends 2λ commitments of messages $((\alpha_{1,0}, \alpha_{1,1}), \ldots, (\alpha_{\lambda,0}, \alpha_{\lambda,1}))$ and in the third message, it opens commitments of messages $(\alpha_{1,b_1}, \ldots, \alpha_{\lambda,b_\lambda})$, where $b_1, \ldots, b_\lambda$ are the challenge bits sent by the prover in the second message. If the verifier does not abort with non-negligible probability then there exists an index i such that the verifier opens to each value $\alpha_{i,0}, \alpha_{i,1}$ with non-negligible probability. The second issue is on non-malleability. The prover could launch a malleability attack by leveraging the commitments sent by the verifier in the first message to cheat the verifier in the WI phase. A first attempt is to make the prover commit to the witness to be used in the WI phase. But even this is susceptible to the malleability attack. We use a technique explored in a recent work [5], where the prover commits to some randomness $\mathbf{r}^*$ at the very beginning even before it sees any message from the verifier. At a later point in time, when the prover commits to the witness, it is expected to use this randomness $\mathbf{r}^*$. This prevents the mauling attack since if the prover computed its own commitment by mauling the commitment by the verifier, it would not have the knowledge of the randomness contained in its commitment. Once we incorporate these fixes, we have a complete description of our protocol and we can prove its space-bounded (Channel Black-box) ZK.

We also notice that in this simple example, since the memory is bounded to logarithmic, all simulation could be classical. However, in a more general case, we need quantum simulators to handle non-uniform quantum advice.

Zero-Knowledge Against Super-Logarithmic Quantum Space Verifiers. In the previous result, we restricted our attention to zero-knowledge against logarithmic quantum space verifiers. We now justify the restriction on the quantum space of the verifiers by showing the following: assuming post-quantum one-way functions, there exist protocols that are space-bounded channel black-box QZK against super-logarithmic quantum space verifiers only for languages in BQP.

This is shown by first proving that any channel black-box QZK protocol against super-logarithmic quantum space verifiers should have a straight-line simulator. We design verifier V' that is composed of channels $\Phi_1, \ldots, \Phi_k$, where

k is the number of rounds in the protocol and Φ_i is used to compute the ith round query and suppose $M = \omega(\log(\lambda))$. We argue that any simulator simulating this verifier should be of a specific form: it should first make a successful query to Φ_1, then make a successful query to Φ_2 and so on. For any i, a query made by the simulator to Φ_i is deemed successful[10] if Φ_i does not abort on that query. Note that a straightline simulator could make many unsuccessful queries to any Φ_j (i.e., queries leading to abort answers) in between two successful queries.

Once we prove that the simulator is straightline, we then show that the language $\mathcal{L}$ associated with the protocol has to be in BQP. This step is relatively more standard and follows similar ideas employed in prior works [27]. We use the straightline simulator to come up with a malicious prover $\widetilde{P}$ who is able to convince the verifier to accept an instance in $\mathcal{L}$ with probability close to 1; for now, assume that the protocol satisfies perfect completeness. At the same time, when given a NO instance, due to the soundness property, $\widetilde{P}$ can convince the verifier to accept only with negligible probability. Thus, using $\widetilde{P}$ and the honest verifier, we can construct a quantum polynomial time algorithm that decides $\mathcal{L}$.

Forcing Simulator to be Straightline. All that is left is to show that the simulator has to be straightline with respect to the contrived verifier V' that we will design below. Since the simulator has complete control over the intermediate states of the verifier in-between different rounds of the protocol, it seems challenging to prevent the simulator from making multiple successful queries to the same channel Φ_i, for some i, where $(\Phi_1, \ldots, \Phi_k)$ are as defined above. We leverage the principles of quantum information to our advantage. Specifically, we use *subspace states* [1], as intermediate private states of the verifier. Subspace states are known to be unclonable and have been instrumental in constructing public-key quantum money [1,45].

In more detail, V' is composed of the channels $(\Phi_1, \ldots, \Phi_n)$, where Φ_i is defined as:

- It takes as input a state ρ_i and the ith round message from the prover.
- It checks if ρ_i is indeed the state $|S_{i-1}\rangle\langle S_{i-1}|$, where S_{i-1} is a random $\frac{M}{2}$-dimensional subspace of $\mathbb{Z}_2^M$ and $|S_{i-1}\rangle = \sum_{x \in S_{i-1}} \sqrt{2^{-|S_{i-1}|}}|x\rangle$. The description of the subspace S_{i-1} is hardwired in Φ_i.
- If the check fails, Φ_i aborts.
- Otherwise, V' computes the next message using the honest verifier and outputs this message along with another subspace state $|S_i\rangle$, where S_i is a random $\frac{M}{2}$-dimensional subspace of $\mathbb{Z}_2^M$. The description of S_i is hardwired in Φ_i (and Φ_{i+1}).

Let us look at the different possible queries a simulator can submit to $(\Phi_1, \ldots, \Phi_k)$.

Out-of-Order Queries: If the simulator tries to query V' out-of-order, for example, submit a query to Φ_{i+1} before querying Φ_i, it would not have the valid subspace state $|S_i\rangle$ and thus, Φ_{i+1} will most likely abort.

10 In the technical sections, we call such queries non-abort queries (Definition 12).

Repeated Queries: If the simulator queries the same Φ_i twice then we claim that there can only be at most one query that passes the subspace state test. If the simulator makes two successful queries to Φ_i then we argue that it must have two copies of $|S_{i-1}\rangle$, thus violating the unclonability property of subspace states. We first argue this for $i = 1$: this follows from the fact that the simulator has only one copy of $|S_0\rangle$. Assuming that at most only successful query can made to all Φ_j, for $j < i$, we can then invoke the unclonability of $|S_{i-1}\rangle$ to argue that there can be at most one successful query to Φ_i.

One has to be careful when violating the unclonability property: the simulator can make many unsuccessful queries before making the two successful queries to Φ_i. The reduction that violates the hardness of subspace states needs to be able to discern whether the adversary has submitted a successful query or not. Moreover, the reduction only receives as input a single copy of $|S_{i-1}\rangle$ and in particular, does not receive as input a description of S_{i-1}. Thus, the reduction does not have the capability to distinguish successful versus unsuccessful queries. We overcome this issue by giving the reduction access to an oracle that tests if a given state is $|S_{i-1}\rangle$. It was shown by [1] that as long as the subspace has super-logarithmic dimension, unclonability still holds even if the reduction gets access to the membership oracle.

Missing Queries: There might exist some i such that the simulator never submits a successful query to Φ_i. By using similar arguments as in the previous cases, we can then argue that it cannot submit a successful query to the last round, i.e., Φ_k. From this, we can come up with a distinguisher that can distinguish the real world and the ideal world.

From the above cases, we can argue that a successful simulator can only submit successful queries *in-order* and moreover, can only submit exactly one successful query for Φ_i, for every $i \in [k]$.

However, there are a couple of issues we need to take into consideration while designing the straightline simulator to ensure that $\tilde{P}$ is successful. Firstly, we need to modify V' so that it encrypts its internal state with a symmetric-key encryption scheme, whose secret key is also hardcoded in all Φ_i. Otherwise, the straightline simulator would expect the internal state in the clear and $\tilde{P}$ would be unable to provide this information to the simulator. Secondly, we need that the internal state chosen by the simulator on query Φ_i to be exactly the same as the internal state after the query to Φ_{i-1}. To solve this issue, V' uses a digital signature scheme to sign its classical internal state. This forces the simulator to use the internal state chosen by the simulator on query Φ_i to be the internal state after the query to Φ_{i-1}, otherwise we could violate the unforgeability of the digital signature scheme.

1.3 Related Work

Knowledge Tightness and Precise Zero-Knowledge. Analogous questions have been explored in the classical literature. However, the main focus has been on designing zero-knowledge simulators whose runtime is closely related to the runtime of the verifiers.

Goldreich, Micali and Widgerson [25] (also, [23]) explore the notion of knowledge tightness which is the ratio of the running time of the simulator and the running time of the verifier. Some existing protocols [11,26,28] already achieve constant knowledge tightness. Along the lines of knowledge tightness, Pass and Micali [34] formalized a notion called precise zero-knowledge where the simulator's runtime is closely related to the runtime of the verifier. Many followup works [19,22,36] study precise zero-knowledge in different settings.

Of relevance is the work by Ning and Du [21] who consider a stronger notion of precise zero-knowledge, where the simulator's space complexity also needs to be closely related to the space complexity of the verifier. However, they study this notion only in the context of zero-knowledge against classical verifiers.

Space-Bounded Verifiers. Another related model considers proof systems where the verifier, even the honest one, has bounded space. Some works [7,37] have proposed feasibility results in this model. We remind the reader that in our proof system, we don't limit the amount of classical space a malicious QPT verifier can have.

Post-Quantum Zero-Knowledge. Watrous [43] presented the first construction of zero-knowledge for NP against quantum verifiers. In the past few years, we have seen remarkable progress in understanding the feasibility of QZK. Bitansky and Shmueli [10] presented the first construction of quantum zero-knowledge in constant rounds. They prove that their construction satisfies QZK in the non-black box simulation setting. In fact, it was shown by Chia, Chung, Liu and Yamakawa [16] that constant round black box quantum zero-knowledge is impossible. This negative result was circumvented by a recent work by Lombardi, Ma and Spooner [33] who achieved purified black-box constant round QZK in the coherent simulation setting. Relaxations of QZK systems have been considered in some recent works [5,17]. Post-quantum zero-knowledge under composition have been studied [2,3,32]. Finally, zero-knowledge for quantum complexity classes such as QMA have also been studied [12,13].

1.4 Future Directions

Non-Black-Box Quantum Space-Bounded Simulation with Superlogarithmic Qubits. Our result in Sect. 4 shows that channel black-box $(\omega(\log\lambda),\cdot)$-space-bounded quantum zero-knowledge is impossible, and as we discussed in Sect. 2.3, purified black-box $(\cdot,p)$-space bounded quantum zero-knowledge is impossible for any polynomial p. We leave as an open problem to explore the feasibility of non-black black-box quantum $(\omega(\log\lambda),p)$-space-bounded simulation for some polynomial p.

New Definitions of "NISQ"-Safe Zero-Knowledge Protocols. In this work, we initiated the study of classical zero-knowledge protocols, whose security is still guaranteed against *weaker* quantum adversaries.[11] We focus here on the num-

[11] As we discussed, since the adversaries are weaker, we can morally break the zero-knowledge property that have much more power than the verifier.

ber of qubits allowed in the simulation and we leave as an open question the proposal of other meaningful definitions such as verifiers/simulators that use a fixed non-universal gateset, a fixed architecture, or verifiers in the recently NISQ complexity class defined recently in [14].

Space-Bounded/channel black-box Simulation. Another interesting direction is to explore the new notions of simulation that we introduce in this work in other cryptographic protocols. Specifically, we could explore the feasibility of channel black-box simulation and space-bounded simulation in both classical protocols and also protocols that use quantum resources such as quantum OT and quantum MPC protocols [2,8,29,30].

1.5 Organization

We discuss the different notions of black-box zero-knowledge and define space-bounded zero-knowledge in Sect. 2.3. We prove our positive result in Sect. 3 and our negative result in Sect. 4.

We assume basic knowledge in quantum computation and cryptographic primitives.

2 Space-Bounded Quantum Zero-Knowledge: Definitions

We present the definition of quantum zero knowledge with space bounded simulation. First, we will revisit the definition of zero-knowledge in Sect. 2.1. Towards defining space-bounded simulation, we present the computational model in Sect. 2.2. This model will explicitly capture the interaction between the classical memory and the quantum memory. We then define space-bounded quantum zero-knowledge in Sect. 2.3.

2.1 Defining Quantum Zero-Knowledge

We discuss the different types of quantum zero-knowledge below. We first start with the notion of quantum zero-knowledge, referred to as *black-box* quantum zero-knowledge, considered in the literature.

Quantum Analog of Classical Black-Box ZK. Classically, we say that a zero-knowledge protocol is black-box if the simulator has only black-box access to the verifier functionalities. More concretely, we model the verifier with the following functions $(m_i, v_i) \leftarrow V_i(p_i, v_{i-i})$, where p_i is the i-th message sent by the prover,[12] m_i is the verifier's ith message and v_{i-1} is the verifier's internal state before receiving the ith message (and in particular v_0 is the verifier's side-information). The simulator interacts with the verifier as follows:

[12] We assume here that the prover sends the first message without loss of generality.

1. The simulator chooses i and p_i.
2. If $v_{i-1} = \perp$, answer $\perp$ to the simulator
3. If $v_{i-1} \neq \perp$, compute $(m_i, v_i) \leftarrow V_i(p_i, v_{i-i})$, store v_i, set $v_j = \perp$ for all $j \neq i$, and answer m_i to the simulator

If we try to define a quantum analog of such definition, in which v_i would be replaced by a quantum state ρ_i, we would face the following problem: when we query i and the state $\rho_{i-1} \neq \perp$, this copy of the state is consumed in the computation $V_i(p_i, \rho_{i-1})$, and in this case, it does not make sense for the simulator to query on i again since there is no ρ_{i-1} left. So in order to have a feasible quantum analog of the classical definition, we would have to do as follows:

1. The simulator chooses i and p_i.
2. If $\rho_{i-1} = \perp$ answer $\perp$ to the simulator
3. If $\rho_{i-1} \neq \perp$, compute $(m_i, \rho_i) \leftarrow V_i(p_i, \rho_{i-i})$, store ρ_i, set $\rho_j = \perp$ for all $j > i$ and answer m_i to the simulator

In this case, the queries with non-$\perp$ answers consists of a sequence of calls $V_1, ..., V_k$. Notice that in this case, the prover could use this simulator a provide an accepting transcript to the verifier by running the simulator and replace these queries by messages sent to the verifier. We can show that in this case the problem is in BQP, which trivializes the protocol.

Therefore, in order to consider "black-box-ish" reductions, we have to relax the model. In previous results, the simulator is given access to the purified unitary that implements the verifier and its inverse. In our work, we call this model as purified black-box. As we discuss shortly, this model is not ideal for space-bounded simulations, and therefore we define a new model, that we call channel black-box, where we give access to the channel that computes the verifier's operations, and we are also given access to the verifier's internal state. We discuss now both of these models.

Purified Black-Box QZK. Consider the following two definitions.

Definition 1 (Canonical purification). *Let V be a quantum channel that is implemented with quantum gates, intermediate measurements and trace-out operations. We denote the canonical purification of V as $\mathscr{P}(V)$, which consists of the unitary circuit that performs all the measurements coherently and replaces all the trace-out operations with identity gates.*

Any circuit can be expressed as its purification followed by measurements and trace out operations.

Definition 2. *Let V be a party in a k-round interactive protocol. We define $\mathscr{C}(V) = (\Phi_1, ..., \Phi_k)$, where $\Phi_i : \mathcal{M}_i \times \mathcal{V}_i \rightarrow \mathcal{M}_{i+1} \times \mathcal{V}_{i+1}$ is the quantum channel corresponding to the computation performed by V on the ith round of the protocol, and where $\mathcal{V}_i$ is the Hilbert space corresponding to the memory of V on round i and $\mathcal{M}_i$ is the Hilbert space corresponding to message sent in round i.*

We let $\mathscr{P}(V) = (\mathscr{P}(\Phi_1), \ldots, \mathscr{P}(\Phi_k))$ and $\mathscr{P}(V)^\dagger = (\mathscr{P}(\Phi_1)^\dagger, \ldots, \mathscr{P}(\Phi_k)^\dagger)$, where $\mathscr{C}(V) = (\Phi_1, \ldots, \Phi_k)$ and $\mathscr{P}$ is as defined in Definition 1.

Most of the recent works [3,15–17,33,43] consider the following definition of quantum zero-knowledge.

Definition 3 (Purified Black-Box Quantum Zero-Knowledge). *A proof (resp., argument) system (P, V) for an NP relation $\mathcal{R}$ is purified black-box quantum zero-knowledge if there exists a QPT simulator* Sim *such that for every QPT verifier V^*, for every $(x, w) \in \mathcal{R}$, for every* $\text{poly}(|x|)$*-qubit state ρ,*

$$\mathsf{View}_{V^*}\left(\langle P(x,w), V^*(x,\rho)\rangle\right) \approx_{\mathcal{Q},\varepsilon(|x|)} \mathsf{Sim}^{\mathscr{P}(V^*),\mathscr{P}(V^*)^{\dagger}}(x,\rho),$$

where Sim *having oracle access to $\mathscr{P}(V^*)$ and $\mathscr{P}(V)^{\dagger}$ is denoted by* $\mathsf{Sim}^{\mathscr{P}(V^*),\mathscr{P}(V^*)^{\dagger}}$*, $\mathscr{P}(\cdot)$ is as defined in Definitions 1 and 2 and* $\varepsilon(|x|) = \mathsf{negl}(|x|)$.

We stress that this notion is usually called "black box QZK" in the literature, but we find more apropriate to call it "purified black-box" in our context.

Channel Black-Box QZK. We consider a new definition that resembles the black-box definition in the classical setting. We call this definition channel black-box QZK. Here, the simulator in the channel black-box QZK only gets oracle access to the verifier circuit, and not the purified version as considered in Definition 3.

We now present our definition of channel black-box zero-knowledge.

Definition 4 (Channel Black-Box Quantum Zero-Knowledge). *A proof (resp., argument) system (P, V) for an NP relation $\mathcal{R}$ is channel black-box quantum zero-knowledge if there exists a QPT simulator* Sim *such that for every QPT malicious verifier V^*, for every $(x, w) \in \mathcal{R}$, for every state ρ,*

$$\mathsf{View}_{V^*}\left(\langle P(x,w), V^*(x,\rho)\rangle\right) \approx_{\mathcal{Q},\varepsilon(|x|)} \mathsf{Sim}^{\mathscr{C}(V^*)}(x,\rho),$$

where Sim *having oracle access to $\mathscr{C}(V^*)$ is denoted by* $\mathsf{Sim}^{\mathscr{C}(V^*)}$*, $\mathscr{C}(\cdot)$ is as defined in Definition 2 and $\varepsilon(|x|)$ is negligible in $|x|$.*

Non Black-Box QZK. We can also define the most general definition of QZK where the simulator can depend arbitrary on the code of the verifier. We call this non black box QZK. This definition was considered in a few recent works [5,9,10].

Definition 5 (Non Black-Box Quantum Zero-Knowledge). *A proof (resp., argument) system (P, V) for an NP relation $\mathcal{R}$ is non black-box quantum zero-knowledge if for every QPT verifier V^*, there exists a QPT simulator* Sim*, for every $(x, w) \in \mathcal{R}$, for every* $\text{poly}(|x|)$*-qubit state ρ,*

$$\mathsf{View}_{V^*}\left(\langle P(x,w), V^*(x,\rho)\rangle\right) \approx_{\mathcal{Q},\varepsilon(|x|)} \mathsf{Sim}(x,\rho),$$

where $\varepsilon(|x|)$ is negligible in $|x|$.

2.2 Computational Model

Towards defining space-bounded simulation, we define the model of quantum computation albeit using a different terminology. The new terminology is necessary to carefully model the interaction between the classical memory and the quantum memory since we are explicitly measuring the amount of quantum memory required for any computation.

First, we start with a weaker computational model. The following definition considers quantum circuits that take as input a unitary and a state and output the computation of the unitary on the state.

Definition 6 (M-qubit programmable quantum computer). *We say that Q is an M-qubit programmable quantum computer, if Q receives as an input an M-qubit quantum state $|\psi\rangle$, the (classical) description of an M-qubit unitary U and it outputs the state $U|\psi\rangle$. We depict such a quantum device in Fig. 2.*

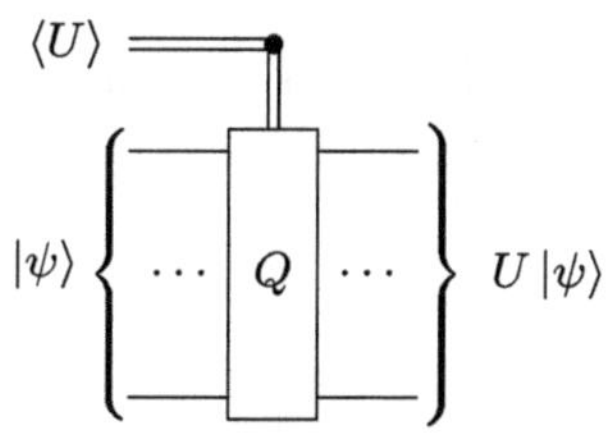

Fig. 2. M-qubit programmable quantum computer

We now generalize the above model in the following way. After the computation of the unitary, we allow for some classical preprocessing. This is enabled by measuring a subset of the qubits of the state obtained after the unitary computation and the resulting measurement outcomes can be used to choose the function to be applied on the classical memory.

This entire computation is considered to be a block of computation. Later, we will consider the most general model where the computation is defined to a sequence of blocks.

Definition 7 (M-qubit of unitary quantum computation with classical post-processing). *An M-qubit of unitary quantum computation with classical post-processing is defined by a tuple $(c, \langle U\rangle, \ell, |\psi\rangle, f)$, where $c \in \{0,1\}^L$ is a classical register, $\langle U\rangle$ is the description of an M-qubit unitary, $\ell \in [M+1]$ is the number of qubits that will be measured, $|\psi\rangle$ is the input state of the quantum computation and f is a classical function used for post-processing.*

The computation proceeds as follows:

1. *Using an M-qubit programmable quantum computer Q, we run the unitary U on the state $|\psi\rangle$,*

2. *We measure the first ℓ qubits of the output, having outcome o and the state on the last $M - \ell$ qubits is $|\phi_o\rangle$,*
3. *We apply a classical function f on $(c, \langle U\rangle, \ell, o)$, resulting in $(c', \langle U'\rangle, \ell')$,*
4. *The first ℓ qubits are reset to $|0\rangle$,*
5. *The output of the computation is $(c', \langle U'\rangle, \ell', |\psi'\rangle)$, where $|\psi'\rangle = |0^\ell\rangle|\phi_o\rangle$.*

We depict such a computation in Fig. 3.

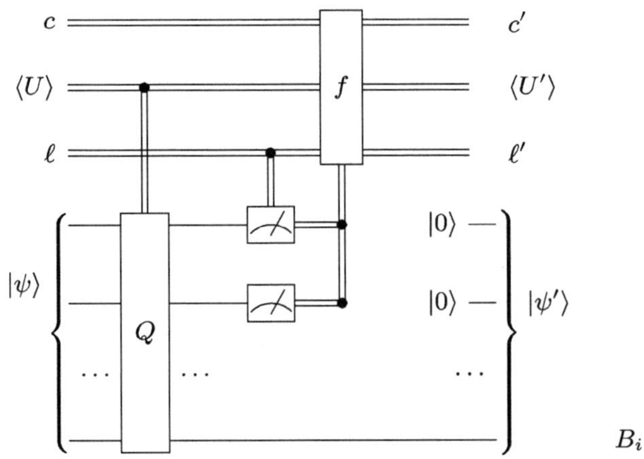

Fig. 3. M-qubit of unitary quantum computation with classical post-processing.

Our Model. We are now ready to define the model that we consider in this work. The model below comprises of a sequence of blocks of computation, where each block is an M-qubit of unitary computation with classical post-processing.

Definition 8 (M-qubit quantum channel). *An M-qubit of quantum computation with classical post-processing is defined by a tuple $(c_0, \langle U_0\rangle, \ell_0, |\psi_0\rangle, f)$, where $c \in \{0,1\}^L$ is a classical register, $\langle U_0\rangle$ is the description of an M-qubit unitary, $\ell_0 \in [M+1]$ is the number of qubits that will be measured, $|\psi_0\rangle$ is the input state of the quantum computation and for f is a classical function used for post-processing.*

The computation proceeds as follows: We run an M-qubit of unitary quantum computation with classical post-processing (Definition 7) defined by $(c_i, \langle U_i\rangle, \ell_i, |\psi_i\rangle, f)$ and we let the output of the computation be $(c_{i+1}, \langle U_{i+1}\rangle, \ell_{i+1}, |\psi_{i+1}\rangle)$. If $\langle U_{i+1}\rangle = \perp$, this process stops and output c', ℓ' and $|\psi'\rangle$.

We depict such a computation in Fig. 4.

We consider M-qubit channels that are efficiently implementable.

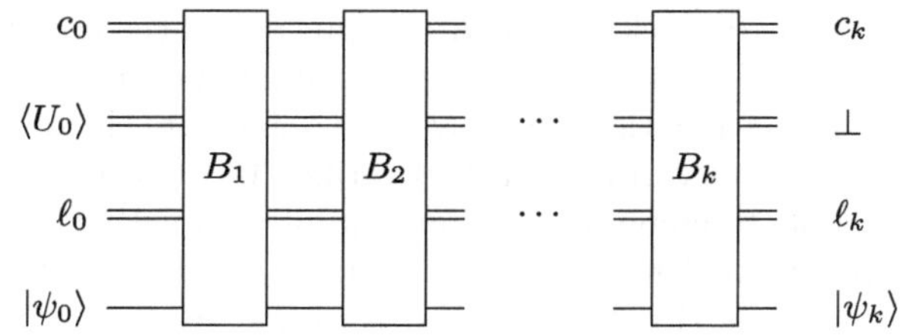

Fig. 4. M-qubit quantum computation with classical post-processing. Each block B_i corresponds to the circuit in Fig. 3 with the corresponding choices of input and classical post-processing f_i.

Definition 9 (M-qubit Quantum Polynomial Time Algorithm). *A (non-uniform) quantum polynomial algorithm C is said to be an M-qubit (resp. non-uniform) strict quantum polynomial-time algorithm if it is an M-qubit quantum channel and there is a polynomial p such that each of the blocks runs in time at most $p(|x|)$ and after $p(|x|)$ rounds, the procedure stops (i.e., there exists some $k \leq p(|x|)$ such that $\langle U_k \rangle = \perp$).*

A (non-uniform) quantum polynomial algorithm C is said to be an M-qubit (resp. non-uniform) expected quantum polynomial-time algorithm if it is an M-qubit quantum channel and there is a polynomial p such that each of the blocks runs in time at most $p(|x|)$ and the expected number of rounds of the procedure is $p(|x|)$ (i.e., $\mathbb{E}[k \mid \langle U_k \rangle = \perp] \leq p(|x|)$, where the expectation is over the measurement outcomes of the procedure).

Oracle Access. In order to discuss space-bounded black-box zero-knowledge, we need to define how the to give oracle access to an M-qubit quantum channel and how the memory of the overall channel is counted.

If an M_A-qubit quantum channel A has oracle access to an M_B-qubit quantum channel B, for $M_A \geq M_B$, then A prepares a classical register $\mathbf{B_C}$ and M_B-qubit quantum register $\mathbf{B_Q}$, and then runs the channel B on input registers $\mathbf{B_C}$ and B_Q. A then has access to the output of B, consisting again of a classical register and an M_B-qubit quantum register.

2.3 Space-Bounded Quantum Zero-Knowledge

Equipped with the computational model described in Sect. 2.2, we state the definition of space-bounded quantum zero-knowledge. Roughly speaking, the definition states that the number of qubits consumed by the simulator should be a fixed polynomial in the number of qubits consumed by the verifier.

Definition 10 ((s,p)-space-bounded QZK). *Let $\mathcal{X} \in$ {channel black-box, purified black box, non black box}. An $\mathcal{X}$ QZK proof (resp., argument) system (P, V) for a language $\mathcal{L}$ is said to be (s, f)-space-bounded $\mathcal{X}$ QZK proof (resp., argument) system if the following property is satisfied: Suppose V^* is an ℓ_{V^*}-qubit QPT (Definition 9), where $\ell_{V^*} = s(|x|)$. Then, Sim is an ℓ_{Sim}-qubit QPT, where $\ell_{\mathsf{Sim}} \leq f(s(|x|))$.*

In the case of purified black box QZK (Definition 3), the amount of quantum memory utilized by Sim is compared against the amount of quantum memory utilized by V^* before its purification. Moreover, by definition, the quantum memory of Sim contains the memory of the purified verifier V^*. For any polynomial $f(\cdot)$, for any s, it is possible to come up with an s-qubit channel[13] (Definition 8) such that purifying this channel would require strictly more than $f(s)$ qubits. This means that any black box simulator against a verifier represented as this s-qubit channel would utilize more than $f(s)$ qubits. Hence, (s, f)-space bounded black box QZK, for any polynomial f, is impossible to achieve. On the other hand, for superpolynomial $f(\cdot)$, existing works demonstrate that (s, f)-space bounded QZK exists.

From the above discussion, it follows that the meaningful notions of space-bounded QZK to consider are channel black-box QZK and non-black box QZK.

Remark 1. Towards circumventing the negative result of (s,p)-purified black-box QZK, one might wonder whether we can modify the definition of purified black box QZK in such a way that the purification is not necessarily canonical. Unfortunately, one can still come up with counterexamples where, irrespective of the purification algorithm, the negative result still holds. To see why consider the following example: suppose there is a channel that solves many instances of factoring sequentially and stores the outputs in some classical memory. In more detail, a k-qubit channel could be solving N instances of factoring, where $N \gg k$. Any canonical purification of this channel would need significantly large amount of memory, as large as N. Suppose there is a unitary that is still able to solve these N instances with small amount of memory, say $n \ll N$, then one can come up with a classical algorithm that breaks all N instantiations of factoring with probability inverse exponential in n. This approach can be formalized into a negative result by leveraging the notion of direct product one-way functions by [31], who demonstrate that any adversary can only break N instantiations of these functions with probability close to inverse exponential in N.

3 Zero-Knowledge Against Logarithmic Quantum Space Verifiers

We present the construction of an argument system Π for the NP relation $R(\mathcal{L})$ which is space-bounded channel black-box zero-knowledge against $O(\log(\lambda))$-qubit quantum channels (Definition 8).

[13] For example, consider an s-qubit channel contains $f(s)$ bits of classical memory. After canonical purification, the overall amount of quantum memory would be more than $f(s)$ qubits. Note that we don't rule out other types of purification which critically use the structure of the s-qubit channel to not increase the quantum memory significantly. However, this is not in the spirit of black box QZK and we consider such variants to be closer to non-black box QZK.

We use the following tools in our construction.

- Statistically-binding and quantum-concealing commitment protocol, denoted by $(\mathsf{Comm}, \mathsf{Receiver}, \mathsf{Open})$.
- Four round quantum witness-indistinguishable proof system Π_{wi}. The relation associated with Π_{wi}, denoted by $\mathcal{R}(\mathcal{L}_{\mathsf{wi}})$, is defined as follows:

$$\mathcal{R}(\mathcal{L}_{\mathsf{wi}}) = \Bigg\{ \Big(\Big(x, \mathbf{c}^*, \mathbf{c}^{**}, \{\alpha_{i,b}\}_{i\in[\lambda],b\in\{0,1\}} \Big) ; (w, \mathbf{r}^*, r, i^*) \Big) : (x, w) \in \mathcal{R}(\mathcal{L}) \text{ or}$$

$$\mathsf{Open}(\mathbf{c}^*) = (\mathbf{r}^*, r) \text{ and } \mathsf{Open}(\mathbf{c}^{**}) = ((i^*, \alpha_{i^*,0} \oplus \alpha_{i^*,1}), \mathbf{r}^*) \Bigg\}$$

We present the construction of Π in Fig. 5. The completeness of Π follows from the completeness of Π_{wi}, and we prove now its soundness.

Proposition 1. *The protocol Π in Fig. 5 satisfies soundness.*

Proof. Let P^* be a (non-uniform) malicious prover. Let $x \in \{0,1\}^*$ be such that $x \notin \mathcal{L}$. We claim that $\Pr[\mathsf{Accept} \leftarrow \langle P^*(x), V(x) \rangle] \leq \mathsf{negl}(\lambda)$.

From the soundness of Π_{wi}, the following holds:

$$\Pr[\mathsf{Accept} \leftarrow \langle P^*(x), V(x) \rangle] \leq \Pr[\mathbf{x}_{\mathsf{wi}} \in \mathcal{L}_{\mathsf{wi}}] + \mathsf{negl}(\lambda), \quad (1)$$

where x_{wi} is a random variable that is assigned the WI instance sampled in the execution of $P^*(x)$.

Thus, to prove soundness, it suffices upper bound the value

$$\varepsilon := \Pr[\mathbf{x}_{\mathsf{wi}} \in \mathcal{L}_{\mathsf{wi}}]\mathsf{negl}(\lambda), \quad (2)$$

Since from Eqs. 1 and 2, we have $\Pr[\mathsf{Accept} \leftarrow \langle P^*(x), V(x) \rangle] \leq \mathsf{negl}(\lambda)$.

Let $\mathbf{x}_{\mathsf{wi}} = \Big(x, \mathbf{c}^*, \mathbf{c}^{**}, \{\alpha_{i,b}\}_{i\in[\lambda],b\in\{0,1\}} \Big)$ be the Π_{wi} instance computed during the execution of $P^*(x)$ and $V(x)$. Define the following event, parameterized by a set of values:

Event $\mathbf{E}\left[\{\alpha_{i,b}\}_{i\in[\lambda],b\in\{0,1\}}\right]$: Output 1 if there exists an $\mathbf{i} \in [\lambda]$ such that the commitment $\mathbf{c}^{**}$ sent by P^* is a commitment of $(\alpha_{\mathbf{i},0} \oplus \alpha_{\mathbf{i},1})$ computed using the randomness $\mathbf{r}^*$.

Consider the following hybrid argument.

$\underline{\mathsf{H}_0}$: This corresponds to the execution of $P^*(x)$ and $V(x)$.

Let $\{\alpha_{i,b}\}_{i\in[\lambda],b\in\{0,1\}}$ be the values committed by V in Step 2. Since $x \notin \mathcal{L}$, the following holds:

$$\Pr\left[\mathbf{E}\left[\{\alpha_{i,b}\}_{i\in[\lambda],b\in\{0,1\}}\right] = 1 \text{ in } \mathsf{H}_0\right] = \Pr[\mathbf{x}_{\mathsf{wi}} \in \mathcal{L}_{\mathsf{wi}}] = \varepsilon$$

$\underline{\mathsf{H}_1}$: We modify the description of $V(x)$ as follows. Sample $\alpha_i \xleftarrow{\$} \{0,1\}^\lambda, \alpha_{i,b} \xleftarrow{\$} \{0,1\}^\lambda$ such that $\alpha_i = \alpha_{i,0} \oplus \alpha_{i,1}$.

Input of P: Instance $x \in \mathcal{L}$ along with witness w.
Input of V: Instance $x \in \mathcal{L}$.

Trapdoor Phase:

1. $P \leftrightarrow V$: P and V engage in an execution of the commitment protocol, where P plays the role of the committer and V plays the role of the receiver. P commits to $\mathbf{r}^*$, where $\mathbf{r}^* \xleftarrow{\$} \{0,1\}^\lambda$. Denote the commitment to be $\mathbf{c}^*$. Let the randomness used by P in the commitment protocol be r.
2. $V \leftrightarrow P$: P and V run 2λ parallel executions of the commitment protocol, with V playing the role of the committer and P playing the role of the receiver. We index the executions using the notation (i, b), where $i \in [\lambda]$ and $b \in \{0,1\}$. In the $(i,b)^{th}$ execution, V commits to $\alpha_{i,b}$, where $\alpha_{i,b} \xleftarrow{\$} \{0,1\}^\lambda$. Denote the commitments by $\left(\{\mathbf{c}_{i,b}\}_{i\in[\lambda],b\in\{0,1\}}\right)$.
3. $P \rightarrow V$: P sends $\mathbf{b}_1, \dots, \mathbf{b}_\lambda$, where $\mathbf{b}_i \xleftarrow{\$} \{0,1\}^\lambda$.
4. $V \rightarrow P$: V sends the openings of all the commitments $\left(\{\mathbf{c}_{i,\mathbf{b}_i}\}_{i\in[\lambda]}\right)$. Denote the opening of the $(i, \mathbf{b}_i)^{th}$ commitment to be $o_{i,\mathbf{b}_i} = \mathsf{Open}(\mathbf{c}_{i,\mathbf{b}_i})$. If any of the openings are invalid, P rejects. Otherwise, P parses $o_{i,\mathbf{b}_i}$ as $(\alpha_{i,\mathbf{b}_i}, r_{i,\mathbf{b}_i})$.
5. $P \leftrightarrow V$: P and V engage in another execution of the commitment protocol, where P plays the role of the committer and V plays the role of the receiver. P commits to 0, using the randomness $\mathbf{r}^*$. Denote the commitment to be $\mathbf{c}^{**}$.
6. $V \rightarrow P$: V sends the rest of the openings of $\left(\{\mathbf{c}_{i,b}\}_{i\in[\lambda],b\in\{0,1\}}\right)$. That is, it sends $\{o_{i,1-\mathbf{b}_i}\}_{i\in[\lambda]}$, where $o_{i,1-\mathbf{b}_i} = \mathsf{Open}(\mathbf{c}_{i,1-\mathbf{b}_i})$. If any of the openings are invalid, P rejects. Otherwise, P parses $o_{i,1-\mathbf{b}_i}$ as $(\alpha_{i,1-\mathbf{b}_i}, r_{i,1-\mathbf{b}_i})$.

WI Phase: P and V engage in Π_{wi} with the common input being the following:

$$\mathbf{x}_{\mathsf{wi}} = \left(x, \mathbf{c}^*, \mathbf{c}^{**}, \{\alpha_{i,b}\}_{i\in[\lambda],b\in\{0,1\}}\right)$$

Additionally, P uses the witness $(w, \bot, \bot, \bot)$.

Fig. 5. Description of the protocol Π.

The two hybrids H_0 and H_1 are identical. Thus, we have the following:

$$\mathsf{Pr}\left[\mathbf{E}\left[\{\alpha_{i,b}\}_{i\in[\lambda],b\in\{0,1\}}\right] = 1 \text{ in } \mathsf{H}_1\right] = \varepsilon$$

<u>$\mathsf{H}_{2.(i^*,b^*)}$ for $i^* \in [2\lambda], b^* \in \{0,1\}$:</u> The verifier behaves as in H_1 except for the following: for every $i \in [\lambda]$, it additionally samples $\beta_{i,0} \xleftarrow{\$} \{0,1\}^\lambda, \beta_{i,1} \xleftarrow{\$} \{0,1\}^\lambda$. Furthermore, for every $i \le i^*$, $b \le b^*$, the $(i,b)^{th}$ committed value by V in Step 2 is $\beta_{i,b}$. We emphasize that for every $i \in [\lambda]$, it still samples $\alpha_{i,0} \xleftarrow{\$} \{0,1\}^\lambda, \alpha_{i,1} \xleftarrow{\$} \{0,1\}^\lambda$.

We state the following lemma that we prove in the full version of the paper [4].

Lemma 1. *Assuming the quantum-concealing property of* $(\mathsf{Comm}, \mathsf{Receiver}, \mathsf{Open})$, *there exists a negligible function* $\nu(\lambda)$ *such that the following holds:*

1. *For every* $i^* \in [\lambda]$,

$$\left|\Pr\left[\mathbf{E}\left[\{\alpha_{i,b}\}_{i\in[\lambda],b\in\{0,1\}}\right] \textit{ in } \mathsf{H}_{2.(i^*.0)}\right] - \Pr\left[\mathbf{E}\left[\{\alpha_{i,b}\}_{i\in[\lambda],b\in\{0,1\}}\right] \textit{ in } \mathsf{H}_{2.(i^*.1)}\right]\right| \leq \nu(\lambda)$$

2. *For every* $i^* \in [\lambda - 1]$,

$$\left|\Pr\left[\mathbf{E}\left[\{\alpha_{i,b}\}_{i\in[\lambda],b\in\{0,1\}}\right] \textit{ in } \mathsf{H}_{2.(i^*-1.1)}\right] - \Pr\left[\mathbf{E}\left[\{\alpha_{i,b}\}_{i\in[\lambda],b\in\{0,1\}}\right] \textit{ in } \mathsf{H}_{2.(i^*.0)}\right]\right| \leq \nu(\lambda),$$

3. $$\left|\Pr\left[\mathbf{E}\left[\{\alpha_{i,b}\}_{i\in[\lambda],b\in\{0,1\}}\right] \textit{ in } \mathsf{H}_1\right] - \Pr\left[\mathbf{E}\left[\{\alpha_{i,b}\}_{i\in[\lambda],b\in\{0,1\}}\right] \textit{ in } \mathsf{H}_{2.(1.0)}\right]\right| \leq \nu(\lambda)$$

As a corollary and from the fact that $\Pr\left[\mathbf{E}\left[\{\alpha_{i,b}\}_{i\in[\lambda],b\in\{0,1\}}\right] = 1 \text{ in } \mathsf{H}_1\right] = \varepsilon$, we have the following.

Corollary 1.

$$\left|\Pr\left[\mathbf{E}\left[\{\alpha_{i,b}\}_{i\in[\lambda],b\in\{0,1\}}\right] \textit{ in } \mathsf{H}_{2.(\lambda.1)}\right]\right| \geq \varepsilon - (2\lambda)\cdot\nu(\lambda)$$

Proof. Follows by applying triangle inequality on Lemma 1. □

Lemma 2. $\Pr\left[\mathbf{E}\left[\{\alpha_{i,b}\}_{i\in[\lambda],b\in\{0,1\}}\right] = 1 \textit{ in } \mathsf{H}_{2.(\lambda.1)}\right] \leq \frac{\lambda}{2^\lambda}$.

Proof. In $\mathsf{H}_{2.(\lambda.1)}$, $\{\alpha_{i,b}\}_{i\in[\lambda],b\in\{0,1\}}$ is information-theoretically hidden from $P^*(x)$. Thus, for any given $i \in [\lambda]$, the probability that $\alpha_{i,0} \oplus \alpha_{i,1}$ is committed by P^* in bullet 5 of Π is $\frac{1}{2^\lambda}$. By union bound, the proof of the claim follows. □

From Corollary 1 and Lemma 2, ε is a negligible function in λ. □

3.1 Proof of Quantum Zero-Knowledge

Proposition 2. *Let* $M = O(\log \lambda)$ *and* $f(M) = 2M$. *The protocol described in Fig. 5 is* (M, f)*-space bounded QZK.*

Proof. Suppose V^* be a malicious QPT (non-uniform) verifier with M-qubit quantum space. We describe a QPT simulator Sim such that the output distribution of Sim is computationally indistinguishable from the output distribution of the real world.

Let $\mathbf{R}$ and $\mathbf{X}$ be two M-qubit quantum registers. We will denote $\mathbf{Y}$ to be the classical memory. The registers $\mathbf{X}$ and $\mathbf{Y}$ are V^*'s private registers whereas $\mathbf{R}$ is an auxiliary register maintained by the simulator. We describe the simulator Sim in Fig. 6.

We defer the proof that Sim indeed runs in expected QPT to the full version of this work [4]. We show now that the output distribution of Sim is computationally indistinguishable from the real world.

1. By taking the role of the honest prover, run the first four steps in Figure 5. That is, until the simulator receives $\{(\alpha_{i,\mathbf{b}_i}, r_{i,\mathbf{b}_i})\}_{i\in[\lambda]}$. Abort if V^* aborts at any point. We emphasize that V^* is executed on the quantum register $\mathbf{X}$ and the classical memory $\mathbf{Y}$. Denote ρ to be the quantum residual state and denote $\mathbf{st}$ to be the classical state after this step.
   1.1. Sim and V^* engage in an execution of the commitment protocol, where Sim commits to $\mathbf{r}^*$, which is sampled as $\mathbf{r}^* \xleftarrow{\$} \{0,1\}^\lambda$. Denote the commitment to be $\mathbf{c}^*$.
   1.2. Sim and V^* run 2λ number of executions of the commitment protocol. Denote the commitments in all the 2λ executions by $(\{\mathbf{c}'_{i,b}\}_{i\in[\lambda],b\in\{0,1\}})$. Denote ρ_{res} to be the quantum residual state and denote $\mathbf{st}'$ to be the classical state after this step.
   1.3. Sim sends $\mathbf{b}_1,\ldots,\mathbf{b}_\lambda$, where $\mathbf{b}_i \xleftarrow{\$} \{0,1\}^\lambda$, to V^*.
   1.4. Sim receives the openings of all the commitments $(\{\mathbf{c}_{i,\mathbf{b}_i}\}_{i\in[\lambda]})$. Denote the opening of the $(i,\mathbf{b}_i)^{th}$ commitment to be $o_{i,\mathbf{b}_i} = \mathsf{Open}(\mathbf{c}_{i,\mathbf{b}_i})$. If any of the openings are invalid, reject. Otherwise, parse $o_{i,\mathbf{b}_i}$ as $(\alpha_{i,\mathbf{b}_i}, r_{i,\mathbf{b}_i})$.
2. Repeat the following forever:
   2.1. Initialize the register $\mathbf{R}$ with the maximally mixed state $\frac{I}{2^M}$. Initialize $\mathbf{Y}$ with $\mathbf{st}'$.
   2.2. Run the third and fourth steps of Figure 5, where V^* is executed on the registers $\mathbf{R}$ and $\mathbf{Y}$. That is, send $\mathbf{b}'_1,\ldots,\mathbf{b}'_\lambda \xleftarrow{\$} \{0,1\}^\lambda$. Receive the openings from V^*, denoted by $\{(\alpha_{i,\mathbf{b}'_i}, r_{i,\mathbf{b}'_i})\}_{i\in[\lambda]}$. Abort the loop if V^* did not abort and $\exists i \in [\lambda]$ such that $\mathbf{b}_i \neq \mathbf{b}'_i$. Otherwise, continue.
3. Discard the register $\mathbf{R}$. From here on, continue (from Step 1) the execution of V^* on the registers $\mathbf{X}$ and $\mathbf{Y}$. Specifically, run V^* on (ρ, st).
4. The simulator commits to $(i^*, \alpha_{i^*,0} \oplus \alpha_{i^*,1})$, where $i^* \in [\lambda]$ is such that $\mathbf{b}_{i^*} \neq \mathbf{b}'_{i^*}$. Denote the commitment to be $\mathbf{c}^{**}$ and let $\mathbf{r}^*$ be the randomness used in $\mathbf{c}^{**}$.
5. It runs the last step of the trapdoor phase by emulating the execution of the honest prover.
6. Finally, Sim runs the WI phase with V^*. Let the instance be $\mathsf{x}_{\mathsf{wi}} = \left(x, \mathbf{c}^*, \mathbf{c}^{**}, \{\alpha_{i,b}\}_{i\in[\lambda],b\in\{0,1\}}\right)$, where $\mathbf{c}^*$ be the commitment sent by Sim in the beginning of the protocol. Sim emulates the honest prover except the witness used is $(\bot, \mathbf{r}^*, r, i^*)$, where r is the randomness used in the commitment of $\mathbf{c}^*$.

Fig. 6. (Expected) QPT Simulator Sim.

Lemma 3. *Let $(x, w) \in \mathcal{R}(\mathcal{L})$. Let ρ be the auxiliary state of V^*. We have that* $\{\mathsf{View}_{V^*}(\langle P(x,w), V^*(x,\rho)\rangle)\} \approx_Q \{\mathsf{Sim}(x,\rho)\}$.

Proof. Consider the following hybrid argument.

$\underline{\mathsf{H}_0}$: The output distribution of this hybrid is $\mathsf{View}_{V^*}(\langle P(x,w), V^*(x,\rho)\rangle)$.

$\underline{\mathsf{H}_1}$: We define a hybrid simulator that essentially behaves like an honest prover except it keeps rewinding until it finds two accepting transcripts. We emphasize that, just like the honest prover, the hybrid simulator still uses the witness w in the WI phase. Formally, we consider a hybrid simulator $\mathsf{H}_1.\mathsf{Sim}(x, w)$ defined as follows:

1. Execute steps 1 through 3 of Sim in Fig. 6.
   1.1. Run the following steps:
      i Engage in an execution of the commitment protocol with V^*, by committing to $\mathbf{r}^*$, which is sampled as $\mathbf{r}^* \xleftarrow{\$} \{0,1\}^\lambda$. Denote the commitment to be $\mathbf{c}^*$.
      ii Execute 2λ number of executions of the commitment protocol with V^*, with V^* playing the role of the committer. Denote the commitments in all the 2λ executions by $(\{\mathbf{c}'_{i,b}\}_{i\in[\lambda],b\in\{0,1\}})$. Denote ρ_{res} to be the quantum residual state and denote $\mathbf{st}'$ to be the classical state after this step.
      iii Send $\mathbf{b}_1,\ldots,\mathbf{b}_\lambda$, where $\mathbf{b}_i \xleftarrow{\$} \{0,1\}^\lambda$, to V^*.
      iv Receive the openings of all the commitments $(\{\mathbf{c}_{i,\mathbf{b}_i}\}_{i\in[\lambda]})$. Denote the opening of the $(i,\mathbf{b}_i)^{th}$ commitment to be $o_{i,\mathbf{b}_i} = \mathsf{Open}(\mathbf{c}_{i,\mathbf{b}_i})$. If any of the openings are invalid, reject. Otherwise, parse $o_{i,\mathbf{b}_i}$ as $(\alpha_{i,\mathbf{b}_i}, r_{i,\mathbf{b}_i})$.
   1.2. Repeat the following forever:
      i. Initialize the register $\mathbf{R}$ with the maximally mixed state $\frac{I}{2^M}$. Initialize $\mathbf{Y}$ with $\mathbf{st}'$.
      ii. Run the third and fourth steps of Fig. 5, where V^* is executed on the registers $\mathbf{R}$ and $\mathbf{Y}$. That is, send $\mathbf{b}'_1,\ldots,\mathbf{b}'_\lambda \xleftarrow{\$} \{0,1\}^\lambda$. Receive the openings from V^*, denoted by $\{(\alpha_{i,\mathbf{b}'_i}, r_{i,\mathbf{b}'_i})\}_{i\in[\lambda]}$. Abort the loop if V^* did not abort and $\exists i \in [\lambda]$ such that $\mathbf{b}_i \neq \mathbf{b}'_i$. Otherwise, continue
   1.3. Discard the register $\mathbf{R}$. From here on, continue (from Step 1) the execution of V^* on the registers $\mathbf{X}$ and $\mathbf{Y}$. Specifically, run V^* on (ρ, st), where (ρ, st) is the private state of the verifier after the execution of Step iv.
2. Execute steps 5 and 6 of Π in Fig. 5. Also, execute the WI phase.
   2.1. Engage in another execution of the commitment protocol by committing to 0, using the randomness $\mathbf{r}^*$. Denote the commitment to be $\mathbf{c}^{**}$.
   2.2. V^* output the rest of the openings of $\left(\{\mathbf{c}_{i,b}\}_{i\in[\lambda],b\in\{0,1\}}\right)$. That is, it sends $\{o_{i,1-\mathbf{b}_i}\}_{i\in[\lambda]}$, where $o_{i,\mathbf{b}_i} = \mathsf{Open}(\mathbf{c}_{i,1-\mathbf{b}_i})$. If any of the openings are invalid, P rejects. Otherwise, P parses $o_{i,1-\mathbf{b}_i}$ as $(\alpha_{i,1-\mathbf{b}_i}, r_{i,1-\mathbf{b}_i})$.
   2.3. Engage in Π_{wi} with V^* on the following common input:

$$\mathbf{x}_{\mathsf{wi}} = \left(x, \mathbf{c}^*, \mathbf{c}^{**}, \{\alpha_{i,b}\}_{i\in[\lambda],b\in\{0,1\}}\right)$$

   Additionally, use the witness $(w, \perp, \perp, \perp)$ in Π_{wi}.

The output of $\mathsf{H}_1.\mathsf{Sim}(x, w)$ is the view of V^* in H_1.

We have the following lemma that shows that H_0 and $\mathsf{H}_1.\mathsf{Sim}(x, w)$ are statistically indistinguishable. We defer its proof to the full version of our paper [4].

Lemma 4. *The trace distance between* H_0 *and* $\mathsf{H}_1.\mathsf{Sim}(x, w)$ *is at most* $\mathsf{negl}(\lambda)$.

$\underline{\mathsf{H}_2}$: We define a hybrid simulator $\mathsf{H}_2.\mathsf{Sim}$ which behaves like $\mathsf{H}_1.\mathsf{Sim}$, except in:

1.1.i Engage in an execution of the commitment protocol with V^*, by committing to 0. Denote the commitment to be $\mathbf{c}^*$.
Note: in bullet 2.1 of H_1, $\mathbf{c}^{**}$ is still a commitment computed using the randomness $\mathbf{r}^*$, where $\mathbf{r}^* \xleftarrow{\$} \{0,1\}^\lambda$.

The rest of the steps is the same as $\mathsf{H}_1.\mathsf{Sim}$. The output of $\mathsf{H}_2.\mathsf{Sim}$ is the view of V^* in H_2.

The output distributions of $\mathsf{H}_1.\mathsf{Sim}$ and $\mathsf{H}_2.\mathsf{Sim}$ are computationally indistinguishable from the quantum-concealing property of $(\mathsf{Comm}, \mathsf{Open}, \mathsf{Receiver})$.

$\underline{\mathsf{H}_3}$: We define a hybrid simulator $\mathsf{H}_3.\mathsf{Sim}$ which behaves like $\mathsf{H}_2.\mathsf{Sim}$, except in the following steps:

2.1 Engage in an execution of the commitment protocol with V^* by committing to $(i^*, \alpha_{i^*,0} \oplus \alpha_{i^*,1})$, where $i^* \in [\lambda]$ is such that $\mathbf{b}_{i^*} \neq \mathbf{b}'_{i^*}$. Denote the commitment to be $\mathbf{c}^{**}$.

The rest of the steps is the same as $\mathsf{H}_2.\mathsf{Sim}$. The output of $\mathsf{H}_3.\mathsf{Sim}$ is the view of V^* in H_3.

The output distributions of $\mathsf{H}_2.\mathsf{Sim}$ and $\mathsf{H}_3.\mathsf{Sim}$ are computationally indistinguishable from the quantum-concealing property of $(\mathsf{Comm}, \mathsf{Open}, \mathsf{Receiver})$.

$\underline{\mathsf{H}_4}$: We define a hybrid simulator $\mathsf{H}_4.\mathsf{Sim}$ which behaves like $\mathsf{H}_3.\mathsf{Sim}$, except in the following steps:

1.1.i Engage in an execution of the commitment protocol with V^*, by committing to $\mathbf{r}^*$, which is sampled as $\mathbf{r}^* \xleftarrow{\$} \{0,1\}^\lambda$. Denote the commitment to be $\mathbf{c}^*$.

The rest of the steps is the same as $\mathsf{H}_3.\mathsf{Sim}$. The output of $\mathsf{H}_4.\mathsf{Sim}$ is the view of V^* in H_4.

The output distributions of $\mathsf{H}_3.\mathsf{Sim}$ and $\mathsf{H}_4.\mathsf{Sim}$ are computationally indistinguishable from the quantum-concealing property of $(\mathsf{Comm}, \mathsf{Open}, \mathsf{Receiver})$.

$\underline{\mathsf{H}_5}$: The output of this hybrid is the output of $\mathsf{Sim}(x, \rho)$.

The only difference between $\mathsf{H}_4.\mathsf{Sim}$ and Sim is in the WI phase. The computational indistinguishability of H_4 and H_5 follows from the witness indistinguishability property of Π_{wi}. □

□

4 $\omega(\log(\lambda))$-Quantum Space Verifiers: Impossibility Result

In this section, we whow that there does not exist any quantum ZK protocol with channel black-box simulation for languages outside BQP against super-logarithmic quantum space verifiers in the Channel Black-box setting.

Lemma 5. *Let $s(\lambda) = \omega(\log(\lambda))$ and f be any polynomial. Assume the existence of post-quantum one-way functions. Suppose there exists a channel black-box (s, f)-space bounded quantum ZK protocol for a language $\mathcal{L}$. Then, $\mathcal{L}$ is in* BQP.

Proof. Consider a language $\mathcal{L}$. Suppose there exists a k-round channel black-box (s, f)-space bounded quantum zero-knowledge protocol $\mathcal{L}$ for some $s(\lambda) = \omega(\log(\lambda))$ and for some polynomial f.

We describe a malicious verifier V' below. In addition to subspace states [1], we use the following additional tools:

- Symmetric-key encryption with post-quantum CPA (chosen plaintext attack) security, denoted by $(\mathsf{Setup}, \mathsf{Enc}, \mathsf{Dec})$.
- Post-quantum secure digital signatures satisfying existential unforgeability property, denoted by $(\mathsf{Gen}, \mathsf{Sign}, \mathsf{Verify})$.

Both of these primitives can be built from post-quantum OWFs [23,35].

Description of V'. Consider the following QPT verifier V' such that the quantum memory of V' is $M = \omega(\lambda)$ qubits. Hardwired in its code are k random $\frac{M}{2}$-dimensional subspaces S_0,...,S_k, where $S_i \subseteq \mathbb{F}_2^M$, a secret-key sk_{enc} for a symmetric-key encryption scheme, sampled as $sk_{\text{enc}} \leftarrow \mathsf{Setup}(1^\lambda)$, and a secret-key and verification keys $(sk_{\text{sign}}, vk_{\text{sign}})$ for a digital signature scheme, sampled as $(sk_{\text{sign}}, vk_{\text{sign}}) \leftarrow \mathsf{Gen}(1^\lambda)$. V' receives as input M-qubit subspace state $|S_0\rangle$, which is initialized in the register $\mathbf{Y}$.

In the first round of the protocol, V' does the following with its two input registers $\mathbf{X}$, $\mathbf{Y}$:

1. Measure the register $\mathbf{X}$ to obtain α_1.
2. Check if the state held in $\mathbf{Y}$ is $|S_0\rangle\langle S_0|$. That is, perform the projective measurement $\{\underbrace{|S_0\rangle\langle S_0|}_{\text{outcome}=0}, \underbrace{I - |S_0\rangle\langle S_0|}_{\text{outcome}=1}\}$ on the register $\mathbf{Y}$. This is possible since V' has the description of S_0 hardwired in its code.
3. If the measured outcome is 1, abort.
4. Run the first round of V on α_1 to obtain β_1. Abort if V aborts.
5. Re-initialize the register $\mathbf{X}$ with $|\beta_1\rangle\langle\beta_1|$.
6. Re-initialize the register $\mathbf{Y}$ with a new M-qubit subspace state $|S_1\rangle\langle S_1|$ in the memory.
7. Using the hardcoded sk_{enc}, initialize the register $\mathbf{Z}$ with the $c_1 = \mathsf{Enc}(sk_{\text{enc}}, \gamma_1)$, where γ_1 is the state of V after the answer.
8. Using the hardcoded sk_{sign}, initialize $\mathbf{T}$ with the signature of c_1, i.e., $\mathsf{Sign}(sk_{\text{sign}}, c_1)$.
9. Output the registers $\mathbf{X}$, $\mathbf{Y}$, $\mathbf{Z}$ and $\mathbf{T}$.

In the ith round of the protocol, V' gets as input four registers $\mathbf{X}$, $\mathbf{Y}$, $\mathbf{Z}$ and $\mathbf{T}$ and does the following:

1. Measure the register $\mathbf{X}$ to obtain α_i.

2. Check if the state held in $\mathbf{Y}$ is $|S_{i-1}\rangle\langle S_{i-1}|$. That is, perform the projective measurement $\{\underbrace{|S_{i-1}\rangle\langle S_{i-1}|}_{\text{outcome}=0}, \underbrace{I - |S_{i-1}\rangle\langle S_{i-1}|}_{\text{outcome}=1}\}$ on the register $\mathbf{Y}$. This is possible since V' has the description of S_i hardwired in its code.
3. If the measured outcome is 1, abort.
4. Using the hardcoded vk_{sign}, check if $\mathbf{T}$ contains the signature of the value in register $\mathbf{Z}$. If the verification does not pass, abort.
5. Using the hardcoded sk_{enc}, decrypt $\mathbf{Z}$ leading to value γ_{i-1}
6. Run the ith round of V on α_i with internal state γ_{i-1} a to obtain β_i. Abort if V aborts.
7. Re-initialize register $\mathbf{X}$ with $|\beta_i\rangle\langle\beta_i|$.
8. Re-initialize the register $\mathbf{Y}$ with a new M-qubit subspace state $|S_i\rangle\langle S_i|$ in the memory.
9. Using the hardcoded sk_{enc}, re-initialize the register $\mathbf{Z}$ with the $c_i = \mathsf{Enc}(sk_{\text{enc}}, \gamma_i)$, where γ_i is the state of V after the answer.
10. Using the hardcoded sk_{sign}, initialize $\mathbf{T}$ with $\mathsf{Sign}(sk_{\text{sign}}, c_i)$.
11. Output the registers $\mathbf{X}$, $\mathbf{Y}$, $\mathbf{Z}$ and $\mathbf{T}$.

Note that the quantum memory of V' takes M qubits.

Let $\mathscr{C}(V') = (\Phi_1, \cdots, \Phi_k)$ be the quantum channels corresponding to the operations of V' as defined in Sect. 2.1. Since Π satisfies channel black-box (M, f)-space bounded QZK, there exists a QPT simulator $\mathsf{Sim}^{\mathscr{C}(V')}$, taking space at most $p(M)$ qubits, simulating the interaction of V' with the honest prover P. In particular, $\mathsf{Sim}^{\mathscr{C}(V')}$ does not abort with probability $1 - \mathsf{negl}(\lambda)$, in which case it outputs $|S_k\rangle$.

Helpful Definitions. We state some useful definitions below.

Definition 11 (State-successful queries). *A query $\rho_{\mathbf{X}\otimes\mathbf{Y}\otimes\mathbf{Z}\otimes\mathbf{T}}$ made by* Sim *to Φ_i, for some $i \in [k]$, is said to be* state-successful *if $\Phi_i(\rho_{\mathbf{X}\otimes\mathbf{Y}\otimes\mathbf{Z}\otimes\mathbf{T}})$ does not abort on step* 3.

In particular, a state-successful query made by Sim could lead to abort if the other registers $\mathbf{X}, \mathbf{Z}$ and $\mathbf{T}$ are not of a specific form.

Definition 12 ((Non-)abort queries). *A query $\rho_{\mathbf{X}\otimes\mathbf{Y}\otimes\mathbf{Z}\otimes\mathbf{T}}$ made by* Sim *to Φ_i, for some $i \in [k]$, is said to be* non-abort *if $\Phi_i(\rho_{\mathbf{X}\otimes\mathbf{Y}\otimes\mathbf{Z}\otimes\mathbf{T}})$ does not abort. Similarly, we say that it is an abort query if $\Phi_i(\rho_{\mathbf{X}\otimes\mathbf{Y}\otimes\mathbf{Z}\otimes\mathbf{T}})$ aborts.*

Note that a non-abort query is also a state-successful query.

Definition 13 (Successful simulation). *We say that* Sim *is* successful, *if it does not abort.*

We now state an important claim regarding the properties of queries made by Sim to $\Phi_1, ..., \Phi_k$ that is proved in the full version of the paper [4].

Lemma 6. *Except with* $\mathsf{negl}(\lambda)$ *probability, the following events do not occur:*

1. *for some i,* Sim *has a state-successful query to Φ_i without a previous non-abort query to Φ_{i-1};*
2. *for some $i \leq j$,* Sim *has a state-successful query to Φ_i after having a state-successful query to Φ_j.*
3. *for some i,* Sim *is successful without a non-abort query to Φ_i.*
4. *for some i,* Sim *has a non-abort query to Φ_i with an input value on register* **Z** *different from the output value on register* **Z** *of a non-abort query to Φ_{i-1}.*

We finish now the proof of Lemma 5.

Proof (of Lemma 5). We start by showing that there exists a prover $\tilde{P}$ that runs in expected poly-time and makes the V accept any $x \in \mathcal{L}$ with probability $1 - \mathsf{negl}(\lambda)$.

Intuitively, $\tilde{P}$ will execute Sim and simulate the queries to V' by exchanging messages with V. Henceforth, we will assume that the registers $\mathbf{X}, \mathbf{Z}$ and $\mathbf{T}$ are measured in the computational basis just before making queries to Φ_i: this does not affect the analysis since they are anyway measured in the channel Φ_i.

In more detail, $\tilde{P}$ proceeds as follows: $\tilde{P}$ chooses random subspaces S_i for $0 \leq i \leq k$, samples a secret-key sk_{enc} corresponding to a symmetric-key encryption scheme and samples a secret-key-verification key pair $(sk_{\text{sign}}, vk_{\text{sign}})$ corresponding to a digital signature scheme.

$\tilde{P}$ then runs Sim on input $|S_0\rangle$. For every query of Sim to Φ_i, $i > 1$, $\tilde{P}$ answers the query with abort. For a query made to Φ_1, on input $|\alpha_1\rangle\langle\alpha_1|_{\mathbf{X}} \otimes \rho_{1\mathbf{Y}}$, $\tilde{P}$ first checks if ρ_1 corresponds to $|S_0\rangle$ by measuring ρ_1 with respect to $\{|S_0\rangle\langle S_0|, I - |S_0\rangle\langle S_0|\}$. If the check fails, $\tilde{P}$ responds with an abort and continues the execution of $\tilde{P}$ with the same oracle responses as before. Otherwise, $\tilde{P}$ will:

1. Send the message α_1 to the verifier,
2. Receive the message β_1 from the verifier,
3. Compute $c_1 = \mathsf{Enc}(sk_{\text{enc}}, 0)$ and $t_1 = \mathsf{Sign}(sk_{\text{sign}}, c_1)$
4. Answer the query from Sim with $|\beta_1\rangle\langle\beta_1|_{\mathbf{X}} \otimes |S_1\rangle\langle S_1|_{\mathbf{Y}} \otimes |c_1\rangle\langle c_1|_{\mathbf{Z}} \otimes |t_1\rangle\langle t_1|_{\mathbf{T}}$,
5. Set $r = 2$ and continues executing Sim, simulating the queries to $\Phi_1, ..., \Phi_k$ as described below.

For every query of Sim to Φ_i, for $i \neq r$, $\tilde{P}$ answers the query with abort. For a query made to Φ_r, on input $|\alpha_r\rangle\langle\alpha_r|_{\mathbf{X}} \otimes \rho_{r\mathbf{Y}} \otimes |c'_r\rangle\langle c'_r|_{\mathbf{Z}} \otimes |t'_r\rangle\langle t'_r|_{\mathbf{T}}$, $\tilde{P}$ first checks if ρ_r corresponds to $|S_{r-1}\rangle$ by measuring ρ_r with respect to $\{|S_{r-1}\rangle\langle S_{r-1}|, I - |S_{r-1}\rangle\langle S_{r-1}|\}$. We now consider the following three cases: First, if the check fails, $\tilde{P}$ answers the query with abort and continues the execution of Sim. Secondly, if the check succeeds and $c_{r-1} \neq c'_r$ then $\tilde{P}$ aborts. Finally, if the check succeeds and the signature t'_r is a correct signature for c'_r then $\tilde{P}$ will do the following:

1. Send the message α_r to the verifier,
2. Receive the message β_r from the verifier,
3. Compute $c_r = \mathsf{Enc}(sk_{\text{enc}}, 0)$ and $t_r = \mathsf{Sign}(sk_{\text{sign}}, c_r)$ (with fresh randomness),
4. Answer the query from Sim with $|\beta_r\rangle\langle\beta_r|_{\mathbf{X}} \otimes |S_r\rangle\langle S_r|_{\mathbf{Y}} \otimes |c_r\rangle\langle c_r|_{\mathbf{Z}} \otimes |t_r\rangle\langle t_r|_{\mathbf{T}}$,

5. Increment r by 1, i.e., set $r = r + 1$, and continue executing Sim by answering the queries with the updated value of r.

We now prove that $\tilde{P}$ makes V accept any instance $x \in \mathcal{L}$ with $1 - \mathsf{negl}(\lambda)$ probability. For that we consider the following hybrids:

$\underline{\mathsf{H}_0}$: The execution of Sim with access to $\Phi_1, ..., \Phi_k$ that come from V'.

$\underline{\mathsf{H}_1}$: The execution of a simulator Sim' which has the same behaviour as Sim, except Sim' aborts if any of the events of the items of Lemma 6 happen.

From Lemma 6, the events happen with probability at most $\mathsf{negl}(\lambda)$ and therefore the output of H_0 and H_1 are statistically close.

$\underline{\mathsf{H}_2}$: In this hybrid, we consider the interaction of Sim' with access to $\Phi'_1, ..., \Phi'_k$, which are controlled by a stateful party P'. At the beginning, for all $j > 1$, P' answers Φ'_j with an abort. On the query to Φ'_1, P' will store the value of the output registers $\mathbf{Z}$ and $\mathbf{T}$, which we denote by c_1 and t_1, and replace them by $d_1 = \mathsf{Enc}(sk_{\text{enc}}, 0)$ and its signature $\mathsf{Sign}(sk_{\text{sign}}, d_1)$. P' will set $r = 2$ and starts answering the queries as below.

On a query to Φ_j, for $j \neq r$, P' answers with an abort. On a query to Φ_r, P' works as follows. P' will check if the content of input register $\mathbf{Z}$ is equal to d_{r-1}. If it is not, P' answers with abort. Otherwise, P' re-initializes the contents of the input registers $\mathbf{Z}$ and $\mathbf{T}$ with c_{r-1} and t_{r-1}. Then P' execute the original channel of Φ_r. P' will store the value of the output registers $\mathbf{Z}$ and $\mathbf{T}$, which we denote by c_r and t_r, and replace them by $d_r = \mathsf{Enc}(sk_{\text{enc}}, 0)$ and its signature $\mathsf{Sign}(sk_{\text{sign}}, d_r)$. P' increments r and answers the queries as described above with the updated value of r.

Given the IND-CPA security of the encryption scheme, the output of H_1 and H_2 are computationally close.

$\underline{\mathsf{H}_3}$: We consider the interaction of Sim' with the prover $\tilde{P}$ of the protocol.

The output of the simulator in H_2 and H_3 are the same, since Sim' does not have access to any value that depends on the internal state of V in H_2, and $\tilde{P}$ simulates all operations of V'.

We show now that the successful output of the simulator in H_3 implies that V accepts in the protocol. The key observation is that, as described above, if the simulator does not abort, any state-successful query to Φ_k is also non-abort. But by construction, this is only possible if V accepts in the protocol. Therefore, since Sim does not abort with probability at least $1 - \mathsf{negl}(\lambda)$, V accepts with the same probability when interacting with $\tilde{P}$ on a yes-instance.

We also notice that for any no-instance x, by the soundness of the protocol, we have that such a $\tilde{P}$ makes V accept with probability at most $\mathsf{negl}(\lambda)$.

Finally, we need to discuss the runtime of $\tilde{P}$. So far, we have that there is a polynomial q such that the expected runtime of $\tilde{P}$ if $q(\lambda)$. However, we can consider a prover $\tilde{P}'$ that terminates the execution of $\tilde{P}$ after $q(\lambda)^2$ steps and in this case, the probability that $\tilde{P}'$ convinces the honest verifier is still a constant. In this case, both $\tilde{P}'$ and V runs in polynomial-time, which can be simulated by a BQP algorithm, which finishes the proof.

Acknowledgements. We thank Kai-Min Chung and Fermi Ma for their insightful discussions, especially regarding the definitions of space-bounded quantum zero-knowledge. This work was done (in part) while the authors were visiting the Simons Institute for the Theory of Computing. This research was supported in part by the National Science Foundation under Grant No. NSF PHY-1748958. ABG is supported by ANR JCJC TCS-NISQ ANR-22-CE47-0004. This work is part of HQI initiative1 and is supported by France 2030 under the French National Research Agency award number ANR-22-PNCQ-0002.

References

1. Aaronson, S., Christiano, P.: Quantum money from hidden subspaces. Theory Comput. **9**, 349–401 (2013)
2. Agarwal, A., Bartusek, J., Goyal, V., Khurana, D., Malavolta, G.: Post-quantum multi-party computation in constant rounds. arXiv preprint arXiv:2005.12904 (2020)
3. Ananth, P., Chung, K.-M., Placa, R.L.L.: On the concurrent composition of quantum zero-knowledge. In: Malkin, T., Peikert, C. (eds.) CRYPTO 2021. LNCS, vol. 12825, pp. 346–374. Springer, Cham (2021). https://doi.org/10.1007/978-3-030-84242-0_13
4. Ananth, P., Grilo, A.B.: Post-quantum zero-knowledge with space-bounded simulation. arXiv preprint arXiv:2210.06093 (2022)
5. Ananth, P., La Placa, R.L.: Secure quantum extraction protocols. In: Pass, R., Pietrzak, K. (eds.) TCC 2020. LNCS, vol. 12552, pp. 123–152. Springer, Cham (2020). https://doi.org/10.1007/978-3-030-64381-2_5
6. Arute, F., et al.: Quantum supremacy using a programmable superconducting processor. Nature **574**, 505–510 (2019)
7. Aumann, Y., Feige, U.: One message proof systems with known space verifiers. In: Stinson, D.R. (ed.) CRYPTO 1993. LNCS, vol. 773, pp. 85–99. Springer, Heidelberg (1994). https://doi.org/10.1007/3-540-48329-2_8
8. Bartusek, J., Coladangelo, A., Khurana, D., Ma, F.: One-way functions imply secure computation in a quantum world. In: Malkin, T., Peikert, C. (eds.) CRYPTO 2021. LNCS, vol. 12825, pp. 467–496. Springer, Cham (2021). https://doi.org/10.1007/978-3-030-84242-0_17
9. Bitansky, N., Kellner, M., Shmueli, O.: Post-quantum resettably-sound zero knowledge. In: Nissim, K., Waters, B. (eds.) TCC 2021. LNCS, vol. 13042, pp. 62–89. Springer, Cham (2021). https://doi.org/10.1007/978-3-030-90459-3_3
10. Bitansky, N., Shmueli, O.: Post-quantum zero knowledge in constant rounds. In: Proceedings of the 52nd Annual ACM SIGACT Symposium on Theory of Computing, pp. 269–279 (2020)
11. Blum, M.: How to prove a theorem so no one else can claim it. In: Proceedings of the International Congress of Mathematicians, vol. 1, p. 2. Citeseer (1986)
12. Broadbent, A., Grilo, A.B.: Zero-knowledge for QMA from locally simulatable proofs. arXiv preprint arXiv:1911.07782 (2019)
13. Broadbent, A., Ji, Z., Song, F., Watrous, J.: Zero-knowledge proof systems for QMA. In: 2016 IEEE 57th Annual Symposium on Foundations of Computer Science (FOCS), pp. 31–40. IEEE (2016)
14. Chen, S., Cotler, J., Huang, H.Y., Li, J.: The complexity of NISQ (2022)

15. Chia, N.H., Chung, K.M., Liang, X., Yamakawa, T.: Post-quantum simulatable extraction with minimal assumptions: black-box and constant-round. arXiv preprint arXiv:2111.08665 (2021)
16. Chia, N.H., Chung, K.M., Liu, Q., Yamakawa, T.: On the impossibility of post-quantum black-box zero-knowledge in constant round. In: 2021 IEEE 62nd Annual Symposium on Foundations of Computer Science (FOCS), pp. 59–67. IEEE (2021)
17. Chia, N.-H., Chung, K.-M., Yamakawa, T.: A black-box approach to post-quantum zero-knowledge in constant rounds. In: Malkin, T., Peikert, C. (eds.) CRYPTO 2021. LNCS, vol. 12825, pp. 315–345. Springer, Cham (2021). https://doi.org/10.1007/978-3-030-84242-0_12
18. Chiesa, A., Ma, F., Spooner, N., Zhandry, M.: Post-quantum succinct arguments: breaking the quantum rewinding barrier. In: 2021 IEEE 62nd Annual Symposium on Foundations of Computer Science (FOCS), pp. 49–58. IEEE (2022)
19. Chung, K.-M., Pass, R., Tseng, W.-L.D.: The knowledge tightness of parallel zero-knowledge. In: Cramer, R. (ed.) TCC 2012. LNCS, vol. 7194, pp. 512–529. Springer, Heidelberg (2012). https://doi.org/10.1007/978-3-642-28914-9_29
20. Dieks, D.G.B.J.: Communication by EPR devices. Phys. Lett. A **92**(6), 271–272 (1982)
21. Ding, N., Gu, D.: Precise time and space simulatable zero-knowledge. In: Boyen, X., Chen, X. (eds.) ProvSec 2011. LNCS, vol. 6980, pp. 16–33. Springer, Heidelberg (2011). https://doi.org/10.1007/978-3-642-24316-5_4
22. Ding, N., Gu, D.: On constant-round precise zero-knowledge. In: Chim, T.W., Yuen, T.H. (eds.) ICICS 2012. LNCS, vol. 7618, pp. 178–190. Springer, Heidelberg (2012). https://doi.org/10.1007/978-3-642-34129-8_16
23. Goldreich, O.: The Foundations of Cryptography - Volume 1: Basic Techniques (2001)
24. Goldreich, O., Krawczyk, H.: On the composition of zero-knowledge proof systems. SIAM J. Comput. **25**(1), 169–192 (1996)
25. Goldreich, O., Micali, S., Wigderson, A.: Proofs that yield nothing but their validity and a methodology of cryptographic protocol design. In: 27th Annual Symposium on Foundations of Computer Science, pp. 174–187. IEEE (1986)
26. Micali, S., Goldreich, O., Wigderson, A.: How to play any mental game. In: STOC (1987)
27. Goldreich, O., Oren, Y.: Definitions and properties of zero-knowledge proof systems. J. Cryptol. **7**(1), 1–32 (1994). https://doi.org/10.1007/BF00195207
28. Goldwasser, S., Micali, S., Rackoff, C.: The knowledge complexity of interactive proof-systems. In: STOC, pp. 291–304 (1985)
29. Grilo, A.B., Lin, H., Song, F., Vaikuntanathan, V.: Oblivious transfer is in MiniQCrypt. In: Canteaut, A., Standaert, F.-X. (eds.) EUROCRYPT 2021. LNCS, vol. 12697, pp. 531–561. Springer, Cham (2021). https://doi.org/10.1007/978-3-030-77886-6_18
30. Hallgren, S., Smith, A., Song, F.: Classical cryptographic protocols in a quantum world. In: Annual Cryptology Conference, pp. 411–428. Springer (2011)
31. Holmgren, J., Lombardi, A.: Cryptographic hashing from strong one-way functions (or: one-way product functions and their applications). In: 2018 IEEE 59th annual symposium on Foundations of Computer Science (FOCS), pp. 850–858. IEEE (2018)
32. Jain, R., Kolla, A., Midrijanis, G., Reichardt, B.W.: On parallel composition of zero-knowledge proofs with black-box quantum simulators. arXiv preprint quant-ph/0607211 (2006)

33. Lombardi, A., Ma, F., Spooner, N.: Post-quantum zero knowledge, revisited (or: how to do quantum rewinding undetectably). arXiv preprint arXiv:2111.12257 (2021)
34. Micali, S., Pass, R.: Local zero knowledge. In: Proceedings of the Thirty-Eighth Annual ACM Symposium on Theory of Computing, pp. 306–315 (2006)
35. Naor, M., Yung, M.: Universal one-way hash functions and their cryptographic applications. In: Proceedings of the Twenty-First Annual ACM Symposium on Theory of Computing, pp. 33–43 (1989)
36. Pandey, O., Pass, R., Sahai, A., Tseng, W.-L.D., Venkitasubramaniam, M.: Precise concurrent zero knowledge. In: Smart, N. (ed.) EUROCRYPT 2008. LNCS, vol. 4965, pp. 397–414. Springer, Heidelberg (2008). https://doi.org/10.1007/978-3-540-78967-3_23
37. Santis, A., Persiano, G., Yung, M.: One-message statistical zero-knowledge proofs and space-bounded verifier. In: Kuich, W. (ed.) ICALP 1992. LNCS, vol. 623, pp. 28–40. Springer, Heidelberg (1992). https://doi.org/10.1007/3-540-55719-9_61
38. Sasson, E.B., et al.: Zerocash: decentralized anonymous payments from bitcoin. In: 2014 IEEE Symposium on Security and Privacy, pp. 459–474. IEEE (2014)
39. Shor, P.W.: Polynomial-time algorithms for prime factorization and discrete logarithms on a quantum computer. SIAM Rev. **41**(2), 303–332 (1999)
40. Unruh, D.: Quantum proofs of knowledge. In: Pointcheval, D., Johansson, T. (eds.) EUROCRYPT 2012. LNCS, vol. 7237, pp. 135–152. Springer, Heidelberg (2012). https://doi.org/10.1007/978-3-642-29011-4_10
41. Unruh, D.: Everlasting multi-party computation. In: Canetti, R., Garay, J.A. (eds.) CRYPTO 2013. LNCS, vol. 8043, pp. 380–397. Springer, Heidelberg (2013). https://doi.org/10.1007/978-3-642-40084-1_22
42. Van De Graaf, J.: Towards a formal definition of security for quantum protocols. Citeseer (1997)
43. Watrous, J.: Zero-knowledge against quantum attacks. SIAM J. Comput. **39**(1), 25–58 (2009)
44. Wootters, W.K., Zurek, W.H.: A single quantum cannot be cloned. Nature **299**(5886), 802–803 (1982)
45. Zhandry, M.: Quantum lightning never strikes the same state twice. Or: quantum money from cryptographic assumptions. J. Cryptol. **34**(1), Paper No. 6, 56 (2021)
46. Zhandry, M.: The space-time cost of purifying quantum computations. arXiv preprint arXiv:2401.07974 (2024)
47. Zhong, H.-S., et al.: Quantum computational advantage using photons. Science (2021)

Adaptive UC NIZK for Practical Applications

Anna Lysyanskaya[1] and Leah Namisa Rosenbloom[2](✉)

[1] Brown University, Providence, RI 02906, USA
anna_lysyanskaya@brown.edu
[2] Northeastern University, Boston, MA 02115, USA
l.rosenbloom@northeastern.edu

Abstract. Non-interactive zero-knowledge proofs of knowledge (NIZK-PoK) serve as a key building block in many important cryptographic protocols. In practice, NIZKPoK are often constructed from Σ-protocols based on the discrete logarithm assumption, and proven secure in the random-oracle model (ROM). Recent work and standardization initiatives have highlighted the importance of concurrent security of NIZKPoK against adversaries who are capable of adaptive corruption.

In this paper, we focus explicitly on Σ-protocols from linear function families, which include those for proving discrete-logarithm based relations. We define a natural adaptivity property for this class of Σ-protocols and show that, given any straight-line compiler which preserves the adaptivity property, it is possible to transform these protocols into adaptive, universally composable (UC) NIZKPoK in the global ROM. We then prove that the most efficient known construction of a straight-line compiler, Kondi and shelat's randomized version of Fischlin's transform [33,40], preserves the adaptivity property. Our construction avoids introducing any additional cryptographic primitives, and, following Kondi and shelat, requires only a polylogarithmic number of repetitions of the underlying Σ-protocol.

1 Introduction

Cryptographic protocols that maintain security under concurrent composition and against adversaries who can corrupt participants adaptively are vital to the formation of cryptographic standards that capture real-world threat models. Our foremost consideration is achieving concurrent, adaptive security in non-interactive zero-knowledge proofs of knowledge (NIZKPoK) on the verge of adoption within larger cryptographic systems [26,49]. NIZKPoK are widely employed in group [8,17], blind [37], threshold [4], aggregate [40], and multi- [4,29] signatures, cryptographic shuffles [42,53] and accumulators [2,13], anonymous networks [27], credentials [12,14,15,50], e-cash [11], e-token [10], and voting [42,45,48], distributed ledgers [45], verifiable secret sharing [48] and encryption schemes [8,16], and in bootstrapping multi-party protocols secure in the "honest-but-curious" model (in which participants are guaranteed to act according to the protocol) into those secure in the more realistic "malicious" model (in which the adversary can adaptively corrupt and execute arbitrary code).

D. Escudero and I. Damgård (Eds.): LATINCRYPT 2025, LNCS 16129, pp. 76–108, 2026.
https://doi.org/10.1007/978-3-032-06754-8_3

Achieving concurrent and adaptive security for Σ-protocol-based NIZKPoK deployed in the above systems is notoriously difficult [6,32,43,52]. Yet, Σ-protocols made non-interactive in the ROM are being embedded into real-world systems [26]. Constructing universally composable (UC) NIZKPoK that can withstand adaptive corruptions in the universal composition with global subroutines (UCGS) framework [1,19] (where the global subroutine is a random oracle) is therefore a natural and well-motivated problem.

Canetti, Sarkar, and Wang [23] developed a compiler that leverages UC non-interactive commitments and a correlation intractable hash function to obtain adaptive Σ-protocol-based UC NIZKPoK from standard assumptions. They consider Σ-protocols in the $\mathcal{F}_{\mathsf{NICOM}}$-CRS-hybrid model, where the first message of the Σ-protocol is transformed into a UC non-interactive commitment using equivocable commitments, CCA-2-secure public key encryption with oblivious ciphertext sampling, and a (non-programmable) common reference string (CRS). Non-interactivity and extractability are achieved using the correlation intractable hash function. These additional cryptographic building blocks are difficult to realize efficiently, so it is of theoretical interest only.

In this paper, we ask the question: can we achieve adaptively secure UC NIZKPoK in the global ROM from Σ-protocols efficiently? Specifically, existing constructions that are considered for standardization rely on Σ-protocols as a building block. Can we achieve a simple compiler that would make this building block into adaptively secure UC NIZKPoK in the global ROM, without paying a high price in efficiency?

Our Main Results. For Σ-protocols that can be described as linear function families [37], we show that our new adaptively-secure version of Kondi and shelat's randomized Fischlin transform [34,40] gives us such a compiler. Efficiency wise, our compiler inherits the same overhead as the standard version, thereby outperforming other known techniques (which we discuss further below).

In the programmable global ROM, we achieve adaptive UC NIZKPoK using our compiler alone; in the non-programmable global ROM, we modify Lysyanskaya and Rosenbloom's OR-protocol transformation [41] for the adaptive corruption setting. Along the way, we define formally the natural adaptivity property of Σ-protocols from linear function families, and also extend the definition to adaptive witness indistinguishability for OR-protocols. We show that proofs of knowledge of a discrete logarithm [47] and proofs of knowledge and equality of representations of a set of group element in a set of bases [16,18,31,49] are Σ-protocols from linear function families, and can therefore be efficiently transformed using our techniques into adaptive UC NIZKPoK in both global ROMs. Since the latter Σ-protocols are the main building block in numerous constructions in the area of privacy-preserving authentication (just to mention a few, see [3,7,14,15,38,50]), our main result will enable the realization of these constructions in a composable way in the adaptive corruption model.

Other Related Work. Prior work has shown that straight-line extraction is necessary to obtain UC NIZKPoK [41]. The overhead of the standard, randomized, and now our adaptive version of the Fischlin transform is—in terms of prover computation and communication complexity—polylogarithmic ($O(\texttt{polylog}(\lambda))$ in the security parameter λ. The cut-and-choose technique due to Pass [46] and adopted by Unruh [51] incurs an overhead of λ^2 (see Kondi and shelat [40, p. 3] for discussion), while the commit-and-open technique due to Camenisch and Damgård [8] and adopted by Canetti, Sarkar, and Wang [23] is in the CRS model rather than the ROM, and incurs an overhead of $O(\lambda)$.

Other proposals for adaptive UC NIZKPoK such as those based on the construction of Groth, Ostrovsky, and Sahai [36], are not optimized to transform Σ-protocols in the ROM. Rather, they are in the CRS model and involve representing the NP statement to be proven as a circuit C, encrypting (and more) each bit of the witness making C satisfiable, and doing a NIZK proof that the computations are correct with respect to the witness and some randomness. Groth, Ostrovsky, and Sahai's original construction incurred an overhead of $O(\lambda)$; more recent constructions such as the one due to Cohen, shelat, and Wichs [25] use new techniques to increase the efficiency, however the overhead is still substantial (in Cohen, shelat, and Wichs' construction, the proof size is $|w| \cdot \texttt{poly}(\lambda, d)$, where $|w|$ is the size of the witness and d is the circuit depth).

Garay, MacKenzie, and Yang [35] developed an efficient compiler for creating adaptive UC *interactive* ZK PoK from Σ-protocols. Lysyanskaya and Rosenbloom showed how to create UC NIZKPoK in the global ROM, but did not consider adaptive security [41]. Crites, Komlo, and Maller [30] achieved threshold signatures from Schnorr's Σ-protocol with strong notions of adaptive and concurrent security in the algebraic group model with random oracles; this work considers unforgeability and does not employ "full-strength" NIZKPoK.

Similarly, many of the protocols undergoing implementation and standardization focus on signatures from Σ-protocols in the ROM, and circumvent the need for NIZKPoK. Part of this seems to be because (as in the work of Crites, Komlo, and Maller) NIZKPoK are "overly strong" in some cases [30, p. 8]. However, the difficulty of achieving strong security notions for NIZKPoK from Σ-protocols in the ROM has also been a significant limiting factor. In the FROST-Interactive protocol, for example, Komlo and Goldberg opted for one-time verifiable random functions "because of the difficulty of simulating [NIZKPoK] in a concurrent setting" [39, p.28]. Our work not only demonstrates that Σ-protocols can be transformed into universally composable, adaptively-secure NIZKPoK in the global ROM, but in such a way that is "plug-and-play" with existing infrastructure (i.e. by repeating various steps of widely-implemented Σ-protocols rather than by introducing new cryptographic primitives). We hope to set the stage for readily deployable, "full-strength" NIZKPoK for new cryptographic applications on the horizon. In the remainder of the introduction, we provide necessary high-level context for understanding our results.

Adaptive Σ-Protocols. A standard Σ-protocol [31,49] is a three-move, public coin zero-knowledge proof system over a binary NP relation R, where statements x are proven to be in the language L_R using a "witness" w such that $(x, w) \in R$. V accepts or rejects the proof transcript $(x, \texttt{com}, \texttt{chl}, \texttt{res})$. This proof system must be *complete*, *special honest-verifier zero-knowledge* (SHVZK), and *special* *sound* (SS). Completeness says that if P forms a proof using the three-move form on input $(x, w) \in R$, then V accepts. SHVZK requires a *simulator* algorithm $\texttt{SimProve}$ that, on input $(x, \texttt{chl})$ (but no witness) produces a proof transcript that looks indistinguishable from that of a "real" prover P. SS implies an *extractor* algorithm $\texttt{Extract}$ that can compute a witness w from any two valid proofs $(\texttt{com}, \texttt{chl}, \texttt{res})$, $(\texttt{com}', \texttt{chl}', \texttt{res}')$ of a statement x with the same first message $\texttt{com} = \texttt{com}'$ but different verifier challenges $\texttt{chl} \neq \texttt{chl}'$. In an OR-type Σ-protocol [28,31], P proves that either it knows a witness w_0 to a statement x_0, or else it knows a witness w_1 to a statement x_1. The proof of the chosen witness w_b is computed according to the "real" prove algorithm of Σ_b, while the proof of $w_{\bar{b}}$ is computed according to the $\texttt{SimProve}$ algorithm of $\Sigma_{\bar{b}}$. OR-protocols have a property called witness indistinguishability (WI), which states that the adversary cannot tell from seeing a proof whether the prover used w_b or $w_{\bar{b}}$.

In the adaptive corruption setting, the adversary can corrupt P after P has already issued proofs, revealing the entirety of P's random tape. We say that a Σ-protocol is adaptive SVHZK (adSHVZK) if it has an additional simulator algorithm, $\texttt{SimRand}$, that generates randomness that P could have used to produce a given (simulated) proof on input a given witness. Adaptive WI (adWI) additionally requires an algorithm $\texttt{RealToSim}$, which allows the simulator to "equivocate" the randomness used in a "real" proof of a witness w_b to make it look simulated (while $\texttt{SimRand}$ is used on the simulated proof of $w_{\bar{b}}$ to make it look "real"). We show that popular Σ-protocols for proving discrete-logarithm-based relations are adaptive according to these definitions.

Universal Composition with Global Subroutines. The security experiment in the UC framework [1,19] tests a session of a cryptographic protocol Π in the presence of arbitrary concurrent protocols, which are modeled using an adversarial "environment" machine $\mathcal{Z}$. $\mathcal{Z}$ controls the corrupted protocol participants through an adversary machine, and can also send inputs to honest protocol participants and observe their outputs. In the "real-world" security experiment, the honest parties form their outputs according to the protocol Π, and interact with a malicious adversary $\mathscr{A}$ that can be an arbitrary polynomial-time algorithm. In the "ideal-world" experiment, honest parties are just placeholder "dummies" who pass all of their inputs to an ideal functionality $\mathcal{F}$ (in our case, the ideal functionality $\mathcal{F}_{\texttt{aNIZK}}$ for adaptive NIZKPoK), which acts according to an "ideal" version of the protocol. The adversary $\mathscr{A}$ is replaced with an "ideal adversary" $\mathcal{S}$, who acts like $\mathscr{A}$ when talking to $\mathcal{Z}$, but also communicates with $\mathcal{F}$ and simulates the view of the corrupted parties. When $\mathcal{Z}$ wishes to adaptively corrupt a protocol participant P, $\mathcal{F}$ hands over any relevant information about P to $\mathcal{S}$, and all future communications with P are handled through $\mathcal{S}$. If $\mathcal{Z}$ cannot distinguish its interaction with "real" parties running Π in the presence of the "real" adversary $\mathscr{A}$ from its interaction with "ideal" (dummy) parties running $\mathcal{F}$ in the presence of the "ideal" adversary, then Π is said to "UC-realize" (or be UC-secure with respect to) $\mathcal{F}$ in the presence of $\mathcal{Z}$.

The universal composition with global subroutines (UCGS) model developed by Badertscher, Canetti, Hesse, Tackmann, and Zikas [1] accomodates a *global subroutine protocol* $\mathcal{G}$, which is wrapped into a joint body with the test protocol session π by a "shell" protocol $\mathtt{M}$. The global subroutines of interest to our work are the restricted programmable observable global RO $\mathcal{G}_{\mathtt{rpoRO}}$ of Camenisch, Drijvers, Gagliardoni, Lehmann, and Neven [9] and the restricted observable (non-programmable) global RO $\mathcal{G}_{\mathtt{roRO}}$ of Canetti, Jain, and Scafuro [20].

Adaptive Straight-Line Compilers. A straight-line compiler (SLC) [41] is an algorithm $\mathtt{SLC}$ that takes as input any Σ-protocol Σ_R for relation R (as described above) and produces as output a *non-interactive, straight-line extractable* (NISLE) proof system $\Pi_R^{\mathtt{SLC}}$ for R in the ROM. A proof system is straight-line extractable if the challenger in the security experiment can obtain the two proofs needed to run the $\mathtt{Extract}$ algorithm (and thereby compute a witness for the statement x) immediately after an adversarial prover issues a single proof, i.e. without any further interaction with the prover. In the ROM, the security experiment has access to the adversary's queries to the RO; therefore, as long as an adversarial prover is forced to query the RO on two proof transcripts with the same first message but different challenges, the $\mathtt{Extract}$ algorithm can immediately compute a witness for the prover's statement. The randomized Fischlin transform [34,40] sets the proof repetition parameters such that the prover is guaranteed to issue two such transcripts to the RO.

We define an *adaptive* SLC as an SLC that preserves the adaptive security properties of the underlying Σ-protocol—that is, the resulting proof system $\Pi_R^{\mathtt{SLC}}$ is also secure against adaptive corruptions. Specifically, we define new adaptive versions of the non-interactive multiple SHVZK (NIM-SHVZK) and special simulation-soundness (NI-SSS) properties guaranteed by the regular SLC, and show these properties (including completeness, Definitions 9-11) are both *necessary* and *sufficient* to obtain adaptive UC NIZKPoK in the global ROM.

Putting it all Together. Consider the Σ-protocol for proving knowledge and equality of discrete logarithm representations in prime-order groups. It is used often in applied cryptography constructions and was put forth for standardization [49]. Our results give a recipe for obtaining an adaptively secure UC NIZKPoK in the global ROM for equality of discrete logarithm representations, as follows: First, we show that this Σ-protocol is already an adaptively secure one, i.e. we give the algorithm $\mathtt{SimRand}$ (Sect. 3). Next, we show that compiling it with an adaptive SLC such as the adaptive randomized Fischlin transform (Sect. 4) yields an adaptively secure UC NIZKPoK in the programmable $\mathcal{G}_{\mathtt{rpoRO}}$-hybrid model; we also show that in the non-programmable $\mathcal{G}_{\mathtt{roRO}}$-$\mathcal{F}_{\mathtt{CRS}}$-hybrid model, we obtain an adaptively secure UC NIZKPoK by compiling a slightly modified version of the Σ-protocol with an adaptive SLC (Sect. 5).

2 Preliminaries

The Global Random Oracle Model(s). We will demonstrate how to obtain adaptive UC NIZKPoK in two global random oracle models: the restricted *observable* global ROM of Canetti et al. [22] and the restricted *programmable* observable global ROM of Camenisch et al. [9]. The global ROs in both models have a traditional random function interface, $\mathtt{Query}$, which takes an any-length string as input and returns a uniformly random ℓ-bit string as output [5]. The "global" designation refers to the fact that there exists a single instance of the oracle for all sessions of a protocol (as opposed to one functionality per protocol session, as in the standard UC model [19]). In order to be considered a global subroutine in the UCGS model [1], the global RO must be *subroutine respecting* and *regular* with respect to the challenge protocol. Both global ROs are subroutine respecting since the "extended instance" of each includes querying parties in any session, and no oracle subroutines interact directly with the querent. They are also regular with respect to the challenge protocol, since they neither invoke new NIZKPoK protocol participants nor run them as subroutines.

The observable-only RO $\mathcal{G}_{\mathtt{roRO}}$ [9,22] records all "illegitimate" queries made for a session s by parties with an $\mathtt{sid} \neq s$, which captures all of the environment's direct queries (since the environment is external to all legitimate protocol sessions by definition). The observability property is captured by the interface $\mathtt{Observe}$, which takes a session s as input and produces a list of illegitimate queries $\mathcal{Q}_s$ for s as output. Since the only queries in $\mathcal{Q}_s$ are adversarial, we model $\mathcal{Q}_s$ as completely public—$\mathcal{G}_{\mathtt{roRO}}$ can release it to anyone who asks [9].

The *programmable* version $\mathcal{G}_{\mathtt{rpoRO}}$ [9] builds on the observable-only functionality with an $\mathtt{IsProgrammed}$ interface, which reveals the programmed entries for a session s to any parties in the same session. Since the environment is external to all legitimate protocol sessions by definition, it will not be able to query the $\mathtt{IsProgrammed}$ interface directly, and must instead ask through the corrupted session participants (in the ideal world, the simulator can always return "false" to corrupted session participants' $\mathtt{IsProgrammed}$ queries). Unlike the "illegitimate queries" of the observation interface, the list of programmed queries cannot be made public to everyone (or the environment could trivially distinguish the real from ideal experiments). We include formalizations of both definitions in the full version of the paper.

The $\mathcal{G}_{\mathtt{roRO}}$*-*$\mathcal{F}_{\mathtt{CRS}}$*-Hybrid Model.* In the observable-only $\mathcal{G}_{\mathtt{roRO}}$-hybrid model, the $\mathtt{SimProve}$ algorithm has no additional power over a regular prover, since it cannot program $\mathcal{G}_{\mathtt{roRO}}$. Thus, NIZKPoK in the plain $\mathcal{G}_{\mathtt{roRO}}$-hybrid model are impossible [9,20–22,46]. To work around this impossibility result and construct UC NIZKPoK while avoiding the session-localized $\mathtt{IsProgrammed}$ interface of $\mathcal{G}_{\mathtt{rpoRO}}$, Lysyanskaya and Rosenbloom introduce the $\mathcal{G}_{\mathtt{roRO}}$-$\mathcal{F}_{\mathtt{CRS}}$-hybrid model [41], where $\mathcal{F}_{\mathtt{CRS}}$ is the (local) ideal common reference string (CRS) functionality.

In the real-world execution of the $\mathcal{G}_{\mathtt{roRO}}$-$\mathcal{F}_{\mathtt{CRS}}$-hybrid model, $\mathcal{F}_{\mathtt{CRS}}$ has one interface, $\mathtt{Query}$, that simply returns a consistent CRS to the participants of a particular session s. In the ideal-world experiment, the simulator plays the role of $\mathcal{F}_{\mathtt{CRS}}$, and can generate $\mathtt{CRS}_s$ for each session s with a secret trapdoor $\mathtt{trap}_s$. Provers in the $\mathcal{G}_{\mathtt{roRO}}$-$\mathcal{F}_{\mathtt{CRS}}$-hybrid model prove via an OR-protocol [28, 31] that *either* they know a real witness to a statement, *or* they know the trapdoor $\mathtt{trap}_s$ to $\mathtt{CRS}_s$. This allows the simulator in the ideal-world experiment to "simulate" proofs of statements without witnesses using its extra power—the CRS trapdoor—which a real-world prover will never have.

In order to make the CRS statement compatible with the definition of Σ-protocols, it must be drawn from a *samplable-hard relation* S—that is, generating the CRS must be efficient, and, given any $\mathtt{CRS}_s \in L_S$, it must be overwhelmingly difficult to generate a $\mathtt{trap}_s$ such that $S(\mathtt{CRS}_s, \mathtt{trap}_s) = 1$ [41]. The relation S must additionally be *Σ-friendly*: it must have a corresponding *efficient*—and in our case *adaptive* and *witness equivocable* (according to the definitions given in Sect. 3)—Σ-protocol Σ_S. Proofs in the $\mathcal{G}_{\mathtt{roRO}}$-$\mathcal{F}_{\mathtt{CRS}}$-hybrid model are therefore well-specified as OR-protocols $\Sigma_{R \vee S}$, where R is the relation of the original Σ-protocol Σ_R, and S is the relation underlying Σ_S. Formal definitions of $\mathcal{F}_{\mathtt{CRS}}$ and context-friendly properties are given in the full veresion of the paper.

UC with Global Subroutines and Adaptive Corruptions. Informally, a protocol Π qualifies as adaptive UC with respect to an ideal functionality $\mathcal{F}$ (i.e. Π "aUC-emulates" $\mathcal{F}$) in the global ROM if for all efficient players in the security experiment, no adaptively-corrupting environment can distinguish the real-world experiment (with Π and $\mathscr{A}$) from the ideal-world experiment (with $\mathcal{F}_{\mathtt{aNIZK}}$ and $\mathcal{S}$). In other words, adaptive UC is just standard UC with an adaptive corruption flag set, but to maintain the clarity of our results we call any protocol that satisfies the UC security definition with adaptive corruptions aUC for short. We review the specifics of adaptive corruption in the UC experiment in the full version of the paper. Briefly, $\mathcal{Z}$ is allowed to issue a command $(\textbf{Corrupt}, P)$ during the protocol execution which reveals a full internal view of a party P.

In the UC with global subroutines (UCGS) model, Π UC-emulates $\mathcal{F}$ *in the presence of a global subroutine* $\mathcal{G}$ if $\mathtt{M}[\Pi, \mathcal{G}]$ UC-emulates $\mathtt{M}[\mathcal{F}, \mathcal{G}]$, where $\mathtt{M}$ is the "shell" wrapper mentioned in the introduction. Badertscher et al. [1] show that as long as the global subroutine is subroutine respecting and regular with respect to the challenge protocol, and that the challenge protocol is subroutine respecting *except in its interactions with* $\mathcal{G}$ (i.e. it is $\mathcal{G}$-subroutine respecting), then $\mathtt{M}[\Pi, \mathcal{G}]$ (resp. $\mathtt{M}[\mathcal{F}, \mathcal{G}]$) are subroutine respecting and behave just like Π and $\mathcal{G}$ (resp. $\mathcal{F}$ and $\mathcal{G}$) would behave as individual entities. We argued in earlier in this section that both $\mathcal{G}_{\mathtt{rpoRO}}$ and $\mathcal{G}_{\mathtt{roRO}}$ qualify as global subroutines, and as $\mathcal{G}_{\mathtt{rpoRO}}$ and $\mathcal{G}_{\mathtt{roRO}}$ are the only global subroutines in our experiments, Π and $\mathcal{F}_{\mathtt{aNIZK}}$ are $\mathcal{G}_{\mathtt{rpoRO}}$- and $\mathcal{G}_{\mathtt{roRO}}$-subroutine respecting. Therefore, without loss of generality, we consider our UC experiments "in the presence of global subroutines" $\mathcal{G}_{\mathtt{rpoRO}}$ and $\mathcal{G}_{\mathtt{roRO}}$—or in the $\mathcal{G}_{\mathtt{rpoRO}}$- and $\mathcal{G}_{\mathtt{roRO}}$-hybrid models—and omit the notation $\mathtt{M}$.

We review the standard UC-security definition with respect to a generic global subroutine $\mathcal{G}$, and instantiate the individual versions (i.e. with the generic global RO $\mathcal{G}_{\mathtt{RO}}$, $\mathcal{G}_{\mathtt{rpoRO}}$, $\mathcal{G}_{\mathtt{roRO}}$, and $\mathcal{F}_{\mathtt{CRS}}$) as needed throughout the paper.

Definition 1 (aUC Protocols in the $\mathcal{G}$-hybrid Model). *A protocol Π with security parameter λ* aUC-realizes the ideal functionality $\mathcal{F}$ with adaptive corruptions in the $\mathcal{G}$-hybrid model *if for all efficient $\mathscr{A}$, there exists an ideal adversary $\mathcal{S}$ efficient in expectation such that for all efficient environments $\mathcal{Z}$ that can issue adaptive corruptions,* $\mathsf{IDEAL}^{\mathcal{G}}_{\mathcal{F},\mathcal{S},\mathcal{Z}}(1^\lambda, \mathtt{aux}) \approx_c \mathsf{REAL}^{\mathcal{G},*}_{\Pi,\mathscr{A},\mathcal{Z}}(1^\lambda, \mathtt{aux})$, *where $\mathcal{G}$ is a global subroutine,* $\mathtt{aux}$ *is any auxiliary information provided to the* *environment, and $*$ represents any additional local functionality included in the real-world experiment.*

3 Adaptive Σ-Protocols and Friends

Adaptive Σ-Protocols. Recall from the introduction that a Σ-protocol for a binary NP relation R is a three-move public-coin protocol between a prover P and a verifier V, after which V is convinced that P has a witness w for some statement x such that $R(x, w) = 1$. P is assumed to be a *probabilistic* (polynomial-time) Turing Machine (TM)—that is, P is assumed to have a random tape, from which it can sample (polynomially-many) random bits. We make this random tape explicit, denoting it as a random string r of length λ_r.

The basic three-move form of a Σ-protocol is generally described as an interactive "protocol template" τ [31,41]. The algorithmic version of the protocol template definition consists of the following algorithms: τ.`Setup`, τ.`Commit`, τ.`Challenge`, τ.`Respond`, and τ.`Decision` [41]. We modify the τ.`Setup` algorithm such that the public parameters contain the prover's *randomness security parameter* λ_P, derived from the overall security parameter λ, that specifies the amount of randomness necessary to compute the first message `com`. In particular, we assume the randomness r that is given as input to τ.`Commit` is sampled uniformly at random from $\{0,1\}^{\lambda_P}$, representing a λ_P-length section of P's random tape. The algorithms τ.`Challenge`, τ.`Respond`, and τ.`Decision` are unchanged. We include a formal description of the adaptive Σ-protocol template in the full version of the paper.

In addition to the protocol template, Σ-protocols are defined with respect to three fundamental properties: completeness, special honest-verifier zero-knowledge (SHVZK), and special soundness (SS). In the adaptive corruption setting, the zero-knowledge simulator must additionally be able to produce a view of the prover's randomness that is consistent with the proofs generated by the `SimProve` algorithm. We therefore introduce a new algorithm—`SimRand`—which, given its own section of random tape $r_{\texttt{Sim}}$ of size λ_S, a statement, a proof, some auxiliary information produced by `SimSetup` and `SimProve`, and *the witness that was supposedly used to compute the proof*, outputs some simulated randomness r. This algorithm captures the intuition that an adaptive Σ-protocol simulator must be able to generate convincing randomness for the prover's random tape *after the proof has already been generated* and the prover is corrupted.

Definition 2 (Adaptive Σ-protocol). *An* adaptive Σ-protocol for a relation R *based on adaptive protocol template τ (see full version for details) is a tuple of efficient procedures $\Sigma_{R,\tau}$ =* (`Setup`, `Prove`, `Verify`, `SimSetup`, `SimProve`, `SimRand`, `Extract`)*, defined as follows.*

- `ppm` $\leftarrow$ `Setup`(1^λ)*: Given a security parameter 1^λ, invoke τ.*`Setup`(1^λ) *to obtain the public parameters* `ppm`*, which include randomness security parameters λ_P and $\lambda_{\texttt{Sim}}$ for the prover and simulator, respectively.*

- $\pi \leftarrow \texttt{Prove}((\texttt{ppm}, x, w, r), (\texttt{ppm}, x, \texttt{chl}))$: *Let the first (resp. second) argument to* Prove *be the input to* P *(resp.* V*), where both parties get* ppm *and the statement* x*, but only* P *gets witness* w *and randomness* $r \leftarrow_\$ \{0,1\}^{\lambda_P}$*.* P *and* V *run* τ.Commit, τ.Challenge, *and* τ.Respond*. Output* $\pi = (\texttt{com}, \texttt{chl}, \texttt{res})$.
- $\{0,1\} \leftarrow \texttt{Verify}(\texttt{ppm}, x, \pi)$: *Given a proof* π *for statement* x*, parse* π *as* $(\texttt{com}, \texttt{chl}, \texttt{res})$ *and output the result of running* τ.Decision *on input* $(x, \texttt{com}, \texttt{chl}, \texttt{res})$. Verify *must satisfy the* completeness property *(see full version for details of the basic completeness property).*
- $(\texttt{ppm}, z_{\texttt{Sim}}) \leftarrow \texttt{SimSetup}(1^\lambda)$: *Generate* ppm *and simulator state information* $z_{\texttt{Sim}}$*. Together,* SimSetup, SimProve, *and* SimRand *must satisfy the* adaptive special honest-verifier zero-knowledge property *(see full version for details of the basic HVZK property).*
- $(\pi, z_\pi) \leftarrow \texttt{SimProve}(\texttt{ppm}, z_{\texttt{Sim}}, x, \texttt{chl}, r_{\texttt{Sim}})$: *Given public parameters* ppm*, state* $z_{\texttt{Sim}}$*, statement* x*, challenge* chl*, and randomness* $r_{\texttt{Sim}} \leftarrow \{0,1\}^{\lambda_{\texttt{Sim}}}$*, produce a proof* $\pi = (\texttt{com}, \texttt{chl}, \texttt{res})$ *and proof state information* z_π.
- $r \leftarrow \texttt{SimRand}(\texttt{ppm}, z_{\texttt{Sim}}, z_\pi, x, \pi, w, r_{\texttt{Sim}})$: *Given public parameters* ppm*, simulator state* $z_{\texttt{Sim}}$*, proof state* z_π*, proof* π *for statement* x*, a witness* w *such that* $R(x, w) = 1$*, and randomness* $r_{\texttt{Sim}}$*, produce randomness* r.
- $w \leftarrow \texttt{Extract}(\texttt{ppm}, x, \pi, \pi')$: *Given two proofs* $\pi = (\texttt{com}, \texttt{chl}, \texttt{res})$ *and* $\pi' = (\texttt{com}, \texttt{chl}', \texttt{res}')$ *for a statement* x*, output a witness* w*.* Extract *must satisfy the* two-special soundness property *(see full version for the basic two-special soundness property).*

For convenience and when the meaning is clear, we use Σ_R *to represent* $\Sigma_{R,\tau}$ *and omit* ppm *from the input of the algorithms.*

Standard definitions of completeness and two-special soundness are given in the full version; our new definition of adaptive SHVZK is given below.

Definition 3 (Adaptive Special Honest-Verifier Zero-Knowledge). *A* Σ*-protocol* Σ_R *for relation* R *is statistical (resp. computational)* adaptive special honest-verifier zero-knowledge (adaptive SHVZK) *if there exist algorithms* SimSetup, SimProve, *and* SimRand *such that for any security parameter* λ*, any adversary (resp. any* PPT *adversary)* $\mathscr{A}$*, and a bit* $b \leftarrow_\$ \{0,1\}$*, there exists some negligible function* negl *such that* $\Pr[b' = b] \leq \frac{1}{2} + \mathsf{negl}(\lambda)$*, where* b' *is the result of running the game* $\mathsf{adSHVZK}_{\mathscr{A},\Sigma_R}(1^\lambda, b)$ *from Fig. 1. We say* $\mathscr{A}$ *wins the* adSHVZK *game if* $\Pr[b' = b] > \frac{1}{2} + \mathsf{negl}(\lambda)$.

OR-Protocols. An OR-protocol [31,41] is a Σ-protocol over a disjunctive relation: the prover shows that *either* it knows a witness w_0 for a statement x_0 such that $R_0(x_0, w_0) = 1$, *or* it knows a witness w_1 for a statement x_1 such that $R_1(x_1, w_1) = 1$. The structure of the proof produced by an OR-protocol prover is $\Phi = (\pi_0, \pi_1, \texttt{CHL})$, where one of the proofs π_b is computed according to the Σ_b.Prove algorithm and the other is according to the $\Sigma_{\bar{b}}$.SimProve algorithm.

Recall from the introduction that an OR-protocol Σ_{OR} must have a property called *witness indistinguishability*, which (in the non-adaptive setting) follows directly from the special honest-verifier zero-knowledge property of Σ_0 and Σ_1

$\mathsf{adSHVZK}_{\mathscr{A},\Sigma_R}(1^\lambda, 0)$: REAL	$\mathsf{adSHVZK}_{\mathscr{A},\Sigma_R}(1^\lambda, 1)$: IDEAL
$\texttt{ppm} \leftarrow \Sigma_R.\texttt{Setup}(1^\lambda)$	$(\texttt{ppm}, z_{\texttt{Sim}}) \leftarrow \Sigma_R.\texttt{SimSetup}(1^\lambda)$
$(x, w, \texttt{st}) \leftarrow \mathscr{A}(1^\lambda, \texttt{ppm})$	$(x, w, \texttt{st}) \leftarrow \mathscr{A}(1^\lambda, \texttt{ppm})$
if $R(x, w) = 1$:	**if** $R(x, w) = 1$:
$\quad r \leftarrow_\$ \{0,1\}^{\lambda_P}$	$\quad r_{\texttt{Sim}} \leftarrow_\$ \{0,1\}^{\lambda_{\texttt{Sim}}}$
$\quad \texttt{chl} \leftarrow \{0,1\}^\ell$	$\quad \texttt{chl} \leftarrow \{0,1\}^\ell$
$\quad \pi \leftarrow \Sigma_R.\texttt{Prove}((x, w, r), (x, \texttt{chl}))$	$\quad (\pi, z_\pi) \leftarrow \Sigma_R.\texttt{SimProve}(z_{\texttt{Sim}}, x, \texttt{chl}, r_{\texttt{Sim}})$
	$\quad r \leftarrow \Sigma_R.\texttt{SimRand}(z_{\texttt{Sim}}, z_\pi, x, \pi, w, r_{\texttt{Sim}})$
else :	**else** :
$\quad \pi \leftarrow \perp$	$\quad \pi \leftarrow \perp$
$b' \leftarrow \mathscr{A}(\texttt{st}, \pi, r)$	$b' \leftarrow \mathscr{A}(\texttt{st}, \pi, r)$
return b'	**return** b'

Fig. 1. Adaptive Special Honest-Verifier Zero-Knowledge (adSHVZK) Game.

[31]. We introduce an *adaptive* OR-protocol formalization, which we will need for the proof of Theorem 8. Since $\Sigma_{OR}.\texttt{SimProve}$ computes both halves of the proof according to $\Sigma_b.\texttt{SimProve}$ and $\Sigma_{\overline{b}}.\ \texttt{SimProve}$, respectively, in order to make the simulated random tape look "real", $\Sigma_{OR}.\texttt{SimRand}$ must produce real-looking randomness for the proof π_b corresponding to the witness w_b that was supposedly used to run $\Sigma_{OR}.\texttt{Prove}$.

This is not enough, however: we know from Damgård that the zero knowledge property for Σ-protocols implies the witness indistinguishability property for OR-type Σ-protocols [31]. Informally, our *adaptive* witness indistinguishability property states that $\mathscr{A}$ cannot tell whether a prover used w_b or $w_{\overline{b}}$, even upon learning either the prover's true random tape, or an alternative random tape that the prover might have had if it were using the other witness. Conversely, if our adaptive Σ-protocols do not afford witness indistinguishability when composed in an OR-protocol, they cannot satisfy zero knowledge. Therefore, we introduce an algorithm to capture the idea that the simulator, after issuing a *real proof* for the witness w_b, must be able to reveal its random coins as if it used $w_{\overline{b}}$.

Let $\texttt{RealToSim}$ be an algorithm that takes as input a proof π for statement x computed according to $\Sigma.\texttt{Prove}$ using witness w and randomness r, and outputs simulated random coins $r_{\texttt{Sim}}$. In order to express that the simulator is able to effectively equivocate the prover's random tape in either direction (such that the proof could have been computed according to w_b or $w_{\overline{b}}$), we say that a Σ-protocol is *randomness equivocable* if there does not exist an $\mathscr{A}$ which can distinguish a simulated proof accompanied by the simulator's actual random tape $r_{\texttt{Sim}}$ and a real proof accompanied by the output of $\texttt{RealToSim}$ with non-negligible advantage. For clarity we keep the $\texttt{SimRand}$ and $\texttt{RealToSim}$ algorithms separate for OR-protocols, but intuitively if one considers the OR-protocol as any other Σ-protocol, one can think of wrapping both of these algorithms together into an overarching $\Sigma_{OR}.\texttt{SimRand}'$ algorithm (as specified in Definition 2) which produces the contents of the prover's random tape given either scenario (i.e. making a fully-simulated proof look real, or equivocating the witness used).

Definition 4 (Randomness Equivocability). *A Σ-protocol Σ_R for relation R is* randomness equivocable (RE) *if there exist algorithms* `SimSetup`, `SimProve`, `SimRand`, *and* `RealToSim` *such that Σ_R is adaptive special honest-verifier zero-knowledge (Definition 3) and for any security parameter λ, any adversary (resp. any* PPT *adversary) $\mathscr{A}$, and a bit $b \leftarrow_{\$} \{0,1\}$, there exists some negligible function* negl *such that $\Pr[b' = b] \leq \frac{1}{2} + \mathsf{negl}(\lambda)$, where b' is the result of running the game $\mathsf{RE}_{\mathscr{A},\Sigma_R}(1^\lambda, b)$ from Fig. 2. We say $\mathscr{A}$ wins the* RE *game if* $\Pr[b' = b] > \frac{1}{2} + \mathsf{negl}(\lambda)$.

$\mathsf{RE}_{\mathscr{A},\Sigma_R}(1^\lambda, 0)$	$\mathsf{RE}_{\mathscr{A},\Sigma_R}(1^\lambda, 1)$
$(\mathtt{ppm}, z_{\mathtt{Sim}}) \leftarrow \Sigma_R.\mathtt{SimSetup}(1^\lambda)$	$(\mathtt{ppm}, z_{\mathtt{Sim}}) \leftarrow \Sigma_R.\mathtt{SimSetup}(1^\lambda)$
$(\mathtt{Prove}, x, w, \mathtt{st}) \leftarrow \mathscr{A}(1^\lambda, \mathtt{ppm})$	$(\mathtt{Prove}, x, w, \mathtt{st}) \leftarrow \mathscr{A}(1^\lambda, \mathtt{ppm})$
if $R(x, w) = 1$:	**if** $R(x, w) = 1$:
$\quad r \leftarrow_{\$} \{0,1\}^{\lambda_P}$	$\quad r_{\mathtt{Sim}} \leftarrow \{0,1\}^{\lambda_{\mathtt{Sim}}}$
$\quad \mathtt{chl} \leftarrow \{0,1\}^{\ell}$	$\quad \mathtt{chl} \leftarrow \{0,1\}^{\ell}$
$\quad \pi \leftarrow \Sigma_R.\mathtt{Prove}((x, w, r), (x, \mathtt{chl}))$	$\quad (\pi, z_\pi) \leftarrow \Sigma_R.\mathtt{SimProve}(z_{\mathtt{Sim}}, x, \mathtt{chl}, r_{\mathtt{Sim}})$
$\quad r_{\mathtt{Sim}} \leftarrow \Sigma_R.\mathtt{RealToSim}(\mathtt{ppm}, z_{\mathtt{Sim}}, x, \pi, w, r)$	
else :	**else** :
$\quad \pi \leftarrow \perp$	$\quad \pi \leftarrow \perp$
$b' \leftarrow \mathscr{A}(\mathtt{st}, \pi, r_{\mathtt{Sim}})$	$b' \leftarrow \mathscr{A}(\mathtt{st}, \pi, r_{\mathtt{Sim}})$
return b'	**return** b'

Fig. 2. Randomness Equivocability (RE) Game.

When plugged into an OR-protocol, the `SimRand` and `RealToSim` algorithms allow the simulator to equivocate the witness used to compute a real proof from w_b to $w_{\bar{b}}$ by fabricating a "real" prover's random tape for the previously simulated proof $\pi_{\bar{b}}$ (according to $\Sigma_{\bar{b}}$.`SimRand`) *and* the simulator's random tape for the previously "real" proof π_b (according to Σ_b.`RealToSim`). We call this OR-protocol algorithm `EquivRand`.

Definition 5 (Adaptive OR-Protocol). *An* adaptive OR-protocol *for a relation $R_{OR} = R_0 \vee R_1$ based on adaptive Σ-protocols Σ_{R_0,τ_0} and Σ_{R_1,τ_1} (Definition 2) is a tuple of procedures $\Sigma_{OR} =$* (`Setup`, `Prove`, `Verify`, `SimSetup`, `SimProve`, `SimRand`, `Extract`), *defined as follows.*

- $\mathtt{PPM} \leftarrow \mathtt{Setup}(1^\lambda)$*: Given a security parameter 1^λ, run $\Sigma_{R_0}.\mathtt{Setup}(1^\lambda)$ to obtain* $\mathtt{ppm}_0$ *and $\Sigma_{R_1}.\mathtt{Setup}(1^\lambda)$ to obtain* $\mathtt{ppm}_1$. *Let $\lambda_P = \lambda_{\mathtt{Sim}} = \lambda_{r_0} + \lambda_{\mathtt{Sim}_0} + \lambda_{r_1} + \lambda_{\mathtt{Sim}_1}$. Output* $\mathtt{PPM} = (\mathtt{ppm}_0, \mathtt{ppm}_1, \lambda_P, \lambda_{\mathtt{Sim}})$.

- $\Phi \leftarrow \texttt{Prove}((\texttt{PPM}, X, W, T), (\texttt{PPM}, X, \texttt{CHL}))$: *Parse* $X = (x_0, x_1)$, $W = (w, b)$, *and* $T = (r_b, r_{\texttt{Sim}_b}, r_{\bar{b}}, r_{\texttt{Sim}_{\bar{b}}})$, *and let* b *be the bit such that* $(x_b, w) \in R_b$. P *computes* $\texttt{com}_b$ *according to* $\tau_b.\texttt{Commit}(x_b, w, r_b)$. P *chooses* $\texttt{chl}_{\bar{b}}$ *at random and generates* $(\texttt{com}_{\bar{b}}, \texttt{chl}_{\bar{b}}, \texttt{res}_{\bar{b}})$ *by running* $\Sigma_{R_{\bar{b}}}.\texttt{SimProve}(x_{\bar{b}}, z_{\bar{b}}, \texttt{chl}_{\bar{b}}, r_{\texttt{Sim}_{\bar{b}}})$. P *sends* V $\texttt{Com} = (\texttt{com}_0, \texttt{com}_1)$ *and* V *sends* P *a random* ℓ*-bit string* $\texttt{CHL}$. P *sets* $\texttt{chl}_b = \texttt{CHL} \oplus \texttt{chl}_{\bar{b}}$ *and computes* $\texttt{res}_b$ *according to* $\tau_b.\texttt{Respond}(x_b, w, \texttt{com}_b, \texttt{chl}_b)$. P *sends* $(\texttt{Chl}, \texttt{Res}) = (\texttt{chl}_0, \texttt{chl}_1, \texttt{res}_0, \texttt{res}_1)$ *to* V.
- $\{0,1\} \leftarrow \texttt{Verify}(\texttt{PPM}, X, \Phi)$: *Parse* Φ *as* $(\pi_0, \pi_1, \texttt{CHL})$, *where* $\pi_b = (\texttt{com}_b, \texttt{chl}_b, \texttt{res}_b)$ *for* $b \in \{0,1\}$. *If* $\tau_0.\texttt{Decision}(x_0, \texttt{com}_0, \texttt{chl}_0, \texttt{res}_0) = \tau_1.\texttt{Decision}(x_1, \texttt{com}_1, \texttt{chl}_1, \texttt{res}_1) = 1$ *and* $\texttt{chl}_0 \oplus \texttt{chl}_1 = \texttt{CHL}$, *return 1 (accept). Otherwise, return 0 (reject).*
- $(\texttt{PPM}, Z_{\texttt{Sim}}) \leftarrow \texttt{SimSetup}(1^\lambda)$: *Compute* $(\texttt{ppm}_0, z_{\texttt{Sim}_0}) \leftarrow \Sigma_{R_0}.\texttt{SimSetup}(1^\lambda)$ *and* $(\texttt{ppm}_1, z_{\texttt{Sim}_1}) \leftarrow \Sigma_{R_1}.\texttt{SimSetup}(1^\lambda)$. *Return* $(\texttt{PPM}, Z)$ *where* $\texttt{PPM} = (\texttt{ppm}_0, \texttt{ppm}_1)$ *and* $Z_{\texttt{Sim}} = (z_{\texttt{Sim}_0}, z_{\texttt{Sim}_1})$.
- $(\Phi, Z_\Phi) \leftarrow \texttt{SimProve}(\texttt{PPM}, X, Z_{\texttt{Sim}}, \texttt{CHL}, T_{\texttt{Sim}})$: *Parse* $\texttt{PPM} = (\texttt{ppm}_0, \texttt{ppm}_1)$, $X = (x_0, x_1)$, $Z_{\texttt{Sim}} = (z_{\texttt{Sim}_0}, z_{\texttt{Sim}_1})$, *and* $T_{\texttt{Sim}} = (r_{\texttt{Sim}_0}, r_{\texttt{Sim}_1})$. *Generate* $\texttt{chl}_0$ *uniformly at random and set* $\texttt{chl}_1 = \texttt{chl}_0 \oplus \texttt{CHL}$. *Compute* $(\pi_0, z_{\pi_0}) \leftarrow \Sigma_{R_0}.\texttt{SimProve}(x_0, \texttt{chl}_0, r_{\texttt{Sim}_0})$ *and* $(\pi_1, z_{\pi_1}) \leftarrow \Sigma_{R_1}.\texttt{SimProve}(x_1, \texttt{chl}_1, r_{\texttt{Sim}_1})$. *Return* (Φ, Z_Φ) *where* $\Phi = (\pi_0, \pi_1, \texttt{CHL})$ *and* $Z_\Phi = (z_{\pi_0}, z_{\pi_1})$.
- $T' \leftarrow \texttt{SimRand}(\texttt{PPM}, Z_{\texttt{Sim}}, X, \Phi, Z_\Phi, W, T_{\texttt{Sim}})$: *Parse* $\texttt{PPM} = (\texttt{ppm}_0, \texttt{ppm}_1)$, $Z_{\texttt{Sim}} = (z_{\texttt{Sim}_0}, z_{\texttt{Sim}_1})$, $X = (x_0, x_1)$, $\Phi = (\pi_0, \pi_1, \texttt{CHL})$, $Z_\Phi = (z_{\pi_0}, z_{\pi_1})$, $W = (w, b)$, *and* $T_{\texttt{Sim}} = (r_{\texttt{Sim}_0}, r_{\texttt{Sim}_1})$. *Compute* $r_b \leftarrow \Sigma_{R_b}.\texttt{SimRand}(\texttt{ppm}_b, z_{\texttt{Sim}_b}, x_b, z_{\pi_b}, w, r_{\texttt{Sim}_b})$ *and let* $r_{\bar{b}} = r_{\texttt{Sim}_{\bar{b}}}$. *Return* $T = (r_0, r_1)$.
- $T^* \leftarrow \texttt{EquivRand}(\texttt{PPM}, Z_{\texttt{Sim}}, X, \Phi, Z_\Phi, W, T)$: *Parse* $\texttt{PPM} = (\texttt{ppm}_0, \texttt{ppm}_1)$, $Z_{\texttt{Sim}} = (z_{\texttt{Sim}_0}, z_{\texttt{Sim}_1})$, $X = (x_0, x_1)$, $\Phi = (\pi_0, \pi_1, \texttt{CHL})$, $Z_\Phi = (z_{\pi_0}, z_{\pi_1})$, $W = (w, b)$, *and* $T = (r_b, r_{\texttt{Sim}_b}, r_{\bar{b}}, r_{\texttt{Sim}_{\bar{b}}})$. *Compute* $r'_{\bar{b}} \leftarrow \Sigma_{R_b}.\texttt{RealToSim}(\texttt{ppm}_b, x_b, \pi_b, w, r_b)$ *and* $r'_b \leftarrow \Sigma_{R_{\bar{b}}}.\texttt{SimRand}(\texttt{ppm}_b, z_{\texttt{Sim}_{\bar{b}}}, x_b, \pi_b, z_{\pi_{\bar{b}}}, w, r_{\texttt{Sim}_{\bar{b}}})$. *Return* $T = (r'_0, r'_1)$.
- $W \leftarrow \texttt{Extract}(\texttt{PPM}, X, \Phi, \Phi')$: *Parse* $X = (x_0, x_1)$, $\Phi = (\pi_0, \pi_1)$, *and* $\Phi' = (\pi'_0, \pi'_1)$. *Compute* $w_0 \leftarrow \Sigma_{R_0}.\texttt{Extract}(x_0, \pi_0, \pi'_0)$ *and* $w_1 \leftarrow \Sigma_{R_1}.\texttt{Extract}(x_1, \pi_1, \pi'_1)$. *Return* $W = (w_0, w_1)$.

Adaptive Witness Indistinguishability. Finally, we formalize the definition of adaptive witness indistinguishability for OR-protocols and prove that as long as the underlying Σ-protocols Σ_0 and Σ_1 are both adaptive special honest-verifier zero-knowledge *and* randomness equivocable, the OR-protocol based on Σ_0 and Σ_1 is adaptive witness indistinguishable.

Definition 6 (Adaptive Witness Indistinguishability). *An adaptive OR-protocol* $\Sigma_{OR} = (\texttt{Setup}, \texttt{Prove}, \texttt{Verify}, \texttt{SimSetup}, \texttt{SimProve}, \texttt{SimRand}, \texttt{Extract})$ *(Definition 5) based on two adaptive* Σ*-protocols* Σ_{R_0} *and* Σ_{R_1} *(Definition 2) is* adaptive witness indistinguishable (adWI) *if there exists an algorithm* $\texttt{EquivRand}$ *such that for all security parameters* 1^λ, *all PPT* $\mathscr{A}$, *and a bit*

$b \leftarrow_{\$} \{0,1\}$, *there exists some negligible function* negl *such that* $\Pr[b' = b] \leq \frac{1}{2} + \mathsf{negl}(\lambda)$, *where* b' *is the result of running the game* $\mathsf{adWI}_{\mathscr{A},\Sigma_{OR}}(1^\lambda, b)$ *from Fig. 3. We say* $\mathscr{A}$ *wins the* adWI *game if* $\Pr[b' = b] > \frac{1}{2} + \mathsf{negl}(\lambda)$.

$\mathsf{adWI}_{\mathscr{A},\Sigma_{OR}}(1^\lambda, 0)$	$\mathsf{adWI}_{\mathscr{A},\Sigma_{OR}}(1^\lambda, 1)$
$\mathtt{PPM} \leftarrow \Sigma_{OR}.\mathtt{Setup}(1^\lambda)$	$\mathtt{PPM} \leftarrow \Sigma_{OR}.\mathtt{Setup}(1^\lambda)$
$(x_0, x_1, w_0, w_1, b, \mathtt{st}) \leftarrow \mathscr{A}(1^\lambda, \mathtt{ppm})$	$(x_0, x_1, w_0, w_1, b, \mathtt{st}) \leftarrow \mathscr{A}(1^\lambda, \mathtt{ppm})$
if $R_0(x_0, w_0) = R_1(x_1, w_1) = 1$:	**if** $R_0(x_0, w_0) = R_1(x_1, w_1) = 1$:
$\quad$ Set $W = (w_b, b)$	$\quad$ Set $W = (w_{\bar{b}}, \bar{b})$
$\quad T \leftarrow_{\$} \{0,1\}^{\lambda_P}$	$\quad T' \leftarrow_{\$} \{0,1\}^{\lambda_{\mathtt{Sim}}}$
$\quad \mathtt{CHL} \leftarrow \{0,1\}^\ell$	$\quad \mathtt{CHL} \leftarrow \{0,1\}^\ell$
$\quad \Phi \leftarrow \Sigma_{OR}.\mathtt{Prove}((X, W, T), (X, \mathtt{CHL}))$	$\quad \Phi \leftarrow \Sigma_{OR}.\mathtt{Prove}((X, W, T'), (X, \mathtt{CHL}))$
	$\quad T \leftarrow \Sigma_{OR}.\mathtt{EquivRand}(Z, X, \Phi, W, T')$
else :	**else** :
$\quad \Phi \leftarrow \bot$	$\quad \Phi \leftarrow \bot$
$b' \leftarrow \mathscr{A}(\Phi, T, \mathtt{st})$	$b' \leftarrow \mathscr{A}(\Phi, T, \mathtt{st})$
return b'	**return** b'

Fig. 3. Adaptive Witness Indistinguishability (adWI) Game.

Theorem 1 (adSHVZK and RE Imply Adaptive WI). *Let* Σ_{OR} *be an OR-protocol (Definition 5) based on two* Σ*-protocols* Σ_{R_0,τ_0} *and* Σ_{R_1,τ_1} *(Definition 2). If* Σ_{OR} *is adaptive special honest-verifier zero-knowledge (Definition 3) and randomness equivocable (Definition 4), then* Σ_{OR} *is adaptive witness indistinguishable (Definition 6).*

Proof. We wish to show that as long as Σ_{OR} is adaptive special honest-verifier zero-knowledge (adSHVZK) and randomness equivocable (RE), $\mathscr{A}$'s advantage in distinguishing the adaptive witness indistinguishability (adWI) experiments is negligible. Without loss of generality, we consider equivalent formulations of the definitions in which the statement $\Pr[b' = b] \leq \frac{1}{2} + \mathsf{negl}(\lambda)$ is replaced with $|\Pr[b' = 0 \mid b = 0] - \Pr[b' = 0 \mid b = 1]| \leq \mathsf{negl}(\lambda)$, where b' represents $\mathscr{A}$'s output in either the $b = 0$ or $b = 1$ experiments.

Let the 0-bit adWI experiment be denoted RS for "real-sim," since the adversary's chosen witness w_b is used as input to $\Sigma_{OR}.\mathtt{Prove}$, i.e. π_b and r_b (resp. $\pi_{\bar{b}}$ and $r_{\bar{b}}$) are computed according to $\Sigma_b.\mathtt{Prove}$ and the prover's randomness(resp. $\Sigma_{\bar{b}}.\mathtt{SimProve}$ and the simulator's randomness). Let the 1-bit adWI experiment be denoted SR for the above scenario's complement, "sim-real," where the only change is that the random tape is equivocated (according to $\Sigma_b.\mathtt{SimRand}$ and $\Sigma_{\bar{b}}.\mathtt{RealToSim}$). We fix $\mathscr{A}$'s probability of outputting 0 in the RS (resp. SR) experiment to be $p^{\mathscr{A}}_{\mathsf{RS}}(\lambda)$ (resp. $p^{\mathscr{A}}_{\mathsf{SR}}(\lambda)$). We will show via a hybrid experiment

SS, or "sim-sim"—in which both halves of the proof are according to SimProve—that for all $\mathscr{A}$, as long as Σ_{OR} is adSHVZK and RE, $|p^{\mathscr{A}}_{\mathsf{RS}}(\lambda) - p^{\mathscr{A}}_{\mathsf{SR}}(\lambda)| \leq \mathsf{negl}(\lambda)$.

In the proof of the first lemma, we show that, as long as both Σ_0 and Σ_1 are adSHVZK, $|p^{\mathscr{A}}_{\mathsf{RS}}(\lambda) - p^{\mathscr{A}}_{\mathsf{SS}}(\lambda)| \leq \mathsf{negl}(\lambda)$. Our reduction proceeds by using an $\mathscr{A}$ such that $|p^{\mathscr{A}}_{\mathsf{RS}}(\lambda) - p^{\mathscr{A}}_{\mathsf{SS}}(\lambda)| > \mathsf{negl}(\lambda)$ as a black-box, forwarding all queries to the adSHVZK challenger for proofs π_b of $\mathscr{A}$'s chosen Σ_b and computing the other half $\pi_{\bar{b}}$ using $\Sigma_{\bar{b}}$.SimProve. In the second lemma we use a similar $\mathscr{A}$ and proof strategy, this time to show that, as long as both Σ_0 and Σ_1 are randomness equivocable, $|p^{\mathscr{A}}_{\mathsf{RS}}(\lambda) - p^{\mathscr{A}}_{\mathsf{SS}}(\lambda)| \leq \mathsf{negl}(\lambda)$. By these two lemmas and the triangle inequality, we conclude that $|p^{\mathscr{A}}_{\mathsf{RS}}(\lambda) - p^{\mathscr{A}}_{\mathsf{SR}}(\lambda)| = |(p^{\mathscr{A}}_{\mathsf{RS}}(\lambda) - p^{\mathscr{A}}_{\mathsf{SS}}(\lambda)) + (p^{\mathscr{A}}_{\mathsf{SS}}(\lambda) - p^{\mathscr{A}}_{\mathsf{SR}}(\lambda))| \leq \mathsf{negl}(\lambda)$. The full details of the proof are available in the full version of the paper. □

Simple Adaptive Σ-Protocol Abstraction. We use the abstraction of Hauck, Kiltz, and Loss [37], and show how it captures simple Σ-protocols. We then give two instantiations: proofs of knowledge of a discrete logarithm and n equivalent representations of m witnesses. As proven in Sect. 5, any Σ-protocol that qualifies as adaptive can be efficiently bootstrapped into an adaptive UC NIZKPoK in both the programmable and non-programmable global ROMs.

Hauck et al.'s construction of canonical identification schemes from pseudo-modules and linear function families [37] describes an abstract three-move identification scheme that bears close resemblance to the three-move form of a Σ-protocol. We remodel their construction as a Σ-protocol template and add new adaptive Σ-protocol-specific abstractions for the SimProve, SimRand, RealToSim, and Extract algorithms. We narrow the focus of our abstraction to modules, and discuss the potential implications of module properties for Σ-protocols in the full version of the paper. We highlight the properties of linear function families that are critical to understanding our results as part of the proof below.

Definition 7 (Simple Adaptive Σ-protocol Candidate). *The* simple adaptive Σ-protocol candidate $\Sigma_{\mathtt{simple}}$ *for relation* R *is a tuple of efficient procedures* $\Sigma_{\mathtt{simple}} = (\mathtt{Setup}, \mathtt{Prove}, \mathtt{Verify}, \mathtt{SimSetup}, \mathtt{SimProve}, \mathtt{SimRand}, \mathtt{RealToSim}, \mathtt{Extract})$ *that adhere to the following format:*

- $\mathtt{ppm} \leftarrow \mathtt{Setup}(1^\lambda)$*: Define the linear function family* $\mathtt{LF} = (\mathtt{PGen}, \mathtt{F})$ *(Definition 3.1 in [37]) such that* $\mathtt{ppm} \leftarrow \mathtt{PGen}(1^\lambda)$ *fixes a statement space* $\mathcal{X}$*, witness space* $\mathcal{W}$*, first message space* $\mathcal{A}$*, challenge space* $\mathcal{C}$*, response space* $\mathcal{B}$*, and randomness space* $\mathcal{R}$ *such that* $\mathcal{W} = \mathcal{R} = \mathcal{B}$*,* $\mathcal{X} = \mathcal{A}$*,* $\mathcal{W}$ *and* $\mathcal{X}$ *form* modules *over* $\mathcal{C}$*,* $|\mathcal{X}| \geq |\mathcal{C}| \geq 2^{2\lambda}$*, and the evaluation function* $\mathtt{F} : \mathcal{W} \rightarrow \mathcal{X}$*.*
- $\pi \leftarrow \mathtt{Prove}((\mathtt{ppm}, x, w, r), (\mathtt{ppm}, x, \mathtt{chl}))$*: P sends V a first message* $\mathtt{com} = \mathtt{F}(r)$*. V replies with a challenge* $\mathtt{chl} \leftarrow_\$ \mathcal{C}$*. P responds with* $\mathtt{res} = \mathtt{chl} \cdot w + r$*.*
- $\{0,1\} \leftarrow \mathtt{Verify}(\mathtt{ppm}, x, \pi)$*: Parse π as* $(\mathtt{com}, \mathtt{chl}, \mathtt{res})$*. If* $\mathtt{F}(\mathtt{res}) = \mathtt{chl} \cdot x + \mathtt{com}$*, output 1 (accept). Otherwise, output 0 (reject).*
- $\mathtt{ppm} \leftarrow \mathtt{SimSetup}(1^\lambda)$*: Invoke* $\mathtt{Setup}(1^\lambda)$ *and return* $\mathtt{ppm}$.
- $\pi \leftarrow \mathtt{SimProve}(\mathtt{ppm}, x, \mathtt{chl}, r')$ *: Parse* $r' = \mathtt{res}$ *and compute* $\mathtt{com} = F(\mathtt{res} - \mathtt{chl} \cdot w)$*. Return* $\pi = (\mathtt{com}, \mathtt{chl}, \mathtt{res})$.

- $r \leftarrow \texttt{SimRand}(\texttt{ppm}, x, \pi, w)$: *Parse* $\pi = (\texttt{com}, \texttt{chl}, \texttt{res})$. *Compute and output* $r = \texttt{res} - (\texttt{chl} \cdot w)$.
- $r' \leftarrow \texttt{RealToSim}(\texttt{ppm}, \pi)$: *Parse* $\pi = (\texttt{com}, \texttt{chl}, \texttt{res})$ *and output* $r' = \texttt{res}$.
- $w \leftarrow \texttt{Extract}(\texttt{ppm}, x, \pi, \pi')$: *Given any two proofs* $\pi = (\texttt{com}, \texttt{chl}, \texttt{res})$ *and* $\pi' = (\texttt{com}, \texttt{chl}', \texttt{res}')$ *such that* $\texttt{Verify}(x, \pi) = \texttt{Verify}(x, \pi') = 1$ *and* $\texttt{chl} \neq \texttt{chl}'$, *compute and output* $w = (\texttt{res} - \texttt{res}') \cdot (\texttt{chl} - \texttt{chl}')^{-1}$.

Theorem 2 ($\Sigma_{\texttt{simple}}$ is Adaptive). *The simple adaptive Σ-protocol candidate given above (Definition 7) is an adaptive Σ-protocol (Definition 3) with randomness equivocability (Definition 4).*

Proof. The proof relies on two core properties of the evaluation function $\texttt{F}$, described below (for details in context, see Definition 4.1 [37]). First, the *pseudo-module homomorphism* (PMH) property states that for all $y, z \in \mathcal{W}$, $\texttt{F}(\texttt{chl} \cdot y + z) = \texttt{chl} \cdot \texttt{F}(y) + \texttt{F}(z)$. Second, the *smoothness property* guarantees that for all $y \in \mathcal{W}$, $\texttt{F}(y)$ is uniformly distributed over $\mathcal{X}$. (Recall these properties hold as well for $\mathcal{W} = \mathcal{R} = \mathcal{B}$ and $\mathcal{X} = \mathcal{A}$.) Verifying that the simple Σ-protocol format above satisfies the necessary completeness, adaptive special honest-verifier zero-knowledge, special soundness, and randomness equivocability properties is straight-forward; we defer the details to the full version of the paper.

Adaptive Proof of Knowledge of Discrete Logarithm. Proofs of knowledge of discrete logarithm (PoK DL), also known as Schnorr proofs [47], are the backbone of many practical constructions of group [8,17], threshold [4], blind [37], and multi- [4,29] signatures. See full version for the proof of:

Theorem 3 (Σ_{DL} is Simple Adaptive). *A proof of knowledge of discrete logarithm can be described as a simple adaptive Σ-protocol with randomness equivocability (Definition 7).*

Adaptive Proof of Knowledge of Equality of n Representations. Proofs of knowledge of equality of n representations of m witnesses (PoK EqRep) are essential building blocks in the construction of cryptographic shuffles [42,53], accumulators [2,13], and anonymous credentials [12], which form the basis of anonymous networks, voting, payment, and identification systems. Note also that PoK EqRep is a generalization of other common Σ-protocols such as standard PoK of representation [16,18] and Okamoto-Schnorr [44], and that the following result holds for those narrower instantiations as well. See full version for the proof of:

Theorem 4 ($\Sigma_{\texttt{EqRep}}$ is Simple Adaptive). *A proof of knowledge of equality of n representations can be described as a simple adaptive Σ-protocol with randomness equivocability (Definition 7).*

4 Adaptive Straight-Line Compilers

Recall from the introduction that an adaptive straight-line compiler is a straight-line compiler [41] that preserves the adaptive security properties of the Σ-protocol under transformation. A regular straight-line compiler $\mathtt{SLC}$ takes a Σ-protocol Σ_R for a relation R as input and produces a new proof system $\Pi_R^{\mathtt{SLC}}$ that is a tuple of (non-interactive) *algorithms* ($\mathtt{Setup}^H, \mathtt{Prove}^H, \mathtt{Verify}^H, \mathtt{SimSetup}, \mathtt{SimProve}, \mathtt{Extract}$), where H is a traditional RO. In order to be considered a straight-line compiler, $\Pi_R^{\mathtt{SLC}}$ must have the following properties: overwhelming completeness (i.e. a negligibly small completeness error is allowed), non-interactive multiple special honest-verifier zero-knowledge (NIM-SHVZK), and non-interactive special simulation soundness (NI-SSS) [41]. Our *adaptive* SLC, denoted $\mathtt{aSLC}$, says that $\Pi_R^{\mathtt{aSLC}}$ must have *adaptive* NIM-SHVZK and *adaptive* NI-SSS properties—that is, NIM-SHVZK and NI-SSS must hold even when the adversary gets to compare the prover's internal tapes with the output of $\mathtt{SimRand}$.

Definition 8 (Adaptive Straight-Line Compiler). *An algorithm* $\mathtt{SLC}$ *is an* adaptive straight-line compiler (adaptive SLC) *in the random-oracle model if given any adaptive Σ-protocol Σ_R for relation R (Definition 2) as input, it outputs a tuple of* algorithms $\Pi_R^{\mathtt{SLC}} = (\mathtt{Setup}^H, \mathtt{Prove}^H, \mathtt{Verify}^H, \mathtt{SimSetup}, \mathtt{SimProve}, \mathtt{SimRand}, \mathtt{Extract})$ *based on Σ_R that satisfy the following properties: overwhelming completeness (Definition 9), adaptive non-interactive multiple special honest-verifier zero-knowledge (Definition 10), and adaptive non-interactive special simulation soundness (Definition 11).*

We refer to $\Pi_R^{\mathtt{aSLC}} \leftarrow \mathtt{aSLC}(\Sigma_R)$ as an adaptive and non-interactive straight-line extractable (adaptive NISLE) proof system for R, and proofs generated by $\Pi_R^{\mathtt{aSLC}}$ as adaptive and non-interactive straight-line extractable zero-knowledge proofs of knowledge (adaptive NISLE ZKPoK).

Definition 9 (Overwhelming Completeness). *An adaptive NISLE proof system $\Pi_R^{\mathtt{aSLC}}$ for relation R in the random-oracle model has the* overwhelming completeness *property if for any security parameter λ, any $(x, w) \in R$, and any proof $\pi \leftarrow \Pi_R^{\mathtt{aSLC}}.\mathtt{Prove}^H(x, w)$, $\Pr[\Pi_R^{\mathtt{aSLC}}.\mathtt{Verify}^H(x, \pi) = 1] \geq 1 - \mathsf{negl}(\lambda)$.*

To capture the difference between a standard random oracle (modeled as a truly random function) and its programmable version (modeled as a data structure that can be edited by the security experiment), the RO H_f is parameterized by a function $f \leftarrow_\$ F$ selected from random function family F, while the RO H_L is parameterized by an initially empty list L that the challenger in the security experiment can program via an interface $\mathtt{Prog}_L$. When programming does not occur, the list oracle simply selects a return value uniformly at random from the output space. In order to maintain indistinguishability between the experiments and satisfy the (adaptive) NIM-SHVZK property, the ideal-world challenger must program the RO imperceptibly.[1] For convenience the interface

[1] To satisfy NIM-SHVZK when $\Sigma_R.\mathtt{SimProve}$ involves programming, the first message $\mathtt{com}$ will need entropy that is superlogarithmic in the security parameter [34,41].

Prog is included in the definitions of NIM-SHVZK and NI-SSS below; in non-programmable models, one can replace $\texttt{Prog}_L$ with H_L.

Definition 10 (Adaptive Non-Interactive Multiple SHVZK). *An adaptive NISLE proof system $\Pi_R^{\mathtt{aSLC}}$ for relation R in the random-oracle model has the* adaptive non-interactive multiple special honest-verifier zero-knowledge (adNIM-SHVZK) *property if there exist algorithms $\Pi_R^{\mathtt{SLC}}.\mathtt{SimSetup}$, $\Pi_R^{\mathtt{SLC}}.\mathtt{SimProve}$, and $\Pi_R^{\mathtt{SLC}}.\mathtt{SimRand}$ such that for any security parameter λ, any* PPT *adversary $\mathscr{A}$, and a bit $b \leftarrow_\$ \{0,1\}$, there exists some negligible function* negl *such that* $\Pr[b' = b] \leq \frac{1}{2} + \mathsf{negl}(\lambda)$, *where b' is the result of running the game* $\mathsf{adNIM\text{-}SHVZK}_{\mathscr{A},\Pi_R^{\mathtt{SLC}}}^{H_*,*}(1^\lambda, b)$ *from Fig. 4.*

$\mathsf{adNIM\text{-}SHVZK}_{\mathscr{A},\Pi_R^{\mathtt{SLC}}}^{H_*,F}(1^\lambda, 0)$: REAL	$\mathsf{adNIM\text{-}SHVZK}_{\mathscr{A},\Pi_R^{\mathtt{SLC}}}^{H_*,\mathtt{Prog}}(1^\lambda, 1)$: IDEAL
$f \leftarrow_\$ F$	$L \leftarrow \bot$
$\mathtt{ppm} \leftarrow \Pi_R^{\mathtt{SLC}}.\mathtt{Setup}^{H_f}(1^\lambda)$	$(\mathtt{ppm}, z_{\mathtt{Sim}}) \leftarrow \Pi_R^{\mathtt{SLC}}.\mathtt{SimSetup}^{\mathtt{Prog}_L}(1^\lambda)$
$\mathtt{st} \leftarrow \mathscr{A}^{H_f}(1^\lambda, \mathtt{ppm})$	$\mathtt{st} \leftarrow \mathscr{A}^{H_L}(1^\lambda, \mathtt{ppm})$
while $\mathtt{st} \notin \{0,1\}$:	**while** $\mathtt{st} \notin \{0,1\}$:
$(\mathtt{Prove}, x, w, \mathtt{st}) \leftarrow \mathscr{A}^{H_f}(\mathtt{st})$	$(\mathtt{Prove}, x, w, \mathtt{st}) \leftarrow \mathscr{A}^{H_L}(\mathtt{st})$
if $R(x,w) = 1$:	**if** $R(x,w) = 1$:
$r \leftarrow_\$ \{0,1\}^{\lambda_r}$	$(\pi, z_\pi) \leftarrow \Pi_R^{\mathtt{SLC}}.\mathtt{SimProve}^{\mathtt{Prog}_L}(z_s, x)$
$\pi \leftarrow \Pi_R^{\mathtt{SLC}}.\mathtt{Prove}^{H_f}(x, w, r)$	$r \leftarrow \Pi_R^{\mathtt{SLC}}.\mathtt{SimRand}^{\mathtt{Prog}_L}(z_{\mathtt{Sim}}, z_\pi, x, \pi, w)$
else :	**else** :
$\pi, r \leftarrow \bot$	$\pi, r \leftarrow \bot$
$\mathtt{st} \leftarrow \mathscr{A}^{H_f}(\mathtt{st}, \pi, r)$	$\mathtt{st} \leftarrow \mathscr{A}^{H_L}(\mathtt{st}, \pi, r)$
return st	**return** st

Fig. 4. Adaptive Non-Interactive Multiple SHVZK (adNIM-SHVZK) Game.

Definition 11 (Adaptive Non-Interactive SSS). *An adaptive NISLE proof system $\Pi_R^{\mathtt{SLC}}$ for relation R in the random-oracle model has the* adaptive non-interactive special simulation sound (adNI-SSS) *property if there exists an algorithm $\Pi_R^{\mathtt{SLC}}.\mathtt{Extract}$ such that for any security parameter λ and any* PPT *adversary $\mathscr{A}$,* $\Pr[\mathtt{Fail} \leftarrow \mathsf{adNI\text{-}SSS}_{\mathscr{A},\Pi_R^{\mathtt{SLC}}}^{H}(1^\lambda)] \leq \mathsf{negl}(\lambda)$, *where H is any random oracle and* adNI-SSS *is the game described in Fig. 5.*

The randomized Fischlin transform [34,40] rFis is a (standard) straight-line compiler that transforms any Σ-protocol with certain general properties into a non-interactive, straight-line extractable proof system $\Pi_R^{\mathtt{aFis}}$ in the ROM [41]. The prover in rFis essentially rewinds itself, computing proofs on repeated commitments (but different challenges) until it is guaranteed with overwhelmingly probability that there are at least two transcripts queried to the RO with the

$\mathsf{adNI\text{-}SSS}^{H_L,\mathtt{Prog}_L}_{\mathscr{A},\Pi_R^{\mathtt{SLC}}}(1^\lambda)$

$L, \mathtt{pflist}, \mathtt{Response}, \mathtt{st} \leftarrow \bot;$

$(\mathtt{ppm}, z_{\mathtt{Sim}}) \leftarrow \Pi_R^{\mathtt{SLC}}.\mathtt{SimSetup}^{\mathtt{Prog}_L}(1^\lambda)$

$\textbf{while } (\mathtt{Query}, \mathcal{Q}_{\mathscr{A}}, \mathtt{st}) \leftarrow \mathscr{A}^{H_L}(1^\lambda, \mathtt{ppm}, \mathtt{st}) \neq \textbf{halt} :$

$\quad \textbf{if } \mathtt{Query} = (\mathtt{Prove}, x, w) \wedge R(x, w) = 1 :$

$\quad\quad \mathtt{chl} \leftarrow_\$ \{0,1\}^\ell; r_{\mathtt{Sim}} \leftarrow_\$ \{0,1\}^{\lambda_{\mathtt{Sim}}}$

$\quad\quad (\pi, z_\pi) \leftarrow \Pi_R^{\mathtt{SLC}}.\mathtt{SimProve}^{\mathtt{Prog}_L}(z_{\mathtt{Sim}}, x, \mathtt{chl}, r_{\mathtt{Sim}})$

$\quad\quad \mathtt{pflist}.\mathbf{append}(x, \pi)$

$\quad\quad r \leftarrow \Pi_R^{\mathtt{SLC}}.\mathtt{SimRand}^{\mathtt{Prog}_L}(z, z_\pi, x, \pi, w, r_{\mathtt{Sim}})$

$\quad\quad \mathtt{Response} \leftarrow (x, \pi, r)$

$\quad \textbf{elseif } \mathtt{Query} = (\mathtt{Challenge}, x, \pi)$

$\quad\quad \textbf{if } \Pi_R^{\mathtt{SLC}}.\mathtt{Verify}^{H_L}(x, \pi) = 1 \wedge (x, \pi) \notin \mathtt{pflist} :$

$\quad\quad\quad w \leftarrow \Pi_R^{\mathtt{SLC}}.\mathtt{Extract}(x, \pi, \mathcal{Q}_{\mathscr{A}})$

$\quad\quad\quad \textbf{if } R(x, w) = 0 : \textbf{return Fail}$

$\quad \mathtt{st} \leftarrow \mathscr{A}^{H_L}(\mathtt{st}, \mathtt{Response})$

$\textbf{return } \mathtt{Success}$

Fig. 5. Adaptive Non-Interactive Special Simulation Soundness (adNI-SSS) Game.

same commitment but different challenges. The rFis extractor takes these proofs as input (via the adversary's oracle query history $\mathcal{Q}_{\mathscr{A}}$), and can therefore extract witnesses for adversarially-created proofs without rewinding the prover.

In the remainder of this section, we extend rFis for the adaptive setting, and prove that our construction satisfies the definition of an adaptive straight-line compiler. In particular, we will show that the *adaptive* randomized Fischlin transform aFis, which extends rFis with a SimRand functionality, preserves the adaptive security property of the underlying Σ-protocol: as long as Σ_R is adaptive and conforms to the standard requirements of rFis (reviewed in the full version of the paper), aFis is an adaptive SLC. The $\Pi_R^{\mathtt{aFis}}$.SimRand functionality, which is in charge of producing a convincing version Q of the prover's random tape, works as follows.

In order to reconstruct the random "first-message" section of Q (i.e. the section used to run τ.Commit), the $\Pi_R^{\mathtt{aFis}}$.SimRand algorithm runs $\Sigma_{R,\tau}$.SimRand using auxiliary output from $\Pi_R^{\mathtt{aFis}}$.SimProve. To simulate the random "challenge-selection" section of Q (i.e. the section used to generate the prover's random selection of challenges), $\Pi_R^{\mathtt{aFis}}$.SimRand first gathers the random coins corresponding to all of the challenges sampled by $\Pi_R^{\mathtt{aFis}}$.SimProve. Note that in order for (not only the challenges in the proof tuple) but *all* of the challenges included in Q to agree with the output of the RO, $\Pi_R^{\mathtt{aFis}}$.SimRand must be able to simulate the prover's entire sequence of challenges. In the adaptive setting, generating a convincing version of the prover's entire challenge sequence is non-trivial, and in particular requires a simulation technique other than the dynamic programming strategy of the original and randomized Fischlin transforms [34,40].

Fortunately, Kondi and shelat's randomization of the challenge space allows the $\Pi_R^{\mathtt{aFis}}.\mathtt{SimRand}$ algorithm to finish the challenge section of the prover's random tape by computing transcripts using the real witness, sampling a fresh challenge-to-output mapping, and inserting the challenge used to compute the simulated transcript as the first input to produce the all-zero string. We assume that the challenge space ℓ is exponential, or on the order of 2^λ, with respect to security parameter λ. This is true of many Σ-protocols, and in particular discrete logarithm-based protocols that are the primary focus of this work. For those that do not have this property a priori, the security parameter can be sufficiently increased using parallel repetition of the proof process, trading linear multiplicative overhead for adaptive security. We predict that this restriction can be relaxed, but leave the exploration of those techniques to future work.

Construction 1 (Adaptive Randomized Fischlin Transform). Let $\Sigma_{R,\tau}$ be any adaptive Σ-protocol for relation R (Definition 2) based on protocol template τ (see full version for details) with the required properties for $\mathtt{rFis}$ (see full version for details). Let H be any random oracle and $\mathtt{trunc}_b$ be a truncation algorithm which returns the first b bits of $H(x)$ for some input x. Then the *adaptive randomized Fischlin transform* of $\Sigma_{R,\tau}$, denoted $\mathtt{aFis}$, is an algorithm that takes $\Sigma_{R,\tau}$ as input and creates a tuple of algorithms $\Pi_R^{\mathtt{aFis}} = (\mathtt{Setup}^H, \mathtt{Prove}^H, \mathtt{Verify}^H, \mathtt{SimSetup}, \mathtt{SimProve}, \mathtt{SimRand}, \mathtt{Extract})$, defined as follows.

- $\mathtt{ppm} \leftarrow \mathtt{Setup}^H(1^\lambda)$: H is fixed. Let b, n, t be set according to the randomized Fischlin transform [34,40]: $bn = \omega(\log\lambda)$, $2^{t-b} = \omega(\log\lambda)$, $b, n, t = O(\log\lambda)$ and $b \leq t$, where we use n in place of r repetitions to avoid confusion with the notation for randomness. Let $\ell = O(2^\lambda)$. The compound randomness security parameters are $\lambda_Q = \lceil n(\lambda_r + 2^t\ell)\rceil$ and $\lambda_{Q'} = \lceil n(\lambda_r' + \ell) + n(\lambda_r + 2^t\ell)\rceil$, where λ_r and $\lambda_{r'}$ are the randomness security parameters of $\Sigma_{R,\tau}$. Run $\mathtt{ppm}_\Sigma \leftarrow \tau.\mathtt{Setup}(1^\lambda)$. Output the public parameters $\mathtt{ppm} = (\mathtt{ppm}_\Sigma, b, n, t, \ell, \lambda_Q)$.
- $(x, \Phi) \leftarrow \mathtt{Prove}^H(x, w, Q)$: Compute the vector of n first messages $\overline{\mathtt{com}} = \langle \mathtt{com}_1, \dots, \mathtt{com}_n\rangle$ by running $\tau.\mathtt{Commit}(x, w, r_i)$ for $1 \leq i \leq n$, where each r_i consumes λ_r bits of the random tape Q. To compute each proof π_i, sample challenges $\mathtt{chl}_j$ from Q and compute $\mathtt{res}_j \leftarrow \tau.\mathtt{Respond}(x, w, \mathtt{com}_i, \mathtt{chl}_j)$ until $\mathtt{trunc}(H(x, \overline{\mathtt{com}}, i, \mathtt{chl}_j, \mathtt{res}_j)) = 0^b$, then set $\pi_i = (\mathtt{com}_i, \mathtt{chl}_j, \mathtt{res}_j)$. Finally, return (x, Φ), where $\Phi = (\pi_1, \dots, \pi_n)$.
- $\{0,1\} \leftarrow \mathtt{Verify}^H(x, \Phi)$: Parse $\Phi = (\pi_1, \dots, \pi_n)$. Output 1 (accept) if and only if $\Sigma_R.\mathtt{Verify}(x, \pi_i) = 1$ and $\sum_{i=1}^n \mathtt{trunc}(H(x, \overline{\mathtt{com}}, i, \mathtt{chl}_i, \mathtt{res}_i)) = 0^b$ for $1 \leq i \leq n$. Otherwise, output 0 (reject).
- $(\mathtt{ppm}, z_s) \leftarrow \mathtt{SimSetup}(1^\lambda)$: Fix H and generate b, n, t the same as in $\mathtt{Setup}$. Generate $\mathtt{ppm}_\Sigma$ and simulator state information z_s by running $\Sigma_{R,\tau}.\mathtt{SimSetup}$. Set $\mathtt{ppm} = (\mathtt{ppm}_\Sigma, b, n, t, \lambda_R)$ and return $(\mathtt{ppm}, z_s)$.

- $(x, \Phi, Z_\Phi) \leftarrow \texttt{SimProve}(x, z_s, Q')$: For each proof $1 \leq i \leq n$, sample a random r_i and a random challenge $\texttt{chl}_i$ from Q'. Then run $\Sigma_{R,\tau}.\texttt{SimProve}(x, z_s, \texttt{chl}_i, r_i)$ to obtain $\pi_i = (\texttt{com}_i, \texttt{chl}_i, \texttt{res}_i)$ and z_{π_i}. For each proof, program the truncated output of H on input $(x, \overline{\texttt{com}}, i, \texttt{chl}_i, \texttt{res}_i)$ to be 0^b. Finally, output the proof tuple (x, Φ) and auxiliary information Z_Φ, where $\Phi = (\Phi_1, \ldots, \Phi_n)$ and $Z_\Phi = (z_{\pi_1}, \ldots, z_{\pi_n})$.
- $Q \leftarrow \texttt{SimRand}(\texttt{ppm}, z_s, Z_\Phi, x, \Phi, w, Q')$: Parse $\Phi = (\pi_1, \ldots, \pi_n)$ and $Z_\Phi = (z_{\pi_1}, \ldots, z_{\pi_n})$. For each proof $\pi_i = (\texttt{com}_i, \texttt{chl}_i, \texttt{res}_i)$, run $\Sigma_{R,\tau}.\texttt{SimRand}(\texttt{ppm}, z_s, z_{\pi_i}, x, \pi_i, w)$ to obtain r_i, and concatenate it to Q. Then, sample a fresh random challenge $\texttt{chl}_j$ from Q' and compute $\texttt{res}_j \leftarrow \tau.\texttt{Respond}(\texttt{ppm}, x, w, \texttt{com}_j, \texttt{chl}_j)$. If $\texttt{trunc}(H(x, \overline{\texttt{com}}, j, \texttt{chl}_j, \texttt{res}_j)) = 0^b$, concatenate $\texttt{chl}_i$ to Q and move on to the next proof π_{i+1}; otherwise, concatenate $\texttt{chl}_j$ to Q and continue sampling challenges until the condition is met. Finally, return Q.
- $w \leftarrow \texttt{Extract}(X, \Phi, \mathcal{Q}_\mathscr{A})$: Parse $\Phi = (\pi_1, \ldots, \pi_n)$ and each $\pi_i = (\texttt{com}_i, \texttt{chl}_i, \texttt{res}_i)$. Given a list $\mathcal{Q}_\mathscr{A}$ the adversary's queries to H, search for two queries $(x, \overline{\texttt{com}}, i, \texttt{chl}_i, \texttt{res}_i)$ and $(x, \overline{\texttt{com}}, i, \texttt{chl}'_i, \texttt{res}'_i)$ such that $(\texttt{chl}_i, \texttt{res}_i) \neq (\texttt{chl}'_i, \texttt{res}'_i)$ and $\Sigma_R.\texttt{Verify}(x, \pi_i) = \Sigma_R.\texttt{Verify}(x, \pi'_i) = 1$. If no such queries exist, output $\texttt{Fail}$. Otherwise, obtain w by running $\Sigma_R.\texttt{Extract}(x, \pi, \pi')$.

We now prove that as long as the Σ-protocol used as input to the transform is adaptive special honest-verifier zero-knowledge (adSHVZK), aFis is an adaptive SLC. We will show in Sect. 5 that any adaptive SLC is sufficient to bootstrap adaptive Σ-protocols into adaptive UC NIZKPoK in the global ROM(s).

Theorem 5 (aFis is an Adaptive SLC). *Let $\Sigma_{R,\tau}$ be an adaptive Σ-protocol based on protocol template τ for relation R (Definition 2) with the required properties for* rFis *(see full version of the paper for details), and $H : \{0,1\}^* \rightarrow \{0,1\}^b$ be any random oracle. Then the adaptive randomized Fischlin transform* aFis *(Definition 1) is an adaptive straight-line compiler for $\Sigma_{R,\tau}$ (Definition 8) in the ROM.*

Proof. Recall that an adaptive straight-line compiler according to our definition must create protocols that are overwhelmingly complete, adaptive non-interactive multiple special honest-verifier zero-knowledge (adNIM-SHVZK), and adaptive non-interactive special simulation-sound (adNI-SSS).

First, note that since the specification of $\Pi_R^{\texttt{aFis}}.\texttt{Prove}$ does not functionally change between rFis and aFis (as our explicit treatment of the prover's randomness is syntactic), aFis is as complete as rFis [34,40]. We first construct a series of hybrid arguments to show that if $\Pi_R^{\texttt{aFis}}$ is not adNIM-SHVZK, then Σ_R cannot be regular adaptive special honest-verifier zero-knowledge (adSHVZK), contradicting the assumption in the theorem statement.

Hybrid 0. This is the "real-world" experiment, where honest parties compute proofs using $\Pi_R^{\texttt{aFis}}.\texttt{Prove}$, verify proofs using $\Pi_R^{\texttt{aFis}}.\texttt{Verify}$, reveal their random tapes upon corruption, and the random oracle is setup in "random-function" mode (as in the $b = 0$ experiment of the adNIM-SHVZK game in Fig. 4).

Hybrid 1. The random oracle is setup by an experiment "challenger" in "list" mode, where all queries are recorded in a list. The challenger draws the oracle's response to new queries uniformly at random from the response space, then "programs" them (this is still mostly the $b = 0$ experiment in the adNIM-SHVZK from Fig. 4, but rather than using function f the security experiment is using list L, and the resulting oracle is denoted H_L). Hybrids 0 and 1 are statistically indistinguishable as the challenger has essentially replaced the "real-world" oracle with a statistically identical process of choosing random values and storing them in a function table.

We now wish to construct a reduction $\mathscr{B}$ that uses an algorithm $\mathscr{A}$ that can win the adNIM-SHVZK game (Definition 10) parameterized over $\Pi_R^{\mathtt{aFis}}$ with non-negligible advantage as a black-box in order to win the adSHVZK game (Definition 3) parameterized over Σ_R with non-negligible advantage. Note that the adSHVZK challenger is expecting exactly one Prove query (i.e. it is not *multi*-adaptive), and will issue only one proof in return (as opposed to the tuple of proofs returned by $\Pi_R^{\mathtt{aFis}}$.Prove). We therefore modify $\mathscr{A}$ to distinguish two hybrids, $(1, i, j)$ and $(1, i, j + 1)$.

Hybrid $(1, i, j)$**.** For $0 < i < \mathtt{max}$ and any $0 \leq j \leq n$ where $\mathtt{max} = \mathsf{poly}(\lambda)$ is the maximum number of Prove queries, the first $i - 1$ responses to $\mathscr{A}$'s Prove queries are all formed using the $\Pi_R^{\mathtt{aFis}}$.Prove algorithm, and starting with the $(i + 1)^{st}$ query, $\Pi_R^{\mathtt{aFis}}$.SimProve is used (along with the setup parameters from the $\Pi_R^{\mathtt{aFis}}$.SimSetup algorithm). The corresponding randomness of these proofs are computed using the $\Pi_R^{\mathtt{aFis}}$.SimRand algorithm. For the ith Prove query, the response is a hybrid in which the first j proofs are computed using the Σ.Prove algorithm, while the rest are computed using the Σ.SimProve algorithm (again with setup from Σ.SimProve and randomness according to Σ.SimRand). Hybrid $(1, \mathtt{max}, n)$ is identical to Hybrid 1 and Hybrid $(1, 0, 0)$ is identical to the $b = 1$ adNIM-SHVZK experiment from Fig. 4.

Note that as part of the simulation algorithms for both Σ and $\Pi_R^{\mathtt{aFis}}$, $\mathscr{B}$ may need to program the RO H using the interface $\mathtt{Prog}_L$. Because H is set up in "list" mode, the security experiment allows programming from authorized parties, which in this case is the adSHVZK challenger and also $\mathscr{B}$ after the $(i, j+1^{st})$ proof is fixed. Without loss of generality we can imagine the reduction returns each completed proof in the tuple sequentially, as each one is computed and fixed independently once the commitment vector is generated. Note also that since all programmed points are generated independently, the ability of $\mathscr{B}$ to program at this stage does not give $\mathscr{B}$ any insight into what has been programmed previously (i.e. $\mathscr{B}$ does not have an advantage in determining whether the challenger programmed the oracle as part of its answer to the $j + 1^{st}$ prove query).

We argue that Hybrid $(1, i, j)$ is computationally indistinguishable from Hybrid $(1, i, j + 1)$ as long as Σ is adSHVZK. Assume for a contradiction that it is not. The reduction $\mathscr{B}$ proceeds as follows.

At the beginning of the experiment, $\mathscr{B}$ receives 1^λ and $\texttt{ppm}$ from the adSHVZK challenger. Note that the $\texttt{ppm}$ associated with Σ (i.e. other than the $\texttt{aFis}$ parameters (b, n, t)) are exactly the same between $\Sigma.\texttt{Setup}$, $\Sigma.\texttt{SimSetup}$, $\Pi_R^{\texttt{aFis}}.\texttt{Setup}$, and $\Pi_R^{\texttt{aFis}}.\texttt{SimSetup}$; the only difference is that the challenger in the adSHVZK and adNIM-SHVZK experiments might additionally generate some initial state information $z_{\texttt{Sim}}$ that it might use while simulating future proofs. The fact that the challenger has or has not generated $z_{\texttt{Sim}}$ is obviously not revealed to $\mathscr{B}$, but note that the value is deterministic with respect to the security parameter—$\mathscr{B}$ will generate the same $\texttt{ppm}, z_{\texttt{Sim}}$ upon running $\texttt{SimSetup}$ itself. The way the game is defined states that the adversary receives 1^λ and $\texttt{ppm}$ from the challenger, but equivalently, you could think of the adversary receiving 1^λ only, and generating the same $\texttt{ppm}$ itself.

Up to the ith query $(\texttt{Prove}, x, w)$ from $\mathscr{A}$, the reduction runs the $\Pi_R^{\texttt{aFis}}.\texttt{Setup}$ algorithm itself to obtain $\texttt{ppm}$ and computes proofs entirely on its own: $\mathscr{B}$ samples randomness $Q \leftarrow \{0,1\}^{\lambda_Q}$, runs $\Pi_R^{\texttt{aFis}}.\texttt{Prove}(x, w, Q)$, and returns (Φ, Q) to $\mathscr{A}$. On $\mathscr{A}$'s i^{th} query $(\texttt{Prove}, x^*, w^*)$, $\mathscr{B}$ passes $(\texttt{Prove}, x^*, w^*)$ to the adSHVZK challenger and receives (π^*, r^*) for $\pi^* = (\texttt{com}^*, \texttt{chl}^*, \texttt{res}^*)$ that is either the result of running $\Sigma_R.\texttt{Prove}$ on randomness r^* or the result of running $\Sigma_R.\texttt{SimProve}$ and $\Sigma_R.\texttt{SimRand}$. Recall that $\mathscr{A}$ is expecting more proofs than just π^*, as the output of $\Pi_R^{\texttt{aFis}}.\texttt{Prove}$ and $\Pi_R^{\texttt{aFis}}.\texttt{SimProve}$ should actually be a tuple of proofs $\Phi_i = \pi_1, \ldots, \pi_n$. Moreover, since each proof in the tuple $\pi_j \in \Phi_i$ requires the prover to make $2^t - 1$ secret queries to the RO, $\mathscr{A}$ is expecting more randomness than just r^*. Without loss of generality, we define each chunk Q_j of the prover's random tape Q to be a λ_r-length segment corresponding to the first-message randomness for π_j, followed by a 2^t-length segment corresponding to the random challenges for each RO query, where t is the total number of queries the prover makes to the RO in the process of producing π_j. $\mathscr{B}$ constructs the hybrid proof tuple Φ_i from the challenge query as follows.

Let the jth commitment $\texttt{com}_j = \texttt{com}^*$, and $\pi_j = \pi^* = (\texttt{com}^*, \texttt{chl}^*, \texttt{res}^*)$. Since it must have the entire tuple $\texttt{com}_1, \ldots, \texttt{com}_n$ of commitments before running $\Pi_R^{\texttt{aFis}}.\texttt{Prove}$, $\mathscr{B}$ starts by running the steps of $\Pi_R^{\texttt{aFis}}.\texttt{SimProve}$ $n-j$ times to obtain $\pi_{j+1}, \ldots, \pi_n$. $\mathscr{B}$ then samples each $r_1, \ldots r_{j-1}$ from Q' and runs $\tau.\texttt{Commit}$ $j-1$ times to obtain $\texttt{com}_1, \ldots, \texttt{com}_{j-1}$. It then finalizes the commitment vector $\overline{\texttt{com}} = \texttt{com}_1, \ldots, \texttt{com}_n$ and programs the truncated output of H to output 0^b on input $(x, \overline{\texttt{com}}, k, \texttt{chl}_k, \texttt{res}_k)$ for each simulated proof π_k, where $k \in [j+1, n]$. $\mathscr{B}$ computes each proof $\pi_1, \ldots, \pi_{j-1}$ by running the steps of $\Pi_R^{\texttt{aFis}}.\texttt{Prove}$ starting right after the generation of the commitment vector. $\mathscr{B}$ generates the prover's hybrid random tape Q for the proof tuple Φ as follows. For each of the first chunks $Q_m \in Q_1, \ldots, Q_{j-1}$, $\mathscr{B}$ concatenates the first-message randomness r_m and challenge randomness $\texttt{chl}_1, \ldots, \texttt{chl}_t$ it used in the execution of $\Pi_R^{\texttt{aFis}}.\texttt{Prove}$. The jth chunk, which must contain the bits corresponding to the challenge proof $\pi^* = \pi_j$, are generated as follows. $\mathscr{B}$ sets the first λ_r bits to be the value r^* returned by the adSHVZK challenger. $\mathscr{B}$ then samples a fresh random challenge $\texttt{chl}_m$, computes $\texttt{res}_m \leftarrow \tau.\texttt{Respond}(\texttt{ppm}, x, w, \texttt{com}^*, \texttt{chl}_m)$, and checks whether $\texttt{trunc}(H(x, \overline{\texttt{com}}, j, \texttt{chl}_m, \texttt{res}_m)) = 0^b$. If it does, $\mathscr{B}$ concatenates $\texttt{chl}^*$ to Q and moves on to the next step. Otherwise, $\mathscr{B}$ concatenates $\mathtt{chl}_m$ to Q and continues sampling challenges until the condition is met. Finally for the remaining chunks $Q_m \in Q_{j+1}, \ldots, Q_n$, $\mathscr{B}$ concatenates the first-message randomness r_m and challenge randomness $\mathtt{chl}_1, \ldots, \mathtt{chl}_t$ returned by executing $\Pi_R^{\mathtt{aFis}}.\mathtt{SimRand}$ on input the proofs $\pi_{j+1}, \ldots, \pi_n$ and auxiliary information $z_{\pi_{j+1}}, \ldots, z_{\pi_n}$ output by its execution of $\mathtt{SimProve}$. $\mathscr{B}$ then returns Φ and Q to $\mathscr{A}$. From the ith $\mathtt{Prove}$ query onward, $\mathscr{B}$ computes proofs according to $\Pi_R^{\mathtt{aFis}}$. $\mathtt{SimProve}$ (with setup according to $\Pi_R^{\mathtt{aFis}}.\mathtt{SimSetup}$) and returns randomness according to $\Pi_R^{\mathtt{aFis}}.\mathtt{SimRand}$.

For the analysis, consider that $\mathscr{B}$'s execution of the proofs $\pi_1, \ldots, \pi_j$ and $\pi_{j+2}, \ldots, \pi_n$ and corresponding randomness is exactly what $\mathscr{A}$ expects in either hybrid. It remains to show that the challenge proof π_{j+1} and corresponding randomness is also formatted according to what $\mathscr{A}$ expects. If the adSHVZK challenger is playing with bit $b = 0$ and generated (π^*, r^*) according to $\Pi_R^{\mathtt{aFis}}.\mathtt{Prove}$ and the prover's random tape, then π_{j+1} and the first-message section of Q_{j+1} corresponding to r_{j+1} (i.e. the randomness used to generate $\mathtt{com}^* = \mathtt{com}_{j+1}$) will be exactly what $\mathscr{A}$ expects from Hybrid $(1, i, j+1)$. If π^*, r^* were generated according to $\Pi_R^{\mathtt{aFis}}.\mathtt{SimProve}$ and $\Pi_R^{\mathtt{aFis}}.\mathtt{SimRand}$ respectively, then $\mathscr{A}$'s view of π_{j+1} and r_{j+1} in Q_j will be according to Hybrid $(1, i, j)$.

For the challenge section of Q_{j+1}, note that the challenge selection process of $\Pi_R^{\mathtt{aFis}}.\mathtt{Prove}$ is identical to that of $\Pi_R^{\mathtt{aFis}}.\mathtt{SimRand}$ up to the challenge in the tth transcript—the $\mathtt{Prove}$ and $\mathtt{SimRand}$ algorithms sample challenges and compute responses using the real witness until they find a transcript that causes the RO to return a truncated output of 0^b. When this condition occurs, the $\mathtt{Prove}$ algorithm returns the accepting transcript computed using the challenge it sampled, while the $\mathtt{SimRand}$ algorithm inserts the challenge and transcript generated by $\mathtt{SimProve}$. For the challenge section of Q_{j+1}, $\mathscr{B}$ samples challenges according to either algorithm and when it finds a transcript that returns 0^b, it inserts the challenge $\mathtt{chl}^*$ from the adSHVZK challenger. $\mathscr{A}$'s view of the challenge selection section in the case that $b = 0$ is therefore identical to Hybrid $(1, i, j+1)$, while if $b = 1$, its view is identical to Hybrid $(1, i, j)$. Therefore, if $\mathscr{B}$ outputs 0 when $\mathscr{A}$ outputs "Hybrid $(1, i, j+1)$" and 1 when $\mathscr{A}$ outputs "Hybrid $(1, i, j)$," it succeeds with the same probability as $\mathscr{A}$. Because i is bounded by the number of prove queries and j is bounded by the parameter n, the number of hybrids is polynomial in the security parameter, and $\mathscr{B}$'s summed advantage over all of the hybrids is negligible, completing the proof that $\Pi_R^{\mathtt{aFis}}$ must be adNIM-SHVZK.

We now use the fact that $\Pi_R^{\mathtt{aFis}}$ is adNIM-SHVZK to argue that $\Pi_R^{\mathtt{aFis}}$ must also be adaptive non-interactive special simulation-sound (adNI-SSS). Consider a new reduction $\mathscr{B}$ that uses an adversary $\mathscr{A}$ that can win the adNI-SSS game (Definition 11), as well as a second adversary $\mathscr{A}'$ that can win the regular non-interactive special soundness (NI-SS) game (a weaker version of adNI-SSS where $\mathscr{A}$ cannot query the simulator; see full version of the paper for details) with non-negligible advantage as black boxes to win the adNIM-SHVZK game (Definition 10). $\mathscr{B}$ forwards all of $\mathscr{A}$'s $\mathtt{Prove}$ queries to and from the adNIM-SHVZK challenger, and all of $\mathscr{A}$'s random oracle queries to and from H. Similarly, $\mathscr{B}$ forwards all of $\mathscr{A}'$'s oracle queries to and from H. Whenever $\mathscr{A}$ produces a fresh (non-simulated) proof (x, Φ) such that $\Pi_R^{\mathtt{aFis}}.\mathtt{Verify}(x, \Phi) = 1$, $\mathscr{B}$ computes $w \leftarrow \Pi_R^{\mathtt{aFis}}.\mathtt{Extract}(x, \Phi, \mathcal{Q}_{\mathscr{A}})$ and checks whether $R(x, w) = 0$, which happens with non-negligible probability by assumption. $\mathscr{B}$ does the same for $\mathscr{A}'$'s proofs (x', Φ'). (The argument that there must be sufficient queries in $\mathcal{Q}_{\mathscr{A}}$ or $\mathcal{Q}_{\mathscr{A}'}$ to invoke $\Pi_R^{\mathtt{aFis}}.\mathtt{Extract}$ in the first place is identical to the arguments given by Kondi and shelat [40]; in brief, the strong special soundness property stops $\mathscr{A}$ from being able to "tweak" an old proof to create a forgery).

If the adNIM-SVHZK challenger is playing with bit $b = 1$ and the proofs and randomness being passed to $\mathscr{A}$ are according to $\Pi_R^{\mathtt{aFis}}.\mathtt{SimProve}$ and $\Pi_R^{\mathtt{aFis}}.\mathtt{SimRand}$, this is exactly what $\mathscr{A}$ expects from the adNI-SSS game, and $\mathscr{B}$'s advantage is the same as $\mathscr{A}$'s. If the adNIM-SHVZK challenger is playing with bit $b = 0$, then $\mathscr{A}$'s advantage reduces to $\mathscr{A}'$'s advantage in the standard NI-SS game (since $\mathscr{A}'$ can always generate honest proofs and randomness according to $\Pi_R^{\mathtt{aFis}}.\mathtt{Prove}$ itself). Assume for a contradiction that there is a non-negligible difference between the extraction failures produced by $\mathscr{A}$ when $b = 1$ and $\mathscr{A}/\mathscr{A}'$ when $b = 0$. If $\mathscr{B}$ observes a difference in output between $\mathscr{A}$ and $\mathscr{A}'$, $\mathscr{B}$ knows $\mathscr{A}$ has an extra advantage due to seeing simulated proofs and randomness and outputs 1; otherwise if there is no difference, $\mathscr{B}$ outputs 0. Therefore, the difference must be negligible: as long as $\Pi_R^{\mathtt{aFis}}$ is adNIM-SHVZK (as proven in the preceding paragraphs) and NI-SS (which follows directly from the special soundness of $\Sigma_{R,\tau}$ and the randomness of H), $\Pi_R^{\mathtt{aFis}}$ must be adNI-SSS. □

5 Constructing Adaptive, Efficient UC NIZKPoK

In this section, we show that the adaptive non-interactive multiple special honest-verifier zero-knowledge (adNIM-SHVZK) and adaptive non-interactive special simulation-soundness (adNI-SSS) properties afforded by an adaptive SLC are *necessary* to achieve adaptive UC NIZKPoK in any global ROM, and that they are *sufficient* to transform any Σ-protocol into an adaptive UC NIZKPoK in the $\mathcal{G}_{\mathtt{rpoRO}}$-hybrid model. For our construction in the $\mathcal{G}_{\mathtt{roRO}}$-$\mathcal{F}_{\mathtt{CRS}}$-hybrid model, we adapt Lysyanskaya and Rosenbloom's OR-protocol compiler [41].

Recall from the introduction that ideal functionalities $\mathcal{F}$ in the UC model operate on behalf of the honest "dummy parties" in the ideal-world experiment [19]. Upon receiving instructions from the ideal adversary $\mathcal{S}$ and setting up any necessary parameters, $\mathcal{F}_{\mathtt{aNIZK}}$ proves statements for honest parties using the `SimSetup` and `SimProve` algorithms (which do not take witnesses as input) and verifies proofs using the `Extract` algorithm. If the algorithms from $\mathcal{S}$ do not function as $\mathcal{F}_{\mathtt{aNIZK}}$ intends, for instance if `SimProve` produces proofs that do not verify or `Extract` outputs invalid witnesses, $\mathcal{F}_{\mathtt{aNIZK}}$ outputs `Fail`. During its processing, $\mathcal{F}_{\mathtt{aNIZK}}$ stores information about the proofs it has computed on each dummy party's behalf. $\mathcal{S}$ retrieves this information via $\mathcal{F}_{\mathtt{aNIZK}}$'s **Corrupt** interface whenever an honest party is corrupted by the environment. The style of our definition follows the standard introduced by Chase and Lysyanskaya [24].

Definition 12 (Adaptive NIZKPoK Ideal Functionality). *The ideal functionality* $\mathcal{F}_{\mathtt{aNIZK}}$ *of an* adaptive non-interactive zero-knowledge proof of knowledge (adaptive NIZKPoK) *for a particular session s is defined as follows, where all outputs are returned to the calling party.*

Setup: *Initialize an empty list* C *of corrupted parties. Upon receiving a request* $(\texttt{Setup}, P)$ *from a party* $P = (\texttt{pid}, \texttt{sid})$*, check whether* $\texttt{sid} = s$ *and* $P \notin C$*. If either check fails, output* $\perp$*. Otherwise, if this is the first time a request* $(\texttt{Setup}, P)$ *was received from an uncorrupted party with* $\texttt{sid} = s$*, do as follows: pass* $(\texttt{Setup}, s)$ *to the ideal adversary* $\mathcal{S}$*, receive and store* $(\texttt{Algorithms}, \texttt{Setup}, \texttt{Prove}, \texttt{Verify}, \texttt{SimSetup}, \texttt{SimProve}, \texttt{Extract})$*. Then run* SimSetup *and store* $(\texttt{ppm}, z_{\texttt{Sim}})$ *where* ppm *are public parameters and* $z_{\texttt{Sim}}$ *is any auxiliary output of* SimSetup*, and output* Success*. Otherwise, output* $\perp$*.*

Prove: *Upon receiving a request* $(\texttt{Prove}, x, w)$ *from a party* $P = (\texttt{pid}, \texttt{sid})$*, check that* $\texttt{sid} = s$*,* $P \notin C$*, and* $R(x, w) = 1$*. If any check fails, output* $\perp$*. Otherwise, set* w *aside, compute* π *according to the* SimProve *algorithm, and check that* $\texttt{Verify}(x, \pi) = 1$*. If it doesn't, output* Fail*. Otherwise, record the tuple* $(\texttt{Proof}, P, x, w, \pi, z_{\texttt{Sim}}, z_\pi)$*, where* z_π *is any auxiliary output of the* SimProve *algorithm. Output* $(\texttt{Proof}, P, x, \pi)$*.*

Verify: *Upon receiving a request* $(\texttt{Verify}, x, \pi)$ *from a party* $P = (\texttt{pid}, \texttt{sid})$*, first check that* $\texttt{sid} = s$ *and* $P \notin C$*. If either check fails, output* $\perp$*. If there exists a tuple* $(\texttt{Proof}, P, x, w, \pi, z_{\texttt{Sim}}, z_\pi)$ *already stored, output* $(\texttt{Verification}, P, x, \pi, 1)$*. Else if* $\texttt{Verify}(x, \pi) = 0$*, output* $(\texttt{Verification}, P, x, \pi, 0)$*. Otherwise, compute* w *according to the* Extract *algorithm. If* $R(x, w) = 1$*, output* $(\texttt{Verification}, P, x, \pi, 1)$ *for a successful extraction. Else if* $R(x, w) = 0$*, output* Fail*.*

Corrupt: *Upon receiving a request* (**Corrupt**, P) *from* $\mathcal{S}$*, add* P *to* C *and return all of the stored tuples* $(\texttt{Proof}, P, *)$*, if they exist. Otherwise, output* $\perp$*.*

We begin by showing that any adaptive UC NIZKPoK must be adaptive NIM-SHVZK and adaptive NI-SSS. Because this result holds for any choice of global RO with the minimal Query functionality (as described in Sect. 2), we use the generic $\mathcal{G}_{\texttt{RO}}$ to represent the global RO. See the full version of the paper for the proof of:

Theorem 6 (Required Properties for aUC NIZKPoK). *Let* Π *be a protocol that aUC-realizes* $\mathcal{F}_{\texttt{aNIZK}}$ *in the* $\mathcal{G}_{\texttt{RO}}$*-hybrid model (Definition 1 where* $\mathcal{G}$ *is replaced with* $\mathcal{G}_{\texttt{RO}}$*) with adaptive corruptions. Then* Π *must be overwhelmingly complete (Definition 9), adaptive NIM-SHVZK (Definition 10), and adaptive NI-SSS (Definition 11).*

Next, we show that running any adaptive Σ-protocol Σ_R for relation R through any adaptive straight-line compiler (adaptive SLC) results in adaptive UC NIZKPoK for relation R in the (programmable) $\mathcal{G}_{\texttt{rpoRO}}$-hybrid model. Our proof techniques are covered in Theorem 8; we therefore leave details to the full version of the paper.

Theorem 7 (aUC NIZKPoK in the $\mathcal{G}_{\mathtt{rpoRO}}$-hybrid Model). *Let Σ_R be any adaptive Σ-protocol for relation R (Definition 2), $\mathcal{G}_{\mathtt{rpoRO}}$ be the restricted programmable observable global random oracle (see full version for details) and* SLC *be any adaptive straight-line compiler (Definition 8). Then the NISLE proof system $\Pi_R^{\mathtt{SLC}} \leftarrow \mathtt{SLC}(\Sigma_R)$ aUC-realizes $\mathcal{F}_{\mathtt{aNIZK}}$ in the $\mathcal{G}_{\mathtt{rpoRO}}$-hybrid model (Definition 1 where $\mathcal{G}$ is replaced with $\mathcal{G}_{\mathtt{rpoRO}}$).*

Our final theorem shows that any adaptive SLC in conjunction with our adaptive OR-protocol compiler is sufficient to create adaptive UC NIZKPoK in the $\mathcal{G}_{\mathtt{rpoRO}}$-$\mathcal{F}_{\mathtt{CRS}}$-hybrid model. Recall from Sect. 2 that $\mathcal{F}_{\mathtt{CRS}}$ must be parameterized over a samplable-hard, adaptive Σ-friendly relation S.

Construction 2 (Candidate Compiler). Let Σ_R be any adaptive Σ-protocol for relation R (Definition 2), $\mathcal{G}_{\mathtt{roRO}}$ be the restricted observable global random oracle, Σ_S be an efficient Σ-protocol for samplable-hard relation S, $\mathcal{F}_{\mathtt{CRS}}$ be the ideal CRS functionality (see full version for details) where $\mathtt{GenCRS} := \kappa_S$, and aSLC be any adaptive straight-line compiler (Definition 8). Then our *candidate compiler* auc is an algorithm that, on input Σ_R and aSLC, produces a tuple of algorithms $\Pi_{\mathtt{R}\vee\mathtt{S}}^{\mathtt{auc}} = (\mathtt{Setup}^{\mathcal{G}_{\mathtt{roRO}}}, \mathtt{Prove}^{\mathcal{G}_{\mathtt{roRO}},\mathcal{F}_{\mathtt{CRS}}}, \mathtt{Verify}^{\mathcal{G}_{\mathtt{roRO}},\mathcal{F}_{\mathtt{CRS}}}, \mathtt{SimSetup}, \mathtt{SimProve}, \mathtt{SimRand}, \mathtt{Extract})$, defined in Fig. 6.

Theorem 8 (aUC NIZKPoK in the $\mathcal{G}_{\mathtt{roRO}}$-$\mathcal{F}_{\mathtt{CRS}}$-Hybrid Model). *Let Σ_R be any adaptive Σ-protocol for relation R (Definition 2) with randomness equivocability (Definition 4), $\mathcal{G}_{\mathtt{roRO}}$ be the restricted observable global random oracle (see full version for details), Σ_S be an efficient Σ-protocol for adaptive Σ-friendly relation S (see full version), $\mathcal{F}_{\mathtt{CRS}}$ be the ideal CRS functionality (see full version),* aSLC *be any adaptive straight-line compiler (Definition 8), and* auc *be the candidate compiler (Construction 2). Then $\Pi_{\mathtt{R}\vee\mathtt{S}}^{\mathtt{auc}} \leftarrow \mathtt{auc}(\Sigma_R, \mathtt{aSLC})$ aUC-realizes $\mathcal{F}_{\mathtt{aNIZK}}$ in the $\mathcal{G}_{\mathtt{roRO}}$-$\mathcal{F}_{\mathtt{CRS}}$-hybrid model (Definition 1 where $\mathcal{G} := \mathcal{G}_{\mathtt{roRO}}$ and $* := \mathcal{F}_{\mathtt{CRS}}$).*

Proof. We begin with the construction of the ideal adversary. When $\mathcal{S}$ receives $(\mathtt{Setup}, s)$ from $\mathcal{F}_{\mathtt{aNIZK}}$, $\mathcal{S}$ returns the tuple of algorithms $\Pi_{\mathtt{R}\vee\mathtt{S}}^{\mathtt{auc}}$. When $\mathcal{Z}$ issues a query $(\mathbf{Corrupt}, P)$ for a party $P = (\mathtt{pid}, \mathtt{sid})$, $\mathcal{S}$ sends $(\mathbf{Corrupt}, P)$ to $\mathcal{F}_{\mathtt{aNIZK}}$ to obtain the stored tuples $(\mathtt{Proof}, P, x_1, w_1, \pi_1, z_{\mathtt{Sim}}, z_1), \ldots, (\mathtt{Proof}, P, x_q, w_q, \pi_q, z_{\mathtt{Sim}}, z_q)$ corresponding to each query $(\mathtt{Prove}, P, x_i, w_i)$ that $\mathcal{Z}$ issued to P (who forwarded them to $\mathcal{F}_{\mathtt{aNIZK}}$). $\mathcal{S}$ then runs $r_i \leftarrow \Pi_{\mathtt{R}\vee\mathtt{S}}^{\mathtt{auc}}.\mathtt{SimRand}(z_s, z_{\pi_i}, x, \pi, w)$ to obtain simulated randomness r_i. To reconstruct the prover's random tape R, $\mathcal{S}$ concatenates $R = r_1 || \ldots || r_q$ and returns R to $\mathcal{Z}$. Otherwise, $\mathcal{S}$ acts as a "dummy adversary" [19], forwarding all communications to and from $\mathcal{Z}$.

Our proof of UC-security proceeds via a series of hybrids, starting in the real-world experiment and replacing each piece of the real-world adaptive NISLE OR-protocol $\Pi_{\mathtt{R}\vee\mathtt{S}}^{\mathtt{auc}}$ with the functionality of $\mathcal{F}_{\mathtt{aNIZK}}$ and $\mathcal{S}$.

Hybrid 1. First, we replace all of the environment's and adversary's connections to the real-world protocol participants with the "challenger" of our reduction, $\mathcal{C}$. This difference is syntactic, so Hybrid 1 is identical to the real-world experiment.

auc Compiler Parameters

$1^\lambda, R, \Sigma_R, \lambda_R, \lambda_{R'}, S, \Sigma_S, \lambda_S, \lambda_{S'}, \mathsf{aSLC}, \mathcal{G}_{\mathtt{roRO}}, \mathcal{F}_{\mathtt{CRS}}$ with $\mathtt{GenCRS} := (x, w) \leftarrow \kappa_S(1^\lambda)$

$\Pi^{\mathsf{auc}}_{\mathtt{R\vee S}}.\mathtt{Setup}^{\mathcal{G}_{\mathtt{RO}}}(1^\lambda)$

$\quad \mathsf{PPM} \leftarrow \Pi^{\mathsf{aSLC}}_{\mathtt{R\vee S}}.\mathtt{Setup}^{\mathcal{G}_{\mathtt{RO}}}(1^\lambda)$
$\quad$ **return** PPM

$\Pi^{\mathsf{auc}}_{\mathtt{R\vee S}}.\mathtt{SimSetup}(1^\lambda)$

$\quad \mathsf{PPM}, Z' \leftarrow \Pi^{\mathsf{aSLC}}_{\mathtt{R\vee S}}.\mathtt{SimSetup}(1^\lambda)$
$\quad \mathtt{simcrs} \leftarrow \bot$
$\quad Z = (Z', \mathtt{simcrs})$
$\quad$ **return** (PPM, Z)

$\Pi^{\mathsf{auc}}_{\mathtt{R\vee S}}.\mathtt{Prove}^{\mathcal{G}_{\mathtt{RO}}, \mathcal{F}_{\mathtt{CRS}}}(\mathsf{PPM}, s, x, w, T, T')$

$\quad$ **if** $R(x, w) \neq 1$:
$\qquad$ **return** $\bot$
$\quad \mathsf{CRS}_s \leftarrow \mathcal{F}^s_{\mathtt{CRS}}.\mathtt{Query}(s)$
$\quad X \leftarrow (x, \mathsf{CRS}_s)$
$\quad W \leftarrow (w, 0)$
$\quad \Phi \leftarrow \Pi^{\mathsf{aSLC}}_{\mathtt{R\vee S}}.\mathtt{Prove}^{\mathcal{G}_{\mathtt{RO}}}(\mathsf{PPM}, X, W, T, T')$
$\quad$ **return** (s, X, Φ)

$\Pi^{\mathsf{auc}}_{\mathtt{R\vee S}}.\mathtt{SimProve}(\mathsf{PPM}, Z, s, x, w, T, T')$

$\quad$ **if** $R(x, w) \neq 1$:
$\qquad$ **return** $\bot$
$\quad$ **if** $\nexists(\mathsf{CRS}_s, \mathtt{trap}_s)$ **s.t.**
$\qquad (s, \mathsf{CRS}_s, \mathtt{trap}_s) \in \mathtt{simcrs}$:
$\qquad (\mathsf{CRS}_s, \mathtt{trap}_s) \leftarrow \kappa_S(1^\lambda)$
$\qquad \mathtt{simcrs.append}(s, \mathsf{CRS}_s, \mathtt{trap}_s)$
$\quad X \leftarrow (x, \mathsf{CRS}_s)$
$\quad W \leftarrow (\mathtt{trap}_s, 1)$
$\quad \Phi \leftarrow \Pi^{\mathsf{aSLC}}_{\mathtt{R\vee S}}.\mathtt{Prove}^{\mathcal{G}_{\mathtt{RO}}}(\mathsf{PPM}, X, W, T, T')$
$\quad$ **return** $(s, X, \Phi, \mathtt{simcrs})$

$\Pi^{\mathsf{auc}}_{\mathtt{R\vee S}}.\mathtt{Verify}^{\mathcal{G}_{\mathtt{RO}}, \mathcal{F}_{\mathtt{CRS}}}(\mathsf{PPM}, s, X, \Phi)$

$\quad$ **parse** $X = (x, \mathsf{CRS}_s)$
$\quad \mathsf{CRS}'_s \leftarrow \mathcal{F}_{\mathtt{CRS}}.\mathtt{Query}(s)$
$\quad$ **if** $\mathsf{CRS}_s = \mathsf{CRS}'_s \wedge$
$\qquad \Pi^{\mathsf{aSLC}}_{\mathtt{R\vee S}}.\mathtt{Verify}^{\mathcal{G}_{\mathtt{RO}}}(\mathsf{PPM}, X, \Phi) = 1$:
$\qquad$ **return** 1
$\quad$ **else** :
$\qquad$ **return** 0

$\Pi^{\mathsf{auc}}_{\mathtt{R\vee S}}.\mathtt{Extract}(\mathsf{PPM}, X, \Phi, \mathcal{Q}_{P^*})$

$\quad W \leftarrow \Pi^{\mathsf{aSLC}}_{\mathtt{R\vee S}}.\mathtt{Extract}(X, \Phi, \mathcal{Q}_{P^*})$
$\quad$ **parse** $X = (x, \mathsf{CRS}_s)$
$\quad$ **parse** $W = (w, \mathtt{trap}_s)$
$\quad$ **if** $R_{\mathtt{R\vee S}}(X, W) = 1 \wedge R(x, w) = 0$:
$\qquad$ **return** $\mathtt{Fail}$
$\quad$ **else** :
$\qquad$ **return** W

$\Pi^{\mathsf{auc}}_{\mathtt{R\vee S}}.\mathtt{SimRand}(\mathsf{PPM}, Z, X, \Phi, W, T')$

$\quad$ **parse** $\mathsf{PPM} = (\mathsf{ppm}_0, \mathsf{ppm}_1), Z = (z_0, z_1), X = (x, \mathsf{CRS}_s)$
$\quad$ **parse** $\Phi = (\pi_0, \pi_1, \mathsf{CHL}), W = (w, 0), T' = (r'_0, r'_1)$
$\quad r^*_0 \leftarrow \Sigma_R.\mathtt{SimRand}(\mathsf{ppm}_0, z_0, x, \pi_0, w, r'_0)$
$\quad r^*_1 \leftarrow \Sigma_S.\mathtt{RealToSim}(\mathsf{ppm}_1, z_1, \mathsf{CRS}_s, \pi_1, \mathtt{trap}_s, r'_1)$
$\quad T^* = (r^*_0, r^*_1)$
$\quad$ **return** T^*

Fig. 6. Compiler $\Pi^{\mathsf{auc}}_{\mathtt{R\vee S}} \leftarrow \mathsf{auc}(\Sigma_R, \mathsf{SLC})$ for Σ_R in the $\mathcal{G}_{\mathtt{roRO}}$-$\mathcal{F}_{\mathtt{CRS}}$-hybrid Model.

Hybrid 2. In the second hybrid, we replace $\mathcal{C}$'s real-world `Prove` functionality with the original straight-line compiled OR-protocol simulator algorithms $\Pi^{\mathtt{aSLC}}_{\mathtt{R\vee S}}$.`SimSetup`, $\Pi^{\mathtt{aSLC}}_{\mathtt{R\vee S}}$.`SimProve`, and $\Pi^{\mathtt{aSLC}}_{\mathtt{R\vee S}}$.`SimRand`, and show that Hybrids 1 and 2 are indistinguishable as long as $\Pi^{\mathtt{aSLC}}_{\mathtt{R\vee S}}$ is adNIM-SHVZK. We bound $\mathcal{Z}$'s probability of distinguishing the hybrids based on the proofs and randomness by constructing a reduction to the adNIM-SHVZK property as follows. Whenever $\mathcal{Z}$ issues a query $(\mathtt{Prove}, P, x_i, w_i)$ to $\mathcal{C}$, $\mathcal{C}$ forwards the query to the adNIM-SHVZK challenger from Fig. 4, who returns (Φ_i, T_i). $\mathcal{C}$ forwards Φ_i to $\mathcal{Z}$ and stores (P, Φ_i, T_i) for later. If $\mathcal{Z}$ issues a query $(\mathbf{Corrupt}, P)$, $\mathcal{C}$ retrieves all of the tuples (P, Φ_i, T_i) and sets the random tape T to be the concatenation of all T_i in the order they were stored. It then returns T to $\mathcal{C}$. For $\mathcal{Z}$'s queries $(\mathtt{Verify}, X, \Phi)$, $\mathcal{C}$ returns the result of $\Pi^{\mathtt{aSLC}}_{\mathtt{R\vee S}}.\mathtt{Verify}(X, \Phi)$. $\mathcal{C}$ then outputs whatever $\mathcal{Z}$ outputs.

Note that if the adNIM-SHVZK challenger is running the 0-bit experiment (using $\Pi^{\mathtt{aSLC}}_{\mathtt{R\vee S}}$.`Prove` and the prover's randomness), $\mathcal{C}$ simulates $\mathcal{Z}$'s exact view of the experiment in Hybrid 1. Else if the adNIM-SHVZK challenger is running the 1-bit experiment (using $\Pi^{\mathtt{aSLC}}_{\mathtt{R\vee S}}$.`SimProve` and $\Pi^{\mathtt{SLC}}_{\mathtt{R\vee S}}$.`SimRand`), $\mathcal{C}$ simulates $\mathcal{Z}$'s view of Hybrid 2. Therefore, $\mathcal{C}$ succeeds at winning the adNIM-SHVZK game with the same probability that $\mathcal{Z}$ can distinguish the hybrids, proving Hybrid 1 is computationally indistinguishable to Hybrid 2.

Hybrid 3. In the third hybrid, we replace $\mathcal{C}$'s `Verify` functionality with the **Verify** functionality of $\mathcal{F}_{\mathtt{aNIZK}}$, and show the environment's views are indistinguishable between Hybrids 2 and 3 as long as $\Pi^{\mathtt{SLC}}_{R}$ is adaptive non-interactive special simulation-sound (adaptive NI-SSS) *and* S is a hard relation (i.e. given $\mathtt{CRS}_s$, the probability of finding $\mathtt{trap}_s$ such that $S(\mathtt{CRS}_s, \mathtt{trap}_s) = 1$ is negligible). $\mathcal{Z}$'s adaptive corruption queries are handled identically to those in Hybrid 2 (i.e. $\mathcal{S}$ patches together the prover's random tape by concatenating the outputs of $\Pi^{\mathtt{aSLC}}_{\mathtt{R\vee S}}$.`SimRand` returned by the adaptive NI-SSS challenger). $\mathcal{C}$ plays the role of the adversary in the adaptive NI-SSS game, forwarding $\mathcal{Z}$'s queries to its challenger. When $\mathcal{Z}$ produces a valid proof that causes $\Pi^{\mathtt{auc}}_{\mathtt{R\vee S}}$.`Extract` to output `Fail` (which happens with non-negligible probability by assumption, as the failure condition is the only difference between the hybrids), either R is not satisfied and $\mathcal{C}$ wins the adaptive NI-SSS game, or S is not satisfied and $\mathcal{C}$ breaks the hardness property of S.

Hybrid 4. In the fourth hybrid, $\mathcal{C}$ goes back to using $\Pi^{\mathtt{auc}}_{\mathtt{R\vee S}}$.`Prove` and revealing the real prover's random tape upon corruption. As the only difference between Hybrids 3 and 4 is to reverse the transition between real and simulated proofs made in Hybrid 2, the proof is an almost identical reduction to the adNIM-SHVZK property of $\Pi^{\mathtt{SLC}}_{\mathtt{R\vee S}}$, with one caveat: we must argue that $\mathcal{Z}$ is not able to use its interactions with the $\Pi^{\mathtt{auc}}_{\mathtt{R\vee S}}$.`Extract` algorithm to help it distinguish between the real and simulated proofs. Following Lysyanskaya and Rosenbloom [41], we note that since $\Pi^{\mathtt{auc}}_{\mathtt{R\vee S}}$.`Extract` operates using only information that $\mathcal{Z}$ already knows (its externalized proofs and RO queries), it cannot possibly gain any new insight from interacting with the extractor. Therefore, the only way for $\mathcal{Z}$ to distinguish between Hybrids 3 and 4 is to break the adNIM-SHVZK property, which follows from the same reduction used to prove indistinguishability between Hybrids 1 and 2.

Hybrid 5. In the penultimate hybrid, $\mathcal{C}$ replaces the proof process with $\Pi^{\mathtt{auc}}_{\mathtt{RVS}}.\mathtt{SimSetup}$, $\Pi^{\mathtt{auc}}_{\mathtt{RVS}}.\mathtt{SimProve}$, and $\Pi^{\mathtt{auc}}_{\mathtt{RVS}}.\mathtt{SimRand}$. Recall that $\Pi^{\mathtt{auc}}_{\mathtt{RVS}}.\mathtt{SimProve}$ is essentially $\Pi^{\mathtt{auc}}_{\mathtt{RVS}}.\mathtt{Prove}$, except that $\mathcal{C}$ generates and stores pairs $(\mathtt{CRS}_s, \mathtt{trap}_s)$ for each protocol session s in the list $\mathtt{simcrs}$, and uses the witness $\mathtt{trap}_s$ as input to $\Pi^{\mathtt{auc}}_{\mathtt{RVS}}.\mathtt{Prove}$ rather than a "real" witness w. We show that Hybrid 4 is indistinguishable from Hybrid 5 as long as Σ_{OR} is adaptive witness indistinguishable (adWI) according to Theorem 1. Note that since Σ_R is given to be adSHVZK and randomness equivocable in the theorem statement and that Σ_S is an adaptive Σ-friendly relation and therefore also randomness equivocable and adSHVZK, adaptive witness indistinguishability of Σ_{OR} follows from Theorem 1. Since the adWI game captures only a single $\mathtt{Prove}$ query, we consider a hybrid experiment in which the first i queries (and corresponding sections of the prover's random tape) are answered according to Hybrid 4, and the $i + 1^{st}$ query onwards are answered according to Hybrid 5. Our reduction $\mathscr{B}$ will use an environment $\mathcal{Z}$ that can distinguish between the i and $i + 1^{st}$ hybrids with non-negligible advantage to win the adWI game from Fig. 3 with non-negligible advantage as follows.

$\mathscr{B}$ answers $\mathcal{Z}$'s RO queries as usual. For up to and including the ith $\mathtt{Prove}$ query that $\mathcal{Z}$ issues for a party P, $\mathscr{B}$ computes and returns proofs using $\Pi^{\mathtt{auc}}_{\mathtt{RVS}}.\mathtt{Prove}$, exactly as $\mathcal{Z}$ expects from Hybrid 4; past the $i + 1^{st}$ query, $\mathscr{B}$ computes and returns proofs using $\Pi^{\mathtt{auc}}_{\mathtt{RVS}}.\mathtt{SimProve}$, exactly as $\mathcal{Z}$ expects from Hybrid 5. $\mathscr{B}$ stores all tuples (P, Φ_i, T_i). When $\mathcal{Z}$ issues the $i + 1^{st}$ query $(\mathtt{Prove}, P, s, x_{i+1}, w_{i+1})$ for some party P in session s, $\mathscr{B}$ constructs a query $(\mathtt{Prove}, x_{i+1}, \mathtt{CRS}_s, w_{i+1}, \mathtt{trap}_s, 0, \mathtt{st})$ and forwards it to the adWI challenger, who returns a response $(\Phi, T, \mathtt{st})$. $\mathscr{B}$ stores the tuple $(P, \Phi_{i+1}, T_{i+1}) = (P, \Phi, T)$, programs the RO to agree with Φ, then returns Φ to $\mathcal{Z}$. If $\mathcal{Z}$ issues a query $(\mathbf{Corrupt}, P)$, $\mathscr{B}$ gathers all (P, Φ_i, T_i) and returns the concatenation of all T_i to $\mathcal{Z}$. If $\mathcal{Z}$ outputs "Hybrid 3" then $\mathscr{B}$ outputs 0; otherwise if $\mathcal{Z}$ outputs "Hybrid 4" then $\mathscr{B}$ outputs 1.

Note that if the adWI challenger is running the 0-bit experiment, it computed the proof Φ_{i+1} using the real witness w_{i+1} for x_{i+1} using tape T_{i+1}, which is exactly what $\mathcal{Z}$ expects from Hybrid $i + 1$. Otherwise if the adWI challenger is running the 1-bit experiment then it computed the proofs using the opposite witness $\mathtt{trap}_s$ for statement $\mathtt{CRS}_s$, then "equivocated" the random tape to look like it used w_{i+1}, which is exactly what $\mathcal{Z}$ expects from Hybrid i. Therefore, $\mathscr{B}$ succeeds in winning the adWI game with the same probability as $\mathcal{Z}$ succeeds in distinguishing Hybrids i and $i + 1$. Since the number of $\mathtt{Prove}$ queries must be polynomial in the security parameter, $\mathscr{B}$'s total advantage in winning the adWI game over all of the proofs is still non-negligible, completing the proof.

Hybrid 6. The final hybrid replaces $\mathcal{C}$ with $\mathcal{F}_{\mathtt{aNIZK}}$ and $\mathcal{S}$. Note that since $\mathcal{C}$ now runs all of $\mathcal{F}_{\mathtt{aNIZK}}$ and $\mathcal{S}$'s procedures, this is again a syntactic difference, and Hybrid 5 is identical to Hybrid 6. □

Acknowledgments. This research was supported by NSF Grants 2312241, 2154170, and 2247305.

References

1. Badertscher, C., Canetti, R., Hesse, J., Tackmann, B., Zikas, V.: Universal composition with global subroutines: capturing global setup within plain UC. In: Pass, R., Pietrzak, K. (eds.) TCC 2020. LNCS, vol. 12552, pp. 1–30. Springer, Cham (2020). https://doi.org/10.1007/978-3-030-64381-2_1
2. Baldimtsi, F., et al.: Accumulators with applications to anonymity-preserving revocation. In: 2017 IEEE European Symposium on Security and Privacy (EuroS&P), pp. 301–315. IEEE (2017)
3. Baldimtsi, F., Lysyanskaya, A.: Anonymous credentials light. In: Proceedings of the 2013 ACM SIGSAC Conference on Computer & Communications Security, pp. 1087–1098 (2013)
4. Bellare, M., Crites, E., Komlo, C., Maller, M., Tessaro, S., Zhu, C.: Better than advertised security for non-interactive threshold signatures. In: Dodis, Y., Shrimpton, T. (eds.) CRYPTO 2022. LNCS, vol. 13510, pp. 517–550. Springer, Cham (2022). https://doi.org/10.1007/978-3-031-15985-5_18
5. Bellare, M., Rogaway, P.: Random oracles are practical: a paradigm for designing efficient protocols. In: Proceedings of the 1st ACM Conference on Computer and Communications Security, pp. 62–73 (1993)
6. Benhamouda, F., Lepoint, T., Loss, J., Orrù, M., Raykova, M.: On the (in)security of ROS. In: Canteaut, A., Standaert, F.-X. (eds.) EUROCRYPT 2021. LNCS, vol. 12696, pp. 33–53. Springer, Cham (2021). https://doi.org/10.1007/978-3-030-77870-5_2
7. Boneh, D., Boyen, X., Shacham, H.: Short group signatures. In: Franklin, M. (ed.) CRYPTO 2004. LNCS, vol. 3152, pp. 41–55. Springer, Heidelberg (2004). https://doi.org/10.1007/978-3-540-28628-8_3
8. Camenisch, J., Damgård, I.: Verifiable encryption, group encryption, and their applications to separable group signatures and signature sharing schemes. In: Okamoto, T. (ed.) ASIACRYPT 2000. LNCS, vol. 1976, pp. 331–345. Springer, Heidelberg (2000). https://doi.org/10.1007/3-540-44448-3_25
9. Camenisch, J., Drijvers, M., Gagliardoni, T., Lehmann, A., Neven, G.: The wonderful world of global random oracles. In: Nielsen, J.B., Rijmen, V. (eds.) EUROCRYPT 2018. LNCS, vol. 10820, pp. 280–312. Springer, Cham (2018). https://doi.org/10.1007/978-3-319-78381-9_11
10. Camenisch, J., Hohenberger, S., Kohlweiss, M., Lysyanskaya, A., Meyerovich, M.: How to win the clonewars: efficient periodic n-times anonymous authentication, pp. 201–210. ACM (2006)
11. Camenisch, J., Hohenberger, S., Lysyanskaya, A.: Compact E-cash. In: Cramer, R. (ed.) EUROCRYPT 2005. LNCS, vol. 3494, pp. 302–321. Springer, Heidelberg (2005). https://doi.org/10.1007/11426639_18
12. Camenisch, J., Lysyanskaya, A.: An efficient system for non-transferable anonymous credentials with optional anonymity revocation. In: Pfitzmann, B. (ed.) EUROCRYPT 2001. LNCS, vol. 2045, pp. 93–118. Springer, Heidelberg (2001). https://doi.org/10.1007/3-540-44987-6_7

13. Camenisch, J., Lysyanskaya, A.: Dynamic accumulators and application to efficient revocation of anonymous credentials. In: Yung, M. (ed.) CRYPTO 2002. LNCS, vol. 2442, pp. 61–76. Springer, Heidelberg (2002). https://doi.org/10.1007/3-540-45708-9_5
14. Camenisch, J., Lysyanskaya, A.: A signature scheme with efficient protocols. In: Cimato, S., Persiano, G., Galdi, C. (eds.) SCN 2002. LNCS, vol. 2576, pp. 268–289. Springer, Heidelberg (2003). https://doi.org/10.1007/3-540-36413-7_20
15. Camenisch, J., Lysyanskaya, A.: Signature schemes and anonymous credentials from bilinear maps. In: Franklin, M. (ed.) CRYPTO 2004. LNCS, vol. 3152, pp. 56–72. Springer, Heidelberg (2004). https://doi.org/10.1007/978-3-540-28628-8_4
16. Camenisch, J., Shoup, V.: Practical verifiable encryption and decryption of discrete logarithms. In: Boneh, D. (ed.) CRYPTO 2003. LNCS, vol. 2729, pp. 126–144. Springer, Heidelberg (2003). https://doi.org/10.1007/978-3-540-45146-4_8
17. Camenisch, J., Stadler, M.: Efficient group signature schemes for large groups. In: Kaliski, B.S. (ed.) CRYPTO 1997. LNCS, vol. 1294, pp. 410–424. Springer, Heidelberg (1997). https://doi.org/10.1007/BFb0052252
18. Camenisch, J., Stadler, M.: Proof systems for general statements about discrete logarithms. Technical Report/ETH Zurich, Department of Computer Science, p. 260 (1997)
19. Canetti, R.: Universally composable security: a new paradigm for cryptographic protocols. In: Proceedings 42nd IEEE Symposium on Foundations of Computer Science, pp. 136–145. IEEE (2001)
20. Canetti, R., Dodis, Y., Pass, R., Walfish, S.: Universally composable security with global setup. In: Vadhan, S.P. (ed.) TCC 2007. LNCS, vol. 4392, pp. 61–85. Springer, Heidelberg (2007). https://doi.org/10.1007/978-3-540-70936-7_4
21. Canetti, R., Fischlin, M.: Universally composable commitments. In: Kilian, J. (ed.) CRYPTO 2001. LNCS, vol. 2139, pp. 19–40. Springer, Heidelberg (2001). https://doi.org/10.1007/3-540-44647-8_2
22. Canetti, R., Jain, A., Scafuro. A.: Practical UC security with a global random oracle. In: Proceedings of the 2014 ACM SIGSAC Conference on Computer and Communications Security, pp. 597–608 (2014)
23. Canetti, R., Sarkar, P., Wang, X.: Triply adaptive UC NIZK. In: Agrawal, S., Lin, D. (eds.) ASIACRYPT 2022. LNCS, vol. 13792, pp. 466–495. Springer, Cham (2022). https://doi.org/10.1007/978-3-031-22966-4_16
24. Chase, M., Lysyanskaya, A.: On signatures of knowledge. In: Dwork, C. (ed.) CRYPTO 2006. LNCS, vol. 4117, pp. 78–96. Springer, Heidelberg (2006). https://doi.org/10.1007/11818175_5
25. Cohen, R., Shelat, A., Wichs, D.: Adaptively secure MPC with sublinear communication complexity. In: Boldyreva, A., Micciancio, D. (eds.) CRYPTO 2019. LNCS, vol. 11693, pp. 30–60. Springer, Cham (2019). https://doi.org/10.1007/978-3-030-26951-7_2
26. Connolly, D., Komlo, C., Goldberg, I., Wood, C.A.: RFC 9591: the flexible round-optimized Schnorr threshold (frost) protocol for two-round Schnorr signatures (2024)
27. Corrigan-Gibbs, H., Boneh, D., Mazières, D.: Riposte: an anonymous messaging system handling millions of users. In: 2015 IEEE Symposium on Security and Privacy, pp. 321–338. IEEE (2015)
28. Cramer, R., Damgård, I., Schoenmakers, B.: Proofs of partial knowledge and simplified design of witness hiding protocols. In: Desmedt, Y.G. (ed.) CRYPTO 1994. LNCS, vol. 839, pp. 174–187. Springer, Heidelberg (1994). https://doi.org/10.1007/3-540-48658-5_19

29. Crites, E., Komlo, C., Maller, M.: How to prove schnorr assuming schnorr: security of multi-and threshold signatures. ePrint Archive (2021)
30. Crites, E., Komlo, C., Maller, M.: Fully adaptive schnorr threshold signatures. In: Handschuh, H., Lysyanskaya, A. (eds.) CRYPTO 2023. LNCS, vol. 14081, pp. 678–709. Springer, Cham (2023). https://doi.org/10.1007/978-3-031-38557-5_22
31. Damgård, I.: On σ-protocols. University of Aarhus, Department of Computer Science (2002)
32. Drijvers, M., et al.: On the security of two-round multi-signatures. In: 2019 IEEE Symposium on Security and Privacy, pp. 1084–1101. IEEE (2019)
33. Fischlin, M.: Communication-efficient non-interactive proofs of knowledge with online extractors. Manuscript (2005). http://www.cryptoplexity.informatik.tu-darmstadt.de/media/crypt/publications_1/fischlinonline-extractor2005.pdf
34. Fischlin, M.: Communication-efficient non-interactive proofs of knowledge with online extractors. In: Shoup, V. (ed.) CRYPTO 2005. LNCS, vol. 3621, pp. 152–168. Springer, Heidelberg (2005). https://doi.org/10.1007/11535218_10
35. Garay, J.A., MacKenzie, P., Yang, K.: Strengthening zero-knowledge protocols using signatures. In: Biham, E. (ed.) EUROCRYPT 2003. LNCS, vol. 2656, pp. 177–194. Springer, Heidelberg (2003). https://doi.org/10.1007/3-540-39200-9_11
36. Groth, J., Ostrovsky, R., Sahai, A.: New techniques for noninteractive zero-knowledge. J. ACM (JACM) **59**(3), 1–35 (2012)
37. Hauck, E., Kiltz, E., Loss, J.: A modular treatment of blind signatures from identification schemes. In: Ishai, Y., Rijmen, V. (eds.) EUROCRYPT 2019. LNCS, vol. 11478, pp. 345–375. Springer, Cham (2019). https://doi.org/10.1007/978-3-030-17659-4_12
38. Kohlweiss, M., Lysyanskaya, A., Nguyen, A.: Privacy-preserving blueprints. In: Hazay, C., Stam, M. (eds.) EUROCRYPT 2023. LNCS, vol. 14005, pp. 594–625. Springer, Cham (2023). https://doi.org/10.1007/978-3-031-30617-4_20
39. Komlo, C., Goldberg, I.: FROST: flexible round-optimized schnorr threshold signatures. In: Dunkelman, O., Jacobson, Jr., M.J., O'Flynn, C. (eds.) SAC 2020. LNCS, vol. 12804, pp. 34–65. Springer, Cham (2021). https://doi.org/10.1007/978-3-030-81652-0_2
40. Kondi, Y., Shelat, A.: Improved straight-line extraction in the random oracle model with applications to signature aggregation. In: Agrawal, S., Lin, D. (eds.) ASIACRYPT 2022. LNCS, vol. 13792, pp. 279–309. Springer, Cham (2022). https://doi.org/10.1007/978-3-031-22966-4_10
41. Lysyanskaya, A., Rosenbloom, L.N.: Universally composable σ-protocols in the global random-oracle model. In: Kiltz, E., Vaikuntanathan, V. (eds.) TCC 2022. LNCS, vol. 13747, pp. 203–233. Springer, Cham (2022). https://doi.org/10.1007/978-3-031-22318-1_8
42. Neff, C.A.: A verifiable secret shuffle and its application to e-voting. In: Proceedings of the 8th ACM Conference on Computer and Communications Security, pp. 116–125 (2001)
43. Nick, J., Ruffing, T., Seurin, Y.: MuSig2: simple two-round schnorr multi-signatures. In: Malkin, T., Peikert, C. (eds.) CRYPTO 2021. LNCS, vol. 12825, pp. 189–221. Springer, Cham (2021). https://doi.org/10.1007/978-3-030-84242-0_8
44. Okamoto, T.: Provably secure and practical identification schemes and corresponding signature schemes. In: Brickell, E.F. (ed.) CRYPTO 1992. LNCS, vol. 740, pp. 31–53. Springer, Heidelberg (1993). https://doi.org/10.1007/3-540-48071-4_3
45. Panja, S., Roy, B.: A secure end-to-end verifiable e-voting system using blockchain and cloud server. J. Inf. Secur. Appl. **59**, 102815 (2021)

46. Pass, R.: On deniability in the common reference string and random oracle model. In: Boneh, D. (ed.) CRYPTO 2003. LNCS, vol. 2729, pp. 316–337. Springer, Heidelberg (2003). https://doi.org/10.1007/978-3-540-45146-4_19
47. Schnorr, C.P.: Efficient signature generation by smart cards. J. Cryptol. **4**(3), 161–174 (1991). https://doi.org/10.1007/BF00196725
48. Schoenmakers, B.: A simple publicly verifiable secret sharing scheme and its application to electronic voting. In: Wiener, M. (ed.) CRYPTO 1999. LNCS, vol. 1666, pp. 148–164. Springer, Heidelberg (1999). https://doi.org/10.1007/3-540-48405-1_10
49. Proposal: Σ-protocols. Stephan krenn and michele orrù (2021)
50. Tessaro, S., Zhu, C.: Revisiting BBS signatures. In: Hazay, C., Stam, M. (eds.) EUROCRYPT 2023. LNCS, vol. 14008, pp. 691–721. Springer, Cham (2023). https://doi.org/10.1007/978-3-031-30589-4_24
51. Unruh, D.: Non-interactive zero-knowledge proofs in the quantum random oracle model. In: Oswald, E., Fischlin, M. (eds.) EUROCRYPT 2015. LNCS, vol. 9057, pp. 755–784. Springer, Heidelberg (2015). https://doi.org/10.1007/978-3-662-46803-6_25
52. Wagner, D.: A generalized birthday problem. In: Yung, M. (ed.) CRYPTO 2002. LNCS, vol. 2442, pp. 288–304. Springer, Heidelberg (2002). https://doi.org/10.1007/3-540-45708-9_19
53. Wikström, D.: A commitment-consistent proof of a shuffle. In: Boyd, C., González Nieto, J. (eds.) ACISP 2009. LNCS, vol. 5594, pp. 407–421. Springer, Heidelberg (2009). https://doi.org/10.1007/978-3-642-02620-1_28

Fast Elliptic Curve Scalar Multiplications in SN(T)ARK Circuits

Liam Eagen[1], Youssef El Housni[2(✉)], Simon Masson[3], and Thomas Piellard[2]

[1] Alpen Labs, New York, USA
liameagen@protonmail.com
[2] Linea, New York, USA
{youssef.elhousni,thomas.piellard}@consensys.net
[3] ZKNox, Paris, France
simon.masson@protonmail.com

Abstract. Proof systems of arbitrary computations have found many applications in recent years. However, the proving algorithm has a consequent complexity tied to the size of the computation being proved. Thus, proving large computations is quite inefficient. One of these large computations is the scalar multiplication over an elliptic curve. In this work, we provide new techniques for reducing the time corresponding to proving a scalar multiplication, using integer lattice reduction or a (half) extended Euclidean algorithm in a ring of integers. We investigate optimizations in the case of small (complex multiplication) discriminant curves, and its generalization for multi scalar multiplications as used in signature verification. We provide an optimized Golang implementation for different elliptic curves in different proof systems settings. The speed-up in proving time is between 22% and 53% compared to the previous state-of-the-art.

Keywords: SNARK · STARK · proof systems · elliptic curves · scalar multiplication

1 Introduction

Over the past few years, proof systems have become an essential primitive for privacy-preserving and scalable applications in blockchains. A proof system is an interactive protocol in which one party, referred to as the prover, seeks to convince another party, known as the verifier, of the truth of a given statement. Proof systems are classified as non-interactive when no communication is required between the prover and the verifier beyond the transmission of the proof itself. Within the category of non-interactive proofs, particularly notable concepts for demonstrating computational integrity are the Succinct Non-interactive ARgument of Knowledge (SNARK) and Scalable Transparent ARgument of Knowledge (STARK). SNARKs and STARKs offer computationally sound proofs that are efficient to verify and compact in size relative to the statement being proved. Proof systems were first introduced in [18] and have since been extensively studied in both theoretical and practical contexts [5,17,20,25]. Recent advancements

D. Escudero and I. Damgård (Eds.): LATINCRYPT 2025, LNCS 16129, pp. 109–129, 2026.
https://doi.org/10.1007/978-3-032-06754-8_4

have explored a wide range of settings, including cryptographic assumptions, asymptotic efficiency, implementation performance, and diverse applications. In this work, we use the terms SNARK and STARK interchangeably, as the techniques presented are agnostic to the specific choice of proof system. In the context of blockchain technology, the computations being proved are often large, making the proving algorithm computationally expensive and a critical target for optimization. One prominent example of such a resource-intensive computation is scalar multiplication over an elliptic curve. This operation is fundamental to applications such as blockchain rollups[1], Verkle tries[2], account abstraction[3], and proof recursion [8,9,27]. While efficient computation of scalar multiplication over elliptic curves is a well-established problem in cryptography, proving scalar multiplication using a SNARK introduces a novel challenge that paves the way for new research directions and implementation strategies.

Contributions. In this work, we investigate optimizations for proving scalar multiplications with a SNARK. Given the pre-computed resulting point Q (called a hint), and leveraging lattice reduction in $\mathbb{Z}$, we show how to turn proving a n-bit scalar multiplication $[k]P \stackrel{?}{=} Q$ in a curve E into mainly proving a $n/2$-bit double-scalar-multiplication $[k_1]P - [k_2]Q \stackrel{?}{=} 0_E$, regardless of the existence of an efficient endomorphism. When it exists, we show how to turn proving a n-bit scalar multiplication into mainly a $n/4$-bit quadruple-scalar-multiplication. Alternatively to using a lattice reduction in $\mathbb{Z}$, we propose a novel use in cryptography of the (half) extended Euclidean algorithm (rational reconstruction) in an order $\mathcal{O}$ of an Euclidean imaginary quadratic field, e.g. Eisenstein integers for elliptic curves of j-invariant 0. This alternative algorithm speeds up the witness generation (scalar decomposition) at the cost of slowing down the proof generation (increasing the decomposed sub-scalars bounds). This is useful in use-cases where a prover cannot invoke arbitrary hints. Finally, we provide a fast implementation in Golang using the `gnark` library for different elliptic curves in different proof systems settings. The circuit size speed-up from this work is summarized in Table 1.

Table 1. Scalar multiplication constraint speed-up using our work.

Circuit	Curve	Groth16 speed-up	PLONK speed-up
Emulated	small discriminant	24%	42%
	generic	52%	50%
Native	small discriminant	48%	53%
	generic	22%	28%

[1] https://ethereum.org/en/developers/docs/scaling/zk-rollups/.
[2] https://ethereum.org/en/roadmap/verkle-trees/.
[3] https://ethereum.org/en/roadmap/account-abstraction/.

Organization of the Paper. In Sect. 2, we explain what are SNARK circuits and how to optimize them and we recall basics about elliptic curves and (multi) scalar multiplications. We also recall facts about the decomposition of scalars, useful for the results of Sect. 3, which is the core of this paper. We provide some comparison of the new circuits with the previous state-of-the-art implementation in Sect. 4, and conclude this work in Sect. 5.

2 Background

The results of this paper are related to the cost of elliptic curve scalar multiplication in SNARK circuits. In this section, we explain what are SNARK circuits and recall results about elliptic curves, in particular for simple and multi scalar multiplications. We present two techniques for decomposing scalars from a general point of view. These techniques allow the well-known GLV decomposition [16], that splits a scalar into two sub-scalars in order to reduce the cost of a scalar multiplication for small discriminant curves.

2.1 SNARK Circuits

Given a public non-deterministic polynomial (NP) program F and inputs b, c, such that the program F satisfies the relation $F(b) = c$, a SNARK consists in proving this relation succinctly. It consists mainly of the `Prove` and `Verify` algorithms. The first algorithm requires generating an execution trace of the program F. This step is called witness generation. In this paper, we are interested in optimizing the `Prove` algorithm for the program F corresponding to a scalar multiplication over an elliptic curve. We do this by expressing F as an arithmetic circuit as efficiently as possible (low number of gates). This step is called *the arithmetization* of the program F.

Our techniques are valid for any SNARK (or STARK) but we implemented our work (see Sect. 4) for two widely used schemes: Groth16 [19] and PLONK [13]. Considering w the number of wires, m the number of multiplication gates, a the number of addition gates, $\ell =$ number of public inputs and $\mathtt{M}_{\mathbb{G}}$ a multiplication in $\mathbb{G}$, the cost of the `Prove` algorithm is given by $(3m + w - \ell)\ \mathtt{M}_{\mathbb{G}}$ for Groth16, and $9(m + a)\ \mathtt{M}_{\mathbb{G}}$ for PLONK. Note that we omit the number of FFTs in this estimation, as $\mathbb{G}$ multiplications dominate the overall cost of `Prove`. The better we arithmetize F, the faster the `Prove` algorithm is.

Arithmetization. The first step in proving an arbitrary program is to *arithmetize* it, that is to reduce the computation satisfiability to an intermediate representation satisfiability. Many problems in cryptography can be expressed as the task of computing some polynomials. Arithmetic circuits are the most standard model for studying the complexity of such computations.

An arithmetic circuit over the field $\mathbb{F}$ and the set of variables $X = \{x_0, \ldots, x_n\}$ is a directed acyclic graph such that the vertices are called gates, while the edges are called wires. Arithmetic circuits of interest to many proof

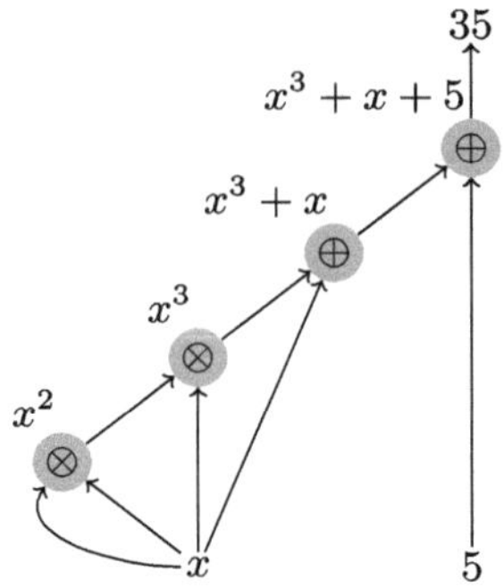

Fig. 1. Arithmetic circuit encoding the computation $x^3 + x + 5 = 35$ for which the (secret) solution is $x = 3$.

systems and most applicable to this work are those with two incoming wires and one out-coming wire (cf. Fig. 1 for an example).

SNARK-Friendly Computations. Many proof systems (e.g. Groth16 and PLONK) arithmetize programs as arithmetic circuits. The number of gates is what determines the prover complexity. For example, Groth16 prover complexity is dominated by some multi scalar multiplications in $\mathbb{G}$ of sizes m (the number of multiplication gates). With this in mind, multiplications by constants in $\mathbb{F}$, which are usually expensive in hardware, are essentially free. While more traditional hardware-friendly computations (e.g. XORing 32-bit numbers) are far more costly in this model. The following two observations, noted in earlier works [21], are the key to lower the number of gates of a circuit:

- The multiplication by constants in $\mathbb{F}$ is free,
- The verification can be sometimes simpler than forward computation. The circuits do not always have to compute the result, but can instead represent a verification algorithm. For example a multiplicative inversion circuit ($1/x \stackrel{?}{=} y$) does not have to arithmetize the computation of the inversion ($1/x$) but can instead consist of a single multiplication gate ($x \cdot y$) on the value provided (pre-computed) by the prover (y) and checks the equality ($x \cdot y \stackrel{?}{=} 1$).

This is basically a computation model where inversions cost as much as multiplications.

2.2 Elliptic Curves

In this work, E is an ordinary elliptic curve defined over $\mathbb{F}_p$ for a large characteristic p. From Hasse theorem [29, page 138], the $\mathbb{F}_p$-rational points form a finite abelian group of order $\#E(\mathbb{F}_p) = p + 1 - t$ where t is the trace of the curve and satisfies $|t| \leq 2\sqrt{p}$. We consider a subgroup of prime order r on $E(\mathbb{F}_p)$, i.e. r divides $p+1-t$. In other words, let $P \in E(\mathbb{F}_p)$ a point of prime order r and $\mathbb{G}$ the cyclic subgroup generated by P. We define the scalar multiplication as $[k]P$ for an integer $k < r$. In this work, N denotes the bit-size of r, and D the Complex Multiplication (CM) discriminant associated to E, i.e. the discriminant of the order $\mathrm{End}(E)$, the endomorphism ring of the curve as an order in the integer ring of $\mathbb{Q}(\sqrt{t^2 - 4p})$. We refer to [29] for a deeper introduction to the theory of elliptic curves.

2.3 Computing Scalar Multiplications

Single Scalar Multiplication. A scalar multiplication is the computation of $[k]P = P + \ldots + P$ (k times). The double-and-add technique given in Algorithm 1 has a complexity linear in N, the bit-size of the scalar k. We provide here an algorithm reading bits from the Most Significant Bit (MSB) to the Least Significant Bit (LSB).

Algorithm 1: ScalarMultiplication(k, P)

Input. A scalar k of N bits,
A point P.
Output. $Q = [k]P$.

```
R ← P
for b bit of k read from second MSB to LSB
do
  R ← [2]R
  if b = 1 then
    R ← R + P
  end if
end for
return R
```

In cryptographic schemes where k is a secret, this algorithm is often computed in constant-time, and the conditional $R \leftarrow R + P$ is implemented consistently. In the context of SNARK circuits, conditional branching is not possible and an addition is always computed at every step of the loop. In total, the cost of a scalar multiplication is given by $(N-1)\mathbf{Add} + (N-1)\mathbf{Dbl}$.

Multi Scalar Multiplication. We consider two points P_1 and P_2, and two scalars k_1, k_2. In order to compute $[k_1]P_1 + [k_2]P_2$, it is possible to scan the bits of both scalars simultaneously and compute the result at the cost of one scalar multiplication (and an extra pre-computation). This improvement was originally proposed in [30] and [12], and it can be generalized to a multi scalar multiplication with n points, but the pre-computation cost increases. We provide Algorithm 2 for the generic case of n scalar multiplication.

Algorithm 2: MultiScalarMultiplication$((k_1, P_1), \ldots, (k_n, P_n))$

Input. A list of scalars $k_1, \ldots, k_n$ of N bits,
A list of points $P_1, \ldots, P_n$.
Output. $Q = [k_1]P_1 + \ldots + [k_n]P_n$.

Pre-computation table T.
for j between 0 and $2^n - 1$ **do**
  $T[j] \leftarrow \sum_{i=1}^{n} [e_i]P_i$ where $j = \sum_{i=1}^{n} e_i 2^{i-1}$.
end for

Main loop.
$R \leftarrow 0_E$
for $(b_1, \ldots, b_n)$ bits of $k_1, \ldots, k_n$ read from MSB to LSB **do**
  $R \leftarrow [2]R$
  $R \leftarrow R + T\left[\sum_{i=1}^{n} b_i 2^{i-1}\right]$
end for
return R

The cost of this algorithm is split into two: a pre-computation table of $2^n - n - 1$ elliptic curve additions (**Add**), and a main loop with $N-1$ steps including a doubling (**Dbl**) and an addition. Adding the neutral element may occur with probability 2^{-n}, but in the context of SNARK circuits (as well as for constant time algorithms), additions will always be computed so we decided to keep $(N-1)$**Add** for the cost estimation. From now, we denote MSM(n, N) to be the cost of a multi scalar multiplication of n points and scalars of N bits:

$$\mathrm{MSM}(n, N) = (2^n - n - 1 + N - 1) \cdot \mathbf{Add} + (N - 1) \cdot \mathbf{Dbl}.$$

We recall in the next section a technique that speeds up a scalar multiplication by computing it as a multi scalar multiplication with halve size scalars. It was introduced in [16] by Gallant, Lambert and Vanstone.

GLV Scalar Multiplication. Let $\mathrm{End}(E) = \mathbb{Z} + \psi\mathbb{Z}$, and $\psi(P) \equiv [\lambda]P$, i.e. λ is the eigenvalue of ψ seen as a linear application on $E(\mathbb{F}_p)[r]$, the order-r subgroup defined over $\mathbb{F}_p$. The method introduced in [16] turns $[k]P$ into $[k_1]P + [k_2]\psi(P)$ with ψ efficiently computable. This applies to elliptic curves with small CM discriminant, where the endomorphism ψ has a tiny degree. The scalars k_1, k_2 can be constructed of size around $\sqrt{r}$. We dig the details of this decomposition from a generic point of view in Sect. 2.4. Note that for computing the multi scalar multiplication, it is required to compute $[\lambda]P = \psi(P)$, and it is expensive when the degree of ψ is large. The GLV technique is implemented in many libraries, and leads to almost 40% speed-up for scalar multiplication.

Example 1. Consider an elliptic curve defined over $\mathbb{F}_p$ by $y^2 = x^3 + b$. There is an efficient endomorphism $\psi : E \to E$ defined by $(x, y) \mapsto (\omega x, y)$ (and $0_E \mapsto 0_E$)

such that $\psi(P) = [\lambda]P$, where both ω and λ are cubic roots of unity in $\mathbb{F}_p$ and $\mathbb{F}_r$ respectively. Evaluating this endomorphism costs only one multiplication over $\mathbb{F}_p$. Using ψ, it is possible to turn $[k]P$ into $[k_1]P + [k_2]\psi(P)$ which costs $\mathrm{MSM}(2, N/2)$.

In the next sections, we dig the decomposition of a scalar from a general point of view. The GLV method can be obtained from it as a special case, and the results of Sect. 3 also use this technique.

2.4 Scalar Decomposition Using Lattice Reduction

In this section, we consider the generic decomposition of a scalar k. We look for a small solution $(x, y, z, t) \in \mathbb{Z}^4$ of

$$x + \lambda y - k(z + \lambda t) = 0 \bmod r,$$

where λ is fixed. Note that when λ is the eigenvalue of the endomorphism, finding a solution with $z = 1$ and $t = 0$ leads to the GLV decomposition.

We look for *small* solutions to this problem. The set of solutions is a lattice of small dimension, and it is possible to use algorithms of reduction in order to find *small* solutions. Minkowski's theorem ensure that in a lattice $\mathcal{L}$ of rank n, there exists a vector v of norm $|v|_\infty \leq \mathrm{Vol}(\mathcal{L})^{1/n}$, where $\mathrm{Vol}(\mathcal{L})$ is the volume of the lattice and can be computed as $\sqrt{\det(MM^t)}$ for a matrix M defining the lattice. If the lattice is described by a full rank matrix, the volume is simply the determinant. Finding a short vector of the lattice can be computed in polynomial time using for instance [23], but the obtained vector can be slightly larger. The obtained bound is $\mathrm{Vol}(\mathcal{L})^{1/n}/(\delta - 1/4)^{(n-1)/n}$, where δ is a parameter usually set to a value close to 1, often $\delta = 0.99$. However, we consider here only dimension up to 6 and algorithms such as LLL [23] work also well for this range of dimensions [26]. Though, the obtained vectors are short with respect to the Euclidean norm. While this computation is done out-of-circuit during the witness generation, it might be expensive depending on the context (see Sect. 4.1). We consider an alternative approach in Sect. 2.5 for a witness/proof generation trade-off that is easier to implement. We consider now specific values of the parameter λ that will be useful in Sect. 3.

Integer Fraction Decomposition. When $\lambda = 0$, the equation is simply $x - kz = 0 \bmod r$. It corresponds to a fraction decomposition of $k = x/z$ in $\mathbb{Z}/r\mathbb{Z}$. In this case, the solutions form a lattice of dimension 2 defined with

$$\begin{pmatrix} r & 0 \\ k & 1 \end{pmatrix}$$

After reducing this matrix, the resulting scalars are expected to be bounded by $r^{1/2}/(\delta - 1/4)^{1/2} \approx 1.16 r^{1/2}$ for $\delta = 0.99$. This case is studied in Sect. 3.1.

Simultaneous Fraction Decomposition. It is possible to solve two equations simultaneously, namely for two scalars k_1, k_2, we consider the equations $x_1 - k_1 z = 0 \bmod r$ and $x_2 - k_2\,\mathrm{z} = 0 \bmod r$. In other words, we write k_1 and k_2 as fractions modulo r with the same denominator z, and it corresponds to a lattice of dimension 3 defined with

$$\begin{pmatrix} r & 0 & 0 \\ 0 & r & 0 \\ k_1 & k_2 & 1 \end{pmatrix}$$

and the resulting scalars are expected to be bounded by $r^{2/3}/(\delta - 1/4)^{2/3} \approx 1.22 r^{2/3}$ for $\delta = 0.99$. This case is studied in Sect. 3.2.

Fraction Decomposition in a Quadratic Extension. The solutions of the original equation $x + \lambda y - k(z + \lambda t) = 0 \bmod r$ is a lattice of dimension 4 defined with

$$\begin{pmatrix} r & 0 & 0 & 0 \\ -\lambda & 1 & 0 & 0 \\ k & 0 & 1 & 0 \\ 0 & 0 & -\lambda & 1 \end{pmatrix}$$

and a solution corresponds to a rational fraction $k = (x + \lambda y)/(z + \lambda t) \bmod r$, i.e. a fraction in $(\mathbb{Z}/r\mathbb{Z})[\lambda]$. Using a lattice reduction, the scalars are expected to be bounded by $r^{1/4}/(\delta - 1/4)^{3/4} \approx 1.25 r^{1/4}$ for $\delta = 0.99$. This case is studied in Sect. 3.3.

Simultaneous Fraction Decomposition in a Quadratic Extension. Generalizing this to two equations simultaneously is also possible. The two equations $(x_1 + \lambda y_1) - k_1(z + \lambda t) = 0 \bmod r$ and $(x_2 + \lambda y_2) - k_2(z + \lambda t) = 0 \bmod r$ define a lattice of dimension 6 defined by

$$\begin{pmatrix} r & 0 & 0 & 0 & 0 & 0 \\ -\lambda & 1 & 0 & 0 & 0 & 0 \\ 0 & 0 & r & 0 & 0 & 0 \\ 0 & 0 & -\lambda & 1 & 0 & 0 \\ k_1 & 0 & k_2 & 0 & 1 & 0 \\ 0 & 0 & 0 & 0 & -\lambda & 1 \end{pmatrix}$$

and the resulting scalars are expected to be bounded by $r^{2/6}/(\delta - 1/4)^{5/6} \approx 1.28 r^{1/3}$. We study this case in Sect. 3.4.

In the next section, we investigate how to compute a scalar decomposition without lattice reduction. Instead, we consider the extended Euclidean algorithm in different rings. First, we recall how it works in $\mathbb{Z}$, and then apply the same idea on the norm Euclidean rings $\mathbb{Z}[j]$ and $\mathbb{Z}[\sqrt{-2}]$.

2.5 Scalar Decomposition Using the (Half) Extended Euclidean Algorithm

A fraction decomposition can be obtained using the extended Euclidean algorithm (EEA), as described in [16, Sec. 4].

Decomposition in $\mathbb{Z}$. Running the extended Euclidean algorithm on (r, k) in $\mathbb{Z}$ produces a sequence of numbers s_i, t_i, r_i, starting with

$$s_0 = 1, t_0 = 0, r_0 = r,$$
$$s_1 = 0, t_1 = 1, r_1 = k,$$

and verifying

1. $s_i r + t_i k = r_i$
2. $r_i > r_{i+1} \geq 0$ for $i \geq 0$,
3. $|s_i| < |s_{i+1}|$ for $i \geq 1$,
4. $|t_i| < |t_{i+1}|$ for $i \geq 0$,
5. $r_i|t_{i+1}| + r_{i+1}|t_i| = r$ for $i \geq 1$.

Stopping the algorithm at the last step m where $r_m \geq \sqrt{r}$ ensures that $|t_{i+1}| < \sqrt{r}$. Since $r_{m+1} < \sqrt{r}$, we obtain $(x, z) := (r_{m+1}, t_{m+1})$ such that $x - zk = 0 \bmod r$, and $|(x, z)|_\infty < \sqrt{r}$.

This method allows in fact to find a short vector in the lattice $\mathcal{L}$, the kernel of

$$\begin{aligned} \mathbb{Z} \times \mathbb{Z} &\longrightarrow \mathbb{Z}/r\mathbb{Z} \\ (x, y) &\longrightarrow x + ky \end{aligned}$$

Note that the short vector that is found is below the Minkowski bound $\mathrm{Vol}(\mathcal{L})^{1/2} = \sqrt{r}$.

Decomposition in a Norm Euclidean Imaginary Quadratic Ring. In an imaginary quadratic ring $\mathcal{O}$ which is norm Euclidean (meaning that we can run the Greatest Common Divisor (GCD) algorithm using the norm $\mathcal{N}$ in the complex sense), if an ideal (r) splits as a product of two distinct prime ideals I_1 and I_2, we can apply the same idea as in $\mathbb{Z}$ to find a short vector in the kernel (which is a lattice $\mathcal{L}$) of

$$\begin{aligned} \mathcal{O} \times \mathcal{O} &\longrightarrow \mathcal{O}/I_1 \cong \mathbb{Z}/r\mathbb{Z} \\ (x, y) &\longrightarrow x + ky \end{aligned}$$

Running the extended Euclidean algorithm on (r, k) in $\mathcal{O}$ produces a sequence of values s_i, t_i, r_i, starting with

$$s_0 = 1, t_0 = 0, r_0 = r,$$
$$s_1 = 0, t_1 = 1, r_1 = k,$$

and verifying

1. $s_i r + t_i k = r_i$
2. $\mathcal{N}(r_i) > \mathcal{N}(r_{i+1}) \geq 0$ for $i \geq 0$,
3. $\mathcal{N}(s_i) < \mathcal{N}(s_{i+1})$ for $i \geq 1$,
4. $\mathcal{N}(t_i) < \mathcal{N}(t_{i+1})$ for $i \geq 0$,
5. $\pm(r_i t_{i+1} - r_{i+1} t_i) = r$ for $i \geq 1$.

As in $\mathbb{Z}$, if we stop the algorithm at the last step m where $\mathcal{N}(r_m) \geq \sqrt{\mathcal{N}(r)} = \sqrt{r}$, we can find a short vector (t_{m+1}, r_{m+1}) satisfying $r_{m+1} - t_{m+1}k = 0 \bmod r$, where $\mathcal{N}(r_{m+1}) \leq \sqrt{\mathcal{N}(r)}$. From $\pm(r_{i-1}t_i - r_i t_{i-1}) = r$ for $i \geq 1$ and $\mathcal{N}(r_{i-1}) > \mathcal{N}(r_i)$ we have

$$\mathcal{N}(r) \geq \mathcal{N}(r_{i-1})\mathcal{N}(t_i) - \mathcal{N}(r_i)\mathcal{N}(t_{i-1}) \geq \mathcal{N}(r_{i-1})(\mathcal{N}(t_i) - \mathcal{N}(t_{i-1}))$$

Since $\mathcal{N}(r_i) \geq \sqrt{r}$ for $i \geq m$, we have for $i \geq m$

$$\sqrt{\mathcal{N}(r)} \geq (\mathcal{N}(t_i) - \mathcal{N}(t_{i-1}))$$

Since this inequality is true for all the first m steps and since $t_0 = 0$, summing all those inequalities gives

$$c\sqrt{\mathcal{N}(r)} \geq \mathcal{N}(t_i)$$

where c is the number of steps before we stop the algorithm. The number of steps when running the extended Euclidean algorithm on (a, b) with $\mathcal{N}(a) > \mathcal{N}(b)$ is at worst $\log_2(\mathcal{N}(a))$.

The bound $\sqrt{r}$ is far from the theoretical Minkowski bound $\mathrm{Vol}(\mathcal{L})^{1/4} = \sqrt[4]{r}$. To remedy to this, instead of running the extended Euclidean algorithm on (r, k), we can run it on (w, k) where w is a short vector in I_1, of size below $\sqrt{r}$, which is possible since I_1, I_2 are lattices of rank 2 and volume r. In this case, running the extended Euclidean algorithm on (w, k) would produce (t_{m+1}, r_{m+1}) such that

$$\mathcal{N}(t_{m+1}) < c\sqrt{\mathcal{N}(w)}$$
$$\mathcal{N}(r_{m+1}) < \sqrt{\mathcal{N}(w)}$$

and

$$r_{m+1} - t_{m+1}k = 0 \bmod w$$

and since w is I_1, this gives that

$$r_{m+1} - t_{m+1}k = 0 \bmod I_1$$

Decomposition in $\mathbb{Z}[j]$. In the ring of Eisenstein integers, the ideal (r) splits as the product of $I_1 := (r, j - \lambda)$ and $I_2 := (r, j - \lambda^2)$. To find a short vector w in I_1, we apply the half-GCD method for the decomposition in $\mathbb{Z}$ on (r, λ). It produces a vector (w_0, w_1) such that

$$w := w_0 + jw_1 \in I_1$$

since in $\mathbb{Z}[j]/(r, j - \lambda)\mathbb{Z} \cong \mathbb{Z}/r\mathbb{Z}$, $w = 0$. Also $|(w_0, w_1)|_\infty < \sqrt{r}$.

Now, running the extended Euclidean algorithm on (w, k) produces $x, y \in \mathbb{Z}[j]$ such that

$$x - kz = 0 \bmod (r, j - \lambda)$$

and such that $\mathcal{N}(x) < \sqrt{\mathcal{N}(w)}$ and $\mathcal{N}(z) < N\sqrt{\mathcal{N}(w)}$ where N is the bit-size of k.

For implementation purposes, we need to know the bit-size of the scalars x and z. For that we need to compare the norm $\mathcal{N}$ and maximum norm defined by $|a + jb|_\infty = \max\{|a|, |b|\}$. The comparison of those norms is described in the Appendix A. We obtain that

$$|x|_\infty \leq 2\sqrt{2}\sqrt[4]{r},$$
$$|z|_\infty \leq 2\sqrt{2}N\sqrt[4]{r}.$$

Decomposition in $\mathbb{Z}[\sqrt{-2}]$. When r splits in $\mathbb{Z}[\sqrt{-2}]$ as $I_1 := (r, \sqrt{-2} - \mu)$, $I_2 := (r, \sqrt{-2} - \nu)$, we proceed exactly in the same way as in $\mathbb{Z}[j]$, that is we first find a short vector $w \in I_1$ such that $|w|_\infty < \sqrt{r}$, and then we run the extended Euclidean algorithm on (w, k) in $\mathbb{Z}[\sqrt{-2}]$ to find (x, z) such that $x - kz = 0 \bmod (r, r - \mu)$ and such that $\mathcal{N}(x) < \sqrt{\mathcal{N}(w)}$ and $\mathcal{N}(z) < N\sqrt{\mathcal{N}(w)}$ where N is the bit-size of k. Again, comparing the norm $\mathcal{N}$ and the maximum norm defined by $|a + b\sqrt{-2}|_\infty = \max\{|a|, |b|\}$ (see Appendix A) shows that

$$|x|_\infty \leq 2\sqrt[4]{2}\sqrt[4]{r},$$
$$|z|_\infty \leq 2\sqrt[4]{2}N\sqrt[4]{r}.$$

3 Proving Scalar Multiplications

In this section, we explain how to apply scalar decomposition in order to speed up proving scalar multiplications in SNARKs. In the traditional context, when an efficient endomorphism is available, one can turn a single scalar multiplication i.e. MSM$(1, N)$ into a MSM$(2, N/2)$. In Sects. 3.1 and 3.2, we present a technique to turn any MSM$(1, N)$ into a MSM$(2, N/2)$ regardless if the elliptic curve is equipped with an efficient endomorphism. In Sects. 3.3 and 3.4, when the curve is equipped with a GLV endomorphism, we show how to turn a MSM$(1, N)$ into a MSM$(4, N/4)$.

3.1 Hinted Simple Scalar Multiplication

In the context of SNARKs, the scalar multiplication $[k]P$ is rather *verified* than computed. In this context it is possible to hint the output $Q = [k]P$, that is the prover computes the scalar multiplication outside of the SNARK circuit. Then the verifier checks whether if $[k]P - Q = 0_E$ inside the SNARK circuit. This way, it is possible to write k as $x/z \bmod r$ with x, z small as in Sect. 2.4.

$$[k]P = Q \iff [x]P - [z]Q = 0$$

This computation can be done with a double scalar multiplication as in Sect. 2.3. From Sect. 2.4, the resulting scalars x, z are expected to be bounded by $1.16\sqrt{r}$. However, the verifier has to additionally check that the decomposition is correct, i.e. $k \cdot z = x \bmod r$.

In the traditional context of computing $[k]P$, the GLV endomorphism is a way to introduce a second point $\phi(P)$ which is cheap to compute to turn $[k]P$ into $[k_1]P + [k_2]\phi(P)$ where k_1, k_2 are small. In the SNARK context, we use the resulting point Q as this second point to achieve the same speed-up. In terms of cost, this technique enables a verification in almost MSM$(2, N/2)$. We note that a similar idea for verifying signatures was introduced in [2] in a different context. In the next section, we investigate how to use this technique for a double scalar multiplication.

Example 2. Consider the following toy elliptic curve: $E/\mathbb{F}_{103} : y^2 = x^3 + 5$. It forms a group of prime order 97. Let $P = (38, 94)$ be a point on the curve. Given $Q = [11]P = (95, 27)$, proving $[11]P = Q$ is equivalent to proving $[2]P - [9]Q = 0_E$.

3.2 Hinted Double Scalar Multiplication

The previous technique can be generalized for a *double* scalar multiplication. The computation of $[k_1]P_1 + [k_2]P_2$ can be decomposed using the simultaneous fraction decomposition of Sect. 2.4 in order to write $k_1 = x_1/z \bmod r$ and $k_2 = x_2/z \bmod r$. Then,

$$[k_1]P_1 + [k_2]P_2 = Q \iff [x_1]P_1 + [x_2]P_2 - [z]Q = 0$$

and the scalars x_1, x_2 and z are expected to be bounded by $1.22r^{2/3}$. The computation of the MSM of size 2 can be done using a MSM of size 3 with scalar of size almost 2/3 of the original scalar size. We estimate that this leads to a 25% improvement for a signature verification. In the next section, we investigate the case of GLV optimization.

Example 3. Let $P_1 = (38, 94)$ and $P_2 = (31, 82)$ be two points on the curve $E(\mathbb{F}_{103})$. Given $Q = [75]P_1 + [35]P_2 = (8, 38)$, proving $[75]P_1 + [35]P_2 = Q$ is equivalent to proving $[-18]P_1 + [11]P_2 + [8]Q = 0_E$.

3.3 Hinted GLV Scalar Multiplication

It is possible to use the technique described in Sect. 3.1 together with the GLV speed-up. Instead of writing $k = x/z \bmod r$, we decompose the scalar in $(\mathbb{Z}/r\mathbb{Z})[\lambda]$ as in Sect. 2.4:

$$k = \frac{x + \lambda y}{z + \lambda t} \bmod r$$

leading to a four-dimensional multi scalar multiplication:

$$[k]P = Q \iff [x]P + [y]\psi(P) - [z]Q - [t]\psi(Q) = 0$$

Using a lattice reduction, a solution (x, y, z, t) can be found with expected norm bounded by $1.25\sqrt[4]{r}$. Finally, we obtain an overall cost of almost MSM(4, $N/4$), improving the scalar multiplication verification for small discriminant curves.

Example 4. The curve $E(\mathbb{F}_{103})$ has the same form as Example 1. Hence, it has an efficient endomorphism ψ with $\lambda = 61$ and $\omega = 46$. Let $P = (38, 94) \in E$. Given $Q = [56]P = (8, 65)$, proving $[56]P = Q$ is equivalent to proving $[1]P + [1]\psi(P) + [1]Q - [1]\psi(Q) = 0_E$.

3.4 Hinted GLV Double Scalar Multiplication

An approach similar to Sect. 3.2 can be combined with the GLV optimization. As in Sect. 2.4, we write

$$k_1 = \frac{x_1 + \lambda y_1}{z + \lambda t} \bmod r, \qquad k_2 = \frac{x_2 + \lambda y_2}{z + \lambda t} \bmod r$$

and so

$$[k_1]P_1 + [k_2]P_2 = Q \iff [x_1]P_1 + [y_1]\psi(P_1) + [x_2]P_2 + [y_2]\psi(P_2) - [z]Q - [t]\psi(Q) = 0.$$

From Sect. 2.4, we expect x_i, y_i, z, t to be bounded by $1.28r^{1/3}$. The final cost is almost MSM(6, N/3), slightly better than MSM(4, $N/2$) when the double scalar multiplication is computed using the GLV optimization.

Example 5. Let $P_1 = (38, 94)$ and $P_2 = (31, 82)$ in $E(\mathbb{F}_{103})$. Given $Q = [16]P_1 + [92]P_2 = (57, 2)$, proving $[16]P_1 + [92]P_2 = Q$ is equivalent to proving $[2]P_1 + [-1]\psi(P_1) + [1]P_2 + [-2]\psi(P_2) - [2]Q - [1]\psi(Q) = 0_E$.

Note 1. In this section, we only focused on elliptic curves defined over $\mathbb{F}_p$. Galbraith, Lin, and Scott [14,15] generalized the GLV method for a large class of elliptic curves over $\mathbb{F}_{p^2}$, referred to as GLS curves. Our technique applies similarly to this generalization. It can turn proving a N-bit scalar multiplication over a GLS curve into proving a $N/8$-bit multi scalar multiplication of size 8.

Note 2. The difference between our method and the (traditional) GLV method is threefold:

1. In GLV, for the scalar decomposition, we usually start by pre-computing a short basis using a lattice reduction given the curve order r and the endomorphism eigenalue λ. This is a one-time setup per elliptic curve. Then we find a close vector to the scalar k in the lattice using Babai rounding. In our case, it is the lattice reduction that gives us directly the scalar decomposition. The reduction takes k and r as inputs and has to be performed for every new scalar multiplication.
2. In GLV, the scalar decomposition (Babai rounding) is part of the running time of the scalar multiplication algorithm. In our case, the SNARK circuit only verifies that the (pre-computed) decomposition is correct.
3. In 2-dimensional GLV, we need an efficient endomorphism. In our case, we don't. In 4-dimensional GLV, we need two endomorphisms. In our case, we only need one.

4 Implementation Results

For the implementation, we choose two widely used proof systems: Groth16 and PLONK. As shown in Sect. 2.1, we are interested in reducing the number of gates of the arithmetic circuit corresponding to a scalar multiplication. For Groth16, we only consider multiplication gates and for PLONK we consider both addition and multiplication gates.

4.1 Considerations

Arithmetizing computations for SNARK proving is different than traditionally carrying plain computations as shown in Sect. 2.1.

Arithmetizing Elliptic Curve Operations. Since inversions cost as much as multiplications here, we use affine coordinates to double and add points on the elliptic curve in short Weierstrass form. When a doubling is followed by an addition i.e. $[2]R+P$ we instead compute $(R+P)+R$ omitting the computation of the y-coordinate of $R+P$ as pointed out in [10].

With these considerations, we can implement Algorithm 1 in a SNARK but conditional branching (If/Else) is not possible in SNARK circuits so this is replaced by constant window table lookups inside the circuit. This can be achieved using polynomials which vanish at the constants that aren't being selected, i.e. a 1-bit table lookup $R \leftarrow k_i \cdot R + (1 - k_i) \cdot (R + P)$. Hence this double-and-add algorithm requires N doubling, N additions and N 1-bit table lookup where N is the bit-size of the scalar. This can be extended to windowed double-and-add, i.e. scanning more than a bit per iteration using larger window tables, but the number of gates of the lookup table increases exponentially.

Since we start with $R \leftarrow 0_E$ it is infeasible to avoid conditional branching because affine formulas are incomplete. Instead, we scan the bits right-to-left and assume that the first bit k_0 is 1 (so that we start at $R \leftarrow P$), we double the input point P in the accumulator T in this algorithm and finally conditionally subtract (using the 1-bit lookup) P if k_0 was 0, as shown in Algorithm 3.

Algorithm 3: ScalarMultiplication(k, P)

Input. A scalar k of N bits,
A point P.
Output. $Q = [k]P$.
$R \leftarrow P$
$T \leftarrow [2]P$
for b bit of k read from second LSB to MSB **do**
  $R \leftarrow b \cdot R + (1 - b) \cdot (R + T)$
  $T \leftarrow [2]T$
end for
$k_0 \leftarrow k \bmod 2$
$R \leftarrow k_0 \cdot R + (1 - k_0) \cdot (R - P)$
return R

With these considerations, implementing the GLV scalar multiplication in a SNARK is also feasible as demonstrated in [9, Alg. 1]. We further extend this technique by using a 16-bit lookup, as show in the attached code (See Sect. 4.2). While the cost of lookups grows in SNARK circuits, we empirically found that, in the case of emulated arithmetic (elliptic curve base field is different from the SNARK field), it yields the best performances. The scalar decomposition is verified inside the SNARK circuit. However, sub-scalars can be negative. In this case the hint returns positive sub-scalars and a bit to indicate when to inverse points instead using a 1-bit lookup.

When the curve is endomorphism-equipped, we implement a MSM of size 4 using the 16-bit lookup as shown in the attached code (See Sect. 4.2).

For curves in twisted Edwards form, since formulae are complete, we implement a 2-bit windowed scalar multiplication as shown in [31] and [3, Alg. 17]. For a MSM of size 4, the cost of the 16-bit lookup is expensive in native arithmetic compared to the cost of point arithmetic. This makes the algorithm in Sect. 3.3 costlier than the one in Sect. 3.1 for Bandersnatch curve as shown in Table 6. In native SNARK circuits, we it is better to always use Sect. 3.1 regardless of the existence of an efficient endomorphism.

Proving and Witness Generation Times Trade-Off. In blockchain applications, e.g. StarkNet[4], to prevent Denial of Service (DOS) attacks, arbitrary hints are not allowed. A malicious prover can run an infinite loop as a hint and cause a DOS. Only whitelisted hints by StarkNet are allowed. A developer submits their hint as a transaction calldata[5] which costs fees and is limited in size, inherently limiting the DOS surface. In this case, we would like to trade off the cost of the witness generation for the cost of the proving. In this case, for the scalar decomposition hint, we use the half-GCD algorithm in $\mathbb{Z}[j]$ developed in Sect. 2.5 instead of the lattice reduction techniques shown in Sect. 2.4. However, this increases the bounds on the sub-scalars as seen in Sect. 2.5 resulting in slower proving but cheaper calldata per transaction.

4.2 Implementation and Benchmarks

Our code is available in the following GitHub repository:

https://github.com/yelhousni/scalarmul-in-snark.

We choose to implement our work for some of the widely used elliptic curves in SNARKs and blockchains (See Table 2).

We use the `gnark` library [6] in Golang to implement the circuits. We refer by r1cs (rank-1 constraint system) to Groth16 constraints and by scs (sparse constraint system) to the PLONK constraints. We consider two settings:

---
[4] https://www.starknet.io/.

[5] https://learnevm.com/chapters/fn/calldata.

Table 2. Some elliptic curves used in SNARKs and blockchains.

Curve[a]	Endomorphism?	Form
BN254 (Ethereum)	✓	Weierstrass
BLS12-381 [7]	✓	Weierstrass
BW6-761 [11]	✓	Weierstrass
Secp256k1 (Bitcoin)	✓	Weierstrass
P-256 (SEC 2)	✗	Weierstrass
P-384 (SEC 2)	✗	Weierstrass
Jubjub [31]	✗	twisted Edwards
Bandersnatch [24]	✓	twisted Edwards

[a] The parameters of the elliptic curves can be found in https://neuromancer.sk/std/.

- Setting (i): The emulated case. We use a SNARK over an arbitrary field and we prove scalar multiplication over a given elliptic curve by emulating the base field arithmetic in the SNARK arbitrary field (see [1,22] for details on field emulation in SNARKs). Table 3 reports our results for curves with an efficient endomorphism (setting (i)-a) and Table 4 for curves without endomorphism (setting (i)-b).
- Setting (ii): The native case. We use a SNARK over a fixed field that matches the base field of the given elliptic curve we want to prove scalar multiplications over. Table 5 reports our results for curves with an efficient endomorphism (setting (ii)-a) and Table 6 for curves without endomorphism (setting (ii)-b).

Table 3. Implementation results for setting (i)-a.

Curve	Previous work ([9, Alg. 1])	This work (Sect. 3.3)	Speed-up
BN254	381467 scs	220436 scs	42%
	78246 r1cs	59351 r1cs	24%
BLS12-381	539973 scs	307045 scs	43%
	110928 r1cs	84508 r1cs	24%
BW6-761	1367067 scs	765544 scs	44%
	295194 r1cs	212659 r1cs	28%
Secp256k1	385461 scs	223188 scs	42%
	78940 r1cs	60089 r1cs	24%

Table 4. Implementation results for setting (i)-b.

Curve	Previous work (Alg. 3)	This work (Sect. 3.1)	Speed-up
P-256	612759 scs	294128 scs	52%
	157685 r1cs	78940 r1cs	50%
P-384	1233998 scs	588942 scs	52%
	325974 r1cs	159073 r1cs	51%

Table 5. Implementation results for setting (ii)-a.

Curve	Previous work ([3, Alg. 17])	This work (Sec. 3.1)	Speed-up
Jubjub	5863 scs	4549 scs	22%
	3314 r1cs	2401 r1cs	28%

Table 6. Implementation results for setting (ii)-b.

Curve	Previous work ([24, Sec. 4.3])	This work (Sect. 3.3)	slow-down
Bandersnatch	4712 scs	8519 scs	**80%**
	2621 r1cs	4038 r1cs	**54%**

Table 7. In-circuit scalar multiplication cost.

Algorithm	Previous work		This work	
	Cost	Scalar bound	Cost	Scalar bound
SM	$\text{MSM}(1, N)$	r	$\text{MSM}(2, \lceil N/2 \rceil)$	$1.16 \cdot r^{1/2}$
GLV SM	$\text{MSM}(2, \lceil N/2 \rceil)$	$1.16 \cdot r^{1/2}$	$\text{MSM}(4, \lceil N/4 \rceil)$	$1.25 \cdot r^{1/4}$
2MSM	$\text{MSM}(2, N)$	r	$\text{MSM}(3, \lceil 2N/3 \rceil)$	$1.22 \cdot r^{2/3}$
GLV 2MSM	$\text{MSM}(4, \lceil N/2 \rceil)$	$1.16 \cdot r^{1/2}$	$\text{MSM}(6, \lceil N/3 \rceil)$	$1.28 \cdot r^{1/3}$

In this section, we only implemented single scalar multiplication circuits. The practical and the theoretical speed-ups roughly match, but the number of constraints is slightly more complicated to analyse. The look-up table access has a cost in SNARKs that becomes significant when the table size increases. Moreover, for the emulated case, the cost of the non-native arithmetic operations become predominant. We did not investigate the implementation for multi scalar multiplications as SNARK circuit in **gnark**, but expect to get a speed-up only for $n = 2$. In systems such as PLONK or Groth16, reading points of the precomputation table requires some constraints, and the overall circuit size may

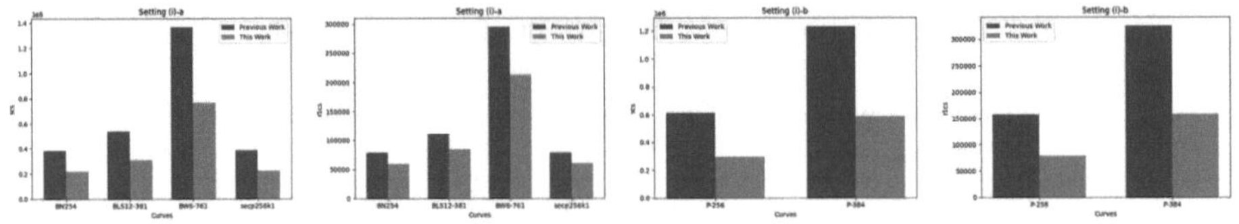

(a) Setting (i)-a scs (b) Setting (i)-a r1cs (c) Setting (i)-b scs (d) Setting (i)-b r1cs

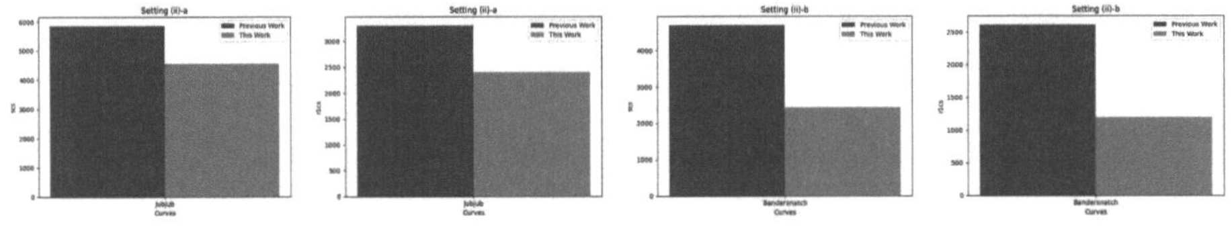

(e) Setting (ii)-a scs (f) Setting (ii)-a r1cs (g) Setting (ii)-b scs (h) Setting (ii)-b r1cs

Fig. 2. Implementation results.

increase in consequence. A similar result is expected for scalar multiplication using GLS decomposition, where the scalar can be decomposed with 8 sub-scalars.

5 Conclusion

In this work, we investigate new techniques for proving scalar multiplications in the context of generic proof systems. While the computation of scalar multiplications has been optimized in the last decades, the case of a verification has not been investigated. Using the hint of the output point, it is possible to apply decomposition of the scalars in order to speed up the proving time. Table 7 provides the expected size of scalars and cost for simple and double scalar multiplications (SM and 2MSM resp.) in the case of small (GLV) and large (generic) discriminant curves. The obtained scalar sizes were obtained using a reduction of the lattice with respect to the Euclidean norm. Thus, the maximum norm is slightly larger than the Minkowski bound. A refined lattice reduction would be possible in order to reduce further the scalar sizes.

We implemented the different techniques for elliptic curves used in production in blockchains and obtained significant speed-ups, as shown in Fig. 2.

As we have shown in Sect. 2.3, multi scalar multiplications based on Strauss's [30] trick speeds up the algorithmic cost but the pre-computation table cost grows exponentially in n. Hence, we expect to benefit from our optimizations for a double scalar multiplication ($n = 2$) but not for higher multi scalar multiplication ($n \geq 3$). However, for future work, considering in SNARK circuits different algorithms for larger sizes such as Pippenger's [4, Sec. 4] or Bos–Coster's [28, Sec. 4] algorithms may lead to promising results.

Acknowledgments. We express our gratitude to 0xPARC since this work partially started while the first and second authors (in alphabetical order) were at the 0xPARC residency in San Francisco. We would also like to thank Renaud Dubois and Olivier Bégassat for fruitful discussions.

A Comparison of Norms

A.1 Comparison of $\mathcal{N}$ and the Maximum Norm in $\mathbb{Z}[j]$

We compare both norms with $|\cdot|_2$ defined by $|x+jy|_2 = \sqrt{x^2+y^2}$. Recall that $\mathcal{N}(a+jb) = \sqrt{a^2+b^2-ab}$, so it is the norm in the complex sense. From the triangle inequality, followed by Cauchy inequality, we obtain that

$$|a+jb|_\infty \leq |a|_\infty|1|_\infty + |b|_\infty|1|\infty \leq \sqrt{2}|a+jb|_2,$$
$$\mathcal{N}(a+jb) \leq \mathcal{N}(1)\mathcal{N}(a) + \mathcal{N}(1)\mathcal{N}(b) \leq \sqrt{2}|a+jb|_2.$$

Now, on the circle $|x|_2 = 1$, the norm $\mathcal{N}$ reaches its minimum $\frac{1}{\sqrt{2}}$ at $\frac{1}{\sqrt{2}} + \frac{j}{\sqrt{2}}$, and so

$$\frac{1}{\sqrt{2}}|\cdot|_2 \leq \mathcal{N}(\cdot).$$

The same reasoning shows that

$$\frac{1}{\sqrt{2}}|\cdot|_2 \leq |\cdot|_\infty.$$

A.2 Comparison of $\mathcal{N}$ and the Maximum Norm in $\mathbb{Z}[\sqrt{-2}]$

Here again, $|a+b\sqrt{-2}|_\infty = \max\{|a|,|b|\}$ and $\mathcal{N}(a+\sqrt{-2}b) = \sqrt{a^2+2b^2}$. Again, the triangle inequality and the Cauchy inequality shows that

$$\mathcal{N}(x) \leq \sqrt{2}|x|_2,$$
$$|x|_\infty \leq \sqrt{2}|x|_2.$$

Now, on the circle $|x|_2 = 1$, we see that the norm $\mathcal{N}$ reaches its minimum 1 at $1+0\sqrt{-2}$, and $|\cdot|_\infty$ reaches its minimum $\frac{1}{\sqrt{2}}$ at $\frac{1}{\sqrt{2}}+\sqrt{-2}\frac{1}{\sqrt{-2}}$, and so we obtain

$$|\cdot|_2 \leq |\cdot|_\infty,$$
$$\frac{1}{\sqrt{2}}|\cdot|_2 \leq \mathcal{N}(\cdot).$$

References

1. Ambrona, M., Firsov, D., Querejeta-Azurmendi, I.: Efficient foreign-field arithmetic in PLONK. Cryptology ePrint Archive, Paper 2025/695 (2025). https://eprint.iacr.org/2025/695

2. Antipa, A., Brown, D.R.L., Gallant, R., Lambert, R., Struik, R., Vanstone, S.A.: Accelerated verification of ECDSA signatures. In: Preneel, B., Tavares, S. (eds.) SAC 2005. LNCS, vol. 3897, pp. 307–318. Springer, Berlin, Heidelberg (2006). https://doi.org/10.1007/11693383_21
3. Aranha, D.F., El Housni, Y., Guillevic, A.: A survey of elliptic curves for proof systems. DCC **91**(11), 3333–3378 (2023). https://doi.org/10.1007/s10623-022-01135-y
4. Bernstein, D.J., Doumen, J., Lange, T., Oosterwijk, J.J.: Faster batch forgery identification. In: Galbraith, S.D., Nandi, M. (eds.) INDOCRYPT 2012. LNCS, vol. 7668, pp. 454–473. Springer, Berlin, Heidelberg (2012). https://doi.org/10.1007/978-3-642-34931-7_26
5. Bitansky, N., Canetti, R., Chiesa, A., Tromer, E.: From extractable collision resistance to succinct non-interactive arguments of knowledge, and back again. In: Goldwasser, S. (ed.) ITCS 2012, pp. 326–349. ACM (January 2012). https://doi.org/10.1145/2090236.2090263
6. Botrel, G., Piellard, T., El Housni, Y., Kubjas, I.: Consensys/gnark: v0.12.0 (January 2025). https://doi.org/10.5281/zenodo.5819104
7. Bowe, S.: BLS12-381: new zk-SNARK elliptic curve construction. Zcash blog (2017). https://blog.z.cash/new-snark-curve/
8. Bowe, S., Chiesa, A., Green, M., Miers, I., Mishra, P., Wu, H.: ZEXE: enabling decentralized private computation. In: 2020 IEEE Symposium on Security and Privacy, pp. 947–964. IEEE Computer Society Press (May 2020). https://doi.org/10.1109/SP40000.2020.00050
9. Bowe, S., Grigg, J., Hopwood, D.: Halo: recursive proof composition without a trusted setup. Cryptology ePrint Archive, Report 2019/1021 (2019). https://eprint.iacr.org/2019/1021
10. Eisenträger, K., Lauter, K., Montgomery, P.L.: Fast elliptic curve arithmetic and improved Weil pairing evaluation. In: Joye, M. (ed.) CT-RSA 2003. LNCS, vol. 2612, pp. 343–354. Springer, Berlin, Heidelberg (2003). https://doi.org/10.1007/3-540-36563-X_24
11. El Housni, Y., Guillevic, A.: Optimized and secure pairing-friendly elliptic curves suitable for one layer proof composition. In: Krenn, S., Shulman, H., Vaudenay, S. (eds.) CANS 20. LNCS, vol. 12579, pp. 259–279. Springer, Cham (2020). https://doi.org/10.1007/978-3-030-65411-5_13
12. ElGamal, T.: On computing logarithms over finite fields. In: Williams, H.C. (ed.) CRYPTO'85. LNCS, vol. 218, pp. 396–402. Springer, Berlin, Heidelberg (1986). https://doi.org/10.1007/3-540-39799-X_28
13. Gabizon, A., Williamson, Z.J., Ciobotaru, O.: PLONK: permutations over Lagrange-bases for oecumenical noninteractive arguments of knowledge. Cryptology ePrint Archive, Report 2019/953 (2019). https://eprint.iacr.org/2019/953
14. Galbraith, S.D., Lin, X., Scott, M.: Endomorphisms for faster elliptic curve cryptography on a large class of curves. In: Joux, A. (ed.) EUROCRYPT 2009. LNCS, vol. 5479, pp. 518–535. Springer, Berlin, Heidelberg (2009). https://doi.org/10.1007/978-3-642-01001-9_30
15. Galbraith, S.D., Lin, X., Scott, M.: Endomorphisms for faster elliptic curve cryptography on a large class of curves. J. Cryptol. **24**(3), 446–469 (2010). https://doi.org/10.1007/s00145-010-9065-y
16. Gallant, R.P., Lambert, R.J., Vanstone, S.A.: Faster point multiplication on elliptic curves with efficient endomorphisms. In: Kilian, J. (ed.) CRYPTO 2001. LNCS, vol. 2139, pp. 190–200. Springer, Berlin, Heidelberg (2001). https://doi.org/10.1007/3-540-44647-8_11

17. Gentry, C., Wichs, D.: Separating succinct non-interactive arguments from all falsifiable assumptions. In: Fortnow, L., Vadhan, S.P. (eds.) 43rd ACM STOC, pp. 99–108. ACM Press (2011).https://doi.org/10.1145/1993636.1993651
18. Goldwasser, S., Micali, S., Rackoff, C.: The knowledge complexity of interactive proof systems. SIAM J. Comput. **18**(1), 186–208 (1989). https://doi.org/10.1137/0218012
19. Groth, J.: On the size of pairing-based non-interactive arguments. In: Fischlin, M., Coron, J.-S. (eds.) EUROCRYPT 2016. LNCS, vol. 9666, pp. 305–326. Springer, Heidelberg (2016). https://doi.org/10.1007/978-3-662-49896-5_11
20. Kilian, J.: A note on efficient zero-knowledge proofs and arguments (extended abstract). In: 24th ACM STOC, pp. 723–732. ACM Press (May 1992). https://doi.org/10.1145/129712.129782
21. Kosba, A., et al.: C∅c∅: a framework for building composable zero-knowledge proofs. Cryptology ePrint Archive, Report 2015/1093 (2015). https://eprint.iacr.org/2015/1093
22. Kubjas, I.: Notes about optimizing emulated pairing (part 1) (2023). https://hackmd.io/@ivokub/SyJRV7ye2
23. Lenstra, H.j., Lenstra, A., Lovász, L.: Factoring polynomials with rational coefficients. Math. Annal. **261**, 515–534 (1982). http://eudml.org/doc/182903
24. Masson, S., Sanso, A., Zhang, Z.: Bandersnatch: a fast elliptic curve built over the bls12-381 scalar field. DCC **92**(12), 4131–4143 (2024). https://doi.org/10.1007/s10623-024-01472-0
25. Micali, S.: CS proofs (extended abstracts). In: 35th FOCS, pp. 436–453. IEEE Computer Society Press (1994). https://doi.org/10.1109/SFCS.1994.365746
26. Nguyen, P.Q., Stehlé, D.: Low-dimensional lattice basis reduction revisited. ACM Trans. Algorithms **5**(4) (2009). https://doi.org/10.1145/1597036.1597050
27. Prover, L.: Linea prover documentation. Cryptology ePrint Archive, Paper 2022/1633 (2022). https://eprint.iacr.org/2022/1633
28. de Rooij, P.: Efficient exponentiation using procomputation and vector addition chains, pp. 389–399 (1995). https://doi.org/10.1007/BFb0053453
29. Silverman, J.H.: The Arithmetic of Elliptic Curves, Graduate Texts in Mathematics, vol. 106. Springer, New York (1986). https://doi.org/10.1007/978-0-387-09494-6
30. Strauss, E.G.: Addition chains of vectors (problem 5125). Amer. Math. Monthly **70**(114), 806–808 (1964)
31. ZCash: What is jubjub? (2021). https://z.cash/technology/jubjub/

Great-LaKeys: An Improved Threshold-PRF and a Novel Exponent-VRF from LWR

Matthias Geihs(✉)

Consensys, Fort Worth, USA
matthias.geihs@consensys.net

Abstract. Building on the recently proposed LWR-based threshold-PRF LaKey (USENIX'24), we propose two new PRF constructions. First, we present an optimized variant of the LaKey threshold-PRF with significantly reduced round and communication complexity. We achieve this by improving the efficiency of the underlying bit truncation protocol, which may be of independent interest, and by providing tighter parameter bounds. Second, we show that the underlying LWR-based PRF can be proven efficiently in zero-knowledge, and thereby yields a novel and practically efficient exponent-VRF. We provide prototype implementations of both of our constructions and evaluate their concrete performance.

1 Introduction

MPC-friendly PRFs are important building blocks in cryptographic protocols. They enable applications like scalable decentralized key management [GM24] and secure encryption in MPC [GØS+23]. We refer to [GØS+23] for a more comprehensive list of applications.

Moreover, the same PRF constructions are often also useful in zero-knowledge (ZK) protocols, as their structure often also allows for efficient ZK proof generation [AABS+20]. The recently proposed notion of an exponent VRF [BHL24] indeed shows that efficiently provable PRFs are a powerful tool, facilitating efficient threshold key generation and signing protocols.

Here we present two new PRF constructions based on the Learning-With-Rounding (LWR) assumption and inspired by the LaKey PRF design [GM24]: An improved Threshold PRF and a novel, practically efficient Exponent VRF.

1.1 Improved Threshold-PRF

Firstly, we present a variant of the LaKey threshold PRF [GM24] with significantly reduced round and communication complexity. We achieve this mainly by improving the efficiency of the underlying bit truncation protocol. Concretely, we show how previously separate and sequential bit truncation protocols for

M. Geihs—Work done while at Torus Labs.

D. Escudero and I. Damgård (Eds.): LATINCRYPT 2025, LNCS 16129, pp. 130–142, 2026.
https://doi.org/10.1007/978-3-032-06754-8_5

higher order and lower order bit truncation can be merged into a single protocol that requires the same amount of communication as just the previous higher order bit truncation protocol, essentially cutting communication cost in half. We also improve the analysis of the parameter sizes and thereby are able to further reduce the communication. We provide an open-source implementation of our threshold PRF (tPRF) construction using the MP-SPDZ library [Kel20] and compare it with the previous work.

1.2 Novel Exponent-VRF

Building on the LWR-based PRF construction underlying LaKey, we observe that it lends itself well to be turned into an efficient exponent VRF (eVRF), using Bulletproofs [BBB+17] as the proof system. The main observation is that almost all operations of the PRF are linear, and thereby basically free to prove, except for the bit truncations. These, however, we also know how to efficiently prove using Bulletproofs. The resulting eVRF is relatively simple in its construction, supports arbitrary target groups, and is expected to have comparable performance to the recently proposed DDH-based eVRF from [BHL24], which, to the best of our knowledge, does not have an open-source implementation and only works for target groups that have a matching source group (see [BHL24], Sect. 5, *Practical considerations*). We provide an open-source implementation of our eVRF construction using the `zkcrypto/bulletproofs` library [Zer24] and practically demonstrate its performance.

1.3 Organization

We present preliminaries in Sect. 2. Then we present our threshold-PRF optimizations in Sect. 3. Next, we present our novel LWR-based exponent-VRF in Sect. 4. Finally, we evaluate the performance of our constructions in Sect. 5. We also outline some directions for future work in Sect. 6.

2 Preliminaries

2.1 Notation

For two probability distributions X and Y over a finite domain D, we define their statistical distance as

$$\Delta(X,Y) = \frac{1}{2} \sum_{a \in D} |\Pr[X = a] - \Pr[Y = a]| \ .$$

By $U(D)$ we denote the uniform distribution over a finite domain D.

2.2 LaKey PRF

A *pseudorandom function* (PRF) [GGM86] is an efficiently computable function $F : \mathcal{K} \times \mathcal{X} \to \mathcal{Y}$ such that for a uniform k in $\mathcal{K}$ and a uniform function $f : \mathcal{X} \to \mathcal{Y}$, an oracle for $F(k, \cdot)$ is computationally indistinguishable from an oracle for $f(\cdot)$.

Let $l, m, \bar{q}, \bar{p}, \tilde{p} \in \mathbb{N}$, where $\bar{q} > \bar{p}$, set $q = 2^{\bar{q}}, p = 2^{\bar{p}}$, and let $H : \{0,1\}^* \to \mathbb{Z}_q^{l \times m}$ be a cryptographic hash function. The LaKey PRF [GM24] is defined as

$$F_{\mathsf{LaKey}} : \mathbb{Z}_q^m \times \{0,1\}^* \to \mathbb{Z}_{\tilde{p}}; (\mathbf{k}, x) \mapsto \mathsf{Acc}(\mathsf{Trunc}(H(x) \cdot \mathbf{k})) \ ,$$

where $\mathsf{Trunc} : \mathbb{Z}_q^l \to \mathbb{Z}_p^l; x \mapsto \lfloor (x \bmod q)/(q/p) \rfloor$ truncates the highest and lowest bits (below bit $\bar{q} - \bar{p}$ and above bit $\bar{q}$), and $\mathsf{Acc} : \mathbb{Z}_p^l \to \mathbb{Z}_{\tilde{p}}; (x_1, \ldots, x_l) \mapsto \sum_{i=1}^{l} x_i \cdot p^{i-1}$ maps a vector of integers in $\mathbb{Z}_p$ onto a single integer in $\mathbb{Z}_{\tilde{p}}$.

2.3 Bit Truncation in MPC

[CdH10] features two deterministic bit truncation protocols for MPC. The first one is for truncating higher order bits (referred to by $\mathsf{Mod2m}$ in their paper, here referred to as $\mathsf{TruncHi}$, shown in Algorithm 1). The second one is for truncating lower order bits (referred to by Trunc in their paper, here referred to as $\mathsf{TruncLo}$, Algorithm 2). Both of these protocols rely on protocols PRandM and BitLT as building blocks, whose functionality and properties we will outline below. In the protocol descriptions, $[a]$ denotes a secret-sharing of a.

Protocol $\mathsf{PRandM}(k, m) \to ([r''], [r'], [r'_{m-1}], \ldots, [r'_0])$ is a protocol that outputs two random secret-shared integers in $[r'']$ and $[r']$, and a vector of secret-shared random bits $[r'_{m-1}], \ldots, [r'_0]$ such that $r'' \in [0, 2^{k+\kappa-m}]$, $r' \in [0, 2^m]$, and $r' = \sum_{i=0}^{m-1} r'_i * 2^i$. Here, κ refers to a globally fixed statistical security parameter. To generate random integers within a certain range, PRandM consumes pre-shared random bits. Concretely, an invocation of $\mathsf{PRandM}(k, m)$ consumes $k + \kappa - m + m = k + \kappa$ pre-shared random bits.

$\mathsf{BitLT}(a, [b_{l-1}], \ldots, [b_0]) \to [c]$ is a protocol that compares a cleartext integer a with a secret-shared integer in binary form $[b_{l-1}], \ldots, [b_0]$ (where $[b_i] \in \{[0], [1]\}$). It outputs $[c] = [1]$ if $a < \sum_{i=0}^{l-1} b_i * 2^i$ and $[c] = [0]$ otherwise. There are various possible implementations of BitLT, but for our purposes we will rely on an implementation that runs in $\log(m)$ online rounds and balances communication with round complexity.

We remark that there is also a constant round version of the comparison protocol at the cost of added communication complexity. However, for our smaller parameter sizes, the round count of the constant-round protocol is the same as the logarithmic round protocol, and for the larger parameter sizes the round count difference is still small (within 1 or 2 rounds).

2.4 Exponent VRFs

An exponent VRF [BHL24] is defined by a set of algorithms ($\mathsf{KeyGen}, \mathsf{Eval}$, Verify), associated with a cyclic group generated by a group element G, with the following properties.

Algorithm 1. $\mathsf{TruncHi}([a], k, m) \to [a']$

$([r''], [r'], [r'_{m-1}], \ldots, [r'_0]) \leftarrow \mathsf{PRandM}(k, m)$
$c \leftarrow \mathsf{Output}(2^{k-1} + [a] + 2^m[r''] + [r'])$
$c' \leftarrow c \bmod 2^m$
$[u] \leftarrow \mathsf{BitLT}(c', [r'_{m-1}], \ldots, [r'_0])$
$[a'] \leftarrow c' - [r'] + 2^m[u]$
return $[a']$

Algorithm 2. $\mathsf{TruncLo}([a], k, m) \to [a'']$

$[a'] \leftarrow \mathsf{TruncHi}([a], k, m)$;
$[a''] \leftarrow ([a] - [a'])/2^m$;
return $[a'']$;

$\mathsf{KeyGen}() \to (k, vk)$: The key generation algorithm randomly generates a secret evaluation key k and a public verification key vk.

$\mathsf{Eval}(k, x) \to (y, Y, \pi)$: On input an evaluation key k, and a message x, the evaluation algorithm outputs (y, Y, π), where y is a pseudorandom value in the target domain, $Y = G * y$, and π is a proof for the correct evaluation.

$\mathsf{Verify}(vk, x, Y, \pi) \to \{0, 1\}$: On input a verification key vk, a message x, an exponent output Y, and a proof π, the verification algorithm outputs 1 if π certifies that Y is the correct output for input x, and 0 otherwise.

In addition, an exponent VRF must satisfy consistency, pseudo-randomness, and simulatable verifiability. For consistency, we require that Eval yields consistent outputs (i.e., $Y = G * y$). For pseudo-randomness, we require that (KeyGen, Eval) is a secure PRF (w.r.t. the first output y). For simulatable verifiability, we require that one cannot generate two conflicting proofs for the same input x (i.e., $(vk, x, Y_0, \pi_0, Y_1, \pi_1)$ such that $\mathsf{Verify}(vk, x, Y_0, \pi_0) = \mathsf{Verify}(vk, x, Y_1, \pi_1) = 1$ and $Y_0 \neq Y_1$) and that a proof does not leak anything beyond the correctness of the statement. We refer to [BHL24], Sect. 3, for a more formal definition.

2.5 Bulletproofs

Bulletproofs [BBB+17] is an efficient zero-knowledge proof system based on elliptic-curve cryptography. In short, it allows a prover to efficiently generate a short proof for an arbitrary computation (e.g., expressed as a Rank-1 Constraint System or R1CS) such that a verifier can verify the correctness of the computation much more efficiently than recomputing it themselves. Moreover, the prover can choose to hide some of the inputs of the computation but still convince the verifier that it knows corresponding inputs that satisfy certain constraints. For example, a prover could convince the verifier that it knows the secret key belonging a public key without revealing anything other than the truthfulness of that statement.

We will use the following algorithmic notation when working with Bulletproofs and assume fixed group generators $\mathsf{Bul}.G$ and $\mathsf{Bul}.H$ with a corresponding set of scalars $\mathsf{Bul}.S$.

$\mathsf{Bul.Com}(k, d) \rightarrow K$: The commit algorithm computes a Pedersen commitment $K = \mathsf{Bul}.G * k + \mathsf{Bul}.H * d$ to a secret scalar k using blinding value d.
$\mathsf{Bul.Prove}(C, X, W) \rightarrow \pi$: The prove algorithm generates a proof π for a constraint system C to be satisfied by input X and witness W.
$\mathsf{Bul.Verify}(C, X, \pi) \rightarrow \{0, 1\}$: The verify algorithm checks the correctness of a proof π for a constraint system C and input X.

2.6 Schnorr Proofs

Schnorr proofs [Sch90] are a zero-knowledge proof system based on elliptic-curve cryptography. In short, given a group element Y and a group generator G, it allows a prover to generate a zero-knowledge proof of knowledge of a scalar y such that $Y = G * y$. Here we refer to the non-interactive variant of Schnorr proofs [Hao17]. We will use the following algorithmic notation when working with Schnorr proofs.

$\mathsf{Schnorr.Prove}(Y, y) \rightarrow \pi$: The prove algorithm generates a proof π for a group element Y and a group scalar y such that $Y = G * y$.
$\mathsf{Schnorr.Verify}(Y, \pi) \rightarrow \{0, 1\}$: The verify algorithm checks the correctness of a proof π for a group element Y.

3 Improvements to Threshold-PRF

We present our two improvements to the LaKey threshold PRF construction. The first one is an improved bit truncation protocol, which lies at the heart of LaKey and significantly reduces rounds and communication. The second one is a tighter bound on the statistical distance between the intermediate LWR-based PRF output and the target distribution, which allows us to choose smaller parameters and further reduces the computation and communication requirements of LaKey. We will evaluate the impact of these improvements in Sect. 5.

3.1 Bit Truncation with Fewer Rounds and Communication

We present our improved bit truncation protocol in Algorithm 3. The main observation is that the existing protocols TruncHi and TruncLo (Subsect. 2.3) can be merged into a single protocol TruncHiLo that enjoys the same round and communication complexity as just running TruncHi.

Algorithm 3. $\mathsf{TruncHiLo}([a], k, m, n) \to [a']$

$([r''], [r'], [r'_{n-1}], \ldots, [r'_0]) \leftarrow \mathsf{PRandM}(k, n)$
$c \leftarrow \mathsf{Output}(2^{k-1} + [a] + 2^n[r''] + [r'])$ ▷ *1 round*
for $x \in \{m, n\}$ **do** ▷ *Can run in parallel.*
  $c' \leftarrow c \bmod 2^x$
  $[u] \leftarrow \mathsf{BitLT}(c', [r'_{x-1}], \ldots, [r'_0])$ ▷ $\log(x)$ *rounds*
  $[r'] \leftarrow \sum_{j=0}^{x-1} 2^j [r'_j]$
  $[a'_x] \leftarrow c' - [r'] + 2^x[u]$
$[a'] \leftarrow ([a'_n] - [a'_m])/2^m$
return $[a']$

Correctness. We need to show that for all valid $([a], k, m, n)$,

$$\mathsf{TruncHiLo}([a], k, m, n) = \lfloor (a \bmod 2^n)/2^m \rfloor \ .$$

Let $[a'] = \mathsf{TruncHiLo}([a], k, m)$. Observe that $[a'] = ([a'_n] - [a'_m])/2^m$ by the construction of TruncHiLo, where $[a'_n] = [a] \bmod 2^n$ and $[a'_m] = [a] \bmod 2^m$ by the construction of TruncHi. Finally, we observe that we have

$$(([a] \bmod 2^n) - ([a] \bmod 2^m))/2^m = \lfloor ([a] \bmod 2^n)/2^m \rfloor \ ,$$

because $n \geq m$ and therefore $([a] \bmod 2^n) - ([a] \bmod 2^m)$ is divisible by 2^m.

Security. We need to show that the protocol does not leak anything about the secret value a. Our analysis follows the analysis of [CdH10], Sect. 2, *Security*. The only value that is revealed in the protocol is $c = 2^{k-1} + [a] + 2^n[r''] + [r']$. We observe that $a \in \mathbb{Z}_{2^k}$ and that $r = 2^n[r''] + [r']$ is a random element in $\mathbb{Z}_{2^{k+\kappa}}$. By Theorem 2 of [CdH10] it follows that $a + r$ is κ-statistically-close to the uniform distribution over $\mathbb{Z}_{2^{k+\kappa}}$.

Efficiency. Running $\mathsf{TruncHiLo}([a], k, m, n)$ takes $\log(n) + 1$ online rounds and consumes $k + \kappa$ pre-shared random bits.

3.2 Exact Bound on Statistical Distance to Target Distribution

For LaKey to be pseudorandom over $\mathbb{Z}_{\tilde{p}}$, we require that the statistical distance between $\mathsf{Acc}(U(\mathbb{Z}_p^l)) \bmod \tilde{p}$ and $U(\mathbb{Z}_{\tilde{p}})$ is negligible. In [GM24], it was established that the distance is bounded by $\tilde{p}/p^l$. The following Lemma 1 establishes a tighter bound and thereby allows for choosing smaller l.

Lemma 1. *For* $m, n \in \mathbb{N}$,

$$\Delta(U(\mathbb{Z}_m), U(\mathbb{Z}_n) \bmod m) = \left| \frac{(n \bmod m)^2 - (n \bmod m)m}{nm} \right| \ .$$

Proof. Writing out the definition, we have

$$\Delta(X,Y) = \frac{1}{2} \sum_{a \in \mathbb{Z}_m} |\Pr[X = a] - \Pr[Y = a]| \enspace .$$

For $a \in \mathbb{Z}_m$, we have $\Pr[X = a] = 1/m$ and

$$\Pr[Y = a] = \begin{cases} \frac{n-(n \bmod m)}{nm} & \text{if } a \geq n \bmod m, \\ \frac{n-(n \bmod m)+m}{nm} & \text{if } a < n \bmod m. \end{cases}$$

Denote $r = (n \bmod m)$. It follows that

$$\begin{aligned} \Delta(X,Y) &= \frac{1}{2}\left(\left(\sum_{a \in \mathbb{Z}_m : a < r} \left|\frac{1}{m} - \frac{n-r+m}{nm}\right|\right) + \left(\sum_{a \in \mathbb{Z}_m : a \geq r} \left|\frac{1}{m} - \frac{n-r}{nm}\right|\right)\right) \\ &= \frac{1}{2}\left(r\left|\frac{1}{m} - \frac{n-r+m}{nm}\right| + (m-r)\left|\frac{1}{m} - \frac{n-r}{nm}\right|\right) \\ &= \left|\frac{r^2 - rm}{nm}\right| \enspace . \end{aligned}$$

□

4 Novel Exponent-VRF

We present our novel exponent VRF eLaKey in Definition 1. It is constructed by composing the LaKey PRF together with an efficient proof system for its correct evaluation, which we realize using Bulletproofs and Schnorr Proofs.

Definition 1 (LaKey-eVRF). *Let* LaKey *denote the LaKey PRF (Subsect. 2.2), let* Bul *denote the BulletProofs proof system (Subsect. 2.5), and let* Schnorr *denote the Schnorr proof system (Subsect. 2.6). Given (K, x, Y), let C_{LaKey} be a constraint system for $Y = \mathsf{LaKey.Eval}(K, x)$, which we further describe in Subsect. 4.2. The* eLaKey *exponent-VRF is defined as follows.*

$\mathsf{eLaKey.KeyGen}() \to (k, vk)$.

1. *Compute* $k_{\mathsf{PRF}} \leftarrow \mathsf{LaKey.KeyGen}()$.
2. *For* $i \in \{1, \ldots, \mathsf{LaKey}.m\}$, *sample* $d_i \leftarrow U(\mathsf{Bul}.S)$ *and compute* $K_i \leftarrow \mathsf{Bul.Com}(k_{\mathsf{PRF},i}, d_i)$.
3. *Set* $K \leftarrow (K_1, \ldots, K_m)$ *and* $d \leftarrow (d_1, \ldots, d_m)$.
4. *Set* $k \leftarrow (k_{\mathsf{PRF}}, d)$ *and* $vk \leftarrow (K)$.

$\mathsf{eLaKey.Eval}(k, x) \to (y, Y, \pi)$.

1. *Parse* $(k_{\mathsf{PRF}}, d) \leftarrow k$ *and compute* $K \leftarrow \mathsf{Bul.Com}(k_{\mathsf{PRF}}, d)$.
2. *Compute* $y \leftarrow \mathsf{LaKey.Eval}(k_{\mathsf{PRF}}, x)$ *and* $Y \leftarrow \mathsf{Bul.Com}(y, 0)$.
3. *Compute* $\pi_{\mathsf{Bul}} \leftarrow \mathsf{Bul.Prove}(C_{\mathsf{LaKey}}, [K, x, Y], k_{\mathsf{PRF}})$.
4. *Compute* $\pi_{\mathsf{Schnorr}} \leftarrow \mathsf{Schnorr.Prove}(Y, y)$.
5. *Set* $\pi \leftarrow (\pi_{\mathsf{Bul}}, \pi_{\mathsf{Schnorr}})$.

$\mathsf{eLaKey.Verify}(vk, x, Y, \pi) \rightarrow b.$

1. *Parse* $(K) \leftarrow vk$ *and* $(\pi_{\mathsf{Bul}}, \pi_{\mathsf{Schnorr}}) \leftarrow \pi$.
2. *Compute* $b_{\mathsf{Bul}} \leftarrow \mathsf{Bul.Verify}(C_{\mathsf{LaKey}}, [K, x, Y], \pi_{\mathsf{Bul}})$.
3. *Compute* $b_{\mathsf{Schnorr}} \leftarrow \mathsf{Schnorr.Verify}(Y, \pi_{\mathsf{Schnorr}})$.
4. *Compute* $b \leftarrow b_{\mathsf{Bul}} \wedge b_{\mathsf{Schnorr}}$.

4.1 Security

In the following we show that eLaKey satisfies consistency, pseudo-randomness, and simulatable verifiability.

For consistency it suffices to show that for all k, x and $(y, Y, \pi) \leftarrow \mathsf{Eval}(k, x)$, we have $Y = G * y$. This is obviously the case as Y is computed as $Y \leftarrow \mathsf{Bul.Com}(y, 0) = \mathsf{Bul}.G * y + \mathsf{Bul}.H * 0 = G * y$.

For pseudo-randomness, we need to show that (KeyGen, Eval) is a secure PRF when restricted to output y. This also immediately follows from the fact that y is computed as $y \leftarrow \mathsf{LaKey.Eval}(k_{\mathsf{PRF}}, x)$ and assuming LaKey is a secure PRF.

For simulatable verifiability, we need to show that eLaKey is verifiable and simulatable. Simulatability follows from the fact that Bulletproofs and Schnorr proofs are zero knowledge and that the eLaKey proof π emitted by eLaKey.Eval reveals nothing beyond π_{Bul} and π_{Schnorr}.

For verifiability, we observe that eLaKey.Verify asserts that

$$\mathsf{Bul.Verify}(C_{\mathsf{LaKey}}, [K, x, Y], \pi_{\mathsf{Bul}}) = 1 \tag{1}$$

and

$$\mathsf{Schnorr.Verify}(Y, \pi_{\mathsf{Schnorr}}) = 1 \tag{2}$$

By (1) and the soundness of Bul, it follows that

$$Y = \mathsf{Acc}'(\mathsf{Trunc}'(\mathsf{BitDecomp}(H(x) * K))) \tag{3}$$

for some k and d with $K_i = \mathsf{Bul.Com}(k_i, d_i)$ and $i \in \{1, \ldots, \mathsf{LaKey}.m\}$. By (2) and the soundness of Schnorr, it follows that

$$Y = G * y \tag{4}$$

for some y. By (3) and (4), we obtain

$$y = \mathsf{Acc}(\mathsf{Trunc}(H(x) * k)) = \mathsf{LaKey.Eval}(k, x) \ .$$

4.2 Efficient Realization of Constraint System

We now describe how the constraint system C_{LaKey} can be efficiently realized as a rank-1 constraint system (R1CS). The main observation is that most of the operations of LaKey.Eval are linear, except for the bit truncation. Bit truncation, however, can be efficiently realized via bit decomposition, which we know can be efficiently represented as an R1CS ([BBB+17], Sect. 4). Figure 1 describes the C_{LaKey} constraint system in more detail. Here, BitDecomp denotes an algorithm that on input $(X; x)$, where $X = (X_1, \ldots, X_m)$ is a commitment vector and $x = (x_1, \ldots, x_m)$ is a witness vector such that X_i is a commitment to x_i, outputs (C, B), where C is a constraint system and B is a commitment matrix, such that each row i of B is a commitment vector to a bit decomposition of x_i.

In the description of the constraint system we use the following conventions. By Acc' and Trunc' we refer to the algorithms Acc and Trunc from Subsect. 2.2 but with group elements as input. Because Trunc is a non-linear operation, we first apply $\mathsf{BitDecomp}$ and then apply Trunc' on the bit decomposition. Finally, when we refer to a constraint $Y = \mathsf{LaKey.Eval}(K, x)$ where K is a commitment vector, we mean a constraint system for $Y = \mathsf{Acc}'(\mathsf{Trunc}'(\mathsf{BitDecomp}(A * K)))$. We refer to Subsect. 5.2 for a concrete implementation.

Input: $K = (K_1, \ldots, K_m), x, Y; k_{\mathsf{PRF}} = (k_1, \ldots, k_m)$.
Output: Constraints for $Y = \mathsf{LaKey.Eval}(K, x)$.
Procedure:
1. Let $A = \mathsf{LaKey}.H(x)$ and set $(C_1, Y_1) \leftarrow \mathsf{BitDecomp}(A * K; A \cdot k_{\mathsf{PRF}})$.
2. Let $Y_2 = \mathsf{Acc}'(\mathsf{Trunc}'(Y_1))$ and set $C_2 \leftarrow (Y = Y_2)$.
3. Output C_1, C_2.

Fig. 1. R1CS for eLaKey.

4.3 Comparison with eVRFs from [BHL24]

[BHL24] proposes two eVRF constructions, one based on DDH and another one based on Paillier. Both of their constructions require some tricks to make them work for practical use cases.

For their DDH-based eVRF, they describe how to instantiate the eVRF when the target group $\mathbb{G}_T$ is either `secp256k1` or `ed25519`. For the case of `secp256k1`, the target group needs to be the standard group of points on curve $y^2 = x^3 + 7$ over some prime field $\mathbb{F}_p$. To find a corresponding source group, they observe that, due to a theorem by Silverman and Stange [SS11], curve $y^2 = x^3 + 7$ over $\mathbb{F}_q$, for some q, has prime order p, and can therefore be used as the source group. A different observation is made to find a corresponding source group for the target group `ed25519`. We remark that no such tricks are required for instantiating our eVRF eLaKey as we do not need to find a matching source group.

For their Paillier-based eVRF, they remark that efficient range proofs for Paillier require a trusted setup, which is a relatively strong assumption in itself that rules out certain pratical use cases where such a setup procedure is not feasible. Again, our eVRF eLaKey does not have such a limitation.

5 Evaluation

5.1 Threshold-PRF

We implemented our improved threshold PRF LaKey2 using MP-SPDZ [Kel20]. The code is available at github.com/torusresearch/lakey-tprf. As in [GM24], we target a 256-bit prime field and fix the lattice dimension to 512. As modulo parameter sets we use ($\bar{q} = 12, \bar{p} = 8$) and ($\bar{q} = 32, \bar{p} = 24$). The corresponding scheme instances are denoted as LaKey_{12} and $\mathsf{LaKey2}_{12}$, and LaKey_{32} and $\mathsf{LaKey2}_{32}$, respectively. Due to our improved lower bound on the statistical distance of the output distribution, we are able to reduce the size of the integral parameter l from $l = 37$ for LaKey_{12} and $l = 13$ for LaKey_{32} to $l = 32$ for $\mathsf{LaKey2}_{12}$ and $l = 11$ for $\mathsf{LaKey2}_{32}$, which in turn reduces the number of LWR instances we need to evaluate in parallel and thereby reduces computation as well as communication costs.

Table 1 gives an overview of the performance measurements for LaKey2 compared with LaKey. Here, the parameters with a subscript K correspond to the communication-optimized LaKey variant denoted by OPT in [GM24]. The measurements have been performed on a machine with a 10-core M1 Pro CPU and 32 GB RAM, simulating 3 parties with a reconstruction threshold of 2, and using protocol `mal-shamir`.

We observe that LaKey2 significantly outperforms LaKey on all measures. Computation is reduced by 12% to 17%. Online communication is reduced by 14% to 16% and total communication by 35% to 41% in case of the regular construction and by 15% to 16% in case of the communication-optimized construction. Round count is reduced significantly to 5 or 6 rounds, depending on the parameter choice, from previously 8 or 10, respectively. The reduction of the number of required pre-shared random bits is reflected by the lower communication cost. We also show the difference in key sizes between the regular and the communication-optimized variant of LaKey. Due to the much improved communication complexity of LaKey2, the communication-optimized variant can almost be considered obsolete due to the much larger key size.

Table 1. Comparison of LaKey and LaKey2 threshold PRFs.

Protocol	Computation (ms)	Communication (MB, online/total)	Rounds	Random Bits	Key Size (B)
		LaKey			
LaKey_{12}	11.34	0.41 / 6.01	8	4625	768
LaKey_{32}	8.06	0.43 / 3.85	10	2405	768
LaKey_{K12}	24.79	0.33 / 3.85	8	2753	28416
LaKey_{K32}	12.86	0.36 / 2.79	10	1541	28416
		LaKey2			
$\mathsf{LaKey2}_{12}$	9.80	0.35 / 3.56	5	2336	768
$\mathsf{LaKey2}_{32}$	6.68	0.36 / 2.49	6	1243	768
$\mathsf{LaKey2}_{K12}$	21.84	0.29 / 3.29	5	2336	24576
$\mathsf{LaKey2}_{K32}$	10.78	0.31 / 2.33	6	1243	24576

5.2 Exponent-VRF

We implemented our novel exponent VRF eLaKey using the `bulletproofs` Rust library [Zer24]. As scheme parameters we use $m = 512$, $\bar{q} = 12$, and $\bar{p} = 8$, and we target a 255-bit prime field, concretely the scalar field of `curve25519`. The source code can be found at github.com/torusresearch/lakey-evrf.

Benchmarks are run on a machine with a 10-core M1 Pro CPU and 32 GB RAM. The results can be found in Table 2. We observe that key generation and verification are both well below 100 ms. Evaluation is a bit more costly and takes around 260 ms. The proof size is around 1 kB. We expect that these figures can further be tweaked by experimenting with different parameter sets. Overall, we expect these figures to suffice for many practical applications, like distributed key generation and threshold signing.

Comparison to [BHL24]**.** In comparison to the eVRFs proposed in [BHL24], we observe the following. For their DDH-based eVRF, the number of constraints is between 1282 and 1537, and they estimate a proof size of about 900 bytes, and proving and verification times of a "few tens of milliseconds". For their Pallier-based eVRF, the authors estimate the proving time at about 375 ms and the verification time at about 168 ms. They do not make any statements about the proof size. We note that, to the best of our knowledge, both of their proposed eVRFs have not been implemented and the provided numbers are therefore only theoretical estimates. It is likely that performance in an actual implementation would be lower than these theoretical estimates. Moreover, we remark that these estimations have been stripped from later versions of [BHL24].

Table 2. Exponent-VRF eLaKey evaluation results.

	eLaKey
Key generation	56 ms
Evaluation	264 ms
Verification	27 ms
Proof size	1185B
Constraints	2145
Multipliers	1056

6 Open Questions

We foresee at least two interesting future lines of work.

The first question is whether we can also build an oblivious PRF from the same underlying PRF construction. The main obstacle here is that the LaKey threshold PRF as a first step requires each protocol participants to map the public input x onto a random matrix A in $\mathbb{Z}_q^{l \times m}$. In our construction, we use a random oracle for that mapping which we can instantiate using a hash function like SHA2 or SHA3. If the input is secret, as required for an OPRF, we would need to find an efficient way to compute this mapping in MPC.

The second question is whether our underlying PRF construction can be efficiently evaluated in FHE. We have observed that the construction lends itself well to be run in MPC as well as in ZK proof systems, but while FHE systems share some similarities, it is currently unclear what the concrete efficiency of an implementation in FHE would be. Such a construction would be interesting, as it could also be the basis for an OPRF construction, as shown in [ADD+23], with the benefit that the security of our PRF is reducible to standard LWE. First steps in this direction have been made in [DJL+24].

Acknowledgements. Thanks to Andreas Erwig for proposing the idea to investigate LaKey further in the context of exponent-VRFs, and thanks to Hart Montgomery for his continued guidance around the topic of LWR-based PRFs.

References

AABS+20. Aly, A., Ashur, T., Ben-Sasson, E., Dhooghe, S., Szepieniec, A.: Design of symmetric-key primitives for advanced cryptographic protocols. IACR Trans. Symmetric Cryptol. **2020**(3), 1–45 (2020)

ADD+23. Albrecht, M.R., Davidson, A., Deo, A., Gardham, D.: Crypto dark matter on the torus: oblivious prfs from shallow prfs and fhe. Cryptology ePrint Archive, Paper 2023/232, 2023. https://eprint.iacr.org/2023/232

BBB+17. Bünz, B., Bootle, J., Boneh, D., Poelstra, A., Wuille, P., Maxwell, G.: Bulletproofs: short proofs for confidential transactions and more. Cryptology ePrint Archive, Paper 2017/1066, 2017. https://eprint.iacr.org/2017/1066

BHL24. Boneh, D., Haitner, I., Lindell, Y.: Exponent-VRFs and their applications. Cryptology ePrint Archive, Paper 2024/397, 2024. https://eprint.iacr.org/2024/397

CdH10. Catrina, O., de Hoogh, S.: Improved primitives for secure multiparty integer computation. In: Garay, J.A., De Prisco, R. (eds.) Security and Cryptography for Networks. SCN 2010. LNCS, vol. 6280, pp. 182–199. Springer, Berlin, Heidelberg (2010). https://doi.org/10.1007/978-3-642-15317-4_13

DJL+24. Deo, A., Joye, M., Libert, B., Curtis, B.R., de Bellabre, M.: Homomorphic evaluation of LWR-based PRFs and application to transciphering. Cryptology ePrint Archive, Paper 2024/665, 2024. https://eprint.iacr.org/2024/665

GGM86. Goldreich, O., Goldwasser, S., Micali, S.: How to construct random functions. J. ACM **34**(4), 792–807 (1986)

GM24. Geihs, M., Montgomery, H.: LaKey: efficient lattice-based distributed prfs enable scalable distributed key management. In: 33rd USENIX Security Symposium (USENIX Security 24), pp. 4319–4335, Philadelphia, PA, August 2024. USENIX Association

GØS+23. Grassi, L., Oygarden, M., Schofnegger, M., Walch, R.: From farfalle to megafono via ciminion: the PRF Hydra for MPC applications. In: Hazay,

C., Stam, M. (eds.) Advances in Cryptology – EUROCRYPT 2023. EUROCRYPT 2023. LNCS, vol. 14007, pp. 255–286. Springer, Cham (2023). https://doi.org/10.1007/978-3-031-30634-1_9
Hao17. Hao, F.: Schnorr Non-interactive Zero-Knowledge Proof. RFC 8235, September 2017
Kel20. Keller, M.: MP-SPDZ: a versatile framework for multi-party computation. In: Proceedings of the 2020 ACM SIGSAC Conference on Computer and Communications Security, 2020
Sch90. Schnorr, C.P.: Efficient identification and signatures for smart cards. In: Brassard, G. (eds.) Advances in Cryptology – CRYPTO' 89 Proceedings. CRYPTO 1989. Lecture Notes in Computer Science, vol. 435, pp. 239–252. Springer, New York (1990). https://doi.org/10.1007/0-387-34805-0_22
SS11. Silverman, J.H., Stange, K.E.: Amicable pairs and aliquot cycles for elliptic curves. Exp. Math. **20**(3), 329–357 (2011)
Zer24. Zero-knowledge Cryptography in Rust. Bulletproofs, 2024. https://github.com/zkcrypto/bulletproofs

Quantum and Post-quantum Cryptography

Orient Express: Using Frobenius to Express Oriented Isogenies

Wouter Castryck[1(✉)], Riccardo Invernizzi[1], Gioella Lorenzon[1], Jonas Meers[2], and Frederik Vercauteren[1]

[1] COSIC, KU Leuven, Leuven, Belgium
wouter.castryck@esat.kuleuven.be
[2] CASA, Ruhr-Universität Bochum, Bochum, Germany

Abstract. In this paper we study supersingular elliptic curves primitively oriented by an imaginary quadratic order, where the orientation is determined by an endomorphism that factors through the Frobenius isogeny. In this way, we partly recycle one of the main features of CSIDH, namely the fact that the Frobenius orientation can be represented for free. This leads to the most efficient family of ideal-class group actions in a range where the discriminant is significantly larger than the field characteristic p. Moreover, if we orient with a non-maximal order $\mathcal{O} \subset \mathbb{Q}(\sqrt{-p})$ and we assume that it is feasible to compute the ideal-class group of the maximal order, then also the ideal-class group of $\mathcal{O}$ is known and we recover the central feature of SCALLOP-like constructions.

We propose two variants of our scheme. In the first one, the orientation is by a suborder of the form $\mathbb{Z}[f\sqrt{-p}]$ for some f coprime to p, so this is similar to SCALLOP. In the second one, inspired by the work of Chenu and Smith, the orientation is by an order of the form $\mathbb{Z}[\sqrt{-dp}]$ where d is square-free and not a multiple of p. We give practical ways of generating parameters, together with a proof-of-concept SageMath implementation of both variants, which shows the effectiveness of our construction.

Keywords: Isogeny-based cryptography · class group action · Frobenius endomorphism

1 Introduction

In recent years, there has been a surging interest in the cryptographic use of finite abelian group actions. This concept extends exponentiation in finite cyclic groups, while maintaining the flexibility needed for generalizing several discrete logarithm-based cryptographic constructions, with the Diffie–Hellman key exchange protocol as the main example. The primary motivation for this generalization is that there exist group actions which, unlike exponentiation, are believed to be hard to invert by quantum adversaries.

Unfortunately, we know of one family of such post-quantum finite abelian group actions only: ideal-class groups of imaginary quadratic orders acting on

D. Escudero and I. Damgård (Eds.): LATINCRYPT 2025, LNCS 16129, pp. 145–173, 2026.
https://doi.org/10.1007/978-3-032-06754-8_6

sets of elliptic curves over finite fields via isogenies,[1] a construction originating from the theory of complex multiplication. Their cryptographic potential was first recognized by Couveignes [16] and, independently, by Rostovtsev and Stolbunov [35]. While the original proposal was to work with ordinary elliptic curves, the research focus has shifted entirely to supersingular elliptic curves. This is mainly for reasons of efficiency, but there is also greater flexibility: through the theory of orientations [14,30], supersingular elliptic curves admit actions by ideal-class groups of (infinitely) many different imaginary quadratic orders.

The most practical instantiation is CSIDH [10], coming from the so-called Frobenius orientation. Here one acts with the ideal-class group of a quadratic order containing $\mathbb{Z}[\sqrt{-p}]$ on the set of supersingular elliptic curves $E/\mathbb{F}_p$ up to $\mathbb{F}_p$-isomorphism, where p denotes a large prime number; the required order of magnitude to achieve security is debated (see Sect. 6 for a discussion). Under this orientation the ring element $\sqrt{-p}$ corresponds to the p-th power Frobenius endomorphism $\pi_p : E \to E : (x, y) \mapsto (x^p, y^p)$. There are three main reasons why the (supersingular) Frobenius orientation stands out in terms of efficiency:

1. all curves and isogenies that one encounters during the group action evaluation are defined over $\mathbb{F}_p$;
2. it is easy to choose parameters such that there exist many prescribed ideals that are very easy to act with (e.g., having a small norm and ideal kernels consisting of $\mathbb{F}_p$-rational points),
3. representing the orientation comes at no cost, i.e., when given an elliptic curve $E/\mathbb{F}_p$, it is immediate how to evaluate the endomorphism π_p corresponding to $\sqrt{-p}$ on it.

Reason 2 distinguishes the supersingular case from the ordinary case and was the main selling point of CSIDH. The focus of this article is on reason 3: this is a very powerful feature which was not recognized until other orientations started entering the picture, where the lack of this property is often an important bottleneck.

For the sake of flexibility in current and future applications of cryptographic group actions, it is desirable to cultivate a pool of practical orientations that is as diverse as possible. Indeed, there are good reasons for studying orientations by imaginary quadratic orders $\mathcal{O} \not\supseteq \mathbb{Z}[\sqrt{-p}]$. For example, certain applications like CSI-FiSh [6] require knowledge of the order (or even the structure) of the ideal-class group $\mathrm{cl}(\mathcal{O})$. In general, this is very hard to compute: our fastest known (classical) methods run in sub-exponential time [23]. Here, the leading family of proposals is SCALLOP [2,12,20], where $\mathcal{O}$ is chosen to be an order with large conductor in an imaginary quadratic field having a small(ish) class number. However, unlike the Frobenius case, representing such orientations is non-trivial. This situation was greatly improved through the use of higher-dimensional isogeny representations [12], but the cost remains really substantial.

[1] The cryptographic use of ideal-class group actions on abelian varieties of higher dimension has seen preliminary exploration only [36].

Orientations Factoring Through Frobenius

Inspired by the "higher-degree" supersingular group actions introduced by Chenu and Smith [13], in this paper we study orientations by orders $\mathcal{O}$ containing $\mathbb{Z}[\sqrt{-dp}]$ with $p \nmid d$. On an $\mathcal{O}$-oriented supersingular elliptic curve $E/\mathbb{F}_{p^2}$, the endomorphism corresponding to $\sqrt{-dp}$ necessarily factors through the Frobenius isogeny:

$$E \xrightarrow{\tau} E^{(p)} \xrightarrow{\pi_p} E, \qquad \deg(\tau) = d.$$

Our motivation for studying this kind of orientations is easy to state: in order to represent the endomorphism $\pi_p \circ \tau$, it suffices to represent the isogeny τ since the Frobenius part comes for free. As such, we recover a part of the selling point highlighted in feature 3. The isogeny τ can then be represented in terms of interpolation data, i.e., by the images of a basis of $E[N]$ for some smooth integer $N \approx \sqrt{d}$ (which in practice is of the form 2^a). Without the Frobenius boost, this lower bound would grow to $\sqrt{dp}$, negatively affecting

- the speed: longer higher-dimensional isogeny chains would need to be computed;
- the design flexibility: the N-torsion is expected to be defined over $\mathbb{F}_{p^2}$, putting severe constraints on p.

A nice by-product of orientations factoring through Frobenius is that the ideal class group actions are transitive, since by construction p ramifies in $\mathcal{O}$. Recall from [30] that, in the inert case, the class group action has two orbits.

Comparison with Other Frameworks

The smaller bound on N allows to work in a regime where the discriminant $|\Delta_{\mathcal{O}}|$ of the orienting order $\mathcal{O}$ is significantly larger than p. As far as we are aware, the only other practical instantiations of an orientation breaking through the p-barrier are

- the first version of SCALLOP, but our construction is simpler and orders of magnitude faster,
- a very recent construction due to Houben [24], also based on factoring endomorphisms into isogenies, but his construction does not account for factorizations through Frobenius, and thus does not benefit from the associated performance gains (that said, Houben's construction is orthogonal to ours and could be improved by also incorporating Frobenius as a factor).

We believe that the large-discriminant range deserves further study, because for a given class group size (i.e., a given security level) it allows to work over smaller finite fields. In turn, this may lead to increased efficiency, or to greater flexibility in applications where the field size is constrained. Moreover, as soon as $|\Delta_{\mathcal{O}}| \approx p^2$, it seems reasonable to expect that, when forgetting about the orientation, the class group action samples close-to-uniformly from the entire set of supersingular elliptic curves over $\mathbb{F}_{p^2}$, which may be seen as a security feature (although this requires further study and justification). Note that in the key exchange protocol from [24], the orientation is dropped from the final shared secret.

When compared to CSIDH, orientations factoring through Frobenius do not offer any efficiency gains (yet?), but the following asymptotic trade-off is a glimmer on the horizon. Let us say that we are targeting a class group size having $S/2$ bits, then we want $\log_2 d + \log_2 p \approx S$. If (as usual) one works with curve models satisfying

$$E(\mathbb{F}_{p^2}) \cong \frac{\mathbb{Z}}{(p+1)\mathbb{Z}} \times \frac{\mathbb{Z}}{(p+1)\mathbb{Z}}$$

and $\mathbb{F}_{p^2}$-rational interpolation data, then we must have $N \mid p+1$. If we allow N to take up almost all of $p+1$, then this means that we can let d grow up to about p^2, meaning that $\log_2 p \approx \frac{1}{3}S$. In other words, the bit size of our base field $\mathbb{F}_{p^2}$ is about $2\log_2 p \approx \frac{2}{3}S$, whereas in CSIDH the bit size of the base field $\mathbb{F}_p$ is invariably $\log_2 p \approx S$.

Remark 1. As mentioned, unfortunately, the cheaper field arithmetic does not result in an overall speed-up because it is negatively compensated by a larger number of field operations (mainly due to the computation of two-dimensional isogeny chains). Moreover, we stress that this is an aymptotic trade-off, which kicks in beyond the concrete class group sizes that are currently being proposed. The reason is that $p+1$ must leave room for a constant number of small prime divisors, needed for an efficient evaluation of the class group action.

When compared to the second-generation versions of SCALLOP [2,12], orientations factoring through Frobenius are quite a bit more efficient, thanks to the shorter isogeny chains and the smaller base field. Moreover, by letting $d = f^2$ be a square, we orient by a non-maximal order of $\mathbb{Q}(\sqrt{-p})$ and, if the class group structure of the maximal order is known, then also the class group structure of this suborder is known. Thus, in ranges where computing the class group of the maximal order of $\mathbb{Q}(\sqrt{-p})$ is feasible, we recover the main selling point of SCALLOP. Unfortunately, because of the constraint $N \mid p+1$, we cannot merely recycle the record class group computation from [6], but at least it shows that $\log_2 p \approx 512$ is well within reach. As explained above, this allows to take $d = f^2$ up to bit size 1024, apart from the space allocated for the small primes needed for evaluating the class group action. So this roughly covers the concrete parameter sizes that were proposed in [2]. Asymptotically, this selling point evaporates because computing the class group of the maximal order of $\mathbb{Q}(\sqrt{-p})$ becomes too costly. This being said, in most applications where $\mathrm{cl}(O)$ must be known, one also wants to work with genuinely effective group actions (EGAs, see Sect. 2.1), which neither the SCALLOP family nor our orientations can offer: indeed, with the current methods, acting with arbitrary class group elements comes at the cost of approximate closest-vector-problem computations in lattices of growing dimension [32].

This brings us to our final comparison: we work in the restricted effective group action (REGA) model. Using an exponential-time precomputation (i.e., lattice reduction), this can be turned into an EGA, but at any rate this is a point where it cannot compete with the Clapoti-family of proposals [31,33], which recently culminated in the efficient EGA framework PEGASIS [18]. But these constructions strongly rely on the bound $|\Delta_{\mathcal{O}}| \lessapprox p$.

2 Background

2.1 Group-Action Based Cryptography

We recall the definition of a (restricted) effective group action from [1].

Definition 1 (Abelian Group Action). *Let $(\mathcal{G}, \cdot)$ be an abelian group with identity $1 \in \mathcal{G}$ and $\mathcal{X}$ a set. A map $\star : \mathcal{G} \times \mathcal{X} \to \mathcal{X}$ is called a* group action *if it satisfies the following properties:*

- *Identity: $1 \star x = x$ for all $x \in \mathcal{X}$.*
- *Compatibility: $(g \cdot h) \star x = g \star (h \star x)$ for all $g, h \in \mathcal{G}$ and $x \in \mathcal{X}$.*

Definition 2 (Effective Group Action (EGA)). *An abelian group action $(\mathcal{G}, \mathcal{X}, \star)$ is called* effective *if the following properties are satisfied:*

- *$\mathcal{G}$ is finite and there exists efficient (PPT) algorithms for membership testing, equality testing, (random) sampling, group operation and inversion.*
- *$\mathcal{X}$ is finite and there exist efficient algorithms for membership testing and for computing a unique representation.*
- *There exists a distinguished element $\widetilde{x} \in \mathcal{X}$ with known representation.*
- *There exists an efficient algorithm to evaluate the group action, i.e. to compute $g \star x$ given g and x.*

In practice, the requirements of an effective group action are too strong. In particular, most isogeny-based instantiations of group actions lack the property of efficiently evaluating the group action for every $g \in \mathcal{G}$. Notable exceptions are Clapoti [31], its successor KLaPoTi [33] and PEGASIS [18]. All other (isogeny-based) group actions only satisfy the following weaker notion where the group action can only be efficiently evaluated for a generating set of small cardinality.

Definition 3 (Restricted Effective Group Action (REGA)). *Let $(\mathcal{G}, \mathcal{X}, \star)$ be an abelian group action and let $\mathbf{g} = \{g_1, \ldots, g_n\}$ be a generating set for $\mathcal{G}$. The action is said to be* $\mathbf{g}$-restricted *effective if the following properties are satisfied:*

- *$\mathcal{G}$ is finite and $n = \operatorname{poly}\log|\mathcal{G}|$.*
- *$\mathcal{X}$ is finite and there exist efficient algorithms for membership testing and for computing a unique representation.*
- *There exists a distinguished element $\widetilde{x} \in \mathcal{X}$ with known representation.*
- *There exists an efficient algorithm to evaluate the group action $g_i \star x$ and $g_i^{-1} \star x$ for all $i \in [n]$ and $x \in \mathcal{X}$.*

We remark, however, that a REGA can often be turned into an EGA through some expensive precomputations. For more details, we refer to [12,20].

2.2 Oriented Elliptic Curves and Their Class Group Actions

Up to our knowledge, all current candidate post-quantum abelian group actions involve isogenies between elliptic curves. This comes from the theory of complex multiplication. We give a quick theoretical overview; the statements below can be found in [14,30,37,39]. Let K be an imaginary quadratic number field and let E be an elliptic curve over an algebraically closed field k of characteristic $p \geq 0$. A K-orientation on E is an embedding

$$\iota : K \hookrightarrow \mathrm{End}^0(E) = \mathrm{End}(E) \otimes_{\mathbb{Z}} \mathbb{Q}$$

of K into the endomorphism algebra of E (such an embedding may not exist). The couple (E, ι) is called a K-oriented elliptic curve. For an order $\mathcal{O} \subseteq K$, we say that ι is a primitive $\mathcal{O}$-orientation if $\mathcal{O} = \iota^{-1}\,\mathrm{End}(E)$. We denote by $\mathcal{O}_K$ the ring of algebraic integers of K, which is the maximal order with respect to inclusion.

If $\varphi : E \to E'$ is an isogeny, then there is a corresponding push-forward K-orientation on E' given by

$$\iota' : K \hookrightarrow \mathrm{End}^0(E') : u \mapsto \frac{\varphi\iota(u)\hat{\varphi}}{\deg \varphi},$$

and we say that $\varphi : (E, \iota) \to (E', \iota')$ is an isogeny of K-oriented elliptic curves. If $\deg \varphi = 1$ then this is called an isomorphism, and we write $(E, \iota) \cong (E', \iota')$. If both ι and ι' are primitive $\mathcal{O}$-orientations then the isogeny φ is called horizontal.

For any imaginary quadratic order $\mathcal{O}$, its ideal-class group $\mathrm{cl}(\mathcal{O})$ acts freely on

$$\mathcal{E}\!\ell\ell_k(\mathcal{O}) = \{\text{elliptic curves } E/k \text{ along with a primitive } \mathcal{O}\text{-orientation } \iota\} / \cong \tag{1}$$

via horizontal isogenies, as soon as this set is non-empty. More concretely, for any ideal class $[\mathfrak{a}] \in \mathrm{cl}(\mathcal{O})$, represented by an invertible ideal $\mathfrak{a}$ whose norm is not divisible by p (which can be assumed w.l.o.g.), and every $(E, \iota) \in \mathcal{E}\!\ell\ell_k(\mathcal{O})$, one defines $[\mathfrak{a}](E, \iota)$ as the codomain of the separable isogeny

$$\varphi_{\mathfrak{a}} : E \to E/E[\mathfrak{a}], \qquad E[\mathfrak{a}] = \bigcap_{u \in \mathfrak{a}} \ker \iota(u),$$

equipped with its induced K-orientation; it can be argued that such isogenies are indeed horizontal, and all separable horizontal isogenies arise in this way.

If $p = 0$ then this group action is sometimes called the complex multiplication torsor. Here, all curves in $\mathcal{E}\!\ell\ell_k(\mathcal{O})$ can be defined over a fixed number field (namely, the ring class field $L \supseteq K$ of $\mathcal{O}$), and the action is transitive. If $p > 0$ then there are four cases:

(i) If p splits in $\mathcal{O}$ then all curves in $\mathcal{E}\!\ell\ell_k(\mathcal{O})$ are ordinary and defined over a fixed finite field $\mathbb{F}_q$, and again the action is transitive.

(ii) If p ramifies in $\mathcal{O}$ but does not divide $[\mathcal{O}_K : \mathcal{O}]$ then all curves in $\mathcal{E}\ell\ell_k(\mathcal{O})$ are supersingular and can therefore be defined over $\mathbb{F}_{p^2}$; here too, the action is transitive.

(iii) If p divides $[\mathcal{O}_K : \mathcal{O}]$ then $\mathcal{E}\ell\ell_k(\mathcal{O})$ is empty.

(iv) If p is inert in $\mathcal{O}$ then all curves in $\mathcal{E}\ell\ell_k(\mathcal{O})$ are supersingular and thus definable over $\mathbb{F}_{p^2}$, but in this case there are two orbits. The Frobenius map $(E, \iota) \to (E^{(p)}, \iota^{(p)})$ jumps back and forth between these two orbits.

Remark 2. In the above statements, whenever we claim that all curves in $\mathcal{E}\ell\ell_k(\mathcal{O})$ can be defined over a fixed non-algebraically closed field (the ring class field L, or a finite field $\mathbb{F}_q$), then this also applies to their endomorphism rings, in particular to all endomorphisms in $\iota(\mathcal{O})$. However, we emphasize that in (1), the isomorphism $\cong$ remains to be interpreted over the algebraic closure.

2.3 Higher-Dimensional Isogeny Representations

Kani's Lemma [26] gives a tool for computing isogenies of dimension one using isogenies of dimension two. It was at the heart of the recent SIDH attacks [8, 28,34], but it quickly turned into a powerful building block for isogeny-based protocols.

Theorem 1 (Kani). *Let d_1, d_2 and N be pairwise coprime integers such that $N = d_1 + d_2$, and let E_1, E_2, F_1, and F_2 be elliptic curves connected by the following diagram of isogenies:*

$$\begin{array}{ccc} E_1 & \xrightarrow{\varphi_1} & F_1 \\ \downarrow{\scriptstyle \psi_2} & & \downarrow{\scriptstyle \varphi_2} \\ F_2 & \xrightarrow{\psi_1} & E_2 \end{array}$$

such that $\deg(\varphi_1) = \deg(\psi_1) = d_1$, $\deg(\varphi_2) = \deg(\psi_2) = d_2$ *and* $\varphi_2 \circ \varphi_1 = \psi_1 \circ \psi_2$. *Then the map*

$$\Phi = \begin{pmatrix} \varphi_1 & \hat{\varphi}_2 \\ -\psi_2 & \hat{\psi}_1 \end{pmatrix} : E_1 \times E_2 \to F_1 \times F_2$$

is an (N, N)-isogeny of (principally polarized) abelian varieties with kernel

$$\ker(\Phi) = \{(\hat{\varphi}_1(P), \varphi_2(P)) \mid P \in F_1[N]\}.$$

Assuming that N is powersmooth, the isogeny Φ can be efficiently evaluated at any point on $E_1 \times E_2$. In practice, if $N = 2^a$ for some $a \geq 1$ (which will always be the case for us) one can use algorithms given in [19].

Kani's Lemma is mostly used in isogeny-based cryptography to represent isogenies of a given degree, leading to the following definition.

Definition 4 (2dim-Representation). *A* 2dim*-representation for an isogeny* $\varphi = \varphi_2 \circ \varphi_1$ *of degree* $d = d_1 \cdot d_2$ *and with domain* E *is a tuple*

$$(E, a, u, v, P, Q, \varphi(P), \varphi(Q))$$

where $u, v \in \mathbb{N}$ *under the condition that* $ud_1 + vd_2 = 2^a$ *and* (P, Q) *a basis of* $E[2^a]$.

Definition 4 leverages the following result, which appeared in different shapes in the literature and that we report for convenience.

Proposition 1. *Let* $(E_1, a, u, v, P, Q, \varphi(P), \varphi(Q))$ *be a* 2dim*-representation for an isogeny* $\varphi = \varphi_2 \circ \varphi_1 : E_1 \to E_2$, *where* $\varphi_1 : E_1 \to F_1$ *has degree* d_1, $\varphi_2 : F_1 \to E_2$ *has degree* d_2, *and*

$$ud_1 + vd_2 = 2^a \tag{2}$$

where degree-u *isogenies from* E_1 *and degree-*v *isogenies from* E_2 *are efficiently computable. Assume moreover* d_1, d_2, u *and* v *odd. Then we can efficiently evaluate:*

1. φ_1 *on any point on* E_1 *with order coprime with* u;
2. $\hat{\varphi}_2$ *on any point on* E_2 *with order coprime with* v;
3. φ *on any point on* E_1, *with order coprime with* uv.

Proof. Equation (2) implies $\gcd(ud_1, vd_2) = 1$ and in particular $\gcd(d_1, d_2) = 1$. We have the following commuting square:

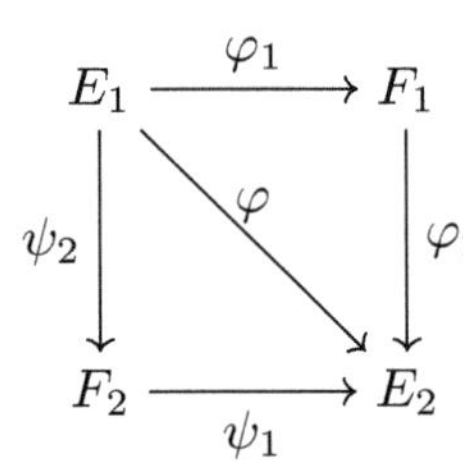

where ψ_1 is the pushforward of φ_1 and ψ_2 is the pullback of φ_2. In particular, $\deg(\varphi_1) = \deg(\psi_1) = d_1$ and $\deg(\varphi_2) = \deg(\psi_2) = d_2$. With the assumption that we can compute u-isogenies and v-isogenies from E_1 and E_2 respectively, and thanks to Eq. (2), we can apply Theorem 1 to a new diagram, of the following form:

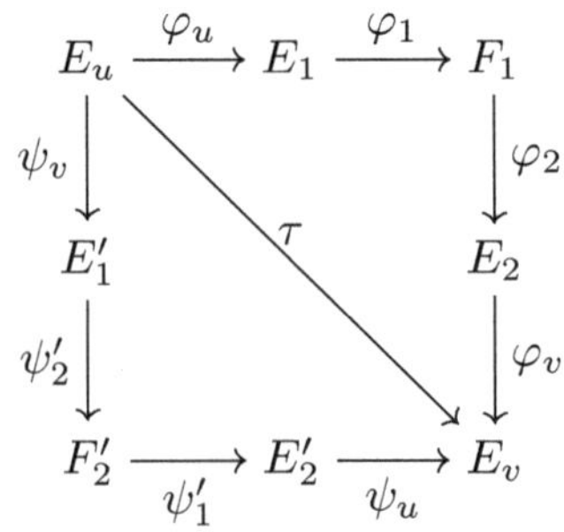

where φ_u and φ_v are any degree u and v isogenies, and $\tau = \varphi_v \circ \varphi_2 \circ \varphi_1 \circ \varphi_u = \varphi_v \circ \varphi \circ \varphi_u$. The map $\psi_u \circ \psi_1'$ is the pushforward of $\varphi_1 \circ \varphi_u$ and $\psi_2' \circ \psi_v$ is the pullback of $\varphi_v \circ \varphi_2$. Then, the map

$$\Phi = \begin{pmatrix} \varphi_1 \circ \varphi_u & \hat{\varphi}_2 \circ \hat{\varphi}_v \\ -\psi_2' \circ \psi_v & \hat{\psi}_1' \circ \hat{\psi}_u \end{pmatrix} : E_u \times E_v \to F_1 \times F_2$$

is a $(2^a, 2^a)$-isogeny with kernel

$$\ker(\Phi) = \{(\hat{\varphi}_u \circ \hat{\varphi}_1(P), \varphi_v \circ \varphi_2(P)) \mid P \in F_1[2^a]\} = \{([ud_1]P, \tau(P)) \mid P \in E_u[2^a]\}.$$

Thus, from the torsion point information and the knowledge of φ_u and φ_v we can compute $\ker(\Phi)$ and consequently evaluate Φ. Now for given points $R \in E_u$ and $S \in E_v$, we have that

$$\Phi(R, 0) = (\varphi_1 \circ \varphi_u(R), -\psi_2' \circ \psi_v(R)), \quad \Phi(0, S) = (\hat{\varphi}_2 \circ \hat{\varphi}_v(S), \hat{\psi}_1' \circ \hat{\psi}_u(S)).$$

From the first components of these points, and with the knowledge of φ_u and φ_v, we can recover φ_1 and $\hat{\varphi}_2$ on any point of order coprime with u and v respectively. This proves (1) and (2).

Now let l be a prime and $R \in E_u[l^e]$, for some positive integer e. Let us assume that l is coprime with vd_2 (otherwise it will be coprime with ud_1). We can compute

$$\Phi(R, 0) = (\varphi_1 \circ \varphi_u(R), -\psi_2' \circ \psi_v(R)),$$

obtaining $R' = \varphi_1 \circ \varphi_u(R)$. We can now use the map

$$\hat{\Phi} = \begin{pmatrix} \hat{\varphi}_u \circ \hat{\varphi}_1 & -\hat{\psi}_v \circ \hat{\psi}_2' \\ \varphi_v \circ \varphi_2 & \psi_u \circ \psi_1' \end{pmatrix} : F_1 \times F_2 \to E_u \times E_v$$

that we can evaluate since its kernel consists of the image under Φ of the 2^a-torsion points of $E_1 \times E_2$. We can then compute

$$\hat{\Phi}(R', 0) = (\hat{\varphi}_u \circ \hat{\varphi}_1(R'), \varphi_v \circ \varphi_2(R')),$$

obtaining $\varphi_v \circ \varphi_2(R') = \varphi_v \circ \varphi_2 \circ \varphi_1 \circ \varphi_u(R) = \tau(R)$. With the knowledge of φ_u and φ_v, and consequently of their duals, we can recover the evaluation of φ on points of order coprime with uv from the evaluation of $\tau = \varphi_v \circ \varphi \circ \varphi_u$, which proves (3). □

This technique was first introduced in QFESTA [29], where the degree of φ was restricted to the shape $q(2^a - q)$ (i.e. $u = v = 1$). Notably, together with the `RepresentInteger` algorithm of [21], this method allows us to find an endomorphism of degree $q(2^a - q)$ and hence find and evaluate isogenies of given (not necessarily smooth) degree q from a curve with $j = 1728$, as long as the 2^a-torsion is accessible. Building on this result, other works generalized it to the current form, most notably [4,31]. We refer to these papers for a more detailed exposition.

To efficiently compute degree u (and v) isogenies from a given curve E, we generally have three options:

- if u is smooth, a degree-u isogeny can be computed from any curve;
- if u is not smooth, we can compute a u-isogeny from E with the technique from [29] mentioned above, assuming some additional information on E (generally, the knowledge of the endomorphism ring is enough);
- if u is non smooth and $\mathrm{End}(E)$ is unknown, there is no known way of efficiently computing a u-isogeny from E. A workaround consists in computing a (u, u)-isogeny in dimension 2, and moving the entire construction from Proposition 1 to dimension 4. This technique is explained in [18], and, while concretely feasible, it is significantly slower than the first two.

3 Orientations Factoring Through Frobenius

In this paper, we study case *(ii)* from the classification in Sect. 2.2. That is, we study primitively $\mathcal{O}$-oriented supersingular elliptic curves $E/\mathbb{F}_{p^2}$ in the case where p ramifies in $\mathcal{O}$ but does not divide the conductor $[\mathcal{O}_K : \mathcal{O}]$. Necessarily $\mathcal{O}$ contains an element of the form

$$\sigma = \sqrt{-dp}$$

for some positive integer d coprime with p. We take σ such that d is as small as possible, for reasons of efficiency (see below).

Remark 3. It may not be possible to pick σ such that it generates $\mathcal{O}$, as it could be that $\mathcal{O} = \mathbb{Z}[(1 + \sqrt{-dp})/2]$. Nevertheless a primitive orientation $\iota : \mathcal{O} \hookrightarrow \mathrm{End}(E)$ is completely determined by $\iota(\sigma)$. To simplify notation, we will just assume that $\mathcal{O} = \mathbb{Z}[\sqrt{-dp}]$, since this has no effect on any of our conclusions. Only if we wanted to act with ideals of norm 2, as in CSURF [7], then it would be important to be more careful. But in our case the 2-torsion is used for representing the orientation.

Since $[p]$ is purely inseparable, there must exist a degree-d isogeny

$$\tau : E \xrightarrow{\tau} E^{(p)}$$

such that $\iota(\sigma) = \pi_p \circ \tau$, where $\pi_p : E \to E^{(p)}$ denotes the p-th power Frobenius isogeny. Clearly, in order to represent $\iota(\sigma)$, it suffices to represent the isogeny τ, i.e. the degree-p part of $\iota(\sigma)$ comes for free: this is the central observation on which this entire paper builds. E.g., using higher-dimensional isogeny representations, it suffices to specify how τ acts on a basis of $E[N]$ with $N > 2\sqrt{d}$. Clearly, this becomes more efficient for smaller values of d, which is why we take d as small as possible for a given instance of $\mathcal{O}$.

Of course, the case $d = 1$ just corresponds to CSIDH [10], where we can always take $\tau = \mathrm{Id}$ and the orientation representation becomes totally implicit. (But one can also take $\tau = -\mathrm{Id}$ which leads to the twisted version of CSIDH.) Higher values of d were studied by Chenu and Smith in [13], where they mainly focused on the cases $d = 2, 3$, but such small factors do not provide any additional security (in view of genus theory attacks, see Sect. 6.4); in contrast, the cases studied in this paper will correspond to large values of d without small prime factors. From [13, Lemma 1] we recycle the following useful fact:

Lemma 1. $\hat{\tau} = \tau^{(p)}$.

Proof. We calculate

$$\tau^{(p)}\tau = \frac{-1}{p}\tau^{(p)}\pi^2\tau = \frac{-1}{p}\pi\tau\pi\tau = \frac{-1}{p}(\pi\tau)^2 = \frac{dp}{p} = d$$

and conclude by composing on the right with $\frac{1}{d}\hat{\tau}$. □

From now on, when no confusion is possible, we will suppress the orientation ι from the notation and just write σ instead of $\iota(\sigma)$.

3.1 Representing the Orientation

To instantiate the framework described above, we will need an efficient way to encode and evaluate the isogeny τ, which will be of large non-smooth degree. The only currently known method to do so is to embed them into 2-dimensional isogenies as described in Sect. 2.3. This will naturally put a constraint on the degrees we will choose for our orientation. In particular, we need to be able to solve Eq. (2) where d_1 and d_2 are related to the generator σ of the order determining our orientation. In Sect. 4 and Sect. 5 we will discuss in more detail how this is done in practice.

3.2 Evaluating the Action

Given an efficient way of evaluating τ (and consequently σ), we can proceed to evaluate the group action. This is completely analogous to [12, Algorithm 3].

We start from an ideal $\mathfrak{a} = (m, \sigma - \lambda)$ of $\mathcal{O}$ of odd prime norm m, coprime to pd, and an oriented curve (E, σ). The first step is to compute the kernel $E[\mathfrak{a}]$ of $\mathfrak{a}$ on E. Let X, Y be points of E such that $\langle X, Y\rangle = E[m]$, $\sigma(X) = \lambda X$ and $\sigma(Y) = -\lambda Y$, where we note that $(m) = \mathfrak{a}\bar{\mathfrak{a}} = (m, \sigma - \lambda)(m, \sigma + \lambda)$. Notice that the existence of X, Y follows by decomposing $E[m]$ into eigenspaces. Any non-zero multiple of X will generate $E[\mathfrak{a}]$. If we sample a random point $P \in E[m]$, we will have $P = aX + bY$ for some (unknown) a, b and hence

$$\sigma(P) + \lambda P = a(\sigma(X) + \lambda X) + b(\sigma(Y) + \lambda\ Y) = 2a\lambda X.$$

Thus, if $a \neq 0$, $\sigma(P) + \lambda P$ generates the kernel of $\mathfrak{a}$. If $a = 0$ (which will happen with probability $1/m$), then $\sigma(P) + \lambda P = 0$ and we will try again with another point P'. In particular, by choosing P' to be independent from P, we can ensure $\sigma(P') + \lambda P' = 2a'\lambda X$ with $a' \neq 0$.

Remark 4. This first step can be done on multiple ideals at the same time. Given ideals $\mathfrak{a}_i = (m_i, \sigma - \lambda_i)$ (with m_i pairwise coprime), we sample a point $P \in E[\prod m_i]$ and define λ to be an integer such that $\lambda \equiv \lambda_i \bmod m_i$ via the Chinese Reminder Theorem. We can then compute $R = \sigma(P) + \lambda P$ with a single evaluation of σ (and in particular of τ). By iterating the argument above, $(\prod_{j \neq i} m_j)R \in E[m_i]$, if non-zero, generates $\mathfrak{a}_i$.

Once a point P generating the kernel $E[\mathfrak{a}]$ is found, the corresponding isogeny $\varphi_{\mathfrak{a}} : E \to E' \cong E/\langle P \rangle$ can be computed using Vélu's formulae. Finally, we need to recover the orientation $\sigma' = \pi' \circ \tau'$ on E'. The involved isogenies respect the following diagram:

$$\begin{array}{ccccc} E & \xrightarrow{\tau} & E^{(p)} & \xrightarrow{\pi} & E \\ \downarrow{\scriptstyle \varphi_{\mathfrak{a}}} & & \downarrow{\scriptstyle \varphi_{\mathfrak{a}}^{(p)}} & & \downarrow{\scriptstyle \varphi_{\mathfrak{a}}} \\ E' & \xrightarrow{\tau'} & E'^{(p)} & \xrightarrow{\pi'} & E' \end{array}$$

and we have interpolation data of the form $(P, \tau(P))$ for $P \in E[2^a]$. Then, interpolation data for τ' is given by $(\varphi_{\mathfrak{a}}(P), -\frac{1}{p}\pi' \circ \varphi_{\mathfrak{a}} \circ \sigma(P))$.

Remark 5. At this step it is important not to publish $(\varphi_{\mathfrak{a}}(P), \varphi_{\mathfrak{a}}(Q))$ directly, where (P, Q) is a basis of $E[2^a]$, as the secret isogeny $\varphi_{\mathfrak{a}}$ can otherwise be recovered by an attacker. However, a random linear transformation of the basis is enough to hide $\varphi_{\mathfrak{a}}$. In particular, picking a random basis on E' and publishing its images under τ' does not leak any information about $\varphi_{\mathfrak{a}}$.

3.3 Easily Acting Ideal Classes

As a byproduct of our construction, we obtain ideals that are very easy to act with, namely ideals of the form $I_l = (l, \sqrt{-dp})$ with $l | d$. Notice that in general l will be a big prime, so acting with this ideal via a kernel computation is very expensive. First of all, we observe that such an ideal is 2-torsion (and typically has exact order 2) in the class group of $\mathbb{Z}[\sqrt{-dp}]$, since $I_l^2 = (l)$. To interpret the action of such an ideal, let us restrict to the case $d = l_1 l_2$ with l_1, l_2 distinct primes and $l_1 + l_2 = 2^a$. This will exactly match the setting of Sect. 5, but the argument can be adapted to work in general. When evaluating τ using the machinery from Sect. 2.3, we end up with the following diagram:

$$\begin{array}{ccc} E & \xrightarrow{\varphi_1} & F_1 \\ \downarrow{\scriptstyle \psi_2} & & \downarrow{\scriptstyle \varphi_2} \\ F_2 & \xrightarrow{\psi_1} & E^{(p)} \end{array}$$

where $\deg(\varphi_i) = \deg(\psi_i) = l_i$. Here we have $\tau = \varphi_2 \circ \varphi_1$. But recall from Lemma 1 that $\hat{\tau} = \tau^{(p)}$, so $\tau = \hat{\tau}^{(p)} = \hat{\varphi}_1^{(p)} \circ \hat{\varphi}_2^{(p)}$ is a factorization of τ into an ℓ_2-isogeny followed by an ℓ_1-isogeny: therefore, this is precisely the other side of the diagram, i.e., we can rewrite

$$\begin{array}{ccc} E & \xrightarrow{\varphi_1} & F_1 \\ \Big\downarrow{\scriptstyle \hat{\varphi}_2^{(p)}} & & \Big\downarrow{\scriptstyle \varphi_2} \\ F_1^{(p)} & \xrightarrow{\hat{\varphi}_1^{(p)}} & E^{(p)} \end{array}$$

Our goal is now to show that $I_1 = (l_1, \sqrt{-dp})$ corresponds to φ_1. This follows from the fact that $I_\tau = (d, \sqrt{-dp}) \subset I_1$, and so $\ker(I_1) \subset \ker(\tau)$ and I_1 has norm l_1. This shows that if we act with I_1 on E we land on F_1. Moreover, the new orientation is given by

$$\sigma' = \frac{1}{l_1}\varphi_1 \sigma \hat{\varphi}_1 = \frac{1}{l_1}\varphi_1 \pi \varphi_2 \varphi_1 \hat{\varphi}_1 = \pi \varphi_1^{(p)} \varphi_2.$$

We proved that acting with I_1 effectively corresponds to flipping the diagram. In the same way, acting with I_2 correspond to flipping in the other direction (we land on $F_1^{(p)}$), and acting with $I_p = (p, \sqrt{-dp})$ mirrors it (landing on $E^{(p)}$). Since to evaluate the action we have to construct all sides of the diagram anyway, we obtain three ideals whose action can be computed almost for free. However, all these ideals have order at most 2 (but typically equal to 2) in the class group since their squares are principal. So each I_l provides only one bit of extra key space each. Moreover, their product is always trivial: we can see it directly in this case (e.g. acting with I_1 and then I_2 is the same as acting with I_p), but this is true more generally if we consider all the factors of dp. In conclusion: if there are n different factors of d whose corresponding isogeny appears in the evaluation of τ, we have $n+1$ extra ideals of order 2 that we can evaluate efficiently, and consequently n extra bits of key space. An alternative use of these bonus ideal classes lies in countering genus-theory attacks on the Decisional Diffie–Hellman problem (DDH), as discussed in Sect. 6.4.

3.4 Split Primes and Exponents

In this work we focus on the key exchange setting, i.e. two parties (Alice and Bob) acting with small-norm ideals from a starting curve E_0. For an instantiation of our protocol we need to provide a list of small-norm ideals that we can easily act with. Typically, these will be of the form $\mathfrak{m}_i = (m_i, \sigma - \lambda_i)$ where m_i is a small odd prime. A secret key then consists of a list of random exponents, one for each $\mathfrak{m}_i$, ranging in an interval $[-B, B]$ for some bound B; here, a negative exponent will correspond to a repeated application of $\overline{\mathfrak{m}}_i = (m_i, \sigma + \lambda_i)$ which is in the inverse ideal class of $\mathfrak{m}_i$. If we denote by R the number of such (conjugated pairs of) small-norm ideals, B and R will be crucial in determining the (classical) security of our key exchange protocol, as the size of the key space is $(2B+1)^R$. However, they will have no impact on the size of the class group, and hence on our quantum security, as argued in [11]. To prevent meet-in-the-middle attacks and guarantee 128 bits of security, we need $(2B+1)^R \approx 2^{256}$. On the other hand, we want to keep B as small as possible, since it will determine the average number of times each party will need to compute an action. For a fixed B, we also choose R to be as small as possible, while providing enough security, as it poses less constraints on parameter generation. The values for B and R reported in Table 1 are taken from [11, Tbl. 3] (we are in the OAYT setting).

Table 1. Exponent choices for 128 bits of security taken from [11, Tbl. 3]. R is the number of acting ideals of small norm, with exponents in the interval $[-B, B]$.

B	1	2	3	4	5
R	139	95	79	70	64

Remark 6. As described here, our construction is a Restricted Effective Group Action (REGA). As is the case for many similar constructions, it can be turned into an Effective Group Action (EGA) through some expensive precomputations, as was already mentioned in Sect. 2. We remark that such a choice will not alter our overall construction, but only eventually affect parameter choices.

4 The Square Case

In this section we consider orientations by $\sigma = \sqrt{-dp}$ with $d = f^2$, hence $\mathcal{O} = \mathbb{Z}[f\sqrt{-p}]$, where we recall the convention made in Remark 3. To facilitate parameter generation, we take $f = f_0 f_1$ the product of two large primes. This setting resembles SCALLOP-HD [12], where $\mathcal{O} = \mathbb{Z}[f\sqrt{-k}]$ for some small $k \in \mathbb{N}$. However, differently from SCALLOP-HD, we consider $k = p$, thus achieving much larger class groups while minimizing the size of the available 2-torsion required to represent the orientation. Indeed, the size of the class group of $\mathcal{O}$ in this setting is $h(\mathcal{O}) \approx \sqrt{dp} = f\sqrt{p}$. However, $d = f^2$ will have to satisfy some constraints. Let $\sigma = \pi_p \circ \tau = \sqrt{-dp} = f\sqrt{-p}$, where $\deg(\tau) = d = f^2$. To instantiate a class group action-based key exchange protocol as described in Sect. 3, we need to:

- represent τ with 2-dimensional isogenies;
- find ideals that are split in $\mathbb{Z}[f\sqrt{-p}]$ and easy to evaluate.

The first requirement imposes that the 2^a-torsion points are defined over the base field, with $2^a > \sqrt{d} = f$. This forces $2^a \mid p+1$. The second requirement, namely finding split ideals which are easy to evaluate, can be fulfilled by using the same strategy as in CSIDH. Imposing $m_i \mid p+1$ for a number of small primes m_i ensures that the m_i-torsion points are defined over the base field and that they split in $\mathbb{Z}[f\sqrt{-p}]$, as we will detail in the next section.

4.1 Parameter Generation

Choosing the Conductor. As in the case of all SCALLOP variants, we require that f_0, f_1 are large primes to avoid certain security issues, e.g., discussed in Sect. 6.3. For efficiency reasons, we additionally require that the isogeny τ of degree f^2 can be represented via a higher dimensional isogeny, as described in Sect. 2.3. Hence, we introduce two positive coprime integers $u, v \in \mathbb{N}$ and we require that Equation (2) is satisfied, namely, for fixed u, v we define the binary quadratic form $Q_{u,v}(x, y) = ux^2 + vy^2$ and look for integer solutions to the equation $Q_{u,v}(x, y) = 2^a$. We can iterate over all combinations of u, v for a fixed a, determined by the desired size of the class group, yielding candidates $x = f_0$, $y = f_1$ for the factors of the conductor f.

Lastly we choose u, v small since we need to compute isogenies of degree u and v when evaluating τ. This is not a strict requirement, as we will explain in Sect. 4.3.

Choosing the Characteristic p. In order to represent the orientation via a $(2^a, 2^a)$-isogeny, we need 2^a-torsion points to be defined over the base-field, hence we require $2^a \mid p+1$, with $2^a > f$. Note that this last condition is already ensured for any a such that $uf_0^2 + vf_1^2 = 2^a$. Additionally, the representation requires auxiliary isogenies, hence rational u, v-torsion points. Finally, for the computation of the class group action we need rational m_i-torsion points, hence $m_i \mid p + 1$, for small odd primes m_i that split in $\mathbb{Z}[f\sqrt{-p}]$. Then, we take $p = 2^a c \prod m_i - 1$, where $uv \mid \prod m_i$ and where c is a cofactor that ensures p is prime; this way, all primes m_i split in $\mathbb{Z}[f\sqrt{-p}]$. Indeed, $-p \equiv 1 \bmod m_i$ and thus the order discriminant $\Delta = -4f^2p$ is always a square modulo m_i.

4.2 Computing a Starting Curve and Finding the Orientation

To compute an $\mathcal{O}$-oriented starting curve (E, ι_E), we need to compute a descending f-isogeny starting from an elliptic curve that is oriented by $\mathbb{Z}[\sqrt{-p}]$, that is, a curve defined over $\mathbb{F}_p$.

To this end, we make use of the QFESTA technique [29] already mentioned in Sect. 2.3. In particular, we pick the elliptic curve $E_{1728} : y^2 = x^3 + x$, defined over $\mathbb{F}_p$ and use the `RepresentInteger` algorithm to compute a degree-f isogeny φ_f from E_{1728}. The algorithm yields a solution as long as $f(2^a - f) > p$. Depending on the choice of parameters, this condition might not hold, e.g. this is the case for the first parameter sets in Table 2. To circumvent this issue, we can make use of a variant introduced in [5], where `RepresentInteger` is used to find an endomorphism of degree $f(2^a - f)t$ for some smooth cofactor $t \mid p + 1$; since we can always compute smooth-degree isogenies from E_{1728}, the degree-t part can then be removed. For more details on this strategy, we refer to [5].

The obtained f-isogeny $\varphi_f : E_{1728} \to E$ will be descending with overwhelming probability. Indeed, if f_0, f_1 are both inert in $\mathbb{Z}[\sqrt{-p}]$ we are guaranteed that any f-isogeny is descending and hence E is primitively oriented by the order $\mathbb{Z}[f\sqrt{-p}]$. On the other hand, even if $\left(\frac{-p}{f_i}\right) = 1$ for either factor $f_i \mid f$,

Algorithm 1: GenStartCurve

Input: A prime $p = 2^a c \prod \ell_i - 1$ and a conductor f
Output: A 2dim-representation for an $\mathcal{O}$-oriented curve (E, ι_E), where $\mathcal{O} = \mathbb{Z}[f\sqrt{-p}]$

Let $E_{1728}/\mathbb{F}_{p^2}$ be the curve with $j = 1728$
Compute random isogeny $\varphi_f : E_{1728} \to E$ of degree f via [29, Algorithm 2]
Choose deterministic bases (R_0, S_0) of $E_{1728}[2^a]$ and (R, S) of $E[2^a]$
Compute a matrix $\mathbf{A} \in \mathrm{GL}(2, 2^a)$ such that $(R_0, S_0) = \mathbf{A}(\pi_p(\hat{\varphi}_f(R)), \pi_p(\hat{\varphi}_f(S)))^\top$
$(R', S') \leftarrow -\mathbf{A}(\pi_p(\varphi_f(R_0)), \pi_p(\varphi_f(S_0)))^\top \in E^{(p)}[2^a]$
return (E, R', S')

there are exactly 2 horizontal and $f_i - 1$ descending isogenies. Since f_0, f_1 are large primes, a random f-isogeny is descending with overwhelming probability.

Once we have computed φ_f, we can take τ to be the composition of its dual $\hat{\varphi}_f$ with the Frobenius conjugate $\varphi_f^{(p)}$. To this end, we only need to evaluate φ_f and $\varphi_f^{(p)}$ on a basis (P_0, Q_0) of $E_{1728}[2^a]$, followed by a base change to a canonical basis of $E[2^a]$; these steps are summarized in Algorithm 1. Note that the algorithm is correct because $\pi_p \circ \varphi_f \circ \pi_p \circ \hat{\varphi}_f = [p] \circ \varphi_f^{(p)} \circ \hat{\varphi}_f$ and $p \equiv -1 \bmod 2^a$.

The algorithm provides a 2dim-representation of τ, which is based on Proposition 1 and relies on auxiliary u and v-isogenies, as illustrated in Fig. 1. Indeed, note that $\tau = \varphi_f^{(p)} \circ \hat{\varphi}_f$ has degree $f^2 = f_0^2 f_1^2$, hence can be seen as a composition of an f_0^2-isogeny and an f_1^2-isogeny, whose degrees are chosen to satisfy Eq. (2).

4.3 Parameter Choices

For a targeted discriminant bit size, which we denote by S, we need to find

- a prime $p = 2^a c \prod m_i - 1$;
- two primes f_0, f_1, such that $uf_0^2 + vf_1^2 = 2^a$ for some positive integers u, v that are odd and coprime.

The number of primes m_i is determined by the classical security of our protocol and by efficiency considerations, i.e. it depends on the number of times we will have to evaluate the action, as discussed in Sect. 3.4. Note that we must take into account that small prime divisors of u, v are not usable for the class group action, as the corresponding torsion points will be needed to produce the auxiliary isogenies for the representation of τ. Therefore, we will have $p = 2^a cM - 1$ with M being the product of the first $R + n$ odd primes, where n is the number of prime divisors of uv among the first R odd primes.

In order to find parameters for a discriminant Δ of expected bit size S, which gives rise to a class number $h(\mathcal{O}) \approx \sqrt{|\Delta|} = 2f\sqrt{p}$ of bit size roughly $S/2$, according to our previous discussions we first estimate a range of corresponding

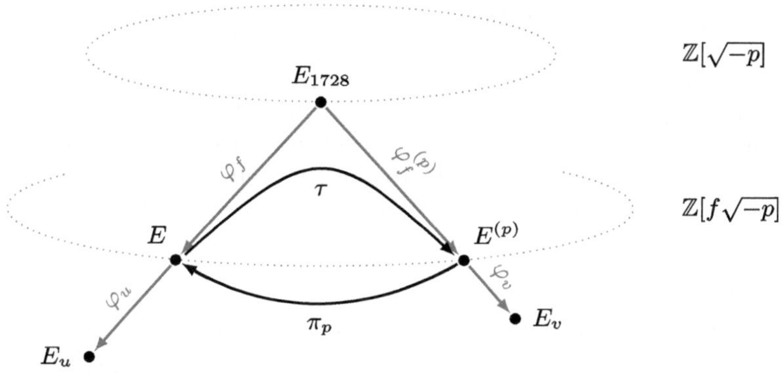

Fig. 1. An isogeny volcano with auxiliary isogenies φ_u, φ_v for the `2dim`-representation of τ.

values of a. Recall that $f \approx 2^a$ hence in general, for a given S and M we have $a \approx (S - \log_2 M)/3$. Note that, since f_0 and f_1 will have roughly the same bit size, it is enough to ensure $\log_2(f) > 128$ to avoid attacks via evaluation of prime-degree f_i-isogenies, as we will discuss in Sect. 6.3. Then, for a chosen value of a, iterating on pairs u, v we look for integer prime solutions f_0, f_1 to $Q_{u,v}(x, y) = 2^a$, of appropriate size. The values of u, v are picked so that they are coprime and have few and small prime divisors. It is not a strict requirement that u, v are of this form, as we could compute auxiliary isogenies from the starting curve and its Frobenius conjugate as push-forwards of u and v-isogenies from E_0; then, during the action computation it suffices to compute their push-forwards through the isogeny we are acting with and its Frobenius conjugate.

In Table 2 we report on parameter sets that allow us to choose $B = 5$ and $B = 2$. For each set, M is the product of all primes from 3 to the last prime reported in the table. We then set $p = 2^a cM + 1$. We set $d = f^2$, with $f = f_0 f_1$ where f_0 and f_1 are prime integer solutions to $2^a = uf_0^2 + vf_1^2$, not dividing M. The values of c, chosen to be coprime to u, v, are reported in the table, together with the size of p and of the discriminant of the orienting discriminant (recall the class group size is half of the discriminant size).

Table 2. Parameter sets for the case $d = f^2$ with $f = f_0^2 f_1^2$, where f_0, f_1 are solutions to $uf_0^2 + vf_1^2 = 2^a$. The prime field characteristic is $p = 2^a cM - 1$, where M is the product of distinct primes m_i such that $m_1 = 3 \leq m_i \leq m_L$. Parameter B is chosen to allow for 128 bit classical security.

Discriminant size (bits)	p size (bits)	a	m_L	B	c	u, v
1438	780	333	331	5	59	5, 3
4242	1897	1184	521	2	5	173, 83

5 The Square-Free Case

Let d square-free, and $\mathcal{O} = \mathbb{Z}[\sqrt{-dp}]$. This setting was firstly studied in [13] for small d. The size of the class group of $\mathcal{O}$ in this setting is $h(\mathcal{O}) \approx \sqrt{dp}$. This means that by allowing d to grow we can act with a larger class group for the same field size p. However, d cannot grow indefinitely. Let $\sigma = \pi_p \circ \tau = \sqrt{-dp}$, where $\deg(\tau) = d$. To instantiate a CSIDH-like protocol in this setting we want to be able to

- represent τ with 2-dimensional isogenies;
- find ideals that are split for σ and easy to evaluate.

The first requirement imposes the same conditions as in the previous case, which are described in Sect. 4: to represent τ we need access to the 2^a torsion, with $2^a > \sqrt{d}$, forcing $2^a \mid p+1$ and giving us a lower bound on the size of p. The best result we can obtain with this approach is hence $d \approx p^2$, for a class group of size $\sqrt{dp} \approx \sqrt{p^3}$ over a field of size p^2.

However, we still have to take care of the second requirement, namely find split ideals which are easy to evaluate. The most natural way is again to adapt the CSIDH approach to our setting: by imposing $m_i \mid p+1$ for enough small primes m_i we gain access to the rational m_i torsion. We still have to make sure that the ideal (m_i) is split in $\mathcal{O}$ for all such m_i, but that can be achieved by a careful choice of d. On the other hand, this method imposes further constraints on p, forcing it to be bigger that the optimal size $\sqrt{d}$. Since the number of small ideals that we can evaluate is only relevant to the classical security of our scheme, and not the quantum one [11, Sec. 4], this effect is mitigated for higher quantum security levels. However, for small parameters this will become a significant limiting factor.

5.1 Finding the Orientation

A concrete way to instantiate the above setting is the following. Let us start by taking E_0 as the curve $y^2 = x^3 + 1$ in characteristic $p \equiv 2 \bmod 3$. Given a primitive 3rd root of unity $\omega \in \mathbb{F}_{p^2} \setminus \mathbb{F}_p$, the map $(x, y) \mapsto (\omega x, y)$ is an endomorphism on E_0, that we denote (with a slight abuse of notation) ω as well; in other terms, $\mathbb{Z}[\omega]$ naturally embeds into $\mathrm{End}(E_0)$. By [17, Prop. 4.7], a prime $l \neq 3$ appears as a norm of an element in $\mathbb{Z}[\omega]$ if and only if $l \equiv 1 \bmod 3$. As a consequence, for every prime $l \equiv 1 \bmod 3$ we can find an endomorphism on E_0 of degree l. We cannot choose d to be prime, since we need to write it as $u(2^t - u)$ to embed τ into a 2-dimensional isogeny. The next natural choice is to look for $d = l_1 l_2$, with $l_1 \equiv l_2 \equiv 1 \bmod 3$. Let us fix a even. Then $l_1 = 2^a - 3x$ and $l_2 = 2^a + 3x$ are both 1 mod 3, for any value of x. We can hence set $d = l_1 l_2 = l_1(2^{a+1} - l_1)$. Since in principle we have no restriction on x, we can try multiple values until both l_1 and l_2 are primes. We can then find elements $\alpha_1, \alpha_2 \in \mathbb{Z}[\omega]$ of norm l_1, l_2 respectively and define $\tau = \alpha_1 \alpha_2$.

There is still an aspect that we need to assess, namely how to access enough small ideals to act with. As already observed, by enforcing $m_i \mid p+1$ we can access the rational m_i torsion for small primes. This also implies $-p \equiv 1 \bmod m_i$ is a square. To make sure that the ideal (m_i) is split, we then need $\left(\frac{d}{m_i}\right) = 1$. If we impose $m_i \mid x$, we get $d = l_1 l_2 \equiv 2^{2a} \bmod m_i$, and so d is a square modulo all the m_i as required.

5.2 Parameter Generation

With the notation of the previous section, let us define $M = \prod_{i=1}^{R} m_i$. For a given S, denoting the bit size of the discriminant, we need to find

- a prime $p = 2^{a+1}cM - 1$;
- two primes $l_1 = 2^a - 3x$ and $l_2 = 2^a + 3x$, such that $\left(\frac{d}{m_i}\right) = 1$ for all m_i.

The value of R, and consequently of M, is determined by the classical security of our protocol and by efficiency considerations (the number of times we will have to evaluate the action), as discussed in Sect. 3.4. Asymptotically, the value of M is just a constant, and should not impact the method outlined in Sect. 5.1. However, if the security parameter S is not big enough compared to M, we may run into trouble. In general, for a given S and M we would like to compute a as $\lceil (S - \log_2 M)/3 \rceil$, then set $p = 2^{a+1}cM - 1$ (for a small cofactor c) and $d \approx 2^{2a}$ as outlined above. If we set $l_i = 2^a \pm x$ where $M \mid x$ this method will fail as soon as $\log_2 M > a$, or $S < 4 \log_2 M$, strongly limiting our parameter choices. Notice that for fixed M and a we have roughly $2^a/M$ choices for l_1 and l_2; since the probability of a number l being prime is $1/\log l$, assuming independence between l_1 and l_2 the probability that they are both prime is roughly $1/a^2$, meaning that we need $2^a/M > a^2$ to find a valid pair (this estimate is extremely conservative; see Remark 7). If this is not true, we can relax the condition $M \mid x$ and replace it with $M' \mid x$, where $M' = \prod_{i=1}^{R'} m_i$ with $R' = R - k$. In this way, the condition $\left(\frac{d}{m_i}\right) = 1$ is automatically satisfied only by the m_i for $i < R'$; this means that the number of attempts to find a valid pair l_1, l_2 grows by a factor 2^k. On the other hand, the number of possibilities grows by a factor $\prod_{i=R'}^{R} m_i$, i.e. the product of the last k primes. This product is certainly bigger than 2^k, and generally by some margin. For instance, the last prime if we pick $B = 1$ in Table 1 is 809, which is 10 bits. This greatly improves our chance of finding valid parameters. While the choice of k is limited by our computational capabilities, this is a one time computation.

We show the effectiveness of our method by computing a parameter set for a discriminant size of 1500 bits where $B = 5$ and so M is 424 bits, way above the limit $S/4$. To investigate the scalability of our protocol we also provide a parameter with $S = 4000$, but there $B = 2$ and so we get $a > \log_2 M$. These parameters are reported in Table 3. The prime is $p = 2^{a+1}cM - 1$, and $d = l_1 l_2$ where $l_i = 2^a \pm xM'$, with M' defined as above.

Remark 7. The probability (loosely speaking) that a random number n is prime is asymptotic to $1/\log n$. Hence, the probability that two random numbers

Table 3. Parameter sets for the case $d = l_1 l_2$ square-free, where $l_i = 2^a \pm xM'$ and M' is the product of primes m_i such that $3 \le m_i \le m_{L-k}$. The prime field characteristic is $p = 2^{a+1}cM - 1$, where M is the product of distinct primes m_i such that $m_1 = 3 \le m_i \le m_L$. Parameter B is chosen to allow for 128 bit classical security.

Discriminant size (bits)	p size (bits)	a	m_L	B	c	x	k
1506	786	360	313	5	2	2308855	11
4006	1802	1102	503	2	51	8075	0

$n_1, n_2 \approx n$ are prime at the same time is $1/(\log n)^2$. However, we are working with numbers of the form $2^a \pm xM$, with M a product of many small primes. This already ensures that l_1 and l_2 are not divisible by all the m_i, greatly boosting their probability of being prime. Moreover, they are coprime with each other, making the probability slightly higher. Determining the number of representations of a number as a sum of two primes is a famous open problem in mathematics, known as the *extended Goldbach's conjecture*; a more detailed treatment of the matter is outside the scope of this work. However, from this preliminary discussion we can already conclude that the estimate $1/a^2$ provided above is conservative.

5.3 Protocol Setup

Unlike in the square case, we can setup our protocol already on $E_0 : y^2 = x^3 + 1$, the curve of j-invariant 0. We can then efficiently evaluate $\tau = \alpha_1\alpha_2$ (where α_1 and α_2 are the endomorphisms of norm l_1 and l_2 described above) as an endomorphism. Notice that τ could also be represented by a 2-dimensional isogeny, namely

$$\Phi : E_0 \times E_0 \to E_0 \times E_0 = \begin{pmatrix} \alpha_1 & \hat{\alpha}_2 \\ -\alpha_2 & \hat{\alpha}_1 \end{pmatrix},$$

as detailed in Sect. 3.1. This representation is used to evaluate the orientation away from E_0. For this reason, the first step of the action from E_0 (namely, the first step of the public key generation) will be much faster than the subsequent ones.

Moreover, we observe the following interesting fact. Recall that, by construction, $\alpha_1, \alpha_2 \in \mathbb{Z}[\omega]$.

Proposition 2. *Let*

$$\Phi : E_0 \times E_0 \to E_0 \times E_0 = \begin{pmatrix} \alpha_1 & \hat{\alpha}_2 \\ -\alpha_2 & \hat{\alpha}_1 \end{pmatrix}$$

be a $(2^n, 2^n)$-isogeny, with $\alpha_1, \alpha_2 \in \mathbb{Z}[\omega]$. Then we can write Φ as a composition of n $(2,2)$-isogenies $\Psi_i : E_0 \times E_0 \to E_0 \times E_0$, $i = 1, \dots, n$, of the form

$$\Psi_i = \begin{pmatrix} \gamma & 1 \\ -1 & \hat{\gamma} \end{pmatrix}$$

with $\gamma \in \mathbb{Z}[\omega]^\times$.

Proof. We proceed by induction. The first step is to prove that if Φ is a $(2,2)$-endomorphism of $E_0 \times E_0$, it can always be expressed in the form above, up to post-composition with an isomorphism, or in other words up to multiplication on the left with an invertible matrix. Since $N(\alpha_1) + N(\alpha_2) = 2$, and $\mathbb{Z}[\omega]$ does not contain elements of norm 2 ([17, Prop. 4.7]), we must have $N(\alpha_1) = N(\alpha_2) = 1$. In particular α_1, α_2 are isomorphisms, and their inverses coincide with the dual. Then, using that α_1 and α_2 commute as elements of $\mathbb{Z}[\omega]$,

$$\begin{pmatrix} \alpha_2 & 0 \\ 0 & \hat{\alpha}_2 \end{pmatrix} \begin{pmatrix} \alpha_1 & \hat{\alpha}_2 \\ -\alpha_2 & \hat{\alpha}_1 \end{pmatrix} = \begin{pmatrix} \alpha_2\alpha_1 & 1 \\ -1 & \hat{\alpha}_1\hat{\alpha}_2 \end{pmatrix}$$

and the matrix on the right corresponds to Ψ_1 with $\gamma = \alpha_2\alpha_1$.

For the induction step, given the matrix Φ with $N(\alpha_1) + N(\alpha_2) = 2^n$, we want to write it as

$$\begin{pmatrix} \alpha_1 & \hat{\alpha}_2 \\ -\alpha_2 & \hat{\alpha}_1 \end{pmatrix} = \begin{pmatrix} \beta_1 & \hat{\beta}_2 \\ -\beta_2 & \hat{\beta}_1 \end{pmatrix} \begin{pmatrix} \gamma & 1 \\ -1 & \hat{\gamma} \end{pmatrix}$$

with the additional condition $N(\beta_1) + N(\beta_2) = 2^{n-1}$ and $N(\gamma) = 1$. By expanding the product, we obtain two equations

$$\begin{cases} \alpha_1 = \beta_1\gamma - \hat{\beta}_2 \\ \alpha_2 = \beta_2\gamma + \hat{\beta}_1 \end{cases}$$

that we can rearrange into

$$\begin{cases} \alpha_1 - \gamma\hat{\alpha}_2 = -2\hat{\beta}_2 \\ \alpha_1 + \gamma\hat{\alpha}_2 = 2\beta_1\gamma. \end{cases}$$

We are left with proving that there exists $\gamma \in \mathbb{Z}[\omega]^\times = \{\pm 1, \pm\omega, \pm\omega^2\}$ such that $\alpha_1 + \gamma\hat{\alpha}_2 \equiv 0 \bmod 2$ for any given α_1, α_2 such that $N(\alpha_1) + N(\alpha_2) = 2^n$. Let us assume this is not true. We can then write down $\alpha_1, \alpha_2 \in \mathbb{Z}[\omega]$, and compute $\alpha_1 + \gamma\hat{\alpha}_2 \bmod 2$ for each $\gamma \in \mathbb{Z}[\omega]^\times$. We get a set of 4 binary equations (three choices for γ plus the norm condition) which have to hold at the same time. Direct calculation shows that this is not possible. From the above system,

$$N(\beta_1) + N(\beta_2) = \frac{1}{4}(N(\alpha_1 - \gamma\alpha_2) + N(\alpha_1 + \gamma\alpha_2)) = \frac{1}{4}(2N(\alpha_1) + 2N(\alpha_2))$$

from which we conclude that $N(\beta_1) + N(\beta_2) = 2^{n-1}$. □

As a consequence, our starting orientation Φ on $E_0 \times E_0$ can be written as a composition of $(2,2)$-endomorphisms. This ceases to be true as we move away from E_0, since we do no longer see all elements of $\mathbb{Z}[\omega]^\times$ as endomorphisms.

6 Security

As for the hardness of the vectorization problem, i.e., the problem of retrieving the secret ideal class $[\mathfrak{a}]$ connecting two public oriented elliptic curves (E, ι) and $(E', \iota') = [\mathfrak{a}](E, \iota)$, we largely fall back on the discussion from [11], which is restricted to Frobenius orientations aka CSIDH, but the analysis carries over to all orientations as long as one works in the REGA framework. In a nutshell, to achieve classical 128-bit security, the size of the key space should be in the order of 256 bits due to meet-in-the-middle attacks. It is believed that this also suffices against a quantum adversary; Grover-type speed-ups over the standard meet-in-the-middle algorithm have been proposed in the past but are now considered unrealistic [11,25]. However, a much bigger quantum threat is Kuperberg's algorithm (and its descendants) for hidden-shift finding, which runs in time $L_{|\Delta|}(1/2)$. For this reason the discriminant Δ should be large (in absolute value). How large exactly is a topic of debate. Two of the main fuzzy factors are the cost of an oracle query and the cost of using quantum random access classical memory (QRACM). For NIST level 1, the authors of [11] propose a discriminant of 4096 bits, which is why these orders of magnitude were included in Table 2 and Table 3, along with the more aggressive choice $|\Delta| \approx 1596$.

Let us now discuss some (non-)threats that are specific to our proposal.

6.1 Known Endomorphisms

A priori, a security concern could be that the orientation gives away *two* endomorphisms of E in interpolation form, thereby potentially revealing a full-rank subring of $\mathrm{End}(E)$: indeed, an eavesdropper has access to

$$\tau^{(p)} \circ \tau \qquad \text{and} \qquad \pi \circ \tau.$$

However, this was resolved in Lemma 1: the first map is just the multiplication-by-d map. Thus, we only leak an embedding of $\mathcal{O}$, and this is the same as for all known class group actions.

6.2 Acting on Conjugate Pairs

Recall from Sect. 3.3 that the ideal class $[(p, \sqrt{-dp})]$ acts by Frobenius conjugation. Therefore, the action of $\mathrm{cl}(\mathbb{Z}[\sqrt{-dp}])$ on our set of oriented elliptic curves $E \xrightarrow{\tau} E^{(p)}$ induces a well-defined action of

$$\frac{\mathrm{cl}(\mathbb{Z}[\sqrt{-dp}]}{\langle[(p, \sqrt{-dp})]\rangle} \quad \text{on the set of conjugate pairs} \quad E \xrightarrow{\tau} E^{(p)}, E^{(p)} \xrightarrow{\tau^{(p)}} E.$$

Of course, this is just a special case of a general statement: for every subgroup $H \subset \mathrm{cl}(\mathcal{O})$, the quotient group $\mathrm{cl}(\mathcal{O})/H$ acts on the set of orbits under H. However, despite the size of $\mathrm{cl}(\mathcal{O})/H$ being smaller, in general this does not lead to a simpler vectorization problem: it is very hard to represent the orbits in a way that allows for the desired quantum state collapses in Kuperberg's algorithm. But in the case of conjugate pairs this is much more natural, so it could allow for a faster run of Kuperberg's algorithm. Since this just reduces the size of $\mathrm{cl}(\mathcal{O})$ by 1 bit, the effect is minimal.

6.3 Walking Up the Volcano

In the setting of Sect. 4, namely when the orientation comes from $\mathbb{Z}[f\sqrt{-p}]$, a potential attack consists in walking up the isogeny volcano to solve the vectorization problem in a larger suborder of $\mathbb{Z}[\sqrt{-p}]$ (with smaller class group) instead. In our case $f = f_0 f_1$, so the cost of walking up is lower bounded by the cost of computing an f_0 (or f_1) isogeny from a random curve. Computing isogenies of large prime degree d is considered cryptographically hard, with the best known classical algorithms running in $\widetilde{O}(d^2)$, assuming that points of order d can be found over an extension of the base field of degree $O(d)$ only [3, Section 4.4]. Moreover, no quantum speed-up on such algorithms is currently known. To protect against such an attack it is thus sufficient to ensure $f_0, f_1 \approx 2^{64}$, which is way below the sizes we need for quantum security.

The assumption that points of order d can be found over an extension of the base field of degree $O(d)$ is true with overwhelming probability, and can be verified explicitly by checking that the multiplicative order of $p \bmod d$ only has large factors. If this condition was violated, computing a d-isogeny would be more efficient, as detailed in [22, Section 2.3], [15, Section 2.5].

6.4 Genus Theory Attacks

Another potential attack consists in breaking the Decisional Diffie-Hellman (DDH) assumption using genus theory. Let $\mathcal{O}$ be the order giving the orientation, and $\Delta = -2^a m_1^{e_1} \cdots m_r^{e_r}$ its discriminant, factored into powers of distinct primes. For any odd prime factor m_i we have a well-defined assigned character

$$\chi_{m_i} : \mathrm{cl}(\mathcal{O}) \to \{\pm 1\} : [I] \mapsto \left(\frac{N(I)}{m_i}\right)$$

where $[I]$ is assumed to be represented by an ideal of norm coprime with m_i. If $\Delta = -4n$ is even and $n \not\equiv 3 \bmod 4$ then this list is extended with one or two additional characters. Moreover, there is a unique non-trivial relation among the characters [9, Eq. (3)]. The authors of [9] give a way to evaluate such an assigned character on an ideal class $[I]$ given access only to (E, ι) and $[I](E, \iota)$. The cost of this evaluation is exponential in the size of m_i, meaning that we can only evaluate characters for small prime factors of the discriminant (and also the additional characters in case they occur). Being able to evaluate a non-trivial character effectively breaks the DDH assumption in our setting.

The discriminant of $\mathbb{Z}[\sqrt{-dp}]$ is $-4dp$. Since both d and p do not have small prime factors, the only characters that we have to avoid are the additional ones. In the concrete set-up from Sect. 4, $p \equiv 3 \bmod 4$ and $d = f^2 \equiv 1 \bmod 4$, so

$dp \equiv 3 \bmod 4$ and there are no additional characters. In the set-up from Sect. 5, $p \equiv 3 \bmod 4$, and $l_1 \equiv -l_2 \bmod 4$ implying $d \equiv 3 \bmod 4$. As a consequence, $dp \equiv 1 \bmod 4$ and in this case there is a unique additional character

$$\delta : \mathrm{cl}(\mathcal{O}) \to \{\pm 1\} : [I] \mapsto (-1)^{(N(I)-1)/2}$$

(where now $[I]$ is assumed represented by an ideal of odd norm) which is non-trivial and whose action is easy to evaluate [9, Prop. 1]. Thus in this case the DDH assumption does not apply. One way out is to act with keys sampled from the subgroup $\ker \delta \subset \mathrm{cl}(\mathcal{O})$. This is easy to control: when acting with a key $(e_1, \ldots, e_R)$ representing an ideal class $[\mathfrak{m}_1]^{e_1} \cdots [\mathfrak{m}_R]^{e_R}$, one should verify that

$$e_1 \frac{m_1 - 1}{2} + \ldots + e_R \frac{m_R - 1}{2} \equiv 0 \bmod 2 \tag{3}$$

and try another key if this is violated. Unless $m_i \equiv 1 \bmod 4$ for all i (in which case we are automatically sampling from $\ker \delta$), this reduces the size of the key space by about 1 bit. An alternative option is to also act with $[(p, \sqrt{-dp})]$, which just amounts to flipping as was explained in Sect. 3.3, whenever (3) is violated. This ideal class indeed has δ-value equal to -1 because $p \equiv 3 \bmod 4$, so it multiplies any other ideal class with δ-value -1 into $\ker \delta$.

6.5 Validating the Starting Curve

In this section we briefly discuss how to validate a starting curve, namely to verify that it was honestly generated. In our setting, the starting curve is a curve together with an orientation, and it is honestly generated if the orientation is by $\mathbb{Z}[\sqrt{-dp}]$ and primitive. Indeed, if the orientation was not primitive, the parties engaging in the protocol would act by ideals of a generally bigger order than $\mathbb{Z}[\sqrt{-dp}]$, hence by elements of a smaller ideal class group. The class number of a suborder $\mathcal{O}' \subset \mathcal{O}$ of index f is indeed roughly f times bigger than the class number of $\mathcal{O}$, as proven in [17, Theorem 7.24] and [27, Theorem 5.4].

We note that in the case where $\mathbb{Z}[\sqrt{-dp}]$ is a maximal order, namely when d is square-free and $-dp \not\equiv 1 \bmod 4$, the starting curve must be honestly generated as long as the orientation generates an order of the correct discriminant. This is always the case in the setting of Sect. 5, where we have $p \equiv 3 \bmod 4$ and $l_1 \equiv -l_2 \bmod 4$, implying $d = l_1 l_2 \equiv 3 \bmod 4$ and hence $-dp \equiv 3 \bmod 4$. We mention that, even if $\mathbb{Z}[\sqrt{-dp}]$ with d square-free was not maximal, it would be a suborder of conductor 2 in the maximal order $\mathbb{Z}[(1 + \sqrt{-dp})/2]$; in this case, either 2 is inert, hence the class number of the suborder is the same as that of the maximal order, or 2 is split, hence the class number of the suborder is three times the size of that of the maximal order. Thus, a non-primitive orientation in this setting would either provide no advantage to an attacker, or reduce the security of only roughly 1 bit.

To check that the discriminant of the order generated by $\sigma : E \to E$, given a `2dim`-representation of τ, is correct, one has to check that $|\Delta| = 4\deg(\sigma) - \mathrm{tr}(\sigma)^2 = 4dp$. Computing a Weil pairing $e_{2^a}(\tau(P), \tau(Q)) = e_{2^a}(P, Q)^{\deg(\tau)}$ where

P, Q form a basis of $E[2^a]$, and a discrete logarithm, one recovers $\deg(\tau) \bmod 2^a$, and actually the correct value of the degree since $\deg(\tau) < 2^a$ as required by the `2dim`-representation of τ. Then one checks that $\deg(\tau) = d$, hence $\deg(\sigma) = \deg(\tau)p = dp$. It is then left to check that $\operatorname{tr}(\sigma) = 0$. It follows from $4\deg(\sigma) - \operatorname{tr}(\sigma)^2 \geq 0$ that if one computes $\operatorname{tr}(\sigma)$ modulo at least $2\sqrt{\deg \sigma} = 2\sqrt{dp}$, this yields the exact value of the trace. One can then check correctness of the value of the trace modulo $p + 1 > 2\sqrt{dp}$, as $d \leq p/4$. By definition, $[\operatorname{tr}(\sigma)] = \sigma + \hat{\sigma} = \pi \circ \tau + \hat{\tau} \circ \hat{\pi}$. Hence, one can check that $\pi \circ \tau(P) + \hat{\tau} \circ \hat{\pi}(P) = \pi \circ \tau(Q) + \hat{\tau} \circ \hat{\pi}(Q) = 0$, where P, Q form a basis of $E[p + 1]$ (we can compute both τ and $\hat{\tau}$ on the $p + 1$ torsion given a `2dim`-representation of τ).

We are then going to discuss the setting of Sect. 4, where $\mathbb{Z}[\sqrt{-dp}]$ with $d = f^2$ has a non-trivial conductor $f = f_0 f_1$, and f_0 and f_1 are distinct primes. We recall that f-isogenies from a curve that is primitively oriented by $\mathbb{Z}[f\sqrt{-p}]$ are descending with overwhelming probability, as explained in Sect. 4.2. In particular, a starting curve that is computed via Algorithm 1 will always be honestly generated with overwhelming probability.

In order to validate the starting curve, one should first check that the given orientation σ generates an order with the correct discriminant via pairings, as explained above, and then verify that the orientation is primitive by checking that σ does not factor through multiplication by f_0 or f_1. For this second step, one can consider the given `2dim`-representation of τ and the corresponding isogeny diagram illustrated in Sect. 2.3, where τ is viewed as composition of f_0^2 and f_1^2-isogenies. According to Proposition 1, the codomain curve of the isogeny of degree f_0^2 can be computed; if it is equal to the domain then τ, hence σ, has to factor through multiplication by f_0; similarly, if the codomain of the isogeny of degree f_1^2 equals its domain, then the orientation factors through multiplication by f_1.

We remark that the above considerations apply in the same way to public-key validation, which would be required to protect against active attacks on encryption schemes based on our construction in a static setting.

7 Implementation

We provide a proof-of-concept implementation of our protocol in SageMath [38], to show feasibility and allow for a rough comparison with other existing schemes. We stress that many known optimizations are still possible, especially in the setting of key exchange discussed in the paper. Unfortunately, we are not able to provide direct timing comparisons, as there is no available SageMath key-exchange implementation for SCALLOP in a REGA setting, which would be the most appropriate comparison.

Our implementation can be found at https://github.com/KULeuven-COSIC/OrientExpress. We ran our implementation on Ubuntu 24.04 with an Intel(R) Core(TM) Ultra 7 165H CPU, and timings are reported in the next sections.

7.1 Timings for the Case $d = f^2$

We report timings of an action computation from a starting curve in Table 4 for parameter sets from Table 2.

Table 4. Timings for the case $d = f^2$. Average timing for an action computation.

Discriminant size	Avg. action	B
1438	47.8 s	5
4242	297 s	2

7.2 Timings for the Case d Square-Free

As already discussed, in the maximal order case the first step of the action computed from E_0 is much faster than the other ones, since on E_0 evaluating the orientation does not require 2-dimensional isogenies. We report timings in Table 5, highlighting this difference. We compare timings for the first step of the action when starting from E_0 and from a random curve E; we then report timings for the remaining $B-1$ steps, which are all done from a random curve, separately. Notice that in general the last $B-1$ steps will be each on average faster than the first step from a random curve, since the exponents are progressively smaller.

A key generation will consist in a step from E_0 together with the remaining $B-1$ steps, while the key exchange will include a step from a given E and the remaining $B-1$ steps. Notice that in the latter case the first step can sometimes be precomputed and included in the public key, as discussed in Sect. 7.3.

7.3 Sizes

A public key consists in two pair of points, $(P_1, Q_1) \in E$ and $(P_2, Q_2) = (\tau(P_1), \tau(Q_1)) \in E^{(p)}$. Recall that we are working over the prime field $\mathbb{F}_{p^2}$, where p is of the form $p = 2^a cM - 1$. In general, we can always assume (P_1, Q_1) to be a deterministic basis of E, and to be working with Montgomery curves. To send this information there are two main strategies:

Table 5. Timings for the case d square-free. Average timing of the first step of an action computation from E_0, average timing of the first step of an action computation from a random curve E and average timing of the last $B-1$ steps of an action computation.

Discriminant size	Avg. first step from E_0	Avg. first step from E	Avg. $B-1$ last steps	B
1506	3.77 s	9.17 s	26.82 s	5
4006	25.18 s	93.24 s	74.57 s	2

- sending the points (P_2, Q_2) directly; this allows us to recover the Montgomery coefficient of E, and compute P_1, Q_1 from there. We can stretch this a bit more, and send P_2 and only the x-coordinate of Q_2, together with a bit denoting the sign of its y coordinate. Moreover, in this case the points (P_i, Q_i) do not need to be a basis of the respective 2^a-torsion, but can instead be points of $p+1$-torsion at no additional cost. This allows Alice to precompute one step of the action of Bob, and publish that in the public data. The size in this case is $6p$;
- sending the Montgomery coefficient of E together with 4 coefficients in $\mathbb{Z}_{2^a}$, representing the coordinates of P_2 and Q_2 in terms of a deterministic basis of $E^{(p)}$. If we are mainly concerned about sizes, we can send only 3 such coefficients and recover the fourth one using pairings. The size in this case is $2p + 3a$.

Acknowledgments. We thank Marc Houben and the anonymous reviewers for helpful comments on an earlier version of this paper, and Luciano Maino for help in the implementation of 2D isogenies. This work is supported by the European Research Council (ERC) under the European Union's Horizon 2020 research and innovation programme (grant agreement ISOCRYPT – No. 101020788), by the Research Council KU Leuven grant C14/24/099, by CyberSecurity Research Flanders with reference number VR20192203, by the Deutsche Forschungsgemeinschaft (DFG, German Research Foundation) under Germany's Excellence Strategy – EXC 2092 CASA – 390781972, and by Fonds voor Wetenschappelijk Onderzoek (FWO) with reference numbers 1138925N and 1139225N.

References

1. Alamati, N., Feo, L., Montgomery, H., Patranabis, S.: Cryptographic group actions and applications. In: Moriai, S., Wang, H. (eds.) ASIACRYPT 2020, Part II. LNCS, vol. 12492, pp. 411–439. Springer, Cham (2020). https://doi.org/10.1007/978-3-030-64834-3_14
2. Allombert, B., et al.: Faster SCALLOP from non-prime conductor suborders in medium sized quadratic fields. In: Public-Key Cryptography – PKC 2025. Lecture Notes in Computer Science, vol. 15676, pp. 333–363 (2025)
3. Basso, A., et al.: PRISM: simple and compact identification and signatures from large prime degree isogenies. In: Public-Key Cryptography – PKC 2025. Lecture Notes in Computer Science, vol. 15676, pp. 300–332 (2025)
4. Basso, A., Dartois, P., Feo, L., Leroux, A., Maino, L., Pope, G., Robert, D., Wesolowski, B.: Sqisign2d-west - the fast, the small, and the safer. In: Chung, K.-M., Sasaki, Yu. (eds.) ASIACRYPT 2024, Part III. LNCS, vol. 15486, pp. 339–370. Springer, Singapore (2024)
5. Basso, A., Maino, L.: POKÉ: a compact and efficient PKE from higher-dimensional isogenies. In: Advances in Cryptology – Eurocrypt 2025 Part II. Lecture Notes in Computer Science, vol. 15602, pp. 94–123. Springer (2025)
6. Beullens, W., Kleinjung, T., Vercauteren, F.: CSI-FiSh: efficient isogeny based signatures through class group computations. In: Galbraith, S.D., Moriai, S. (eds.) ASIACRYPT 2019. LNCS, vol. 11921, pp. 227–247. Springer, Cham (2019). https://doi.org/10.1007/978-3-030-34578-5_9

7. Castryck, W., Decru, T.: CSIDH on the surface. In: Ding, J., Tillich, J.-P. (eds.) PQCrypto 2020. LNCS, vol. 12100, pp. 111–129. Springer, Cham (2020). https://doi.org/10.1007/978-3-030-44223-1_7
8. Castryck, W., Decru, T.: An efficient key recovery attack on SIDH. In: Hazay, C., Stam, M. (eds.) EUROCRYPT 2023, Part V. LNCS, vol. 14008, pp. 423–447. Springer, Cham (2023)
9. Castryck, W., Houben, M., Vercauteren, F., Wesolowski, B.: On the decisional Diffie-Hellman problem for class group actions on oriented elliptic curves. Res. Number Theory **4**(8), Article 99 (2022). Proceedings of ANTS-XV
10. Castryck, W., Lange, T., Martindale, C., Panny, L., Renes, J.: CSIDH: an efficient post-quantum commutative group action. In: Peyrin, T., Galbraith, S. (eds.) ASIACRYPT 2018. LNCS, vol. 11274, pp. 395–427. Springer, Cham (2018). https://doi.org/10.1007/978-3-030-03332-3_15
11. Chávez-Saab, J., Chi-Domínguez, J.-J., Jaques, S., Rodríguez-Henríquez, F.: The sqale of csidh: sublinear vélu quantum-resistant isogeny action with low exponents. J. Cryptogr. Eng. **12**(3), 349–368 (2022)
12. Chen, M., Leroux, A., Panny, L.: SCALLOP-HD: group action from 2-dimensional isogenies. In: Tang, Q., Teague, V. (eds.) PKC 2024, Part II. LNCS, vol. 14603, pp. 190–216. Springer, Cham (2024)
13. Chenu, M., Smith, B.: Higher-degree supersingular group actions. Math. Cryptol. **1**, 85–101 (2021)
14. Colò, L., Kohel, D.: Orienting supersingular isogeny graphs. Cryptology ePrint Archive, Report 2020/985 (2020)
15. Corte-Real Santos, M., Eriksen, J.K., Meyer, M., Reijnders, K.: Aprèssqi: extra fast verification for sqisign using extension-field signing. In: EUROCRYPT 2024, pp. 63–93. Springer (2024)
16. Couveignes, J.-M.: Hard homogeneous spaces. Cryptology ePrint Archive, Paper 2006/291 (2006)
17. Cox, D.A.: Primes of the Form x^2+ny^2: Fermat, Class Field Theory, and Complex Multiplication. Pure and Applied Mathematics: A Wiley Series of Texts, Monographs and Tracts. Wiley (2013)
18. Dartois, P., et al.: PEGASIS: practical effective class group action using 4-dimensional isogenies. In: Advances in Cryptology – Crypto 2025. Lecture Notes in Computer Science (2025, to appear)
19. Dartois, P., Maino, L., Pope, G., Robert, D.: An algorithmic approach to (2, 2)-isogenies in the theta model and applications to isogeny-based cryptography. In: Chung, K.-M., Sasaki, Yu. (eds.) ASIACRYPT 2024, Part III. LNCS, vol. 15486, pp. 304–338. Springer, Singapore (2024)
20. Feo, L.D., et al.: SCALLOP: scaling the CSI-FiSh. In: Boldyreva, A., Kolesnikov, V. (eds.) Public-Key Cryptography – PKC 2023, Part I. LNCS, vol. 13940, pp. 345–375. Springer, Cham (2023)
21. De Feo, L., Kohel, D., Leroux, A., Petit, C., Wesolowski, B.: SQISign: compact post-quantum signatures from quaternions and isogenies. In: Moriai, S., Wang, H. (eds.) ASIACRYPT 2020. LNCS, vol. 12491, pp. 64–93. Springer, Cham (2020). https://doi.org/10.1007/978-3-030-64837-4_3
22. Eriksen, J.K., Panny, L., Sotáková, J., Veroni, M.: Deuring for the people: supersingular elliptic curves with prescribed endomorphism ring in general characteristic. In: LuCaNT 2023. Contemporary Mathematics, vol. 796, pp. 339–373. American Mathematical Society (2024)
23. Hafner, J.L., McCurley, K.S.: A rigorous subexponential algorithm for computation of class groups. J. Am. Math. Soc. **2**(4), 837–850 (1989)

24. Houben, M.: Isogeny-based key exchange from orientations of large discriminant. In: Advances in Cryptology – Crypto 2025. Lecture Notes in Computer Science (2025, to appear)
25. Jaques, S., Schrottenloher, A.: Low-gate quantum golden collision finding. In: Dunkelman, O., Jacobson, Jr., M.J., O'Flynn, C. (eds.) SAC 2020. LNCS, vol. 12804, pp. 329–359. Springer, Cham (2021). https://doi.org/10.1007/978-3-030-81652-0_13
26. Kani, E.: The number of curves of genus two with elliptic differentials. Journal für die reine und angewandte Mathematik **485**, 93–122 (1997)
27. Kopp, G.S., Lagarias, J.C.: Class field theory for orders of number fields (2022)
28. Maino, L., Martindale, C., Panny, L., Pope, G., Wesolowski, B.: A direct key recovery attack on SIDH. In: Hazay, C., Stam, M. (eds.) EUROCRYPT 2023, Part V. LNCS, vol. 14008, pp. 448–471. Springer, Cham (2023)
29. Nakagawa, K., Onuki, H.: QFESTA: efficient algorithms and parameters for FESTA using quaternion algebras. In: Reyzin, L., Stebila, D. (eds.) CRYPTO 2024, Part V. LNCS, vol. 14924, pp. 75–106. Springer, Cham (2024)
30. Onuki, H.: On oriented supersingular elliptic curves. Finite Fields Appl. **69**, Article No. 101777 (2021)
31. Page, A., Robert, D.: Introducing clapoti(s): evaluating the isogeny class group action in polynomial time. Cryptology ePrint Archive, Paper 2023/1766 (2023)
32. Panny, L.: CSI-FiSh really isn't polynomial-time (2023). Blah post available at https://yx7.cc/blah/2023-04-14.html
33. Panny, L., Petit, C., Stopar, M.: KLaPoTi: an asymptotically efficient isogeny group action from 2-dimensional isogenies. Cryptology ePrint Archive, Report 2024/1844 (2024)
34. Robert, D.: Breaking SIDH in polynomial time. In: Hazay, C., Stam, M. (eds.) EUROCRYPT 2023, Part V. LNCS, vol. 14008, pp. 472–503. Springer, Cham (2023)
35. Rostovtsev, A., Stolbunov, A.: Public-Key Cryptosystem Based On Isogenies. Cryptology ePrint Archive, Report 2006/145 (2006)
36. Sanon, S.P.: Endomorphism rings of ordinary abelian varieties. Ph.D. thesis, TU Kaiserslautern (2022)
37. Schoof, R.: Nonsingular plane cubic curves over finite fields. J. Comb. Theory Ser. A **46**(2), 183–211 (1987)
38. The Sage Developers. SageMath, the Sage Mathematics Software System (Version 10.6.beta7) (2025). https://www.sagemath.org
39. Waterhouse, W.C.: Abelian varieties over finite fields. Annales Scientifiques de l'École Normale Supérieure **2**(4), 521–560 (1969)

Improved Algorithms for Ascending Isogeny Volcanoes, and Applications

Steven D. Galbraith[1], Valerie Gilchrist[2(✉)], and Damien Robert[3]

[1] University of Auckland, Auckland, New Zealand
[2] Université Libre de Bruxelles, Brussels, Belgium
valerie.gilchrist@ulb.be
[3] Inria Bordeaux, Institut de Mathématiques de Bordeaux, Bordeaux, France

Abstract. Given two elliptic curves over $\mathbb{F}_q$, computing an isogeny mapping one to the other is conjectured to be classically and quantumly hard. This problem plays an important role in the security of elliptic curve cryptography. In 2024, Galbraith applied recently developed techniques for isogenies to improve the state-of-the-art for this problem.

In this work, we focus on computing ascending isogenies with respect to an orientation. Our results apply to both ordinary and supersingular curves. We give a simplified framework for computing self-pairings, and show how they can be used to improve upon the approach from Galbraith to recover these ascending isogenies and eliminate a heuristic assumption from his work. We show that this new approach gives an improvement to the overall isogeny recovery when the curves have a small crater (super-polynomial in size). We also study how these self-pairings affect the security of the (PEARL)SCALLOP group action, gaining an improvement over the state-of-the-art for some very particular parameter choices. The current SCALLOP parameters remain unaffected.

1 Introduction

Tate's isogeny theorem [30] states that two elliptic curves defined over $\mathbb{F}_q$ have the same number of points if and only if they are isogenous. To date, it is thought to be a hard problem to recover an isogeny between two fixed elliptic curves. The case where these two curves are supersingular greatly concerns modern-day isogeny-based cryptography, however, the case where they're ordinary still remains pertinent to elliptic curve cryptography and pairing cryptography. In 1999, Galbraith [13] gave algorithms solving the ordinary case, and then improved upon the worst case complexities in [14] using Kani's lemma.

Authors listed in alphabetical order: see https://www.ams.org/profession/leaders/CultureStatement04.pdf. Valerie Gilchrist is supported by a FRIA grant by the National Fund for Scientific Research (F.N.R.S.) of Belgium. Damien Robert is supported by the France 2030 program under grant agreement ANR-22-PETQ-0008 PQ-TLS. Date of this document: 2025-08-25.

D. Escudero and I. Damgård (Eds.): LATINCRYPT 2025, LNCS 16129, pp. 174–208, 2026.
https://doi.org/10.1007/978-3-032-06754-8_7

In the later work, given elliptic curves on the floor of an isogeny volcano, Galbraith solves the problem by first computing paths up to the crater from each curve, and then solving a meet-in-the-middle search on the crater to complete the path. In this work we focus on how to compute the paths up to the crater, these paths are called *vertical* or *ascending* isogenies. In Sect. 3.2 we give a new method to determine an ascending isogeny when the endomorphism ring is known. In Sect. 4, we make use of the work from Castryck et al. [5], extended by Macula and Stange in [20], that shows how *self-pairings* can be used to recover unknown *horizontal* isogenies. These are pairings that can be evaluated using only one elliptic curve point and give a non-trivial output, i.e. $e(P, P) \neq 1$. We give a simplified framework for these pairings, and show how they can be used to recover vertical isogenies as well. In Sect. 4.2 we give a simplified proof of a special case of a result from [20] where we use only the standard Weil pairing rather than sesquilinear pairings. This proof is designed to be accessible to non-experts. We carefully characterize the cases when the order of the torsion subgroup does or does not divide the conductor, as well as the additional case when it divides the overall degree of the secret isogeny. This increases the available torsion subgroups on which we can gain *partial* information about how the isogeny acts. We then show how to encode the *missing* information into a conic equation, and treat the case of degenerate and non-degenerate conics individually.

With this new toolkit to compute unknown vertical isogenies, we consider the computational isogeny problem on certain curves with large volcanos (for example, pairing-friendly ordinary elliptic curves). In this case, the isogeny volcano is tall and the crater is very small (usually of size 1). The main result of [14] is to show that this case can be solved in $\tilde{O}(q^{1/4})$ field operations. In Sect. 5 we first show how to eliminate a heuristic assumption (about Elkies primes) from Galbraith's work using our pairing construction. We then detail an algorithm for solving the computational isogeny problem in volcanoes that are tall but with crater larger than polynomial size. Denote by Δ the discriminant of the maximal order and suppose $|\Delta| = q^a$ for some $0 < a < 1$. Write $t^2 - 4q = N^2\Delta$, where the curves in the isogeny class have $q + 1 - t$ points. The state-of-the-art algorithm from Galbraith [14] has complexity $\tilde{O}(h_0 N^{1/2})$ operations over $\mathbb{F}_q$ when the class number, h_0, is small enough, which works out as $\tilde{O}(q^{(1+a)/4})$ operations when a is small. Our new approach using self-pairings gives an improved complexity of $\tilde{O}(q^{(1-a)/4})$ operations, for most integers Δ.

In addition, in Sect. 2.4, we consider the case of volcanoes with small (but super-polynomial) conductor. The result is implicit in [13] but has not been explicitly stated anywhere. We show these two improvements compared to [14] in Fig. 1.

Lastly, in Sect. 6, we demonstrate a second application of our approach to computing vertical isogenies. In this section our focus is on supersingular curves. Namely, we outline an attack on the SCALLOP group action for maximal orders with (almost) smooth discriminants. We show that if the fundamental discriminant Δ has a smooth factor of size at least $\Delta^{1/2+\epsilon}$, then our isogeny recovery approach from self-pairings potentially gives an improvement over the state-of-

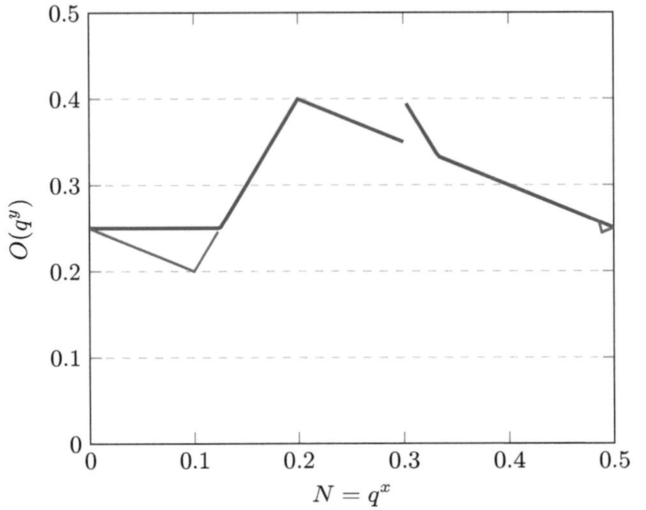

Fig. 1. The state-of-the-art from Galbraith is plotted in blue. The two improvements that will be presented in this paper are plotted in red. (Color figure online)

the-art *classical* attacks. The exact complexity of our attack depends on the exact number and size of the prime factors of the smooth part of Δ.

Self pairings were introduced in [5] as a way to attack isogeny class group actions; they were then extended in [20]. However, they only apply when the degree d of the unknown isogeny $\phi : E_0 \to E_1$ is known. A key feature of our attacks in Sect. 5 and Sect. 6 is that we use the self-pairings only to ascend the volcano, and use this to compute an isogeny whose degree is not known. We can always recover the degree of the going up isogeny (and it is usually part of the SCALLOP parameter anyway).

2 Isogeny Graphs and Previous Results on Ascending Isogenies

We study elliptic curves over a finite field $\mathbb{F}_q$. In some sections of the paper the focus is on ordinary curves and in some sections on supersingular curves.

In the ordinary case, the fundamental problem is to construct an isogeny $\phi : E_0 \to E_1$ between two given curves E_0, E_1 over $\mathbb{F}_q$. We are mainly interested in the case when ϕ is a vertical degree-N isogeny, which means one of the orders $\mathrm{End}(E_0), \mathrm{End}(E_1)$ has index N in the other.

We will sometimes use the notation that $\mathrm{End}(E_0)$ and $\mathrm{End}(E_1)$ have discriminants Δ_0, Δ_1 respectively, and write Δ for the discriminant of the imaginary quadratic field $K = \mathrm{End}(E_0) \otimes \mathbb{Q}$. Note that $\Delta_i = f_i^2 \Delta$ for $i = 0, 1$ and the integer f_i is called the conductor of the ring $\mathrm{End}(E_i)$. Sometimes we will abuse notation and talk of the discriminant of a curve E when we mean the discriminant of $\mathrm{End}(E)$.

We write π_q for the q-power Frobenius map on E_0 and E_1. If R is a quadratic imaginary order, we will also often denote by $\Delta_R = \Delta(R)$ its discriminant, and likewise if $\gamma \in R$ we will denote by $\Delta_\gamma = \Delta(\gamma)$ the discriminant of its minimal polynomial (which is also the discriminant of $\mathbb{Z}[\gamma]$).

When we talk about supersingular curves we will always take them to be defined over $\mathbb{F}_{p^2}$ and we will assume that we are in the isogeny class of maximal curves, meaning that $\#E(\mathbb{F}_{p^2}) = (p+1)^2$.

2.1 Isogeny Volcanos

Let E_0 be an elliptic curve over $\mathbb{F}_q$. Let S be a set of primes ℓ coprime to the characteristic of $\mathbb{F}_q$. The isogeny graph of E_0 with isogeny degrees in S is the graph whose vertex set is elliptic curves E over $\mathbb{F}_q$ that are isogenous to E_0, and there is an edge $\{E, E'\}$ if there exists an isogeny $\psi : E \to E'$ such that $\deg(\psi) \in S$. In the case $S = \{\ell\}$ we call the graph the ℓ-isogeny graph.

The connected components of the ℓ-isogeny graphs of ordinary elliptic curves have a specific structure. They constitute a cycle where each vertex of the cycle is the root of a tree. As can be seen in the example given in Fig. 2, this structure resembles a volcano.

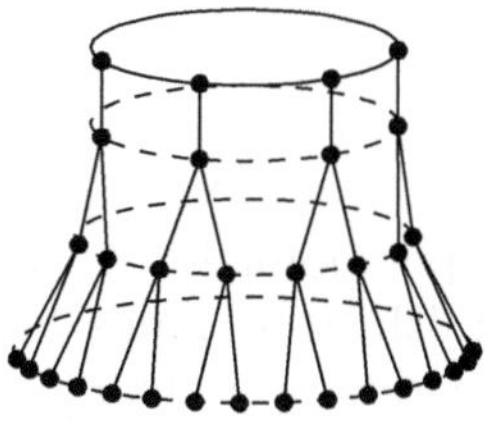

Fig. 2. Example 2-isogeny volcano of depth 3.

The vertices forming the top cycle of the volcano are often called the *crater*, or the *surface* of the volcano. The leaf vertices of the trees are called the *floor* of the volcano. A set of vertices at the same distance from the crater are called a level. The distance of a vertex on the floor from the cycle is called the *depth*. Vertices in the same level correspond to curves whose endomorphism ring has the same discriminant. Vertices on the crater correspond to curves whose discriminant is equal to the fundamental discriminant, Δ (or at least to a ring whose conductor is not divisible by ℓ). In an ℓ-isogeny volcano, a vertex in level k will correspond to a curve with discriminant $\Delta' = \ell^{2k}\Delta$.

In the ordinary case we will also consider volcanos with respect to a set S consisting of all primes dividing the conductor of the ring $\mathbb{Z}[\pi_q]$.

The Computational Isogeny Problem asks to recover an isogeny between two given elliptic curves, E_0, E_1. Taking a walk in the ℓ-isogeny volcano, where the starting point is the vertex associated to E_0 and the ending point is the vertex associated to E_1, can be seen as a special case of this problem where the recovered isogeny is a power of ℓ.

2.2 The 1999 Algorithm

In [13] Galbraith gave an algorithm that computes an isogeny between two ordinary elliptic curves. For two elliptic curves E_0, E_1, the approach used was to take a path starting at each of these curves that climbs up to the crater using modular polynomials. Once on the crater, a meet-in-the-middle computation determines how to join the two paths. If N is the largest prime divisor of the conductor and h is the class number of the maximal order then equation (5) of Sect. 6 of [13] states the complexity of the algorithm as

$$O(N^3(\log(N) + \log(q)) + \sqrt{h}(\log(h)^2 + \log(h)\log(q)^5) \\ + \log(h)\log(q)^6 + \log(q)^8/\log\log(q)) \quad (1)$$

field operations. When N is constant or polynomial in $\log q$, the complexity is $\tilde{O}(q^{1/4})$. The worst case is when h is small and $N \approx q^{1/2}$, in which case the complexity is $\tilde{O}(q^{3/2})$ operations over $\mathbb{F}_q$.

2.3 The 2024 Algorithm

Recently, Kani's lemma [18] was leveraged in some attacks [3,21,26] that were able to reconstruct a secret isogeny given some information about how the isogeny acts on a sufficiently large torsion group. Galbraith used this idea constructively in his recent paper [14] where he improves upon the worst case complexity of his previous work [13].

Instead of using modular polynomials to walk up the volcano from each of E_0, E_1 to the crater, Galbraith uses Kani's lemma to reconstruct the path. Suppose that N divides the conductor and that E_0 is directly above E_1 in the sense that there is a descending N-isogeny $\phi : E_0 \to E_1$ (see Fig. 3). Then if we know ϕ on $E_0[M]$ for some suitable torsion group, the Kani construction can provide a representation of ϕ. Since we do not have any way to compute ϕ on $E_0[M]$, the method requires guessing how the isogeny acts on some torsion points. In other words, for several small primes $\ell \mid M$, given an ℓ-torsion basis (P_0, Q_0) on E_0, we need to guess $\phi(P_0), \phi(Q_0)$. It is explained in [14] that we need $M \approx N^{1/2}$.

To get the desired complexity we need the number of guesses for $\phi(P_0), \phi(Q_0)$ to be at most $O(M)$. Since there are M^2 choices for each M-torsion point, this seems to be a challenge. In [14] it is suggested to choose M to be a product of Elkies primes ℓ, namely primes such that $E_0[\ell]$ has a Frobenius eigenbasis with distinct eigenvalues, so $\pi_q(P_0) = uP_0$ and $\pi_q(Q_0) = qu^{-1}Q_0$ where π_q is the q-power Frobenius and $u \in (\mathbb{Z}/\ell\mathbb{Z})^*$. By choosing P_1 and Q_1 in the appropriate eigenspaces of $E_1[\ell]$, we know that $P_1 = [\lambda]\phi(P_0)$ and $Q_1 = [\nu]\phi(Q_0)$ for some integers λ, ν. Using the Weil pairing one can reduce to a single unknown integer, hence reducing the problem to trying $O(\ell)$ values. The drawback of this approach is that one needs to apply heuristic assumptions about the distribution of Elkies primes, see [14, Assumption 1] or [3, Section 10]).

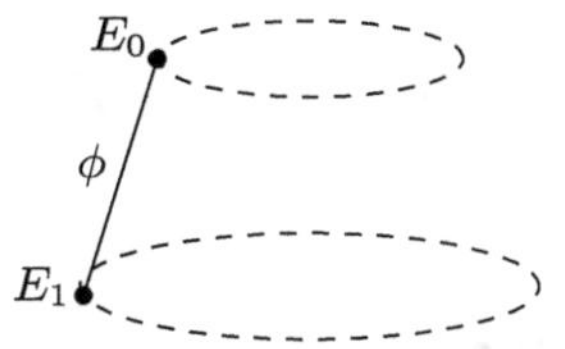

Fig. 3. Two curves at different levels of a volcano.

For each guess, we run the Kani attack. If it returns a viable isogeny, then we can stop. Otherwise we repeat with a new guess. To run the Kani attack we have to choose our integer M so that $M - N$ is the sum of integer squares. One can write all positive integers as a sum of 4 squares, but the attack is faster if one can write $M - N$ as a sum of two squares.

2.4 Precise Analysis in the Case of Small Conductor

One of the observations in [14] is that it is sometimes more efficient to compute descending isogenies than ascending isogenies. Hence, [14] advocates descending to the floor, and solving the isogeny problem there using a meet-in-the-middle algorithm. This results in complexity $\tilde{O}(q^{1/4})$ operations for all conductors up to $q^{1/8}$. This is seen in Fig. 1 with the flat blue line on the left hand side of the figure.

However, as already implied by Eq. (1), one can do better. We reproduce the analysis in this case.

First we recall the process for computing ascending and descending isogenies. In [13] ascending was done using modular polynomials and required cubic complexity. In [14] it is shown how to compute descending isogenies more efficiently (at least, asymptotically) when the group order is known by generating random kernel points. Given a curve over $\mathbb{F}_q$ with $q+1-t$ points and such that $\ell^4 \mid t^2 - 4q$, computing an ascending ℓ-isogeny may require $\tilde{O}(\ell^3)$ field operations, while computing a descending ℓ-isogeny takes $\tilde{O}(\ell^2)$ operations (see [14, Sect. 2.3] for details). It is possible, however, to compute the ascending isogeny in $\tilde{O}(\ell^2)$ operations as well. This will be detailed in Sect. 3.2. Now recall that we are trying to recover an isogeny, $\phi : E_0 \to E_1$ where $[\mathrm{End}(E_0) : \mathrm{End}(E_1)] = N$ and $\mathrm{End}(E_0) = \mathcal{O}_K$, i.e. E_0 lies on the crater. The approach from [13] is to take a walk up to the crater and then solve the problem there using meet-in-the-middle.

Suppose $N = q^b$ for a number $0 < b < 1/2$. As noted in [14, Section 2.3], walking up to the crater can always be done in $\tilde{O}(q^{2b})$ finite field operations (even with the $\tilde{O}(\ell^3)$ ascending algorithm from [14]). Call this ending curve E_2, so we have recovered the ascending isogeny $\varphi : E_1 \to E_2$ (see Fig. 4 for reference).

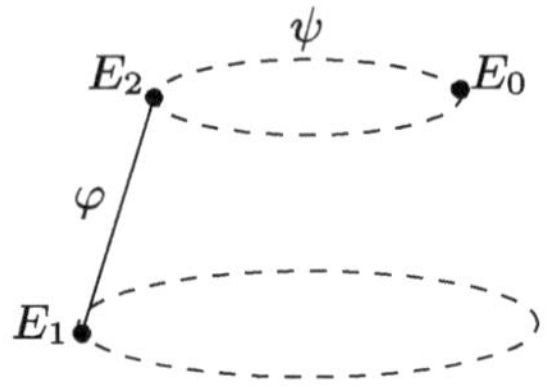

Fig. 4. Volcano where E_0 is not directly above E_1.

The class number of the crater is around $\sqrt{|\Delta_0|}$. Thus since $N^2\Delta_0 = t^2 - 4q$, we get that the class number will be $h_0 = \tilde{O}(\sqrt{q/N^2}) = \tilde{O}(q^{(1-2b)/2})$. Hence the meet-in-middle computation to recover the map $\psi : E_2 \to E_0$ on the crater will cost $\sqrt{h_0} = \tilde{O}(q^{(1-2b)/4})$.

The total complexity to recover $\hat{\varphi} \circ \hat{\psi} : E_0 \to E_1$ therefore comes from the cost to walk up to the crater and then conduct meet-in-the-middle which is $\tilde{O}(q^{2b}) + \tilde{O}(q^{(1-2b)/4})$ operations over $\mathbb{F}_q$. When $0 < b < 1/10$, we get that the meet-in-the-middle computation is dominating, giving a total complexity of $\tilde{O}(q^{(1-2b)/4})$. Otherwise, when $b \geq 1/10$, the total complexity will be $\tilde{O}(q^{2b})$ operations. The details are given in Algorithm 1.

Algorithm 1: Isogeny recovery in volcanoes with small conductor

Input : elliptic curves E_0, E_1 such that $\mathrm{End}(E_0) = \mathcal{O}_K$ and $[\mathrm{End}(E_0) : \mathrm{End}(E_1)] = N$

Output: $\phi : E_0 \to E_1$

Compute the unique ascending path $\varphi : E_1 \to E_2$ by sampling N-torsion points in E_1 and applying the formulas from Vélu ;

Compute an isogeny $\psi : E_2 \to E_1$ via meet-in-the-middle ;

Compute $\phi = \hat{\varphi} \circ \hat{\psi}$;

return ϕ ;

We gain an improvement over [13] when $0 < b < 1/8$. Suppose, for example, that $b = 1/14$. Then we get a complexity proportional to $q^{(1-2b)/4} \approx q^{0.21}$ operations over $\mathbb{F}_q$ which is better than $q^{0.25}$ operations. We outline this range of improvement in Fig. 5.

3 Orientations

One can find a volcano structure in the supersingular isogeny graph over $\mathbb{F}_{p^2}$ when we endow the supersingular elliptic curves with an *orientation.* This terminology was introduced by Colo and Kohel [8].

The terminology and notions in this section apply to both the ordinary and supersingular case. So let E be any elliptic curve over $\mathbb{F}_q$.

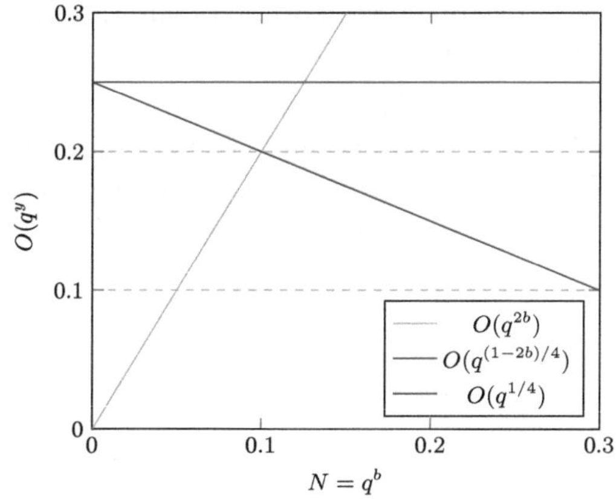

Fig. 5. The algorithmic complexity given in [14] is plotted in red. The complexity of the algorithm described in Sect. 2.4 is plotted in blue and green. Here we see that for $N < q^{1/8}$, the approach from Sect. 2.4 gives an improvement.

Definition 3.1 (K-orientation). *Let $K = \mathbb{Q}(\sqrt{d})$ be a quadratic imaginary field. We say an elliptic curve E is K*-oriented *if there exists a ring homomorphism*

$$\iota : K \hookrightarrow \mathrm{End}(E) \otimes_{\mathbb{Z}} \mathbb{Q}.$$

The pair (E, ι) is called a K-oriented elliptic curve.
If $R \subseteq K$ is a ring and $\iota(R) \subseteq \mathrm{End}(E)$ then we say E is R-oriented.

Suppose ι is the orientation on such a curve E. There exists a unique quadratic order $\mathcal{O} \subset K$ such that $\iota(\mathcal{O}) = \mathrm{End}(E) \cap \iota(K)$. Then we call ι a *primitive $\mathcal{O}$-orientation*, and we say that E is $\mathcal{O}$-orientable.

For any suborder $\mathcal{O}' \subset \mathcal{O}$, ι still induces an orientation on $\mathcal{O}'$, which is no longer primitive. Conversely, given an orientation ι on $\mathcal{O}'$, it extends uniquely to a K-orientation, and if $\mathcal{O}$ is the associated primitive orientation, we have $\mathcal{O}' \subset \mathcal{O}$. We call $\mathcal{O}$ the *saturation* of the orientation on E. We have $\Delta(\mathcal{O}') = \Delta(\mathcal{O})f^2$, and if m is an integer, we say that $\mathcal{O}'$ is *m-locally primitive* if m is coprime to f.

An oriented isogeny between two $\mathcal{O}$-oriented elliptic curves is an isogeny which commutes with the orientations. We will often drop the ι from our notation.

Example 3.1. The advantage of the above framework is that it applies just as well to ordinary curves.

If $E/\mathbb{F}_q$ is ordinary, there is a unique possible quadratic field K given by $K = \mathbb{Q}(\pi_q)$, and we will always use the natural orientation ι on K which sends π_q to the Frobenius endomorphism on E.

In particular, E is always oriented by the order $\mathbb{Z}[\pi_q]$, and the saturation of the orientation is simply given by $R = \mathrm{End}(E)$.

Finally, an oriented isogeny between ordinary elliptic curves with the natural Frobenius orientation is simply an $\mathbb{F}_q$-rational isogeny.

The class group $Cl(\mathcal{O})$ acts freely and transitively on the set of primitive $\mathcal{O}$-oriented curves up to isomorphisms (and Galois conjugacy in the special case where p is inert in $\mathcal{O}$, which can only happen in the supersingular case). A proof of this statement is given by Onuki in [23, Thm. 3.4]. This gives rise to a group action

$$\mathfrak{a} \star (E, \iota) = (E_{\mathfrak{a}}, \iota_{\mathfrak{a}})$$

where $\mathfrak{a}$ is an invertible $\mathcal{O}$-ideal coprime to the conductor of $\mathcal{O}$. To define it concretely, let $E[\mathfrak{a}] := \bigcap_{\alpha \in \mathfrak{a}} \ker \iota(\alpha)$, and denote by $\varphi_{\mathfrak{a}}^E$ the isogeny whose kernel is $E[\mathfrak{a}]$. Then

$$\varphi_{\mathfrak{a}}^E : E \to E_{\mathfrak{a}} = E/E[\mathfrak{a}] \text{ and } \iota_{\mathfrak{a}}(x) = \frac{1}{n(\mathfrak{a})} \varphi_{\mathfrak{a}}^E \circ \iota(x) \circ \hat{\varphi}_{\mathfrak{a}}^E.$$

If we also allow isogenies between $\mathcal{O}$-oriented curves, relaxing the primitive condition, then Colo and Kohel [8] show that there is a volcano structure just like the ordinary case: if E_1 is oriented by $\mathcal{O}$, and $\mathcal{O}_1$ is its saturation in E_1, and we have an order $\mathcal{O}_2$ containing $\mathcal{O}_1$ such that $\mathcal{O}_1$ is of conductor f in $\mathcal{O}_2$, then there is a unique "ascending" isogeny $\phi : E_1 \to E_2$ of degree f such that E_2 is primitively oriented by $\mathcal{O}_2$.

3.1 The Module Structure of the Rational Points of an Oriented Elliptic Curve

In this section we let R be a quadratic imaginary ring, and we assume that we have an orientation $R \to \mathrm{End}(E)$ of an elliptic curve $E/\mathbb{F}_q$. Recall that the orientation is said to be primitive whenever R is saturated in $\mathrm{End}(E)$ (i.e., $R = (\mathrm{End}(E) \otimes_{\mathbb{Z}} \mathbb{Q}) \cap R$), or equivalently $\mathrm{End}(E)/R$ is torsion free. We call $E[n]$ a cyclic R-module if there is some $P \in E[n]$ such that $E[n] = RP = \{\phi(P) : \phi \in R\}$, in which case we call P and R-generator.

Theorem 3.1. *Let n be prime to the characteristic, and assume that the orientation R on E is primitive. Then $E[n]$ is a cyclic R-module.*

In particular, if $P \in E[n]$ is any R-generator, and $\gamma \in R$ is of discriminant $\Delta(\gamma) = f^2 \Delta_R$, then $\mathbb{Z}[\gamma]P$ is of cardinality $n^2/\gcd(n, f)$. So $E[n]$ is a cyclic $\mathbb{Z}[\gamma]$ module if and only if $\gcd(n, f) = 1$. It also follows that the Weil pairing $e_n(P, \gamma P)$ is a root of unity of exact order $n/\gcd(n, f)$.

Proof. The first statement is [20, Theorem 3]. For the second one, if $R = \mathbb{Z}[\omega]$, then we can write $\gamma = a + f\omega$. We have that $P, \omega P$ is a $\mathbb{Z}/n\mathbb{Z}$ basis of $E[n]$, and $\mathbb{Z}[\gamma]P$ is generated by P and $f\omega P$, and the latter is a point of order $n/\gcd(n, f)$. Finally $e_n(P, \gamma P) = e_n(P, \omega P)^f = \zeta^f$ is of order $n/\gcd(n, f)$ since $e_n(P, \omega P)$ is of exact order n. □

We can restate Theorem 3.1 as saying that $E[n]$ is R-cyclic if and only if R is n-locally primitive.

Corollary 3.1. *With the hypothesis of Theorem 3.1, $E[n]$ is isomorphic as an R-module to R/nR.*

Proof. By Theorem 3.1, $E[n]$ is a cyclic R-module, and if P is a generator, $E[n]$ is isomorphic to $R/\mathrm{ann}(P)$ where $\mathrm{ann}(P)$ is the annihilator of P. If $\gamma \in \mathrm{ann}(P)$, then since $\gamma(P) = 0$, R is commutative, and P generates $E[n]$ as an R-module, we find that $\gamma = 0$ on $E[n]$, so γ is divisible by $[n]$. The converse is obvious, so $\mathrm{ann}(P) = nR$, and $E[n] \simeq R/nR$. □

Corollary 3.2. *Let $n = \ell^e$ be prime to the characteristic, and assume that the orientation $R = \mathbb{Z}[\omega_R]$ on E is primitive. Let u be the degree of the field of definition of the geometric points of $E[\ell^e]$. Then $u \leq \ell^{e+1}$ in the ordinary case, and $u \leq \ell^e$ in the supersingular case.*

We can find an R-generator $P \in E[n]$, normalised such that $e_n(P, \omega_R P) = \zeta$, in time $\tilde{O}(\ell + u^2 \log^2 q + \log^{O(1)} q)$ (which can be improved to $\tilde{O}(\ell^{1/2} + u^2 \log^2 q + \log^{O(1)} q)$ in the supersingular case, or if ℓ is not inert in R).

For a general n, if R is n-locally primitive, we can find a basis (P_1, P_2) or an R-generator P of $E[n]$ in time $\tilde{O}(n^4 \log^2 q + \log^{O(1)} q)$ (resp. $\tilde{O}(n^2 \log^2 q + \log^{O(1)} q)$ in the supersingular case), by factorising n and applying the result above.

Proof. Assume for now that $E/\mathbb{F}_q$ is an ordinary curve (this is the harder case). We first explain how to find u. Recall that we can compute the discriminant of π_q acting on E in polynomial time in $\log q$ by point counting algorithms, and that we can use the endomorphism ring algorithm of [25] to also compute the ℓ-saturation R of $\mathbb{Z}[\pi_q]$ in E in polynomial time in $\log q$, so that R is ℓ-locally primitive in E. Now $E[\ell^e] \simeq R/\ell^e$ by Corollary 3.1, and u is the order of $\pi_q \in R/\ell^e$.

Finding u reduces to the computation of the order of elements in $\mathbb{F}_\ell$ if ℓ is ramified or split in R, and in $\mathbb{F}_{\ell^2}$ if ℓ is inert in R, hence costs $\tilde{O}(e \log \ell + \sqrt{\ell})$ or $\tilde{O}(e \log \ell + \ell)$ respectively. In the worst case $u \leq \ell^{e+1}$ (this can be improved to $u \leq \ell^e$ if ℓ is split in R).

Now $\pi_q^u - 1$ is divisible by ℓ^e in R. Write $\pi_q^u - 1 = \ell^e \gamma$, we have $N(\gamma) \leq q^u$. We can sample uniform points in $E[\ell^e]$ as follows. First we sample uniformly random points on $E(\mathbb{F}_{q^u})$ by computing square roots; this costs $\tilde{O}(u^2 \log^2 q)$ [24]. Then we apply γ to get uniformly random points on $E[\ell^e]$. This costs $\tilde{O}(u^2 \log^2 q + \log^{O(1)}(q))$. One then discards points that do not have the required order $n = \ell^e$. Finally, one takes pairs (P_1, P_2) and checks whether the Weil pairing $e_{\ell^e}(P_1, P_2)$ is of full order in μ_{ℓ^e}, in which case (P_1, P_2) is a basis. This requires generating $O(1)$ points and checking $O(1)$ conditions. Hence the overall cost is $\tilde{O}(\log(\ell^e) \log(q^u)) = \tilde{O}(eu \log \ell \log q)$ (because $\mu_{\ell^e} \subset \mathbb{F}_{q^u}$).

Once we have a basis, we know that either P_1 or P_2 is a generator of $E[\ell^e]$ as an R-module, and find it by evaluating ω_R followed by a Weil pairing. The total cost, since $\ell^e < q^u$, is then $\tilde{O}(\ell + u^2 \log^2 q + \log^{O(1)} q)$ to find a basis (P_1, P_2) and an R-generator P of $E[\ell^e]$.

If $E/\mathbb{F}_{p^2}$ is a maximal supersingular curve, then $E(\mathbb{F}_{p^{2u}}) \simeq \mathbb{Z}/(p^u+1) \times \mathbb{Z}/(p^u+1)$, and so u is the order of p^2 modulo n. In particular, $u < n = \ell^e$.

We can also easily sample uniform points in $E[n]$ by sampling them in $E(\mathbb{F}_{q^u})$ and multiplying by the scalar cofactor (no need to use an endomorphism here). This costs $\tilde{O}(u^2 \log^2 q)$ operations. Then we use pairings to extract a basis (P_1, P_2), and then we apply ω_R and pairings again to find an R-generator R. The total cost is thus $\tilde{O}(\ell^{1/2} + u^2 \log^2 q)$ to find a basis (P_1, P_2) of $E[\ell^e]$, to which we need to add an endomorphism evaluation of $\tilde{O}(\log^{O(1)} q)$ to extract an R-generator P.

Finally we mention the case of general n. We simply handle each power of ℓ in turn and apply the Chinese remainder theorem to compute the point. The worst case is when $n = \ell$ is prime, in which case $u = O(n^2)$ and $u^2 = O(n^4)$, giving the stated complexity. □

Example 3.2. Let $E/\mathbb{F}_q$ be an ordinary curve. Specializing to the case $n = \ell$, we have three (well known) possibilities.

The first one is when ℓ splits in $\mathbb{Z}[\pi_q]$ (ℓ is Elkies), $\mathbb{Z}[\pi_q]/\ell\mathbb{Z}[\pi_q] \simeq \mathbb{F}_\ell^2$, π_q acts diagonally, and $u \mid \ell - 1$.

If ℓ is inert in $\mathbb{Z}[\pi_q]$ (ℓ is Atkin), $\mathbb{Z}[\pi_q]/\ell\mathbb{Z}[\pi_q] \simeq \mathbb{F}_{\ell^2}$, so $u \mid \ell^2 - 1$.

Finally, if ℓ is ramified in $\mathbb{Z}[\pi_q]$, then either π_q acts as a diagonal matrix $\begin{pmatrix} \lambda & 0 \\ 0 & \lambda \end{pmatrix}$ (so $u \mid \ell - 1$) on $E[\ell]$, or as $\begin{pmatrix} \lambda & 1 \\ 0 & \lambda \end{pmatrix}$ (so $u \mid \ell(\ell - 1)$). But the diagonal matrix case can happen if and only if $\pi_q - \lambda$ is divisible by ℓ in $\mathrm{End}(E)$, which is equivalent to $\mathbb{Z}[\pi_q]$ being of conductor divisible by ℓ in R. And the second case happens precisely when $\mathbb{Z}[\pi_q]$ is ℓ-locally primitive. Similar analysis holds for $n = \ell^e$, see for instance [22] for some results.

Remark 3.1. As a consequence of the proof above, we remark that in the ordinary case, if $\phi : E_0 \to E_1$ is an ascending oriented isogeny, so that $R_0 \subset R_1$, and u_i denotes the degree of the field of definition of the points in $E_i[n]$, then $u_1 < u_0$, because u_i is the order of π_q in R_i/nR_i.

Definition 3.2. *Let R be a quadratic order of discriminant Δ_R. We define the canonical (up to sign) imaginary element ω_R as follows. If $\Delta_R \equiv 1 \mod 4$, we let $\omega_R = \sqrt{\Delta_R}$; in that case $\mathbb{Z}[\omega_R]$ is of conductor 2 in R. Otherwise, $\Delta_R \equiv 0 \mod 4$, and we let $\omega_R = \sqrt{\Delta_R}/2$; which means $R = \mathbb{Z}[\omega_R]$.*

Corollary 3.3. *Let E be an elliptic curve oriented by R, $n \mid \Delta_R$, and assume that the orientation is n-locally primitive. We let ω_R be as in Definition 3.2.*

Then $E[n, \omega_R]$ is cyclic, and there exists a basis $(P, \omega_R(P))$ of $E[n]$.

Furthermore, if either n is odd, or $n \mid \Delta_R/4$, the matrix of ω_R on this basis is given by

$$\begin{pmatrix} 0 & 0 \\ 1 & 0 \end{pmatrix}$$

In particular, for this n, $E[n, \omega_R] = \omega_R(E[n])$.

Proof. If R is a primitive orientation on E, then $E[\omega_R]$ is cyclic because ω_R is not divisible by any integer in R by construction, so $E[\omega_R]$ cannot contain any subgroups $E[\ell]$. It follows that $E[n, \omega_R]$ is still cyclic if R is just n-locally primitive.

If n is even, then Δ_R has to be divisible by 4, so $R = \mathbb{Z}[\omega_R]$. If n is odd, $\mathbb{Z}[\omega_R]$ might be of index 2 in R, but it is still n-locally primitive.

We deduce that there exists a basis $(P, \omega_R(P))$ of $E[n]$. Since ω_R^2 is either Δ_R or $\Delta_R/4$, under our assumptions $\omega_R^2 = 0 \mod n$, so we get the form of the matrix. □

3.2 The Kernel of an Ascending Isogeny

This section gives new results that allow to compute an ascending isogeny in certain situations. These results extend previous work by Kohel [19] and Ionica and Joux [16].

Kohel [19] pointed out that for ordinary curves E over $\mathbb{F}_q$, if one is on the floor with respect to a prime ℓ, then there is only one $\mathbb{F}_q$-rational ℓ-isogeny from E and it is automatically ascending. This is linked to the fact that the ℓ-torsion is $\mathbb{Z}[\pi_q]$-cyclic for such a curve. Since the cyclic subgroup corresponding to the kernel of the isogeny is fixed by Frobenius, the kernel of the isogeny is $E[\ell, \pi_q - \lambda]$ for some integer λ. In other words, the ascending isogeny has kernel $E[\ell, \pi_q - \lambda]$, and this is a special case of our main result.

Ionica and Joux [16] extended this further, by showing how pairings can, in some situations, identify which subgroup of $E[\ell]$ leads to an ascending isogeny. Their results apply to ordinary curves, and require certain self-pairings to be non-trivial, which does not always hold.

Our result in this section is much more general. It shows that, if we are given a basis of $E[\ell]$, defined over some extension $\mathbb{F}_{q^d}$, we can find the kernel of the ascending isogeny in polynomial time in $\log \ell$ and $d \log q$. It applies in all ordinary settings. It also applies to the oriented supersingular case (provided we have an effective representation of the orientation). It is important to stress that the notion of "ascending" isogeny is not well-defined for supersingular curves in general. Instead, one must consider supersingular curves with an orientation, and it is the orientation that specifies whether or not an isogeny is ascending. This is exactly the information provided by the SCALLOP system.

Theorem 3.2. *Let $\phi : E_0 \to E_1$ be an ascending R-oriented cyclic isogeny of degree d. Let R_i be the saturation of R on E_i, let f be the conductor of R_0 in R_1. Then $f \mid d$, and ϕ factorizes uniquely as $\phi = \phi_2 \circ \phi_1$ where ϕ_1 is a purely ascending isogeny of degree f and ϕ_2 is an R_1-horizontal oriented isogeny.*

Furthermore, for any ω_1 such that $R_1 = \mathbb{Z}[\omega_1]$ (i.e. such that $\Delta_{\omega_1} = \Delta_{R_1}$), $R_0 = \mathbb{Z}[f\omega_1]$ and the kernel of ϕ_1 is given by $E_0[f\omega_1, f]$.

Proof. The unicity of the decomposition comes from the volcano structure.

The form of the kernel is an easy consequence of the general equivalence of categories described in [17,27], which implies that the kernel of the ascending isogeny is given by the action of the conductor ideal. We give a direct proof in a special case that is sufficient for our applications.

Let $\phi_1 : E_0 \to E_0'$ be our strictly ascending f-isogeny. Since ω_1 is an endomorphism on E_0', we have that $f\omega_1$ is 0 on $E_0'[f]$. Since $f\omega_1 \in R_0$ and ϕ_1 is R_0-oriented, if $P \in E_0$ is such that $\phi_1(P) \in E_0'[f]$, then $\phi(f\omega_1 P) = f\omega_1\phi(P) = 0$. In particular, $\ker\phi_1$ contains $(f\omega_1)E_0[f]$.

We also remark that $E_0[f, f\omega_1]$ does not depend on the choice of generator ω_1 for R_1: another generator will be of the form $\omega_1' = a \pm \omega_1$ with $a \in \mathbb{Z}$, so $E_0[f, f\omega_1] = E_0[f, f\omega_1']$. In fact, the argument shows that we can even take $\omega_1' = a + b\omega_1$, of discriminant $\Delta(\omega_1') = b^2\Delta_R$, as long as b is coprime to f.

So we can take ω_1 to be the canonical imaginary element of R_1 from Definition 3.2. Now for simplicity, we assume that f is odd or that Δ_0 is even. In that case, $f\omega_1$ is the canonical imaginary element of R_0, and by Corollary 3.3 there is a basis $(P, f\omega_1 P)$ of $E_0[f]$ and $(f\omega_1)^2$ is zero on $E_0[f]$. It follows that $(f\omega_1)E_0[f] = E_0[f, f\omega_1]$, and so $\ker\phi_1$ contains $E_0[f, f\omega_1]$. But ϕ_1 is of degree f, and the above basis shows that $E_0[f, f\omega_1]$ is too. □

Looking at the proof of the theorem above, we can give another description of a generator of the kernel of ϕ_1, more useful for algorithmic applications:

Corollary 3.4. *With the notations above, assume that R is f-locally primitive in E_0, and let ω_R be the canonical imaginary element from Definition 3.2.*

If either f is odd, or Δ_1 is even, then the kernel K of ϕ_1 is given by $E_0[\omega_R, f]$. If P is any generator of $E_0[f]$ as an R-module, then $\omega_R P$ is a generator of this kernel K.

We can compute the ascending isogeny $\phi_1 : E_0 \to E_0'$ in $\tilde{O}(u^2 \log f \log^2 q + uB_f^{1/2} \log f \log q + \log f \log^{O(1)} q) = \tilde{O}(f^2 \log^2 q + \log f \log^{O(1)} q)$ operations, where B_f is a bound on the largest prime divisor of f, and $u < f$ a bound on the degrees of the field extensions where the points of $(\ker\phi)[\ell_i]$ live, for $f = \prod \ell_i^{e_i}$.

Proof. If $\omega_0, \omega_1, \omega_R$ are the canonical imaginary elements of R_0, R_1, R respectively, then the proof of Theorem 3.2 shows that under our assumptions, we have $\omega_0 = f\omega_1$ and $\omega_R = u\omega_0$ for u coprime to f. From the R module structure of $E_0[f]$, we see that the kernel of ϕ_1, given by $E_0[f, \omega_R]$, is generated by $\omega_R P$ for any R-generator P of $E_0[f]$.

Now, to compute ϕ_1, we will work prime divisor by prime divisor of f (recall that we assumed that we know the factorisation of f_R, hence of f); there are at most $O(\log f)$ such primes. So in what follows we can assume that f is prime.

As in Corollary 3.2, in the ordinary case, we can determine the field extension where the points of the kernel of ϕ_1 are defined by determining the smallest u such that $\pi_q^u = 1$ in $R_0/(f\omega_1, f)$. Since the kernel is of order f, we have $u \mid f-1$. We also remark at this point that, as in Remark 3.1, since the saturation of R in E_0' will contain R_0, the degrees we will subsequently obtain on E_0' when we work prime by prime will be smaller than on E_0.

Now if $E_0[f](\mathbb{F}_{q^u})$ is cyclic, it is automatically equal to $\ker\phi_1$ since the kernel is rational. Sampling a point in $E_0(\mathbb{F}_{q^u})$ and multiplying by the (scalar) cofactor now gives a uniform point in the kernel.

The second case is that $E_0[f](\mathbb{F}_{q^u})$ is the full f-torsion. We can apply Corollary 3.2 to sample a generator P of $E_0[f]$ as an R-module. Then, in the situation of Corollary 3.4, we can apply ω_R to P to get a generator of $\ker \phi_1$.

Finally, computing ϕ_1 from a generator of the kernel can be done in $\tilde{O}(f^{1/2} u \log q)$ operations as shown in [2]. All in all, we can compute ϕ_1 in $\tilde{O}(u^2 \log f \log^2 q + u f^{1/2} \log q + \log^{O(1)} q)$ operations.

The supersingular case works as above, except that this time u is automatically also the degree of the field of definition of the full f-torsion. □

Remark 3.2. The only case not covered by Corollary 3.4 is when Δ_1 is odd and $f = 2f'$ is even. Then we can write ϕ_1 as an f_0-ascending isogeny $E_0 \to E_0''$ with R' the saturation of R in E_0'', of discriminant $4\Delta_1$, followed by a 2-isogeny $E_0'' \to E_0'$. We can apply Corollary 3.4 to the isogeny $E_0 \to E_0''$. And by Theorem 3.2, since $R' = \mathbb{Z}[\frac{1+\sqrt{\Delta_1}}{2}]$, the kernel of the 2-isogeny $E_0'' \to E_0'$ is given by $E_0''[1 + \sqrt{\Delta_1}, 2]$.

4 Recovering an Oriented Isogeny of Known Degree

In this section we study the following problem: let R be a quadratic imaginary order. Let $\phi : E_0 \to E_1$ be an R-oriented cyclic isogeny of known degree d between elliptic curves defined over $\mathbb{F}_q$. Our goal is, given R, E_0, E_1 and d, to recover ϕ. Following [14] we are going to do this by trying to determine ϕ on $E[n]$ for suitable n. In this paper the key tools are self-pairings.

We recall from Sect. 3 that this encompasses two cases. If $E_0/\mathbb{F}_q$ is ordinary, we can take $R = \mathbb{Z}[\pi_q]$ and we will always use the natural Frobenius orientation on E_0, E_1. This is the case we will consider for the (ordinary) computational isogeny problem. We remark that point counting algorithms give Δ_R in polynomial time in $\log q$. The other case is when E_0, E_1 are maximal supersingular elliptic curves defined over $\mathbb{F}_{p^2}$. In that case, ϕ is also automatically rational over $\mathbb{F}_{p^2}$. This is the case we will consider for the SCALLOP group action.

Let R_i be the saturation of R in $\mathrm{End}(E_i)$, and Δ_i the discriminant of R_i. We assume that ϕ is "ascending", meaning that $R_0 \subset R_1$, and we let $f = [R_1 : R_0]$ be the conductor of R_0 in R_1. We will say that ϕ is purely ascending if $f = d$. We remark that ϕ is automatically R_0-oriented: if $\gamma \in R_0$, there is some multiple $m\gamma$ in R, so since ϕ is R-oriented we have $[m]\gamma \circ \phi = \phi \circ [m]\gamma = [m]\phi \circ \gamma$. Dividing by $[m]$, we get $\gamma \circ \phi = \phi \circ \gamma$.

We will make the following assumptions for our complexity analysis:

- First, for simplicity, we will assume that $\log \Delta_R$ is polynomial in $\log q$. This is automatic in the ordinary case, since $|\Delta_{\pi_q}|$ is at most $4q$; and is also the case in all currently proposed instances of a supersingular oriented group action. All statements in this section are still valid in the general case if we replace the $O(\log q^{O(1)})$ in the complexity statements by $O((\log q + \log \Delta_R)^{O(1)})$.

- The orientation R is effective on both E_0 and E_1, meaning that we can evaluate any endomorphism $\gamma \in R$ on a point P using a polynomial in $\log N(\gamma)$ arithmetic operations over the field of definition of P.
  We can refine this as follows: we fix $\omega_R = \sqrt{\Delta_R}/2$ if $\Delta_R \equiv 0 \mod 4$, and $\omega_R = (1+\sqrt{\Delta_R})/2$ if $\Delta_R \equiv 1 \mod 4$. In both cases $N(\omega_R) \leq |\Delta_R|$, and if $\gamma = a + b\omega_R$, $a, b \leq \sqrt{2N(\gamma)}$. If we have an efficient representation of ω_R, then evaluating γ on P requires the evaluation of ω_R, scalar multiplication by $[a], [b]$ and a sum. This thus costs $O(\log(|a|) + \log(|b|) + \log^{O(1)} \Delta_R) = O(\log(N(\gamma)) + \log^{O(1)} \Delta_R)$ arithmetic operations over the field of definition of P.
  As an aside, by adapting point counting algorithms, given an efficient representation of ω_R we can recover Δ_R in polynomial time. From now on, for our complexity analysis, whenever we pick up a generator ω_R of R, we will always assume that ω_R is a generator like the above, such that $N(\omega_R) = O(\Delta_R)$. This prevents silly situations like using $a + \omega_R$ for a very large a.
- As a consequence, the orientations by R_0 and R_1 are also effective. If γ_0 is an element of R_0, then some multiple n_0 of γ_0 is in R, hence can be efficiently evaluated (since $n_0 \mid \Delta_R$ cannot be too large). Now to evaluate γ_0 on a point P, we would like to find a point P' such that $P = [n_0]P'$; then $\gamma_0 P = (n_0\gamma_0)P'$. Such a point can be very expensive to compute for large, non-smooth n_0 since we would require a large extension field. Instead, Robert shows in [25, Sect. 2.3] how to efficiently divide an endomorphism by using higher dimensional isogenies.
  If γ_0 is any generator of R_0, we can thus find an efficient representation of γ_0, and use this efficient representation to evaluate the other endomorphisms. Finding this efficient representation involves the evaluation of an endomorphism of R, but this is a precomputation that only needs to be done once.
  Similar techniques also allow us to push forward the R-representation through an explicit R-isogeny $\phi' : E_0 \to E_0'$, by computing the image by ϕ' of $(P, \omega_R P)$ for several points P. This allows to find an efficient representation of the R-orientation on E_0' through a polynomial in $\log \Delta_R$ number of calls to the evaluation of ϕ'.
- Finally, we will assume that the factorisation of Δ_R is known. As a consequence, we can write $\Delta_R = \Delta f_R^2$ where Δ is a fundamental discriminant and the factorisation of f_R is known. We also have $\Delta_0 = \Delta f_0^2$ and $\Delta_1 = \Delta f_1^2$, with $f_0 = f f_1$. Then thanks to [25], we can recover f_0 and f_1, hence R_0 and R_1 in polynomial time in $\log \Delta_R + \log q$.

4.1 The General Strategy

We will adapt the strategy of [14], which consists in guessing the image of ϕ on suitable subgroups of E_0, typically the image on the ℓ-torsion $E_0[\ell]$ for several small primes ℓ, and then reconstructing ϕ using a higher dimensional isogeny.

There are a number of different ways to reduce the number of guesses required to determine ϕ on $E_0[\ell]$ and we give a high level overview of them now.

- *The case of Elkies primes.* We can adapt the strategy of Sect. 2.3 to the general oriented case as follows. If $\ell \nmid \Delta_R$ splits as $\ell = \mathfrak{f}_1\mathfrak{f}_2$, then $E_0[\mathfrak{f}_i]$ is cyclic of order ℓ with generator P_i. Likewise, $E_1[\mathfrak{f}_i]$ is cyclic of order ℓ with generator Q_i. Since ϕ is R-oriented, $\phi(E_0[\mathfrak{f}_i]) \subset E_1[\mathfrak{f}_i]$, so we have $\phi(P_i) = a_i Q_i$, for some unknown scalars a_1, a_2 modulo ℓ. The Weil pairing gives us some information on a_1, a_2: we have $e_\ell(\phi(P_1), \phi(P_2)) = e_\ell(P_1, P_2)^d = e_\ell(Q_1, Q_2)^{a_1 a_2}$. So, provided discrete logarithms are easy in the multiplicative group μ_ℓ of ℓ-th roots of unity in $\overline{\mathbb{F}}_q$, we can compute c such that $e_\ell(Q_1, Q_2) = e_\ell(P_1, P_2)^c$, and we know that $a_1 a_2 = d/c$ modulo ℓ.
  In the special case that $\ell \mid d$, then either a_1 or a_2 is 0, and $E_0[\mathfrak{f}_1]$ or $E_0[\mathfrak{f}_2]$ is in the kernel of ϕ. So we recover part of the kernel of ϕ up to a choice. Otherwise, $\ell \nmid d$, and there are $\ell - 1$ possibilities for a_1, and then a_2 is completely determined by a_1.
- *Using self-pairings.* If $\ell \mid \Delta_R$, and R is a ℓ-locally primitive orientation on E_0, E_1, then we follow the insight of [5] that there exists a self-pairing that gives the image of ϕ up to a sign on a cyclic subgroup of $E_0[\ell]$. In [20, § 8], Macula and Stange give a more efficient construction of this self-pairing (see in particular [20, Example 3]), and we use a slight variant of their approach.
- *Using sesquilinear self-pairings.* If $\ell \nmid \Delta_R$, then $E[\ell]$ is a cyclic R-module, and Macula and Stange show in [20, Theorem 6] that there exists an R-sesquilinear self-pairing. While this gives less information than the previous case of self pairing, this still allows them to reduce the number of choices for the action of ϕ on $E_0[\ell]$ to $\ell - 1$ (if ℓ splits) or $\ell + 1$ (if ℓ is inert), see [20, Theorem 8 and 9]. In particular, this subsumes the previous special case of Elkies primes.
- The remaining case, at least if $R = R_0$ which we can assume from our hypotheses, is when $\ell \mid f$. In that case, R is not an ℓ-locally primitive orientation on E_1, and we cannot follow the pairing approach. Since we are speaking at the moment about small ℓ, this case is treated in [13,14] as an easy case, because one can ascend in the volcano efficiently using the methods in those papers. We have shown in Sect. 3.2 an improved method to compute $(\ker \phi)[\ell]$ directly.

In summary, we will show that the self-pairings approaches of [5,20], which were mainly used in the horizontal case, work just as well for the ascending case. The main difference compared to [20, Theorem 9] (which treats the case $\ell \nmid \Delta_R$) and [20, Theorem 11] (which treats the case $\ell \mid \Delta_R$) is that we also treat the case when ℓ divides d. This gives more flexibility in our choice of ℓ.

We also give in Sect. 4.2 a simplified and unified construction of "self-pairings", which only requires the standard Weil pairing (but is heavily inspired by the sesquilinear pairings used in [20]). By contrast, in [20] two different pairing constructions are given, depending on whether $\ell \mid \Delta_R$ or not. Our approach is similar to the use of the distortion map in pairing based cryptography. We refer to the end of Sect. 4.2 for a more detailed comparison of our approaches with the approach of [5,20]. We also remark that the use of the distortion map was also explored in [12] as a way to determine whether an ℓ-isogeny was descending.

Finally, since we will apply self-pairings to large-ish ℓ, we will present some precise complexity statements that will be needed for the analysis in Sect. 5 and Sect. 6.

4.2 Pairings and Distortion Maps

We can reduce the computation of ϕ to the computation of the purely ascending isogeny ϕ_1 and an horizontal isogeny ϕ_2. We might not want to compute the purely ascending isogeny ϕ_1 fully, especially if the conductor f has large prime factors.

Section 3.2 can be seen as recovering partial information on the action of ϕ on $E[n]$ when $n \mid f$. But in this section, we focus on the case n coprime to f. More precisely, we explain how we can combine pairings with the orientation R to recover partial information about the image of ϕ on a basis of $E[n]$.

Recall that a pairing is a bilinear and non-degenerate map. Let E be an elliptic curve over $\mathbb{F}_q$ and m an integer co-prime to q. The most well-known and familiar pairing in elliptic curve cryptography is the Weil pairing

$$e_m : E[m] \times E[m] \to \mu_m \subseteq \bar{\mathbb{F}}_q^*$$

where μ_m is the multiplicative group of order m.

An important property of pairings, which has been widely used in isogeny cryptography and cryptanalysis, is that if $\phi : E_0 \to E_1$ is an isogeny of elliptic curves of degree d and $P, Q \in E_0[m]$ then

$$e_m(\phi(P), \phi(Q)) = e_m(P, Q)^d$$

where the first pairing is being computed on E_1 and the second pairing on E_0. Sometimes this property is used to learn information about the degree of an unknown isogeny. Other times, and this is how we use it, knowing d, one can use the above property to constrain the possible values for $\phi(P)$. These approaches have been used in a number of papers, including [5,14,20].

As mentioned in the introduction, an important set of techniques about self-pairings was given in [5], however in some contexts (including in our application) this requires a large field extension to be computed. Macula and Stange [20] showed a different approach that enables to obtain the same results without enlarging the fields over which one is working. Of particular importance for us will be [20, Theorem 8], which treats the case when n is coprime to Δ_R (this is a hidden hypothesis which comes from the invocation of Theorem 6 and Theorem 11 of [20] which treats the case when $n \mid \Delta_R$). Since [20] treats sesquilinear pairings and other advanced topics, the proof of this theorem may not be easily accessible to some researchers. Hence we take the opportunity to give an elementary proof of the result in a special case, and also note that the condition of supersingularity is not required.

Here is our version of "self-pairings".

Theorem 4.1. *Let $\phi : E_0 \to E_1$ be an R-oriented cyclic isogeny of degree d, let $n = \ell^e$ be an integer coprime to d, and assume that R is n-locally primitive on E_0 and E_1. Assume that we are also given $P_0 \in E_0[n], P_1 \in E_1[n]$ cyclic R-generators, and write $\phi(P_0) = \gamma(P_1)$ for some unknown endomorphism $\gamma \in R/nR$.*

Then we can compute $v = \deg(\gamma) \pmod n$ in time $\tilde{O}(ue \log \ell \log q + u'e\sqrt{\ell} \log q)$, where u is the degree of the field of definition of $E_0[\ell^e]$, and $u' \mid u$ the degree of the field of definition of μ_{ℓ^e}.

Proof. Take ω_R a generator of R, of norm bounded by $|\Delta_R|$ so that we can evaluate it efficiently. Since ϕ is oriented, it commutes with ω_R. Furthermore, since $RP_0 = E_0[n]$ it follows that $\{P_0, \omega_R(P_0)\}$ generates $E_0[n]$ and so $e_n(P_0, \omega_R(P_0))$ is an exact n-th root of unity. Similarly, $e_n(P_1, \omega_R(P_1))$ is an exact n-th root of unity. (The endomorphism ω_R here is performing the role of a "distortion map".) Suppose $\phi(P_0) = \gamma(P_1)$.

By compatibility of the Weil pairing with isogenies, we have

$$\begin{aligned} e_n(P_1, \omega_R(P_1))^{\deg(\gamma)} &= e_n(\gamma(P_1), \gamma\omega_R(P_1)) \\ &= e_n(\phi(P_0), \omega_R(\phi(P_0))) \\ &= e_n(P_0, \omega_R(P_0))^{\deg(\phi)}. \end{aligned}$$

Thus by computing these two pairings in $\tilde{O}(ue \log \ell \log q)$ and solving the discrete logarithm problem in $\tilde{O}(u'e\sqrt{\ell} \log q)$, one can compute $\deg(\gamma)$ modulo the order of $e_n(P_0, \omega_R(P_0))$, which is n. □

By combining Corollary 3.2 and Theorem 4.1, we see that sampling P_0, P_1 dominates the complexity:

Corollary 4.1. *With the notations above, we can sample cyclic R-generators $P_0 \in E_0[n], P_1 \in E_1[n]$, and compute $\deg \gamma \pmod n$ where $\gamma(P_1) = \phi(P_0)$ in $\tilde{O}(\ell + u^2 \log^2 q + \log^{O(1)} q)$.*

Let $\gamma = a + b\omega_R \in R \subseteq \operatorname{End}(E_1)$ be such that $\phi(P_0) = \gamma(P_1)$. Then $\deg(\gamma) = N(\gamma) = a^2 + ab \operatorname{Tr}(\omega_R) + b^2 N(\omega_R)$.

From now on, we will suppose that n is coprime to d, since the non-coprime case is easier and will be treated in Sect. 4.3, so that $v = \deg(\gamma) \neq 0 \pmod n$.

For our applications it will not be enough to know $\deg(\gamma)$. We will need to know the integers a and b, because we want to actually compute $\phi(P_0)$ by computing $\gamma(P_1)$. (From this we will also be able to compute $\phi(Q_0)$ where $\{P_0, Q_0\}$ is a basis for $E_0[n]$, by taking $Q_0 = \omega_R(P_0)$ and $\phi(Q_0) = \omega_R(\phi(P_0))$.) To find these integers we need to solve the conic equation

$$x^2 + xy \operatorname{Tr}(\omega_R) + y^2 N(\omega_R) = v \pmod n. \quad (2)$$

In practice it is usually simpler to separately solve the conic modulo each prime dividing n, and then use Hensel lifting and the Chinese remainder theorem to compute the set of solutions. We remark that this conic is of discriminant $\Delta(\omega_R) = \Delta_R$.

There are two cases of relevance in our paper. The first is when n is coprime to Δ_R and the conic is non-singular. In this case there are $O(n)$ solutions. To find solutions one calculates a rational parameterization of the conic and hence one can easily enumerate all solutions. The second case is when $n \mid \Delta_R$ and the conic degenerates, typically as the union of lines. In this case, as long as n does not have too many distinct prime factors, we can obtain a lot of useful information. We explain in more detail below.

The Case of a Non-degenerate Conic. We suppose here for simplicity that $n = \ell$ is a prime, and that $\ell \nmid \Delta_R$.

By assumption, we know there exists an endomorphism γ, hence a solution of Eq. (2) for $x, y \in \mathbb{Z}/\ell\mathbb{Z}$. Thus, the homogenised conic $X^2 + XY\,\mathrm{Tr}(\omega_R) + Y^2 N(\omega_R) - vZ^2$ is isomorphic to $\mathbb{P}^1$ over $\mathbb{Z}/\ell\mathbb{Z}$.

At infinity, $Z = 0$, we have 2 or 0 rational solutions $(X : Y : 0)$ depending on whether Δ_R is a square or not modulo ℓ. We deduce that if ℓ splits in R, the conic has $\ell - 1$ solutions (x, y), and if ℓ is inert in R, the conic has $\ell + 1$ solutions (x, y).

The Case of a Degenerate Conic. In this subsection, we assume that $n \mid \Delta_R$.

Theorem 4.2. *Let ω_R be the canonical imaginary element of R as defined in Definition 3.2. Let $n \mid \Delta_R$ be coprime to d, and such that $n \mid \Delta_R/4$ if n is even. Let $P_0 \in E_0[n]$ be a cyclic generator, and same for P_1. Let $Q_0 = \omega_R(P_0)$ and $Q_1 = \omega_R(P_1)$. Then $\phi(Q_0) = \alpha Q_1$, where $\alpha^2 = v \mod n$, where v is computed using pairings as in Theorem 4.1.*

Proof. As in Corollary 3.3, if n is even then $R = \mathbb{Z}[\omega_R]$, otherwise n is odd and $\mathbb{Z}[\omega_R]$ may be of index 2. In both cases, $\mathbb{Z}[\omega_R]/n\mathbb{Z}[\omega_R] = R/nR$, so we may assume that $\gamma = x + y\omega_R$ is such that $\phi(P_0) = \gamma(P_1)$. Now since ω_R is imaginary, the norm is $N(\gamma) = x^2 + \Delta_{\omega_R} y^2$. And by hypothesis, $n \mid \Delta_{\omega_R}$. So our conic degenerates to $x^2 = v \mod n$. The solutions are given by (α, y) for any α such that $\alpha^2 = v$.

We now recall that $\omega_R^2 = 0$ modulo n by Corollary 3.3. So if $\gamma = \alpha + y\omega_R$, then $\phi Q_0 = \phi\omega_R P_0 = \omega_R \phi P_0 = \omega_R(\gamma P_1) = \omega_R(\alpha P_1 + y\omega_R P_1) = \alpha\omega_R P_1 = \alpha Q_1$. In particular, the image of ϕ on Q_0 only depends on the possible solutions α. □

We remark that the equation $\alpha^2 = v$ has at most 2^{m+1} solutions, where m is the number of distinct prime factors of n. More precisely, since there exists at least one solution by hypothesis, there are exactly 2^{m-1}, 2^m or 2^{m+1} solutions according to whether $v_2(n) = 1$, $v_2(n) = 0, 2$, or $v_2(n) > 2$ respectively.

This means that while the image of Q_0 is fairly constrained (if n has not too many prime factors), the conic itself actually has $\approx 2^m n$ solutions, rather than just $O(n)$ (because it is not irreducible). We will call this version of self-pairing the cyclic version, because it gives information on a cyclic subgroup of $E_0[n]$.

Comparison with Self-pairings. As mentioned in [20], the sesquilinear pairings used in that article can be seen as a neat way to package together the pairing data $e_n(P,Q), e_n(\omega_R P, Q), e_n(P, \omega_R Q), e_n(\omega_R P, \omega_R Q)$ together into an R-sesquilinear Weil pairing. (In [20] Macula and Stange look at the R-sesquilinear Tate pairing rather than the sesquilinear Weil pairing, but the sesquilinear Weil pairing works similarly and was constructed in [29]).

Unfortunately, this sesqulinear pairing becomes degenerate when $n \mid \Delta_R$, so to handle this situation, in [20] the authors look at $(P,Q) \mapsto (t_n(\omega_R P, Q), t_n(P,Q))$ where t_n is the Tate pairing. Theorem 4.1 is almost the same, except that using the Weil pairing e_n instead of the Tate pairing allows us to only use $e_n(P, \omega_R Q)$, because the Weil pairing is alternating, and to use the same construction both for $n \mid \Delta_R$ and n coprime to Δ_R. We remark that the same phenomena was present in [6], where the authors remarked that it is often more convenient to use the Weil pairing than the Tate pairing to evaluate the "character" associated to an horizontal isogeny. This is not surprising: as explained in [5, § 6.2], this character evaluation can be done through self-pairings computation.

Finally, still for the case $n \mid \Delta_R$, the authors of [5] construct a self-pairing on the cyclic subgroup $E_0[n, \omega_R]$, using an "oriented" version of the Tate pairing [5, § 5.1]. By the discussion of [5, § 5.3], we see that a way to compute these self-pairings is via the distorted pairing $e_n(P, \omega_R Q)$ from Theorem 4.1. We refer to Appendix A for a generalisation of this result.

4.3 Putting Everything Together

In this section, we summarise the torsion information we can guess on ϕ, and how to use it to reconstruct ϕ. Recall that we assume $d = \deg(\phi)$ is known and is large, and we are choosing suitable $n = \ell^e$, where ℓ is a small prime, and attempting to deduce candidates for ϕ on $E_0[n]$.

We have developed tools for a number of cases.

1. The case $n = \ell$ is a prime dividing d. In this article, we will be interested in the case where ℓ furthermore divides the conductor f. Then we can use Sect. 3.2 to compute the associated ascending ℓ-isogeny $\phi_1 : E_0 \to E_0'$. We have $\phi = \phi_2 \circ \phi_1$, and we are reduced to recovering $\phi_2 : E_0' \to E_1$ of degree d/ℓ. We remark that the case where n divides d but not f is standard: we can write as above $\phi = \phi_2 \circ \phi_1$ where this time ϕ_1 is an horizontal ℓ-isogeny, and there are at most two such isogenies.
2. The case n is coprime to Δ_R and d. Then by Sect. 4.2, we have $O(n)$ possible choices for the action of ϕ on $E_0[n]$, which we can recover in $\tilde{O}(\ell + u^2 \log^2 q + eu \log \ell \log q + \log^{O(1)} q) = \tilde{O}(n^4 \log^2 q + \log^{O(1)} q)$. Here, u is the degree of the field extension of the points in $E_0[n]$. Indeed, this dominates both the cost of finding the conic equation Eq. (2), and the cost of finding all solutions of this conic.
3. The case $n \mid \Delta_R$, but with n coprime to d (hence also to f). For simplicity, we will assume that $n \mid \Delta_R/4$ if n is even. Then by Sect. 4.2, we have $O(2^m)$

possible choices for the action of ϕ on a specific point Q of $E_0[n]$ (with the notation of Theorem 4.2, the image by ω_R of an R-generator of $E_0[n]$), where m is the number of distinct prime divisors of n. These choices can be computed in $\tilde{O}(\ell + u^2 \log^2 q + eu \log \ell \log q + \log^{O(1)} q) = \tilde{O}(n^4 \log^2 q + \log^{O(1)} q)$.

We now explain how to use the torsion information from cases 2 and 3, which are the main cases of interest since d is coprime to n for these cases and so we are not directly getting information about the kernel of ϕ.

The method in [14] was based on the Kani attack [3,21,26], which needed the full torsion information (as provided by case 2). Namely, knowing the torsion information of ϕ on the n-torsion for $n^2 > 4d$ is enough to recover ϕ. This involves computing an n^2-isogeny $\Phi : E_0^r \times E_1^r \to E_0^r \times E_1^r$ in higher dimension $g = 2r$. The higher dimensional isogeny Φ is built out of an $(d, n^2 - d)$-isogeny diamond, involving the isogeny $\phi \mathrm{Id}_r$ with $r = 1, 2, 4$ and auxiliary isogenies ϕ', ρ, ρ' in dimension r of polarised degree $d, n^2 - d, n^2 - d$ respectively. Then Φ will be an isogeny of polarised degree n^2 in dimension $2r$.

The reason we need to move from dimension 1 to r is to be able to compute ψ, ψ' of the correct degree efficiently. Namely, if $n^2 - d = \sum_{i=1}^{r} a_i^2$ is the sum of $r = 1$, 2 or 4 squares, we can build the auxiliary isogenies in dimension r by using suitable $r \times r$ integer matrices. We know by Lagrange's theorem that we can always find a sum of 4 squares (and finding an explicit decomposition is efficient), so we can always work in dimension $g = 8$.

The Kani construction is well-documented in many papers so we do not give all the details. We remind the reader that $\ker \Phi$ may be computed as

$$\{(\hat{\phi}(P), -\rho'(P)) : P \in E_1^r[n^2]\}$$

where we view $\hat{\phi} : E_1^r \to E_0^r$ as a diagonal map, and where $\rho' : E_1^r \to E_1^r$ is coming from the matrix associated with the sum of squares. To compute $(\ker \Phi)[\ell]$ it suffices to know a basis (P, Q) for $E_0[\ell]$ and the values $(\phi(P), \phi(Q)) \in E_1[\ell]$ and everything else follows.

Finally, we mention that in practice, Φ is not computed directly, rather we write it as $\Phi = \Phi_2 \circ \Phi_1$ where Φ_i is of polarised degree n and we compute the two isogenies Φ_1 and $\tilde{\Phi}_2$ from $E_0^r \times E_1^r$ and $E_1^r \times E_0^r$ respectively and meet in the middle. It suffices to know ϕ on $E_0[n]$ to be able to compute the kernel of both these higher dimensional isogenies.

Remark 4.1. To handle case 3 we use an approach that was presented in an invited talk at ANTS in 2024 by Castryck [4]. At a high level, the result is that one can recover an unknown isogeny of degree d given interpolation data coming from a group of size $O(d)$.

We briefly recall the ideas from [4], which apply in a simplified form for our case 3. Reusing the notation and arguments from Theorem 4.2, we have points P_0, Q_0, P_1, Q_1 such that $\phi(P_0) = \gamma P_1$, for some $\gamma = \alpha + y\omega_R$, where α is constrained by an equation $\alpha^2 = v \pmod{n}$, but y can be arbitrary. From this we know that $\alpha Q_1 = \alpha \omega_R(P_1) = \phi(Q_0)$, but $\phi(P_0) = \alpha P_1 + y Q_1$. The idea is to compose ϕ with an isogeny $\psi : E_1 \to E_2$ of kernel $\langle Q_1 \rangle$, so that

$$\psi(\phi(P_0)) = \psi(\alpha P_1 + y Q_1) = \alpha \psi(P_1).$$

We remark that $\ker \psi = E_1[n, \omega_R]$, so ψ is R-oriented, and does not depend on α. Now consider $\phi_2 = \psi \circ \phi$, of degree nd. Then we know that $\phi_2(P_0) = \psi(\alpha P_1 + y\omega_R P_1) = \alpha\psi(P_1)$. Since P_0 is an R-generator of $E_0[n]$, this allows to recover how ϕ_2 acts on the full n-torsion of $E_0[n]$.

In conclusion, we now have an isogeny ϕ_2 of degree dn and we know how ϕ_2 acts on the full group $E_0[n]$. We can then proceed with existing techniques.

All in all, let n_1 be the product of all prime powers we use for case 2, and n_2 the product of all prime powers we use for case 3. Let $n = n_1 n_2$. We build a n_2-isogeny $\psi : E_1 \to E_2$ using the method in the previous paragraph to obtain a $n_2 d$-isogeny $\phi_2 = \psi \circ \phi : E_0 \to E_2$ for which we know the action on the full $E_0[n]$-torsion. We need $n_1^2 n_2 > 4d$ to be able to recover ϕ_2 hence ϕ, via a $n_1^2 n_2^2$-isogeny $\Phi : E_0^r \times E_2^r \to E_0^r \times E_2^r$ in dimension $g = 2r$ (see Fig. 6). Here the dimension r will depend on whether we can find a solution with $r = 1, 2, 4$ to $n_1^2 n_2^2 - n_2 d = \sum_{i=1}^r a_i^2$. Because of the common factor n_2, we require n_2 to be a sum of two squares to be able to work in dimension $g = 4$ (i.e., $r = 2$). In general we will need to work with $r = 4$ and so dimension 8 Abelian varieties.

Remark 4.2. Let E_0 be an ordinary elliptic curve over $\mathbb{F}_q$ with $q+1-t$ points and let $\mathrm{End}(E_0)$ have discriminant Δf^2. If t is odd then $\Delta f^2 = t^2 - 4q \equiv 1 \pmod 4$ and so $|\Delta| \equiv 3 \pmod 4$. So we know Δ is divisible by a prime congruent to 3 modulo 4. So a bad case is when t is odd and $|\Delta|$ is a prime.

Furthermore, while ψ does not depend on the torsion possibilities, we need to compute Φ for all the possibilities of the torsion we have. As explained before, in practice we compute two $n_1 n_2$-isogenies Φ_1, Φ_2 from $E_0^r \times E_2^r$. As a technical detail: to find the kernel of Φ_2 we need to know how $\tilde{\phi}_2$ acts on the n-torsion; this can be done from the knowledge of how ϕ_2 acts on the n-torsion through pairings and DLPs, because $\tilde{\phi}_2$ is the adjoint of ϕ_2 for the Weil pairing.

The complexity of the computation of the isogenies ψ, Φ itself will depend on the dimension where Φ lives, and if $n = \prod \ell_i^{e_i}$, of the largest prime ℓ_i and the degrees u_i of the field generated by the $\ell_i^{e_i}$-torsion points. More precisely, by [28, Lemma 5.7], if $n = \prod_{i=1}^a \ell_i^{e_i}$, computing an n-isogeny in dimension g can be done in time $\tilde{O}(ae\ell^g u \log q)$, where ℓ (resp. e) is a bound on the ℓ_i (resp. e_i), and u is a bound on the $lcm(u_i, u_j)$ where u_i is the degree of the field extension defined by the points of the $\ell_i^{e_i}$-torsion (so $u \leq n^2$).

The choice of prime power ℓ^e to use in practice will be a delicate balance between the size of ℓ, the degree of the field extension where the ℓ^e-torsion is defined, and the number of possibilities, mainly whether we are in case 2 or 3.

Remark 4.3. There is a non-trivial way to save time: rather than computing Φ from scratch from every possible choice of torsion information, we remark that we can reuse part of our construction of Φ.

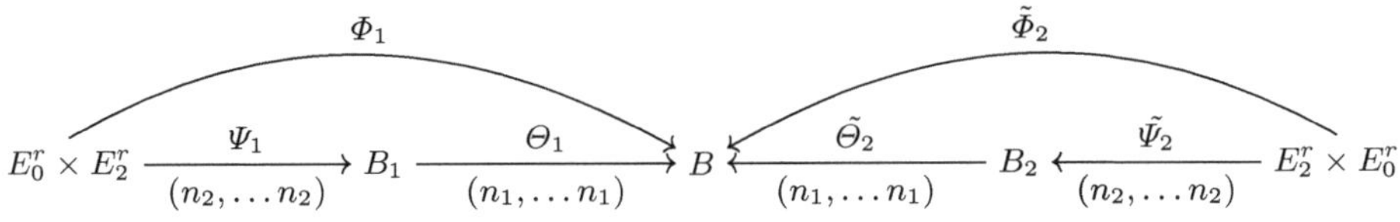

Fig. 6. This isogeny diagram corresponds to the explanation of how to address case 3. We use our knowledge of the $E_0[n]$ torsion group to compute the (probably non-smooth) $(n_2, \dots n_2)$-isogeny and guess the remaining (smooth) $(n_1, \dots n_1)$-isogeny ϕ_2 using a meet-in-the-middle computation (as detailed in Remark 4.3).

First, we can assume that we are given the torsion information of $\phi_2 : E_0 \to E_2$ in terms of matrices acting on basis elements (P_0, Q_0), (P_1', Q_1') of the $\ell_i^{e_i}$-torsion. We remark that the pairing information from Sect. 4.2 already gives this information on E_1, we have P_i a cyclic R-generator, and $Q_i = \omega_R P_i$, and the torsion information is expressed as a constraint on an endomorphism $\gamma \in R/\ell_i^{e_i}$, which we can recast as a matrix. We propagate this information through ψ, this involves sampling a new basis; we may pick P_1' a cyclic generator of $E_2[\ell_i^{e_i}]$ and let $Q_1' = \omega_R P_1'$ to simplify the computations. Then $\psi(P_1') = cQ_1'$, and we determine c by pairings and DLPs as in Sect. 4.2.

Now we have several choices of matrices for the action of ϕ_2 on $\ell_1^{e_1}$. We pick one choice, and use it to build the $\ell_1^{e_1}$-component of the kernel of Φ_1, Φ_2. We push the other $\ell_i^{e_i}$-basis points (using a product basis); this is where the compositum of the field of definition of the $\ell_1^{e_1}$ and $\ell_i^{e_i}$ torsion comes in. Then we make a choice of matrix for the action on $\ell_2^{e_2}$, determine the kernel of the next $\ell_2^{e_2}$ higher dimensional isogenies, and so on.

The key remark is that if we change our choice of matrix for $\ell_m^{e_m}$, we need to recompute the subsequent $\ell_i^{e_i}$ isogenies for $i \geq m$, but we can keep the ones already computed for $i < m$.

We illustrate this with a small example: assume that we want to use $n_1 = \ell_1 \ell_2$ with ℓ_1 split and ℓ_2 inert, and $n_2 = \ell_3 \ell_4$ a product of two different primes. We have $\ell_1 - 1$ possible choices for the action of ϕ on $E_0[\ell_1]$, $\ell_2 + 1$ possible choices for the action of ϕ on $E_0[\ell_1]$, and 2 possible choices for the action of ϕ on a subgroup of order ℓ_i of $E_0[\ell_i]$ for $i = 3, 4$. We can choose in which order to treat our primes, and it makes sense to pick them up by decreasing size. So suppose for instance that $\ell_3 > \ell_1 > \ell_2 > \ell_4$. Then via the above strategy, to compute all possibilities for Φ_1, we will compute in total $2(\ell_1 - 1)(\ell_2 + 1)2$ ℓ_4-isogenies, $2(\ell_1 - 1)(\ell_2 + 1)$ ℓ_2-isogenies, $2(\ell_1 - 1)$ ℓ_1-isogenies, and 2 ℓ_1-isogenies.

We have all the tools to bound the cost of recovering ϕ.

Theorem 4.3. *Let the notation and hypothesis be as at the beginning of Sect. 4. Specifically, let $\phi : E_0 \to E_1$ be an ascending R-oriented isogeny of degree d. Let $m \mid \Delta_R$ be a factor of Δ_R. Assume that R is m-locally primitive on E_0, and let $m = \prod \ell_i^{e_i}$. Denote the number of square roots of* 1 *modulo m by T, B a bound on the largest prime divisor ℓ_i of m, and u a bound on the $\mathrm{lcm}(u_i, u_j)$, where u_i is the degree of the field of definitions of the points of $E_0[\ell_i^{e_i}]$.*

Then we can recover $\phi : E_0 \to E_1$ *in time* $\tilde{O}((TuB^8 + T\sqrt{d/m})(\log q + \log d)^{O(1)})$.

Proof. First, dividing m by 2 or 4 if necessary, we can assume that $m \mid \Delta_R/4$. We can also assume that we know the factorisation of m, since we know the one of Δ_R.

If m is not coprime to d, we use standard tools such as case 1.

Following the notation used above, we take $n_2 = m$, and for n_1 a B'-powersmooth number coprime to Δ_R and of size $\Theta(\sqrt{d/m})$. We can always take a smoothness bound B' polynomial in $\log q + \log d$.

We compute the torsion information on the n_1 and n_2 torsion using Sect. 4.2. There are T possibilities for the n_2-torsion by Theorem 4.2, and $\tilde{O}(n_1)$ possibilities for the action on the n_1-torsion. By Corollaries 3.2 and 4.1 the cost of recovering this information is not the dominating step.

Computing the n_2-isogeny $\psi : E_1 \to E_2$ as in Remark 4.1 takes $\tilde{O}(Bu)$ field operations.

We apply the strategy of Remark 4.3 by computing the n_2-isogeny first, followed by the n_1-isogeny. We assume that we are in the worst case and that we need to work in dimension 8. The first n_2-isogeny costs $\tilde{O}(uB^8 \log^2(n_2) \log q)$. We also need to push the torsion information on the n_1-torsion, which costs $\tilde{O}(u'B^8 \log n_2 \log n_1 \log q)$. Here u' is a bound on the degree of the compositum field of the $\ell_i^{e_i}$-torsion and the $\ell_j^{e_j}$ torsion for $\ell_i \mid n_2$ and $\ell_j \mid n_1$, so since n_1 is B'-powersmooth, we have $u' \leq u(B')^2$. We need to perform these computations T times.

Then we need to compute the remaining n_1-isogeny and decide if we meet in the middle. This costs $\tilde{O}(B'^4 B'^8 \log^2(n_1) \log q)$. We need to do this computation $\tilde{O}(Tn_1)$ times. This gives us our final complexity result. ◻

Remark 4.4.

- A bound on u is given by $u = \min(O(m^2), O(B^4))$ in the ordinary case and $u = \min(O(m), O(B^2))$ in the supersingular case.
- In practice for our applications, the term $TuB^8 + T\sqrt{d/m}$ will be large enough to absorb the $\log q + \log d$ part into the $\tilde{O}$ factor, and we will use $\tilde{O}(TuB^8 + T\sqrt{d/m})$ as our complexity.
- If m is a sum of two squares, then heuristically we can work in dimension 4, and replace the term TuB^8 by TuB^4.
- If $\phi : E_0 \to E_1$ is an R-oriented cyclic descending isogeny of degree d, we can follow the same approach, *except* for case 2: ℓ is a prime dividing the conductor. Indeed, in that case, $K = (\ker \phi)[\ell]$ is a kernel of a strictly descending isogeny, but there are between $\ell - 1$ and $\ell + 1$ descending isogenies, so many more possibilities for K than in the case of a purely ascending isogeny when K is unique. Of course, the better strategy is to reconstruct the dual $\tilde{\phi} : E_1 \to E_0$ instead, which is ascending.

5 Improving the Computational Isogeny Problem When the Conductor Is Large

In this section we apply the techniques from Sect. 4 to the ordinary isogeny problem. In particular, we will show how to use the pairings from Sect. 4.2 to improve the algorithm from [14]. Our main application is the case of volcanoes with a small crater.

5.1 Improved Computation of an Ascending Isogeny

Let E_0 and E_1 be ordinary elliptic curves over $\mathbb{F}_q$ with $q+1-t$ points. Let $t^2-4q = f^2\Delta$, where Δ is a fundamental discriminant and $f>1$. Suppose $\mathrm{End}(E_1)$ has discriminant $\Delta_1 = \Delta f_1^2$, $\mathrm{End}(E_0)$ has discriminant $\Delta_0 = \Delta f_0^2$ with $f_0 = Nf_1$. We want to recover the ascending $\mathbb{F}_q$-rational N-isogeny $\phi : E_0 \to E_1$ of degree $N|f$. Since ϕ is $\mathbb{F}_q$-rational we have $\phi \circ \pi_q = \pi_q \circ \phi$, where π_q denotes the q-power Frobenius maps on E_0 and E_1, so ϕ is $\mathbb{Z}[\pi_q]$-oriented. In this section we will neglect factors polynomial in $\log q$.

Galbraith in [14, Theorem 2] gives an algorithm that can compute ϕ in $\tilde{O}(N^{1/2})$ operations over $\mathbb{F}_q$. Our first improvement concerns a heuristic assumption used in the algorithm. As explained in Sect. 2.3, a key task of the 2024 algorithm is to guess $\phi(P_0), \phi(Q_0)$ for a suitable basis P_0, Q_0 of $E_0[\ell]$. This was done in [14] by choosing P_0 and Q_0 to be Elkies primes (i.e., eigenvectors for the q-power Frobenius). But by Theorem 4.1, we can use inert primes just as well as split primes. This removes the need for an assumption about the distribution of Elkies primes.

Our second main improvement will come from cyclic self-pairings (or from our point of view, the use of degenerate conics), coming from a factor $m \mid \Delta_1$. The details of the self-pairings algorithm is outlined in Algorithm 2.

In that algorithm we restrict for simplicity to the case where m is odd and $\gcd(m,f)=1$. This is because in that case we can directly use the Frobenius π_q to get the self-pairing information. Indeed, define $\tau = 2\pi_q - t$, which will be interpreted depending on the context as lying in $\mathrm{End}(E_0)$ and $\mathrm{End}(E_1)$. Note that $\tau = \phi \circ \alpha \circ \hat{\phi}$, where $\alpha \in \mathrm{End}(E_0)$ is the endomorphism corresponding to $\sqrt{\Delta}$. We also have that $\mathrm{Tr}(\tau) = 2\,\mathrm{Tr}(\pi_q) - 2t = 0$ and $\Delta(\tau) = \tau^2 = t^2 - 4q$, $N(\tau) = 4q - t^2$. In particular τ is, up to a factor 2, our canonical imaginary element for $\mathbb{Z}[\pi_q]$ from Definition 3.2. We can thus apply Sect. 4.2, using $\omega_R = \tau$. Since $e_m(P, \tau Q) = e_m(P, \pi_q Q)^2$, the situation is simplified because we can simply evaluate the Frobenius rather than a more general endomorphism of the form τ/b. We refer to Theorem 4.2 for the general case, when m may have a common factor with f.

We then illustrate how to use the self-pairing information to recover ϕ in Algorithm 3. This algorithm calls two functions $\mathsf{Guess}()$ and $\mathsf{Kani}()$.

As already explained, we need to compute $(\ker \Phi)[\ell]$ for various primes ℓ, and this is fully determined by a basis (P, Q) for $E_0[\ell]$ and the corresponding image $(P', Q') \in E_2[\ell]$ under $\psi \circ \phi$.

In our applications we will have a point $P_0 \in E_0[\ell]$ such that $RP_0 = E_0[\ell]$ and a point $P_1 \in E_1[\ell]$ such that $RP_1 = E_1[\ell]$. We know that $\phi(P_0) = \gamma(P_1)$ for some $\gamma = a + b\omega_R$, but we don't know (a, b). Indeed, we will extend this to $P_2 \in E_2[\ell]$ such that $\psi \circ \phi(P_0) = \gamma(P_2)$, using the fact that ψ is also R-oriented. The function Guess() will produce a list of candidates for the unknown coefficients (a, b) in γ. To be precise, it will take as input torsion information as a sequence of data $(P_0, P_2) \in E_0[\ell] \times E_2[\ell]$, and it will output a list of items, each of which is a tuple of candidates for the correct $(a, b) \in (\mathbb{Z}/\ell\mathbb{Z})^2$.

The notation A_ℓ represents the data needed for the Kani construction. For example, $A_{n_2} = (n_2, (P_0, Q_0), (S, 0)))$ represents the information that (P_0, Q_0) is a basis for $E_0[n_2]$ and that $\psi \circ \phi(P_0) = S$ and $\psi \circ \phi(Q_0) = 0$.

The function Kani() takes as input the torsion data $\ell, (P_0, P_2) \in E_0[\ell] \times E_2[\ell]$ and a candidate (a, b) and constructs some prefix of the map Φ of degree $(\ell, \ell, \ldots, \ell)$, by computing the ℓ-part of $\ker \Phi$. An extra detail is that we will apply this to an abelian variety B_1 that is already part-way along the path of Φ. This is handled by calculating the image of $\psi \circ \phi(P_0) = (a + b\omega_R)(P_2)$ on B_1 by working with the images of the points P_0 and P_2 on B_1. We will also abuse notation and use the function Kani() for computing the ℓ-part of $\ker \tilde{\Phi}$ corresponding to the right hand side of Fig. 6.

Algorithm 3 puts everything together. It describes how to recover an ascending isogeny between two fixed elliptic curves by making use of the partial information gained from self-pairings and then using Guess() and Kani() to recover the remaining part.

Applying Theorem 4.3 to our situation, we obtain the following complexity.

Proposition 5.1. *Let E_0 and E_1 be ordinary elliptic curves over $\mathbb{F}_q$. Suppose* $\mathrm{End}(E_1)$ *has discriminant Δ_1 and* $\mathrm{End}(E_0)$ *has discriminant $\Delta_0 = \Delta_1 N^2$. Suppose there is an N-isogeny $\phi : E_0 \to E_1$ (in other words E_1 is directly above E_0 in the volcano). Suppose Δ_1 has a large divisor $m = q^a$ which has $O(\log(\log(q)))$ distinct prime factors.*

Then we can recover ϕ using

$$\max\Big(\tilde{O}(q^{10a}), \tilde{O}(q^{(1-3a)/4})\Big)$$

operations over $\mathbb{F}_q$.

Proof. In the notation of Theorem 4.3, we have $d = N$, and since $N^2|\Delta| = O(q)$, we have $N = O(q^{(1-a)/2})$. We also have $m = O(q^a)$ since $m \mid \Delta$, so $\sqrt{d/m} = O(q^{(1-3a)/4})$. We also take the trivial upper bounds $B = m$ and $u = m^2$. Finally $T = O(\log q)$ because of our assumptions on the number of distinct prime factors of m. Then we can bound the term TuB^8 by $\tilde{O}(q^{10a})$, and the term $T\sqrt{d/m}$ by $\tilde{O}(q^{(1-3a)/4})$. □

Remark 5.1. It remains to address the question of whether $|\Delta_1|$ contains a large divisor m with $O(\log \log q)$ distinct prime factors. Unfortunately this may not

Algorithm 2: Torsion recovery via self-pairings

Input : Ordinary elliptic curves E_0, E_1 over $\mathbb{F}_q$ such that $[\mathrm{End}(E_0) : \mathrm{End}(E_1)] = N$, an odd integer m such that $m \mid \Delta_1$, $(m, f) = 1$;

Output : $S_0 \in E_0(\mathbb{F}_q), \{S_j\}_{j=1}^T$ such that $\phi(S_0) = S_j$ for one $j \in [1, T]$.

1 Sample $P_i \in E_i[m]$ that is a generator for the $\mathbb{Z}[\pi_q]$-module $E_i[m]$ for $i = 0, 1$;
2 Define $\tau = 2\pi_q - t$ and set $Q_i = \tau(P_i)$ for $i = 0, 1$;
3 Compute the following pairings: $T_i = e_m(P_i, Q_i), i = 0, 1$;
4 Compute all possible $\{a_j\}_{j=1}^T$ such that $(T_1)^{a_j^2} = (T_0)^N$;
5 **return** $\big((P_0, Q_0, P_1, Q_1), \{a_j\}_{j=1}^T\big)$;

always be the case. If $|\Delta_1|$ is a primorial then divisors of it, even of size only $|\Delta_1|^{1/2}$, will have too many distinct prime factors.

However, it is well-known (see Theorem 430 of Sect. 22.10 of Hardy and Wright [15]) that the average number of distinct prime factors of integers up to X is $\log\log(X)$. Hence the required condition on m applies to most integers Δ_1 and our claim holds on average.

We also consider the *very* special case that Δ_1 has a large powersmooth factor in the following corollary.

Proposition 5.2. *Let notation and hypotheses be as in Proposition 5.1. In addition, suppose the discriminant Δ_1 has a factor $m \mid \Delta_1$ of size q^a which is B-powersmooth. Denote the number of square roots of* 1 *modulo m by T.*

Then we can recover $\phi : E_0 \to E_1$ in time

$$\max\Big(\tilde{O}(TB^{12}), \tilde{O}(T \cdot q^{(1-3a)/4})\Big)$$

Proof. This is immediate from Theorem 4.3 using the bound $u = B^4$ and the analysis from Proposition 5.1. □

5.2 Volcanoes with Small Crater

Let E_0 and E_1 be ordinary elliptic curves over $\mathbb{F}_q$ with $q + 1 - t$ points where $t^2 - 4q = f^2\Delta$ where Δ is the fundamental discriminant, and $|\Delta| = q^a$ with $a > 0$ small. We want to find an isogeny between them, but this time we do not assume that E_0 is directly below E_1.

If E_0 is on the crater and E_1 on the floor then the approach in Galbraith [14] has complexity $\tilde{O}(h_0 f^{1/2})$ operations over $\mathbb{F}_q$, where h_0 is the class number of Δ. Since $f = O(q^{(1-a)/2})$ and $h_0 = \tilde{O}(\sqrt{|\Delta_0|}) = \tilde{O}(q^{a/2})$, we get that $\tilde{O}(h_0 f^{1/2}) = \tilde{O}(q^{a/2} q^{(1-a)/4}) = \tilde{O}(q^{(1+a)/4})$. The approach in [14] dealt with the cases when

Algorithm 3: Vertical isogeny recovery in volcanoes with small crater

Input : Ordinary elliptic curves E_0, E_1 such that $[\mathrm{End}(E_0) : \mathrm{End}(E_1)] = N$

Output : A representation of $\phi : E_0 \to E_1$

Choose $n_2 \in \mathbb{Z}$ dividing the discriminant Δ that satisfies the conditions in Algorithm 2;

Choose t small distinct primes $\ell_1, \ldots \ell_t$ and a (small) integer s such that $N < 3^s \cdot n_2 \cdot \prod_{i\in[1,t]} \ell_i^2 < 2N(c + 2t\log(t))^2)$ for a small constant c;

Set $n_1 = 4 \cdot 3^{\lceil s/2 \rceil} \ell_1 \cdots \ell_t$;

Write $3^s n_2^2 (\ell_1 \cdots \ell_t)^2 - n_2 N > 0$ as a sum of squares;

Run Algorithm 2 to get $(P_0, Q_0, P_1, Q_1, \{a_j\}_{j=1}^T)$ such that $\phi(Q_0) = a_j Q_1$ for one of the $j \in [1, T]$;

Compute $\psi : E_1 \to E_2$ with kernel $\langle Q_1 \rangle$;

Set up torsion information $S_\ell = (P_{0,\ell}, P_{2,\ell}) \in E_0[\ell] \times E_2[\ell]$ for each ℓ_i, and also $S_{3^{\lceil s/2 \rceil}} \in E_0[3^{\lceil s/2 \rceil}] \times E_2[3^{\lceil s/2 \rceil}]$;

for $j \in [1, T]$ **do**

- Set $A_{n_2} = (n_2, (P_0, Q_0), (a_j \psi(P_1), 0)))$;
- Compute $\Psi_1, B_1 \leftarrow \mathsf{Kani}(E_0^4 \times E_2^4, A_{n_2})$; `// The partial Kani isogenies`
- Compute the kernel of the dual isogeny to Ψ_1 and use Kani to compute the image B_2 of the isogeny $\tilde{\Psi_2} : E_2^4 \times E_0^4 \to B_2$;
- Compute $S'_\ell = \Psi_1((P_0, Q_0, S_j))$ and $S''_\ell = \tilde{\Psi_2}((P_0, Q_0, S_j))$ for each $i = 1, \ldots t$; `// Push the torsion basis`
- Let $M = \tilde{O}(n_1)$ be the number of possible guesses for the images of ϕ on n_1-torsion;
- **for** $i \in [1, M]$ **do**
  - Compute bases $A_{3^{s/2}}, A_{\ell_1}, \ldots, A_{\ell_t}$ from $\mathsf{Guess}(S_{3^{\lceil s/2 \rceil}}, \{S_{\ell_1}, \ldots S_{\ell_t}\})[i]$;
  - $\Theta_1, B \leftarrow \mathsf{Kani}(B_1, n_1, A_{3^{s/2}}, A_{\ell_1}, \ldots, A_{\ell_t})$;
  - Use Kani to compute the corresponding $\tilde{\Theta_2}$ from B_2 and call the codomain B';
  - `// Test if the two Kani isogenies have met in the middle:`
  - **if** $B \cong B'$ **then**
    - **return** $\Psi_2 \circ \Theta_2 \circ \Theta_1 \circ \Psi_1$ as a representation of ϕ;

return $\perp$;

E_0 and E_1 are not on the crater by descending to the floor and solving the isogeny problem in $\tilde{O}(q^{1/4})$ time.

We can improve these results using the results of Sect. 5.1, in the case when Δ has $O(\log\log(q))$ prime factors.

Theorem 5.1. *Assume that $|\Delta| = q^a$ has $O(\log\log(q))$ prime factors, and that $a < 1/41$. Then we can find a connecting isogeny between E_0 and E_1 in time $\tilde{O}(q^{(1-a)/4})$.*

Proof. We will show that we can climb up from E_0 to the crater in $\tilde{O}(q^{(1-a)/4})$ when a is small enough. Doing the same for E_1, we can then solve the isogeny problem in the crater in time $\tilde{O}(h_0^{1/2})$ where $h_0 = \tilde{O}(|\Delta|^{1/2}) = \tilde{O}(q^{a/2})$ is the number of curves on the crater, which is the class number of $\mathbb{Q}(\sqrt{\Delta})$. So $\tilde{O}(h_0^{1/2}) = \tilde{O}(q^{a/4})$, and the dominating step is the climbing up phase (since a is small).

We let $m = |\Delta|/4$ if $4 \mid \Delta$, and $m = |\Delta|$ otherwise. We still have $m = \Theta(q^a)$. If we knew the curve E_0' on the crater directly above E_0, we could apply Proposition 5.1 to climb up in time $\tilde{O}(q^{(1-3a)/4})$, when $a < 1/43$ (for larger a, the dominating complexity becomes $\tilde{O}(q^{10a})$). Since we do not know E_0', we need to test all the curves on the crater, for a total time of $\tilde{O}(h_0 q^{(1-3a)/4}) = \tilde{O}(q^{(1-a)/4})$. This is the dominating complexity over $\tilde{O}(q^{10a})$ when $a < 1/41$. □

Remark 5.2. If all primes dividing $f = O(q^{(1-a)/2})$ are smaller than $q^{a'}$ then one can compute ascending isogenies from E_0, E_1 to the crater in $\tilde{O}(q^{2a'})$ operations and solve the isogeny problem in the crater in $\tilde{O}(|\Delta|^{1/2}) = \tilde{O}(q^{a/2})$ operations, for a total cost of $\tilde{O}(q^{2a'} + q^{a/2})$. So Theorem 5.1 is mainly interesting in the case where f has at least one large enough prime divisor.

6 A Special Case Attack Attempt on SCALLOP

In what follows we outline how the general approach from Sect. 4 might potentially be leveraged to attack the SCALLOP group action when the fundamental discriminant has a large smooth factor. This indicates that any cryptographic protocol using this group action should exclude (almost) smooth discriminants from their parameter selection.

SCALLOP [11] is a group action on oriented supersingular elliptic curves, initially proposed with the purpose of improving upon the CSIDH group action. There have since been two variants: SCALLOP-HD [7] and PEARL-SCALLOP [1], that improve upon some subroutines and parameter choices but rely on similar security assumptions. Our attack will apply in the special case that the discriminant has a large smooth factor, so we will focus on PEARL-SCALLOP, whose parameter generation uses larger fundamental discriminants.

We consider the SCALLOP class group action by a non-maximal order $\mathcal{O} \subset K$ of discriminant $\Delta = \Delta_0 f^2$. Suppose we are given two oriented curves (E_0, ι_0) and $(E_\mathfrak{a}, \iota_\mathfrak{a})$ on the floor. We would like to recover an ideal $\mathfrak{a}$ in $Cl(\mathcal{O})$ such that $\mathfrak{a} \star (E_0, \iota_0) = (E_\mathfrak{a}, \iota_\mathfrak{a})$. In this section, we only look at classical attacks.

Standard Attack. The standard classical attack for this problem is direct meet-in-the-middle [1, Sect. 3.5]. Since the class group is of order $\sqrt{|\Delta|}$ this gives a complexity of $\tilde{O}(|\Delta^{1/4}|) = \tilde{O}(|\Delta_0|^{1/4} f^{1/2})$ field operations. So for a security parameter, λ, we can expect $\log|\Delta| = 4\lambda$ in order to avoid this attack.

The "Climbing Up" Approach. We consider the same attack from Galbraith [14] in the ordinary case, that uses the Kani machinery to climb up to the crater from each curve, and then use meet-in-the-middle on the crater to join the paths (see the figure below).

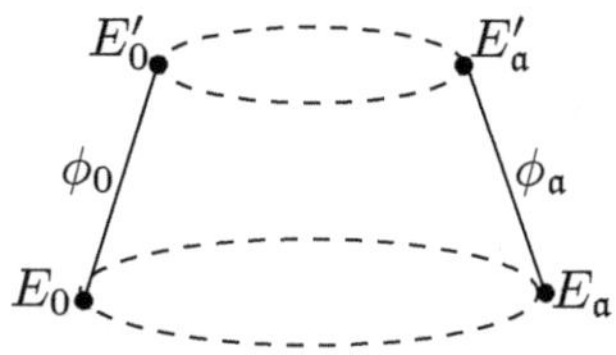

This is the approach we improved in Sect. 5.1 by using self pairings.

Recall, this approach involves guessing which curve on the crater is "directly above" the curves, i.e. the curve $E'_{\mathfrak{a}}$ such that $[\mathrm{End}(E'_{\mathfrak{a}}) : \mathrm{End}(E_{\mathfrak{a}})] = f$. Note that we usually already know E'_0. For brevity we outline how to recover $\phi_{\mathfrak{a}}$, though recovering ϕ_0 follows symmetrically. There are $\tilde{O}(\sqrt{\Delta_0})$ curves that lie on the crater. For each of these candidate curves, we must then guess the action of $\phi_{\mathfrak{a}}$ on some torsion points. Galbraith [14] shows that this guessing requires a complexity of $O(\sqrt{f})$; so in total the approach requires $(|\Delta_0|f)^{1/2}$ field operations to complete.

From here, we compute a meet-in-the-middle search on the crater to get an ideal mapping $E'_0 \to E'_{\mathfrak{a}}$. This requires $\tilde{O}(|\Delta_0|^{1/4})$ field operations. Let $\mathcal{O}_0$ be the maximal order of $\mathcal{O}$. So far we have recovered an ideal $\mathfrak{b}$ such that $\mathfrak{b}\star E'_0 = E'_{\mathfrak{a}}$, but where $[\mathfrak{b}]$ is in $Cl(\mathcal{O}_0)$ instead of $Cl(\mathcal{O})$. Notice that we have an exact sequence

$$0 \to G \to Cl(\mathcal{O}) \to Cl(\mathcal{O}_0) \to 0,$$

where $G := \ker(Cl(\mathcal{O}) \to Cl(\mathcal{O}_0))$ is of order $\Theta(f)$ that has a very explicit description (see Theorem 7.24 and Equation (7.25) of Cox [9]).

Taking an arbitrary preimage of $[\mathfrak{b}]$ in $Cl(\mathcal{O})$, say $[\mathfrak{b}']$, we may still be off from our target ideal by an element in G. With yet another meet-in-the-middle on the G action we recover this element with a complexity of $O(f^{1/2})$ operations.

Thus, to recover the ascending isogeny, compute the meet-in-the-middle on the crater, and recover the necessary element of G, the final complexity is

$$\tilde{O}(|\Delta_0|^{1/2}f^{1/2}) + \tilde{O}(|\Delta_0|^{1/4}) + \tilde{O}(f^{1/2}) = \tilde{O}(|\Delta_0|^{1/2}f^{1/2})$$

field operations. Note, this complexity is worse than the direct meet-in-the-middle attack from before.

Self-pairings Attack. We can follow the same idea as the "Climbing Up" approach, but hope to gain some savings using self-pairings. In the following theorem, we compute the cost of recovering the ascending isogeny as outlined in Algorithm 3.

Theorem 6.1. *Fix an imaginary quadratic order K and a non-maximal order $\mathcal{O} \subset K$ with discriminant $\Delta = \Delta_0 f^2$, where Δ_0 is a fundamental discriminant.*

Further, suppose Δ_0 has a B-smooth factor m. Denote the number of square roots of 1 *modulo m by T.*

Let (E_0, ι_0) and $(E_{\mathfrak{a}}, \iota_{\mathfrak{a}})$ be two oriented curves such that there exists an ideal $\mathfrak{a} \in Cl(\mathcal{O})$ such that $\mathfrak{a} \star (E_0, \iota_0) = (E_{\mathfrak{a}}, \iota_{\mathfrak{a}})$.

Then we can recover $\mathfrak{a}$ in

$$\tilde{O}\left(T|\Delta_0|^{1/2}B^{10} + T(f|\Delta_0|/m)^{1/2}\right)$$

field operations.

Proof. First, suppose we are given two supersingular curves $E_{\mathfrak{a}}, E'_{\mathfrak{a}}$ over $\bar{\mathbb{F}}_p$ such that $[\mathrm{End}(E'_{\mathfrak{a}}) : \mathrm{End}(E_{\mathfrak{a}})] = f$.

Then recovering the isogeny $\phi_{\mathfrak{a}} : E_{\mathfrak{a}} \to E'_{\mathfrak{a}}$ can be done in $\tilde{O}(T(B^{10} + f^{1/2}m^{-1/2})\log(q)^{O(1)})$ field operations by Theorem 4.3 (here we bound u by B^2).

Since we must also guess which curve $E'_{\mathfrak{a}}$ on the crater is above $E_{\mathfrak{a}}$, we must again multiply the complexity above by the number of guesses, which is $\tilde{O}\sqrt{|\Delta_0|}$. This gives a complexity of $\tilde{O}(T|\Delta_0|^{1/2}B^{10} + T(f|\Delta_0|/m)^{1/2})$ field operations.

From here, we have the same task as before of computing the precise ideal $\mathfrak{b}$, requiring yet another meet-in-the-middle computation in the action G. This costs $\tilde{O}(|\Delta_0|^{1/4} + f^{1/2})$ field operations, which is negligible compared to the climbing up phase. □

Let us assume that m has $O(\log\log q)$ distinct factors, so that $T = O(\log q)$. The complexity becomes $\tilde{O}(|\Delta_0|^{1/2}B^{10} + (f|\Delta_0|/m)^{1/2})$ field operations.

We see that for this method to be better than the direct attack on the floor which costs $\tilde{O}(|\Delta_0|^{1/4}f^{1/2})$, we need:

- $|\Delta_0|$ to be not too large compared to f so that $|\Delta_0|^{1/4}B^{10} \ll f^{1/2}$.
- m large enough compared to Δ_0, so that $m \gg |\Delta_0|^{1/2}$, but with few enough prime factors, which forces m not to be too large either: $m \le B^{O(\log\log q)}$. In particular, we need $|\Delta_0|^{1/2} \ll B^{O(\log\log q)}$.

These make for tight restrictions on the choice of Δ_0 and f even when $|\Delta_0| \ll f$.

For instance, if $B^{10} = f^{1/2}|\Delta_0|^{-1/4-\epsilon}$, and $m = |\Delta_0|^{1/2+\epsilon}$ (with few enough prime factors), we obtain a complexity of $O(f^{1/2}|\Delta_0|^{1/4-\epsilon})$.

In the most favourable scenario for our attack, Δ_0 has a large smooth divisor $m = \prod \ell_i$, such that each ℓ_i is congruent to 1 modulo 4 so that we can work in dimension $g = 4$ rather than 8, and $\ell_i \mid p+1$ so the ℓ_i-torsion is already rational. The reason we need ℓ_i congruent to 1 modulo 4 to be able to work in dimension 4 is that this allows us to write a suitable multiple m' of m as a sum of two squares, which allows us to build a suitable m'-isogeny in dimension 2 given by a matrix of integers. But for SCALLOP we also have access to endomorphisms in $\mathcal{O}$, not just integers, and we can build an m'-isogeny in dimension 2 given by $\begin{pmatrix} \gamma_1 & \overline{\gamma_2} \\ -\gamma_2 & \overline{\gamma_1} \end{pmatrix}$ as long as we find $\gamma_1, \gamma_2 \in \mathcal{O}$ such that $m' = N(\gamma_1) + N(\gamma_2)$. This can allow us to relax the conditions on the ℓ_i. The total complexity of the attack would then be $\tilde{O}(|\Delta_0|^{1/2}B^4 + (f|\Delta_0|/m)^{1/2})$.

We finish by an example showing that our attack does not apply to the public SCALLOP parameter sets.

Example 6.1.

- The original version of SCALLOP uses $|\Delta_0| = O(1)$. This is too small to be of use, since it means that m is $O(1)$ and the self-pairings do not provide enough information.
- For $\lambda = 128$ bits of classical security, the authors of PEARL-SCALLOP use a discriminant $\Delta = \Delta_0 f^2$ of 512 bits, where Δ_0 has 6 factors, $\log(|\Delta_0|) = 256$, and $\log(f) = 128$. Here Δ_0 is too large compared to f for our attack to apply: we would have too many curves on the crater to try.
- For $\lambda = 256$ bits of security the authors of PEARL-SCALLOP [1, Sect. 4.1] suggest a discriminant of 1024 bits where Δ_0 has 4 factors, $\log(|\Delta_0|) = 258$, and $\log(f) = 390$.
  The self-pairings attack described above would give an improvement over state-of-the-art for a smoothness bound B such that
  $$|\Delta_0|^{1/2} B^{10} < |\Delta_0|^{1/4} f^{1/2}.$$
  This gives $\log B < 13$ (of course this is a back of the envelope computation, the exact value would depend on the exact hidden factors). Their Δ_0 contains a 2^{16}-smooth factor m of size $\log(m) \approx 33 \ll 258/2$. So Δ_0 is not smooth enough for our attack to apply either.

A Tate-Weil-Cartier Pairings

The goal of this section is to revisit the construction of self pairings from [5].

Consider a commutative diagram of isogenies of abelian varieties:

$$\begin{array}{ccc} A_1 & \xrightarrow{\sigma_1} & A_2 \\ \downarrow{\scriptstyle \psi_1} & & \downarrow{\scriptstyle \psi_2} \\ B_1 & \xrightarrow{\sigma_2} & B_2 \end{array}$$

We know that the Weil-Cartier pairing [10, Ch. 11] is non degenerate: $e_{\sigma_1} : A_1[\sigma_1] \times \hat{A}_2[\hat{\sigma}_1] \to \mathbb{G}_m$, where we denote by $A_1[\sigma_1]$ the kernel of σ_1. By analogy with the standard Tate pairing, we can define a Tate-Weil-Cartier pairing by restricting to the subgroup $A_1[\sigma_1, \psi_1] = A_1[\sigma_1] \cap A_1[\psi_1]$ of $A_1[\sigma_1]$.

Theorem A.1. *There is a well defined Tate-Weil-Cartier pairing:*

$$T_{\psi_1}^{\sigma_1} : A_1[\sigma_1, \psi_1] \times \hat{A}_2[\hat{\sigma}_1] / \hat{\psi}_2(\hat{B}_2[\hat{\sigma}_2]) \to \mathbb{G}_m$$

which can be computed for $P_1 \in A_1[\sigma_1, \psi_1]$ *and* $Q_2 \in \hat{A}_2[\hat{\sigma}_1]$ *by*

$$T_{\psi_1}^{\sigma_1}(P_1, Q_2) = e_{\sigma_1}(P_1, Q_2) = e_{\psi_1}(P_1, \hat{\sigma}_2 Q') \quad (3)$$

where $\hat{\psi}_2 Q' = Q$.

Proof. Let

$$A_1[\sigma_1,\psi_1]^\perp = \{P \in \hat{A}_2[\hat{\sigma}_1] : e_{\sigma_1}(Q,P) = 1 \ \forall\ Q \in A_1[\sigma_1,\psi_1]\}$$

be the orthogonal of $A_1[\sigma_1,\psi_1]$ in $\hat{A}_2[\hat{\sigma}_1]$ for the Weil-Cartier pairing. We then have a well defined pairing:

$$A_1[\sigma_1,\psi_1] \times \hat{A}_2[\hat{\sigma}_1]/A_1[\sigma_1,\psi_1]^\perp \to \mathbb{G}_m$$

It is not hard to see that $\hat{\psi}_2(\hat{B}_2[\hat{\sigma}_2])$ is in this orthogonal, because $e_{\sigma_1}(P_1,\hat{\psi}_2 Q_2) = e_{\psi_2\circ\sigma_1}(P_1,Q_2) = e_{\sigma_2\circ\psi_1}(P_1,Q_2) = e_{\sigma_2}(\psi_1 P_1,Q_2) = 1$, since $\psi_1(P_1) = 0$ when $P_1 \in A_1[\sigma_1,\psi_1]$. Hence $T_{\psi_1}^{\sigma_1}$ is well defined.

We can use the compatibility of the Weil-Cartier pairings with isogenies to prove Eq. (3). Indeed, we have $\hat{\psi}_1\hat{\sigma}_2 Q' = \hat{\sigma}_1\hat{\psi}_2 Q' = 0$, so $e_{\psi_1}(P_1,\hat{\sigma}_2 Q')$ is well defined. And we compute: $e_{\psi_1}(P_1,\hat{\sigma}_2 Q') = e_{\sigma_2\psi_1}(P_1,Q') = e_{\psi_2\sigma_1}(P_1,Q') = e_{\sigma_1}(P_1,\hat{\psi}_2 Q') = e_{\sigma_1}(P_1,Q_2)$. □

Remark A.1.

- The non degenerate pairing on the left $A_1[\sigma_1,\psi_1] \times \hat{A}_2[\hat{\sigma}_1]/\hat{\psi}_2(\hat{B}_2[\hat{\sigma}_2]) \to \mathbb{G}_m$ is also non degenerate on the right whenever $\hat{\psi}_2(\hat{B}_2[\hat{\sigma}_2])$ is the full orthogonal, e.g., when $\#\hat{B}_2[\hat{\sigma}_2] = \#\hat{A}_2[\hat{\sigma}_1]$ and $\#\hat{B}_2[\hat{\sigma}_2,\hat{\psi}_2] = \#A_1[\sigma_1,\psi_1]$.
- The proof of Eq. (3) shows that $Q' \in B_2[\sigma_2\psi_1]$ and that $T_{\psi_1}^{\sigma_1}(P_1,Q_2) = e_{\sigma_2\psi_1}(Q') = e_{\sigma_2\psi_1}(Q')$ which shows that $T_{\psi_1}^{\sigma_1}$ is also induced by the Weil-Cartier pairing $e_{\sigma_2\psi_1}$, which highlight the symmetric role of the ψ_i,σ_i.
- Still by the compatibility of the Weil-Cartier pairing and isogenies, whenever σ_1 is a d-isogeny, that is we have a contragradient isogeny $\tilde{\sigma}_1$ satisfying $\sigma_1 \circ \tilde{\sigma}_1 = \tilde{\sigma}_1 \circ \sigma_1 = [d]$, we have: $e_{\sigma_1}(P,Q) = e_d(P,Q') = e_d(P',Q)$ where $\sigma_1(Q') = Q$ and $\tilde{\sigma}_1(P') = P$.

Example A.1.

- Take $E_1/\mathbb{F}_q$ an elliptic curve defined over a finite field $\mathbb{F}_q$, $\psi_1 = \psi_2 = \psi : E_1 \to E_2$ a rational isogeny, and $\sigma_i = \hat{\pi}_q - 1$ on E_i. Since $E[\hat{\pi}_q - 1] = E[\pi_q - q]$ and $E[\pi_q - 1] = E(\mathbb{F}_q)$, we obtain a non degenerate pairing on the left $E_1[\pi_q - q,\psi] \times E_1(\mathbb{F}_q)/\hat{\psi}(E_2(\mathbb{F}_q)) \to \mathbb{G}_m$. We remark that if $E_1[\psi] \subset E_1[m]$ with $q \equiv 1 \mod m$, then $E_1[\pi_q - q,\psi] = E_1(\mathbb{F}_q)[\psi]$.
  As a further special case, taking $\psi = [m]$ (where m satisfy the above condition), we obtain a non degenerate pairing on the left $e : E_1(\mathbb{F}_q)[m] \times E_1(\mathbb{F}_q)/m(E_1(\mathbb{F}_q)) \to \mathbb{G}_m$, which can be computed as $e(P,Q) = e_{\hat{\pi}_q - 1}(P,Q) = e_m(P,(\pi_q - 1)Q')$ where $mQ' = Q$. We recover the standard Tate pairing.
- Take $E/\mathbb{F}_q$ an elliptic curve, and R a primitive orientation on E by a quadratic imaginary order of discriminant Δ_R. Let ω_R be the canonical imaginary element of Definition 3.2. Since $\hat{\omega} = -\omega$, we have a non degenerate Cartier-Weil pairing $e_{\omega_R} : E[\omega_R] \times E[\omega_R] \to \mathbb{G}_m$. Since $E[\omega_R]$ is cyclic, we see that e_{ω_R} gives a cyclic self pairing.

Now if $N(\omega_R) = m_1 m_2$, then we can construct a commutative diagram as above, by taking $\sigma_1 = \omega_R, \psi_1 = [m_1], \psi_2 = \hat{\omega_R}, \sigma_2 = [m_2]$, to obtain a non degenerate pairing on the left (hence also on the right) $E[\omega_R, m_1] \times E[\omega_R]/\omega_R E[m_2] \to \mathbb{G}_m$, which can be computed as $e_\omega(P, Q) = e_{m_1}(P, m_2 Q')$ where $\omega_R Q' = Q$.
Let P_0 be a $\mathbb{Z}[\omega_R]$-generator of $E[m_1 m_2]$. Then $Q_0 = \omega_R P_0$ is a generator of $E[\omega_R]$, $P = m_2 P_0$ is a $\mathbb{Z}[\omega_R]$-generator of $E[m]$, and $Q = \omega_R P = m_2 \omega_R P_0$ a generator of $E[\omega_R, m_1]$. By the result above, we find that $e_\omega(Q, Q) = e_{m_1}(\omega_R P, P)$. We recover the distorted pairing from Theorem 4.1 (up to a sign), and this is the self pairing built in [5].

References

1. Allombert, B., et al.: Faster SCALLOP from non-prime conductor suborders in medium sized quadratic fields. In: Jager, T., Pan, J. (eds.) PKC 2025. LNCS, vol. 15676, pp. 333–363. Springer, Cham (2025). https://doi.org/10.1007/978-3-031-91826-1_11
2. Bernstein, D.J., De Feo, L., Leroux, A., Smith, B.: Faster computation of isogenies of large prime degree. MSP Open Book Series (2020)
3. Castryck, W., Decru, T.: An efficient key recovery attack on SIDH. In: Hazay, C., Stam, M. (eds.) EUROCRYPT 2023. LNCS, vol. 14008, pp. 423–447. Springer, Cham (2023). https://doi.org/10.1007/978-3-031-30589-4_15
4. Castryck, W., et al.: Isogeny interpolation for elliptic curves, and applications. Presented by Wouter Castryck at the Sixteenth Algorithmic Number Theory Symposium, Massachusetts Institute of Technology, 15 July 2024. https://antsmath.org/ANTSXVI/schedule.html
5. Castryck, W., Houben, M., Merz, S.P., Mula, M., Buuren, S., Vercauteren, F.: Weak instances of class group action based cryptography via self-pairings. In: Handschuh, H., Lysyanskaya, A. (eds.) CRYPTO 2023. LNCS, vol. 14083, pp. 762–792. Springer, Cham (2023). https://doi.org/10.1007/978-3-031-38548-3_25
6. Castryck, W., Houben, M., Vercauteren, F., Wesolowski, B.: On the decisional Diffie-Hellman problem for class group actions on oriented elliptic curves. Res. Number Theory **8**(4), 99 (2022)
7. Chen, M., Leroux, A., Panny, L.: SCALLOP-HD: group action from 2-dimensional isogenies. In: Tang, Q., Teague, V. (eds.) PKC 2024. LNCS, vol. 14603, pp. 190–216. Springer, Cham (2024). https://doi.org/10.1007/978-3-031-57725-3_7
8. Colò, L., Kohel, D.: Orienting supersingular isogeny graphs. J. Math. Cryptol. **14**(1), 414–437 (2020)
9. Cox, D.A.: Primes of the Form $x^2 + ny^2$: Fermat, Class Field Theory, and Complex Multiplication. AMS Chelsea Publishing/American Mathematical Society, 3rd edn. (2022)
10. Edixhoven, B., van der Geer, G., Moonen, B.: Abelian varieties. Book project (2012). http://van-der-geer.nl/~gerard/AV.pdf
11. Feo, L.D., et al.: SCALLOP: scaling the CSI-FiSh. In: Boldyreva, A., Kolesnikov, V. (eds.) PKC 2023. LNCS, vol. 13940, pp. 345–375. Springer, Cham (2023). https://doi.org/10.1007/978-3-031-31368-4_13

12. Fouquet, M., Miret, J.M., Valera, J.: Distorting the volcano. Finite Fields Appl. **49**, 108–125 (2018)
13. Galbraith, S.D.: Constructing isogenies between elliptic curves over finite fields. LMS J. Comput. Math. **2**, 118–138 (1999)
14. Galbraith, S.D.: Climbing and descending tall isogeny volcanos. Res. Number Theory **11**(7) (2025)
15. Hardy, G.H., Wright, E.M.: An Introduction to the Theory of Numbers, 5th edn. Oxford (1979)
16. Ionica, S., Joux, A.: Pairing the volcano. Math. Comput. **82**(281), 581–603 (2013)
17. Jordan, B.W., Keeton, A.G., Poonen, B., Rains, E.M., Shepherd-Barron, N., Tate, J.T.: Abelian varieties isogenous to a power of an elliptic curve. Compositio Mathematica **154**(5), 934–959 (2018)
18. Kani, E.: The number of curves of genus two with elliptic differentials. Journal für die reine und angewandte Mathematik (Crelles Journal) **122–93**, 1997 (1997)
19. Kohel, D.R.: Endomorphism rings of elliptic curves over finite fields. Ph.D. thesis, University of California, Berkeley (1996)
20. Macula, J., Stange, K.E.: Extending class group action attacks via sesquilinear pairings. In: Chung, K.M., Sasaki, Y. (eds.) ASIACRYPT 2024. LNCS, vol. 15486, pp. 371–395. Springer, Singapore (2025). https://doi.org/10.1007/978-981-96-0891-1_12
21. Maino, L., Martindale, C., Panny, L., Pope, G., Wesolowski, B.: A direct key recovery attack on SIDH. In: Hazay, C., Stam, M. (eds.) EUROCRYPT 2023. LNCS, vol. 14008, pp. 448–471. Springer, Cham (2023). https://doi.org/10.1007/978-3-031-30589-4_16
22. Miret, J.M., Moreno, R., Sadornil, D., Tena, J., Valls, M.: An algorithm to compute volcanoes of 2-isogenies of elliptic curves over finite fields. Appl. Math. Comput. **176**(2), 739–750 (2006)
23. Onuki, H.: On oriented supersingular elliptic curves. Finite Fields Their Appl. **69**, 101777 (2021)
24. Pornin, T.: Optimized discrete logarithm computation for faster square roots in finite fields. Cryptology ePrint Archive, Paper 2023/828 (2023)
25. Robert, D.: Some applications of higher dimensional isogenies to elliptic curves (preliminary version). IACR Cryptology ePrint Archive, p. 1704 (2022)
26. Robert, D.: Breaking SIDH in polynomial time. In: Hazay, C., Stam, M. (eds.) EUROCRYPT 2023. LNCS, vol. 14008, pp. 472–503. Springer, Cham (2023). https://doi.org/10.1007/978-3-031-30589-4_17
27. Robert, D.: The module action for isogeny based cryptography. IACR Eprint 2024/1556, October 2024
28. Robert, D.: On the efficient representation of isogenies (a survey). IACR Eprint 2024/1071, June 2024
29. Stange, K.E.: Sesquilinear pairings on elliptic curves. arXiv preprint arXiv:2405.14167 (2024)
30. Tate, J.: Endomorphisms of abelian varieties over finite fields. Invent. Math. **2**, 134–144 (1966)

The Tate Profile

Krijn Reijnders(✉)

COSIC, KU Leuven, Leuven, Belgium
crypto.krijn@gmail.com

Abstract. This work explores the Tate profile and its applications. We show that, framed using Tate profiles, several well-known results on divisibility and basis sampling become natural. Then, having rewritten these results in this more natural setting, we generalize and optimize several use cases: First, we use Tate profiles to generalize entangled basis generation to any Weierstrass curve. Second, we optimize the computation of degree-2 Tate pairings on Kummer surfaces using cubical arithmetic, which allows us to compute the 2-Tate profile in only 6 additions, 10 multiplications, and 4 Legendre symbols. Third, we apply the optimized 2-Tate profile computation to perform subgroup membership testing on the Gaudry–Schost Kummer Surface, smoothly combining these ideas.

Keywords: pairings · isogenies · Kummer surfaces

1 Introduction

Pairings have been ubiquitous in curve-based cryptography, both as an adversarial and constructive tool in elliptic curve cryptography [MVO91, FR94, HSSI99, Jou04], as the main points of interest in pairing-based cryptography [BLS01, BF01, BKLS02, GHS02, Jou02, BGLS03, BLS04, Gal05, Ver09], and again as an adversarial and constructive tool in isogeny-based cryptography [CJL+17, KT18, Reij23, CHM+23, LWXZ24, MS24]. This work specifically looks at the Tate pairing. Often, we look at a single pairing value $t_n(P,Q)$ to learn something about the relation between P and Q, or we use several pairing values and the properties of the Tate pairing to derive a result.

The easiest example of the usability of the Tate pairing is given on Montgomery curves $E_A : y^2 = x^3 + Ax^2 + x$, with $A \in \mathbb{F}_q$, where any point P with non-square x-coordinate x_P must be in the set $E_A \setminus [2]E_A$. It is no coincidence that the quadratic character of x_P is also exactly the value of the degree-2 reduced Tate pairing $t_2(L_0, P)$ where $L_0 = (0,0) \in E_A[2]$. In this example,

This work was supported in part by the European Research Council (ERC) under the European Union's Horizon 2020 research and innovation programme (grant agreement ISOCRYPT - No. 101020788), by the Research Council KU Leuven grant C14/24/099 and by CyberSecurity Research Flanders with reference number VR20192203.
Date of this document: 2025-08-25.

D. Escudero and I. Damgård (Eds.): LATINCRYPT 2025, LNCS 16129, pp. 209–233, 2026.
https://doi.org/10.1007/978-3-032-06754-8_8

the Tate pairing allows us to transform something we know about $E_A[2]$ into something we know about $[2]E_A$. In fact, this correspondence between $E_A[2]$ and $[2]E_A$, or in other words, between the kernel and the image of the endomorphism $[2] : E_A \to E_A$ is one of the core properties of the Tate pairing, and highlights its connection to divisibility.

This study of divisibility by $[\ell]$ quickly leads to useful building blocks in modern isogeny-based cryptography [CJL+17,ZSP+18,CEMR24], which highly impact the practical performance of schemes: When computing isogenies of large smooth degree, for example 2^n, we often rely on Vélu's formulas [Vél71,BDLS20] to compute these isogenies, which often takes a generator K of the kernel as input. To describe K, we may take a basis P, Q of $E[2^n]$ and express K as a linear combination $[a]P+[b]Q$, for some $a, b \in \mathbb{Z}_{2^n}$. Finding such a basis is linked to divisibility, as we must look for these points P and Q in the set $E \setminus [2]E$, i.e., those points that are *not* divisible by [2].

Another example is subgroup membership testing, in the context of elliptic-curve cryptography. Subgroup membership testing asks if a point $P \in E(\mathbb{F}_q)$ is a member of a particular subgroup $G \subset E(\mathbb{F}_q)$. Usually, G is a subgroup of large prime order r of $E(\mathbb{F}_q)$, and we assume the hardness of the discrete logarithm in G to build cryptographic primitives. Optimizing subgroup membership testing is a non-trivial task, but essential to prevent certain *subgroup attacks* [LL97]. For example, a major bug in the Monero cryptocurrency allows for double-spending of coins, and requires a subgroup membership test to prevent this [lS17]. Similarly, pairing-based protocols require subgroup membership testing to ensure that we are working with points in the correct subgroups [BCM+15,Bow19,Sco21]. A recent innovation by Koshelev [Kos23] applies the non-degeneracy of the Tate pairing to subgroup membership testing. For certain curves, this may outperform previous methods when the Tate pairing computation is fast, and the parameters of the elliptic curve are suitable.

In recent years, the Tate pairing has been put into a wider context: Bruin [Bru11] highlights the connection of the Tate pairing to isogenies, and shows that we may define a (generalized) Tate pairing t_ϕ for any isogeny $\phi : E \to E'$,

$$t_\phi : (\ker \phi)(k) \times (\operatorname{coker} \widehat{\phi})(k) \to \mu_n$$

instead of the classical Tate pairing t_n defined with respect to the endomorphism $[n] : E \to E$. Similarly to our initial example, such a generalized Tate pairing is able to transform knowledge of the kernel of ϕ into knowledge of the image of the dual $\widehat{\phi}$, and vice versa. Expanding on this, Robert [Rob23] rephrases the Tate pairing as a map that allows us to study the fibers $\phi^{-1}(P)$ of an isogeny ϕ, as a single abstraction that covers many of the examples given above, and many other results can similarly be phrased in this context [IJ13,Dol18,CDV20].

When placed in this broader context, we find that it is easier to see several individual Tate pairing as a single object instead, which we denote the Tate profile [Rob23,CR24]. Starting with the Tate profile as our essential tool, we study core properties of $\phi^{-1}(P)$, following the theoretical framework of [Rob23].

Contributions.

In this work we explore the Tate profile and its applications. First, in Sect. 3, we derive a result that shows how the Tate profile allows us to transform knowledge of the rational ℓ-torsion into knowledge of the Sylow ℓ-subgroup, that is, the largest rational $\ell^\bullet$-torsion. This result, Theorem 1, lies at the heart of many of the later results, as it shows that thinking in terms of the Tate profile helps us to understand most results that rely on Tate pairings.

Second, in Sect. 4, we rephrase smart torsion basis sampling [CEMR24], entangled basis generation [ZSP+18], and subgroup membership [Kos23] in terms of Tate profiles, which gives us a deeper understanding of these results and their connection to the Tate pairing. This allows us to generalize these results to different curves or higher dimensions.

Third, in Sect. 5, to achieve an efficient computation of the 2-Tate pairing on Kummer surfaces, we study cubical arithmetic [Rob24] to compute such pairings, and highly optimize the computation of the 2-Tate profile. We are able to compute the 2-Tate profile in only 6 additions, 10 multiplications, and 4 Legendre symbols.

Lastly, in Sect. 6, we look at a concrete example in which most of the above comes together: subgroup membership testing on the Gaudry–Schost Kummer surface [GS12]. As a challenge, we try to perform subgroup membership testing on this surface as efficiently as possible, by combining a higher-dimensional application of Koshelev's method [Kos23] with the optimized cubical arithmetic from Robert [Rob24]. Although this approach to subgroup membership testing is significantly faster than other approaches, our main goals are to **a.)** highlight the usefulness of the Tate profile, and **b.)** showcase the effectiveness of cubical arithmetic to compute Tate profiles.

2 Preliminaries

Notation. We work mostly over $\mathbb{F}_p$. An extension is denoted by $\mathbb{F}_q$ for $q = p^m$. Whenever we write $\mathbb{Z}_n$, we mean $\mathbb{Z}/n\mathbb{Z}$, the integers modulo n. We denote exact divisibility by $a \parallel b$. When working with Jacobians $\mathcal{J}/\mathbb{F}_p$, we describe the 2-torsion by $D_{i,j} \in \mathcal{J}[2]$, which refers to element of $\mathcal{J}$ associated to the divisor $(w_i, 0) + (w_j, 0)$, where w_i, w_j are Weierstrass points of the hyperelliptic curve. We assume this curve is in Rosenhain form, and so $w_1 = \infty$, $w_2 = 0$, $w_3 = 1$, $w_4 = \lambda$, $w_5 = \mu$, and $w_6 = \nu$. More details can be found in, for example, [CR24, §2].

On their Kummer surfaces, we denote by $L_{i,j} \in \mathcal{K}[2]$ the point associated to $D_{i,j} \in \mathcal{J}[2]$. The map $Q \mapsto Q + L_{i,j}$ is well-defined for 2-torsion points $L_{i,j}$, and can be given as a (4×4)-matrix, which we denote by $W_{i,j}$.

On Kummer surfaces, we denote a point $Q \in \mathcal{K}$ by $(Q_1 : Q_2 : Q_3 : Q_4) \in \mathbb{P}^3(\mathbb{F}_p)$, which is defined up to scalars. An *affine lift* for Q is denoted by $\widetilde{Q}$, and in this work specifically refers to any choice $(Q_1, Q_2, Q_3, Q_4) \in \mathbb{F}_p^4$ that represents Q. We may normalize such a lift $\widetilde{Q}$ in index k by $Q_i \mapsto Q_i/Q_k$, as long as $Q_k \neq 0$.

Operations in $\mathbb{F}_p$ are denoted by **M** for multiplication, **S** for squaring, **A** for addition, and **L** for the Legendre symbol. Whenever we refer to $\mathbb{F}_p$-operations, we use the model $\mathbf{S} = 0.8\mathbf{M}$ and $\mathbf{A} = 0.05\mathbf{M}$. We estimate $1\mathbf{L}$ at $125\mathbf{S} + 9\mathbf{M}$ using an addition chain [McL21].

Terminology. In this work, we will often refer to a *basis* $(P_1, \dots, P_r)$ for some subgroup $G \subseteq A(k)$ of an abelian variety A, for example, $G = (\ker f)(k)$ for an isogeny $f : A \to B$, or $G = A(k)[n]$ is the rational n-torsion. In the elliptic curve case, we usually do not define what is meant by a basis, as it is understood from the context, but for higher dimensions we need to be a bit more careful.

Definition 1. *Let G be a subgroup of $A(k)$. By the structure theorem, there are unique integers $d_1, \dots, d_r \geq 1$ such that G decomposes into cyclic groups as*

$$G \cong \mathbb{Z}/d_1\mathbb{Z} \times \cdots \times \mathbb{Z}/d_r\mathbb{Z},$$

where $d_1 \mid d_2 \mid \cdots \mid d_r$, with $d_1 \geq 1$ and $d_r = n$. We say that n is the exponent *of G and r is the* rank *of G. We say that a set of points $(P_1, \dots, P_r)$ with $P_i \in A(k)$ is a* basis *for G if there exists an isomorphism*

$$\phi : G \to \mathbb{Z}/d_1\mathbb{Z} \times \cdots \times \mathbb{Z}/d_r\mathbb{Z},$$

where $\phi(P_i) = (0, \dots, 0, 1, 0, \dots, 0)$, with the 1 in the i-th position.

The notation $G = \langle P_1, \dots, P_r \rangle$ is used to denote that $(P_1, \dots, P_r)$ is a basis for G. Often in this article, we consider abelian varieties A of dimension g with $A[n](k) = A[n]$. Then for $G = A[n]$, we get $d_i = n$ for all $1 \leq i \leq r$, and the rank of G is $r = 2g$. Another example that we see often in isogeny-based cryptography is given by $(n, n, \dots, n)$-isogenies $f : (A, \lambda_A) \to (B, \lambda_B)$ of principally polarized abelian varieties, where for $G = \ker f$, we get $d_1 = \cdots = d_r = n$, and $r = g$. Lastly, note that when n is prime, we must similarly have $d_i = n$ for all i. This definition generalizes the usual notions of a basis (P, Q) for the rational n-torsion of an elliptic curve, or a generator K for a cyclic isogeny $E \to E/\langle K \rangle$.

2.1 The Generalized Tate Pairing

This work requires a generalized notion of the original Tate-Lichtenbaum pairing [Tat62,Lic69] on abelian varieties, which was introduced in a cryptographic context by Frey and Rück [FR94]. Over a finite field k, Bruin [Bru11] shows how to generalize the Tate pairing to any isogeny $f : A \to B$ between principally polarized abelian varieties A and B to obtain the generalized Tate pairing

$$T_f : (\ker f)(k) \times (\operatorname{coker} \hat{f})(k) \to k^*/k^{*,n},$$

where $(\operatorname{coker} \hat{f})(k) = A(k)/\hat{f}(B(k))$ and n is the exponent of $\ker f$. This pairing is also referred to as the Tate-Cartier pairing, and is explored by Robert [Rob23]. We slightly abuse notation here, by swapping the roles of f and its dual $\hat{f}$, which allows us to present some results more cleanly. In this work, we will often take for A and B the (Jacobians of) elliptic or hyperelliptic curves. If we take the endomorphism $f = [n]$ of degree n^2 and exponent n on a Jacobian $\mathcal{J}$, we obtain the original Tate pairing

$$T_n : \mathcal{J}[n](k) \times \mathcal{J}(k)/[n]\mathcal{J}(k) \to k^*/k^{*,n}.$$

Over a finite field $k = \mathbb{F}_q$ where n divides $q-1$, we get a unique representative of the class $T_n(P,Q) \in k^*/k^{*,n}$ by raising any representative to the power $\frac{q-1}{n}$, giving us an n-th root of unity $\zeta \in \mu_n$. This combination is the *reduced* Tate pairing of degree n

$$t_n : \mathcal{J}[n](k) \times \mathcal{J}(k)/[n]\mathcal{J}(k) \to \mu_n.$$

Computation. Miller's algorithm [Mil04] enables efficient computation on the Jacobian. Methods to compute the Tate pairing are developed in [Sta07,LR10, LR15,LR16,Rob24]. Computing pairings on the Kummer variety of an abelian variety is more difficult. We discuss this for Kummer surfaces in Sect. 2.3, more generally see [Rob24].

2.2 Kummer Surfaces

Only a few years after the birth of elliptic-curve cryptography [Mil85,Kob87], Koblitz [Kob89] showed that one may just as well use curves of larger genus. In particular, genus-2 hyperelliptic curves, and their Jacobians, seem well-suited for cryptography based on the discrete-logarithm problem.

To improve the efficiency, one may choose to work on the *Kummer surface* of a Jacobian,[1] the higher-dimensional analogue to x-only arithmetic of elliptic curves. Already in 1986, Chudnovsky and Chudnovsky [CC86] realized the efficiency of Kummer surfaces, with the idea to apply this to factorization tests. Gaudry [Gau07] shows that working on the Kummer surface similarly improves cryptography in genus 2 as the Kummer surface has enough structure to allow us to compute $P \mapsto [n]P$. A good introduction to arithmetic in genus 2 can be found in Cassels and Flynn [CF96].

In genus 2, however, it is much harder to find secure curves, compared to genus 1. We want to find a curve such that the Jacobian has a large enough prime-order subgroup, and such that its *twist* has a similarly large prime-order subgroup. Furthermore, several other technical details are important to achieve fast arithmetic on their related Kummer surfaces. Through a large computational search, Gaudry and Schost [GS12] found a nearly perfect Jacobian over the prime $p = 2^{127} - 1$. We briefly describe the Jacobian, and its associated Kummer surface, as given in [BCHL16, §5.5.1]. A more detailed description of Kummer surfaces is given in [CR24, §2].

[1] We choose to use the language of Kummer surfaces, although our work can be interpreted in the language of theta structures of level 2 for abelian surfaces as well.

Example 1 (The Gaudry–Schost Kummer Surface). The fundamental constants $(a^2, b^2, c^2, d^2) = (11, -22, -19, -3) \in \mathbb{F}_p^4$, where $p = 2^{127} - 1$, give us a Kummer surface $\mathcal{K}/\mathbb{F}_p$ which we call the *Gaudry–Schost Kummer surface.* It is the Kummer surface associated to the Jacobian $\mathcal{J}/\mathbb{F}_p$ defined by the Rosenhain invariants

$$\begin{aligned}\lambda &= 28356863910078205288614550619314017618,\\ \mu &= 154040945529144206406682019582013187910,\\ \nu &= 113206060534360680770189432771018826227.\end{aligned}$$

The Jacobian $\mathcal{J}$ has $2^4 \cdot r$ rational points, and its twist $\mathcal{J}^T$ has $2^4 \cdot r'$ rational points, where r and r' are the primes

$$\begin{aligned}r &= 1809251394333065553414675955050290598923508843635941313077767297801179626051,\\ r' &= 1809251394333065553571917326471206521441306174399683558571672623546356726339.\end{aligned}$$

The zero point is $\mathbf{0}_\mathcal{K} = (a^2, b^2, c^2, d^2)$. To do arithmetic on the Kummer surface, we use the usual building blocks: the Hadamard transform, the 4-way squaring, and the 4-way multiply.

Remark 1. A similar Kummer surface over $p = 2^{128} - 34827$ is given in [BCHL16, §5.5.2]. As the group structure is similar, the techniques in this work apply directly to this Kummer surface too.

The Origin of Points on the Kummer Surface. Points $P \in \mathcal{K}(\mathbb{F}_p)$ are either associated to a point $\bar{P} \in \mathcal{J}(\mathbb{F}_p)$ on the Jacobian, or to a point $\bar{P}' \in J^T(\mathbb{F}_p)$ on its twist. In the former case, we say that a point $P \in \mathcal{K}(\mathbb{F}_p)$ *originates from* the Jacobian, whereas in the latter case, P originates from the twist. An algorithm to compute the origin of a point is given in [CR24, §4.1]. For the Gaudry–Schost Kummer surface, checking the origin of a point using this algorithm takes $22\mathbf{M} + 1\mathbf{S} + 13\mathbf{A} + 1\mathbf{L}$.

2.3 Pairings on Kummer Surfaces

For this work, we require level-2 pairings on Kummer surfaces. We quickly discuss two methods in details: first, using a partial map back to the Jacobian [CR24], and second, the more natural approach using cubical arithmetic [Rob24].

Pairings Using a Partial Map to the Jacobian. Intuitively, computing pairings on Jacobians is simpler to understand than on Kummer surfaces, as we can perform Miller's algorithm [Mil04] on the Jacobian. Hence, if we can find an associated $P \in \mathcal{J}(\mathbb{F}_p)$ such that $Q = \rho(P)$ for the map $\rho : \mathcal{J}(\mathbb{F}_p) \to \mathcal{K}(\mathbb{F}_p)$, we can compute the required pairings on $\mathcal{J}(\mathbb{F}_p)$ using P. In particular, for the Tate pairing of degree 2, given $D_{i,j} \in \mathcal{J}[2]$ and $P \in \mathcal{J}(\mathbb{F}_p)$ in Mumford representation

$$D_{i,j} = \langle (x - w_i)(x - w_j), 0 \rangle, \quad P = \langle a(x), b(x) \rangle,$$

with $a(x) \in \mathbb{F}_p[x]$, we can compute the (non-reduced) Tate pairing as the resultant of $(x - w_i)(x - w_j)$ and $a(x)$. Hence, given $Q \in \mathcal{K}(\mathbb{F}_p)$, we only need to recover $a(x)$ from Q to compute the pairings.

Such a map $\mathcal{K}(\mathbb{F}_p) \to \mathbb{F}_p[x]$, with $Q \mapsto a(x)$ is given in [CR24, §2.7], as a partial inverse to the map $\mathcal{J}(\mathbb{F}_p) \to \mathcal{K}(\mathbb{F}_p)$. Given $a(x)$, we may then compute the 2-Tate pairing with respect to $D_{i,j} \in \mathcal{J}[2]$.

Cubical Pairings of Degree 2. In [Rob24], Robert introduces *cubical arithmetic* to compute pairings, specializing to Kummer varieties in §4.7. With this, we compute Tate pairings on Kummer surfaces naturally, without moving to the Jacobian.

The Tate pairing of degree $n = 2$ is special, as it requires almost none of the machinery of cubical arithmetic, beyond *translations*: Given a point $L_{i,j} \in \mathcal{K}[2]$, and any point $Q \in \mathcal{K}(\mathbb{F}_p)$, the point $L_{i,j} + Q$ is well-defined. The map $Q \mapsto L_{i,j} + Q$ is given by a (4×4)-matrix which we denote $W_{i,j}$. These matrices $W_{i,j}$ are given in [CR24, App. A] in terms of the coefficients of $\mathbf{0}_{\mathcal{K}}$ and the Rosenhain invariants of the associated Jacobian.

To compute the pairing $t_2(L_{i,j}, Q)$ using cubical arithmetic[2], we compute two values[3] λ_Q and $\lambda_{L_{i,j}}$ using the translation matrix $W_{i,j}$. The pairing $t_2(L_{i,j}, Q)$ is then given by the Legendre symbol of λ_Q/λ_P. We describe the cubical pairing computation of degree 2 on $\mathcal{K}(\mathbb{F}_p)$ in Algorithm 1, which is slightly adjusted from [Rob24] for easier implementation.

Algorithm 1. Degree-2 cubical pairing computation on $\mathcal{K}(\mathbb{F}_p)$

Input: The point Q as (Q_1, Q_2, Q_3, Q_4), the normalization index n_{ij}, and the matrix $W_{i,j}$.

Output: The reduced Tate pairing $t_2(L_{i,j}, Q) \in \mu_2$.

1: $\widetilde{L_{i,j}} \leftarrow W_{i,j} \cdot \widetilde{\mathbf{0}_{\mathcal{K}}}$
2: $\widetilde{L_{i,j} + Q} \leftarrow W_{i,j} \cdot \widetilde{Q}$ ▷ Compute $L_{i,j} + Q$
3: $\widetilde{2L_{i,j}} \leftarrow W_{i,j} \cdot \widetilde{L_{i,j}}$ ▷ Translate $L_{i,j}$
4: $\left(\widetilde{2L_{i,j} + Q}\right) \leftarrow W_{i,j} \cdot \left(\widetilde{L_{i,j} + Q}\right)$ ▷ Translate $L_{i,j} + Q$
5: $\lambda_{L_{ij}} \leftarrow (\widetilde{2L_{i,j}})_{n_{i,j}} / (\widetilde{L_{i,j}})_{n_{i,j}}$
6: $\lambda_Q \leftarrow (\widetilde{2L_{i,j} + Q})_{n_{i,j}} / (\widetilde{L_{i,j} + Q})_{n_{i,j}}$
7: $\zeta \leftarrow \mathsf{Legendre}(\lambda_Q / \lambda_{L_{ij}})$
8: **return** ζ

---

[2] For full details, see [Rob24, Alg. 5.2]. For a more friendly introduction, see [PRR+25].

[3] More properly speaking, monodromies [Sta07, Rob24].

3 The Tate Profile

In this section we analyze the Tate profile and give a crucial connection between the Tate pairing of degree ℓ and the ℓ-Sylow subgroup of $E(\mathbb{F}_q)$ in Theorem 1, which captures the essence of many subsequent results in this work.

The description in terms of Tate profiles heavily relies on the results in [Rob23, Sec. 5]. We hope that rephrasing those results allows for a more concrete and practical understanding, suitable for applications. Although Sects. 3.1 and 3.2 are written for general abelian varieties to prove Theorem 1, later sections only require such results for elliptic curves or Jacobians of hyperelliptic curves. All isogenies in this section are assumed to be separable, and we are working over a finite field $k = \mathbb{F}_q$ of characteristic p.

3.1 The Tate Profile

The Tate profile [CR24] of an isogeny $f : A \to B$ allows us to study the properties of the Tate pairing T_f in a single object, by evaluating a point $Q \in A(k)$ in a basis of $\ker f$, as defined in Definition 1. The profile rephrases several of the ideas explored in [Rob23, CR24].

Definition 2. *Let $f : A \to B$ be a separable isogeny between abelian varieties A and B over a finite field k, and let n be the exponent of $(\ker f)(k)$ and r its rank. Let $(P_1, \ldots, P_r)$ be a basis for $(\ker f)(k)$, so that P_i has order d_i for all i. The* Tate profile *$t_{\ker f}$ associated to the reduced generalized Tate pairing $t_f : (\ker f)(k) \times (\operatorname{coker} \hat{f})(k) \to \mu_n$ with respect to this basis is the map*

$$\begin{aligned} t_{\ker f} : A(k) &\to \mu_{d_1} \times \ldots \times \mu_{d_r} \\ Q &\mapsto (t_f(P_1, Q), \ldots, t_f(P_r, Q)) \end{aligned}$$

We refer to $t_{\ker f}(Q)$ for $Q \in A(k)$ as the Tate profile of Q. We say that the profile $t_{\ker f}(Q)$ is trivial, *when $t_{\ker f}(Q) = (1, \ldots, 1)$.*

From the bilinearity of the Tate pairing, the Tate profile inherits linearity. When the Tate pairing is non-degenerate, the Tate profile then induces an isomorphism

$$(\operatorname{coker} \hat{f})(k) \xrightarrow{\sim} \mu_{d_1} \times \ldots \times \mu_{d_r}.$$

In essence, the choice of a basis for $(\ker f)(k)$ fixes an isomorphism to this product of roots of unities, which gives us a coordinate system to work with on the cokernel. In practice, we will mostly use the Tate profile either in the case where f is a separable $(n, \ldots, n)$-isogeny between principally polarized abelian varieties, so that we get a map $t_{\ker f} : A(k) \to \mu_n^r$ with $r = g$, or the case $f = [n]$ with $t_{\ker f} : A(k) \to \mu_n^r$ with $r = 2g$ if the $[n]$-torsion is rational. In both these cases, non-degeneracy of the Tate pairing t_f gives us an isomorphism

$$t_{\ker f} : (\operatorname{coker} \hat{f})(k) \xrightarrow{\sim} \mu_n^r, \tag{1}$$

which will be key to the results in this work. A trivial but useful corollary of this definition is the following.

Corollary 1 ([Rob23, Cor. 5.2]). *If the Tate pairing t_f is non-degenerate, then*

$$t_{\ker f}(Q) \text{ is trivial} \quad \Leftrightarrow \quad Q \in \widehat{f}(B(k)).$$

In other words, $\ker t_{\ker f} = \hat{f}(B(k))$.

Many divisibility results require only this corollary, in particular for the Tate pairing t_n associated to scalar multiplication by $[n]$, as we get that $Q \in [n]A(k)$ if the profile $t_{\ker[n]}(Q)$ is trivial. A notable exception is in [CR24, §3], which requires the full isomorphism to identify points with certain properties in $\mathcal{J}[2^f]$ for a specific Jacobian $\mathcal{J}$.

3.2 Sylow ℓ-Torsion of Abelian Varieties

The Tate profile of degree n is a useful tool to analyze divisibility by $[n]$, as its kernel describes precisely those points divisible by $[n]$ on an abelian variety A. Similarly, for ℓ prime, we know that divisibility by ℓ is observable in the subgroup $A[\ell^\infty](\mathbb{F}_q)$. This section describes the close connection between the divisibility by $[\ell]$ and the subgroup $A[\ell^\infty](\mathbb{F}_q)$. To avoid the annoying notation $A[\ell^\infty](\mathbb{F}_q)$, we introduce the following notation.

Definition 3. *Let A be an abelian variety over $\mathbb{F}_q$ and ℓ a prime, coprime to p. The* Sylow ℓ-torsion *of $A(\mathbb{F}_q)$, which we denote $\mathcal{S}_{\ell,q}(A)$, is the unique subgroup $A[\ell^\infty](\mathbb{F}_q)$. As a group, $\mathcal{S}_{\ell,q}(A)$ is isomorphic to*

$$\mathbb{Z}_{\ell^{f_1}} \times \mathbb{Z}_{\ell^{f_2}} \times \ldots \times \mathbb{Z}_{\ell^{f_d}}$$

with $f_i \in \mathbb{N}$ such that $f_1 \geq f_2 \geq \ldots \geq f_d > 0$ and $d \leq 2g$.

The rank d is equal to the rank of the rational ℓ-torsion, as $A[\ell](\mathbb{F}_q) \subseteq \mathcal{S}_{\ell,q}(A)$, and the exponent is ℓ^{f_1}. An isogeny $f : A \to B$ induces a group homomorphism $\mathcal{S}_{\ell,q}(A) \to \mathcal{S}_{\ell,q}(B)$, and, when $\deg f$ and ℓ are coprime, this induced map is an isomorphism.

Example 2. Many of the later results will study $\mathcal{S}_{2,p^2}(E)$ for supersingular Montgomery curves E. When $2^f \parallel p+1$, we have the 'nice' structure

$$\mathcal{S}_{2,p^2}(E) \cong \mathbb{Z}_{2^f} \times \mathbb{Z}_{2^f},$$

whereas more generally we may have $\mathcal{S}_{2,p^2}(E) \cong \mathbb{Z}_{2^f} \times \mathbb{Z}_{2^g}$ for some $g < f$. Examples of sampling of points in this structure using the 2-Tate profile are ample in isogeny-based cryptography, and we revisit some examples in Sect. 4.

Example 3. The Jacobian $\mathcal{J}(\mathbb{F}_p)$ derived from Scholten's construction [Sch03] for supersingular elliptic curves E over $\mathbb{F}_{p^2}$ with $\mathcal{S}_{2,p^2}(E) \cong \mathbb{Z}_{2^f} \times \mathbb{Z}_{2^f}$ has the peculiar structure

$$\mathcal{S}_{2,p}(\mathcal{J}) \cong \mathbb{Z}_{2^{f-1}} \times \mathbb{Z}_{2^{f-1}} \times \mathbb{Z}_2 \times \mathbb{Z}_2.$$

Sampling of points in this structure using the 2-Tate profile is explored in [CR24].

3.3 The Tate Profile and the Sylow ℓ-Torsion

As a concretization of Definition 1, we define what a basis for $\mathcal{S}_{\ell,q}(A)$ means.

Definition 4. *Let* $\mathcal{S}_{\ell,q}(A) \cong \bigoplus_{i=1}^{d} \mathbb{Z}_{\ell^{f_i}}$. *A* basis $\mathcal{B}$ *for* $\mathcal{S}_{\ell,q}(A)$ *is a minimal set of points* $(P_1, \dots, P_d)$ *that generates every point* $Q \in \mathcal{S}_{\ell,q}(A)$ *as a linear combination* $\sum \lambda_i P_i$, *with* $\lambda_i \in \mathbb{Z}_{\ell^{f_i}}$. *We write* $\langle P_1, \dots, P_d\rangle = \mathcal{S}_{\ell,q}(A)$ *to denote that* $(P_1, \dots, P_d)$ *is a basis for* $\mathcal{S}_{\ell,q}(A)$.

From any basis $\mathcal{B} = (P_i)_{i=1}^{d}$ of $\mathcal{S}_{\ell,q}(A)$, we easily find a description of $[\ell]A(\mathbb{F}_q)$, the points divisible by $[\ell]$, as the points

$$Q = \sum \lambda_i [\ell] P_i + R, \quad R \in [\ell^{f_1}]A(\mathbb{F}_q), \lambda_i \in \mathbb{Z}_{\ell^{f_i}}.$$

For principally polarized abelian varieties, the Tate profile of degree ℓ connects $A[\ell](\mathbb{F}_q)$ to $A(\mathbb{F}_q)/[\ell]A(\mathbb{F}_q)$. Given a basis $\mathcal{B} = (P_i)_{i=1}^{d}$ of $\mathcal{S}_{\ell,q}(A)$, we may represent the classes of $A(\mathbb{F}_q)/[\ell]A(\mathbb{F}_q)$, using the description above, by

$$\sum \lambda_i P_i + [\ell]A(\mathbb{F}_q), \quad \lambda_i \in \mathbb{Z}_{\ell}.$$

The following theorem captures the essence of the connection between the kernel $A[\ell]$ and divisibility by $[\ell]$, using the Tate profile. Recall that for $f = [\ell]$, the map $t_{\ker f}$ gives the isomorphism from (1), where r is the rank of $A[\ell](\mathbb{F}_q)$.

Theorem 1. *Let* r *denote the rank of* $A[\ell](\mathbb{F}_q)$, *assume the* ℓ*-Tate pairing is non-degenerate, and define the Tate profile* $t_{\ker[\ell]}$ *with respect to a basis of* $A[\ell](\mathbb{F}_q)$. *Then, for points* $P_1, \dots, P_r \in A(\mathbb{F}_q)$, *we get*

$$A(\mathbb{F}_q)/A[\ell](\mathbb{F}_q) = \langle P_1, \dots, P_r\rangle \quad \textit{if and only if} \quad \mu_\ell^r = \langle t_{\ker[\ell]}(P_1), \dots, t_{\ker[\ell]}(P_r)\rangle.$$

Consequently, for $h = \frac{|A(\mathbb{F}_q)|}{|\mathcal{S}_{\ell,q}(A)|}$ *so that* $[h]P \in \mathcal{S}_{\ell,q}(A)$ *for all* $P \in A(\mathbb{F}_q)$, *we get*

$$\mathcal{S}_{\ell,q}(A) = \langle [h]P_1, \dots, [h]P_r\rangle.$$

Proof. The map $[\ell] : A(\mathbb{F}_q) \to A(\mathbb{F}_q)$ has kernel $A[\ell](\mathbb{F}_q)$ by definition, whose size is ℓ^r by assumption. Thus, there are ℓ^r cosets which we may write as $P_i + [\ell]A(\mathbb{F}_q)$ for some $P_i \in A(\mathbb{F}_q)$. By the non-degeneracy of the ℓ-Tate pairing and Eq. (1), we find that

$$Q \in \sum \lambda_i P_i + [\ell]A(\mathbb{F}_q) \quad \Leftrightarrow \quad t_{\ker[\ell]}(Q) = t_{\ker[\ell]}\left(\sum \lambda_i P_i\right).$$

By linearity, we find that $t_{\ker[\ell]}\left(\sum \lambda_i P_i\right) = \prod t_{\ker[\ell]}(P_i)^{\lambda_i}$. As a result, if the profiles $t_{\ker[\ell]}(P_i)$ span μ_ℓ^r, their combinations span every coset, and vice versa. Consequently, by killing any non-ℓ torsion using $[h]$, we obtain points $[h]P_i$ that are a basis for $\mathcal{S}_{\ell,q}(A)$. □

Concretely, this means that we can find such a basis for the Sylow ℓ-torsion if we have a basis for the kernel $A[\ell]$ and can efficiently compute the Tate profile (i.e., can efficiently compute the required Tate pairings): we sample random points of $A(\mathbb{F}_q)$ and compute their ℓ-Tate profiles until we find r points whose profiles span μ_ℓ^r, and then we clear the cofactor h.

Although Theorem 1 is written in a general setting, most of the results in this work follow from the general idea that we can derive as a consequence: if we know the ℓ-torsion, the ℓ-Tate profile helps us find a basis for the ℓ-Sylow torsion.

Remark 2. In the most practical case, we may apply the above mantra to the case $\ell = 2$, with E a supersingular elliptic curve and $2^f \parallel p+1$. Then, if we know the rational 2-torsion $E[2](\mathbb{F}_{p^2})$ and we want to find points Q whose order is divisible by 2^f, the 2-Tate profile will be the essential tool that connects these Q to $E[2](\mathbb{F}_{p^2})$.

3.4 Single Tate Pairing Results as Profiles

One may wonder how we should handle the case of results that only use a single Tate pairing value $t_n(P,Q)$ for some $P \in E[n]$ and $Q \in E(\mathbb{F}_q)$, which do not seem to fit the above framework of Tate profiles. We argue that such results should be interpreted with respect to the cyclic isogeny $f : E \to E/\langle P\rangle$ and the generalized Tate pairing t_f, instead of the Tate pairing t_n associated to scalar multiplication by $[n]$.

With respect to this isogeny, the single Tate pairing value $t_n(P,Q)$ becomes the full Tate profile $t_{\ker f}(Q) = t_f(P,Q)$ as we have the basis $\ker f = \langle P\rangle$, instead of simply a partial profile with respect to $[n]$. We believe this more clearly demonstrates what the value $t_n(P,Q)$ illustrates: it signifies the position of $Q \in E(\mathbb{F}_q)$ with respect to the decomposition of $E(\mathbb{F}_q)$ into cosets $Q' + \widehat{f}(E'(\mathbb{F}_q))$, where $E' = E/\langle P\rangle$. We illustrate this with a few examples from the literature.

Example 4. Assume we are working with supersingular Montgomery curves over $\mathbb{F}_{p^2}$ with $2^f \mid p+1$ so that $\mathcal{S}_{2,p^2} = \mathbb{Z}_{2^f} \times \mathbb{Z}_{2^f}$. A well-known trick to find points Q whose order is divisible by 2^f is to simply sample a non-square x_Q until it defines a point $Q \in E(\mathbb{F}_{p^2})$ [CJL+17]. This should be interpreted as a non-trivial reduced Tate pairing of degree 2 with $P = (0,0)$, as we have that $t_2(P,Q) = x_Q^{\frac{q-1}{2}}$. Using the above interpretation, we can similarly say that Q has a non-trivial profile with respect to the degree-2 isogeny $f : E \to E'$ where $\ker f = \langle P\rangle$, and so, we find that Q is *not* in the image $\widehat{f}(E'(\mathbb{F}_{p^2}))$. This implies two things:

1. The order of Q is divisible by 2^f. Otherwise, there is an $R \in E(\mathbb{F}_q)$ such that $[2]R = \widehat{f}(f(R)) = Q$, which implies $Q \in \widehat{f}(E'(\mathbb{F}_{p^2}))$
2. The point Q is *not* above $(0,0)$. Namely, if Q is above $(0,0)$, then $f(Q)$ is of order 2^{f-1}, and there is an $R' \in E'(\mathbb{F}_{p^2})$ such that $[2]R' = f(Q)$. But then $\widehat{f}(R') = Q$.

This interpretation of the value $t_2(P,Q)$ gives us slightly more information: we learn something about the *position* of Q instead of only about the *order* of Q.

Example 5. The self-Tate pairing $t_\ell(P,P)$ for $P \in E(\mathbb{F}_q)$ gives us information about the ℓ-volcano structure [IJ13]. Indeed, Robert [Rob23] shows that, rephrased as the Tate profile, triviality of the value $t_\ell(P,P)$ implies that $P \in \widehat{f}(E'(\mathbb{F}_q))$ where $E' = E/\langle P\rangle$. Hence, $E'(\mathbb{F}_q)[\ell]$ must be rank 2: there is a point $P' \in E'[\ell]$ that generates the dual $\widehat{f}$, and some other point $Q' \in E'[\ell]$ that maps back to P under $\widehat{f}$.

4 Improving Known Results Using Tate Profiles

In this section, we improve smart sampling [CEMR24], entangled basis generation [ZSP+18], and subgroup membership testing [Kos23] in terms of Tate profiles. We then generalize entangled basis generation to a wider set of elliptic curves.

Remark 3. This section focuses solely on elliptic curves. In the previous section we computed the profile with respect to a basis of $E[n]$. In this section, when $n = 2$, we will compute the profile with respect to all three points $E[2] \setminus \mathbf{0}_E$, which clarifies some results. For Montgomery curves $E_A : y^2 = x^3 + Ax^2 + x$, we use the notation $L_0 = (0,0)$, $L_1 = (\alpha, 0)$, and $L_2 = (1/\alpha, 0)$ to denote the three 2-torsion points, and we denote by $t_{[2]}(Q)$ the 2-Tate profile

$$t_{[2]}(Q) = (t_2(L_0,Q), t_2(L_1,Q), t_2(L_2,Q)) \in \mu_2^3$$

with respect to these three points. This is only meant to illustrate the results: the third value of the profile can be derived from the first two.

4.1 Smart Torsion Basis Sampling

Theorem 2 of AprèsSQI [CEMR24] shows that the quadratic characters of x, $x-\alpha$ and $x-1/\alpha$ on Montgomery curves contain precise information on points $P \in E[2^f]$, namely, that they are above a certain 2-torsion point L_i.

Lemma 1 **([CEMR24, Thm. 2]).** *Let E_A be a maximal supersingular Montgomery curve over $\mathbb{F}_{p^2}$ with $p = 2^f \cdot h - 1$, written as $E_A : y^2 = x(x-\alpha)(x-1/\alpha)$. Let $P \in E[2^f]$, then*

$$[2^{f-1}]P = L_i \quad \Leftrightarrow \quad t_2(L_i,P) = 1 \text{ and } t_2(L_j,P) = -1 \text{ for } j \neq i.$$

Lemma 1 essentially shows that the profile of P determines the coset of $E(\mathbb{F}_q)/[2]E(\mathbb{F}_q)$ in which P lies. This allows for an even broader interpretation: Any basis (P,Q) for $E[2^f]$ must have P and Q in different, non-trivial, cosets of $E(\mathbb{F}_q)/[2]E(\mathbb{F}_q)$. In simpler terms, if we want a basis P,Q for $E(\mathbb{F}_q)[2^f]$, we need two points P and Q with different non-trivial profiles $t_{[2]}(P)$ and $t_{[2]}(Q)$. The profile interpretation of Lemma 1 tells us that $t_{[2]}(P)$ indicates precisely the coset $P + [2]E(\mathbb{F}_q)$ that lies above a certain 2-torsion point.

Remark 4. In practice, Lemma 1 can be used to avoid certain edge cases: we may want to avoid cyclic 2^f-isogenies with $L_0 = (0,0)$ in their kernel, and so, we can sample P above L_1 or L_2, and Q above L_0. Then, any combination $K = P + sQ$ for $s \in \mathbb{Z}_{2^f}$ gives us an isogeny $E \to E/\langle K \rangle$, whose kernel does not contain L_0.

We rephrase Lemma 1 in terms of the profile of the generalized Tate pairing with respect to the isogenies $E \to E/\langle L_i \rangle$, as described in Sect. 3.4, essentially generalizing Example 4.

Lemma 2. *Let E_A be a maximal supersingular Montgomery curve over $\mathbb{F}_{p^2}$ with $p = 2^f \cdot h - 1$, written as $E_A : y^2 = x(x-\alpha)(x-1/\alpha)$. Let $\phi_i : E \to E/\langle L_i \rangle$. Then,*

$$t_{\ker \phi_i}(P) \neq 1 \quad \Leftrightarrow \quad 2^f \mid \mathrm{Order}(P) \text{ and } [2^{f-1}]P \neq L_i.$$

Proof. The proof is a repetition of Example 4: we have $t_{\ker \phi_i}(P) \neq 1$ only if $P \in E \setminus \widehat{\phi}_i(E'(\mathbb{F}_q))$. By writing out the action of ϕ_i and $\widehat{\phi}_i$ on $E[2^f]$, we find that $P \in E \setminus \widehat{\phi}_i(E'(\mathbb{F}_q))$ only if $2^f \mid \mathrm{Order}(P)$ and P is above L_i, i.e., $[2^{f-1}]P \neq L_i$. □

4.2 Entangled Basis Generation

Entangled basis generation [ZSP+18] allows us to sample a basis for $E[2^f]$ very efficiently, using a modification of the Elligator map [BHKL13]. Due to its efficiency, this approach is often used in practice. Examples are SIDH/SIKE [DJP14, JAC+17] and SQIsign [AAA+25].

Lemma 3 ([ZSP+18]). *Let E_A be a maximal supersingular Montgomery curve over $\mathbb{F}_{p^2}$ with $p = 2^f \cdot h - 1$ for $f \in \mathbb{N}$ and some cofactor h, and $A \neq 0$. Choose a non-square $t \in \mathbb{F}_{p^2}$, such that $x_P = -A/(1+t^2)$ is also non-square, and x_P defines a point $P \in E(\mathbb{F}_{p^2})$.*

Then $x_Q = -x_P - A$ defines a point $Q \in E(\mathbb{F}_{p^2})$, and $([h]P, [h]Q)$ is a basis for $E[2^f]$.

At first, this result feels somewhat magical: there is no good reason why this particular choice of x_Q would define a point on $E(\mathbb{F}_{p^2})$, nor why both points have order divisible by 2^f and together generate $E[2^f]$. Following the mantra, we must look at their 2-Tate profiles $t_{[2]}(P)$ and $t_{[2]}(Q)$.[4]

First, notice that the choice of x_P as a non-square implies that $t_{\ker \phi_i}(L_0, P) \neq 1$, hence from Example 4 P has order divisible by 2^f and is not above $(0,0)$. As $t_{\ker \phi_i}(L_0, P) \neq 1$, we furthermore get that $t_{[2]}(P)$ is non-trivial, so, either $(-1,1,-1)$ or $(-1,-1,1)$. Then, choosing x_Q as $-x_P - A$ ensures two things: First, $x_Q = -x_P - A = t^2 \cdot x_P$ is non-square too, and second, the quadratic character of $x_Q - \alpha$ and $x_Q - 1/\alpha$ can be computed as

$$x_Q - \alpha = -x_P - A - \alpha = -x_P + \alpha + 1/\alpha - \alpha = -(x_P - 1/\alpha),$$

[4] We thank Damien Robert for explaining entangled basis generation in this way.

where we use that $A = -\alpha - 1/\alpha$. Thus, this choice of x_Q ensure two things: x_Q determines a point $Q \in E(\mathbb{F}_{p^2})$ with a non-trivial profile, and this profile $t_{[2]}(Q)$ is the permutation of the profile $t_{[2]}(P)$, as it swaps the last two elements, i.e., mapping either $t_{[2]}(P) = (-1,-1,1) \mapsto t_{[2]}(Q) = (-1,1,-1)$, or vice versa. Although we know neither the profile of P, nor of Q, we know both profiles are different and non-trivial, hence some multiple of P and Q generate $E[2^f]$. Rephrased in Tate profiles, we get the following.

Lemma 4. *Let E_A be a maximal supersingular Montgomery curve over $\mathbb{F}_{p^2}$ with $p = 2^f \cdot h - 1$ for $f \in \mathbb{N}$ and some cofactor h, and $A \neq 0$. Choose a non-square $t \in \mathbb{F}_{p^2}$, such that $x_P = -A/(1+t^2)$ is also non-square, and x_P defines a point $P \in E(\mathbb{F}_{p^2})$. Then $t_{[2]}(P)$ is non-trivial.*

Furthermore, taking $x_Q = -x_P - A$ defines a point $Q \in E(\mathbb{F}_{p^2})$ with $t_{[2]}(Q) \neq t_{[2]}(P)$ and both non-trivial.

We see that the magic is somewhat clarified: the choice of x_Q is determined by the permutation of the profile. This observation allows us to generalize this result in Sect. 4.3.

Remark 5. In contrast to Lemma 1, entangled basis generation does not give us the exact position of P and Q. However, we can still avoid $L_0 = (0,0)$ in the kernel of an isogeny: this only happens when $K = aP + bQ$, with $a, b, \in \mathbb{Z}_{2^f}$ is above $(0,0)$, which can only occur when either both a and b are even (but then K has order smaller than 2^f) or when both a and b are odd. Thus, we can still avoid $(0,0)$ by choosing only one of a or b odd.

4.3 Generalizing Entangled Basis Generation

We now also have enough understanding of profiles to generalize entangled basis generation (Lemma 3) to any Weierstrass curve over $\mathbb{F}_q$ with $q = p^{2k}$, so that -1 is a square, and

$$E : y^2 = (x - \lambda_1)(x - \lambda_2)(x - \lambda_3), \quad \lambda_i \in \mathbb{F}_q.$$

Remark 6. In practice, restricting to Weierstrass curves whose right-hand side factors is not an actual restriction: this implies that the 2-torsion is rational, and so that $\mathcal{S}_{2,q}(E)$ has rank 2. If the right-hand-side does not factor, the Sylow-2 torsion has rank 1, so we just need to find a single generator $P \in E[2^f]$.

In this case, we do not just find a basis for $E[2^f]$, but really for the Sylow 2-torsion, even if $\mathcal{S}_{2,q}(E) \not\cong \mathbb{Z}_{2^f} \times \mathbb{Z}_{2^f}$. We need to find a transformation $x_P \mapsto x_Q$ that ensures we get two different non-trivial profiles $t_{[2]}(P) \neq t_{[2]}(Q)$. Thus, we need to sample x_P in such a way that we do not change the quadratic character of the first (unreduced) Tate pairing $x_P - \lambda_1 = u^2(x_Q - \lambda_1)$ for some $u \in \mathbb{F}_q$, and permute the second and third Tate pairing using $x_Q = -x_P + \lambda_2 + \lambda_3$, as this ensures

$$(x_Q - \lambda_2) = -(x_P - \lambda_3), \quad (x_Q - \lambda_3) = -(x_P - \lambda_2).$$

This gives us two equations in terms of x_P and x_Q and solving these gives us

$$x_P = \frac{\lambda_2 + \lambda_3 - 2 \cdot \lambda_1}{1 + u^2}, \quad u \in \mathbb{F}_q.$$

Thus, if we precompute two lists with values $\frac{1}{1+u^2}$ either squares or non-squares, then by the quadratic character of $\lambda_2 + \lambda_3 - 2 \cdot \lambda_1$, we can ensure we sample x_P as a non-square. By the above equations, when x_P defines a point on E, the derived $x_Q = -x_P + \lambda_2 + \lambda_3$ defines a point $Q \in E$, such that P and Q have different non-trivial 2-profiles, and hence generate the Sylow-2 subgroup for E. Summarizing, we get the following.

Lemma 5. *Let $E : y^2 = (x - \lambda_1)(x - \lambda_2)(x - \lambda_3)$, with $\lambda_i \in \mathbb{F}_q$. Let $P \in E(\mathbb{F}_q)$ with non-square $x_P = \frac{\lambda_2+\lambda_3-2\cdot\lambda_1}{1+u^2}$ for some $u \in \mathbb{F}_q$. Then, $x_Q = -x_P + \lambda_2 + \lambda_3$ defines a second point Q on E such that $[h]P$ and $[h]Q$ generate the Sylow-2 subgroup $\mathcal{S}_{2,q} \cong \mathbb{Z}_{2^f} \times \mathbb{Z}_{2^g}$, with $f \geq g$, for $h = \frac{\#E(\mathbb{F}_q)}{2^{f+g}}$.*

If necessary, we may also permute the profiles in any other permutation. This approach similarly extends to other curve models if we can solve the following linear system, which is underneath the above result: Let $f_i(x)$ denote the unreduced 2-Tate pairing $T_2(L_i, -)$ on the given curve E. Crucially, in the above, we have that x defines a point on $E(\mathbb{F}_{p^2})$ whenever $\prod f_i(x) = 1$, as this is the right-hand side of the curve equation of E. Then, for entangled basis generation, we want a non-trivial profile, i.e., at least some $f_i(x_P)$ is a non-square, and furthermore

$$f_1(x_P) = t_1^2 \cdot f_1(x_Q)$$
$$f_2(x_P) = t_2^2 \cdot f_3(x_Q)$$
$$f_3(x_P) = t_3^2 \cdot f_2(x_Q)$$

where the $t_i \in \mathbb{F}_q^*$ are chosen so that we have slightly more freedom, as they do not affect the profiles. In the above example, if we choose $t_2^2 = -1$, we turn the second equation into $x_P - \alpha = -(x_Q - 1/\alpha)$, from which we find the choice $x_Q = -x_P - A$. The first equation then ensures our choice of x_P must satisfy $x_P = -A/(1 + t_1^2)$, which recovers the original solution in Lemma 3. Note that the third equation is satisfied by these choices.

4.4 Subgroup Membership Testing

Koshelev's method for subgroup membership testing [Kos23, DHK+24] is based on the observation that the subgroup membership problem can, in some cases, be rephrased using the non-degeneracy of the Tate pairing. This is significantly different from other approaches [Sco21].

Theorem 2 ([Kos23, Lem. 1])**.** *Let $E/\mathbb{F}_p$ be an elliptic curve with $E(\mathbb{F}_p) \cong \mathbb{Z}_{e_1} \times \mathbb{Z}_{e_2} \times \mathbb{Z}_r$, with $e_1 \mid e_2$ and both coprime with r, and let G denote the* *subgroup of* $E(\mathbb{F}_p)$ *of order* r*. Let* P_1 *and* P_2 *generate* $E[e_2](\mathbb{F}_p)$*, of order* e_1*, resp.* e_2*. Assume* $e_2 \mid p-1$*, so that the Tate pairing is non-degenerate. Then,*

$$Q \in G \quad \Leftrightarrow \quad t_{e_1}(P_1, Q) = 1 \text{ and } t_{e_2}(P_2, Q) = 1.$$

Rephrased in Tate profiles, Koshelev's subgroup membership test simply says that $Q \in E[r](\mathbb{F}_p)$ if and only if Q has trivial profile $t_{[e_2]}(Q)$. This simple observation makes the generalization to higher dimensions clear: we need to verify the triviality of the n-profile of Q with respect to the cofactor n.

5 Optimized 2-Tate Profile Using Cubical Pairings

In this section we optimize the computation of level-2 cubical pairings on Kummer surfaces. We first discuss generic improvements, which apply in general to improve cubical pairings of degree 2 on Kummer surfaces, before we describe specific improvements that are possible by precomputation given a specific Kummer surface. The starting point is Algorithm 1, which we try to optimize as much as possible to compute the full 2-Tate profile.

In this section, $\mathcal{K}$ denotes a Kummer surface associated to some Jacobian $\mathcal{J}$, and we want to compute the 2-Tate profile with respect to some basis $B_1, \dots, B_4$ of $\mathcal{K}[2]$. We assume this basis is k-rational, for some finite field k. Later, we want to specifically work with the Gaudry–Schost Kummer surface from Example 1, with $k = \mathbb{F}_p$. The result of this section is summarized in the following theorem.

Theorem 3. *Let* $P = (P_1 : P_2 : P_3 : P_4) \in \mathcal{K}(\mathbb{F}_p)$*, originating from* $\mathcal{J}(\mathbb{F}_p)$*. Let* $m_1 := P_1 \cdot \left(\sum_{j=1}^4 M_{1,j} P_i\right)$*,* $m_2 := P_3 \cdot \left(\sum_{j=1}^4 M_{2,j} P_i\right)$*,* $m_3 := P_1 \cdot P_4$*, and* $m_4 := P_1 \cdot P_3$ *where the* $M_{i,j} \in \mathbb{F}_p$ *are precomputed constants. Denote by* ζ_i *the Legendre symbol of* m_i*. Then the 2-Tate profile*

$$t_{[2]}(P) = (\zeta_1, \zeta_2, \zeta_3, \zeta_4),$$

is computed in 6 additions, 10 multiplications, and 4 Legendre symbols over $\mathbb{F}_p$*.*

Remark 7. We should be careful that this profile computation assumes P originates from $\mathcal{J}$, and not $\mathcal{J}^T$, as this could affect some sign differences in the profile computation. Although these are easy and essentially free to correct, they are unnecessary if we simply care if a profile is trivial or not.

5.1 Generic Improvements

Replace Inversions by Multiplications. As inversions are rather costly in finite fields, we prefer to avoid them as much as possible in our computations. Luckily, in Tate pairing computations, our results live in the quotient k^*/k^{*n}, which allows us to remove inversions if n is small enough, using the following observation.

Observation 1. In k^*/k^{*n}, for $\lambda_Q, \lambda_P \in k^*$, we have $\lambda_P^n \in k^*$, hence,

$$\frac{\lambda_Q}{\lambda_P} \equiv \frac{\lambda_Q}{\lambda_P} \cdot \lambda_P^n \equiv \lambda_Q \cdot \lambda_P^{n-1}.$$

In particular, for $n = 2$, we have $\lambda_Q/\lambda_P \equiv \lambda_Q \cdot \lambda_P$.

As we focus only on the degree-2 Tate pairing, we are essentially able to remove most inversions in our cubical arithmetic. For the *reduced* Tate pairing, one can rephrase the above observation: the Legendre symbol of $1/\alpha$ is the same as the Legendre symbol of α.

An Easy Basis of $\mathcal{K}[2]$. We are free to choose our basis $B_1, \dots, B_4$ of $\mathcal{K}[2]$ with respect to which we compute the profile $t_{[2]}(Q) = (t_2(B_i, Q))_{i=1}^4$. We make the following observation.

Observation 2. The matrices $W_{1,2}$, $W_{3,4}$, and $W_{5,6}$ are permutation matrices, hence, their action on $Q = (Q_1 : Q_2 : Q_3 : Q_4) \in \mathcal{K}(\mathbb{F}_p)$ is essentially free. In particular, the computation of $t_2(L_{i,j}, Q)$ is significantly cheaper for $(i,j) \in \{(1,2),(3,4),(5,6)\}$.

Therefore, choosing (arbitrarily) a basis with $B_3 = L_{3,4}$ and $B_4 = L_{5,6}$ saves a significant amount of multiplications in the computation of $t_2(B_3, Q)$ and $t_2(B_4, Q)$, and therefore in the profile $t_{[2]}(Q)$.

Partial Matrix Multiplication. In the computation of λ_Q, we require the action of $W_{i,j}$ on $\widetilde{L_{i,j} + Q} = (l_1, l_2, l_3, l_4)$ to compute the translation. However, in line 6 and later, we only need the k-th index of the result, for some predetermined $1 \le k \le 4$. Hence, if $W_{i,j}^{(k)} = (w_1, w_2, w_3, w_4)$ denotes the k-th row of $W_{i,j}$, we only need to compute the k-th index of $W_{i,j} \cdot \widetilde{L_{i,j} + Q}$ as $m_1 l_1 + m_2 l_2 + m_3 l_3 + m_4 l_4$. This saves a significant number of multiplications in the computation of $t_2(L_{i,j}, Q)$ for $(i,j) \notin \{(1,2),(3,4),(5,6)\}$[5].

5.2 Specific Improvements

We now describe improvements that are possible when working on a specific Kummer surface. An explicit example is given in Sect. 6, where we apply these optimizations to the Gaudry–Schost Kummer surface.

Removing the Action of $W_{i,j}^2$. To compute the λ_Q required for $t_2(L_{i,j}, Q)$, we compute $\widetilde{L_{i,j} + Q}$ using the action of $W_{i,j}$ on $\widetilde{Q}$, and translate the result again by $W_{i,j}$. This can be simplified by the following observation.

[5] The case $(i,j) \in \{(1,2),(3,4),(5,6)\}$ is covered more efficiently by Observation 2.

Observation 3. Let $\widetilde{Q} = (Q_1, Q_2, Q_3, Q_4) \in \mathcal{K}(\mathbb{F}_p)$. Then $\widetilde{L_{i,j} + Q} = W_{i,j} \cdot \widetilde{Q} = (a_1, a_2, a_3, a_4)$ for some $a_i \in \mathcal{K}(\mathbb{F}_p)$. After normalizing $\widetilde{L_{i,j} + Q}$ to a given index $k \in \{1, \ldots 4\}$, we find that $W_{i,j} \cdot a_k \cdot \widetilde{L_{i,j} + Q} = a_k \cdot W_{i,j}^2 \widetilde{Q}$. For every possible (i, j), we have $W_{i,j}^2 = \gamma_{i,j} \cdot I_4$ for some $\gamma_{i,j} \in \mathbb{F}_p$. Hence,

$$\lambda_Q \equiv \left(W_{i,j} \cdot a_k \cdot \widetilde{L_{i,j} + Q}\right)_k \equiv a_k \cdot \left(W_{i,j}^2 \widetilde{Q}\right)_k \equiv a_k \cdot \gamma_{i,j} \cdot Q_k$$

As we can precompute the Legendre symbol of $\gamma_{i,j}$ on a specific Kummer surface, we can significantly simplify the computation of λ_Q: we only need to compute a_k as the k-th index of $W_{i,j} \cdot \widetilde{Q}$, which we can do using the partial matrix multiplication. Combined, these improvements replace two full matrix computations, at 16 multiplications each, by a single row multiplication at 4 multiplications, per pairing $t_2(L_{i,j}, Q)$ for $(i, j) \notin \{(1, 2), (3, 4), (5, 6)\}$.

For pairings with $(i, j) \in \{(1, 2), (3, 4), (5, 6)\}$, we find that we only need to know the permutation given by $W_{i,j}$. For example, as $W_{3,4}$ maps $(a, b, c, d) \mapsto (d, c, b, a)$, a similar derivation shows that we can compute λ_Q as $Q_1 \cdot Q_4$.

Precompute the Legendre Symbol of $\lambda_{L_{i,j}}$. It is clear that $\lambda_{L_{i,j}}$ does not depend on the point Q we are pairing with. Hence, on a given Kummer surface, we may precompute the Legendre symbol of $\lambda_{L_{i,j}}$ for each index pair (i, j). To compute $t_2(L_{i,j}, Q)$, we then simply compute the Legendre symbol of λ_Q and adjust by -1 if $\lambda_{L_{i,j}}$ is non-square.

5.3 Optimized Profiles of Degree 2

We combine all these improvements: We choose the basis $\langle L_{2,3}, L_{3,5}, L_{3,4}, L_{5,6} \rangle$ for $\mathcal{K}[2]$, and, together with the other improvements, we obtain Algorithm 2. This is an algorithmic description of Theorem 3: we can compute the 2-profile $t_{[2]}(Q)$ for $Q \in \mathcal{K}(\mathbb{F}_p)$ in $10\mathbf{M} + 6\mathbf{A} + 4\mathbf{L}$ operations over $\mathbb{F}_p$.

Algorithm 2. Optimized pairing computation on $\mathcal{K}(\mathbb{F}_p)$

Input: The point $\widetilde{Q} = (Q_1, Q_2, Q_3, Q_4)$, row 1 of $W_{2,3}$ as (w_1, w_2, w_3, w_4) with $w_1 = 1$, and row 3 of $W_{3,5}$ as (w_1', w_2', w_3', w_4') with $w_3' = -1$.
Output: The profile $t_{[2]}(Q) \in \mu_2^4$.
1: $T_1 \leftarrow Q_1 \cdot (w_1 Q_1 + w_2 Q_2 + w_3 Q_3 + w_4 Q_4)$
2: $T_2 \leftarrow Q_3 \cdot (w_1' Q_1 + w_2' Q_2 + w_3' Q_3 + w_4' Q_4)$
3: $T_3 \leftarrow Q_1 \cdot Q_4$
4: $T_4 \leftarrow Q_1 \cdot Q_3$
5: For $i \in \{1, 2, 3, 4\}$ do $\zeta_i \leftarrow \mathsf{Legendre}(T_i)$,
6: **return** $(\zeta_1, \zeta_2, \zeta_3, \zeta_4)$

Remark 8. Heuristically, it seems infeasible to compute a profile with fewer than 4 Legendre symbols, as the profile requires 4 bits of information. As the overhead, $10\mathbf{M} + 6\mathbf{A}$, is negligible compared to the cost of the Legendre symbols, we did not pursue further optimizations. If one assumes $\widetilde{Q}$ obtained as a normalized point $(1, Q_2, Q_3, Q_4)$, we save an extra $4\mathbf{M} + 1\mathbf{A}$.

6 Subgroup Membership Testing for Gaudry–Schost's $\mathcal{K}$

This section combines the ideas from Sects. 4.4 and 5 and applies them to highly optimize a specific situation. First, we apply the generalization of subgroup membership testing to Kummer surfaces using Tate profiles to the Gaudry–Schost Kummer surface. Then, we use the optimized 2-Tate profile computation from Sect. 5 to perform this subgroup membership testing.

This section only focuses on this particular Kummer surface, as described in Sect. 2.2. We denote it by $\mathcal{K}$, and the associated Jacobian by $\mathcal{J}$. Furthermore, $G = \mathcal{K}[r](\mathbb{F}_p)$ denotes the subgroup of large prime order r, and so subgroup membership testing asks us to verify $Q \in G$ for $Q = (Q_1 : Q_2 : Q_3 : Q_4) \in \mathcal{K}(\mathbb{F}_p)$.

6.1 The Sylow 2-Torsion Structure of $\mathcal{J}$

For the Gaudry–Schost surface, we know that the order of the associated Jacobian $\mathcal{J}(\mathbb{F}_p)$ is $16 \cdot r$, and of its twist $\mathcal{J}^T(\mathbb{F}_p)$ is $16 \cdot r'$. By construction, $\mathcal{J}$ has rational 2-torsion, which is the perfect set-up for Koshelev's approach to subgroup membership testing using Tate pairings:

Observation 4. Let G be the subgroup of order r of $\mathcal{J}(\mathbb{F}_p)$, and similarly, let G' be the subgroup of order r' of $\mathcal{J}^T(\mathbb{F}_p)$. We have that

$$J(\mathbb{F}_p) = \mathcal{J}[2] \times G, \quad \mathcal{J}^T(\mathbb{F}_p) = \mathcal{J}^T[2] \times G'.$$

In other words, we know that $\mathcal{S}_{2,p}(\mathcal{J}) = \mathcal{J}[2] \cong \mathbb{Z}_2 \times \mathbb{Z}_2 \times \mathbb{Z}_2 \times \mathbb{Z}_2$. From this, we easily find the subgroup membership test, by an application of Corollary 1:

Lemma 6. *For $Q \in \mathcal{J}(\mathbb{F}_p)$, we have*

$$Q \in G \quad \Leftrightarrow \quad t_{[2]}(Q) \text{ is trivial.}$$

Proof. By non-degeneracy of the 2-Tate pairing, we have that a trivial profile $t_{[2]}(Q)$ implies $Q \in [2]\mathcal{J}(\mathbb{F}_p)$, and, from Observation 4 we know that $[2]\mathcal{J}(\mathbb{F}_p) = G$. □

We will abuse notation and write $Q \in G$, when we mean that Q is a point on the Kummer surface $\mathcal{K}$ associated to a point in the subgroup $G = \mathcal{J}[r](\mathbb{F}_p)$.

6.2 Results

To the best of our knowledge, there are no previous attempts in the literature to perform subgroup membership testing on Kummer surfaces. We therefore compare our results against **a.)** the naive approach using a ladder, and **b.)** the approach of Sect. 2.3 to compute the profile. The results are summarized in Table 1.

a.) Verifying $[r]Q = \mathbf{0}_{\mathcal{K}}$ using a ladder takes almost 7000 operations in $\mathbb{F}_p$, whereas the optimized cubical profile takes only 478 operations[6] in $\mathbb{F}_p$.

b.) The dominating cost in both approaches is the overhead of the Legendre symbols, which takes more than 98% in the optimized approach. A more useful metric here is the reduction in overhead, i.e., everything beyond the Legendre symbols. The overhead of the approach of Sect. 2.3 is $76\mathbf{M}+33\mathbf{S}+53\mathbf{A}$, whereas Algorithm 2 computes the profile with an overhead of $10\mathbf{M}+6\mathbf{A}$ operations in $\mathbb{F}_p$. Assuming $\mathbf{S} = 0.8\mathbf{M}$ and $\mathbf{A} = 0.05\mathbf{M}$, the latter takes roughly 10 times fewer operations.

Including Origin Check. Depending on the application, one may need to verify that $Q \in \mathcal{K}(\mathbb{F}_p)$ originates from $\mathcal{J}$ or its twist.

a.) The naive approach verifies the origin from the fact that only a point originating from the Jacobian could have order r, and so, we verify the origin at no extra cost. Including the origin check to the cubical approach adds 140 $\mathbb{F}_p$ operations, bringing the total to 618 operations in $\mathbb{F}_p$. The cubical approach is therefore still more than ten times faster than the naive approach, even including the origin check.

b.) For the pairings from Sect. 2.3, this only requires an extra Legendre symbol, whereas for the cubical pairings, this adds an extra $22\mathbf{M}+1\mathbf{S}+13\mathbf{A}$, beyond the extra Legendre symbol, to the overhead. The resulting overhead is however still three times less.

Table 1. Operation counts for different approaches to subgroup membership testing on the Gaudry–Schost Kummer surface, with and without origin check. Cost model: $\mathbf{M} = 1$, $\mathbf{S} = 0.8$, $\mathbf{A} = 0.05$, Legendre $\mathbf{L} = 125\mathbf{S} + 9\mathbf{M}$.

	M	S	A	L	Overhead	Total
Ladder by $[r]$	4514	2008	8016	0	–	**6992**
On Jacobian (Sect. 2.3)	76	33	53	4	105	**573**
Opt. Cubical (Sect. 5)	10	0	6	4	10	**478**
On Jacobian w/ Origin	76	33	53	5	105	**682**
Opt. Cubical w/ Origin	32	1	19	5	34	**579**

[6] We estimate a Legendre symbol computation at $125\mathbf{S}+9\mathbf{M}$ using an optimal addition chain. In practice, this can be done much faster [Por20, AHST23].

7 Future Work

In this work we have shown that the language of Tate profiles gives a natural description of many results in the literature, and, by placing these results in this language, we are able to generalize several of them. As a consequence, one may similarly rephrase other results in this language in the hope to generalize them.

For example, one may apply the generalization of Koshelev's membership test to other Kummer surfaces, or essentially any (Kummer variety of an) abelian variety, and optimize the required cubical arithmetic.

Furthermore, the optimized cubical profile computation may be used more widely to sample points of order 2^f on Kummer surfaces: by forcing a non-trivial profile during sampling, we force $Q \in \mathcal{K} \setminus [2]\mathcal{K}$. For example, if we initialize Q as $(1, Y, Z, T)$ where Z is any non-square element in $\mathbb{F}_p$, we force $t_2(L_{5,6}, Q) = -1$, which ensures a non-trivial profile. We then look for suitable Y and T to ensure $Q \in \mathcal{K}(\mathbb{F}_p)$. In practice, Tate pairings are often used for basis generation, and so, simpler 2-pairings should apply more broadly to generate a basis of 2^f-torsion, with 2^f maximal.

Lastly, we may hope to generalize entangled basis generation to higher dimensions, using both the techniques from Sect. 4.3 and Sect. 5.

References

[AAA+25] Aardal, M.A., et al.: SQIsign 2.0: Algorithm specifications and supporting documentation. Technical report (2025)

[AHST23] Aranha, D.F., Hvass, B.S., Spitters, B., Tibouchi, M.: Faster constant-time evaluation of the Kronecker symbol with application to elliptic curve hashing. In: Proceedings of the 2023 ACM SIGSAC Conference on Computer and Communications Security, pp. 3228–3238 (2023)

[BCHL16] Bos, J.W., Costello, C., Hisil, H., Lauter, K.: Fast cryptography in genus 2. J. Cryptol. **29**(1), 28–60 (2016)

[BCM+15] Barreto, P.S.L.M., Costello, C., Misoczki, R., Naehrig, M., Pereira, G.C.C.F., Zanon, G.: Subgroup security in pairing-based cryptography. In: Lauter, K., Rodríguez-Henríquez, F. (eds.) LATINCRYPT 2015. LNCS, vol. 9230, pp. 245–265. Springer, Cham (2015). https://doi.org/10.1007/978-3-319-22174-8_14

[BDLS20] Bernstein, D.J., De Feo, L., Leroux, A., Smith, B.: Faster computation of isogenies of large prime degree. In: ANTS-XIV-14th Algorithmic Number Theory Symposium, vol. 4, pp. 39–55. Mathematical Sciences Publishers (2020)

[BF01] Boneh, D., Franklin, M.: Identity-based encryption from the weil pairing. In: Kilian, J. (ed.) CRYPTO 2001. LNCS, vol. 2139, pp. 213–229. Springer, Heidelberg (2001). https://doi.org/10.1007/3-540-44647-8_13

[BGLS03] Boneh, D., Gentry, C., Lynn, B., Shacham, H.: Aggregate and verifiably encrypted signatures from bilinear maps. In: Biham, E. (ed.) EUROCRYPT 2003. LNCS, vol. 2656, pp. 416–432. Springer, Heidelberg (2003). https://doi.org/10.1007/3-540-39200-9_26

[BHKL13] Bernstein, D.J., Hamburg, M., Krasnova, A., Lange, T.: Elligator: elliptic-curve points indistinguishable from uniform random strings. In: Proceedings of the 2013 ACM SIGSAC Conference on Computer & Communications Security, pp. 967–980 (2013)

[BKLS02] Barreto, P.S.L.M., Kim, H.Y., Lynn, B., Scott, M.: Efficient algorithms for pairing-based cryptosystems. In: Yung, M. (ed.) CRYPTO 2002. LNCS, vol. 2442, pp. 354–369. Springer, Heidelberg (2002). https://doi.org/10.1007/3-540-45708-9_23

[BLS01] Boneh, D., Lynn, B., Shacham, H.: Short signatures from the weil pairing. In: Boyd, C. (ed.) ASIACRYPT 2001. LNCS, vol. 2248, pp. 514–532. Springer, Heidelberg (2001). https://doi.org/10.1007/3-540-45682-1_30

[BLS04] Barreto, P.S., Lynn, B., Scott, M.: Efficient implementation of pairing-based cryptosystems. J. Cryptol. **17**(4), 321–334 (2004)

[Bow19] Bowe, S.: Faster Subgroup Checks for BLS12-381. Cryptology ePrint Archive, Paper 2019/814 (2019). https://eprint.iacr.org/2019/814

[Bru11] Bruin, P.: The Tate pairing for abelian varieties over finite fields. J. de theorie des nombres de Bordeaux **23**(2), 323–328 (2011)

[CC86] Chudnovsky, D.V., Chudnovsky, G.V.: Sequences of numbers generated by addition in formal groups and new primality and factorization tests. Adv. Appl. Math. **7**(4), 385–434 (1986)

[CDV20] Castryck, W., Decru, T., Vercauteren, F.: Radical isogenies. In: Moriai, S., Wang, H. (eds.) ASIACRYPT 2020. LNCS, vol. 12492, pp. 493–519. Springer, Cham (2020). https://doi.org/10.1007/978-3-030-64834-3_17

[CEMR24] Corte-Real Santos, M., Eriksen, J.K., Meyer, M., Reijnders, K.: AprésSQI: extra fast verification for SQIsign using extension-field signing. In: Advances in Cryptology - EUROCRYPT 2024 - 43nd Annual International Conference on the Theory and Applications of Cryptographic Techniques (2024)

[CF96] Cassels, J.W.S., Flynn, E.V.: Prolegomena to a Middlebrow Arithmetic of Curves of Genus 2, vol. 230. Cambridge University Press, Cambridge (1996)

[CHM+23] Castryck, W., Houben, M., Merz, S.P., Mula, M., van Buuren, S., Vercauteren, F.: Weak instances of class group action based cryptography via self-pairings. In: Annual International Cryptology Conference, pp. 762–792. Springer, Heidelberg (2023)

[CJL+17] Costello, C., Jao, D., Longa, P., Naehrig, M., Renes, J., Urbanik, D.: Efficient compression of SIDH public keys. In: Coron, J.-S., Nielsen, J.B. (eds.) EUROCRYPT 2017. LNCS, vol. 10210, pp. 679–706. Springer, Cham (2017). https://doi.org/10.1007/978-3-319-56620-7_24

[CR24] Corte-Real Santos, M., Reijnders, K.: Return of the Kummer: a Toolbox for Genus-2 Cryptography. Cryptology ePrint Archive, Paper 2024/948 (2024). https://eprint.iacr.org/2024/948

[DHK+24] Dai, Y., He, D., Koshelev, D., Peng, C., Yang, Z.: Revisiting subgroup membership testing on pairing-friendly curves via the Tate pairing. Cryptology ePrint Archive, Paper 2024/1790 (2024). https://eprint.iacr.org/2024/1790

[DJP14] Feo, L., Jao, D., Plût, J.: Towards quantumresistant cryptosystems from supersingular elliptic curve isogenies. J. Math. Cryptol. **8**(3), 209–247 (2014)

[Dol18] Doliskani, J.: On division polynomial PIT and supersingularity. Appl. Algebra Eng. Commun. Comput. **29**(5), 393–407 (2018)

[FR94] Frey, G., Rück, H.-G.: A remark concerning mdivisibility and the discrete logarithm in the divisor class group of curves. Math. Comput. **62**(206), 865–874 (1994)

[Gal05] Galbraith, S.D.: Pairings. In: London Mathematics Society Lecture Note Series, vol. 317 (2005)

[Gau07] Gaudry, P.: Fast genus 2 arithmetic based on Theta functions. J. Math. Cryptol. **1**(3), 243–265 (2007)

[GHS02] Galbraith, S.D., Harrison, K., Soldera, D.: Implementing the tate pairing. In: Fieker, C., Kohel, D.R. (eds.) ANTS 2002. LNCS, vol. 2369, pp. 324–337. Springer, Heidelberg (2002). https://doi.org/10.1007/3-540-45455-1_26

[GS12] Gaudry, P., Schost, É.: Genus 2 point counting over prime fields. J. Symb. Comput. **47**(4), 368–400 (2012)

[HSSI99] Harasawa, R., Shikata, J., Suzuki, J., Imai, H.: Comparing the MOV and FR reductions in elliptic curve cryptography. In: Stern, J. (ed.) EUROCRYPT 1999. LNCS, vol. 1592, pp. 190–205. Springer, Heidelberg (1999). https://doi.org/10.1007/3-540-48910-X_14

[IJ13] Ionica, S., Joux, A.: Pairing the volcano. Math. Comput. **82**(281), 581–603 (2013)

[JAC+17] Jao, D., et al.: SIKE: supersingular isogeny key encapsulation. Technical report (2017)

[Jou02] Joux, A.: The weil and tate pairings as building blocks for public key cryptosystems. In: Fieker, C., Kohel, D.R. (eds.) ANTS 2002. LNCS, vol. 2369, pp. 20–32. Springer, Heidelberg (2002). https://doi.org/10.1007/3-540-45455-1_3

[Jou04] Joux, A.: A one round protocol for tripartite Diffie-Hellman. J. Cryptol. **17**(4), 263–276 (2004)

[Kob87] Koblitz, N.: Elliptic curve cryptosystems. Math. Comput. **48**(177), 203–209 (1987)

[Kob89] Koblitz, N.: Hyperelliptic cryptosystems. J. Cryptol. **1**, 139–150 (1989)

[Kos23] Koshelev, D.I.: Subgroup membership testing on elliptic curves via the Tate pairing. J. Cryptogr. Eng. **13**(1), 125–128 (2023). https://doi.org/10.1007/S13389-022-00296-9

[KT18] Koshiba, T., Takashima, K.: New assumptions on isogenous pairing groups with applications to attribute-based encryption. In: Lee, K. (ed.) ICISC 2018. LNCS, vol. 11396, pp. 3–19. Springer, Cham (2019). https://doi.org/10.1007/978-3-030-12146-4_1

[Lic69] Lichtenbaum, S.: Duality theorems for curves over p-adic fields. Inventiones mathematicae **7**(2), 120–136 (1969)

[LL97] Lim, C.H., Lee, P.J.: A key recovery attack on discrete log-based schemes using a prime order subgroup. In: Kaliski, B.S. (ed.) CRYPTO 1997. LNCS, vol. 1294, pp. 249–263. Springer, Heidelberg (1997). https://doi.org/10.1007/BFb0052240

[LR10] Lubicz, D., Robert, D.: Efficient pairing computation with theta functions. In: Hanrot, G., Morain, F., Thomé, E. (eds.) ANTS 2010. LNCS, vol. 6197, pp. 251–269. Springer, Heidelberg (2010). https://doi.org/10.1007/978-3-642-14518-6_21

[LR15] Lubicz, D., Robert, D.: A generalisation of Miller's algorithm and applications to pairing computations on abelian varieties. J. Symb. Comput. **67**, 68–92 (2015)

[LR16] Lubicz, D., Robert, D.: Arithmetic on Abelian and Kummer varieties. Finite Fields Appl. **39**, 130–158 (2016). https://doi.org/10.1016/j.ffa.2016.01.009. eprint: 2014/493, HAL: hal-01057467

[lS17] luigi1111 and Riccardo "fluffypony" Spagni. Disclosure of a Major Bug in CryptoNote-Based Currencies (2017). Accessed 23 Apr 2025. https://www.getmonero.org/2017/05/17/disclosure-of-a-major-bug-in-cryptonote-based-currencies.html

[LWXZ24] Lin, K., Wang, W., Xu, Z., Zhao, C.A.: A faster software implementation of SQISign. IEEE Trans. Inf. Theory **70**(9), 6679–6689 (2024)

[McL21] McLoughlin, M.B.: addchain: cryptographic addition chain generation in Go. repository (2021). https://github.com/mmcloughlin/addchain. Version 0.4.0. https://doi.org/10.5281/zenodo.5622943

[Mil04] Miller, V.S.: The Weil pairing, and its efficient calculation. J. Cryptol. **17**(4), 235–261 (2004)

[Mil85] Miller, V.S.: Use of elliptic curves in cryptography. In: Williams, H.C. (ed.) CRYPTO 1985. LNCS, vol. 218, pp. 417–426. Springer, Heidelberg (1986). https://doi.org/10.1007/3-540-39799-X_31

[MS24] Macula, J., Stange, K.E.: Extending class group action attacks via sesquilinear pairings. In: International Conference on the Theory and Application of Cryptology and Information Security, pp. 371–395. Springer, Heidelberg (2024)

[MVO91] Menezes, A., Vanstone, S., Okamoto, T.: Reducing elliptic curve logarithms to logarithms in a finite field. In: Proceedings of the Twenty-Third Annual ACM Symposium on Theory of Computing, pp. 80–89 (1991)

[Por20] Pornin, T.: Faster modular inversion and Legendre symbol, and an X25519 speed record (2020). https://www.nccgroup.com/us/research-blog/faster-modular-inversion-and-legendre-symbol-and-an-x25519-speed-record0/

[PRR+25] Pope, G., Reijnders, K., Robert, D., Sferlazza, A., Smith, B: Simpler and faster pairings from the montgomery ladder. IACR Commun. Cryptol. **2**(2), 29 (2025). https://doi.org/10.62056/AH2I893Y6

[Reij23] Reijnders, K.: Effective pairings in isogeny-based cryptography. In: International Conference on Cryptology and Information Security in Latin America, pp. 109–128. Springer, Heidelberg (2023)

[Rob23] Robert, D.: The geometric interpretation of the Tate pairing and its applications. Cryptology ePrint Archive, Paper 2023/177 (2023). https://eprint.iacr.org/2023/177

[Rob24] Robert, D.: Fast pairings via biextensions and cubical arithmetic. Cryptology ePrint Archive, Paper 2024/517 (2024). https://eprint.iacr.org/2024/517

[Sch03] Scholten, J.: Weil restriction of an elliptic curve over a quadratic extension (2003)

[Sco21] Scott, M.: A note on group membership tests for $\mathbb{G}_1$, $\mathbb{G}_2$ and $\mathbb{G}_T$ on BLS pairing-friendly curves (2021). https://eprint.iacr.org/2021/1130

[Sta07] Stange, K.E.: The tate pairing via elliptic nets. In: Takagi, T., Okamoto, E., Okamoto, T., Okamoto, T. (eds.) Pairing 2007, LNCS, vol. 4575, pp. 329–348. Springer, Heidelberg (2007). https://doi.org/10.1007/978-3-540-73489-5_19

[Tat62] Tate, J.: Duality theorems in Galois cohomology over number fields. In: Proceedings of International Congress Mathematicians (Stockholm, 1962), pp. 288–295 (1962)

[Vél71] Vélu, J.: Isogénies entre courbes elliptiques. In: Comptes- Rendus de l'Académie des Sciences, vol. 273, pp. 238–241 (1971). https://gallica.bnf.fr/ark:/12148/cb34416987n/date

[Ver09] Vercauteren, F.: Optimal pairings. IEEE Trans. Inf. Theory **56**(1), 455–461 (2009)

[ZSP+18] Zanon, G.H., Simplicio, M.A., Pereira, G.C., Doliskani, J., Barreto, P.S.: Faster key compression for isogeny-based cryptosystems. IEEE Trans. Comput. **68**(5), 688–701 (2018)

Extending Regev's Quantum Algorithm to Elliptic Curves

Razvan Barbulescu[1,2(✉)], Mugurel Barcau[1,3], and Vicenţiu Paşol[1,3]

[1] Institute of Mathematics of the Romanian Academy, Bucharest, Romania
razvan.barbulescu@u-bordeaux.fr
[2] Institut de mathématiques de Bordeaux, Talence, France
[3] CertSIGN, Bucharest, Romania

Abstract. Public key cryptography can be based on integer factorization and the discrete logarithm problem (DLP), applicable in multiplicative groups and elliptic curves. Regev's recent quantum algorithm was initially designed for solving the integer factorization problem and was later extended to the DLP in the multiplicative group. In this article, we further extend the algorithm to address the DLP for elliptic curves. Notably, based on celebrated conjectures in Number Theory, Regev's algorithm is asymptotically faster than Shor's algorithm for elliptic curves.

We examine the general framework of Regev's algorithm. This preliminary analysis enables us to certify the success of the algorithm on a particular instance before running it. We prove that the algorithm naturally adapts to the multidimensional DLP.

We pave the way for the implementation of Regev's algorithm on certain NIST-listed elliptic curves. Notably, Bernstein's Curve25519 and the deprecated Koblitz curve K-233 have small coefficients—a key feature in the implementation of Regev's algorithm.

1 Introduction

The threat of quantum computing is still in its infancy but is growing rapidly, with the latest NIST technical report recommending the replacement of pre-quantum cryptosystems by 2031 (see [MPR+24]). However, the report states that the solutions must be adapted to the cost requirements and risk management of each application. For instance, in applications based on RFID as the internet of things and self-checkout, the security levels selected by the cryptographers are in some cases below the NIST recommendations (see e.g. [DSL+24] which achieves 95 bits of security on a classical computer instead of 128).

The discrete logarithm problem (DLP) is one of the most important problem in pre-quantum cryptography and it comes in two variants: over the multiplicative group and over the elliptic curves. To assess the security of the DLP in elliptic curves cryptography (ECC) it is necessary to analyze how well the algorithms which tackle the multiplicative group extend to the elliptic curves. Pollard's rho

D. Escudero and I. Damgård (Eds.): LATINCRYPT 2025, LNCS 16129, pp. 234–266, 2026.
https://doi.org/10.1007/978-3-032-06754-8_9

and Shor's algorithm extend to elliptic curves with the same complexity. However, Index Calculus, which is sub-exponential for the multiplicative group, is slower than Pollard's rho in the case of the elliptic curves [Gau00].

In a recent article [Reg25], Regev introduced a quantum algorithm for integer factorization that requires fewer quantum gates per run than Shor's algorithm [Sho94]. Ekerå and Gärtner [EG24] later extended this algorithm to solve discrete logarithms in multiplicative groups, but its elliptic curve variant has remained unexplored. This is our main objective in this work.

At a high level, Regev's algorithm can be seen as a generalization of Shor's algorithm. Let $\mathbb{G}$ denote the group in which discrete logarithms are computed, using additive notation with g as a generator of $\mathbb{G}$ and n as the bit size of the cardinality of $\mathbb{G}$. In Shor's algorithm one computes in superposition the so-called scalar products

$$[z]g = \underbrace{g + g + \cdots + g}_{z \text{ times}}$$

for all n-bit integers z. In Regev's algorithm one selects a set of elements $g_1, \ldots, g_d$ in $\mathbb{G}$ and computes in superposition the so-called multi-scalar products

$$[z_1]g_1 + \cdots + [z_d]g_d,$$

for all the $\lceil n/d \rceil$-bit integers $z_1, \ldots, z_d$.

Recall that on a classical computer multi-scalar product with exponents of n/d bits are computed using a lookup table in $O(n/d)$ group operations (see [Pip80]), having hence a factor d speed-up with respect to computing a scalar product with an n-bit exponent. The improvement offered by Regev's algorithm is primarily due to two key aspects:

- In the multiplicative group, both for factorization and DLP, one can use small elements $g_1, \ldots, g_{d-2}$ and compute on-the-fly every product $[\varepsilon_1]g_1 + \cdots + [\varepsilon_{d-2}]g_{d-2}$ for any $\varepsilon \in \{0,1\}^{d-2}$.
- There are arguments on the geometry of lattices supporting the use of multi-scalar products with exponents of n/d bits.

For a general group $\mathbb{G}$, the geometric arguments are heuristic and related to the classical Gaussian heuristic. Pilatte [Pil24] eliminated the heuristics in the case of factorization and DLP in the multiplicative group. This increases the confidence that similar results hold in other groups $\mathbb{G}$.

Note that if the inputs of the discrete logarithm problem are g and x, then elements $g_0 = g$ and $g_{d-1} = x$ are not small. However, this is not an issue, as a constant number of additions involving general (non-small) elements in the group can still be performed efficiently. In [EG24], it was proposed to explicitly allow a constant number of such non-small elements. The remaining $d-2$ elements are not part of the input and need to be small in order to ensure the efficiency of the algorithm.

In it's initial form, Regev's algorithm required more qubits than Shor's algorithm. This drawback was addressed by Ragavan and Vaikuntanathan (see

[RV24]) who replaced the squaring operations with alternative computations that significantly reduced the number of ancilla qubits. Additionally, the post-processing step was redesigned to ensure robustness against errors arising in the quantum procedure used by the algorithm [EG24, RV24]).

The DLP problem has two important variations : DLP with pre-computations (see e.g. the logjam attack [ABD+15]) and the multidimensional DLP (see e.g. the seminal paper [Bra93]). We also analyze Regev's algorithm for these variants.

A precise cost estimation of the algorithm was done by Ekerå and Gärtner [EG25], who observed that the point at which Regev's algorithm outperforms Shor's occurs beyond typical cryptographic sizes. Thus, Regev's algorithm requires practical improvements to confirm in practice its asymptotic advantage in the gate count. A precise estimation of the quantum resources for the elliptic curve variant is beyond the scope of this article.

1.1 Brief Presentation of Our Results

We begin by considering variants of the DLP for a general group $\mathbb{G}$. Besides the DLP which was treated in [EG24], we are also interested in two of its variations.

First, we address the DLP with pre-computations. In this context, we highlight the advantages of pre-computations that allow us to determine, for a given challenge, the minimal parameters necessary for Regev's algorithm to succeed.

Then we tackle the multidimensional discrete logarithm problem (multidimensional DLP). Specifically, it was known that the multidimensional DLP has a polynomial complexity on a quantum computer (see [BL95]) but a precise gate estimation is absent. We prove that Regev's complexity analysis of his algorithm readily translates to a complexity analysis of the multidimensional DLP.

The primary focus of this article, however, is the application of Regev's algorithm to elliptic curves (see [Sil09] for comprehensive book on the topic). Recall that if E is an elliptic curve defined over a finite field $\mathbb{F}$ with the equation $y^2 = f(x)$, where f is a cubic polynomial and D is a square in $\mathbb{F}$, then the curve $E_D : Dy^2 = f(x)$ is isomorphic to E. If $\phi : E_D \to E$ is the isomorphism $(x, y) \mapsto (x, y/\sqrt{D})$, then for any $P, Q \in E$

$$\log_{\phi(P)} \phi(Q) = \log_P Q.$$

Although, the equation $Dy^2 = f(x)$ is enough to present our proposition, one can use any twist of the elliptic curve (see [Sil09, Sec X.2]). While this observation has no effect on classical DLP algorithms, it can be exploited in Regev's algorithm where we see E as a curve over $\mathbb{Q}$ and search for $D \in \mathbb{Z}$ whose image in $\mathbb{F}$ is a square. Rubin and Silverberg [RS02] proposed an algorithm for finding twisting constants D such that $\operatorname{rk} E_D \geq r$ for large values of r (see [Sil09, Ch. VIII] for the definition of the Mordell-Weil group and the rank of an elliptic curve defined over the rationals). We incorporated their method in Algorithm 1, which solves the DLP on any elliptic curve. We applied this algorithm to several elliptic curves recommended by the NIST, which are commonly deployed in cryptographic systems. For these curves, we identified four small points, allowing us to set $d = 6$. This effectively reduces the width of the quantum circuit by a factor of 6, potentially providing the necessary speedup to enable practical computations with Regev's algorithm.

Finally, we prove that Regev's algorithm has an asymptotic advantages over Shor's algorithm (in its original form) with respect to the gate complexity. Our proofs are conditional on classical assumptions on Regev's algorithm and on a celebrated conjecture in number theory. The speedup is not as important as in the case of the DLP in the multiplicative group, but is asymptotic in nature.

Algorithm 1. Regev's algorithm for elliptic curves

Input: An elliptic curve E over $\mathbb{Q}$ (resp. $\mathbb{F}_2(t)$), a finite field $\mathbb{F}$ and two points P, Q on $E(\mathbb{F})$.

Output: $\log_P Q$

1: (classical computer) Apply Algorithm 3 to find a value $D \in \mathbb{Q}$ such that $\text{rk} E_D \geq d - 2$.

2: (classical computer) Compute a set of generators $P_1, \ldots, P_{d-2}$ of $E_D(\mathbb{Q})$ by 2-descent (see [Sil09, Ch. X]).

3: (quantum computer) Identify the points $P_1, \ldots, P_d$ with their images in $E_D(\mathbb{F})$. Set $P_{d-1} = \phi(Q)$ and $P_0 = \phi(P)$, where $\phi : E(\mathbb{F}) \to E_D(\mathbb{F})$ is the isomorphism $(x, y) \mapsto (x, y/\sqrt{D})$, and apply Regev's algorithm for $P_0, P_1, \ldots, P_{d-1}$.

4: **return** $\log_{P_0} P_{d-1}$

1.2 Organization of the Paper

In Sect. 2, we recall the general framework of Regev's algorithm and analyze its gate complexity. We demonstrate how these results naturally extend to the multidimensional DLP and how they can be used to certify the DLP with pre-computations.

In Sect. 3, we focus on the application of Regev's algorithm to elliptic curves, introducing Algorithm 1. We conduct numerical experiments to evaluate the heuristic of the algorithm and apply it to the most commonly used elliptic curves from the NIST list [Nat23] and other standardization authorities.

In Sect. 4, we establish that the advantage of Regev's algorithm over Shor's algorithm grows with the size of the input, highlighting its potential for scalability with increasing input sizes.

Finally, in Sect. 5, we propose several directions for future research, including potential improvements and further applications of Regev's algorithm.

2 Three DLP Variants of Regev's Algorithm

After we recall Regev's algorithm (Sects. 2.1 and 2.2) we analyze the cases of the DLP with pre-computations (Sect. 2.3) and the multidimensional DLP (Sect. 2.4).

2.1 General Set-up

Let $f : \mathbb{Z}^d \to X$ be a map whose set of periods

$$\mathcal{L} := \mathcal{L}(f) := \{z \in \mathbb{Z}^d \mid f(a+z) = f(a),\ \forall a \in \mathbb{Z}^d\}$$

is a full-rank sub-lattice of $\mathbb{Z}^d$. The continuous hidden subgroup problem (CHSP), which is related to the hidden subgroup problem (HSP) [Kit96] and the hidden linear function [BL95], asks for the computation of a basis of $\mathcal{L}$. Several number-theoretic problems reduce to CHSP (see e.g. the unit group computation [EHKS14]) and the class group [BS16]).

Regev's algorithm [Reg25] has common features with the CHSP-solvers [EHKS14, dBDF20]:

- a quantum procedure is repeated $d + O(1)$ times;
- a post-processing on a classical computer, based on the LLL algorithm, which combines the results of the multiple runs of the quantum procedure;
- the initial state of the quantum procedure uses the Gaussian distribution.

There is significant interest in solving the particular case of the CHSP given by a homomorphism

$$\begin{aligned} &f : \mathbb{Z}^d \to \mathbb{G} \\ &f(z_1, \ldots, z_d) = \textstyle\sum_{i=1}^d [z_i] g_i, \end{aligned} \tag{1}$$

where $g_1, ..., g_d$ is a set of elements of the commutative group $\mathbb{G}$. In many cases of interest one or several g_i's span $\mathbb{G}$, so the set $\{g_1, \ldots, g_d\}$ is called (sometimes abusively) the set of the generators. Then the period lattice of f is the set

$$\mathcal{L} = \left\{ (z_1, \ldots, z_d) \in \mathbb{Z}^d \;\middle|\; \sum_{i=1}^d [z_i] g_i = 0 \right\}, \tag{2}$$

where $[z]g := g + \cdots + g$ (z times).

Regev's algorithm computes (partial) information about the period lattice $\mathcal{L}$, and in this regard, it is similar to the algorithm that solves CHSP. However, it differs in a significant way: it eliminates the objective to always compute a basis of $\mathcal{L}$.

To fix ideas we call q the order of $\mathbb{G}$ and we let g be a generator. Recall that the discrete logarithm of an element $x \in G$, denoted $\log_g x$, is the smallest non-negative integer z such that $x = [z]g$. The discrete logarithm problem consists in computing $\log_g x$ whereas the DLP with pre-computations is the same problem when the attacker has previously computed $\{\log_g x', x' \in X'\}$ for a set of $X' \subset \mathbb{G}$ of her choice. In the variants of the DLP treated in this article we restrict to the case where q is prime (see the Pohlig-Hellman [PH22] reduction).

To solve the DLP, in [EG24] it was given a condition which ensures that the partial information computed by Regev's algorithm gives actually a basis of $\mathcal{L}$ and further allows to find $\log_g x$. It was later proved in [Pil24] that the condition is true with high probability when $\mathbb{G}$ is the multiplicative group but it remains a heuristic in the general case.

In the case of the DLP with pre-computations, we define:

$$\mathcal{L}_0 = \{(z_1, \ldots, z_d) \in \mathcal{L} \mid z_d \equiv 0 \pmod{q}\}. \tag{3}$$

For any vector $z = (z_1, \ldots, z_d)$ of $\mathcal{L}$, the following holds:

$$\sum_{i=1}^{d} z_i \log_g g_i \equiv 0 \ (\mathrm{mod}\ q). \tag{4}$$

If in addition z is outside $\mathcal{L}_0$ one can rewrite Eq. (4) as follows:

$$\log_g g_d \equiv -z_d^{-1} \left(\sum_{i=1}^{d-1} z_i \log_g g_i \right) \pmod{q}, \tag{5}$$

and since $\log_g g_i$ with $1 \leq i \leq d-1$ are pre-computed, we can determine $\log_g g_d$. Hence, $\mathcal{L}_0$ was defined in such a way that any $(z_1, ..., z_d) \in \mathcal{L} \setminus \mathcal{L}_0$ solves the DLP with pre-computations.

To understand the framework of Regev's algorithm it is enough to know that there is a notion of dual lattice. In this article the dual lattice occurs solely to state Regev's results. For completeness, we give the definition below and we refer the reader to [Reg25] and [dBDF20] for more details.

$$\mathcal{L}^* = \{y \in \mathbb{R}^d \mid <x, y> \in \mathbb{Z},\ \forall x \in \mathcal{L}\}.$$

Additionally, for a set of integers $\{a_2, \ldots, a_d\}$ we set

$$\mathrm{knapsack}(q, \{a_2, \ldots, a_d\}) = \begin{pmatrix} q & a_2 & \ldots & a_d \\ 0 & 1 & & 0 \\ \vdots & & \ddots & \\ 0 & 0 & & 1 \end{pmatrix}. \tag{6}$$

This type of lattice was also studied in the context of Merkle and Hellman's knapsack crypto-system (see e.g. Equation (2.4) in [LO85]).

Observe that, in the discrete logarithm case, $\mathcal{L}$ is generated by the columns of $\mathrm{knapsack}(q, \{a_2, \ldots, a_d\})$, where $a_i = -\log_g g_i$. This directly gives

$$\mathrm{Vol}(\mathcal{L}) = q. \tag{7}$$

2.2 Regev's Algorithm in a Nutshell

Regev's algorithm consists of the following two steps:

1. The quantum procedure (Algorithm 2). The quantum Fourier transform (QFT) is applied to a superposition with coefficients given by a Gaussian function of standard deviation R, truncated over the domain $[-D/2, D/2)^d$. This produces approximations of elements from the dual lattice $\mathcal{L}^*$ (the precise definition is not needed to understand the CHSP framework, but one can refer to [dBDF20] for the details), which are randomly sampled from $\mathcal{L}^*/\mathbb{Z}^d$ with a probability that is uniform, up to an error of approximately order $1/R$;

2. The post-processing procedure. A classical algorithm is applied to the output of $d+4$ runs of the quantum procedure. This yields a linearly independent set of vectors from $\mathcal{L}$, which generates all vectors with lengths shorter than a specified bound T.

Algorithm 2. The quantum procedure of Regev's algorithm

Input: – an integer d and $g_1, \ldots, g_d \in \mathbb{G}$
– parameters T, R and D such that $R = 2^{\lfloor d+n/d \rfloor} T$ and $D = 2^{\lceil \log_2 R \rceil}$

Output: a random vector of $\mathcal{L}^*/\mathbb{Z}^d$ according to the distribution Q in Eq. (8).

Compute the quantum state

$$|\varphi_1\rangle = \sum_{z \in [-D/2, D/2)^d \bigcap \mathbb{Z}^d} \varrho_R(z)|z\rangle|0\rangle$$

then in a multi-scalar manner compute the state

$$|\varphi_2\rangle = \sum_{z \in [-D/2, D/2)^d} \varrho_R(z)|z\rangle|f(z)\rangle,$$

where $f(z_1, \ldots, z_d) = [z_1]g_1 + \cdots + [z_d]g_d$.
Measure the register $|f(z)\rangle$ to obtain, for a value $e \in \mathbb{Z}^d$,

$$|\varphi_3\rangle = \sum_{z \in (e+L) \bigcap [-D/2, D/2)^d} \varrho_R(z)|z\rangle.$$

Compute the quantum Fourier transform of $|\psi_3\rangle$ to obtain

$$|\varphi_4\rangle = \sum_{y \in (\mathbb{Z}/D\mathbb{Z})^d} e^{-2ie \cdot y} \left(\sum_{\ell \in L \bigcap (\frac{1}{D}\mathbb{Z}/\mathbb{Z})^d} e^{-2i\pi \ell \cdot y} \varrho_R(e+\ell) \right) |y\rangle.$$

Measure $|\psi_4\rangle$ to obtain every $y \in \mathcal{L}^*/\mathbb{Z}^d$ with probability $Q(y)$, where

$$Q(y) = (\det \mathcal{L})^{-1} \textstyle\sum_{v \in \mathcal{L}^*/\mathbb{Z}^d} Q_v(y) \text{ and } Q_v(y) = \frac{\varrho_{1/\sqrt{2}R}(v+y+\mathbb{Z}^d)}{\varrho_{1/\sqrt{2}R}(v-D^{-1}\mathbb{Z}^d)}. \quad (8)$$

Ekerå and Gärtner proposed the following hypothesis for family of multiplicative groups $\mathbb{G} = (\mathbb{Z}/p\mathbb{Z})^*$, when p ranges over the set of primes. This is now a theorem [Pil24] in that case, but which can be studied for any commutative group $\mathbb{G}$.

Assumption 1 (see [EG24], Assumption 1). *For a given family of groups $\mathbb{G}$, whose bit size n tends to infinity, and for any parameter $d \leq \sqrt{n}$, there exists an absolute constant K such that the lattice $\mathcal{L}$ defined in Eq.* (2) *has a basis formed of vectors of length less than* $\exp(K\frac{n}{d})$.

This assumption asserts that the lattice $\mathcal{L}$ has a "balanced" basis. Indeed, since $\mathrm{Vol}(L)$ has n bits (see Eq. (7)), the Gaussian heuristic predicts that the shortest vector of $\mathcal{L}$ is of size $\exp(K'\frac{n}{d})$ for some constant K'. Under the assumption, the longest vector of a basis also has size $\exp(K\frac{n}{d})$ but for a different constant K. Given this, Regev's algorithm computes a basis for the lattice $\mathcal{L}$. In particular, if $\mathcal{L}_0 \neq \mathcal{L}$, then one vector of this basis will lie in $\mathcal{L} \setminus \mathcal{L}_0$.

This assumption has received considerable attention in the literature:

- If the g_i are chosen from a specific uniform distribution, Pilatte [Pil24] proved this heuristic for the case when $\mathbb{G}$ is a multiplicative group.
- Under the Gaussian heuristic (see e.g. [HPS11, Sec 5]), $\lambda_1(\mathcal{L}) \geq \exp(O(\frac{n}{d}))$ for a constant K. By Mahler's theorem (see [TV06, Theorem 3.34]), $\mathcal{L}$ has a basis of vectors less than $\exp(O(\frac{n}{d}))$.
- We provide support for the heuristic in the context of elliptic curves in Sect. 3.2.

In general, this assumption is too strong to ensure the algorithm's success. Consequently, a weaker assumption is needed, leading to the concept of *inter-lattice minimal distance*, which quantifies the Euclidean distance between a sublattice and its complement. This proves to be the appropriate measure for estimating the success of Regev's algorithm.

For $\mathcal{L} \subset \mathbb{Z}^d$ a lattice of rank d and $\mathcal{L}_0$ a sublattice of $\mathcal{L}$ (not necessarily of the same rank), we define:

$$\lambda_{\mathcal{L}_0}(\mathcal{L}) := \min\{\|v\| \mid v \in \mathcal{L} \setminus \mathcal{L}_0\}.$$

Note that if $\mathcal{L}_0 \neq \mathcal{L}$, then any basis of $\mathcal{L}$ has a vector outside $\mathcal{L}_0$. Therefore, for any basis B of $\mathcal{L}$

$$\lambda_{\mathcal{L}_0}(\mathcal{L}) \leq \max_{b \in B}\|b\|.$$

In this work we investigate an assumption which is implied by Assumption 1 but which is *a priori* satisfied by more groups $\mathbb{G}$.

Assumption 2. *For a given family of groups $\mathbb{G}$, whose bit size n tends to infinity, and for any parameter $d \leq \sqrt{n}$, there exists a constant $K > 0$ such that*

$$\lambda_{\mathcal{L}_0}(\mathcal{L}) \leq \exp(K\frac{n}{d}).$$

We now formulate a theorem on the complexity of Regev's algorithm. In particular it will encompass the case of multidimensional DLP and the case of the DLP elliptic curves. The core ideas are already present in Regev's original paper (see [Reg25, Sec 3]).

In the following, $M(m)$ denotes the cost of multiplying two m-bit integers. It was recently proven in [HVDH21] that $M(m) = O(m \log m)$, but we express complexities using this notation to facilitate the comparison between Regev's and Shor's algorithms.

Proposition 1. *Let E be a commutative group which can be embedded as an algebraic group over $\mathbb{Q}$ (resp. $\mathbb{F}_2(t)$). Let h be the naive height over $\mathbb{Q}$ (resp. $\mathbb{F}_2(t)$) and its extension to the elements of E (we recall its definition in Eqs.* (12) *and* (13)*, see also [Sil09, Ch. VIII]). Let $\mathbb{F} = \mathbb{F}_p$ for an n-bit prime (resp. $\mathbb{F} = \mathbb{F}_{2^n}$). Let $\mathbb{G}$ be the finite commutative group equal to the reduction of E mod $\mathbb{F}$. We consider the DLP with respect to $\mathbb{G}$. We assume that the group law of $\mathbb{G}$ can be done with $M(n)$ gates.*

Let $2 \leq d \leq \sqrt{n}$ be a parameter, and let $g_1, \ldots, g_d$ be elements of $\mathbb{G}$ such that g_1 generates $\mathbb{G}$. Define

$$m := \max_{\varepsilon \in \{0,1\}^{d-2}} h(\sum_{i=2}^{d-1} [\varepsilon_i] g_i) \tag{9}$$

and assume that any such sum can be computed using $O(M(m)(\log_2 m)^2)$ gates.

Let $T > 0$ be a given parameter. Then Regev's algorithm outputs a list of $\ell \leq d$ vectors $z_1, \ldots, z_\ell \in \mathcal{L}$ of norm at most $\sqrt{d}2^{d/2}T$ with the property that any vector in $\mathcal{L}$ of norm at most T must be an integer combination of them. In other words, the sublattice they generate contains all the vectors in $\mathcal{L}$ of norm at most T.

Finally, one has:

$$\textit{gate complexity} = O\left((\frac{n}{d} + d + \log_2 T) \left(M(n) + \min(dM(n), M(m)(\log_2 m)^2) \right) \right).$$

Proof. Let $C = C(g_2, \ldots, g_{d-1})$ be the maximum cost of computing $\sum_{i=2}^{d-1} [\varepsilon_i] g_i$ when $\varepsilon \in \{0,1\}^{d-2}$. By [Reg25, Section 3, Eq (6)], the cost of Algorithm 2 is given by

$$\text{cost(Algorithm 2)} = \log_2 D \cdot (C + d \log_2 \log_2 D + M(n)) + d \cdot \text{poly}(\log_2 d)\,. \tag{10}$$

By assumption $C = O(M(m)(\log_2 m)^2)$. Finally, the relations among T, R and D imply that

$$O(\log_2 D) = O(\log_2 R) = O\left(\log_2 T + d + \frac{n}{d}\right).$$

As we shall prove in Sect. 4, Proposition 5, the assumptions stated in the previous proposition holds in the case of elliptic curves.

Ekerå and Gärtner [EG24, Th 1] proved that, under Assumption 1, Regev's algorithm allows to compute a basis of $\mathcal{L}$ and then by solving a linear system one finds the discrete logarithms of $g_1, \ldots, g_{d-1}$ and $g_d = x$,

2.3 Regev for the DLP with Pre-computations

In this section, we provide a method to certify that Regev's algorithm succeeds in finding discrete logarithms, within the context of Regev's algorithm with pre-computations, as proposed in [EG24].

This variant of the DLP is the most realistic in DLP-based cryptosystems. To name one example a server can implement ECDSA authentication using the same group $\mathbb{G}$ and generator g for a long period of time. A Regev-based attack can be prepared by selecting $g_i, \ldots, g_{d-1}$ and by computing their discrete logarithm in base g with Shor's algorithm. This step can take a few months or years. When a challenge is given, Regev's attack must be carried out in a few second (also see [ABD+15]).

Recall that $\mathbb{G}$ is a cyclic group of order q, where q is an n-bit prime, and g is a generator (in cryptography q is taken to be prime and in the general case one can use the Pohlig-Hellman [PH22] reduction). In the pre-computation stage, the following quantities $a_i = -\log_g g_i$ for $i = 2, \ldots, d-1$ are computed (for instance, using Shor's algorithm). The challenge in our notations will be $g_d = x$, while $g_1 = g$, and the problem is to compute $a_d = -\log_g(g_d)$ in a short time.

Corollary 1 (under Assumption 2). *We use the hypothesis and notations of Proposition 1.*

Let $\mathcal{L}$ and $\mathcal{L}_0$ be the lattices in Eqs. (2) *and* (3)*, and let $T > 0$ be a parameter such that there exists a vector of norm less than T in $\mathcal{L} \setminus \mathcal{L}_0$. Then Regev's algorithm finds a vector in $\mathcal{L} \setminus \mathcal{L}_0$ with*

$$\textit{gate complexity} = O\left(\left(\frac{n}{d} + d + \log_2 T\right)\left(M(n) + M(m)(\log_2 m)^2\right)\right).$$

Proof. If $\lambda_{\mathcal{L}_0}(\mathcal{L})$ is known then Regev's algorithm with parameter $T = \lambda_{\mathcal{L}_0}(\mathcal{L})$ outputs a set of vectors in $\mathcal{L}$ which are not all in $\mathcal{L}_0$. Since $\log_g g_i$ with $1 \leq i \leq d-1$ are pre-computed, hence known, one finds $\log_g x$ by Eq. (5).

If $\lambda_{\mathcal{L}_0}(\mathcal{L})$ is unknown, one runs Regev's algorithm with $\log_2 T = 2^i$ for $i = 1, 2, \ldots$ and succeeds for $i = \lceil \log_2 \log_2 \lambda_{\mathcal{L}_0}(\mathcal{L}) \rceil$. The cost is then twice the one when the optimal value of T is known in advance.

The rest of the section is dedicated to the following questions: when Assumption 2 is false for part of the elements $x \in \mathbb{G}$, is it possible to know that it is true for a particular element $x \in \mathbb{G}$ before running Regev's algorithm?

The question is relevant if the implmentation of the algorithm requires debugging. It allows to eliminate the possibility of a "theoretical bug".

Now, it is clear that the columns of the following two matrices:

$$\mathcal{L}: \begin{pmatrix} q & a_2 & \cdots & a_{d-1} & a_d \\ & 1 & & & \\ & & \ddots & & \\ & & & 1 & \\ & & & & 1 \end{pmatrix} \qquad \mathcal{L}_0: \begin{pmatrix} q & a_2 & \cdots & a_{d-1} & 0 \\ & 1 & & & \\ & & \ddots & & \\ & & & 1 & \\ & & & & q \end{pmatrix} \tag{11}$$

generate the lattices $\mathcal{L}$ and $\mathcal{L}_0$, respectively.

Since the basis for $\mathcal{L}_0$ has been computed during the pre-computation stage and $d \leq \sqrt{n}$, the shortest vector of $\mathcal{L}_0$ can be found in exponential time with respect to d (see [HS07]), which is sub-exponential with respect to n. Regev's algorithm guaranties to find at least one vector with norm at most T, for some chosen parameter T. Thus, if $\lambda_1(\mathcal{L}_0) > T$, then the vector is guaranteed not to be in $\mathcal{L}_0$.

Note that the shortest vector in $\mathcal{L}_0$ has the same length as the shortest vector in the $(d-1)$-dimensional full-rank lattice generated by the first $d-1$ coordinates of the first $d-1$ vectors in the considered basis of $\mathcal{L}_0$. As a consequence, according to Gaussian heuristic (see [TV06, Theorem 3.34]), we get that the expected first minimum of the lattice $\mathcal{L}_0$ is given by $\lambda_1(\mathcal{L}_0) \approx \sqrt{\frac{d-1}{2\pi e}}\, q^{1/(d-1)}$, while for $\mathcal{L}$ it is known that $\lambda_1(\mathcal{L}) \leq \sqrt{d} q^{1/d}$. The quotient of the two expressions which approximate $\lambda_1(\mathcal{L}_0)$ and $\lambda_1(\mathcal{L})$ is $q^{\frac{1}{d(d-1)}} \sqrt{(d-1)/d}/\sqrt{2\pi e}$, which is larger than 1 when q is sufficiently large compared to d. Hence, heuristically, one can expect that $\lambda_1(\mathcal{L}_0) > \lambda_1(\mathcal{L})$, so that the norm of the shortest vector of $\mathcal{L}$ gives the inter-lattice distance. This implies that Assumption 2 will be satisfied and the algorithm will succeed.

The discussion motivates the following definition:

Definition 1. *Let $\mathcal{L}$ be a full-rank lattice in $\mathbb{Z}^d$ with volume* $\mathrm{Vol}(\mathcal{L}) = q$, *where q is an n-bit integer. If $\mathcal{L}_0$ is a sublattice of $\mathcal{L}$, we say that the pair $(\mathcal{L}, \mathcal{L}_0)$ is certified if $\lambda_1(\mathcal{L}_0) \geq \exp(n/d)$. If $\mathcal{L}_0$ is clear from the context, we simply say that $\mathcal{L}$ is certified.*

The following result shows that the conclusion of the above heuristic is valid under the certified condition.

Proposition 2. *Consider a full-rank lattice $\mathcal{L}$ in $\mathbb{Z}^d$ with volume* $\mathrm{Vol}(\mathcal{L}) = q$, *where q is an n-bit integer. Consider a full rank sublattice $\mathcal{L}_0$ such that $\lambda_1(\mathcal{L}_0) \geq \sqrt{d} q^{1/d}$. Then $\log_2(\lambda_{\mathcal{L}_0}(\mathcal{L})) \leq \frac{n+1}{d} + \frac{1}{2}\log_2 d$. In particular, if $d \leq \sqrt{n}$ and $\mathcal{L}$ is certified, then Regev's algorithm with the parameter $T = \exp(n/d)$ is successful in solving DLP with precomputations.*

Proof. Assuming, for the sake of contradiction, that $\lambda_{\mathcal{L}_0}(\mathcal{L}) > \sqrt{d} 2^{(n+1)/d} > \sqrt{d} q^{1/d}$. Consequently, we have $\lambda_1(\mathcal{L}) > \sqrt{d} q^{1/d}$, since the shortest length vector in $\mathcal{L}$ is either in $\mathcal{L}_0$, which by our assumption is of length at least $\lambda_1(\mathcal{L}_0) > \sqrt{d} q^{1/d}$, or in $\mathcal{L} \setminus \mathcal{L}_0$, which has length at least $\lambda_{\mathcal{L}_0}(\mathcal{L}) > \sqrt{d} q^{1/d}$.

By the second Minkowski theorem, we have $\lambda_1(\mathcal{L}) \leq \sqrt{d}\mathrm{Vol}(\mathcal{L})^{1/d} = \sqrt{d} q^{1/d}$, which leads to a contradiction.

The last part of the proposition follows from the inequality

$$4(\log_2 e - 1)\sqrt{n} > \frac{4}{\sqrt{n}} + \log_2 n,$$

which holds for $n \geq 6$.

Note that, in practice, certifying a pair of lattices as in Eq. (11) is fast, as demonstrated by the following experiment.

Experiment 1. *Let $n = 10000$, $d = 40$ and q the next prime after 2^n. Let $a_2 = 1415 \cdots 940$ be the first n decimal digits of π after the dot, a_2 the next n*

digits and so on until a_d*. Using SageMath one finds in 6.56 s the shortest vector of* $\mathcal{L}_0 :=$*knapsack*$(q, \{a_2, \dots, a_{d-1}\})$*. We obtained* $\lambda_1(\mathcal{L}_0) > 3 \cdot 10^{75} > 1.8 \cdot 10^{75} > \exp(n/d)$*, hence* $\mathcal{L}$ *is certified. By Proposition 2, Regev's algorithm will succeed on this instance of the DLP.*

We end this subsection by addressing the question of whether it is likely for a lattice to be certified. The following experiment demonstrates that a random knapsack lattice is indeed certified.

Experiment 2. *We took* $d = 10, 20, 30, 40, 50$*,* $n = d^2$ *and random* n*-bit integers* q*. We drew* d *random integers* $a_1, \dots, a_d$*, and using SageMath, we found that* 100% *of the sampled knapsack lattices knapsack*$(q, \{a_1, \dots, a_d\})$ *are certified.*

2.4 Regev's Algorithm for the Multidimensional DLP

In 1993, Brands [Bra93] created the first cryptographic application based on an extension of DLP, called multidimensional DLP. The problem constantly receives attention in cryptography (see [GR09, Section 6], [CL15, ZZY+19], and [Kos24]).

Definition 2. *Let* $\mathbb{G}$ *be a commutative group whose order is an* n*-bit integer and let* $g_1, \dots, g_d \in \mathbb{G}$ *be given. The multidimensional discrete logarithm problem consists in finding, if they exist, the* $\lceil n/d \rceil$*-bit integers* z_i*,* $1 \le i \le d$ *such that*

$$[z_1]g_1 + \cdots + [z_d]g_d = 0 \text{ and } z_d \neq 0.$$

The problem can be stated with a fixed coordinate, for example $z_d = 1$. If the solution is unique for a given size of the coordinates then any solution of the multidimensional DLP automatically has this property. If the solution has several solutions, the linearity allows to find new solutions with smaller values of z_d. Hence from a cryptographic point of view the two variants have the same security.

A major question on the multidimensional DLP is whether its complexity is the same, as an expression of n, as the one of the DLP as an expression of $|\mathbb{G}|$:

$$\text{gate complexity (multidimensional DLP)} = O(nM(n))?$$

In the paradigm of classical computers, Galbraith and Ruprai [GR09] extended Pollard's rho to the multidimensional DLP, which is general enough to also apply to the case when $\mathbb{G}$ is an elliptic curve.

In the context of quantum computers, Regev's algorithm applies unchanged to the multidimensional DLP and moreover Assumption 1 is not needed because one has by construction a bound on the solution $(z_1, \dots, z_d)$.

A brutal generalization of Shor's DLP algorithm to the multidimensional case would require a QFT on the group $(\mathbb{Z}/q\mathbb{Z})^d$, whose cardinality is much larger than $q = \mathrm{Vol}\mathcal{L}$, which is the "size of the problem". A generalization of Shor's algorithm which is well-suited to the multidimensional DLP is given in [BL95], but only for fixed d. It was only a few years ago that it was proved that the multidimensional DLP has a gate complexity which is polynomial in d (so d can grow with the input size), thanks to the CHSP-solver [EHKS14,dBDF20]. However, the complexity is overestimated, making the complexity analysis of Regev's algorithm the first to provide an estimate that achieves the same result as Shor's algorithm in the DLP case. This is demonstrated by the following result, where the generators $g_1, \ldots, g_d$ are random elements of the group. The improvement in complexity naturally decreases with the size of the generators, without modifying the algorithm or the proof.

Theorem 1. *Let n and d be integers such that $d \leq \sqrt{n}$. Let $\mathbb{G}$ be a group as in Proposition 1 and consider the multidimensional DLP with generators $g_1, \ldots, g_d$ and exponents of ℓ bits.*

1. *[BL95] If the generators are random elements of $\mathbb{G}$ then Shor's algorithm solves the multidimensional DLP with $n^{O(1)}$ gates.*
2. *Let m be the parameter defined in Eq. (9). If $m \leq n$, then Regev's algorithm solves the multidimensional DLP with*

$$\text{gate complexity} = O\left(\frac{n}{d}(M(n) + \min(dM(n), M(m)\log_2 m))\right).$$

In particular, if the generators g_i, $1 \leq i \leq d$, are random elements of $\mathbb{G}$ the multidimensional DLP can be solved with $O(nM(n))$ gates.

Proof. 1. When d is fixed we apply [BL95, Th 1] to the function f in Eq. (1). The parameters are $k = d$, $m = \mathrm{Vol}\mathcal{L} = q$, and $n = \log_2 q$. Hence we obtained a gate complexity $n^{O(1)}$.

When d is not (necessarily) fixed, we apply [dBDF20, Th 1] and find that the complexity is polynomial with respect to $\log_2 \mathrm{Vol}\mathcal{L} = \log_2 q = n$ and $d = n^{1/2}$, hence $n^{O(1)}$.

2. Definition 2 guarantees that, when the lattices $\mathcal{L}$ and $\mathcal{L}_0$ are as in Eqs. (2) and (3), there exists a vector $(z_1, \ldots, z_d) \in \mathcal{L}\backslash\mathcal{L}_0$ such that $\max_{1 \leq i \leq d} |z_i| \leq 2^{n/d}$. Hence, the value of $\log_2 T$ in Proposition 1 can be taken n/d and, since $d \leq \sqrt{n}$, one has

$$d + \frac{n}{d} + \log_2 T \leq 3\frac{n}{d}.$$

The complexity follows.

Example 1. 1. If $\mathbb{G}$ is the multiplicative group $(\mathbb{Z}/p\mathbb{Z})^*$ for a prime p, Regev proved that the conditions of Proposition 1 are satisfied when g_i is the i-th prime and Pilatte [Pil24] extended the proof to the case when the generators $g_2, \ldots, g_{d-1}$ are randomly drawn $O(d)$-bit integers.
2. If $\mathbb{G}$ is the multiplicative group $\mathbb{F}_{2^n}^*$ for an integer n, Regev's proof translates mot a mot.
3. If $\mathbb{G}$ is the Jacobian of a hyperelliptic curve of genus $g \geq \sqrt{n}$ one can instantiate the multidimensional DLP with the generators of [BB]. Hence point 2. of the above theorem applies.

3 Extending Regev to Elliptic Curves

The aim of this section is to analyse Algorithm 1. In Sect. 3.1 we make precise the folklore conjecture that general elliptic curves over finite fields do not admit points that can be considered small. The main scope of this article is to construct such "small points" in the specific case of certain elliptic curves that are among the most widely used in cryptographic applications. In Sect. 3.2 we make precise the heuristics used by Algorithm 1 and support them with experiments. In Sect. 3.4 we apply the algorithm to curves with cryptographic importance and pave the way for future precise gate number estimations.

A key aspect of our investigation is the number of bits needed to represent a point of an elliptic curve over a prime field (resp. a binary field) and what it means to be "small". For this we recall the naive (or Weil) height of a point of an elliptic curve over the rationals (see [Sil09, VIII.5]):

$$\begin{aligned} h(u/v) &= \max(\log_2|u|, \log_2|v|) \ \forall u, v \in \mathbb{Z}^*, \gcd(u,v) = 1 \\ h(x,y) &= \max(h(x), h(y)) \qquad \forall (x,y) \in E(\mathbb{Q}). \end{aligned} \tag{12}$$

Similarly, the naive height of a rational function in $\mathbb{F}_2(t)$ extends to the elliptic curves (see [Sil09, Sec VIII.6]):

$$\begin{aligned} h(u/v) &= \max(\deg u, \deg v) \ \forall u, v \in \mathbb{F}_2[t]^*, \gcd(u,v) = 1 \\ h(x,y) &= \max(h(x), h(y)) \ \ \forall (x,y) \in E(\mathbb{F}_2(t)). \end{aligned} \tag{13}$$

Clearly, the naive height of a point is between one fourth and one half of the bit size representation of the point.

Given a prime p and an integer $a \in [1, p-1]$, the rational reconstruction of a modulo p is the rational number u/v, where $u, v \in \mathbb{Z}$, with the smallest height such that $u \equiv va \pmod{p}$. This can be computed in polynomial time in the bit size of p by reducing a two-dimensional lattice (see [Wan81] or more recent books of computer arithmetic). The height of an element of $\mathbb{F}_p$ is the height of its corresponding rational reconstruction. A similar result stands for the binary curves. In the following all the results translate from the case of the prime fields to that of the binary fields, but in some cases we omit to specify the analogy.

Recall that the discrete logarithm problem on elliptic curves over finite fields involves two $\mathbb{F}_p$ points P and Q on an elliptic curve E defined over $\mathbb{F}_p$. The goal is to find the positive integer a such that $Q = [a]P$, which we denote as $\log_P Q = a$. In Regev's algorithm one uses auxiliary points $P_2, \ldots, P_{d-1}$ for a parameter d and sets $P_1 = P$ and $P_d = Q$. The algorithm is efficient if the points can be represented using a small number of bits, and if the cost to evaluate all linear combinations $\sum_{i=1}^{d}[\varepsilon_i]P_i$ with $\varepsilon = (\varepsilon_1, \ldots, \varepsilon_d) \in \{0,1\}^d$ remains computationally feasible (see Sect. 4.2). By analogy with the multiplicative case, we seek $d-2$ points $P_i = (x_i, y_i)$ for $i = 2, \ldots, d-1$, whose coordinates can be expressed using $O(\sqrt{n})$ bits, where $n = \lfloor \log_2 p \rfloor$ (here n is approximately the same size as $\log_2|E(\mathbb{F}_p)|$). This is significantly fewer than $2n$ bits required to represent arbitrary points on the curve.

Since Regev's algorithm offers a speed-up by a factor of d compared to Shor's algorithm (Prop. 1), we aim to make d as large as possible.

Since we are interested in elliptic curves that possess at least two small points, we shall restrict to the case where the coefficients of the elliptic curve are bounded by a polynomial in $\log_2 n$ (see Proposition 4 bellow). From a cryptographic perspective, this restriction is not a hindrance, as most elliptic curves chosen for cryptographic implementation already meet this condition.

3.1 Obstacle to a Direct Extension of Regev to Elliptic Curves

The main result of this section asserts that only an exponentially small fraction of elliptic curves defined over a prime field possess points that can be represented using $O(\sqrt{n})$ bits. Such points will henceforth be referred to as *small points*. More precisely, we provide an upper bound on the probability that an elliptic curve

$$E_{a,b} : y^2 z = x^3 + axz^2 + bz^3$$

has small points. In the next proposition we sample random elliptic curves by randomly selecting the pair (a, b), rather than considering isomorphism classes of elliptic curves, as this would introduce unnecessary technicalities without impacting the conclusion of our negative result.

Proposition 3. *Let p be an odd prime, and let α be such that $0 < \alpha < 1/3$. For any pair of integers a, b and positive real H we call $E_{a,b}^{h \leq H}(\mathbb{F}_p)$ the set set of triples $(x, y, z) \in \mathbb{Z}^3$ with $h(x, y, z) \leq H$ such that the reductions modulo p of $(x : y : z)$ belongs to $E(\mathbb{F}_p)$. If integers a and b are drawn randomly with uniform probability from $((-p/2, p/2) \bigcap \mathbb{Z})^2$ then the expected value of the number of points with height less than αn is bounded as follows:*

$$\mathbb{E}\left(\#E_{a,b}^{h \leq \alpha n}(\mathbb{F}_p) \;\middle|\; a, b \in (-p/2, p/2) \text{ random}\right) \leq \frac{8p^{3\alpha}}{p-2}.$$

In particular, the probability that a random elliptic curve has points of height less than αn is less than $\frac{8p^{3\alpha}}{p-2}$.

Proof. Let $X_0 := \{(a, b) \in ((-p/2, p/2) \bigcap \mathbb{Z})^2 \mid 4a^3 + 27b^2 \neq 0\}$ and $X_1 := \{(a, b) \in (-p/2, p/2) \bigcap \mathbb{Z})^2 \mid 4a^3 + 27b^2 = 0\}$. For each $(a, b) \in ((-p/2, p/2) \bigcap \mathbb{Z})^2$, let

$$R_{a,b} := \left\{(x, y, z) \in \left((-p^\alpha, p^\alpha) \bigcap \mathbb{Z}\right)^3 \;\middle|\; (x : y : z) \in E_{a,b}(\mathbb{F}_p) \setminus \{\infty\}\right\}$$

be the set of points of height less than αn on the curve $y^2 z = x^3 + axz^2 + bz^3$, and set $r_{a,b} := |R_{a,b}|$. Then, the expected value will be $(\sum_{(a,b) \in X_0} r_{a,b})/|X_0|$.

Since for each value of a there exist at most 2 values of b such that $(a, b) \in X_1$, we have $|X_1| \leq 2p$. Therefore, $|X_0| \geq p^2 - 2p$. On the other hand, we can upper-bound the numerator $\sum_{(a,b) \in X_0} r_{a,b}$ by summing over all pairs $(a, b) \in X_0 \cup X_1$, as follows: $\sum_{(a,b) \in X_0 \cup X_1} r_{a,b} \leq 8p^{1+3\alpha}$.

Indeed, since there is exactly one value of b for each quadruple (x, y, z, a), the total number of quintuples is at most $8p^{3\alpha} \times p$. Hence, we obtain: $\frac{\sum_{(a,b)\in X_0} r_{a,b}}{|X_0|} \leq \frac{8p^{1+3\alpha}}{p^2-2p} = \frac{8p^{3\alpha}}{p-2}$. Finally, since $r_{a,b}$ is a natural number, we get $\frac{\#\{(a,b)\in X_0 | r_{a,b}\neq 0\}}{|X_0|} \leq \frac{\sum_{(a,b)\in X_0} r_{a,b}}{|X_0|} \leq \frac{8p^{3\alpha}}{p-2}$.

Remark 1. Even though more than a triple (x, y, z) may, in fact, correspond to the same point $(x : y : z)$ on the elliptic curve, the conclusion remains correct.

Observe that by choosing $\alpha = O(\frac{1}{\sqrt{n}})$ in Proposition 3, the points of height less than $\alpha\, n$ are those that can be represented using $O(\sqrt{n})$ bits. Therefore, the probability that a random elliptic curve has small points is less than $\frac{1}{2^{n-O(\sqrt{n})}}$.

Proposition 4. *Let $c > 0$ be a constant, p a prime, and n its bit size. Let $(a, b) \in \mathbb{F}_p$ such that $4a^3 + 27b^2 \neq 0$. If $E_{a,b}$ has two affine points P_1, P_2 with $P_1 \neq \pm P_2$ for which $\max(h(P_1), h(P_2)) \leq c\sqrt{n}$, then a and b have heights less than $3c\sqrt{n} + 2$ and $4c\sqrt{n} + 3$, respectively.*

Proof. Let $P_1(x_1 : y_1 : 1)$ and $P_2(x_2 : y_2 : 1)$ be two affine points as described in the statement. Since $P_1 \neq \pm P_2$, we get that $x_1 \neq x_2$. Then we have

$$a = \frac{(y_1^2 - x_1^3) - (y_2^2 - x_2^3)}{x_1 - x_2}$$
$$b = y_1^2 - x_1^3 - a x_1.$$

The first equation bounds the height of a and then the second bounds the height of b.

We conclude that only curves with small coefficients can have two or more small points. Such curves are even less frequent than the probability given in Proposition 5, which shows that most curves possessing a small point cannot have two such points. In practice, for Regev's algorithm, more than one point is required to achieve observable efficiency, so in the search for Regev-friendly curves, we are compelled to focus on curves with small coefficients. Fortunately, this is the case for all the curves proposed on the NIST list.

To reinforce the conclusion of the above results, we considered an experiment in which we search for affine points $(x, y, 1)$ that can be represented using $O(\sqrt{n})$ bits. To do this, one enumerates all possible values of the x-coordinate and retains randomly one of the two possible values of $y := \sqrt{x^3 + ax + b}$. The results of this experiment show that the values of y are uniformly distributed. This also forbids some other generalizations of Regev's algorithm, e.g. that where the points (x, y) have the x-coordinate small and the y-coordinate close to a constant.

Experiment 3. *We fix a random elliptic curve: $y^2 = x^3 + ax + b$ with $a = 3$ and $b = 11$. We also fix a randomly drawn 50-bit prime: $p = 234094748715283$. We enumerate $x = 1, 2, \ldots, X = 10^5$, take a random value among the two square roots of $x^3 + ax + b$ and place them in one of the intervals $[1, p/10]$, $[p/10, 2p/10]$, $\ldots$, $[9p/10, p]$. We summarize the distribution in Fig. 1. Repeating the process on a sample of 100 primes of 50 bits, the maximum value of the statistical distance to uniform distribution was 0.00648.*

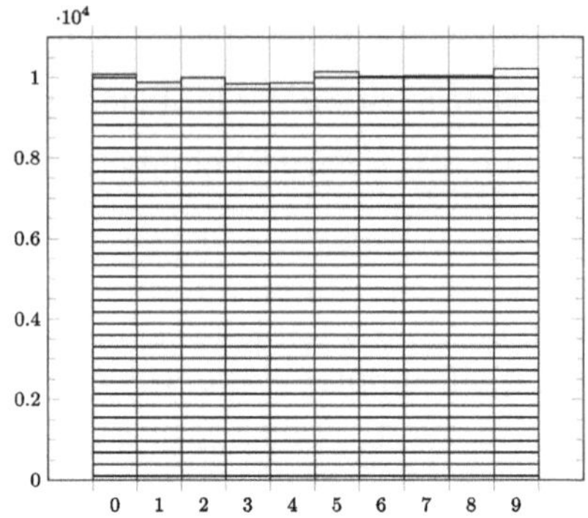

Fig. 1. Distribution of the representatives in $[0, p-1]$ of $\sqrt{x^3 + ax + b}$ in $\mathbb{F}_p$ when x runs through the values $1, 2, \ldots, X$ for a bound X. Here $a = 3$, $b = 11$, $p = 234094748715283$, $X = 10^5$ and the i-th column counts the number of occurrences of the interval $[\frac{i}{p}, \frac{i+1}{p}]$.

3.2 Validity of the Heuristic in Regev's Algorithm for Elliptic Curves

In this subsection we investigate whether Assumption 1 and Assumption 2 are true for lattices defined by points on elliptic curves.

Let E be a curve with rational coefficients (respectively, with coefficients in $\mathbb{F}_2(t)$), and let $P_1, \ldots, P_r$ be points in $E(\mathbb{Q})$ (respectively, $E(\mathbb{F}_2(t))$). Reducing the elliptic curve E modulo a large prime of good reduction, we are interested whether Assumption 1 holds for the lattice defined by the abelian group $E(\mathbb{F})$ ($\mathbb{F} = \mathbb{F}_p$ or $\mathbb{F} = \mathbb{F}_{2^n}$) and the set of points given by the images of $P_1, \ldots, P_r$ in this group.

Note that in cryptographic applications the order of $E(\mathbb{F})$ is prime, so that the set of points generate the whole group, except when the points $P_1, ..., P_r$ are mapped to the identity through the reduction map, i.e. when the prime divides the denominators of all x-coordinates of P_i for all $i \in \{1, \ldots, r\}$.

For the experiments we consider the case where the desired discrete logarithm is $\log_{P_1} P_r$, in other words $d = r$. Since the the generator g and the challenge x are randomly selected, the lattice defined by Eq. (2) is even more likely to satisfy Assumption 1.

Experiment 4. *1. Consider $E_1/\mathbb{Q} : y^2 + y = x^3 - 1076185x + 496031340$, which has $r = 9$ (seeé [Duj24]). For each prime p, we define*

$$B(p) = \min_{\mathcal{B}} \max_{b \in \mathcal{B}} \|b\|,$$

where $\mathcal{B}$ is a basis of the lattice $\mathcal{L}$ corresponding to the reduction modulo p. Next, we let $K(p) = \frac{\log B(p)}{n/d}$, where $d = r$. In Fig. 2 we plot the distribution of $K(p)$ for all the primes less than 10^4.

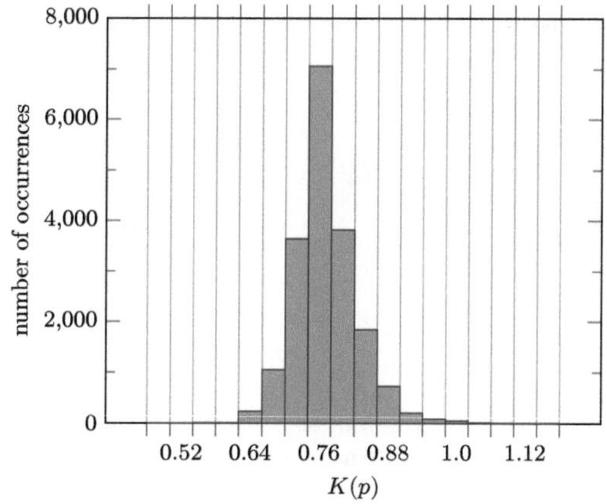

Fig. 2. Distribution of $K(p)$ corresponding to the reduction of E_1 modulo p (see Experiment 4). Equivalently $B(p) \leq \exp(K(p)\frac{n}{d})$ as in Assumption 1.

2. Consider

$$E_2/\mathbb{F}_2(t) : y^2 + \frac{t^6+t^5+t^4+t^3}{t^4+t^3+t^2+t+1}xy + \frac{t^7+t^6+t^4+t+1}{t^4+t^3+t^2+t+1}y = x^3 + \frac{t^6+t^2+t+1}{t^4+t^3+t^2+t+1}x^2 + \frac{t^6+t^5+t^2}{t^4+t^3+t^2+t+1}x + \frac{t^8+t^4+t^2+t}{t^4+t^3+t^2+t+1}.$$

We constructed E_2 by solving a linear system in order to contain a list of small points in $\mathbb{F}_2[t] \times \mathbb{F}_2[t]$.
For each irreducible polynomial $\wp$ of degree less or equal to 40, we define

$$B(\wp) = \min_{\mathcal{B}} \max_{b \in \mathcal{B}} \|b\|$$

where $\mathcal{B}$ is a basis of the lattice $\mathcal{L}$ corresponding to the reduction modulo φ. Next, we let $K(\wp) = \frac{\log B(\wp)}{n/d}$. In Fig. 3 we give the distribution of $K(\wp)$ for all irreducible polynomials with $\deg \wp \in [2, 40]$.
This corroborates with Assumption 1 for elliptic curves.

3.3 Size of the Generators of an Elliptic Curve

In this section we investigate steps 1 and 2 of Algorithm 1, i.e. we are looking to find twists of large rank and compute a basis for their Mordell-Weil group.

The problem has been studied for a long time (see [RS02, Sec 6.1]) for the curve $E : y^2 = x^3 - x$. The general case has been explored by Rubin and Silverberg (see Algorithm 3), as well as by Watkins et al. [WDE+14, Sec 10].

Experiment 5. *Step 1. in Algorithm 1 is done by computing the analytic rank, which is equal to the algebraic rank under the BSD conjecture (see [Sil09, Ch. 16]). In Table 1, we list the computation times for this step. We repeated this subprocedure for all square-free integers D until we found one of rank r. The*

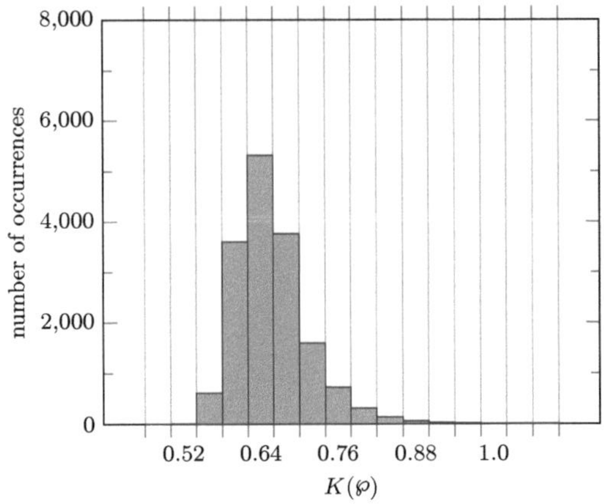

Fig. 3. Distribution of values of $\wp$ having a given value of $K(\wp)$ (see Experiment 4). Equivalently $B(\wp) \leq \exp(K(\wp)\frac{n}{d})$ as in Assumption 1.

Algorithm 3. Rubin-Silverberg [RS02, Sec 9]

Input: an elliptic curve E with rational coefficients and an integer r
Output: an integer D such that the Mordell-Weil rank of E_D is larger or equal to r
 (optional) Make a list of integers D which are likely to have large $\mathrm{rk}(E_D)$.
 repeat
  D=next square-free integer (optionally from the list established in previous step)
  r_D = analytic rank of E_D
 until $r_D \geq r$

---

successful D and implicitly the number of times we repeated the sub-procedure is listed in Table 2.

Step 2. of Algorithm 1 is done by a 2-descent (see [Sto01, Sim02] and their implementations[1] *in KANT and Pari/Gp). We summarize our results in Table 7.*

Table 1. Timings to compute in Magma the analytic rank of $y^2 = x^3 + 7D$ (secp256k1) where D is a random integer of 4 to 14 bits.

$\log_2 D$	time (s)
4	5
10	6
14	7

[1] In a personal communication Simon told the first author that his implementation can be extended to $\mathbb{F}_2(t)$ but it is currently not present in Magma and Sage.

Table 2. Smallest integer D such that E_D has rank r for the curves in Table 5.

curve	secp256k1	BLS 12	BN
$r = 1$	5	2	1
$r = 2$	23	6	53
$r = 3$	61	79	158
$r = 4$	3983	1714	2455
$r = 5$		23659	

3.4 Finding Small Points on Subset of the List Recommended by the NIST [Nat23]

Many of the curves in the NIST list [Nat23] have small coefficients (see Table 5 for some of the most deployed curves). This is no coincidence, as it helps speed up the cryptosystems without reducing the security. Indeed, no attack was known on a classical computer to take advantage of the size of the coefficients. We investigate whether their gate complexity is lower compared to that of curves with large coefficients (see [BCC+15] and [FPRE15] for the importance of this question).

By Proposition 4 any elliptic curve with large coefficients is not affected by Regev's algorithm.

Table 3 makes a list of the elliptic curves in [Nat23, Cer10, ANS11] and indicates whether or not their equations have at least one pseudo-random (large) coefficient.

We stress that the curves are standardized and some are widely deployed, as it is confirmed by the standardization reports. In the following we also give the references to the articles where the curves where introduced.

1. (see [Nat23, Sec 3.2.2]) The recommended Montgomery curves, $By^2 = x^3 + Ax^2 + x$ have $B = 1$ and small A (see [Mon87]). Some examples are: **Curve25519** (see [Ber06]), **Curve383187**, **M-221**, **M-383** and **M-511**. The twisted Edwards curves, $ax^2+ay^2 = 1+dx^2y^2$, the recommended curves have $a = 1$ and small d (see [BBJ+08]). They are different equations for the Montgomery curves and can be treated together when evaluating their security. Some examples are: **Curve1174** (bi-rationally equivalent to Curve25519), **Curve41417**, **E-222**, **E-382**, **Ed448-Goldilocks** and **E-521**.
2. (see [Cer10, 2.4.1]) Some elliptic curves in short Weierstrass form $y^2 = x^3 + ax+b$ have both coefficients a and b small. They include the curve **secp256k1** (see [Kob91]).
3. (see [IEE13]) Part of the elliptic curves in the pairing-based cryptography have small equations, in particular the **BN-254** (sometimes denoted in the literature simply as BN, see [BN05]) and the **BLS-12-381** curves (see [BLS03]). Note that, when the security level varies, the pairings recommended by the standardization agencies belonging to the BN and BLS-12 families have the

Table 3. The list of curves recommended by the NIST in [Nat23] or other authorities as [Cer10, ANS11]. A coefficient is considered large when it has a bit size at least half of that of the group order, as it is the case with large probability when they are randomly drawn during the curve selection.

	type of curves	small coefficients	large-coefficients
1.	Montgomery twisted Edwards	M-221, M-383, M-511 Curve25519, Curve383187 Curve41417, E-222, E-382 Ed448-Goldilocks, E-521	
2.	$y^2 = x^3 + ax + b$ small a, b	secp256k1	
3.	pairings	BLS 12, BN	
4.	Koblitz curves	K-233, K-283 K-409, K-571	
a.	pseudo-random b $y^2 = x^3 + ax + b$		P-224, P-256, P-384 P-521, FRP256v1 brainpoolP256t1 brainpoolP384t1
b.	pseudo-random binary curves		B-233, B-283 B-409, B-571

same equation over different finite fields: $y^2 = x^3 + 3$ for the BN family and $y^2 = x^3 + 4$ for the BLS-12 family.

4. (see [Nat23, Sec 3.3.1] All the curves in Sec 2.4, i.e. binary curves, are indicated as being deprecated). The Koblitz curves include all elliptic curves with coefficients in $\mathbb{F}_2$. The standardized Koblitz curves have equation $y^2 + xy = x^3 + 1$ and are seen as defined over $\mathbb{F}_{2^n}$ where n is the bit size, e.g. the Koblitz curve **K-233** has $n = 233$ (see [Kob90] where the idea to use curves with coefficients in $\mathbb{F}_2$ is attributed to [MV93]). Other examples are **K-283**, **K-409** and **K-571**.

Some elliptic curves have pseudo-random coefficients, which are hence large:

a) (see [Nat23, Sec 3.2.1]) the curves in short Weierstrass form $y^2 = x^3 + ax + b$ with $a = -3$ and b a pseudo-random element of $\mathbb{F}_p$. Examples include: **P-224**, **P-256**, **P-384** (see [CC86]). In addition to the NIST recommendations, see [Cer10] for **brainpoolP256t1**, **brainpoolP384t1** and [ANS11] for **FRP256v1**.

b) (see [Nat23, Sec 3.3.2], also note that all the curves in Sect. 2.4, i.e. binary curves, are indicated as being deprecated) The binary curves other than Koblitz's curves have equation $y^2 + xy = x^3 + x^2 + b$ with large degree $b \in \mathbb{F}_2[t]$ representing an element of $\mathbb{F}_{2^n}$. Examples include: **B-233**, **B-283**, **B-409**, **B-571** (see [Kob90, Sec 2]).

We have established that elliptic curves with large coefficients are impractical for Regev's algorithm. In contrast, for many elliptic curves with small coefficients we found small points, paving the way for an implementation of Regev's algorithm. More precisely, we found twists of large rank and we computed small points on these twists.

Lemma 1. *The curves* ***Curve25519****,* ***BLS-12-231****,* ***BN-254****,* ***secp256k1*** *and* ***K-233*** *have twists of rank between* 3 *and* 4 *and have generators of small height. Hence Algorithm 1 can be run with parameter d between* 5 *and* 6.

Proof. Let E be an elliptic curve over $\mathbb{Q}$ (resp. $\mathbb{F}_2(t)$) and let$\mathbb{F}$ be a prime finite field $\mathbb{F} = \mathbb{F}_p$ (resp. a binary finite field $\mathbb{F} = \mathbb{F}_{2^n} = \mathbb{F}_2[t]/\wp(t)$).

Let ϕ be one of the twists bellow;

- when E is a Montgomery curve defined over $\mathbb{Q}$ and a non-square $D \in \mathbb{Q}^*$ a quadratic twist is as follows:

$$\begin{array}{cccc} \phi : (E_D/\mathbb{Q} : Y^2 = x^3 + ADx^2 + D^2x) & \to & (E/\mathbb{Q} : Y^2 = x^3 + Ax^2 + x) \\ (x, y) & \mapsto & (x/D, y/D^{3/2}) \end{array}$$

- when E is a Mordell curves, defined below, it has a sextic twist as follows:

$$\begin{array}{ccc} \phi : (E_D/\mathbb{Q} : y^2 = x^3 + bD) & \to & (E/\mathbb{Q} : y^2 = x^3 + b) \\ (x, y) & \mapsto & (x.D^{1/3}, y/D^{1/2}) \end{array}$$

- when E is defined over $\mathbb{F}_2(t)$ and $D \in \mathbb{F}_2(t)$

$$\begin{array}{ccc} \phi : (E_D : y^2 + xy = x^3 + Dx^2 + 1) & \to & (E : y^2 + xy = x^3 + 1) \\ (x, y) & \mapsto & (x, y + \alpha x)), \end{array}$$

  where α is a root of the polynomial $\alpha^2 + \alpha + D = 0$.

Note that ϕ is defined over $\mathbb{Q}(\sqrt{D})$ or $\mathbb{Q}(D^{1/6})$ (resp. $\mathbb{F}_2(t, \alpha)$ where α is a root of $\alpha^2 + \alpha = D$). If ϕ is defined over $\mathbb{Q}(\sqrt{D})$ and p is a prime such that D is a non-zero square modulo p then $\phi : E_D(\mathbb{F}_p) \to E(\mathbb{F}_p)$ is a isomorphism. Then, for any $g, x \in E(\mathbb{F})$ one has

$$\log_{\phi(g)} \phi(x) = \log_g x.$$

Hence, one can compute $\log_g x$ by computing $\log_{\phi(g)} \phi(x)$ on $E_D(\mathbb{F})$. Algorithm 1 can be run on $E_D(\mathbb{F})$ using a larger number of generators g_i, i.e. the images of the Mordell-Weil generators of E_D in $E_D(\mathbb{F})$.

In Table 4 we give values of D for which the twists $E_D \to E$ reduce into an isomorphism $E_D(\mathbb{F}) \to E(\mathbb{F})$. The conditions on D can be rapidly verified and this concludes the proof (Tables 6 and 8).

Table 4. Twists of the curves **Curve25519**, **BLS-12-231**, **BN-254**, **secp256k1** and **K-233** on which one can run Regev's algorithm.

curve	rkE_d	D	p	condition on D mod p
Curve25519	3	15	$2^{255} - 19$	square
BLS-12-281	3	9998	0x1a0111ea397fe69a4b1ba7b6434bacd764774b84f38512bf6730d2a0f6b0f6241eabfffeb153ffffb9feffffffffaaab	6-th power
BN-254	3	2143	0x1a0111ea397fe69a4b1ba7b6434bacd764774b84f38512bf6730d2a0f6b0f6241eabfffeb153ffffb9feffffffffaaab	6-th power
secp256k1	3	942	$2^{256} - 2^{32} - 2^9 - 2^8 - 2^7 - 2^6 - 2^4 - 1$	6-th power
K-233	4	$\frac{t^8+t^7+t^5+t+1}{t^4+t}$	any modulus of $\mathbb{F}_{233}$	$\exists\alpha$ $\alpha^2 + \alpha = D$

Table 5. Examples of some of the most used elliptic curves in cryptography (see [App])

equation	name	standard	applications
$y^2 = x^3 + 7$	secp256k1	[Nat23]	Bitcoin, Etherium
$y^2 = x^3 + 486662x^2 + x$	Curve25519	[Nat23]	OpenSSH
$y^2 = x^3 + 4$	BLS-12-381	[Cer10]	BLS signatures
$y^2 = x^3 + 2$	BN-254	deprecated	
$y^2 + xy = x^3 + 1$	Koblitz curves	[Nat23]	hardware

4 Asymptotic Nature of the Speedup

In this section, we demonstrate the theoretical superiority of Regev's algorithm over Shor's algorithm. Specifically, we demonstrate that Algorithm 1 outperforms Shor's algorithm in terms of gate count by a factor that grows without bound as the input size increases.

The complexity analysis reduces to applying Proposition 1. The parameter d must be chosen:

- as large as possible since it corresponds to the speedup,

Table 6. Small points on a twist of Curve25519.

Curve25519
$E_D : y^2 = x^3 + 486662Dx^2 + D^2x, D = 15$ $y^2 = x^3 + 7299930x^2 + 225x$
$P_1 : (\frac{602807829649}{101704078504336}, \frac{-1646772889826139395917}{1025669765879981883584})$
$P_2 : (\frac{2307361}{7396}, \frac{536145478981}{636056})$
$P_3 : (\frac{16646400}{49}, \frac{322073629200}{343})$
$\max_{\varepsilon\in\{0,1\}^5} h(\sum_{i=1}^{5}[\varepsilon_i]P_i) = 115$

Table 7. Small points suited to Regev's algorithm for some curves used in cryptography.

$BLS-12-231$	BN-254	secp256k1
$E_D : y^2 = x^3 + 4D$	$E_D : y^2 = x^3 + 2D$	$E_D : y^2 = x^3 + 7D$
$y^2 = x^3 + 94636$	$y^2 = x^3 + 4910$	$y^2 = x^3 + 27881$
$P_1 : (-43, 123)$	$P_1 : (41/4, 619/8)$	$P_1 : (-28, 77)$
$P_2 : (-18, 298)$	$P_2 : (11, 79)$	$P_2 : (-20, 141)$
$P_3 : (-10, 306)$	$P_3 : (139/9, 2503/27)$	$P_3 : (2, 167)$
$P_4 : (45, 431)$	$P_4 : (131, 1501)$	$P_4 : (7, 168)$
$P_5 : (125, 1431)$		
$h(\sum_{i=1}^r [\varepsilon_i]P_i) = 31$	$h(\sum_{i=1}^r [\varepsilon_i]P_i) = 39$	$h(\sum_{i=1}^r [\varepsilon_i]P_i) = 18$

Table 8. Twists of Koblitz curve K-233. The analytic ranks were computed with Magma. The generators are not given here in absence of a software implementation of the generators computation for curves over $\mathbb{F}_2(t)$.

K-233, K-283 K-409 and K-571 (same lift to $\mathbb{F}_2(t)$)	
$y^2 + xy = x^3 + Dx^2 + 1, D \in \mathbb{F}_2(t)$	
r=1	$D = t^2 + t$
r=2	$D = (t^3 + 1)/t$
r=4	$D = (t^8 + t^7 + t^5 + t + 1)/(t^4 + t)$

- sufficiently small so that, when $r = d - 2$ and the points $P_1, \ldots, P_r$ are as in Algorithm 1, any sum of the form $\sum_{i=1}^r [\varepsilon_i]P_i$, with $\varepsilon \in \{0,1\}^r$, can be computed in time negligible with respect to n.

Let us first analyze the complexity of the addition law on elliptic curves, which is given by rational functions. To fix ideas, we use affine coordinates and put the elliptic curve E in Weierstrass form (this is a common choice in quantum algorithms on elliptic curves [PZ03]). Then the addition law for $P, Q \in E(\mathbb{Q})$ when $x_P \neq x_Q$ is (see e.g. [RS02, Sec 1]):

$$P + Q = \left((\frac{y_Q - y_P}{x_Q - x_P})^2 - x_P - x_Q, (\frac{y_Q - y_P}{x_Q - x_P})x_{P+Q} - \frac{y_P x_Q - y_Q x_P}{x_Q - x_P} \right). \quad (14)$$

Since the operations are done in $\mathbb{Q}$ (resp. $\mathbb{F}_2(t)$ for binary curves), the cost of the multiplications is $M(h_0)$ where $h_0 = \max(h(P), h(Q))$ (here h is the natural height defined in Eq. (12)). The fractions in the coordinates of $P+Q$ are simplified by GCD computations using $O(M(h_0) \log_2 h_0)$ gates (see e.g. [SZ04]).

The size of the generators P_i is given by a conjecture of Lang which is strongly supported by numerical experiments. Contrary to the multiplicative group where the generators are the smallest primes and hence have height $O(\log d)$ (and $\tilde{O}(d)$ is sufficient to make the algorithm work, see [Pil24]), in the case of the elliptic curves we use a bound on the heights which is exponential in d. We show that this implies $d \leq (\log n)^c$ for some explicit constant c. Finally, contrary to the multiplicative group where the height is linear, Eq. (14) implies only that

$$h(P+Q) \leq 8\max(h(P), h(Q)) + 6. \tag{15}$$

When applied recursively to r points, this equation implies that

$$h\left(\sum_{i=1}^{r}[\varepsilon_i]P_i\right) \leq r^3\left(\max_{1\leq i\leq r} h(P_i) + 6\right). \tag{16}$$

In contrast to the multiplicative group, where the factor is r, the factor in this case is r^3.

In Sect. 4.1 we make precise the estimations of $h(P_i)$ with $1 \leq i \leq r$. Then in Sect. 4.2 we show that the properties of the Néron-Tate height allows to improve the inequality in Eq. (15) and we prove the complexity of Regev's algorithm in Theorem 2.

4.1 Size of the Points in Algorithm 1

In this subsection, we establish an upper bound on the height of points on elliptic curves and their twists, relying on number-theoretic heuristics that are rigorously cited. Let r_{an} and N be the analytic rank (see [Sil09, Sec C.16]) and the conductor (see [Sil09, Ch VIII.11]) of an elliptic curve E over $\mathbb{Q}$ (resp. $\mathbb{F}_q(t)$ where q is a prime power).

In [Bru92, Cor 2.11] (resp [Bru92, Prop 6.9] for the curves over function fields) Brumer proved that, assuming GRH (resp. unconditionally), the analytic rank r_{an} of an elliptic curve satisfies

$$r_{\text{an}} \leq \frac{\log N}{\log\log N}, \tag{17}$$

for sufficiently large N. The result requires the Shimura-Taniyama conjecture, which is now a theorem. In the following, we also assume the Birch and Swinnerton-Dyer conjecture (BSD, see [Sil09, Ch. 16]), i.e. $r = r_{\text{an}}$ (resp. a theorem of Tate (see [Zim76]) states that $r \leq r_{\text{an}}$ for curves over $\mathbb{F}_q(t)$).

We note N_D the conductor of the D-twist $E_D : Dy^2 = f(x)$ of E. It is clear that $N_D \leq D^2N$ so that Eq. (17) implies that the smallest D such that $\text{rk}E_D \geq r$ is $D \geq c_E \exp(\frac{1}{2}r\log r)$, for some constant c_E. For a given elliptic curve E defined over $\mathbb{F}_q(t)$ there is a well-studied conjecture stating that the ranks of its twists can be arbitrarily large. The situation differs for elliptic curves defined over $\mathbb{Q}$, where competing conjectures exist regarding whether the rank is bounded (see [PPVW19, Sec 3]).

To formulate the following heuristic, we rely on:

- numerical experiments from Table 2 and [WDE+14, Tab 2];
- an analogy with the case of function fields [Ulm02], where an upper bound on the least quadratic twist is proven for elliptic curves defined over $\mathbb{F}_q(t)$;

- the heuristic that the proven inequality in [HB94, Cor 1] is optimal (see [WDE+14, Sec 14 and footnote 32]).

Heuristic 1. *There exists and absolute constant C such that, for any elliptic curve $E/\mathbb{Q}$, the least integer D such that its quadratic twist by D has rank r is*

$$D \leq \exp(Cr^2).$$

We stress that this heuristic corresponds to the current knowledge of number theorists. We hope that this new cryptographic motivation will stimulate even more efforts to answer this open question. Depending on the exact value of the right hand member, the value of the parameter d in Regev's algorithm for elliptic curve might be smaller or even be bounded by a constant.

For any elliptic curve E given by the equation $y^2 = x^3 + ax + b$, where a and b are integer coefficients, we define $h(E) = \max(h(a), h(b))$. The Neron-Tate height is denoted by $\hat{h}$ (see [Sil09, Sec VIII.9]).

Montgomery (see [Lan83]) proposed extending the GRH to the r-th derivative of the Hasse L-function, leading to a consequence formulated by Lang as follows.

Conjecture 1 (Conjecture 3 in [Lan83]). For a rational elliptic curve E of rank r, there exists a basis $P_1, \ldots, P_r$ of $E(\mathbb{Q})/E_{tors}(\mathbb{Q})$ such that

$$\max_{i=1,\ldots,r} \hat{h}(P_i) \leq 2^{\frac{1}{4}h(E)+c\sqrt{\frac{\log_2 N}{\log_2 \log_2 N}}+cr^2} \tag{18}$$

where c is an absolute constant.

We shall apply this conjecture to the twists E_D of E.

4.2 Asymptotic Complexity

To establish that Regev's algorithm has an elliptic curve version, we show that Regev's algorithm outperforms the asymptotic gate complexity of Shor's algorithm by a factor that tends to infinity.

Theorem 2 (under Heuristics 1, Conjecture 1 and Assumption 1). *Let $\epsilon > 0$ be an absolute constant and let $\mathbb{F}$ be a finite field of n-bit size. Let E be a given elliptic curve defined over $\mathbb{Q}$ (resp. $\mathbb{F}_2(t)$) such that $h(E) \leq (\log_2 n)^{1-\epsilon}$.*

Set $r = r(n) = \lfloor (\log n)^{1/2-\epsilon} \rfloor$, let D be the rational number of the smallest height (resp. the rational function of the smallest height) such that the quadratic D-twist E_D of E has rank r as predicted by Heuristic 1. Let $P_1, \ldots, P_r$ be a set of generators of $E_D(\mathbb{Q})$ (resp. $E_D(\mathbb{F}_2(t))$ with Neron-Tate heights as predicted by Conjecture 1. Additionally, we assume that Assumption 1 holds for $E_D(\mathbb{F})$.

Then Algorithm 1 with parameter $d := r + 2$ is successful in solving the DLP in $E(\mathbb{F})$ and has gate complexity $O(\frac{n}{d} M(n))$. This represents a speedup of a factor of $(\log n)^{\frac{1}{2}-\epsilon}$ with respect to Shor's algorithm.

To proceed with the proof, we first need to establish the following result.

Proposition 5. *Let E be an elliptic curve over $\mathbb{Q}$ (resp. over $\mathbb{F}_2(t)$). Let r be an integer and let D be the rational number of smallest naive height (resp. rational fraction of smallest numerator and denominator degree) such that the D-quadratic twist E_D has r rational points $P_1, \ldots, P_r$. Set*

$$\hat{h}_0 = \max_{1 \leq i \leq r} \hat{h}(P_i) \text{ and } m = r^2 \hat{h}_0 + h(E) + h(D).$$

Then, for any $\varepsilon \in \{0,1\}^r$, the sum $\sum_i^r [\varepsilon_i] P_i$ can be computed with a

$$\text{gate complexity} \leq O(r^2 \log^2 m \cdot \hat{h}_0 + r \log^2 m \cdot (h(E) + h(D))). \qquad (19)$$

Proof. We prove first that for any r' and any $(P'_1, \ldots, P'_{r'}) \in \{P_1, \ldots, P_r\}^{r'}$

$$h\left(\sum_{i=1}^{r'} [\varepsilon_i] P'_i\right) \leq (r')^2 \hat{h}_0 + C(h(D) + h(E)), \qquad (20)$$

where C is an explicit absolute constant, $h(D)$ is the naive height of D and $h(E)$ the naive height of E.

We use the fact that $\hat{h}$ is a quadratic form (it was conjectured by Neron, proven by Tate in an unpublished document, see e.g. [Zim76]). Hence $\sqrt{\hat{h}}$ satisfies the triangle inequality and one has:

$$\begin{aligned} \sqrt{\hat{h}\left(\sum_{i=1}^{r'} [\varepsilon_i] P'_i\right)} &\leq \sum_{i=1}^{r'} \sqrt{\hat{h}(P'_i)} \\ &\leq r' \cdot \max_{1 \leq i \leq r'} \sqrt{\hat{h}(P'_i)} \\ &\leq r' \sqrt{\hat{h}_0} \end{aligned}$$

and equivalently

$$\hat{h}\left(\sum_{i=1}^{r'} [\varepsilon_i] P'_i\right) \leq (r')^2 \hat{h}_0. \qquad (21)$$

By [Zim76, main theorem], for any elliptic curve E and a rational point P of E one has

$$|h(P) - \hat{h}(P)| \leq C' h(E_D) \leq C(h(E) + h(D)),$$

for constants C, C'.

We continue the proof by analyzing the gate count. Let $T(k)$ be the cost of computing the linear combination of 2^k points:

$$T(k) = \max_{(P'_1, \ldots, P'_{2^k}) \in \{P_1, \ldots, P_r\}^{2^k}, \varepsilon \in \{0,1\}^{2^k}} \text{complexity}\left(\sum_{i=1}^{2^k} [\varepsilon_i] P'_i\right).$$

We prove by induction that $T(k) = O(M(m_k) \log(m_k))$ where

$$m_k = 2^{2k} \max_{i=1}^{r} \hat{h}(P_i) + C(h(E) + h(D)).$$

Indeed, we first compute the sums of the points $P_1, \ldots, P_{2^{k-1}}$ and $P_{2^{k-1}+1}, \ldots, P_{2^k}$, referred to as half-sums, and then

$$\sum_{i=1}^{2^k} \varepsilon_i P_i = \left(\sum_{i=1}^{2^{k-1}} \varepsilon_i P_i\right) + \left(\sum_{i=2^{k-1}+1}^{2^k} \varepsilon_i P_i\right). \tag{22}$$

The addition of the two half-sums is done using a constant number of multiplications and of computations of GCD's of integers having the bit size of the two half-sums (see Eq.(14)). By Eq. (20) the bit size is bounded by $O(m_{k-1})$ and therefore the fast GCD cost is bounded by $M(m_{k-1}) \log m_{k-1} = O(m_{k-1} \log^2 m)$ (see [HVDH21]), so that:

$$T(k) \leq 2T(k-1) + O(m_{k-1} \log^2 m). \tag{23}$$

$$\begin{aligned} T(k) &\leq 2\,T(k-1) + O\left(m_{k-1} \log^2 m\right) \\ &= O(\textstyle\sum_{i=0}^{k-1} 2^{k-i-1} \left(m_i \log^2 m\right)) \\ &= \log^2 m \cdot O\left(\textstyle\sum_{i=0}^{k-1} 2^{k-i-1} \left(2^{2i}\hat{h}_0 + C(h(D) + h(E)\right)\right) \\ &= O(2^{2k} \log^2 m \cdot \hat{h}_0 + 2^k \log^2 m \cdot (h(E) + h(D))). \end{aligned}$$

Finally, when applying to $k = \lceil \log_2 r \rceil$, $P'_i = P_i$ for $1 \leq i \leq r$, $\varepsilon_{r+1} = \cdots = \varepsilon_{2^k} = 0$ we obtain Eq. (19).

Proof (of Theorem 2). The theorem is an application of Proposition 1. Since we made Assumption 1, the Algorithm 1 is correct. We claim that the gate complexity given by Proposition 5 is $o(n)$. We use r in place of $r(n)$ as it causes no ambiguity.

By Heuristic 1, we have $h(D) \ll r^2$. Since the conductor is a divisor of the discriminant of the curve, we obtain

$$\log_2 N_D \ll h(E_D) \ll h(D) + h(E) \ll r^2 + (\log n)^{1-\epsilon} \ll (\log n)^{1-\epsilon}.$$

By Conjecture 1, we have

$$\begin{aligned} \hat{h}_0 &\leq 2^{\frac{1}{4}h(E) + c\sqrt{\frac{\log_2 N}{\log_2 \log_2 N}} + cr^2} \\ &\ll 2^{(\log n)^{1-\epsilon}}. \end{aligned}$$

Since $r(n) = (\log n)^{1/2-\epsilon}$

$$r^2 \log^2 m \cdot \hat{h}_0 \ll (\log n)^{O(1)} 2^{(\log_2 n)^{1-\epsilon}} = o(n). \tag{24}$$

Using the estimate of $\hat{h}_0$ in the definition of m (see Proposition 5) we find $m = o(n)$ and hence

$$r(h(E) + h(D)) \log^2 m = (\log n)^{O(1)} = o(n). \tag{25}$$

Finally, the gate complexity computed in Eq. (19) is the sum of the terms that were upper-bounded by $o(n)$ in Eqs. (24) and (25).

In simple words, the condition on the $h(E) = (\log n)^{1-\epsilon}$, states that the coefficients of E must be of size $O(n)$. When the coefficients are not pseudo-random, they are usually the result of a probabilistic search where the expectancy of success is the inverse of the probability of an n-bit integer to be prime. This probability is $1/O(n)$, so the coefficients have size $O(n)$ or equivalently height $O(\log n)$. We conclude that the conditions of the theorem realistic.

5 Conclusion and Open Questions

Theorem 1 states that, when tackling the multidimensional DLP, Regev's algorithm has the same complexity as Shor's algorithm. Its complexity decreases when the generators size is smaller than that of random elements in the group.

This article contains a method to find small points on elliptic curves with small coefficients. When tackling the DLP on elliptic curves with small coefficients, Regev's algorithm is asymptotically faster than all the other known algorithms.

The consequences of Regev's algorithm on the deployment ECC depend on the type of application. Our analysis indicates that Regev's algorithm has no effect on the NIST curve **P-256** whereas Bernstein's **Curve25519** and especially **secp256k1** requires a more precise investigation. More work is needed in order to extend [EG25] to elliptic curves and to propose an implementation of Regev's algorithm on a quantum computer.

The notion of inter-lattice distance which is central in Regev's algorithm has many interesting properties and it was studied in a contemporary work [BBP].

Finally, our work has inspired an adaptation to hyperelliptic curves. In that case, it is ignored whether a conjecture a la Lang, i.e. Conjecture 1 can be formulated based on numerical and theoretical evidences.

Funding. This work was supported by the project "Group schemes, root systems, and related representations" founded by the European Union - NextGenerationEU through Romania's National Recovery and Resilience Plan (PNRR) call no. PNRR-III-C9-2023-I8, Project CF159/31.07.2023, and coordinated by the Ministry of Research, Innovation and Digitalization (MCID) of Romania.
The first author was supported by Agence Nationale de la Recherche under grant ANR-22-PNCQ-0002.

References

[ABD+15] Adrian, D., et al.: Imperfect forward secrecy: how Diffie-Hellman fails in practice. In: Proceedings of the 22nd ACM SIGSAC Conference on Computer and Communications Security–CCS'15, pp. 5–17 (2015)

[ANS11] ANSSI. Avis relatif aux paramètres de courbes elliptiques définis par l'Etat français. Journal officiel de la République Française (2011). https://www.legifrance.gouv.fr/download/pdf?id=QfYWtPSAJVtAB_c6Je5tAv00OY2r1ad3LaVVmnStGvQ=

[App] Some hyperlinks to applications of ECC:. – Bitcoin: https://en.bitcoin.it/wiki/Secp256k1 – Etherium: https://fitsaleem.medium.com/ethereums-elliptic-curve-digital-signature-algorithm-ecdsa-88e1659f4879 – OpenSSH: https://www.openssh.com/specs.html – BLS signature: https://datatracker.ietf.org/doc/html/draft-irtf-cfrg-bls-signature-04 – hardware implementation: https://research.birmingham.ac.uk/en/publications/lightweight-coprocessor-for-koblitz-curves-283-bit-ecc-including-

[BB] Barbulescu, R., Bisson, G.: Regev's attack on hyperelliptic cryptosystems. Cryptology ePrint Archive, Paper 2024 (2004). https://eprint.iacr.org/2024/2004

[BBJ+08] Bernstein, D.J., Birkner, P., Joye, M., Lange, T., Peters, C.: Twisted edwards curves. In: Vaudenay, S. (ed.) AFRICACRYPT 2008. LNCS, vol. 5023, pp. 389–405. Springer, Heidelberg (2008). https://doi.org/10.1007/978-3-540-68164-9_26

[BBP] Barbulescu, R., Barcau, M., Pasol, V.: A comprehensive analysis of Regev's quantum algorithm. Cryptology ePrint Archive, Paper 2024/1758. https://eprint.iacr.org/2024/1758

[BCC+15] Bernstein, D.J.: How to manipulate curve standards: a white paper for the black hat `http://bada55.cr.yp.to`. In: Chen, L., Matsuo, S. (eds.) SSR 2015. LNCS, vol. 9497, pp. 109–139. Springer, Cham (2015). https://doi.org/10.1007/978-3-319-27152-1_6

[Ber06] Bernstein, D.J.: Curve25519: new Diffie-Hellman speed records. In: Yung, M., Dodis, Y., Kiayias, A., Malkin, T. (eds.) PKC 2006. LNCS, vol. 3958, pp. 207–228. Springer, Heidelberg (2006). https://doi.org/10.1007/11745853_14

[BL95] Boneh, D., Lipton, R.J.: Quantum cryptanalysis of hidden linear functions. In: Coppersmith, D. (ed.) CRYPTO 1995. LNCS, vol. 963, pp. 424–437. Springer, Heidelberg (1995). https://doi.org/10.1007/3-540-44750-4_34

[BLS03] Barreto, P.S.L.M., Lynn, B., Scott, M.: On the selection of pairing-friendly groups. In: Matsui, M., Zuccherato, R.J. (eds.) SAC 2003. LNCS, vol. 3006, pp. 17–25. Springer, Heidelberg (2004). https://doi.org/10.1007/978-3-540-24654-1_2

[BN05] Barreto, P.S.L.M., Naehrig, M.: Pairing-friendly elliptic curves of prime order. In: Preneel, B., Tavares, S. (eds.) SAC 2005. LNCS, vol. 3897, pp. 319–331. Springer, Heidelberg (2006). https://doi.org/10.1007/11693383_22

[Bra93] Brands, S.A.: An efficient off-line electronic cash system based on the representation problem. Technical report, Centrum voor Wiskunde en Informatica (CWI) (1993)

[Bru92] Brumer, A.: The average rank of elliptic curves I. Invent. Math. **109**(1), 445–472 (1992)

[BS16] Biasse, J.F., Song, F.: Efficient quantum algorithms for computing class groups and solving the principal ideal problem in arbitrary degree number fields. In: Proceedings of the Twenty-Seventh Annual ACM-SIAM Symposium on Discrete Algorithms, pp. 893–902. SIAM (2016)

[CC86] Chudnovsky, D.V., Chudnovsky, G.V.: Sequences of numbers generated by addition in formal groups and new primality and factorization tests. Adv. Appl. Math. **7**(4), 385–434 (1986)

[Cer10] Certicom research. Standards for efficient cryptography sec 2: Recommended elliptic curve domain parameters (2010). http://www.secg.org/sec2-v2.pdf

[CL15] Costello, C., Longa, P.: FourQ: four-dimensional decompositions on a Q-curve over the mersenne prime. In: Iwata, T., Cheon, J.H. (eds.) ASIACRYPT 2015. LNCS, vol. 9452, pp. 214–235. Springer, Heidelberg (2015). https://doi.org/10.1007/978-3-662-48797-6_10

[dBDF20] Boer, K., Ducas, L., Fehr, S.: On the quantum complexity of the continuous hidden subgroup problem. In: Canteaut, A., Ishai, Y. (eds.) EUROCRYPT 2020. LNCS, vol. 12106, pp. 341–370. Springer, Cham (2020). https://doi.org/10.1007/978-3-030-45724-2_12

[DSL+24] Dhanda, S.S., et al.: A fast and efficient 191-bit elliptic curve cryptographic processor using a hybrid Karatsuba multiplier for IoT applications. IEEE Access (2024)

[Duj24] Dujella, A.: History of elliptic curves rank records (2024). https://web.math.pmf.unizg.hr/~duje/tors/rankhist.html

[EG24] Ekerå, M., Gärtner, J.: Extending Regev's factoring algorithm to compute discrete logarithms. In: Post-Quantum Cryptography–PQC 2024, vol. 14771 of Lecture notes in Computer Science, pp. 211–242. Springer, Heidelberg (2024)

[EG25] Ekerå, M., Gärtner, J.: A high-level comparison of state-of-the-art quantum algorithms for breaking asymmetric cryptography. IACR Commun. Cryptol. **2**(1) (2025)

[EHKS14] Eisenträger, K., Hallgren, S., Kitaev, A., Song, F.: A quantum algorithm for computing the unit group of an arbitrary degree number field. In: Proceedings of the Forty-Sixth Annual ACM Symposium on Theory of Computing, pp. 293–302 (2014)

[FPRE15] Flori, J.P., Plût, J., Reinhard, J.R., Ekerå, M.: Diversity and transparency for ECC. Cryptology ePrint Archive, Paper 2015/659 (2015). https://eprint.iacr.org/2015/659

[Gau00] Gaudry, P.: An algorithm for solving the discrete log problem on hyperelliptic curves. In: Preneel, B. (ed.) EUROCRYPT 2000. LNCS, vol. 1807, pp. 19–34. Springer, Heidelberg (2000). https://doi.org/10.1007/3-540-45539-6_2

[GR09] Galbraith, S., Ruprai, R.S.: An improvement to the gaudry-schost algorithm for multidimensional discrete logarithm problems. In: Parker, M.G. (ed.) IMACC 2009. LNCS, vol. 5921, pp. 368–382. Springer, Heidelberg (2009). https://doi.org/10.1007/978-3-642-10868-6_22

[HB94] Heath-Brown, R.: The size of Selmer groups for the congruent number problem. II. Inventiones Mathematicae **118**(1), 331–370 (1994)

[HPS11] Hanrot, G., Pujol, X., Stehlé, D.: Algorithms for the shortest and closest lattice vector problems. In: Chee, Y.M., et al. (eds.) IWCC 2011. LNCS, vol. 6639, pp. 159–190. Springer, Heidelberg (2011). https://doi.org/10.1007/978-3-642-20901-7_10

[HS07] Hanrot, G., Stehlé, D.: Improved analysis of Kannan's shortest lattice vector algorithm. In: Menezes, A. (ed.) CRYPTO 2007. LNCS, vol. 4622, pp. 170–186. Springer, Heidelberg (2007). https://doi.org/10.1007/978-3-540-74143-5_10

[HVDH21] Harvey, D., Van Der Hoeven, J.: Integer multiplication in time $O(n \log n)$. Ann. Math. **193**(2), 563–617 (2021)

[IEE13] IEEE-SA Standards Board. IEEE standard for pairing-based cryptographic techniques using pairings (2013). https://webpages.charlotte.edu/yonwang/13633-2013.pdf

[Kit96] Kitaev, A.: Quantum measurements and the abelian stabilizer problem. In: Proceedings of the Electronic Colloquium on Computational Complexity–ECCC 1996, vol. TR96-03 of Reports series, p. 1. University of Trier (1996)

[Kob90] Koblitz, N.: Constructing elliptic curve cryptosystems in characteristic 2. In: Menezes, A.J., Vanstone, S.A. (eds.) CRYPTO 1990. LNCS, vol. 537, pp. 156–167. Springer, Heidelberg (1991). https://doi.org/10.1007/3-540-38424-3_11

[Kob91] Koblitz, N.: CM-curves with good cryptographic properties. In: Feigenbaum, J. (ed.) CRYPTO 1991. LNCS, vol. 576, pp. 279–287. Springer, Heidelberg (1992). https://doi.org/10.1007/3-540-46766-1_22

[Kos24] Koshelev, D.: Generation of "independent" points on elliptic curves by means of Mordell-Weil lattices. Math. Cryptol. **4**(1), 11–22 (2024)

[Lan83] Lang, S.: Conjectured diophantine estimates on elliptic curves. In: Arithmetic and Geometry: Papers Dedicated to IR Shafarevich on the Occasion of His Sixtieth Birthday Volume I Arithmetic, pp. 155–171 (1983)

[LO85] Lagarias, J.C., Odlyzko, A.M.: Solving low-density subset sum problems. J. ACM **32**(1), 229–246 (1985)

[Mon87] Montgomery, P.L.: Speeding the Pollard and elliptic curve methods of factorization. Math. Comput. **48**(177), 243–264 (1987)

[MPR+24] Moody, D., Perlner, R., Regenscheid, A., Robinson, A., Cooper, D.: Transition to post-quantum cryptography standards. Technical report, National Institute of Standards and Technology (2024)

[MV93] Menezes, A.J., Vanstone, S.A.: Elliptic curve cryptosystems and their implementation. J. Cryptol. **6**(4), 209–224 (1993). https://doi.org/10.1007/BF00203817

[Nat23] National Institute of Science and Technology, Computer security resource center. Special publication NIST 800-186: Recommendations for discrete logarithm-based cryptography: Elliptic curve domain parameters (2023). https://csrc.nist.gov/pubs/sp/800/186/final

[PH22] Pohlig, S.C., Hellman, M.E.: An improved algorithm for computing logarithms over GF(p) and its cryptographic significance. In: Democratizing Cryptography: The Work of Whitfield Diffie and Martin Hellman, pp. 415–430. ACM (2022)

[Pil24] Pilatte, C.: Unconditional correctness of recent quantum algorithms for factoring and computing discrete logarithms. arXiv preprint arXiv:2404.16450 (2024)

[Pip80] Pippenger, N.: On the evaluation of powers and monomials. SIAM J. Comput. **9**(2), 230–250 (1980)

[PPVW19] Park, J., Poonen, B., Voight, J., Wood, M.M.: A heuristic for boundedness of ranks of elliptic curves. J. Eur. Math. Soc. **21**(9), 1–41 (2019)

[PZ03] Proos, J., Zalka, C.: Shor's discrete logarithm quantum algorithm for elliptic curves. Quant. Inf. Comput. **3**(4), 317–344 (2003)

[Reg25] Regev, O.: An efficient quantum factoring algorithm. J. ACM **72**(1), 1–13 (2025)

[RS02] Rubin, K., Silverberg, A.: Ranks of elliptic curves. Bull. Am. Math. Soc. **39**(4), 455–474 (2002)

[RV24] Ragavan, S., Vaikuntanathan, V.: Space-efficient and noise-robust quantum factoring. In: Advances in Cryptology–CRYPTO 2024, vol. 14925 of Lecture notes in Computer Science, pp. 107–140. Springer, Heidelberg (2024). https://doi.org/10.1007/978-3-031-68391-6_4

[Sho94] Shor, P.W.: Algorithms for quantum computation: discrete logarithms and factoring. In: Proceedings 35th Annual Symposium on Foundations of Computer Science–SFCS'94, pp. 124–134. IEEE (1994)

[Sil09] Silverman, J.H.: The arithmetic of elliptic curves, volume 106 of Graduate Texts in Mathematics. Springer, Heidelberg (2009)

[Sim02] Simon, D.: Computing the rank of elliptic curves over number fields. LMS J. Comput. Math. **5**, 7–17 (2002)

[Sto01] Stoll, M.: Implementing 2-descent for Jacobians of hyperelliptic curves. Acta Arith. **98**(3), 245–277 (2001)

[SZ04] Stehlé, D., Zimmermann, P.: A binary recursive GCD algorithm. In: Buell, D. (ed.) ANTS 2004. LNCS, vol. 3076, pp. 411–425. Springer, Heidelberg (2004). https://doi.org/10.1007/978-3-540-24847-7_31

[TV06] Tao, T., Vu, V.H.: Additive Combinatorics, vol. 105. Cambridge University Press, Cambridge (2006)

[Ulm02] Ulmer, D.: Elliptic curves with large rank over function fields. Ann. Math. 295–315 (2002)

[Wan81] Wang, P.S.: A p-adic algorithm for univariate partial fractions. In: Proceedings of the Fourth ACM Symposium on Symbolic and Algebraic Computation, pp. 212–217 (1981)

[WDE+14] Watkins, M., Donnelly, S., Elkies, N.D., Fisher, T., Granville, A., Rogers, N.F.: Ranks of quadratic twists of elliptic curves. Publications mathematiques de Besancon Algebre et theorie des nombres **2**, 63–98 (2014)

[Zim76] Zimmer, G.H.: On the difference of the Weil height and the Néron-Tate height. Math. Z. **147**, 35–51 (1976)

[ZZY+19] Zhu, Y., Zhuang, J., Yi, H., Lv, C., Lin, D.: A variant of the Galbraith-Ruprai algorithm for discrete logarithms with improved complexity. Des. Codes Crypt. **87**, 971–986 (2019)

The Role of Piracy in Quantum Proofs

Anne Broadbent[1], Alex B. Grilo[2(✉)], Supartha Podder[3], and Jamie Sikora[4]

[1] University of Ottawa, Ottawa, Canada
abroadbe@uottawa.ca
[2] Sorbonne Université, CNRS, LIP6, Paris, France
Alex.Bredariol-Grilo@lip6.fr
[3] Stony Brook University, Stony Brook, USA
supartha@cs.stonybrook.edu
[4] Virginia Tech, Blacksburg, VA, USA
sikora@vt.edu

Abstract. A well-known feature of quantum information is that it cannot, in general, be cloned. Recently, a number of quantum-enabled information-processing tasks have demonstrated various forms of uncloneability; among these forms, *piracy* is an adversarial model that gives maximal power to the adversary in controlling both a *cloning-type* attack, as well as the *evaluation/verification* stage. Here, we initiate the study of *anti-piracy* proof systems, which are proof systems that inherently prevent piracy attacks. We define anti-piracy proof systems, demonstrate such a proof system for an oracle problem, and also describe a candidate anti-piracy proof system for NP. We also study quantum proof systems that are *cloneable* and settle the famous QMA vs. QMA(2) debate in this setting. Lastly, we discuss how one can approach the QMA vs. QCMA question, by studying its cloneable variants.

1 Introduction

The groundbreaking result of Goldwasser, Micali and Rackoff [GMR89] revolutionized the way we think about proofs, by defining a proof system as an interactive game between an unbounded prover and a computationally bounded verifier, where the prover wants to convince the verifier about the truth of some statement. For a proof system to be valid, we want that there is a way that an honest prover can convince the verifier of a true statement, whereas we want that no malicious prover can convince the verifier of a false statement.

This foundational result is adopted as the perfect paradigm for exploring fundamental concepts in many areas, such as in approximability [ALM+98], operator algebras [JNV+20], and, highly relevant to this work, cryptography. Already in [GMR89], a cryptographic version of an interactive proof systems was defined as a *zero-knowledge proof system*. This is an interactive proof system, with the additional property that the verifier does not learn anything new except the fact that the proved statement is indeed true. Such a seemingly paradoxical object has had a profound impact to cryptography, and understanding which problems have zero-knowledge proof systems has had far-reaching applications of

D. Escudero and I. Damgård (Eds.): LATINCRYPT 2025, LNCS 16129, pp. 267–295, 2026.
https://doi.org/10.1007/978-3-032-06754-8_10

theoretical and practical interest. In particular, the definition of zero-knowledge triggered the development of the simulation paradigm, which is fundamental in modern cryptography [Gol04, Lin16].

Starting with the definition of QMA [KSV02] as the quantum analogue of NP, where a *quantum* polynomial-time algorithm verifies a *quantum* proof, the study of proof systems in the quantum world has led to foundational results towards the understanding of quantum information. The notion of a quantum proof has been extended to the interactive setting [Wat03], with multiple provers [KM03, CHTW04], and zero-knowledge [Wat02].

Simultaneously to the above, the area of quantum cryptography has flourished in its study of how quantum resources help in cryptographic protocols. A key property that enables many of these protocols is that quantum states cannot be generically copied [WZ82, Die82]. We note, however that concrete quantum cryptography protocols involve specific distributions of quantum states and that proof techniques for these schemes go well beyond the basic no-cloning principle. Fortunately, many use cases for quantum-cloning in cryptography have been developed, together with their corresponding security notions and proofs. This includes quantum money [Wie83, MVW13a] and new functionalities such as encryption and functionalities with certified deletion and copy-protection (see Sect. 1.1).

Given the importance of proof systems in several domains, including cryptography, and the importance of the uncloneability in quantum cryptography, our work seeks to unify the two theories, by studying uncloneability in proof systems. Our central question is of the existence of such proofs.

Central Question: *Which problems have uncloneable quantum proof systems, and which do not?*

This topic was raised over ten years ago by Aaronson [Aar09], but has remained largely unanswered. Two recent works [JK23, GMR23] consider this question; see more details in Sect. 1.1.

In the remainder of this introduction, we discuss in depth our approaches to these questions and our contributions. In Sect. 1.1, we motivate our study of which problems have uncloneable proof systems by describing our new definition of what we call anti-piracy proof systems, and discuss methods to achieve it; we also compare with recent related work on uncloneable proofs [JK23, GMR23]. In Sect. 1.2, we discuss the other perspective of which problems have cloneable proof systems by examining complexity-theoretic implications of cloneability and showing that in the cloneable setting having multiple unentangled provers does not increase the computational power of QMA.

1.1 Anti-piracy Proof Systems

The first part of our central question asks about the existence of uncloneable proof systems. Towards answering this question, we contribute a new definition that we call *anti-piracy proof systems*; in Sect. 1.1, we motivate this concept and in Sect. 1.1 we detail the definition. We also discuss how to achieve this definition in Sect. 1.1.

Challenges in Defining Uncloneable Proof Systems. As mentioned, the no-cloning principle tells us that unknown quantum states cannot be generically copied; hence it would be reasonable to expect that families of quantum states, such as proofs for QMA, could be shown to be uncloneable. However, such statement requires a careful approach. First, in the context of QMA, any statement regarding the hardness of cloning quantum witnesses cannot be information theoretical: given the input to a problem in QMA, one can find, in exponential time, a quantum proof that satisfies it. Secondly, as quantum witnesses are very structured, one would need to prove the computational uncloneability for such families of states. Examples of such families that appear in cryptography (but not proof systems) are the Wiesner states [Wie83, MVW13a] and the subspace/coset states [AC12, CV22].

Towards understanding the fundamentals of uncloneable proof systems, consider the following candidate for a one-message uncloneable proof system for a promise problem $A = (A_{yes}, A_{no})$.

First Attempt at a Definition for Uncloneable Proof Systems. Given a quantum proof system satisfying completeness and soundness, we require that if $|\psi_x\rangle$ is a witness for $x \in A_{yes}$, then for any polynomial-time adversary $\mathcal{A}$, the probability that $\mathcal{A}(|\psi_x\rangle) = |\psi_x\rangle|\psi_x\rangle$ is negligible.

While our first attempt seems reasonable, below, we describe below multiple shortcomings. (We keep the exposition to product states and equality for simplicity.)

"Cloning a Functionality". Consider an algorithm $\mathcal{A}$ such that $\mathcal{A}(|\psi_x\rangle) = |\phi_A\rangle|\phi_B\rangle$, where both $|\phi_A\rangle$ and $|\phi_B\rangle$ make V accept x with high probability but $|\phi_A\rangle|\phi_B\rangle \neq |\psi_x\rangle|\psi_x\rangle$. Formally speaking, while $\mathcal{A}$ did not "clone" the state $|\psi_x\rangle$, $\mathcal{A}$ is able to "clone its functionality", since $|\phi_A\rangle|\phi_B\rangle$ can be used to convince two independent verifiers that x is a yes-instance. This situation is not ruled out by our first attempt.[1]

"Differing Verifications and Pirate-Verifier Collusions". Consider an algorithm $\mathcal{A}'$ such that $\mathcal{A}'(|\psi_x\rangle) = |\phi'_A\rangle|\phi'_B\rangle$ and a verifier $V' \neq V$ that accepts $|\phi'_A\rangle$ and $|\phi'_B\rangle$ with high probability. As long as such a V' leads to a sound proof system, we believe that such a situation should be disallowed by a correct definition; however our first attempt at a definition does not rule out such a scenario where alternative verification schemes exist, possibly in collusion with the adversarial attack. Two motivating scenarios follow.

- *Quantum-classical proofs:* Consider a proof systems with $|\psi_x\rangle = |\psi_q\rangle|\psi_c\rangle$, where $|\psi_q\rangle$ is an uncloneable quantum state that is independent of A (e.g. Wiesner states or subspace/coset states), and $|\psi_c\rangle$ is a cloneable state

[1] To mitigate the above situation, one approach would be to describe a verifier V such that for every x, there is a single $|\psi_x\rangle$ that makes V accept x with high probability, for instance, as in *Unique* QMA (UQMA) [ABBS22]). For such proof systems, ruling out cloning would also rule out the behaviour of $\mathcal{A}$ described above. However, looking ahead, our next shortcoming would be applicable to this situation.

(for example a classical string) that is used as a classical witness (such as in NP or QCMA). In this case, the proof system might be "uncloneable" for the honest verification which would first verify the quantum state, and proceed to verify the classical state only if the quantum state is deemed authentic. However, it is easy to make this proof system cloneable by considering a pirate that outputs copies of $|\psi_c\rangle$ to valid verifiers that bypass the quantum verification of $|\psi_q\rangle$ and only verify $|\psi_c\rangle$.
- *Collusions between the pirate and verifier.* As a generalization of the above, we note that from the point of view of someone that wants to decide if $x \in A_{yes}$, one obvious approach is to deviate from the honest behaviour V. In this situation, the pirate and the would-be verifier V' are in a collusion, since V' could depend on the actions of the pirate. This situation is similar to what we find in practice with pirated media: users of such media are satisfied as long as the end-result is the same or close enough; for this, bypassing the "honest" decoders that comply with the distributor's requirements is common, and the result is that the method to render the media differs in the intended and pirated setting.

We conclude that our first attempt is insufficient and via the situations described above, we have a better grasp at the subtleties that must be considered towards a robust definition of uncloneability in proof systems.

Our Definition: Anti-piracy Proof Systems. Our work contributes a formal definition of *anti-piracy* proof systems, which, we believe, captures a general sense of uncloneability in proof systems. Since *pirates* are a more powerful case than *cloners*, our choice of terminology emphasises the fundamentally new perspective on uncloneablity in the context of proof systems:

Contribution 1: A formal definition of *anti-piracy* proof systems.

As pointed out in Sect. 1.1, an anti-piracy proof system must not only account for pirates that have access to a proof and attempt to modify it; it must also account for deviations in the verification. To this end, we define a key notion of an *admissible* verifier for a given promise problem A:

A verifier V is *admissible* for A if there exists a prover P such that the resulting proof system (P, V) satisfies completeness and soundness for A.

With this notion in hand, towards defining anti-piracy proof system, we can quantify over "reasonable" verifiers: they want to be convinced in the case that there is a valid proof (there exists a prover that would satisfy completeness), but are not overly gullible (soundness must hold for all possible provers). For instance, this notion lets us exclude verifiers that always reject or always accept. We can now give an informal version of our main definition:

A proof system (P, V) for A is an anti-piracy proof system if, for any $x \in A_{yes}$, any polynomial-time pirate having access to a proof for x and that outputs two registers (R_1, R_2), then for any pair of admissible verifiers (V_1, V_2) for A, the probability that *both* verifiers accept given registers (R_1, R_2), respectively, is negligible.

One problem with the previous definition is that it requires the pirate to perform badly for *all* instances. This is a problem because even for hard problems in worst/average case, there could be a big fraction of the inputs for which it is easy to find a witness. As in the definition of witness hiding [FS90], the solution is to ask for a distribution over the inputs on which the pirate behaves poorly.

Further Remarks. We now mention some additional remarks on our definition:

- The property of being anti-piracy related to a proof system and not a problem/language. Thus, it is conceivable that a language would admit both an anti-piracy proof system and another proof system whose proofs are perfectly cloneable. In particular, our work conjectures the possibility of anti-piracy proof systems for all problems in NP (see Sect. 1.1).
- For simplicity, we focus on *non-interactive* (1-message) proof systems. Moreover, we consider here only *public verification.* If, instead, we had designated verifiers, where the prover and the verifier share private resources such as private keys or EPR pairs, then achieving such a definition would be straightforward. We stress that the pirate should have access to the same resources as the verifiers, and in particular, they can verify the proof. See Sect. 1.3 for further discussion.
- Anti-piracy proof systems are only meaningful for hard problems and instances. In the absence of such hardness, an admissible verifier can disregard any input while ensuring completeness and soundness. We note that this is in stark contrast with zero-knowledge proof systems, where easy problems and instances trivially satisfy the zero-knowledge property. However, as in zero-knowledge, anti-piracy implies witness hiding [FS90]. This is because, in any proof system that is not witness hiding, a pirate should be able to extract a "classical" witness and given its nature, can then clone it.

Schemes that Achieve the Definition. Our definition for anti-piracy proof systems opens a completely new paradigm for uncloneability, that goes beyond the uncloneability of any specific information or functionality, focusing on the intrinsic usefulness of a proof and how quantum information could be used to limit this usefulness to multiple verifiers.

The obvious next question is: *Is it possible to achieve anti-piracy proof systems?* Towards an answer, we note the intrinsic difficulty to the problem, due to the complexity of its definition: because we quantify over *all* possible admissible verifiers (which implicitly quantifies over all possible provers), and then over all possible pirates, achieving a proof is particularly unwieldy.

We thus approach the question stepwise, first showing a conditional result.

Contribution 2: We provide an anti-piracy proof system for an oracle problem. Our oracle anti-piracy proof system makes use of quantum subspace states and subspace membership oracles, as well as a key result from Ben-David and Sattath, on the probability of finding strings in a subspace and their dual given these resources [BS23].

We present our anti-piracy proof systems relative to an oracle in Sect. 3.2. Next, towards an unconditional result on anti-piracy proof systems, we give the following.

Contribution 3: We provide a candidate for uncloneable proof systems for NP. This candidate builds on the idea of the uncloneable subspace state in Contribution 2, but instead of oracles for subspace membership, it uses cryptographic techniques such as obfuscation and non-interactive zero-knowledge proof systems.

In Sect. 3.3, we explain the candidate and explore some challenges towards a proof.

Related Work. We now mention related work on uncloneability in quantum information, comparing with our work.

Uncloneable Proofs. There are two recent results on uncloneable proofs [JK23, GMR23] and we now compare with our work.

In [JK23], the authors define the notion of uncloneable non-interactive zero-knowledge proof systems (NIZKs) which capture the standard notions of completeness, soundness and zero-knowledge, with the additional requirement that, given an honest proof in the protocol, no adversary can pass *two* honest verifications of the proof system (here by honest verification, we mean the verification prescribed by the protocol). In particular, in their proposed protocols, in order to check whether the instance is positive or negative, the verifier only checks classical information. The uncloneable (quantum) piece of the proof is then appended to guarantee uncloneability. While such protocols find their applications elsewhere, we note that they do not satisfy our definition of anti-piracy, since the uncloneable part could be easily removed and the proof would satisfy an admissible verification.

In [GMR23], the authors present two definitions of uncloneable NIZKs. The first one is similar to [JK23] that we have discussed above. In a second definition, called *strong* uncloneable proofs, they require that if the adversary can make two (not necessarily honest) verifiers accept, then we can extract one of the witnesses from the adversary (without the original proof). While [GMR23] demonstrate impossibility results in this model, their results are not applicable to our scenario. The main reason is that [GMR23] allows interaction between a would-be verifier and an adversary (called a "right-receiver" and "MiM" in their work), meaning that a first would-be verifier can return a message to the adversary, who then attempts to convince a second would-be verifier. In contrast, our definition closely models a one-message proof system, enforcing a *simulatenous* evaluation by possibly malicious verifiers.

Copy-Protecting Information. Wiesner's visionary ideas in the late 1960s (but not published until much later [Wie83]) are the foundations of much of present-day quantum cryptography, including quantum key distribution [BB84,Eke91], quantum money [AFG+12], uncloneable encryption [BL20], certified deletion [BI20] and more (for a survey, see [BS16]). These works, however are fundamentally different from uncloneability proofs because the primitives are used for encoding strings (as in encryption), or verify authenticity only (as in money).

Copy-Protecting Software. In groundbreaking work [Aar09] pushed beyond the paradigm of uncloneable information, studying for the first time the idea of uncloneable *functionalities* by defining *quantum copy-protection*, and proposing related schemes. However, this work left many open questions; among them, the question of building *uncloneable quantum software* from standard cryptographic assumptions; follow-up work solved this problem under multiple angles [ALP21, BJL+21,CMP24]. In uncloneable software, there is an explicit input-output behaviour with respect to the evaluator, and this is a key element for the corresponding security game (which relates to challenge distributions, and the limited ability of various parties to correctly predict the outcome of a computation, given an input). In contrast, in anti-piracy proof systems, there is no challenge distribution, which makes the task of even defining such a scheme quite difficult.

Uncloneable Advice. Continuing on the line of work of studying uncloneability and its use, very recently [BKL23] studied uncloneability of quantum advice. They showed that there exist a non-uniform language whose advice states are uncloneable. Following the framework of quantum copy-protection, their definition is given with respect to a challenge distribution. However, in contrast with quantum copy-protection (and more along the lines of anti-piracy quantum proofs), the uncloneable advice state is unkeyed.

Strictly Uncloneable Proofs and Advice. Building on our work and that of [BKL23, CKP24] recently investigated strictly uncloneable variants of QMA, BQP/qpoly, and FEQP/qpoly adopting a stronger notion of uncloneability, where for any family of candidate quantum proofs, no polynomial-time cloning algorithm can produce a state that allows k independent polynomial-time verifiers (for arbitrary polynomial k) to simultaneously accept the proof. Relative to a quantum oracle [AK07a], they showed the existence of languages in strictly uncloneable QMA and strictly uncloneable BQP/qpoly, but not in cloneableQMA [NZ24]. The key distinction from our work lies in the fact that we treat anti-piracy as a property of the proof system, whereas their framework considers it as a property of the language. Moreover, their results apply only in the worst-case setting, while our framework accommodates average-case anti-piracy guarantees.

1.2 Cloneable Proof Systems and Their Implications

We now switch to discussing cloneable proof systems and their implications to complexity theory. A major pressing question in quantum complexity theory, first asked by Aharonov and Naveh [AN02], is to understand the power of quantum proofs over classical proofs. A notorious example is understanding the relationship between QMA and its classical proof counterpart, QCMA. Progress towards answering this question appears in [Wat00, AK07b, KP14, FK15, Kla17, LLPY24, NN24, BK24] however the main question still remains.

One method to separate QCMA and QMA is to find a complexity class that sits between them. For example, in [GKS16], they consider simpler quantum states, called subset states, as witnesses, but they show that this simplification is still strong enough to encompass QMA. Following [NZ24], in this work we consider a different aspect of quantum states which is cloneability. Since classical states are perfectly cloneable, classical witnesses are perfectly cloneable. (There are many interesting complexity classes which are defined with classical witnesses such as NP, its randomized variant MA, and QCMA.) We aim to understand the consequences of general *quantum witnesses* that *can* be copied, which would make them closer to classical in a sense.

More concretely, [NZ24] defines the complexity class cloneableQMA where in the completeness case, the prover can send a state which is *copiable*, up to some fidelity parameter f. Naturally, cloneableQMA is a subset of QMA and a superset of QCMA. Clearly, if cloneableQMA = QMA (or the stronger statement QCMA = QMA), then every problem in QMA has perfectly cloneable proofs. On the other hand, any separation (e.g. oracle) between cloneableQMA and QMA or QCMA and cloneableQMA would give the same type of separation between QMA and QCMA as well. [NZ24] gives a *quantum oracle* separation between cloneableQMA and QMA reproving the result of [AK07b] in the cloneable setting. Moreover if QMA $\neq$ QCMA, then it is intriguing where cloneableQMA lies between them, and which problems outside QCMA admit cloneable proofs [Aar16].

In this work, we push forward the consequences of having cloneable proofs.

Summary of Contributions: Implications of Cloneable Proof Systems. In Sect. 4, we build on the work of [NZ24], which defines and studies the complexity class cloneableQMA, extending it to unentangled provers and studying its behaviour.

> **Contribution 4:** We show that in the uncloneable regime, there is no power of unentanglement. More precisely, we define the analogous class cloneableQMA(k), referring to k unentangled provers, and show that cloneableQMA(k) = cloneableQMA.

Figure 1 depicts cloneableQMA with respect to other variants of QMA. One could ask if any of the containments of QCMA $\subseteq$ cloneableQMA $\subseteq$ QMA $\subseteq$ QMA(2) are strict or not. Resolving this question is of great interest. For one reason, any strict containment between cloneableQMA and any of these other classes

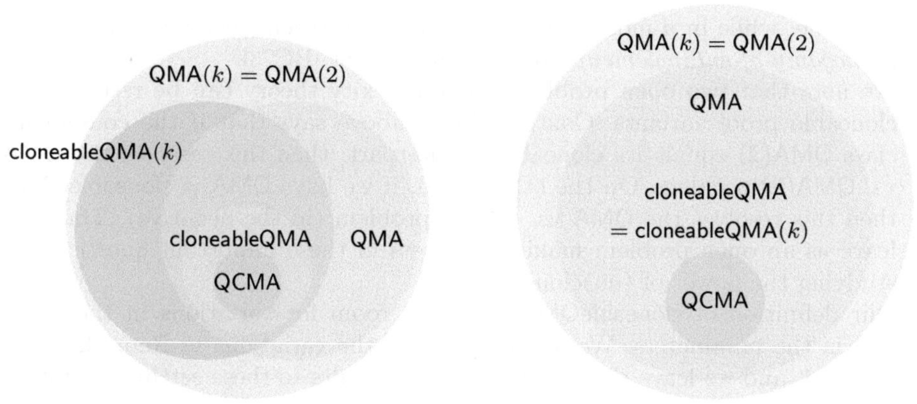

Fig. 1. The QMA landscape with respect to cloneable proof systems. (Left) Immediate/known containments. (Right) Containments following our work.

would separate QCMA from QMA(2), or possibly from QMA, a famous open problem in complexity theory. On the other hand, proving cloneableQMA = QMA implies that QMA witnesses can, in general, forfeit the quantum feature of being uncloneable, yielding great insight towards the nature of quantum proofs. Lastly, proving cloneableQMA(2) = QMA(2) would imply QMA(2) = QMA, settling a longstanding open problem.

1.3 Open Questions and Future Work

After many recent works on uncloneability of quantum states and their applications to cryptography, we are still far from a full understanding. Below is a non-exhaustive list of some of the main open questions that are directly related to our work:

- As we discussed before, the anti-piracy proof system is fundamentally different in nature than the other uncloneable proof systems. Towards its further exploration, can we design anti-piracy proof systems for a more natural problem in NP (or more generally for QMA)? Our work provides a candidate construction for an anti-piracy proof system for all of NP. Can we prove that it satisfies our definition?
- Uncloneable primitives often reduce to one another. It would be interesting to know if the definition of an anti-piracy proof system can imply or can be implied by other uncloneable cryptography primitives? Also, like zero-knowledge, anti-piracy implies witness hiding. Are there further connections of anti-piracy with zero knowledge proof systems?
- We leave for future work the study of uncloneable proof systems where interaction is considered. When multiple rounds are possible, a solution involving first the verification of shared entanglement, followed by teleportation seems

plausible, while in a model without interaction, recent techniques related to *monogamy-of-entanglement* would seem relevant [BC23].
- We note that two open problems in complexity theory can be resolved via cloneable proof variants. Contribution 4 above says that if the complexity class QMA(2) equals its cloneable counterpart, then this resolves the QMA vs. QMA(2) problem. On the other hand, if we have QMA $\neq$ cloneableQMA, then this resolves the QMA vs. QCMA problem (in the negative). Thus, we leave as an open problem making progress in these important questions by studying the power of (un)cloneability.
- Our definition of cloneableQMA(k) leaves room for variations in the setup and in the parameters. We discuss some of the variations in Remark 2 and Sect. 4.4, and we leave the extension of our results to these settings as future work.

1.4 Organization

Our work on anti-piracy proof systems is in Sect. 3, while the complexity-theoretic results of cloneability in QMA proof systems are covered in Sect. 4.

2 Preliminaries

In this section, we review relevant definitions from existing work.

2.1 Quantum Merlin Arthur (QMA) and Related Classes

In the field of computational complexity theory, the class QMA (Quantum Merlin Arthur) [KSV02] is the quantum analog of the non-probabilistic complexity class NP (non-deterministic polynomial) or, more precisely, of the probabilistic complexity class MA (Merlin-Arthur).

Definition 1 (QMA). QMA *is the class of decision problems such that any language* $L \subseteq \{0,1\}^*$ *is in* QMA *if and only if there is a polynomial-time bounded quantum verifier* V *and a polynomial* $p(\cdot)$ *such that:*

- *(Completeness) For every* $x \in L$*, there exists a* $p(n)$*-qubit quantum state* $|\psi\rangle$ *(called the proof or witness), where* $|x| = n$*, such that* $\Pr[V(x, |\psi\rangle) = 1] \geq 2/3$.
- *(Soundness) For every* $x \notin L$*, and for any* $p(n)$*-qubit quantum state* $|\psi\rangle$*, we have that* $\Pr[V(x, |\psi\rangle) = 1] \leq 1/3$.

A variant of QMA is where the witness is restricted to classical strings, resulting in the class QCMA.

Definition 2 (QCMA). QCMA *is the class of decision problems such that any language* $L \subseteq \{0,1\}^*$ *is in* QCMA *if and only if there is a polynomial-time bounded* quantum *verifier* V *and a polynomial* $p(\cdot)$ *such that:*

- *(Completeness) For every $x \in L$, there exists a $p(n)$-bit classical string y (called the proof or witness), where $|x| = n$, such that* $\Pr[V(x, y) = 1] \geq 2/3$.
- *(Soundness) For every $x \notin L$, and for any $p(n)$-length classical string y,* $\Pr[V(x, y) = 1] \leq 1/3$.

We can also define the two-prover version of the class QMA, called QMA(2) [KM03].

Definition 3 (QMA(2)). QMA(2) *is the class of decision problems such that any language $L \subseteq \{0,1\}^*$ is in* QMA(2) *if and only if there is a polynomial-time bounded quantum verifier V and a polynomial $p(\cdot)$ such that:*

- *(Completeness) For every $x \in L$, there exists two $p(n)$-qubit quantum states $|\psi_1\rangle$ and $|\psi_2\rangle$, where $|x| = n$, such that* $\Pr[V(|x\rangle, |\psi_1\rangle, |\psi_2\rangle) = 1] \geq 2/3$.
- *(Soundness) For every $x \notin L$, and for any two $p(n)$-qubit quantum states $|\psi_1\rangle$ and $|\psi_2\rangle$, where $|x| = n$,* $\Pr[V(|x\rangle, |\psi_1\rangle, |\psi_2\rangle) = 1] \leq 1/3$.

We can define the complexity class QMA(k) in an analogous way, where the verification algorithm receives k proofs $|\psi_1\rangle, \ldots, |\psi_k\rangle$.

2.2 Cryptographic Objects

We now give and informal description of the cryptographic objects that we need in Sect. 3.3.

The first object that we will need is non-interactive zero-knowledge proofs (NIZK). Intuitively, this corresponds to non-interactive proofs where the verifier "learns nothing" from the interaction with the prover when the instance is positive. In particular, we will consider NIZKs with a common reference string (CRS) model as a trusted setup. We provide now the formal definition of NIZKs.

Definition 4 (post-quantum NIZKs in the CRS model). *A triple of algorithms (D, P, V) is a post-quantum non-interactive (computational) zero-knowledge proof in the CRS model for a promise problem $A = (A_{yes}, A_{no})$ where D is a probabilistic polynomial time algorithm, V is a probabilistic polynomial time algorithm and P is an unbounded quantum algorithm such that the following conditions follow:*

Completeness: *for every $x \in A_{yes}$, there exists some P*

$$\Pr[\mathit{crs} \leftarrow D(1^{|x|}); \pi \leftarrow P(x, \mathit{crs}); V(x, \mathit{crs}, \pi) = 1] \geq 1 - \text{negl}(n).$$

Soundness: *for every $x \in A_{no}$ and every P*

$$\Pr[\mathit{crs} \leftarrow D(1^{|x|}); \pi \leftarrow P(x, \mathit{crs}); V(x, \mathit{crs}, \pi) = 1] \leq \text{negl}(n).$$

Zero-knowledge: *there is a probabilistic polynomial time algorithm $\mathcal{S}$ such that for every $x \in A_{yes}$, and for every quantum polynomial-time distinguisher $\mathcal{D}$:*

$$\left| \Pr_{\mathsf{crs} \leftarrow D(1^{|x|}); \pi \leftarrow P(x, \mathsf{crs})} [\mathcal{D}(\mathsf{crs}, \pi) = 1] - \Pr_{(\mathsf{crs}, \pi) \leftarrow \mathcal{S}(x)} [\mathcal{D}(\mathsf{crs}, \pi) = 1] \right| = \mathrm{negl}(|x|).$$

The second cryptographic tool that we need is indistinguishability obfuscation, which asks that the obfuscations of two circuits which compute the same function cannot be distinguished. More concretely, we ask the following.

Definition 5. *Let $\mathcal{C}$ be a circuit class. The probabilistic-polynomial time algorithm iO is a post-quantum indistinguishable obfuscation for $\mathcal{C}$ if:*

1. *For any circuit $C \in \mathcal{C}$, $\mathsf{iO}(C)$ computes the same function as C with at most a polynomial slowdown; and*
2. *For any two circuits $C, C' \in \mathcal{C}$ that compute the same function, and for any quantum polynomial-time algorithm $\mathcal{D}$*

$$|\Pr[\mathcal{D}(\mathsf{iO}(C)) = 1] - \Pr[\mathcal{D}(\mathsf{iO}(C')) = 1]| = \mathrm{negl}(|x|).$$

2.3 Subspace States and Quantum Money Schemes

For a subspace $A \subseteq \mathbb{F}_2^n$, for some $n \in \mathbb{N}$, we denote $|A\rangle = \sum_{x \in A} \frac{1}{\sqrt{2^{|A|}}} |x\rangle$. We also denote O^A to be the unitary that maps an $n+1$-qubit state $|A\rangle|y\rangle$ into $|A\rangle|y \oplus 1\rangle$, and for every $|\psi\rangle$ orthogonal to $|A\rangle$, it leaves $|\psi\rangle|y\rangle$ unchanged.

Subspace states have been an essential tool for achieving public-verification quantum money schemes. [AC12] have first introduced them to achieve public-verification quantum money with oracle access to subspace-state oracles.

More concretely, to check if ρ is a subspace state $|A\rangle$ when we have oracle access to O^A and $O^{A^\perp}$:

1. Query the oracle O^A on input $\rho \otimes |0\rangle\langle 0|$.
2. Measure the last qubit, with output b. If $b = 0$, reject.
3. Apply $H^{\otimes n}$ on the first register of the post-measured state, and let it be σ.
4. Query the oracle $O^{A^\perp}$ on input $\sigma \otimes |0\rangle\langle 0|$.
5. Measure the last qubit, with output b. If $b = 0$, reject.
6. Otherwise, accept.

One can easily show that the test above always passes if $\rho = |A\rangle\langle A|$ (see Lemma 3). More interstingly, [AC12] shows that if we pick the subspace A at random, the state $|A\rangle$ is uncloneable by adversaries that make polynomially-many queries to the oracles O^A and $O^{A^\perp}$. Here, we need a stronger version of this theorem proved in [BS23], which shows that one cannot output a pair of inputs $(a, b) \in A \times A^\perp$.

Lemma 1 (Theorem 16 of [BS23]). *Let A be a uniformly random subspace, and let $\varepsilon > 0$ be such that $1/\varepsilon = o(2^{n/2})$. Given one copy of $|A\rangle$ and a quantum membership oracle A and $A^{\perp}$, a counterfeiter needs $\Omega(\sqrt{\varepsilon}2^{n/4})$ queries to output a pair $(a, b) \in A \times A^{\perp}$.*

Subsequently, [Zha19, Zha21] improved this result by providing a cryptographic implementation of the oracle O^A and $O^{A^{\perp}}$ using indistinguishability obfuscation (see Sect. 2.2 for its definition).

Lemma 2 ([Zha19, Zha21], restated). *Let iO be an indistinguishable-obfuscation scheme and let A be a uniformly random subspace. Given one copy of $|A\rangle$ and $\mathsf{iO}(C_A), \mathsf{iO}(C_{A^{\perp}})$, no quantum polynomial-time algorithm can output the state $|A\rangle^{\otimes 2}$, except with negligible probability.*

3 Towards Anti-piracy Proof Systems

In this section, we discuss the possibility of anti-piracy proof systems. We start by providing the definition of anti-piracy proofs in Sect. 3.1. Then, in Sect. 3.2, we show an anti-piracy proof for an oracle problem related to subspace states. Finally, in Sect. 3.3, we provide a candidate for anti-piracy proof systems for all of NP.

3.1 Definition

In order to define anti-piracy proof systems, we start with defining admissible verifiers and non-interactive proof systems.

Definition 6 (Admissible verifier and non-interactive proof system). *Let $A = (A_{yes}, A_{no})$ be a promise problem. We say that a quantum polynomial-time algorithm V is an admissible verifier for A if:*

- ***completeness:*** *if $x \in A_{yes}$, there exists a proof $|\psi\rangle$ such that* $\Pr[V(x, |\psi\rangle) = 1] \geq 1 - \text{negl}(|x|)$.
- ***soundness:*** *if $x \in A_{no}$, for all proofs $|\psi\rangle$ such that* $\Pr[V(x, |\psi\rangle) = 1] \leq \text{negl}(|x|)$.

Moreover, for a possibly unbounded prover P, (P, V) is a non-interactive proof system for A if for all $x \in A_{yes}$, $\Pr[V(x, P(x)) = 1] \geq 1 - \text{negl}(|x|)$.

We notice that we define these notions with negligible completeness and soundness error since these are the relevant parameters in the cryptographic setting, which is our motivation in this section.

As we discussed in the introduction, our notion of anti-piracy proofs only makes sense in average case. For that, we define now a generator of instances as in [FS90].

Definition 7. *A generator G for some promise problem $A = (A_{yes}, A_{no})$ is a randomized polynomial-time algorithm that on input 1^n outputs an $x \in A_{yes}$ such that $|x| = n$.*

We define now the notion of anti-piracy proofs for a generator G.

Definition 8 (Anti-piracy proof for generator G). *Let $A = (A_{yes}, A_{no})$ be a promise problem and G be a generator for A. We say that a non-interactive proof system (P, V) for A is anti-piracy for G, if for every* poly($|x|$)*-bounded adversary $\mathcal{A}$ and admissible verifiers V_1 and V_2 for A, we have that:*

$$Pr_{x \sim G(1^n)}\left[V_1^x \otimes V_2^x(\widetilde{\psi}_{A,B}) = (1,1) \;\middle|\; \begin{array}{c} |\psi\rangle \leftarrow P(x) \\ \widetilde{\psi}_{A,B} \leftarrow \mathcal{A}(x, |\psi\rangle) \end{array}\right] \leq \mathrm{negl}(|x|), \qquad (1)$$

where the probability space is also over the measurement outcomes of V_1 and V_2.

Finally, we can define anti-piracy proof systems for a promise problem.

Definition 9 (Anti-piracy proof for promise problem A). *Let $A = (A_{yes}, A_{no})$ be a promise problem. We say that a proof system (P, V) for A is anti-piracy if there is a generator G such that (P, V) is anti-piracy for G.*

Remark 1. We note that in Definition 9, the proof system could be constructed using oracles or a common reference string (CRS). In this case, we consider that the adversary $\mathcal{A}$ or any admissible verifier for the problem has access to the same resources as the honest verifier. Notice that if the honest prover and verifier pair has access to private resources, such as private keys or EPR pairs, this would lead to a trivial anti-piracy proof system but with a designated verifier. In this work, we focus on proof systems with public verification.

3.2 Anti-piracy Proofs with Subspace Oracles

In this section, we show an oracle problem for which there is an anti-piracy proof using subspace-states (see Sect. 2.3). We start by defining the problem.

Definition 10. *Let $A_n, B_n \in \mathbb{F}_2^n$ be subspaces such that $B \subseteq A^\perp$ and* $\dim(A) = \dim(B) = n/2$, *or* $\dim(A) = n/2$ *and* $\dim(B) = n/4$, *or* $\dim(A) = n/4$ *and* $\dim(B) = n/2$. *Let $A = (A_1, ...)$ and $B = (B_1, ...)$. We define a language $L_{A,B}$ as*

1. $0^n \in L_{A,B}$ *iff* $\dim(A_n) = \dim(B_n) = n/2$
2. $x \notin L_{A,B}$ *for all* $x \neq 0^n$

For each n, we will define the pair of oracles O^{A_n} and O^{B_n} that check membership in A_n and B_n, respectively.

If we want to check that the support of an n-qubit quantum state $|\psi\rangle = \sum_x \alpha_x |x\rangle$ is in A_n, we make an oracle call O^{A_n} on $|\psi\rangle|0\rangle$, which results in $\sum_{x \in A_n} \alpha_x |x\rangle|1\rangle + \sum_{x \notin A_n} \alpha_x |x\rangle|0\rangle$. We can then simply measure the last qubit and if the outcome is 1, then we accept; or if the outcome is 0, then we reject. A similar procedure can be defined for B_n.

Input: input $x \in \{0,1\}^n$ and n-qubit proof $|\psi\rangle$

1. If $x \neq 0^n$, reject.
2. Check if each element of $|\psi\rangle$ belongs to the subspace A_n, reject if not
3. Apply $H^{\otimes n}$ on the state
4. Check if each element of the new state belongs to the subspace B_n, reject if not
5. Accept

Fig. 2. Admissible verification V^* for $L_{A,B}$

Lemma 3. *For any A, B satisfying the properties in Definition 10, let V^* be defined as in Fig. 2, and P^* be the such that on input $x = 0^n$, outputs $|A_n\rangle$. Then (V^*, P^*) is a non-interactive proof system for $L_{A,B}$.*

Proof. For completeness, we have that for all n such that $0^n \in L$, $V^{\mathcal{O}^A,\mathcal{O}^B}$ accepts the proof $|A_n\rangle$ with probability 1: the tests in step 2 and 4 never reject since $H^{\otimes n}|A_n\rangle = |A_n^{\perp}\rangle = |B_n\rangle$.

To prove soundness, the case where $x \neq 0^n$ is trivial. Let us now consider the case where $x = 0^n \notin L$. Let us assume that $\dim(A_n) = n/2$ and $\dim(B_n) = n/4$ (the other case follows analogously).

Let us assume that the first test passes (if it does not pass, the verifier rejects as desired). We denote state of the verifier after the first test as $|\phi\rangle = \sum_{x \in A_n} \alpha_x |x\rangle$, and we use the fact that the first test has passed, so the support of $|\phi\rangle$ is a subset of A_n.

When V applies $H^{\otimes n}$ to $|\phi\rangle$, the resulting state is

$$\frac{1}{2^{n/2}} \sum_{y \in \{0,1\}^n} \sum_{x \in A_n} (-1)^{x \cdot y} \alpha_x |y\rangle, \tag{2}$$

and the probability of measuring $y \in B$ is

$$\sum_{y \in B_n} \left| \frac{1}{2^{n/2}} \sum_{x \in A_n} \alpha_x \right|^2 \tag{3}$$

$$\leq \frac{1}{2^n} \sum_{y \in B_n} \left| 2^{n/2} \frac{1}{2^{n/4}} \right|^2 \tag{4}$$

$$= \frac{1}{2^{n/4}}. \tag{5}$$

Thus, the second test passes with negligible probability.

In order to prove the anti-piracy property, we first prove a result on the queries made by an admissible verifier for the language $L_{A,B}$.

Lemma 4. *Let $V^{\mathcal{O}^{A_n},\mathcal{O}^{B_n}}$ be an admissible verifier for $L_{A,B}$. Let us also fix some n and some polynomial p such that $0^n \in L_{A,B}$ and some state $|\psi\rangle$ such that $V^{\mathcal{O}^{A_n},\mathcal{O}^{B_n}}$ accepts on $|\psi\rangle$ with probability at least $\frac{1}{p(n)}$.*

Then there exists a polynomial q such that for every subspace $B'_n \subseteq A_n^\perp$ of dimension $n/4$, there exists one query to $\mathcal{O}^{B_n}$ that has $\frac{1}{q(n)}$ mass on elements in $B_n \setminus B'_n$. Moreover, for every subspace $A'_n \subseteq A$ of dimension $n/4$, there exists one query to $\mathcal{O}^{A_n}$ that has non-negligible mass on elements in $A_n \setminus A'_n$.

Proof. Let us suppose that the statement is false. In this case, we have that there is a negligible function ε such that every query to $\mathcal{O}^{B_n}$ has $\varepsilon(n)$ mass on elements in $B_n \setminus B'_n$.

We will show that we can replace the oracle B_n with an oracle $B'_n \subseteq A_n^\perp$ of dimension $n/4$, and that $V^{\mathcal{O}^{A_n}, \mathcal{O}^{B'_n}}$ accepts 0^n with probability $\frac{1}{p(n)} - \varepsilon(n)$, contradicting the assumption that $V^{\mathcal{O}^{A_n}, \mathcal{O}^{B'_n}}$ is an admissible verifier of $L_{A,B'}$.

Without loss of generality, we assume that $V^{\mathcal{O}^{A_n}, \mathcal{O}^{B_n}}$ can be decomposed as

$$U_{T+1}\mathcal{O}^{B_n}U_T^B ... \mathcal{O}^{B_n}U_1^B\mathcal{O}^{A_n}U_1^A\mathcal{O}^{B_n}U_0^B\mathcal{O}^{A_n}U_0^A, \tag{6}$$

where U_i^A and U_i^B are arbitrary unitaries.

Let us define

$$|\psi_i\rangle = U_i^B ... \mathcal{O}^{B_n}U_0^B\mathcal{O}^{A_n}U_0^A|x\rangle|\psi\rangle|0\rangle \quad \text{and} \quad |\phi_i\rangle = U_i^B ... \mathcal{O}^{B'_n}U_1^B\mathcal{O}^{A_n}U_1^A\mathcal{O}^{B'_n}U_0^B\mathcal{O}^{A_n}U_0^A|\psi\rangle|0\rangle.$$

We will show by induction that there exists a negligible function $\varepsilon(n)$ such that for every $0 \le i \le T$

$$\| |\psi_i\rangle - |\phi_i\rangle \| \le i\varepsilon(n). \tag{7}$$

Notice that from Eq. (7), we can prove our statement since $|\phi_T\rangle$ is the state of the verifier $V^{\mathcal{O}^{A_n}, \mathcal{O}^{B'_n}}$ on input $|\psi\rangle|0\rangle$. In this case, the acceptance probability of the no-instance 0^n of $L_{A,B'}$ would be $\frac{2}{3} - \mathrm{negl}(n)$ and therefore the verification is not sound, which is a contradiction.

We now prove Eq. (7). For the base case $i = 0$, we have that $|\psi_0\rangle = |\phi_0\rangle$, and therefore the statement holds.

Let us now assume that Eq. (7) holds for some i. Then we have that

$$\begin{aligned}
&\| |\psi_{i+1}\rangle - |\phi_{i+1}\rangle \| \\
&= \| U_{i+1}^B\mathcal{O}^{A_n}U_{i+1}^A\mathcal{O}^{B_n}|\psi_i\rangle - U_{i+1}^B\mathcal{O}^{A_n}U_{i+1}^A\mathcal{O}^{B'_n}|\phi_i\rangle \| \\
&= \| \mathcal{O}^{B_n}|\psi_i\rangle - \mathcal{O}^{B'_n}|\phi_i\rangle \| \\
&\le \| \mathcal{O}^{B_n}|\psi_i\rangle - \mathcal{O}^{B'_n}|\psi_i\rangle \| + \| \mathcal{O}^{B'_n}|\psi_i\rangle - \mathcal{O}^{B'_n}|\phi_i\rangle \| \\
&\le \| \mathcal{O}^{B_n}|\psi_i\rangle - \mathcal{O}^{B'_n}|\psi_i\rangle \| + i\varepsilon(n) \\
&\le \varepsilon(n) + i\varepsilon(n) \\
&= (i+1)\varepsilon(n),
\end{aligned}$$

where the second equality follows by unitary invariance of the norm, the first inequality follows by the triangle inequality, and the second inequality follows from the induction hypothesis. We argue now the third inequality. Notice that by the assumption, all queries to $\mathcal{O}^{B_n}$ have $\varepsilon(n)$ mass on $B_n \setminus B'_n$, i.e., $\sum_{x \in B \setminus B'_n, b, y} |a_{x,b,y}|^2 \le \varepsilon(n)$. In this case, $\| \mathcal{O}^{B_n}|\psi_i\rangle - \mathcal{O}^{B'_n}|\psi_i\rangle \| \le \varepsilon(n)$.

Theorem 1. *Let V^* and P^* be defined as Lemma 3. Then (V^*, P^*) is an anti-piracy proof system for $L_{A,B}$.*

Proof. We will consider a generator G such that $G(1^n)$ outputs 0^n, if $0^n \in L_{A,B}$ or $\perp$ otherwise.

Let n be such $0^n \in L_{A,B}$ and $\mathcal{A}$ be an adversary that receives ψ created by the prover, has oracle access to $\mathcal{O}$, and outputs $\widetilde{\psi}_{A,B}$. Let $\widetilde{V}_1^{\mathcal{O}_{A_n},\mathcal{O}_{B_n}}$ and $\widetilde{V}_2^{\mathcal{O}_{A_n},\mathcal{O}_{B_n}}$ be two admissible verifiers for $L_{A,B}$ with the input 0^n hardcoded. We need to show that

$$Pr\left[\widetilde{V}_1^{\mathcal{O}_{A_n},\mathcal{O}_{B_n}} \otimes \widetilde{V}_2^{\mathcal{O}_{A_n},\mathcal{O}_{B_n}}(\widetilde{\psi}_{A,B}) = (1,1) \;\middle|\; \substack{\mathcal{O},\psi \leftarrow P \\ \widetilde{\psi}_{A,B} \leftarrow \mathcal{A}^{\mathcal{O}_{A_n},\mathcal{O}_{B_n}}(\psi)}\right] \leq \text{negl}(n). \tag{8}$$

Let M be the POVM where we pick one of the queries uniformly at random, measure the input register and accept iff the measurement outcome is a vector in the subspace.

By Lemma 4, we have that

$$Pr\left[M \otimes \widetilde{V}_2^{\mathcal{O}}(\widetilde{\psi}_{A,B}) = (1,1) \;\middle|\; \substack{\mathcal{O},\psi \leftarrow P \\ \widetilde{\psi}_{A,B} \leftarrow \mathcal{A}^{\mathcal{O}}(\psi)}\right] \tag{9}$$

$$\geq \frac{1}{p(n)} \cdot Pr\left[\widetilde{V}_1^{\mathcal{O}} \otimes \widetilde{V}_2^{\mathcal{O}}(\widetilde{\psi}_{A,B}) = (1,1) \;\middle|\; \substack{\mathcal{O},\psi \leftarrow P \\ \widetilde{\psi}_{A,B} \leftarrow \mathcal{A}^{\mathcal{O}}(\psi)}\right]. \tag{10}$$

Notice that since M and $\widetilde{V}_2^{\mathcal{O}}$ commute, we can use Lemma 4 again and we have that

$$Pr\left[M \otimes M(\widetilde{\psi}_{A,B}) = (1,1) \;\middle|\; \substack{\mathcal{O},\psi \leftarrow P \\ \widetilde{\psi}_{A,B} \leftarrow \mathcal{A}^{\mathcal{O}}(\psi)}\right] \tag{11}$$

$$\geq \frac{1}{p(n)} Pr\left[M \otimes \widetilde{V}_2^{\mathcal{O}}(\widetilde{\psi}_{A,B}) = (1,1) \;\middle|\; \substack{\mathcal{O},\psi \leftarrow P \\ \widetilde{\psi}_{A,B} \leftarrow \mathcal{A}^{\mathcal{O}}(\psi)}\right] \tag{12}$$

$$\geq \frac{1}{p(n)^2} \cdot Pr\left[\widetilde{V}_1^{\mathcal{O}} \otimes \widetilde{V}_2^{\mathcal{O}}(\widetilde{\psi}_{A,B}) = (1,1) \;\middle|\; \substack{\mathcal{O},\psi \leftarrow P \\ \widetilde{\psi}_{A,B} \leftarrow \mathcal{A}^{\mathcal{O}}(\psi)}\right]. \tag{13}$$

By Lemma 1, we have that

$$Pr\left[M \otimes M(\widetilde{\psi}_{A,B}) = (1,1) \;\middle|\; \substack{\mathcal{O},\psi \leftarrow P \\ \widetilde{\psi}_{A,B} \leftarrow \mathcal{A}^{\mathcal{O}}(\psi)}\right] \leq \text{negl}(n), \tag{14}$$

and therefore

$$Pr\left[\widetilde{V}_1^{\mathcal{O}} \otimes \widetilde{V}_2^{\mathcal{O}}(\widetilde{\psi}_{A,B}) = (1,1) \;\middle|\; \substack{\mathcal{O},\psi \leftarrow P \\ \widetilde{\psi}_{A,B} \leftarrow \mathcal{A}^{\mathcal{O}}(\psi)}\right] \leq \text{negl}(n), \tag{15}$$

proving our statement.

3.3 Candidates for Anti-piracy Proofs for NP

We propose here a candidate scheme for anti-piracy proofs beyond the oracle model, for any hard language $L \in \mathsf{NP}$.

The starting point is a natural open question if Theorem 1 still holds when we replace the oracle access to O^A and $O^{A^\perp}$ by its indistinguishable obfuscation. More concretely, instead of considering the oracles O^A and O^B, the input to the problem consists of $(\mathsf{iO}(C_A), \mathsf{iO}(C_B))$, where the C_D is the circuit that verifies membership in a subspace D, with the same promise of Definition 10.[2] Completeness and soundness hold similarly, and the key open question here consists on showing the anti-piracy property.

Then, the idea is to interweave this basic scheme, which does not depend on L but has the anti-piracy property, with another part of the proof that allows us to verify L. More concretely, the prover in our candidate scheme first picks a random $A \subseteq \mathbb{F}_2^n$ of dimension $n/2$ and computes $O_1 = \mathsf{iO}(C_A)$ and $O_2 = \mathsf{iO}(C_{A^\perp}))$. Then, the prover also computes a classical proof π that shows that:

1. the string (O_1, O_2) is an obfuscation of two subspace-membership circuits such that one subspace has dimension $n/2$ and the second one has dimention $n/4$; or
2. $x \in L$.

However, we want that the sensitive information that enables anti-piracy to be hidden in π. For example, we do not want the NP-witness used to prove that $x \in L$ to be revealed. For that, π will actually be a NIZK that proves that at least one of the two previous conditions is true. Moreover, we should also to include in the proof that the obfuscations are well-formed even if the first statement is false.

Then, the candidate anti-piracy proof for $x \in L$ consists of

$$((\mathsf{iO}(C_A), \mathsf{iO}(C_{A^\perp})), \pi, |A\rangle),$$

and the verifier checks that NIZK verification accepts π *and* performs the subspace verification using the state $|A\rangle$ and the two obfuscated circuits. We notice that by construction, if the verification of π passes, it means that at least one of the statements 1 and 2 above is true. Moreover, if the subspace verification passes, it means that the statement 1 is false. Thus, if both tests pass, we can conclude that $x \in L$. We formally describe our candidate in Fig. 3.

We provide now the intuition on why we think that such a scheme is an anti-piracy proof system. First, notice that the pirate cannot trivially provide two copies of the proof because the state $|A\rangle$ is uncloneable. Moreover, the zero-knowledge proof alone cannot be used to verify that x belongs to the language since soundness crucially requires checking the subspace state. Therefore, it seems that the quantum subspace state is making the cloneable part of the proof useless on its own.

[2] For technical reasons, we would need coset states instead of subspace-states, but we will keep the exposition with subspace-states for simplicity.

Fix a language $L \in \mathsf{NP}$. We define the language L_{sub} as

$$L_{sub} = \{(x, O_1, O_2) : \exists A, B \subseteq \mathbb{F}_2^n \text{ s.t.} \quad (16)$$
$$O_1 = \mathcal{O}(C_A) \wedge O_2 = \mathcal{O}(C_B) \wedge B \subseteq C^{\perp} \quad (17)$$
$$\wedge\, (\dim(A) = n/2 \vee \dim(B) = n/2) \quad (18)$$
$$\wedge\, (x \in L \vee \dim(A) = n/4 \vee \dim(B) = n/4)\} \quad (19)$$

The scheme that we consider is the following:

1. The Prover and the Verifier have access to a CRS.
2. The Prover chooses a subspace A, computes $O_1 = \mathcal{O}(C_A)$, $O_2 = \mathcal{O}(C_{A^{\perp}})$
3. The Prover computes a NIZK proof π that $(x, O_1, O_2) \in L_{sub}$
4. The Prover sends $(O_1, O_2, \pi, |A\rangle)$ to the Verifier
5. The Verifier accepts iff π passes the ZK verification and $|A\rangle$ passes the verification with O_1 and O_2 (similarly to Figure 2).

Fig. 3. Candidate anti-piracy proof system for NP.

We explain now the difficulties that we have in proving the security of this scheme. First of all, the only assumption that we have from admissible verifiers is completeness and soundness. Therefore, we do not have many handles to argue that one of the verifiers has no useful information on the subspace state.

Moreover, to prove the security of our protocol, we would need to prove that if the cryptographic objects that we use are secure, then either we can break the soundness of the protocol, or the language is easy (i.e. the pirate is cooking up the witness by herself). Proving the first conclusion is hard since the pirate can detect when we move from a yes-instance to a no-instance, or even harder, the pirate has a yes-instance in mind and creates an accepting good witness for a no-instance.

To conclude the easiness of the language, we would need:

1. the state provided to the pirate to be easily generated (instead of the original witness);
2. even with the new state, the pirate outputs a state that passes the admissible verification.

The only route that we can see goes through using the simulation coming from the ZK property, which is done by creating a proof coupled with a simulated CRS. However, the state generated by the pirate would need to pass completeness and soundness using the real CRS.

4 Complexity Implications of Cloneable Proofs

In this section, we discuss the implications of the existence of cloneable proofs for QMA, QMA(2), and, more generally, QMA(k).

4.1 Cloneable Quantum Proofs

Recently, [NZ24] defined the complexity class cloneableQMA to denote the promise problems in QMA that have cloneable witnesses. We reproduce it below.

Definition 11 (cloneableQMA$_p$ [NZ24]). *A decision problem $L = (L_{\text{yes}}, L_{\text{no}})$ is said to be in the class* cloneableQMA(c, f, s) *if there exists a polynomial-time quantum verifier V (uniformly generated), a polynomial time quantum cloner C (also uniformly generated), and a polynomial p, such that*

- ***Completeness:*** *if $x \in L_{\text{yes}}$, then there exists a quantum witness $|\psi\rangle$ on $p(|x|)$ qubits such that $\Pr[V(|x\rangle, |\psi\rangle) = 1] \geq c$, and*
  Cloning fidelity: *when given this same witness, $|\psi\rangle$, as input, C succeeds at producing two independent copies of $|\psi\rangle$ with fidelity at least f. That is,*

$$\langle\psi| \otimes \langle\psi| \, C(|\psi\rangle\langle\psi| \otimes |0\rangle\langle 0|) \, |\psi\rangle \otimes |\psi\rangle \geq f. \tag{20}$$

- ***Soundness:*** *if $x \in L_{\text{no}}$, then for all quantum states $|\psi^*\rangle$ on $p(|x|)$ qubits, we have that $\Pr[V(|x\rangle, |\psi^*\rangle) = 1] \leq s$.*

Since classical proofs are cloneable, we have QCMA (roughly, QMA with classical witnesses) is contained in cloneableQMA. Moreover, cloneableQMA is contained in QMA, by definition. (Technically, we have

$$\mathsf{cloneableQMA}(c, f, s) \subseteq \mathsf{cloneableQMA}(c, f', s) \tag{21}$$

where $f \geq f'$, and the equality

$$\mathsf{QMA}(c, s) = \mathsf{cloneableQMA}(c, 0, s) \tag{22}$$

as well.) Overall, we have the containments

$$\mathsf{QCMA}(c, s) \subseteq \mathsf{cloneableQMA}(c, 1, s) \subseteq \mathsf{cloneableQMA}(c, 0, s) = \mathsf{QMA}(c, s). \tag{23}$$

4.2 Cloneable Unentangled Quantum Proofs

We now consider the similar setting where the proofs are unentangled, defined below.

Definition 12 (cloneableQMA$_p$). *A decision problem $L = (L_{\text{yes}}, L_{\text{no}})$ is said to be in the class* cloneableQMA$_p(k)(c, f, s)$ *if there exists a polynomial-time quantum verifier V (uniformly generated), k polynomial-time quantum cloners $C_1, \ldots, C_k$ (each uniformly generated), such that:*

- ***Completeness:*** *if $x \in L_{\text{yes}}$, then there exists k quantum witnesses $|\psi_1\rangle$, ..., $|\psi_k\rangle$, each on $p(|x|)$ qubits, such that $\Pr[V(|x\rangle, |\psi_1\rangle, ..., |\psi_k\rangle) = 1] \geq c$, and*
Cloning fidelity: *when given these same witnesses, $|\psi_1\rangle$, ..., $|\psi_k\rangle$, as input, C_i succeeds at producing two independent copies of $|\psi_i\rangle$ with fidelity at least f. That is,*

$$\langle\psi_i| \otimes \langle\psi_i| \, C_i(|\psi_i\rangle\langle\psi_i| \otimes |0\rangle\langle 0|) \, |\psi_i\rangle \otimes |\psi_i\rangle \geq f, \quad \textit{for all } i. \tag{24}$$

- ***Soundness:*** *if $x \in L_{\text{no}}$, then for all quantum states $|\psi_1^*\rangle$, ..., $|\psi_k^*\rangle$, each on $p(|x|)$ qubits, $\Pr[V(|x\rangle, |\psi_1^*\rangle, ..., |\psi_k^*\rangle) = 1] \leq s$.*

Remark 2. We make a few observations about the definition.

- First, note that, just like in $\mathsf{QMA}(k)$, there is no soundness guarantee for entangled proofs in $\mathsf{cloneableQMA}(k)$.
- Second, similar to $\mathsf{cloneableQMA}$, we are only interested in cloning "good" proofs, thus the cloning fidelity is only defined in the completeness conditions.
- One could consider alternative definitions of $\mathsf{cloneableQMA}(k)$. For instance, having a separate parameter f_i for each cloning fidelity. This flexibility could find other applications, although it is not needed in this work.
- We have defined the cloners to act on separate proofs as separate circuits and not as a joint circuit. An alternative version with a joint cloner could find application, but one big obstacle in defining the (single) cloner this way is that an imperfect cloner could create entanglement in the proofs. While we do consider perfect cloning in this work, it is important to note that in our proofs below, we do end up applying the cloning circuits to proofs even when $x \in L_{no}$. Since there is no promise how a cloning circuit behaves for such no instances, it could create entanglement and ruin any soundness promises.

We begin by noting some immediate containments. Firstly, we have

$$\mathsf{cloneableQMA}(k)(c, f, s) \subseteq \mathsf{cloneableQMA}(k)(c, 0, s) = \mathsf{QMA}(k). \tag{25}$$

Secondly, we have

$$\mathsf{cloneableQMA}_p(c, f, s) \subseteq \mathsf{cloneableQMA}_p(k)(c, f, s) \tag{26}$$

since if $|\psi\rangle$ is a cloneable proof for QMA, then $|\psi\rangle|0\rangle^{\otimes(k-1)}$ is a cloneable proof for $\mathsf{QMA}(k)$ using the same QMA verification and ignoring the $|0\rangle$ proofs. To summarize the complexity landscape so far, see the left figure in Fig. 1 in Sect. 1.2.

In this section, we investigate the power of the class $\mathsf{cloneableQMA}(k)$ with completeness-soundness gap $c - s \geq 1/q$, where q is a polynomial-bounded function. We only consider cloning fidelity $f = 1$, i.e., perfect cloning. For brevity, we define

$$\mathsf{cloneableQMA}(k) := \mathsf{cloneableQMA}(k)(2/3, 1, 1/3) \tag{27}$$

$$\mathsf{cloneableQMA} := \mathsf{cloneableQMA}(2/3, 1, 1/3). \tag{28}$$

The main result of this section is given in the following theorem.

Theorem 2. *We have*

$$\mathsf{cloneableQMA}(k) = \mathsf{cloneableQMA}. \tag{29}$$

Determining any non-trivial relationship between QMA and QMA(2) = QMA(k) is a big open problem in complexity theory. The above result settles this question in the cloneable setting. More precisely, when the proofs are cloneable, there is no added power from unentanglement.

Corollary 1. *If* cloneableQMA(2) = QMA(2), *that is,* QMA(2) *can always be made to have cloneable proofs, then* QMA(2) = QMA. *Moreover, we would also have* QMA = cloneableQMA.

4.3 Proof of cloneableQMA(k) = cloneableQMA

In this section we prove Theorem 2 that QMA(k) and QMA are equal in the cloneable setting. The main idea of our proof is that we can use the completeness-soundness amplification techniques of [HM13] while maintaining *similarly-sized* proofs. More precisely, we can obtain *strong amplification* for cloneableQMA(2) which, by a result of Brandão (see [ABD+08]), will put it in QMA. By careful observation, this reduction puts it into cloneableQMA by noticing that we are maintaining cloneable proofs throughout the entire series of reductions.

Lemma 5. *If $c - s \geq 1/q$, for some polynomial bounded function q, then we have*

$$\mathsf{cloneableQMA}_p(k)(c, s) \subseteq \mathsf{cloneableQMA}_p(k)\left(1 - 2^{-\ell}, 1 - \frac{1}{2q}\right) \tag{30}$$

for any polynomial-bounded function ℓ.

This follows from standard gap-amplification techniques (e.g., in [KMY03]) with the note that the proofs are still cloneable.

Proof. Choose the function ℓ as described in the lemma. We now take the verification circuit V from the $\mathsf{cloneableQMA}_p(k)(c, s)$ protocol and the cloning circuits C_i and produce a new verification circuit for $\mathsf{cloneableQMA}_p(k)$ $\left(1 - 2^{-\ell}, 1 - \frac{1}{2q}\right)$. These will use the same proofs in the yes case, thus will still be cloneable. The rest follows from standard gap amplification techniques which we sketch below.

The new verification takes the form:

1. Take the k proofs $|\psi_1^*\rangle \otimes \cdots \otimes |\psi_k^*\rangle$ and apply the circuit $C_1 \otimes \cdots \otimes C_k$ to them $N := 2\ell q^2$ times.
2. Apply the verification circuit V in parallel $(N + 1)$ times.
3. Accept if and only if $\left(\frac{c+s}{2}\right) \cdot (N + 1)$ of these $N + 1$ verifications accept.

Using Chernoff and Markov inequalities, we get the desired completeness and soundness bounds.

We now apply the product-state test from [HM13] to reduce the number of provers and to obtain a verification with an accepting POVM which is separable. The latter condition is crucial to amplify the completeness-soundness gap in a following lemma.

Lemma 6. *If $c > s$, we have*

$$\mathsf{cloneableQMA}_p(k)(c, s) \subseteq \mathsf{cloneableQMA}_{kp}^{\mathrm{SEP}}(2)\left(\frac{1+c}{2}, 1 - \frac{(1-s)^2}{100}\right). \tag{31}$$

Here, the SEP superscript means the accepting POVM of the $\mathsf{QMA}(2)$ *verifier is separable.*

This follows immediately from the analogous result in [HM13][3] noting that cloneability is not required in the proof but carries throughout. More precisely, in the new verification, we replace the k proofs $|\psi_i\rangle$ with two proofs, each being $|\psi_1\rangle \otimes \cdots \otimes |\psi_k\rangle$. Since each one is cloneable, then so is $|\psi_1\rangle \otimes \cdots \otimes |\psi_k\rangle$ (the new cloning circuit is $C_1 \otimes \cdots \otimes C_k$).

Lemma 7. *We have*

$$\mathsf{cloneableQMA}_p^{\mathrm{SEP}}(2)(c, s) \subseteq \mathsf{cloneableQMA}_p(2)(c^\ell, s^\ell) \tag{32}$$

for any polynomial-bounded function ℓ.

Again, this follows from the analogous result in [HM13][4], but in this case the size of the proof need not grow thanks to the ability to clone. We also only need it for the case $k = 2$.

Proof. Let V be a $\mathsf{cloneableQMA}_p^{\mathrm{SEP}}(2)(c, s)$ verification and let C_A and C_B be the cloning circuits. We now define a verification for $\mathsf{cloneableQMA}_p(2)$ which does the following. First, it applies the cloning circuits ℓ times, on each respective proof, then it verifies all $\ell+1$ pairs of proofs each using the verification V. Overall, this new verification accepts if and only if all $(\ell + 1)$ V verifications accept.

For completeness, it is straightforward to see that if you send a cloneable proof $|\psi_A\rangle|\psi_B\rangle$, then you will have $\ell+1$ copies afterwards, each of which will be accepted with probability at least $c^{\ell+1}$. Note that since this is the same proof, it is still cloneable.

For soundness, this is a bit trickier since one has to be concerned with the verifications producing entanglement (for which V may not be sound). We can analyze these in sequence. If a verification V accepts, then since the accepting POVM is separable, the post-measured state (upon V accepting) will not produce any entanglement. Therefore, the next set of (unentangled) proofs which are verified by V will be accepted with probability at most s. Repeating this, the new soundness will be at most $s^{\ell+1}$, as desired.

[3] In particular, Lemma 5 in their updated arXiv.org preprint, version 6.

[4] In particular, Lemma 7 in their updated arXiv.org preprint, version 6.

We remark that this proof is similar to the perfect parallel repetition result in [HM13] except that we can use the cloners to produce the $\ell + 1$ copies of the proofs instead of asking the prover to supply them. We also remark that having a separable accepting POVM is crucial in this proof; we are unaware how to prove this claim without this assumption. We do not require this assumption in the rest of the proofs, thus we are not concerned with maintaining it.

We now show that if a BQP verifier is sound against product states, then we can bound the soundness against all (even entangled) states as well. The following two lemmas follow closely from a result of Brandão, found in a footnote in [ABD+08].

Lemma 8. *Suppose M is a positive semidefinite matrix. If $\langle e|\langle f|M|e\rangle|f\rangle \leq \alpha$ for all unit vectors $|e\rangle, |f\rangle \in \mathbb{C}^n$, then $\lambda_{\max}(M) \leq \alpha n$.*

Proof. Since $\langle e|\langle f|M|e\rangle|f\rangle = \|\sqrt{M}|e\rangle|f\rangle\|_2^2$, we have

$$\|\sqrt{M}|e\rangle|f\rangle\|_2 \leq \sqrt{\alpha}, \text{ for all unit vectors } |e\rangle,\ |f\rangle. \tag{33}$$

Let $|\psi\rangle$ be the normalized eigenvector of M corresponding to its greatest eigenvalue. It helps to write $|\psi\rangle = \sum_{i=1}^{n} \sqrt{\lambda_i}|e_i\rangle|f_i\rangle$ in its Schmidt decomposition (so $\lambda_i \geq 0$ and $\sum_{i=1}^{n} \lambda_i = 1$). We can write

$$\begin{aligned} \lambda_{\max}(M) &= \langle\psi|M|\psi\rangle & (34)\\ &= \|\sqrt{M}|\psi\rangle\|_2^2 & (35)\\ &= \left\| \sqrt{M} \left(\sum_{i=1}^{n} \sqrt{\lambda_i}|e_i\rangle|f_i\rangle \right) \right\|_2^2 & (36)\\ &\leq \left(\sum_{i=1}^{n} \sqrt{\lambda_i} \left\| \sqrt{M}|e_i\rangle|f_i\rangle \right\|_2 \right)^2 & (37) \end{aligned}$$

using the triangle inequality. We can now apply Eq. 33 to get

$$\lambda_{\max}(M) \leq \left(\sum_{i=1}^{n} \sqrt{\lambda_i}\sqrt{\alpha} \right)^2 = \alpha \left(\sum_{i=1}^{n} \sqrt{\lambda_i} \right)^2 \leq \alpha n \tag{38}$$

where the last inequality holds by Cauchy-Schwarz.

We use this lemma to prove the following.

Lemma 9. *We have*

$$\mathsf{cloneableQMA}_p(2)(c, s) \subseteq \mathsf{cloneableQMA}_{2p}\left(c, 2^p \cdot s\right). \tag{39}$$

Before we prove this lemma, we remark that we only use this lemma in the case when $c > 2^p \cdot s$.

Proof. Suppose we take a $\mathsf{cloneableQMA}_p(2)(c, s)$ verification. Define the new verification where we remove the "unentangled" constraint. Then in a yes-instance, there exists a cloneable proof which is still accepted with probability c in the new verification (and still cloneable). In a no-instance, by Lemma 8, by adding entanglement, soundness can increase to at most $s \cdot 2^p$. Note that this verification takes a $2p$-qubit proof now since the original verification took *two* proofs, each of size p qubits.

We now put these lemmas together to prove $\mathsf{cloneableQMA}(k) = \mathsf{cloneableQMA}$.

Proof (Proof of Theorem 2). Starting from $\mathsf{cloneableQMA}(k)(2/3, 1, 1/3)$ and for any polynomials p_1 and p_2, we have from Lemmas 5 to 7 that

$$\begin{aligned}&\mathsf{cloneableQMA}(k)_p(2/3, 1, 1/3)\\ &\subseteq \mathsf{cloneableQMA}_{kp}(2)\left((1 - 2^{-p_1(|x|)-1})^{p_2(|x|)}, 1, (1 - 1/3600)^{p_2(|x|)}\right).\end{aligned}$$

By picking p_1 to be any polynomial and $p_2 = \Omega(kp)$, we have from Lemma 9 that

$$\mathsf{cloneableQMA}(k)_p(2/3, 1, 1/3) \subseteq \mathsf{cloneableQMA}_{2kp}\left(1 - \text{negl}(|x|), 1, \text{negl}(|x|)\right).$$

The opposite containment (ignoring proof sizes) has already been mentioned (Eq. (26)).

4.4 Remarks and Future Work Regarding Theorem 2

We first mention that one can define a new class $\mathsf{PirateableQMA}$ where a cloner (now referred to as a pirate) takes as input a quantum proof $|\psi\rangle$ and outputs $|\psi'\rangle|\psi''\rangle$ where $|\psi'\rangle$ and $|\psi''\rangle$ are proofs for *possibly different* verifications (of the same problem instance). We suspect some of our results can be generalized to this setting as well and we leave its analysis as an interesting open problem. Secondly, it would be interesting to see how Theorem 2 behaves in the less-than-perfect cloneability setting. We believe that setting the cloneability parameter to $f = 1 - \text{negl}(|x|)$ should not change the results. This would be beneficial since perfect cloneability (when $f = 1$) does depend on the gate set, whereas $f = 1 - \text{negl}(|x|)$ does not. One issue that arises without having perfect clones is that the output of the cloning circuit need not be product, and thus the use of Chernoff's bound in the proof of Lemma 5 poses an issue. Lastly, we do note that there are implicit lower bounds on the cloning parameter f however, assuming unproven conjectures. For example, we have $\mathsf{cloneableQMA}(k)(c, 0, s) = \mathsf{QMA}(k)(c, s)$, so if $\mathsf{cloneableQMA}(k)(c, 0, s) = \mathsf{cloneableQMA}(c', 0, s')$, for reasonable parameters c' and s', then this would imply $\mathsf{QMA}(k) = \mathsf{QMA}$. This statement can be strengthened to $f = 1/\exp$ since the cloning circuit can just output a maximally mixed state, and thus always exists. Thus, we suspect there is a dichotomy-type theorem classifying the consequences of having f belonging to certain intervals.

Finally, we think it would be interesting to understand the interplay of the parameters (c, f, s) in cloneableQMA-type protocols. In particular, how does completeness-soundness gap amplification protocols affect the cloning fidelity f? And can one amplify f without sacrificing much of the completeness and soundness guarantees? These and other related questions which delve deeper into the power and flexibility of cloneable proof systems are very interesting and we leave them to future work.

Acknowledgements. We would like to thank Barak Nehoran for useful discussions and comments. We acknowledge support of the Natural Sciences and Engineering Research Council of Canada (NSERC). This work was supported by the Air Force Office of Scientific Research under award number FA9550-20-1-0375. S.P. is supported by US Department of Energy (grant no DE-SC0023179) and partially supported by US National Science Foundation (award no 1954311). S.P. thanks the University of Ottawa, where a portion of this work was completed. This work was done in part while ABG was visiting the Simons Institute for the Theory of Computing. ABG is funded by ANR JCJC TCS-NISQ ANR-22-CE47-0004 and by the PEPR integrated project EPiQ ANR-22-PETQ-0007 part of Plan France 2030.

References

[Aar09] Aaronson, S.: Quantum copy-protection and quantum money. In: 24th Annual Conference on Computational Complexity (CCC 2009), pp. 229–242 (2009)

[Aar16] Aaronson, S.: The no-cloning theorem and the human condition. In: After-Dinner Talk Given at the QCRYPT 2016 Conference (2016)

[ABBS22] Aharonov, D., Ben-Or, M., Brandão, F.G.S.L., Sattath, O.: The pursuit of uniqueness: extending Valiant-Vazirani theorem to the probabilistic and quantum settings. Quantum **6**, 668 (2022)

[ABD+08] Aaronson, S., Beigi, S., Drucker, A., Fefferman, B., Shor, P.: The power of unentanglement. In: 23rd Annual IEEE Conference on Computational Complexity (CCC 2008), pp. 223–236 (2008)

[AC12] Aaronson, S., Christiano, P.: Quantum money from hidden subspaces. In: STOC '12: Proceedings of the Fourty-Fourth ACM Symposium on Theory of Computing, pp. 41–60 (2012)

[AFG+12] Aaronson, S., Farhi, E., Gosset, D., Hassidim, A., Kelner, J., Lutomirski, A.: Quantum money. Commun. ACM **55**(8), 84–92 (2012)

[AK07a] Aaronson, S., Kuperberg, G.: Quantum versus classical proofs and advice. In: Twenty-Second Annual IEEE Conference on Computational Complexity (CCC'07), pp. 115–128. IEEE (2007)

[AK07b] Aaronson, S., Kuperberg, G.: Quantum versus classical proofs and advice. In: 22nd Annual Conference on Computational Complexity (CCC 2007), pp. 115–128 (2007)

[ALM+98] Arora, S., Lund, C., Motwani, R., Sudan, M., Szegedy, M.: Proof verification and the hardness of approximation problems. J. ACM **45**(3), 501–555 (1998)

[ALP21] Ananth, P., Placa, R.L.: Secure software leasing. In: Canteaut, A., Standaert, F.-X. (eds.) EUROCRYPT 2021. LNCS, vol. 12697, pp. 501–530. Springer, Cham (2021). https://doi.org/10.1007/978-3-030-77886-6_17

[AN02] Aharonov, D., Naveh, T.: Quantum NP – a survey (2002). E-print arXiv:quant-ph/0210077

[BB84] Bennett, C.H., Brassard, G.: Quantum cryptography: public key distribution and coin tossing. In: International Conference on Computers, Systems and Signal Processing, pp. 175–179 (1984)

[BC23] Broadbent, A., Culf, E.: Uncloneable cryptographic primitives with interaction. E-print arXiv:2303.00048 (2023)

[BI20] Broadbent, A., Islam, R.: Quantum encryption with certified deletion. In: Pass, R., Pietrzak, K. (eds.) TCC 2020. LNCS, vol. 12552, pp. 92–122. Springer, Cham (2020). https://doi.org/10.1007/978-3-030-64381-2_4

[BJL+21] Broadbent, A., Jeffery, S., Lord, S., Podder, S., Sundaram, A.: Secure software leasing without assumptions. In: Nissim, K., Waters, B. (eds.) TCC 2021. LNCS, vol. 13042, pp. 90–120. Springer, Cham (2021). https://doi.org/10.1007/978-3-030-90459-3_4

[BK24] Ben-David, S., Kundu, S.: Oracle separation of QMA and QCMA with bounded adaptivity. In: 51st International Colloquium on Automata, Languages, and Programming (ICALP 2024), pp. 21:1–21:18 (2024)

[BKL23] Broadbent, A., Karvonen, M., Lord, S.: Uncloneable quantum advice. E-print arXiv:2309.05155 (2023)

[BL20] Broadbent, A., Lord, S.: Uncloneable quantum encryption via oracles. In: 15th Conference on the Theory of Quantum Computation, Communication, and Cryptography (TQC 2020), pp. 4:1–4:22 (2020)

[BS16] Broadbent, A., Schaffner, C.: Quantum cryptography beyond quantum key distribution. Des. Codes Crypt. **78**(1), 351–382 (2016)

[BS23] Ben-David, S., Sattath, O.: Quantum tokens for digital signatures. Quantum **7**, 901 (2023)

[CHTW04] Cleve, R., Høyer, P., Toner, B., Watrous, J.: Consequences and limits of nonlocal strategies. In: 19th Annual Conference on Computational Complexity (CCC 2004), pp. 236–249 (2004)

[CKP24] Chatterjee, R., Kundu, S., Podder, S.: Are uncloneable proof and advice states strictly necessary? *arXiv preprint*arXiv:2410.11827 (2024)

[CMP24] Coladangelo, A., Majenz, C., Poremba, A.: Quantum copy-protection of compute-and-compare programs in the quantum random oracle model. Quantum **8**, 1330 (2024)

[CV22] Culf, E., Vidick, T.: A monogamy-of-entanglement game for subspace coset states. Quantum **6**, 791 (2022)

[Die82] Dieks, D.: Communication by EPR devices. Phys. Lett. A **92**(6), 271–272 (1982)

[Eke91] Ekert, A.K.: Quantum cryptography based on Bell's theorem. Phys. Rev. Lett. **67**(6), 661–663 (1991)

[FK15] Fefferman, B., Kimmel, S.: Quantum vs classical proofs and subset verification. E-print arXiv:1510.06750 (2015)

[FS90] Feige, U., Shamir, A.: Witness indistinguishable and witness hiding protocols. In: STOC '90: Proceedings of the Twenty-Second ACM Symposium on Theory of Computing, pp. 416–426 (1990)

[GKS16] Grilo, A.B., Kerenidis, I., Sikora, J.: QMA with subset state witnesses. Chicago J. Theor. Comput. Sci. **2016**(4) (2016)

[GMR89] Goldwasser, S., Micali, S., Rackoff, C.: The knowledge complexity of interactive proof systems. SIAM J. Comput. **18**(1), 186–208 (1989)

[GMR23] Goyal, V., Malavolta, G., Raizes, J.: Unclonable commitments and proofs. Cryptology ePrint Archive, Report 2023/1538 (2023)

[Gol04] Goldreich, O.: Foundations of Cryptography:, vol. 2. Cambridge University Press, Basic Applications (2004)

[HM13] Harrow, A.W., Montanaro, A.: Testing product states, quantum Merlin-Arthur games and tensor optimization. J. ACM **60**(1), 1–43 (2013)

[JK23] Jawale, R., Khurana, D.: Unclonable non-interactive zero-knowledge. E-print arXiv:2310.07118 (2023)

[JNV+20] Ji, Z., Natarajan, A., Vidick, T., Wright, J., Yuen, H.: MIP*=RE. E-print arXiv:2001.04383 (2020)

[Kla17] Klauck, H.: The complexity of quantum disjoiness. In: 42nd International Symposium on Mathematical Foundations of Computer Science—MFCS 2017, pp. 15:1–15:13 (2017)

[KM03] Kobayashi, H., Matsumoto, K.: Quantum multi-prover interactive proof systems with limited prior entanglement. J. Comput. Syst. Sci. **66**(3), 429–450 (2003)

[KMY03] Kobayashi, H., Matsumoto, K., Yamakami, T.: Quantum Merlin-Arthur proof systems: are multiple Merlins more helpful to Arthur? In: 14th International Symposium on Algorithms and Computation (ISAAC 2003), pp. 189–198 (2003)

[KP14] Klauck, H., Podder, S.: Two results about quantum messages. In: 39th International Symposium on Mathematical Foundations of Computer Science—MFCS 2014, pp. 445–456 (2014)

[KSV02] Kitaev, A.Yu., Shen, A., Vyalyi, M.N.: Classical and Quantum Computation. American Mathematical Society (2002)

[Lin16] Lindell, Y.: How to simulate it - a tutorial on the simulation proof technique. Cryptology ePrint Archive, Paper 2016/046 (2016)

[LLPY24] Li, X., Liu, Q., Pelecanos, A., Yamakawa, T.: Classical vs quantum advice and proofs under classically-accessible oracle. In: 15th Innovations in Theoretical Computer Science Conference (ITCS 2024), pp. 72:1–72:19 (2024)

[MVW13a] Molina, A., Vidick, T., Watrous, J.: Optimal counterfeiting attacks and generalizations for Wiesner's quantum money. In: Theory of Quantum Computation, Communication, and Cryptography (TQC 2012), pp. 45–64 (2013)

[NN24] Natarajan, A., Nirkhe, C.: A distribution testing oracle separation between QMA and QCMA. Quantum **8**, 1377 (2024)

[NZ24] Nehoran, B., Zhandry, M.: A computational separation between quantum no-cloning and no-telegraphing. In: 15th Innovations in Theoretical Computer Science Conference (ITCS 2024), pp. 82:1–82:23 (2024)

[Wat00] Watrous, J.: Succinct quantum proofs for properties of finite groups. In: 41st Annual Symposium on Foundations of Computer Science (FOCS 2000), pp. 537–546 (2000)

[Wat02] Watrous, J.: Limits on the power of quantum statistical zero-knowledge. In: 43rd Annual IEEE Symposium on Foundations of Computer Science (FOCS 2002), pp. 459–468 (2002)

[Wat03] Watrous, J.: PSPACE has constant-round quantum interactive proof systems. Theor. Comput. Sci. **292**(3), 575–588 (2003)

[Wie83] Wiesner, S.: Conjugate coding. ACM SIGACT News **15**(1), 78–88 (1983)

[WZ82] Wootters, W.K., Zurek, W.H.: A single quantum cannot be cloned. Nature **299**, 802–803 (1982)

[Zha19] Zhandry, M.: Quantum lightning never strikes the same state twice. In: Ishai, Y., Rijmen, V. (eds.) EUROCRYPT 2019. LNCS, vol. 11478, pp. 408–438. Springer, Cham (2019). https://doi.org/10.1007/978-3-030-17659-4_14

[Zha21] Zhandry, M.: Quantum lightning never strikes the same state twice. Or: Quantum money from cryptographic assumptions. J. Cryptol. **34**(1), 6:1–6:56 (2021)

Symmetric-Key Cryptography and Attacks

(Im)Possibility of Symmetric Encryption Against Coordinated Algorithm Substitution Attacks and Key Exfiltration

Simone Colombo[1(✉)] and Damian Vizár[2]

[1] King's College London, London, UK
simone.colombo@kcl.ac.uk
[2] CSEM, Neuchâtel, Switzerland
damian.vizAr@csem.ch

Abstract. A growing body of work addresses the security of cryptographic systems in the presence of mass surveillance, a threat made concrete by Snowden's revelations and the widespread use of spyware against journalists and activists. In this paper, we investigate the security of symmetric encryption faced with simultaneous algorithm substitution attacks (ASAs) and key exfiltration (KE). The security of symmetric encryption in presence of ASAs or KE alone was established but no result deals with their coordinated deployment. Yet, that is a necessary step to be made if we are to achieve actual security against mass surveillance. We formalize this setting, and prove that no scheme alone stands chance against coordinated ASA and KE, by describing a realistic attack. We then describe a new kind of schemes, which make use of externally supplied randomness. We formalize their security and give a construction which provably resists simultaneous ASAs and KE when paired with a verifiable source of randomness, with security bounds in the concrete security spirit.

Keywords: Provable Security · Mass Surveillance · Symmetric Encryption · Key Exfiltration · Algorithm Substitution

1 Introduction

In this paper, we study the security of symmetric encryption in the presence of *simultaneous* algorithm substitution attacks (ASAs) and key exfiltration (KE) via advanced persistent threats (APTs). Both APTs and ASAs enable adversaries to circumvent encryption, facilitating mass surveillance by resourceful entities, to which we refer as *Big Brother*. The idea of covertly subverting cryptographic systems was first introduced by Young and Yung under the term *kleptography* nearly three decades ago [52,53]. The threat of mass surveillance enabled by sophisticated technical means has been made starkly evident by the Snowden revelations and the widespread deployment of spyware targeting journalists and activists [7,28,29,50]. This concern has also been formally acknowledged by the

D. Escudero and I. Damgård (Eds.): LATINCRYPT 2025, LNCS 16129, pp. 299–332, 2026.
https://doi.org/10.1007/978-3-032-06754-8_11

IACR in its "Copenhagen Resolution" [32]. These developments have prompted a resurgence of interest in kleptographic research [14,18,27,34,42,45–48].

ALGORITHM SUBSTITUTION ATTACKS. In an ASA, the executable code implementing, e.g., an encryption algorithm $\mathcal{E}$ gets replaced by the code of a subversion $\tilde{\mathcal{E}}$. The goal of $\tilde{\mathcal{E}}$ is to break confidentiality of communication, and remain undetected by the user while doing so. The target could be a closed-source cryptographic library [19] or a dedicated crypto-hardware [49], or possibly modifications of open source software at compile time [13].

Bellare, Paterson and Rogaway (BPR) formalized the goals of both Big Brother (to avoid detection by the users) and the users (to prevent the existence of useful subversions) in the context of ASAs against symmetric encryption [13]. They demonstrated an efficient and provably undetectable subversion for any symmetric scheme with randomized encryption algorithm. In the opposite direction, BPR showed that a large class of deterministic and stateful symmetric schemes is provably resistant to ASAs (assuming the subverted algorithm meets a very basic condition of concealment). The results of BPR indicate that *no randomized encryption scheme can resist ASAs.*

KEY EXFILTRATION THROUGH APTS. An APT, e.g., a malware like NSO's Pegasus [50], infests a system for a long period and attempts to exfiltrate a user's secret key [12] to Big Brother, negating the encryption. The Snowden revelations indicate, that the NSA is capable of planting APTs across a wide range of platforms [7]. An APT will however be able to communicate a limited amount of data (say 10 GB) to the outside world without being discovered [3]. This motivates the bounded retrieval model (BRM): with a very big secret key (e.g., 1 TB) the damage done by a limited leakage can be mitigated.

Bellare, Kane and Rogaway (BKR) formalized the security of symmetric encryption with leakage in the BRM [12]. They designed a big-key symmetric scheme that is both practically useful, and provably secure against KE in the random-oracle model (ROM)[1]. A crucial aspect of their scheme's security is that *the encryption algorithm uses randomness* to render prior leakage useless.

THE PROBLEM. We address an open question posed by BKR [12]: "*Whether any defense against ASAs is possible in the big-key setting remains open.*" Indeed, it is implausible that Big Brother would refrain from coordinating its tools in a targeted attack. Yet, the two existing results that address ASAs and KE in isolation seem at odds: resisting ASAs requires determinism, whereas defeating KE necessitates randomness. We set out to answer the open question and find means of thwarting simultaneous ASAs and KE with minimal trust.

OUR CONTRIBUTION. We define SURV-LIND, a notion that captures security of symmetric encryption in face of simultaneous ASAs and KE in the ROM. We then describe the *derandomization* attack, confirming that no scheme, randomized or not, can be SURV-LIND secure. We further give a practical variant of the derandomization attack that can be used e.g. for identification of a subset of

[1] BKR also present a less-efficient variant that achieves standard model security.

users of an online service at the time of login. Through the attack, we identify the Achilles heel of the setup: Big Brother's freedom to manipulate randomness.

To sidestep this impossibility result, we propose a new big-key symmetric encryption scheme that uses external randomness. We formalize security with the RESIST notion in the ROM, which models simultaneous ASAs and key exfiltration, assuming that the randomness used by the encryption algorithm is generated by a subroutine free from attacker influence. We then design a big-key symmetric encryption scheme SES that is provably RESIST-secure in this setting. Our proof provides a concrete security bound [9], yielding a meaningful numerical estimate of actual security in practice.

Seemingly a definitional weakening, the explicit, incorruptible randomness in RESIST serves as model for an incorruptible random beacon, a concept introduced through the unicorn protocol by Lenstra and Wesolowski (LW) [36]. The unicorn protocol allows a variable number of parties to generate a provably uncontestable random value, even if we trust no other party but ourselves. When using unicorn to supply our construction SES with randomness, a user can defeat Big Brother who deploys simultaneous ASAs and APTs.

We finally provide a variant of the notion RESIST that incorporates the security game of unicorn, allowing the attacker to attempt to thwart incorruptible randomness generation. We prove the security of SES under this advanced notion, capturing all relevant attack vectors in a single advantage bound. For the sake of efficiency, we propose a variant of big-key symmetric encryption with external randomness, designed in an API-driven syntax with session support: while using external randomness for every encryption query yields a secure scheme, it is exceedingly inefficient. Our construction amortizes this overhead by reusing the costly randomness within a session. SES can thus be easily instantiated and, when paired with a suitable instance of the unicorn protocol, provides an efficient means of securing communication against mass surveillance. To our knowledge, SES paired with unicorn is the first scheme that provably resists simultaneous ASAs and KE in the ROM.

RELATED WORK. The pioneering work on kleptography was done by Young and Yung [52,53]. BPR gave the first formal treatment of ASAs in symmetric encryption [13]. Bellare, Jaeger, and Kane improved BPR's undetectable ASAs against randomized encryption by making them stateless (even less detectable) and more general [11]. Degabriele, Farshim, and Poettering argued that BPR's assumption about subversions is too strong and relaxed it [23]. Dodis, Mironov, and Stephen-Davidowitz proposed *cryptographic reverse firewalls*, which thwart ASAs by re-randomizing outgoing ciphertexts [24,38]. These could also address the simultaneous ASAs and KE, however they require trusted networking devices. We did not adopt this approach, as our goal is a solution with minimal trust. Austrin et al. show that no security is possible if the random tape of an algorithm is tamperable [6]. Russell et al. investigate security when all algorithms can be subverted [46]. Several works study ASAs on various cryptographic primitives [5,10,14,16,47,48]. The BRM is the result of a sequence of works [1,2,17,22,25,26,39]. BKR presented the first efficient symmetric encryption scheme that is computationally secure in the BRM [12]. We rely on encryption tidiness [40] to argue uniqueness of ciphertexts in our proofs. This is reminiscent of the attack where adversary tries to craft ciphertext tuples that correctly decrypt under two different keys [30], which is not thwarted by tidiness. That scenario is not relevant in our notions, where the adversary tries to exfiltrate a key without controlling it—here tidiness suffices as it implies per-key ciphertext uniqueness for any given key, which remains fixed in our security games. Hoang et al. also use an API-driven interface for symmetric encryption, though for a different purpose [31].

Organization of the Paper. In Sect. 2, we introduce notations and briefly review existing security notions. In Sect. 3, we present the SURV-LIND security notion, describe the derandomization attack, and illustrate its practical impact. In Sect. 4, we introduce the syntax of big-key symmetric encryption with sessions and define RESIST security. In Sect. 5, we describe a scheme paired with an honest source of randomness and prove its RESIST security. In Sect. 6, we present the unicorn protocol, which we prove can securely instantiate the honest source of randomness.

2 Preliminaries and Previous Security Definitions

Notations. We denote the set of all strings of n bits with $\{0,1\}^n$ and with $\{0,1\}^*$ the set of all finite strings. The length of a string s is denoted by $|s|$. The special symbol $\perp$ represents an undefined variable or an error. The empty string is represented by ε. The concatenation of two strings s, s' is denoted by $s \| s'$. By $s[i]$ we denote i^{th} bit of a string s. We represent with $\langle s \rangle$ the efficient and injective encoding of a string s. For a set $\mathcal{V}$, we denote a vector as $\overrightarrow{v} \in \mathcal{V}^q$, with $\overrightarrow{v}[i] \in \mathcal{V}$ its i-th coordinate and with $|\overrightarrow{v}| = q$ its length. For a string s and a vector $\overrightarrow{P} \in (\mathbb{Z}_{|s|})^q$ we let $s[\overrightarrow{P}]$ denote $s[\overrightarrow{P}[1]] \|, \ldots, \| s[\overrightarrow{P}[q]]$. We let $\mathbb{N}$ denote the set $\{0,1,2,\ldots\}$ and $\mathbb{N}_{>0}$ denote $\mathbb{N} \backslash \{0\}$. We let $\mathbb{Z}_n$ denote both the set $\{0,1,\ldots,n-1\}$ and the corresponding ring with n elements. We further let $\mathbb{Z}_n^*$ denote both the multiplicative subgroup of $\mathbb{Z}_n$ and the corresponding set. For a prime p, we let $\mathrm{QR}_p \subset \mathbb{Z}_p^*$ denote the set of quadratic residues modulo p. We let $x \leftarrow\!\!\$\; S$ denote uniform sampling of an element x from a set S (finite or endowed with a uniform distribution). We let $y \leftarrow A(x_1, \ldots; r)$ denote running a randomized algorithm A on inputs $x_1, \ldots$ and coins r to obtain y in a deterministic way, while $y \leftarrow\!\!\$\; A(x_1, \ldots)$ denotes running A with implicit coins. A random oracle $\mathrm{RO}(s, l')$ maps every distinct input $s \in \{0,1\}^*$ to an infinite string of uniformly and independently sampled bits, which is truncated to l' bits. For a set $\mathcal{S}$, we let $\mathrm{Perm}(\mathcal{S})$ denote the set of all permutations over $\mathcal{S}$.

Symmetric Encryption. We use the same syntax and correctness definitions as BPR [13]. A scheme for symmetric encryption is a triple $\Pi = (\mathcal{K}, \mathcal{E}, \mathcal{D})$. The key space $\mathcal{K}$ is a finite nonempty set. The possibly randomized and stateful encryption algorithm $\mathcal{E} : \mathcal{K} \times \mathcal{M} \times \mathcal{A} \times \mathcal{S} \rightarrow \mathcal{C} \times \mathcal{S}$, maps a key K, a message M, associated data A and a state σ from their respective domains, which are all subsets of $\{0,1\}^*$, to a ciphertext and an updated state $(C, \sigma') \leftarrow\$ \mathcal{E}(K, M, A, \sigma)$. The decryption algorithm $\mathcal{D} : \mathcal{K} \times \mathcal{C} \times \mathcal{A} \times \mathcal{S} \rightarrow \mathcal{M} \cup \{\perp\} \times \mathcal{S}$ is a deterministic algorithm mapping a tuple (K, C, A, τ) to a recovered plaintext and an updated state $(M, \tau') \leftarrow \mathcal{D}(K, C, A, \tau)$.

We require that $\forall M \in \mathcal{M} : M \in \{0,1\}^m \Rightarrow \{0,1\}^m \subseteq \mathcal{M}$. We further require that for all $K \in \mathcal{K}$, $M \in \mathcal{M}$, $A \in \mathcal{A}$ and $\sigma \in \mathcal{S}$ we have $|\mathcal{E}(K, M, A, \sigma)| = |M| + \mu$ where μ is a constant called *stretch* of Π. We say that Π is stateless if $\mathcal{S} = \{\varepsilon\}$. In this case, we may drop the state input and output from the notation.

Correctness. A scheme for symmetric encryption is *correct*, if the receiver that decrypts the incoming ciphertexts in the correct order always obtains the same messages as the sender encrypted, i.e., if for all $q > 1$ and all $K \in \mathcal{K}$, $M_1, \ldots, M_q \in \{0,1\}^*$ and $A_1, \ldots, A_q \in \{0,1\}^*$ the following holds:

$$\Pr\left[(\forall i,\ C_i \neq \perp) \wedge (\exists i,\ M_i \neq M'_i) \;\middle|\; \begin{array}{l} \sigma_0, \tau_0 \leftarrow \varepsilon; \\ \textbf{for} i = 1, \ldots, q\, \textbf{do} \\ \quad (C_i, \sigma_i) \leftarrow\$ \mathcal{E}(K, M_i, A_i, \sigma_{i-1}) \\ \quad (M'_i, \tau_i) \leftarrow \mathcal{D}(C_i, A_i, \tau_{i-1}) \end{array}\right] = 0$$

Security of Symmetric Encryption. In this work we use two security definitions for symmetric encryption: left or right (LoR), and real or random (RoR) indistinguishability (IND) under chosen plaintext attack (CPA).

Game IND-CPA$_\Pi^\mathscr{A}$ IND\$-CPA$_\Pi^\mathscr{A}$	Oracle Enc(M_0, M_1, A)	Oracle Enc(M, A)
$b \leftarrow\$ \{0,1\}$; $\sigma \leftarrow \varepsilon$	$(C, \sigma) \leftarrow\$ \mathcal{E}(K, M_b, A, \sigma)$	$(C_0, \sigma) \leftarrow\$ \mathcal{E}(K, M, A, \sigma)$
$K \leftarrow\$ \mathcal{K}$	**return** C	$C_1 \leftarrow\$ \{0,1\}^{\lvert C_0 \rvert}$
$b' \leftarrow \mathscr{A}^{\text{Enc,RO}}(L, \sigma)$		**return** C_b
return $(b = b')$		

Fig. 1. Games used to define security of symmetric encryption. The IND-CPA game uses the *Enc*(M_0, M_1, A) oracle, whereas IND\$-CPA$_\Pi^\mathscr{A}$ uses the Enc(M, A) oracle.

Definition 1 (IND-CPA and IND\$-CPA). *Let* $\Pi = (\mathcal{K}, \mathcal{E}, \mathcal{D})$ *be an encryption scheme. We define the advantage of an adversary* $\mathscr{A}$ *at winning the* IND-CPA *(resp.* IND\$-CPA*) game (Fig. 1) as* $\mathbf{Adv}_\Pi^{\text{ind}}(\mathscr{A}) = 2\Pr[\text{IND-CPA}_\Pi^\mathscr{A} \Rightarrow 1] - 1$ *(resp. as* $\mathbf{Adv}_\Pi^{\text{ind\$}}(\mathscr{A}) = 2\Pr[\text{IND\$-CPA}_\Pi^\mathscr{A} \Rightarrow 1] - 1$*).*

An encryption scheme Π is said to be IND-CPA-secure (resp. IND\$-CPA-secure) when this advantage is small for all adversaries $\mathscr{A}$ with reasonable resources. It is well-known that IND\$-CPA $\Rightarrow$ IND-CPA [8,9,44] and we will use this result in the rest of the paper without proof.

2.1 Algorithm Substitution Attacks

BPR formalize an ASA subverting the encryption algorithm of a symmetric scheme. They assume the subversion to be equipped with a master key, that is used to subliminally communicate with Big Brother, and allow it to decrypt the plaintexts. We summarize the model that BPR use.

SUBVERSIONS. A subversion of a scheme $\Pi = (\mathcal{K}, \mathcal{E}, \mathcal{D})$ is a triple $\tilde{\Pi} = (\tilde{\mathcal{K}}, \tilde{\mathcal{E}}, \tilde{\mathcal{D}})$. The master-key space $\tilde{\mathcal{K}}$ is a finite non-empty set. The subverted encryption algorithm $\tilde{\mathcal{E}} : \tilde{\mathcal{K}} \times \mathcal{K} \times \mathcal{M} \times \mathcal{A} \times \tilde{\mathcal{S}} \times \mathcal{I} \to \mathcal{C} \times \tilde{\mathcal{S}}$, which is possibly randomized and stateful, maps a tuple $(\tilde{K}, K, M, A, \sigma, i)$ to a ciphertext and an updated state (C, σ'), where $i \in \mathcal{I}$ is a public value uniquely identifying a user (e.g., a MAC address). All the domains of input and output arguments are subsets of $\{0,1\}^*$. The plaintext-recovery algorithm $\tilde{\mathcal{D}} : \tilde{\mathcal{K}} \times \mathcal{C}^* \times \mathcal{A}^* \times \mathcal{I} \to \mathcal{M}^* \cup \bot$ takes a master key $\tilde{K}$, a vector of ciphertexts $\overrightarrow{C}$ and of associated data $\overrightarrow{A}$ each, and a user identifier i to a vector messages $\overrightarrow{M}$ or to $\bot$ if the plaintext recovery fails. We do not further discuss how $\tilde{\mathcal{D}}$ can be constructed, but rather study how any such $\tilde{\mathcal{D}}$ can be thwarted.

DECRYPTABILITY. BPR assume any subversion must meet the *decryptability condition* [13], as a basic requirement for concealment; failure do so is likely to lead to detection. A subversion $\tilde{\Pi} = (\tilde{\mathcal{K}}, \tilde{\mathcal{E}}, \tilde{\mathcal{D}})$ satisfies the decryptability condition relative to $\Pi = (\mathcal{K}, \mathcal{E}, \mathcal{D})$ if $\Pi' = (\tilde{\mathcal{K}} \times \mathcal{K}, \tilde{\mathcal{E}}, \mathcal{D}')$ is a correct encryption scheme where $\mathcal{D}'$ is defined by $\mathcal{D}'((\tilde{K}, K), C, A, \sigma) = \mathcal{D}(K, C, A, \sigma)$.

Less stringent variants of the decryptability condition have been proposed (e.g., [4,23]), extending the set of "valid" subversions. We adhere to BPR's definition of decryptability, as we do not focus on the nuances of different decryptability notions, and because BPR's measures defeat subversions under all known variants [23].

DEFEATING ASAS. BPR ask that Big Brother, in possession of the master-key, should not only be unable to decrypt the communication, but rather unable to tell apart the real scheme from the subverted one in a chosen plaintext attack.

Definition 2 (SURV [13]). *Let $\Pi = (\mathcal{K}, \mathcal{E}, \mathcal{D})$ be an encryption scheme and $\tilde{\Pi} = (\tilde{\mathcal{K}}, \tilde{\mathcal{E}}, \tilde{\mathcal{D}})$ its subversion. We define the advantage of Big Brother $\mathscr{B}$ at winning the* SURV *game of Fig. 2 as* $\mathbf{Adv}^{\mathrm{srv}}_{\Pi,\tilde{\Pi}}(\mathscr{B}) = 2\Pr[\mathrm{SURV}^{\mathscr{B}}_{\Pi,\tilde{\Pi}} \Rightarrow 1] - 1$.

An encryption scheme Π is said to be secure against surveillance when this advantage is small for all subversions $\tilde{\Pi}$ of Π that meet the decryptability condition and all adversaries $\mathscr{B}$ with reasonable resources.

BPR showed that any scheme that has *unique ciphertexts* will provably resist to ASAs: if only a single ciphertext decrypts to any message (with other inputs to

Game $\text{SURV}^{\mathscr{B}}_{\Pi,\tilde{\Pi}}$	Oracle $\text{Key}(i)$	Oracle $\text{Enc}(M, A, i)$
$b \leftarrow\$ \{0,1\}$	**if** $(K_i = \bot)$ **then**	**if** $(K_i = \bot)$ **then return** $\bot$
$\tilde{K} \leftarrow\$ \tilde{\mathcal{K}}$	$K_i \leftarrow\$ \mathcal{K}$	**if** $(b = 1)$ **then** $(C, \sigma_i) \leftarrow\$ \mathcal{E}(K_i, M, A, \sigma_i)$
$b' \leftarrow \mathscr{B}^{\text{Key},\text{Enc}}(\tilde{K})$	$\sigma_i \leftarrow \varepsilon$	**else** $(C, \sigma_i) \leftarrow\$ \tilde{\mathcal{E}}(\tilde{K}, K_i, M, A, \sigma_i, i)$
return $(b = b')$	**return** ε	**return** C

Fig. 2. Game used to define surveillance security of subversion [13].

$\mathcal{E}$ fixed), a subversion $\tilde{\mathcal{E}}$ can either implement $\mathcal{E}$ or break the decryptability condition. Thus any scheme Π with unique ciphertexts will have $\mathbf{Adv}^{\text{srv}}_{\Pi,\tilde{\Pi}}(\mathscr{B}) = 0$. Due to the correctness condition, any unique-ciphertext scheme is deterministic.

2.2 Key Exfiltration

BKR model an attack by an APT in the BRM. BKR consider symmetric schemes with a very big key. They formalize the security of such schemes exposed to an APTs in the BRM and design a provably secure, practical construction.

Big-Key Symmetric Encryption. BKR's syntax of big-key symmetric encryption (BKSE) is a special case of the syntax defined for symmetric encryption: BKR consider stateless schemes with no associated data. A scheme for big-key symmetric encryption (BKSE) is a triple $\boldsymbol{\Pi} = (\boldsymbol{\mathcal{K}}, \boldsymbol{\mathcal{E}}, \boldsymbol{\mathcal{D}})$, the key space being $\boldsymbol{\mathcal{K}} = \{0,1\}^k$ with k "big", say 1 TB. We use bold symbols to emphasize the big-key setting. The correctness condition is required to be fulfilled. For the sake of efficiency and usability, BKR also require *locality* of the encryption, i.e. the encryption algorithm should only use a "small" fraction of the big key $\boldsymbol{K}$ upon every invocation.

Security Model for Key Exfiltration Attacks. BKR model the security of BKSE in presence of an APT as a LoR IND-CPA game in the ROM, in which Big Brother $\mathscr{B}$ chooses a leakage function Lk that takes a big key $\boldsymbol{K}$, has access to the random oracle[2] and outputs a leakage L with $|L| = l < k$. The amount of leakage l is a parameter of $\mathscr{B}$. The adversary learns the leakage at the *beginning* of the game which then proceeds as a conventional LoR experiment.

Definition 3 ([12]). *Let* $\boldsymbol{\Pi} = (\boldsymbol{\mathcal{K}}, \boldsymbol{\mathcal{E}}, \boldsymbol{\mathcal{D}})$ *be a big-key encryption scheme. We define the advantage of Big Brother* $\mathscr{B}$ *the* LIND *game defined in Fig. 3 as* $\mathbf{Adv}^{\text{lind}}_{\boldsymbol{\Pi}}(\mathscr{B}) = 2\Pr[\text{LIND}^{\mathscr{B}}_{\boldsymbol{\Pi}} \Rightarrow 1] - 1$.

A big-key encryption scheme $\boldsymbol{\Pi}$ is said to be secure in presence of key exfiltration when this advantage is small for all adversaries $\mathscr{B}$ with reasonable resources.

[2] Letting Lk access the RO is necessary to eliminate pathological constructions [12].

Game $\text{LIND}_{\boldsymbol{\Pi}}^{\mathscr{B}}$	Oracle $\text{Enc}(M_0, M_1)$
$(\mathsf{Lk}, \sigma) \leftarrow \mathscr{B}^{\text{RO}}$; $\boldsymbol{K} \leftarrow_\$ \{0,1\}^k$; $L \leftarrow \mathsf{Lk}^{\text{RO}}(\boldsymbol{K})$	$C \leftarrow_\$ \boldsymbol{\mathcal{E}}^{\text{RO}}(\boldsymbol{K}, M_b)$
$b \leftarrow_\$ \{0,1\}$; $b' \leftarrow \mathscr{B}^{\text{Enc},\text{RO}}(L, \sigma)$	**return** C
return $(b = b')$	

Fig. 3. Game used to define security of a big-key encryption scheme $\boldsymbol{\Pi} = (\boldsymbol{\mathcal{K}}, \boldsymbol{\mathcal{E}}, \boldsymbol{\mathcal{D}})$ in presence of key exfiltration. The adversarial leakage function takes $\boldsymbol{K}$ as input, has access to the RO and outputs a leakage L with $|L| = l$ [12].

KEY ENCAPSULATION. BKR reduce the security of BKSE to the security of big-key encapsulation. A big-key encapsulation algorithm $\boldsymbol{S} : \boldsymbol{\mathcal{K}} \times \{0,1\}^r \rightarrow \{0,1\}^\kappa$ takes a big key $\boldsymbol{K}$ and a selector/seed R to a derived key K with $\kappa < k$. We let $\boldsymbol{S}$ access the random oracle. A big-key encapsulation scheme is secure, if the derived keys are indistinguishable from uniform strings in presence of leakage.

Game $\text{KEY}_{\boldsymbol{S}}^{\mathscr{B}}$	Oracle $\text{Derive}()$	Algorithm $\mathsf{XKEY}_{k,\kappa,P,r}^{\text{RO}}(\boldsymbol{K}, R)$
$(\mathsf{Lk}, \sigma) \leftarrow \mathscr{B}^{\text{RO}}$	$R \leftarrow_\$ \{0,1\}^r$	**for** $i \leftarrow 1, \ldots, P$ **do**
$\boldsymbol{K} \leftarrow_\$ \{0,1\}^k$	**if** $(b = 0)$ **then**	$\quad \mathbf{P}[i] \leftarrow \text{RO}(\langle R, i, 0\rangle,\ \log_2(k))$
$L \leftarrow \mathsf{Lk}^{\text{RO}}(\boldsymbol{K})$	$\quad K \leftarrow_\$ \{0,1\}^\kappa$	$J \leftarrow \boldsymbol{K}[\mathbf{P}]$
$b \leftarrow_\$ \{0,1\}$	**else**	$K \leftarrow \text{RO}(\langle R, J, 1\rangle,\ \kappa)$
$b' \leftarrow \mathscr{B}^{\text{Derive, RO}}(L, \sigma)$	$\quad K \leftarrow \boldsymbol{S}^{\text{RO}}(\boldsymbol{K}, R)$	**return** K
return $(b = b')$	**return** (R, K)	

Fig. 4. (**Left**) Game used to define security of a big-key encapsulation algorithm $\boldsymbol{S}$ in presence of key exfiltration [12]. (**Right**) Provably secure key encapsulation algorithm XKEY. The parameters k, κ, P, r are the length of the big key, the length of the derived key, the number of probed bits of the big key and the size of the selector respectively, and $\langle\cdot\rangle$ is an efficient, injective encoding [12].

Definition 4 (**[12]**). *Let* $\boldsymbol{S} : \boldsymbol{\mathcal{K}} \times \{0,1\}^r \rightarrow \{0,1\}^\kappa$ *be a big-key encapsulation scheme. The advantage of an adversary* $\mathscr{B}$ *at winning the game KEY (Fig. 4) is defined as* $\mathbf{Adv}_{\boldsymbol{S}}^{\text{key}}(\mathscr{B}) = 2\Pr[\text{KEY}_{\boldsymbol{S}}^{\mathscr{B}} \Rightarrow 1] - 1$.

A big-key encapsulation algorithm $\boldsymbol{S}$ is said to be secure in presence of key-exfiltration when this advantage is small for all adversaries $\mathscr{B}$ with reasonable resources. BKR designed a provably secure key encapsulation scheme XKEY (right of Fig. 4), whose security follows from [12, Theorem 12].

RESISTING THE KE. BKR proved that combining a secure big-key encapsulation algorithm $\boldsymbol{S}$ with a secure symmetric encryption Π in a natural way yields a secure BKSE $\mathsf{SE}[\Pi, \boldsymbol{\mathcal{S}}]$, for which $\mathbf{Adv}^{\mathrm{lind}}_{\mathsf{SE}}(\mathscr{B}) \leq \mathbf{Adv}^{\mathrm{key}}_{\boldsymbol{\mathcal{S}}}(\mathscr{A}_2) + q \cdot \mathbf{Adv}^{\mathrm{ind}}_{\Pi}(\mathscr{A}_1)$ for any adversary $\mathscr{B}$ that makes at most q queries to its ENC oracle and leaks at most l bits, such that $\mathscr{A}_1$ makes only a single ENC query and has about the same running time as $\mathscr{B}$. $\mathscr{A}_2$ makes at most q queries DERIVE queries, runs in about the same time as $\mathscr{B}$ and makes the same number of RO queries both before and after receiving the leakage as $\mathscr{B}$.

3 Simultaneous ASAs and KE

A natural goal for any real-world application of symmetric encryption would be to resist both ASAs and KE simultaneously. Yet, the counter-measures against isolated ASAs proposed by BPR and those against isolated KE proposed by BKR seem to be contradicting: it appears that a complex defense against Big Brother is not possible. In this section, we formally confirm this intuition. We define the notion SURV-LIND, a natural extension of BPR's SURV notion that incorporates key exfiltration attacks. We then demonstrate in Sect. 3.4 a generic attack, which attacks *any* BKSE scheme, randomized or not, with high SURV-LIND advantage.

3.1 Equivalent Definitions for Surveillance and KE Security

Before defining the notion SURV-LIND, we present alternative definitions for surveillance security of subversion (Definition 5) and key exfiltration security (Definition 6). The original definitions (Definitions 2 and 3) use a LoR approach, while in this section we present a RoR approach and show that our alternative security notions are equivalent (in the case of surveillance) or imply (in the case of KE security) the original ones. Looking ahead, we will build our SURV-LIND notion on this equivalent definitions.

Definition 5 (SURV\$). *Let* $\Pi = (\mathcal{K}, \mathcal{E}, \mathcal{D})$ *be an encryption scheme and* $\tilde{\Pi} = (\tilde{\mathcal{K}}, \tilde{\mathcal{E}}, \tilde{\mathcal{D}})$ *its subversion. We define the advantage of Big Brother* $\mathscr{B}$ *at winning the game* SURV\$ *(defined in Fig. 5) as* $\mathbf{Adv}^{\mathrm{srv\$}}_{\Pi,\tilde{\Pi}}(\mathscr{B}) = 2\Pr[\mathrm{SURV\$}^{\mathscr{B}}_{\Pi,\tilde{\Pi}} \Rightarrow 1] - 1$.

Game $\mathrm{SURV\$}^{\mathscr{B}}_{\Pi,\tilde{\Pi}}$	Oracle $\mathrm{KEY}(i)$	Oracle $\mathrm{ENC}(M, A, i)$
$b \leftarrow_\$ \{0,1\}$	**if** $(K_i = \bot)$ **then**	**if** $(K_i = \bot)$ **then return** $\bot$
$\tilde{K} \leftarrow_\$ \tilde{\mathcal{K}}$	$\quad K_i \leftarrow_\$ \mathcal{K}$	$(C_0, \sigma_i) \leftarrow_\$ \tilde{\mathcal{E}}(\tilde{K}, K_i, M, A, \sigma_i, i)$
$b' \leftarrow \mathscr{B}^{\mathrm{KEY,ENC}}(\tilde{K})$	$\quad \sigma_i \leftarrow \varepsilon$	$C_1 \leftarrow_\$ \{0,1\}^{\lvert C_0 \rvert}$
return $(b = b')$	**return** ε	**return** C_b

Fig. 5. ROR ciphertext game used to define surveillance security of subversion.

RELATION BETWEEN SURV NOTIONS. Proposition 1 shows that SURV\$ security is equivalent to SURV security.

Proposition 1 (SURV\$ $\xleftrightarrow{\text{IND\$-CPA}}$ SURV). *Let $\Pi = (\mathcal{K}, \mathcal{E}, \mathcal{D})$ be an IND-CPA\$-secure (Definition 1) encryption scheme and $\tilde{\Pi} = (\tilde{\mathcal{K}}, \tilde{\mathcal{E}}, \tilde{\mathcal{D}})$ its subversion. Then for any SURV adversary $\mathscr{B}$, there exists a SURV\$ adversary $\mathscr{B}'$ that makes the same number of KEY and ENC queries as $\mathscr{B}$, has the same data complexity as $\mathscr{B}$ and for which $|\mathbf{Adv}^{\mathrm{srv}}_{\Pi,\tilde{\Pi}}(\mathscr{B}') - \mathbf{Adv}^{\mathrm{srv\$}}_{\Pi,\tilde{\Pi}}(\mathscr{B})| \leq \mathbf{Adv}^{\mathrm{ind\$\text{-}cpa}}_{\Pi}(\mathscr{A})$, where $\mathscr{A}$ is an adversary against the IND\$-CPA game for Π that makes the same number of ENC as $\mathscr{B}$ and has the same data complexity as $\mathscr{B}$.*

Proof. Let $P(\mathrm{G}, \bar{b}) = \Pr[\mathscr{B}^{\mathrm{G}} \Rightarrow 1 | b = \bar{b}]$, i.e., the probability that adversary $\mathscr{B}$ outputs 1 after playing with game G given that b in game G is equal to $\bar{b}$.

By definition we have that $\mathbf{Adv}^{\mathrm{srv}}_{\Pi,\tilde{\Pi}}(\mathscr{B}) = P(\mathrm{SURV}, 1) - P(\mathrm{SURV}, 0)$ and $\mathbf{Adv}^{\mathrm{srv\$}}_{\Pi,\tilde{\Pi}}(\mathscr{B}) = P(\mathrm{SURV\$}, 1) - P(\mathrm{SURV\$}, 0)$. By construction we know that $P(\mathrm{SURV}, 0) = P(\mathrm{SURV\$}, 0)$, as when $b = 0$ the two games are identical. Therefore we have

$$|\mathbf{Adv}^{\mathrm{srv}}_{\Pi,\tilde{\Pi}}(\mathscr{B}) - \mathbf{Adv}^{\mathrm{srv\$}}_{\Pi,\tilde{\Pi}}(\mathscr{B})| = |P(\mathrm{SURV}, 1) - P(\mathrm{SURV\$}, 1)| \leq \mathbf{Adv}^{\mathrm{ind\$\text{-}cpa}}_{\Pi}(\mathscr{A}),$$

where the inequality follows from the observation that the difference between SURV and SURV\$ when $b = 1$ is identical to the IND\$-CPA game of Fig. 1. □

Definition 6 (LIND\$). *Let $\boldsymbol{\Pi} = (\boldsymbol{\mathcal{K}}, \boldsymbol{\mathcal{E}}, \boldsymbol{\mathcal{D}})$ be a big-key encryption scheme. We define the advantage of Big Brother $\mathscr{B}$ at winning the game LIND\$ (defined in Fig. 6) as $\mathbf{Adv}^{\mathrm{lind\$}}_{\boldsymbol{\Pi}}(\mathscr{B}) = 2\Pr[\mathrm{LIND\$}^{\mathscr{B}}_{\boldsymbol{\Pi}} \Rightarrow 1] - 1$.*

Game $\mathrm{LIND\$}^{\mathscr{B}}_{\boldsymbol{\Pi}}$ $\mathrm{LIND\text{-}ROR}^{\mathscr{B}}_{\boldsymbol{\Pi}}$	Oracle $\mathrm{ENC}(M)$	Oracle $\mathrm{ENC}(M)$
$(\mathsf{Lk}, \sigma) \leftarrow \mathscr{B}^{\mathrm{RO}}$	$C_0 \leftarrow\!\!\$\ \boldsymbol{\mathcal{E}}^{\mathrm{RO}}(\boldsymbol{K}, M)$	$C_0 \leftarrow\!\!\$\ \boldsymbol{\mathcal{E}}^{\mathrm{RO}}(\boldsymbol{K}, M)$
$\boldsymbol{K} \leftarrow\!\!\$\ \{0,1\}^k$; $L \leftarrow \mathsf{Lk}^{\mathrm{RO}}(\boldsymbol{K})$	$C_1 \leftarrow\!\!\$\ \{0,1\}^{\lvert C_0 \rvert}$	$M' \leftarrow\!\!\$\ \{0,1\}^{\lvert M \rvert}$
$b \leftarrow\!\!\$\ \{0,1\}$; $b' \leftarrow \mathscr{B}^{\mathrm{ENC,RO}}(L, \sigma)$	**return** C_b	$C_1 \leftarrow\!\!\$\ \boldsymbol{\mathcal{E}}^{\mathrm{RO}}(\boldsymbol{K}, M')$
return $(b = b')$		**return** C_b

Fig. 6. Real-or-random ciphertext games used to define security of a big-key encryption scheme $\boldsymbol{\Pi} = (\boldsymbol{\mathcal{K}}, \boldsymbol{\mathcal{E}}, \boldsymbol{\mathcal{D}})$ in presence of key exfiltration. The game $\mathrm{LIND\text{-}ROR}^{\mathscr{B}}_{\boldsymbol{\Pi}}$ uses the $\mathrm{ENC}(M)$ oracle and it is used in the proof of Proposition 2.

RELATION BETWEEN LIND NOTIONS. Proposition 2 shows that LIND\$ security implies LIND security.

Proposition 2 (LIND\$ $\Longrightarrow$ LIND). *Let the triple $\boldsymbol{\Pi} = (\boldsymbol{\mathcal{K}}, \boldsymbol{\mathcal{E}}, \boldsymbol{\mathcal{D}})$ be a big-key encryption (BKSE) scheme (see Sect. 2.2). Then for any LIND adversary $\mathscr{B}$, there exists a LIND\$ adversary $\mathscr{B}'$ that makes the same number of RO and ENC queries as $\mathscr{B}$, has the same data complexity as $\mathscr{B}$ and has $\mathbf{Adv}^{\mathrm{lind}}_{\boldsymbol{\Pi}}(\mathscr{B}') \leq 4 \cdot \mathbf{Adv}^{\mathrm{lind\$}}_{\boldsymbol{\Pi}}(\mathscr{B})$*

Proof The proofs first proves that $\mathbf{Adv}_{\Pi}^{\text{lind-ror}}(\mathscr{B}) \leq 2 \cdot \mathbf{Adv}_{\Pi}^{\text{lind\$}}(\mathscr{B}')$ and then relies on proof techniques from Bellare et al. [9, Theorem 1] to show that $\mathbf{Adv}_{\Pi}^{\text{lind}}(\mathscr{B}) \leq 2 \cdot \mathbf{Adv}_{\Pi}^{\text{lind-ror}}(\mathscr{B})$. We present the complete proof in the full version [21]. □

3.2 Security Model

SYNTAX AND SUBVERSIONS. A BKSE scheme $\boldsymbol{\Pi} = (\boldsymbol{\mathcal{K}}, \boldsymbol{\mathcal{E}}, \boldsymbol{\mathcal{D}})$ is now a symmetric scheme defined in Sect. 2, but the keyspace $\boldsymbol{\mathcal{K}} = \{0,1\}^k$ is comprised of "big" keys. In particular, it can now be stateful and can process associated data. We require that $\boldsymbol{\Pi}$ meets the constant stretch and correctness properties. A subversion of a BKSE scheme $\boldsymbol{\Pi} = (\boldsymbol{\mathcal{K}}, \boldsymbol{\mathcal{E}}, \boldsymbol{\mathcal{D}})$ is a triple $\tilde{\boldsymbol{\Pi}} = (\tilde{\mathcal{K}}, \tilde{\boldsymbol{\mathcal{E}}}, \tilde{\mathcal{D}})$ defined in Sect. 2.1. The decryptability condition applies as defined in Sect. 2.1.

SECURITY. We capture the security of BKSE in presence of ASAs and key leakage in the notion SURV-LIND in the ROM. It is a multi-key RoR indistinguishability game that allows Big Brother $\mathscr{B}$ to both choose a leakage function to be applied to the users' big keys and also substitute the encryption algorithm. As in BKR, the leakage from every key $\mathscr{B}$ wishes to attack is computed only once, before $\mathscr{B}$ can ask any encryption queries for this key. We leave the study of adaptive leakage to future work. The name SURV-LIND is a nod to the fact that the notion intends to be an extension of the SURV notion via the SURV-ROR notion that incorporates the LIND notion.

Definition 7 (SURV-LIND). *Let* $\boldsymbol{\Pi} = (\boldsymbol{\mathcal{K}}, \boldsymbol{\mathcal{E}}, \boldsymbol{\mathcal{D}})$ *be a BKSE scheme and* $\tilde{\boldsymbol{\Pi}} = (\tilde{\mathcal{K}}, \tilde{\boldsymbol{\mathcal{E}}}, \tilde{\mathcal{D}})$ *its subversion. We define the advantage of Big Brother* $\mathscr{B}$ *at winning the game* SURV-LIND *(Fig. 7) as* $\mathbf{Adv}_{\boldsymbol{\Pi},\tilde{\boldsymbol{\Pi}}}^{\text{srv-lind}}(\mathscr{B}) = 2\Pr[\text{SURV-LIND}_{\boldsymbol{\Pi},\tilde{\boldsymbol{\Pi}}}^{\mathscr{B}} \Rightarrow 1] - 1$.

A BKSE scheme $\boldsymbol{\Pi}$ is said to be secure against surveillance and key-leakage when this advantage is small for all subversions $\tilde{\boldsymbol{\Pi}}$ of $\boldsymbol{\Pi}$ that meet the decryptability condition and all adversaries $\mathscr{B}$ with reasonable resources.

3.3 Relations with Previous Notions

In this section we show that our SURV-LIND notions implies SURV\$ and LIND\$ security. This and the results of Sect. 3.1 imply that SURV-LIND security implies also SURV security and LIND security. The relations in the other directions are clarified by our impossibility result in Sect. 3.4.

RELATION WITH LIND AND LIND-\$ NOTIONS. Proposition 3 shows that SURV-LIND security implies LIND\$ security, formally establishing that SURV-LIND notion extends the LIND\$ notion. Proposition 2 shows that LIND\$ security implies LIND, therefore SURV-LIND $\Longrightarrow$ LIND, i.e., SURV-LIND formally extends the BKR's LIND notion (Definition 3).

Game $\text{SURV-LIND}^{\mathscr{B}}_{\boldsymbol{\Pi},\tilde{\boldsymbol{\Pi}}}$	Oracle $\text{Enc}(M, A, i)$	Oracle $\text{Leak}(i)$
$\tilde{K} \leftarrow\$ \tilde{\mathcal{K}}$	**if** $(\boldsymbol{K}_i = \bot)$ **then return** $\bot$	**if** $(\boldsymbol{K}_i = \bot)$ **then**
$(\mathsf{Lk}, \sigma) \leftarrow \mathscr{B}^{\text{RO}}(\tilde{K})$	$(C_0, \sigma_i) \leftarrow\$ \tilde{\boldsymbol{\mathcal{E}}}^{\text{RO}}(\tilde{K}, \boldsymbol{K}_i, M, A, \sigma_i, i)$	$\quad \boldsymbol{K}_i \leftarrow\$ \{0,1\}^k$
$b \leftarrow\$ \{0,1\}$	$C_1 \leftarrow\$ \{0,1\}^{\lvert C_0 \rvert}$	$\quad \sigma_i \leftarrow \varepsilon$
$b' \leftarrow \mathscr{B}^{\text{Leak,Enc, RO}}(\tilde{K}, \sigma)$	**return** C_b	$\quad L \leftarrow\$ \mathsf{Lk}^{\text{RO}}(\boldsymbol{K}_i)$
return $(b = b')$		$\quad$ **return** L
		return $\bot$

Fig. 7. Game used to define security of a big-key encryption scheme $\boldsymbol{\Pi} = (\boldsymbol{\mathcal{K}}, \boldsymbol{\mathcal{E}}, \boldsymbol{\mathcal{D}})$ in presence of key exfiltration and algorithm substitution by a subversion $\tilde{\boldsymbol{\Pi}}$. The adversarial leakage function takes $\boldsymbol{K}_i$ as input for $i \in \mathcal{I}$, has access to the RO and outputs a leakage L with $|L| = l$.

Proposition 3 (SURV-LIND $\implies$ LIND\$)**.** *Let* $\boldsymbol{\Pi} = (\boldsymbol{\mathcal{K}}, \boldsymbol{\mathcal{E}}, \boldsymbol{\mathcal{D}})$ *be a BKSE scheme with* $\mathcal{S} = \mathcal{A} = \emptyset$*. Then for any* LIND\$ *adversary* $\mathscr{B}$*, there exists a* SURV-LIND *adversary* $\mathscr{B}'$ *that makes a single* Leak *query, the same number of* RO *and* Enc *queries as* $\mathscr{B}$*, has the same data complexity as* $\mathscr{B}$ *and has* $\mathbf{Adv}^{\text{srv-lind}}_{\boldsymbol{\Pi},\tilde{\boldsymbol{\Pi}}}(\mathscr{B}') = \mathbf{Adv}^{\text{lind-ror}}_{\boldsymbol{\Pi}}(\mathscr{B})$*, where* $\tilde{\boldsymbol{\Pi}} = (\tilde{\mathcal{K}}, \tilde{\boldsymbol{\mathcal{E}}}, \tilde{\mathcal{D}})$ *is a dummy subversion with* $\tilde{\mathcal{K}} = \emptyset$*, and* $\tilde{\boldsymbol{\mathcal{E}}}(\tilde{K}, \boldsymbol{K}, M, A, \sigma, i) = \boldsymbol{\mathcal{E}}(\boldsymbol{K}, M, A, \sigma)$*.*

Proof. Adversary $\mathscr{B}'$ gets the leakage function from $\mathscr{B}$ and uses it as its own. It then picks any identifier i, asks $\text{Leak}(i)$ to obtain the leakage L and passes it to $\mathscr{B}$. Then, $\mathscr{B}'$ answers all Enc queries made by $\mathscr{B}$ with its own oracle, using the identifier i. When $\mathscr{B}$ outputs its final decision, $\mathscr{B}'$ simply forwards it. Because the subverted encryption algorithm $\tilde{\boldsymbol{\mathcal{E}}}$ implements the actual big-key encryption $\boldsymbol{\mathcal{E}}$, the simulation of LIND-ROR game for $\mathscr{B}$ is perfect. □

Relation with SURV Notion. Proposition 3 shows that SURV-LIND $\Rightarrow$ SURV\$. Proposition 1 states that SURV\$ security implies SURV, therefore we have that SURV-LIND $\implies$ SURV, i.e., SURV-LIND formally extends BPR's SURV notion (Definition 2).

Proposition 4 (SURV-LIND $\Rightarrow$ SURV\$)**.** *Let* $\boldsymbol{\Pi} = (\boldsymbol{\mathcal{K}}, \boldsymbol{\mathcal{E}}, \boldsymbol{\mathcal{D}})$ *be a BKSE scheme and* $\tilde{\boldsymbol{\Pi}} = (\tilde{\mathcal{K}}, \tilde{\boldsymbol{\mathcal{E}}}, \tilde{\mathcal{D}})$ *its subversion. Then for any* SURV\$ *adversary* $\mathscr{B}$*, there exists a* SURV-LIND *adversary* $\mathscr{B}'$ *that makes a single* Leak *query to initialize a target key, the same number of* RO *and* Enc *queries as* $\mathscr{B}$*, has the same data complexity as* $\mathscr{B}$ *and has* $\mathbf{Adv}^{\text{srv-lind}}_{\boldsymbol{\Pi},\tilde{\boldsymbol{\Pi}}}(\mathscr{B}') = \mathbf{Adv}^{\text{surv}}_{\boldsymbol{\Pi}}(\mathscr{B})$*.*

Proof. Adversary $\mathscr{B}'$ sets a dummy leakage function. Whenever $\mathscr{B}$ queries the Key oracle with i, $\mathscr{B}'$ forwards the query to its own Leak oracle to initialize $\boldsymbol{K}_i$ and ignores the leakage L that the oracle returns. $\mathscr{B}'$ answers all Enc queries made by $\mathscr{B}$ with its own oracle. Because the Enc oracle of $\mathscr{B}'$ is identical to the Enc oracle of $\mathscr{B}$, the simulation of SURV\$ game for $\mathscr{B}$ is perfect. □

3.4 Defeat by Big Brother

We give a generic attack that achieves a high SURV-LIND advantage for *any* BKSE scheme. We call this attack *derandomization* attack we present it in Fig. 8.

Algorithm $\mathscr{B}_{\mathrm{drnd}}(\tilde{K}, \tau)$

if $(\tau = \bot)$ **then**
  $M \leftarrow\!\!\$\ \{0,1\}^{\nu}$
  return $(\mathsf{Lk}_{i,\tilde{K},M}, M)$
else
  $M \leftarrow \tau$
$i \leftarrow\!\!\$\ \mathcal{I}$
$A \leftarrow \varepsilon$
$L \leftarrow \textsc{Leak}(i)$
$C \leftarrow \textsc{Enc}(M, A, i)$
$b' \leftarrow (L \neq \mathrm{RO}(\langle C \rangle, l))$
return b'

Algorithm $\tilde{\boldsymbol{\mathcal{E}}}^{\mathrm{RO}}(\tilde{K}, \boldsymbol{K}_i, M, A, \sigma, i)$

if $(\sigma = \varepsilon)$ **then**
  $\tilde{\sigma} \leftarrow 0;\ \bar{\sigma} \leftarrow \varepsilon$
else
  parse σ as $\tilde{\sigma}, \bar{\sigma}$; $\tilde{\sigma} \leftarrow \tilde{\sigma} + 1$
$r \leftarrow \mathrm{RO}(\langle i, \tilde{K}, \tilde{\sigma} \rangle, |r|)$
$(C, \bar{\sigma}) \leftarrow \boldsymbol{\mathcal{E}}^{\mathrm{RO}}(\boldsymbol{K}_i, M, A, \sigma; r)$
return $C, \langle \tilde{\sigma}, \bar{\sigma} \rangle$

Algorithm $\mathsf{Lk}^{\mathrm{RO}}_{i,\tilde{K},M}(\boldsymbol{K}_i)$

$\sigma \leftarrow \varepsilon$
$r \leftarrow \mathrm{RO}(\langle i, \tilde{K}, 0 \rangle, |r|)$
$(C, \sigma') \leftarrow \boldsymbol{\mathcal{E}}^{\mathrm{RO}}(\boldsymbol{K}_i, M, \varepsilon, \sigma; r)$
return $\mathrm{RO}(\langle C \rangle, l)$

Fig. 8. The adversary, the leakage function and the subverted encryption algorithm that achieve high SURV-LIND advantage against any BKSE scheme. $\langle \cdot \rangle$ is an efficient, injective encoding and $\nu = \min\{|M| \text{ for } M \in \mathcal{M}\}$.

Proposition 5. *For any BKSE scheme* $\boldsymbol{\Pi} = (\boldsymbol{\mathcal{K}}, \boldsymbol{\mathcal{E}}, \boldsymbol{\mathcal{D}})$ *that has the correctness property, the adversary* $\mathscr{B}_{\mathrm{drnd}}$ *defined in Fig. 8 and the subversion* $\tilde{\boldsymbol{\Pi}} = (\tilde{\mathcal{K}}, \tilde{\boldsymbol{\mathcal{E}}}, \tilde{\mathcal{D}})$ *with* $\tilde{\mathcal{K}} = \{0,1\}^{\kappa}$ *and* $\tilde{\boldsymbol{\mathcal{E}}}$ *defined in Fig. 8, we have* $\mathbf{Adv}^{\mathrm{srv\text{-}lind}}_{\boldsymbol{\Pi},\tilde{\boldsymbol{\Pi}}}(\mathscr{B}_{\mathrm{drnd}}) = 1 - 2^{-l}$, *where* $\mathscr{B}_{\mathrm{drnd}}$ *leaks* l *bits and makes a single* Enc *query and* $\tilde{\boldsymbol{\Pi}}$ *meets the decryptability condition relative to* $\boldsymbol{\Pi}$.

Proof. Both the subverted encryption algorithm in the first Enc query, and the leakage function derive the same coins $r \leftarrow \mathrm{RO}(\langle i, \tilde{K}, 0 \rangle, |r|)$. They also use the same big key, state and associated data when executing the original big-key encryption algorithm. Fixing these inputs turns $\boldsymbol{\mathcal{E}}(\boldsymbol{K}, \cdot, A, \sigma; r)$ into a deterministic injective mapping (otherwise $\boldsymbol{\Pi}$ would be incorrect). Therefore, the result of the leakage function L and the output of the RO applied to $\langle C \rangle$ are different strings with probability $1 - 2^{-l}$. The decryptability is trivial, as the subversion internally uses the actual encryption algorithm. □

$\mathsf{Lk}^{\mathrm{RO}}_{i,\tilde{K},\mathcal{V}}(\boldsymbol{K})$

$\sigma \leftarrow \varepsilon;\ r \leftarrow \mathrm{RO}(\langle i, \tilde{K}, 0\rangle, |r|);\ L \leftarrow \varepsilon$

for $i \leftarrow 1, \ldots, u$ **do**

$\quad (C_i, \sigma') \leftarrow \boldsymbol{\mathcal{E}}^{\mathrm{RO}}(\boldsymbol{K}, V_i, \bar{A}, \sigma; r);\ L \leftarrow L \| C_i$

return $\mathsf{left}_l(L)$

Fig. 9. The leakage function $\mathsf{Lk}^{\mathrm{RO}}_{i,\tilde{K},\mathcal{V}}$ for derandomization in practice. For a string X, $\mathsf{left}_l(X)$ returns the l most significant bits of L if $|L| > l$ and returns L otherwise.

DISCUSSION. There are two possible interpretations of this result. Either the model captures a too strong goal and the derandomization attack has no meaningful implications, or thwarting simultaneous ASAs and KE is impossible without additional tools. We argue that the latter is true. The SURV-LIND notion formalizes a very intuitive and rather modest security goal: to protect confidentiality when faced with Big Brother's tools. In addition, the derandomization attack can easily be translated into the following real-world attack.

DERANDOMIZATION IN PRACTICE. Consider a scenario where a high-value secret message is transmitted in a BKSE ciphertext at the beginning of a communication session. This could be e.g. a user ID sent to an online service during login. The target of the attack is then to identify logins with IDs belonging to a set of "tracked" users $\mathcal{V} \subset \mathcal{W}$, a subset of all user IDs in the system $\mathcal{W}$. Assume the set $\mathcal{V}$ has a canonical ordering $\mathcal{V} = \{V_1, \ldots, V_u\}$.

Big Brother can mount a variant of the derandomization attack to achieve this, using the leakage function $\mathsf{Lk}_{\tilde{K},\mathcal{V}}$ described in Fig. 9. The function uses $\mathsf{left}_l(L)$ instead of a query to the random oracle to return only the allowed l bits from the leakage function. We opt for this approach because in practice the output of any "decent" big-key encryption scheme can be truncated to the l most significant bits with a similar advantage compared to RO-hashing. The leakage function proceeds as follows. A secret V is easily recovered; after capturing a ciphertext C encrypting a V-dependent login, Big Brother partitions the leakage L into $C_1, \ldots, C_{u'}$ and tries to find an i s.t. $C = C_i$. If such i exists, then $V = V_i$, otherwise $V \notin \mathcal{V}$ or the attack fails. If $|L| \leq l$, the attack always succeeds. Otherwise, the probability of a false $V \notin \mathcal{V}$ conclusion is $1 - \lfloor l/|L| \rfloor$. With a leakage of 1 GB, size of an individual ciphertext ≤ 4 KB and success probability 1, 2^{18} users can be identified. Detecting the attack would be difficult, provided the users can only observe the inputs and outputs of the encryption algorithm, as the master key $\tilde{K}$ is used as a high-entropy seed for the generation of coins.

4 Resisting Algorithm Substitution Attacks and Key Exfiltration

We ask: what key property enables the devastating derandomization attack? The answer is the subversion's ability to control the random coins, which allows the leakage function to perform useful computations in advance.

One countermeasure is the use of reverse cryptographic firewalls (RFs) [24, 38]. However, using an RF implicitly assumes trust in its *implementation*, which is problematic—especially for individual users who cannot verify that the RF itself has not been subverted.

Instead, we propose extending the setup with an external source of randomness, forcing the subversion to use its outputs. In other words, we add a new assumption to overcome the negative result of the previous section: a honest source of incorruptible randomness is available to both sender and receiver. In this section we show how, given this additional assumption, we can defeat ASAs and key exfiltration when incorporated into a new big-key symmetric encryption scheme. Our security model explicitly includes this honest randomness source, whose instantiation we describe in Sect. 6.

4.1 BKSE with Sessions

As we will show later, outsourcing randomness generation to a trusted external source (one observable by both the encrypting and decrypting parties) prevents the derandomization attack. However, accessing incorruptible random coins is expensive, making it impractical to use such randomness for the encryption of *every* message—as done in the BKSE construction of BKR.

At the same time, the big key should remain usable over an extended period, since exchanging a symmetric key of ≈ 1 TB is costly. We address this by augmenting BKSE communication sessions: the expensive external randomness is used only to establish a session, after which all messages are processed by other means. This approach is efficient and enables reuse of the large symmetric key.

Syntax. We shift to an API-driven variant of symmetric encryption's syntax. Both the encryption and decryption are now a collection of algorithms (or subroutines) which can pass a state to one another. A BKSE scheme with sessions (BKSS) is a triple $\boldsymbol{\Pi} = (\boldsymbol{\mathcal{K}}, \boldsymbol{\mathcal{E}}, \boldsymbol{\mathcal{D}})$ with $\boldsymbol{\mathcal{K}} = \{0,1\}^k$ the big-key space. We define the message space $\mathcal{M} \subseteq \{0,1\}^*$, the ciphertext space $\mathcal{C} \subseteq \{0,1\}^*$, the associated data space $\mathcal{A} \subseteq \{0,1\}^*$, the space of random seeds $\mathcal{R} \subseteq \{0,1\}^*$ and the state space $\mathcal{S} \subseteq \{0,1\}^*$. We require that $\forall M \in \mathcal{M} : M \in \{0,1\}^m \Rightarrow \{0,1\}^m \subseteq \mathcal{M}$.

The collection of encryption algorithms $\boldsymbol{\mathcal{E}}$ contains two subroutines $\boldsymbol{\mathcal{E}}.\mathsf{Init}$ and $\boldsymbol{\mathcal{E}}.\mathsf{Enc}$. The possibly random and stateful algorithm $\boldsymbol{\mathcal{E}}.\mathsf{Init} : \boldsymbol{\mathcal{K}} \times \mathcal{R} \times \mathcal{S} \rightarrow \mathcal{S}$ maps a big-key, a random seed and the current state $(\boldsymbol{K}, R, \sigma)$ to an updated state $\sigma' \leftarrow\$ \boldsymbol{\mathcal{E}}.\mathsf{Init}(\boldsymbol{K}, R, \sigma)$. Its role is to set up a session (e.g. derive a conventional symmetric key) and store the setup in the state σ. The seed R is intended to be obtained from an external source of randomness There is no other output value than the updated state; the decrypting party is assumed to be using the same external source of randomness. The possibly random and possibly stateful algorithm $\mathcal{E}.\mathsf{Enc} : \mathcal{K} \times \mathcal{M} \times \mathcal{A} \times \mathcal{S} \to \mathcal{C} \times \mathcal{S}$ maps a big-key, a plaintext, associated data and the current state $(\boldsymbol{K}, M, A, \sigma)$ to a ciphertext and an updated state $(C, \sigma') \leftarrow\$ \mathcal{E}.\mathsf{Enc}(\boldsymbol{K}, M, A, \sigma)$. Its role is to encrypt a messages in the session. We require that $\forall(\boldsymbol{K}, M, A, \sigma) \in (\mathcal{K}, \mathcal{M}, \mathcal{A}, \mathcal{S}) : (C, \sigma') \leftarrow\$ \mathcal{E}.\mathsf{Enc}(\boldsymbol{K}, M, A, \sigma) \Rightarrow |C| = |M| + \mu$, with $\mu \geq 0$ the stretch of $\boldsymbol{\Pi}$.

The collection of decryption algorithms $\mathcal{D}$ contains two subroutines $\mathcal{D}.\mathsf{Init}$ and $\mathcal{D}.\mathsf{Dec}$. The deterministic and possibly stateful algorithm $\mathcal{D}.\mathsf{Init} : \mathcal{K} \times \mathcal{R} \times \mathcal{S} \to \mathcal{S}$ maps a big-key, a random seed and the current state $(\boldsymbol{K}, R, \tau)$ to a state $\tau' \leftarrow \mathcal{D}.\mathsf{Init}(\boldsymbol{K}, R, \tau)$. The deterministic and possibly stateful algorithm $\mathcal{D}.\mathsf{Dec} : \mathcal{K} \times \mathcal{C} \times \mathcal{A} \times \mathcal{S} \to \mathcal{M} \cup \{\bot\} \times \mathcal{S}$ maps a big-key, a ciphertext, associated data and the current state $(\boldsymbol{K}, C, A, \tau)$ to a recovered plaintext and an updated state $(M, \tau') \leftarrow \mathcal{D}.\mathsf{Dec}(\boldsymbol{K}, C, A, \tau)$.

Game $\mathrm{CORR}_{\boldsymbol{\Pi}}\left(\boldsymbol{K}, q, R_1^q, \vec{q}, \left(M_{i,1}^{i,\vec{q}[i]}\right)_{i\in[1..q]}, \left(A_{i,1}^{i,\vec{q}[i]}\right)_{i\in[1..q]}\right)$

$\sigma, \tau \leftarrow \bot$
for $i \leftarrow 1, \ldots, q$ **do**
  $\sigma \leftarrow\$ \mathcal{E}.\mathsf{Init}(\boldsymbol{K}, R_i, \sigma)$; $\tau \leftarrow \mathcal{D}.\mathsf{Init}(\boldsymbol{K}, R_i, \tau)$
  for $j \leftarrow 1, \ldots, \vec{q}[i]$ **do**
    $(C_{i,j}, \sigma) \leftarrow\$ \mathcal{E}.\mathsf{Enc}(\boldsymbol{K}, M_{i,j}, A_{i,j}, \sigma)$; $(M'_{i,j}, \tau) \leftarrow \mathcal{D}.\mathsf{Dec}(\boldsymbol{K}, C_{i,j}, A_{i,j}, \tau)$
return $(\forall i, j\colon C_{i,j} \neq \bot) \wedge \left(\exists i, j\colon M_{i,j} \neq M'_{i,j}\right)$

Fig. 10. Game used to define correctness of a BKSS scheme $\boldsymbol{\Pi}$. We use the notation $R_1^q = (R_1, \ldots, R_q)$ and $M_{i,1}^{i,\vec{q}[i]} = (M_{i,1}, \ldots, M_{i,\vec{q}[i]})$ for compactness.

Correctness. The algorithms $\mathcal{E}.\mathsf{Init}$ and $\mathcal{D}.\mathsf{Init}$ are assumed to be executed synchronously, i.e., they should always use the same externally-generated seed. This assumption is embedded in the correctness condition; when the encrypting party encrypts a sequence of plaintexts partitioned into sessions and the decrypting party decrypts the resulting sequence of ciphertexts in order, partitioned in the same way and using the same seeds, the decrypting party will get the same sequence of plaintexts. Definition 8 formalizes this concept.

Definition 8 (Correctenss of BKSS). *A scheme* $\boldsymbol{\Pi} = (\mathcal{K}, \mathcal{E}, \mathcal{D})$ *is correct if*

$$\forall \boldsymbol{K} \in \mathcal{K},\ \forall q \in \mathbb{N}_{>0},\ \forall (R_1, \ldots, R_q) \in \mathcal{R}^q,\ \forall \vec{q} \in \mathbb{N}^q,$$
$$\forall((M_{1,1}, \ldots, M_{1,\vec{q}[1]}), \ldots, (M_{1,q}, \ldots, M_{1,\vec{q}[q]})) \in \mathcal{M}^{\vec{q}[1]} \times \ldots \times \mathcal{M}^{\vec{q}[q]},$$
$$\forall((A_{1,1}, \ldots, A_{1,\vec{q}[1]}), \ldots, (A_{1,q}, \ldots, A_{1,\vec{q}[q]})) \in \mathcal{A}^{\vec{q}[1]} \times \ldots \mathcal{A}^{\vec{q}[q]}$$

the $\mathrm{CORR}_{\boldsymbol{\Pi}}$ *game shown in Fig. 10 returns* 1 *with probability zero.*

Subversions. A subversion of a BKSS scheme $\boldsymbol{\Pi}$ is a triple $\tilde{\boldsymbol{\Pi}} = (\tilde{\mathcal{K}}, \tilde{\boldsymbol{\mathcal{E}}}, \tilde{\mathcal{D}})$. $\tilde{\mathcal{K}}$, the space of (conventional) master-keys, is a finite nonempty set.

The collection of subverted encryption algorithms $\tilde{\boldsymbol{\mathcal{E}}}$ contains two subroutines $\tilde{\boldsymbol{\mathcal{E}}}.\mathsf{Init}$ and $\tilde{\boldsymbol{\mathcal{E}}}.\mathsf{Enc}$. The subverted initialization subroutine $\tilde{\boldsymbol{\mathcal{E}}}.\mathsf{Init} : \tilde{\mathcal{K}} \times \boldsymbol{\mathcal{K}} \times \mathcal{R} \times \tilde{\mathcal{S}} \times \mathcal{I} \to \tilde{\mathcal{S}}$ is a possibly randomized and stateful algorithm that maps a six-tuple of strings $(\tilde{K}, \boldsymbol{K}, R, \sigma, \iota)$ to an updated state σ'. The input ι represents some public information from a set of public user-identifiers $\mathcal{I}$. Note that the state space $\tilde{\mathcal{S}}$ of the subversion may differ from the original state space $\mathcal{S}$. The possibly randomized and stateful subverted encryption subroutine $\tilde{\boldsymbol{\mathcal{E}}}.\mathsf{Enc} : \tilde{\mathcal{K}} \times \boldsymbol{\mathcal{K}} \times \mathcal{M} \times \mathcal{A} \times \tilde{\mathcal{S}} \times \mathcal{I} \to \mathcal{C} \times \tilde{\mathcal{S}}$ maps a tuple of strings $(\tilde{K}, \boldsymbol{K}, M, A, \sigma, i)$ to a ciphertext and an updated state (C, σ').

The deterministic plaintext-recovery algorithm $\tilde{\mathcal{D}} : \tilde{\mathcal{K}} \times (\mathcal{C}^*)^* \times (\mathcal{A}^*)^* \times \mathcal{R}^* \times \mathcal{I} \to \mathcal{M}^* \cup \{\perp\}$ now works over vectors of vectors of ciphertexts and of associated data, because the grouping of ciphertexts into sessions can be meaningful for $\tilde{\mathcal{D}}$. It also accepts a vector of random seeds. The goal of the algorithm is to produce a vector of recovered plaintexts. We do not study the plaintext recovery any further, as our main goal is to rule out existence of *any* such $\tilde{\mathcal{D}}$.

Decryptability. We define a BKSS variant of BPR's decryptability condition (Sect. 2.1). A subversion $\tilde{\boldsymbol{\Pi}} = (\tilde{\mathcal{K}}, \tilde{\boldsymbol{\mathcal{E}}}, \tilde{\mathcal{D}})$ is decryptable relative to the original scheme $\boldsymbol{\Pi} = (\boldsymbol{\mathcal{K}}, \boldsymbol{\mathcal{E}}, \boldsymbol{\mathcal{D}})$ if $(\tilde{K} \times \boldsymbol{K}, \tilde{\boldsymbol{\mathcal{E}}}, \boldsymbol{\mathcal{D}}')$ is a correct BKSS scheme, where $\boldsymbol{\mathcal{D}}'.\mathsf{Init}((\tilde{K}, \boldsymbol{K}), R, \tau) = \boldsymbol{\mathcal{D}}.\mathsf{Init}(\boldsymbol{K}, R, \tau)$ and $\boldsymbol{\mathcal{D}}'.\mathsf{Dec}((\tilde{K}, \boldsymbol{K}), C, A, \sigma) = \boldsymbol{\mathcal{D}}.\mathsf{Dec}(\boldsymbol{K}, C, A, \sigma)$.

Security Notion. The security notion RESIST (Definition 9, Fig. 11) formalizes the confidentiality of a BKSS scheme used with *external*, uncontestable randomness in the presence of simultaneous ASAs and key exfiltration in the ROM. Our goal is to relate the (in)security of a BKSS scheme to that of a randomness-generation protocol and an encryption scheme Π. For now, we abstract away the details of the randomness-generation protocol and instead sample honest randomness; we will discuss how to instantiate such a protocol in Sect. 6.

In the RESIST game (Fig. 11), Big Brother $\mathscr{B}$ receives the master key $\tilde{K}$ and has access to the random oracle RO. It first outputs a leakage function Lk and a state τ. Then, $\mathscr{B}$ inputs τ and may query: (1) the Leak oracle to obtain leakage on (possibly multiple) big keys; (2) the Init oracle to initiate sessions; (3) the Enc oracle to make real-or-random (RoR) encryption queries. Finally, $\mathscr{B}$ outputs a guess b'.

When $\mathscr{B}$ makes an Init query, another instance of $\mathscr{B}$ is run to tamper with the protocol that generates the seed for that session. For now, we assume this protocol samples honest randomness and is beyond adversarial control. Later, we show how to ensure incorruptible randomness even when the adversary tampers with the protocol.

To model this, the Generate oracle returns a randomness value R, which may be $\perp$ to reflect adversarial tampering. We assume adversarial tampering at this stage already to generalize our approach and because in Sect. 6 we show how to achieve uncontestable randomness generation using a protocol that the adversary can tamper with. If $\mathscr{B}$ is caught tampering with the protocol, the game aborts and $\mathscr{B}$ loses.

This introduces a technical complication: defining the advantage in the usual way (as in IND-CPA in Sect. 2) is insufficient, because the RESIST game has three possible outcomes: 0, 1, and abort. To address this, we adopt the advantage function from Vaudenay [51], which elegantly accounts for all outcomes: the advantage is small either if $\mathscr{B}$ causes too many aborts or if it performs poorly at guessing b when the game proceeds normally.

Definition 9. *Let $\boldsymbol{\Pi} = (\boldsymbol{\mathcal{K}}, \boldsymbol{\mathcal{E}}, \boldsymbol{\mathcal{D}})$ be a BKSS scheme and $\tilde{\boldsymbol{\Pi}} = (\tilde{\mathcal{K}}, \tilde{\boldsymbol{\mathcal{E}}}, \tilde{\mathcal{D}})$ a corresponding subversion. Let $\mathscr{B}$ be an adversary playing* RESIST, *shown Fig. 11. $\mathscr{B}$'s advantage in winning the game is defined as*

$$\mathbf{Adv}^{\mathrm{resist}}_{\boldsymbol{\Pi},\tilde{\boldsymbol{\Pi}}}(\mathscr{B}) = \Pr\left[\mathrm{RESIST}^{\mathscr{B}}_{\boldsymbol{\Pi},\tilde{\boldsymbol{\Pi}}} \Rightarrow 1\right] - \Pr\left[\mathrm{RESIST}^{\mathscr{B}}_{\boldsymbol{\Pi},\tilde{\boldsymbol{\Pi}}} \Rightarrow 0\right].$$

We say that a BKSS scheme $\boldsymbol{\Pi}$ resists simultaneous ASAs and KE if the advantage $\mathbf{Adv}^{\mathrm{resist}}_{\boldsymbol{\Pi},\tilde{\boldsymbol{\Pi}}}(\mathscr{B})$ is small for all adversaries with reasonable resources and any subversion $\tilde{\boldsymbol{\Pi}}$ that is decryptable with respect to $\boldsymbol{\Pi}$.

Game $\mathrm{RESIST}^{\mathscr{B}}_{\boldsymbol{\Pi},\tilde{\boldsymbol{\Pi}}}$	Oracle $\textsc{Enc}(M, A, i)$
$\vec{\boldsymbol{K}}_i, \sigma_i \leftarrow \bot$ everywhere	**if** $(\sigma_i = \bot)$ **then return** $\bot$
$\tilde{K} \leftarrow\$ \tilde{\mathcal{K}}$	$C_0, \sigma_i \leftarrow\$ \tilde{\boldsymbol{\mathcal{E}}}.\mathsf{Enc}^{\mathrm{RO}}(\tilde{K}, \boldsymbol{K}_i, M, A, \sigma_i, i)$
$(\mathsf{Lk}, \tau) \leftarrow\$ \mathscr{B}^{\mathrm{RO}}(\tilde{K})$	$C_1 \leftarrow\$ \{0,1\}^{\lvert C_0 \rvert}$
$b \leftarrow\$ \{0,1\}$	**return** C_b
$b' \leftarrow\$ \mathscr{B}^{\textsc{Leak},\textsc{Init},\textsc{Enc},\mathrm{RO}}(\tilde{K}, \tau)$	Oracle $\textsc{Init}(i)$
return $(b = b')$	**if** $(\boldsymbol{K}_i = \bot)$ **then return** $\bot$
Oracle $\textsc{Leak}(i)$	$R \leftarrow\$ \textsc{Generate}()$
if $(\boldsymbol{K}_i \neq \bot)$ **then return** $\bot$	**if** $R = \bot$ **then** abort
$\boldsymbol{K}_i \leftarrow\$ \boldsymbol{\mathcal{K}}$	$\sigma_i \leftarrow\$ \tilde{\boldsymbol{\mathcal{E}}}.\mathsf{Init}^{\mathrm{RO}}(\tilde{K}, \boldsymbol{K}_i, R, \sigma_i, i)$
$L \leftarrow\$ \mathsf{Lk}^{\mathrm{RO}}(\boldsymbol{K}_i)$	**return** R
return L	Procedure $\textsc{Generate}()$
	$R \leftarrow\$ \mathcal{R}$
	return R

Fig. 11. The game RESIST.

Discussion. The game RESIST covers both the BKSS security and generation of external randomness, so the adversarial advantage covers all attack vectors of Big Brother. We purposefully avoid to specify the source of randomness at this stage to maintain modularity. We will explore later in this work how to instantiate the scheme with a concrete source of randomness. If the RESIST advantage is provably low for a scheme Π, then Π paired with a protocol that provides incorruptible randomness will resist to any leakage function and any subversion. As BKR, we assume that an APT exfiltrates the leakage *before* all of the communication takes place. This assumption is shared with BKR.

5 A BKSS Construction

We design a BKSS construction SES (for symmetric encryption with sessions). SES combines a symmetric encryption scheme with unique ciphertexts with BKR's key encapsulation algorithm XKEY in a way that is provably RESIST-secure. The high-level intuition is simple: XKEY is used with a honest externally-generated seed to derive a conventional symmetric key, and a symmetric encryption scheme with unique ciphertexts is used with this key to secure a session.

THE SCHEME. SES takes four parameters: a conventional symmetric encryption scheme $\Pi = (\mathcal{K}, \mathcal{E}, \mathcal{D})$ with $\mathcal{K} = \{0,1\}^{\kappa}$, and positive integers k, P, h. The BKSS scheme $\mathsf{SES}[\Pi, k, P] = (\boldsymbol{\mathcal{K}}, \boldsymbol{\mathcal{E}}, \boldsymbol{\mathcal{D}})$ has $\boldsymbol{\mathcal{K}} = \{0,1\}^{k}$ with k a "big" power of two, and the encryption and decryption subroutines as defined in Fig. 12.

Algorithm $\boldsymbol{\mathcal{E}}.\mathsf{Init}^{\mathrm{RO}}(\boldsymbol{K}, R, \sigma)$

$K \leftarrow \mathsf{XKEY}^{\mathrm{RO}}_{k,\kappa,P}(\boldsymbol{K}, R)$
$\sigma \leftarrow K \| \varepsilon$
return σ

Algorithm $\boldsymbol{\mathcal{D}}.\mathsf{Init}^{\mathrm{RO}}(\boldsymbol{K}, R, \tau)$

$K \leftarrow \mathsf{XKEY}^{\mathrm{RO}}_{k,\kappa,P}(\boldsymbol{K}, R)$
$\tau \leftarrow K \| \varepsilon$
return τ

Algorithm $\boldsymbol{\mathcal{E}}.\mathsf{Enc}^{\mathrm{RO}}(\boldsymbol{K}, M, A, \sigma)$

parse $K \| \bar{\sigma} \leftarrow \sigma$
$C, \bar{\sigma} \leftarrow\!\!\$\ \mathcal{E}(K, M, A, \bar{\sigma})$
$\sigma \leftarrow K \| \bar{\sigma}$
return C, σ

Algorithm $\boldsymbol{\mathcal{D}}.\mathsf{Dec}^{\mathrm{RO}}(\boldsymbol{K}, C, A, \tau)$

parse $K \| \bar{\tau} \leftarrow \tau$
$M, \bar{\tau} \leftarrow\!\!\$\ \mathcal{D}(K, C, A, \bar{\tau})$
$\tau \leftarrow K \| \bar{\tau}$
return M, τ

Algorithm $\mathsf{XKEY}^{\mathrm{RO}}_{k,\kappa,P}(\boldsymbol{K}, R)$

for $i \leftarrow 1, \ldots, P$ **do**
  $\overrightarrow{P}[i] \leftarrow \mathrm{RO}(\langle R, i, 0\rangle, \log_2(k))$
$J \leftarrow \boldsymbol{K}[\overrightarrow{P}]$
$K \leftarrow \mathrm{RO}(\langle R, J, 1\rangle, \kappa)$
return K

Fig. 12. The BKSS scheme $\mathsf{SES}[\Pi, k, P] = (\boldsymbol{\mathcal{K}}, \boldsymbol{\mathcal{E}}, \boldsymbol{\mathcal{D}})$ with $\boldsymbol{\mathcal{K}} = \{0,1\}^{k}$ and $\Pi = (\mathcal{K}, \mathcal{E}, \mathcal{D})$ be a conventional symmetric encryption scheme with unique ciphertexts, such that $\mathcal{K} = \{0,1\}^{\kappa}$.

RESIST SECURITY OF SES. Theorem 1 shows that SES teamed-up with an incorruptible source of honest randomness is provably resistant to simultaneous ASA and KE. We refer by "queries made in the first stage" to the queries made by $\mathscr{B}$ to RO before it outputs the leakage function Lk and all queries made by the leakage function Lk to those oracle during all the LEAK queries. The "queries made in the second stage" are all the subsequent queries $\mathscr{B}$ makes to RO.

In the following, we let the term "session" refer to a $\mathscr{B}$'s $\textsc{Init}(\iota, \hat{\tau})$ query and all subsequent $\textsc{Enc}(M, A, \iota)$ queries with the same identifier ι, until another INIT query is made with the same ι; j^{th} session in the RESIST game means the session started by j^{th} INIT query made by $\mathscr{B}$.

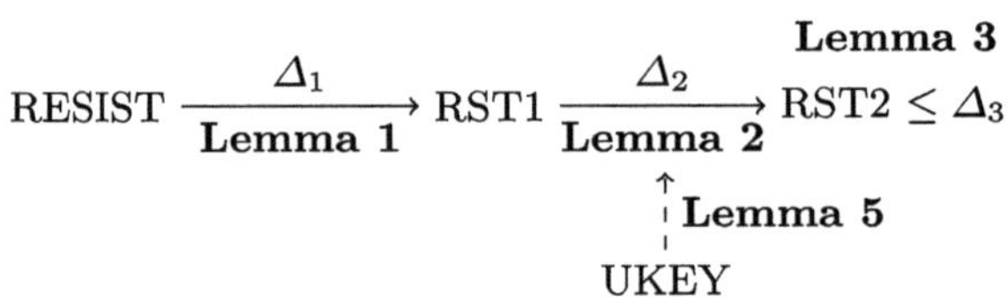

Fig. 13. An overview of the proofs of Theorem 1 and Theorem 2.

Theorem 1. *Let $\Pi = (\mathcal{K}, \mathcal{E}, \mathcal{D})$ be an encryption scheme with unique ciphertexts with $\mathcal{K} = \{0,1\}^{\kappa}$. Let k, P, h be positive integers. Let $\boldsymbol{\Pi} = \mathsf{SES}[\Pi, k, P]$ and Let $\tilde{\boldsymbol{\Pi}} = (\tilde{\mathcal{K}}, \tilde{\boldsymbol{\mathcal{E}}}, \tilde{\mathcal{D}})$ be a subversion of $\boldsymbol{\Pi}$ that meets the decryptability condition. Let $\mathscr{B}$ be an adversary. Then*

$$\mathbf{Adv}^{\text{resist}}_{\boldsymbol{\Pi},\tilde{\boldsymbol{\Pi}},h,p,\ell}(\mathscr{B}) \leq \Delta_1 + \Delta_2 + \Delta_3,$$

with $\Delta_1 = 0$, $\Delta_2 = 2 \cdot q_K \cdot \mathbf{Adv}^{\text{ukey}}_{\mathsf{XKEY}}(\mathscr{A})$, $\Delta_3 = 2 \cdot q_I \cdot \mathbf{Adv}^{\text{ind\$}}_{\Pi}(\mathscr{A}')$, if $\mathscr{B}$ leaks at most l bits, makes at most q_K LEAK queries, at most q_I INIT queries, makes no more than q_E ENC queries which process no more than d bits of data in a session, makes at most q_1 and q_2 queries to RO in the first and the second stage respectively, such that $q = q_1{+}q_2$, and runs in time t. Let $r = (q{+}q_K{+}q_I{+}q_E{+}d)$. The UKEY adversary $\mathscr{A}$ makes at most q_K DERIVE queries and runs in time $t + \gamma \cdot r$ for a positive constant γ. The IND\$-CPA adversary $\mathscr{A}'$ makes at most q_E encryption queries with total data bounded by d bits and runs in time $t + \gamma' \cdot r$ for a positive constant γ'.

Proof. The proof is based on a hybrid argument, with hybrids RST1 and RST2 defined in Fig. 14. The high level overview of the proof is depicted in Fig. 13. Setting RST0 = RESIST, we have

$$\mathbf{Adv}^{\text{resist}}_{\boldsymbol{\Pi},\tilde{\boldsymbol{\Pi}}}(\mathscr{B}) = \Pr\left[\text{RST2}^{\mathscr{B}}_{\boldsymbol{\Pi},\tilde{\boldsymbol{\Pi}}} \Rightarrow 1\right] - \Pr\left[\text{RST2}^{\mathscr{B}}_{\boldsymbol{\Pi},\tilde{\boldsymbol{\Pi}}} \Rightarrow 0\right]$$
$$+ \sum_{i=1}^{2} \sum_{\beta=0}^{1} (-1)^{1-\beta} (\Pr\left[\text{RST}(i-1)^{\mathscr{B}}_{\boldsymbol{\Pi},\tilde{\boldsymbol{\Pi}}} \Rightarrow \beta\right] - \Pr\left[\text{RST}i^{\mathscr{B}}_{\boldsymbol{\Pi},\tilde{\boldsymbol{\Pi}}} \Rightarrow \beta\right]).$$

Theorem 2 follows from triangular inequality after upper-bounding the inner sum for $i = 1$ (Lemma 1 yields Δ_1) and for $i = 2$ (Lemma 2 yields Δ_2), and upper-bounding the term $\Pr[\mathrm{RST2}^{\mathscr{B}}_{\boldsymbol{\Pi},\tilde{\boldsymbol{\Pi}}} \Rightarrow 1] - \Pr[\mathrm{RST2}^{\mathscr{B}}_{\boldsymbol{\Pi},\tilde{\boldsymbol{\Pi}}} \Rightarrow 0]$ (Lemma 3 yields Δ_3). □

Game $\mathrm{RST1}^{\mathscr{B}}_{\boldsymbol{\Pi},\tilde{\boldsymbol{\Pi}}}$, $\boxed{\mathrm{RST2}^{\mathscr{B}}_{\boldsymbol{\Pi},\tilde{\boldsymbol{\Pi}}}}$	Oracle $\textsc{Enc}(M, A, i)$
$\overrightarrow{\boldsymbol{K}}_i, \sigma_i \leftarrow \bot$ everywhere $\tilde{K} \leftarrow\$ \tilde{\mathcal{K}}$ $(\mathsf{Lk}, \tau) \leftarrow\$ \mathscr{B}^{\mathrm{RO}}(\tilde{K})$ $b \leftarrow\$ \{0,1\}$ $b' \leftarrow\$ \mathscr{B}^{\textsc{Leak},\textsc{Init},\textsc{Enc},\mathrm{RO}}(\tilde{K}, \tau)$ **return** $(b = b')$ Oracle $\textsc{Leak}(i)$ **if** $(\boldsymbol{K}_i \neq \bot)$ **then return** $\bot$ $\boldsymbol{K}_i \leftarrow\$ \boldsymbol{\mathcal{K}}$ $L \leftarrow\$ \mathsf{Lk}^{\mathrm{RO}}(\boldsymbol{K}_i)$ **return** L	**if** $(\sigma_i = \bot)$ **then return** $\bot$ $C_0, \sigma_i \leftarrow\$ \boldsymbol{\mathcal{E}}.\mathsf{Enc}^{\mathrm{RO}}(\boldsymbol{K}_i, M, A, \sigma_i)$ $C_1 \leftarrow\$ \{0,1\}^{\lvert C_0 \rvert}$ **return** C Oracle $\textsc{Init}(i, \hat{\tau})$ **if** $(\boldsymbol{K}_i = \bot)$ **then return** $\bot$ $\hat{\tau}, R \leftarrow\$ \textsc{Generate}(\hat{\tau})$ **if** $(R = \bot)$ **then abort** $\sigma_i \leftarrow\$ \boldsymbol{\mathcal{E}}.\mathsf{Init}^{\mathrm{RO}}(\boldsymbol{K}_i, R, \sigma_i)$ $\boxed{K \leftarrow\$ \{0,1\}^{\kappa}; \sigma_i \leftarrow K \Vert \varepsilon}$ **return** $\hat{\tau}, R$ Procedure $\textsc{Generate}(\hat{\tau})$ $R \leftarrow\$ \mathcal{R}$ **return** $\hat{\tau}, R$

Fig. 14. The games RST1 (without the boxed statement) and $\boxed{\text{RST2}}$. The lines that differ from RESIST are marked with in grey. In RST1, we replace $\tilde{\boldsymbol{\Pi}}$ by the original scheme $\boldsymbol{\Pi}$. In RST2, we additionally sample the derived keys uniformly.

Lemma 1. *Let Π be an encryption scheme with unique ciphertexts with $\mathcal{K} = \{0,1\}^{\kappa}$. Let k and P be positive integers. Let $\boldsymbol{\Pi} = \mathsf{SES}[\Pi, k, P]$. Let $\tilde{\boldsymbol{\Pi}} = (\tilde{\mathcal{K}}, \tilde{\boldsymbol{\mathcal{E}}}, \tilde{\mathcal{D}})$ be a subversion of $\boldsymbol{\Pi}$ that meets the decryptability condition. Then for any adversary $\mathscr{B}$ and any $\beta \in \{0,1\}$ we have that*

$$\Pr\left[\mathrm{RESIST}^{\mathscr{B}}_{\boldsymbol{\Pi},\tilde{\boldsymbol{\Pi}}} \Rightarrow \beta\right] = \Pr\left[\mathrm{RST1}^{\mathscr{B}}_{\boldsymbol{\Pi},\tilde{\boldsymbol{\Pi}}} \Rightarrow \beta\right],$$

which implies that $\Delta_1 = 0$.

Proof. The proof shows that a subversion of $\mathsf{SES}[\Pi, k, P]$ for which the decryptability condition holds always outputs the same ciphertexts as the original scheme $\mathsf{SES}[\Pi, k, P]$ would, in any possible sequence of sessions. We present the complete proof in the full version of this work [21]. □

We use the incorruptible randomness R to seed XKEY, a setting that is not treated by BKR. We define the notion UKEY (Definition 10) that captures the security of big-key encapsulation paired with an incorruptible-randomness protocol, that, as before, we abstract away for now by sampling randomness directly in GENERATE. Note that UKEY aborts if $\mathscr{A}$ is caught cheating.

Definition 10. *Let $\boldsymbol{\mathcal{S}}$ be a big-key encapsulation scheme. Let $\mathscr{A}$ be an adversary playing* UKEY *(Fig. 15). $\mathscr{A}$'s advantage in winning the game is defined as*

$$\mathbf{Adv}_{\boldsymbol{\mathcal{S}}}^{\mathrm{ukey}}(\mathscr{A}) = \Pr\left[\mathrm{UKEY}_{\boldsymbol{\mathcal{S}}}^{\mathscr{A}} \Rightarrow 1\right] - \Pr\left[\mathrm{UKEY}_{\boldsymbol{\mathcal{S}}}^{\mathscr{A}} \Rightarrow 0\right].$$

Lemma 2. *Let $\Pi = (\mathcal{K}, \mathcal{E}, \mathcal{D})$ be an encryption scheme with unique ciphertexts with $\mathcal{K} = \{0,1\}^{\kappa}$. Let k and P be positive integers. Let $\boldsymbol{\Pi} = \mathsf{SES}[\Pi, k, P]$. Assume that the Let $\mathscr{B}$ be an adversary that leaks at most l bits, makes at most q_k* LEAK *queries, at most q_I* INIT *queries, no more than q_E* ENC *queries which process no more than d bits of data in a session, makes at most q_1 and q_2 queries to the oracles in $\boldsymbol{\mathcal{O}}$ in the first and the second stage respectively, with $q = q_1 + q_2$, has computational resources limited by c and runs in time t. Then*

$$\left|\sum_{\beta=0}^{1}(-1)^{1-\beta}\left(\Pr\left[\mathrm{RST1}_{\boldsymbol{\Pi},\tilde{\boldsymbol{\Pi}}}^{\mathscr{B}} \Rightarrow \beta\right] - \Pr\left[\mathrm{RST2}_{\boldsymbol{\Pi},\tilde{\boldsymbol{\Pi}}}^{\mathscr{B}} \Rightarrow \beta\right]\right)\right| \leq 2 \cdot q_k \cdot \mathbf{Adv}_{\mathsf{XKEY}_{k,\kappa,P}}^{\mathrm{ukey}}(\mathscr{A})$$

for an adversary $\mathscr{A}$ that leaks at most l bits, makes no more than q_I DERIVE *queries, and makes no more that q_1 and q_2 queries to the oracles in $\boldsymbol{\mathcal{O}}$ in the first and the second phase respectively.*

Proof. The proof is based on a hybrid argument. Assuming that $\mathscr{B}$ queries the LEAK oracle with q_k identifiers, we define $q_k + 1$ hybrids RST1.j for $j = 0, \ldots, q_k$. In the game RST1.j, the queries $\mathrm{INIT}(\hat{\tau}, \iota_u)$ are processed as in RST2 (the derived key K is uniform) for $1 \leq u \leq j$, while for $j < u \leq q_k$ they are processed as in RST1 (K is derived using XKEY). We present the complete proof in the full version [21]. □

Lemma 3. *Let $\Pi = (\mathcal{K}, \mathcal{E}, \mathcal{D})$ be an encryption scheme with unique ciphertexts with $\mathcal{K} = \kappa$. Let k and P be positive integers. Let $\boldsymbol{\Pi} = \mathsf{SES}[\Pi, k, P]$. Let $\mathscr{B}$, be an adversary playing game* RST2 *(Fig. 14) that leaks at most l bits, makes at most q_k* LEAK *queries, at most q_I* INIT *queries, makes no more than q_E* ENC *queries which process no more than d bits of data in a session, makes at most q_1 and q_2 queries to* RO *in the first and the second stage respectively, has computational resources limited by c and runs in time t. Then we have*

$$\Pr\left[\mathrm{RST2}_{\boldsymbol{\Pi},\tilde{\boldsymbol{\Pi}}}^{\mathscr{B}} \Rightarrow 1\right] - \Pr\left[\mathrm{RST2}_{\boldsymbol{\Pi},\tilde{\boldsymbol{\Pi}}}^{\mathscr{B}} \Rightarrow 0\right] \leq 2 \cdot q_I \cdot \mathbf{Adv}_{\Pi}^{\mathrm{ind\$}}(\mathscr{A}),$$

for an IND\$-CPA *adversary $\mathscr{A}$ that makes at most q_E encryption queries with total data complexity bounded by d bits and runs in time $t + \gamma \cdot (q_1 + q_2 + q_K + q_I + q_E + d)$ for some positive constant γ.*

Proof. The proof uses an hybrid argument on the q_I sessions that the adversary spawns by calling the INIT oracle. The complete proof is in the full version [21]. □

Game $\text{UKEY}_{\boldsymbol{S}}^{\mathscr{A}}$	Oracle DERIVE	Procedure GENERATE()
$(\mathsf{Lk}, \sigma) \leftarrow \mathscr{A}^{\boldsymbol{\mathcal{O}}}$	$R \leftarrow_\$ \text{GENERATE}()$	$R \leftarrow_\$ \mathcal{R}$
$\boldsymbol{K} \leftarrow_\$ \{0,1\}^k$	**if** $(R = \bot)$ **then abort**	**return** R
$L \leftarrow \mathsf{Lk}^{\boldsymbol{\mathcal{O}}}(\boldsymbol{K})$	**if** $(b = 0)$ **then**	
$b \leftarrow_\$ \{0,1\}$	$\quad K \leftarrow_\$ \{0,1\}^\kappa$	
$b' \leftarrow \mathscr{A}^{\text{DERIVE}, \mathbf{O}}(L, \sigma)$	**else**	
return $(b = b')$	$\quad K \leftarrow \boldsymbol{S}^{\text{RO}}(\boldsymbol{K}, R)$	
	return R, K	

Fig. 15. Game capturing security of big-key encapsulation with selectors generated by some source of incorruptible randomness, where $\boldsymbol{\mathcal{O}} = \{\text{RO}, \text{RO'}\}$.

6 Uncontestable Random Number Generation

In this section, we show how to design a protocol that enables provably uncontestable random number generation, thus providing the final component needed to achieve security against coordinated algorithm substitution attacks and key exfiltration.

The first concept of a public randomness source was the *random beacon*, introduced by Rabin [43]. A random beacon is an online service that broadcasts unpredictable random values at regular intervals—e.g., the NIST randomness beacon [41]. The problem with such beacons is the lack of verifiability: we cannot tell whether they are secretly controlled by Big Brother and must simply trust them. This trust requirement is unacceptable when facing an adversary with the resources and influence to compromise such infrastructure.

Instead, we adopt a protocol by Lenstra and Wesolowski (LW) [36], called unicorn, which offers *provably uncontestable* randomness generation. The protocol is interactive and allows a variable number of parties to jointly sample a common random value, with each participant able to verify that no tampering occurred—without trusting the others. We adapt unicorn to fit our security model by modifying its syntax, while preserving the underlying computation.

6.1 The unicorn Protocol

ALGORITHMS, PARTICIPANTS AND MESSAGES. In the rest of the section, we let $\mathfrak{P}$ denote the unicorn protocol. $\mathfrak{P}$ uses the following algorithms:

- A hash-based commitment algorithm $\mathfrak{P}.\mathsf{commit}^H : \{0,1\}^* \rightarrow \{0,1\}^h$ that computes a commitment $c \in \{0,1\}^h$ for a seed $s \in \{0,1\}^*$, using a conventional hash function $H : \{0,1\}^* \rightarrow \{0,1\}^h$. commit must be either randomized or use a RO.
- A slow-timed, verifiable hash function $\mathfrak{P}.\mathsf{SH}^{H,p,\ell,\theta} : \{0,1\}^* \rightarrow \{0,1\}^h \times \mathcal{W}$ that maps a seed $s \in \{0,1\}^*$ to a fixed sized output $g \in \{0,1\}^h$ and a

witness from the set of witnesses $w \in \mathcal{W}$. The algorithm SH is parametrized by a conventional hash function $H : \{0,1\}^* \rightarrow \{0,1\}^h$, a prime number p with $p \geq 2^h$ and $p \equiv 3 \pmod 4$, a positive integer ℓ, and a permutation $\theta : \mathbb{Z}_p^* \rightarrow \mathbb{Z}_p^*$.
- A verification algorithm $\mathfrak{P}.\mathsf{ver}^{H,p,\ell,\theta} : \{0,1\}^* \times \{0,1\}^h \times \{0,1\}^h \times \mathcal{W} \rightarrow \{0,1\}$ that takes a seed $s \in \{0,1\}^*$, a commitment $c \in \{0,1\}^h$, a value $g \in \{0,1\}^h$ and a witness $w \in \mathcal{W}$ and outputs a single bit that indicates if $c = \mathsf{commit}(s)$ and $g, w = \mathsf{SH}(s)$. The algorithm ver is parametrized by a conventional hash function $H : \{0,1\}^* \rightarrow \{0,1\}^h$, a prime number p with $\log_2(p) \geq h$, a positive integer ℓ, and a permutation $\theta : \mathbb{Z}_p \rightarrow \mathbb{Z}_p$

The three algorithms used in unicorn are described in detail in full version [21]. We let $\mathfrak{P}^{H,p,\ell,\theta}$ denote the instance of the unicorn protocol parametrized by H, p, ℓ, and θ. We omit some of the parameters, if they are implicit from the context.

There are two types of participants in a $\mathfrak{P}$, a single participant P_0 that carries out the computation, and n seed-contributing participants $P_1, \ldots, P_n$. An execution of a $\mathfrak{P}$ proceeds in three, time-limited phases.

The first is the collection phase, taking place between wall-clock times t_{-1} and t_0, in which each participant sends their seed-contribution to P_0. Next, in the commitment phase, taking place between times t_0 and t_1, P_0 completes the seed with their own contribution, commits to the complete seed and broadcasts the commitment. Finally, in the generation phase which takes place between times t_1 and t_2, P_0 computes the verifiable hash, and broadcasts it along with the witness. The exact execution of $\mathfrak{P}$ is depicted in Fig. 16.

Security Model. LW model the worst case scenario, where all but one participants collude in their *incorruptibility* notion. We extend their notion by allowing the adversary to break the commitment. The corresponding security game, labelled INCORR, is defined in Fig. 17. The conventional hash function is modelled as a RO and the permutation θ as a random permutation. INCORR is parametrized by a time limit δ and a target function $t : \{0,1\}^h \rightarrow \{0,1\}$. The time limit δ models the time between the moment when the last honest seed contribution x appears in the protocol, and the time t_1, when the commitment on the seed has been published and the computation of the value g starts. Before receiving x, the adversary is allowed to do precomputations. The target function t models any property the adversary $\mathscr{A}$ may want to force on the generated value g. The adversary wins the INCORR game if it can produce an incomplete seed $\bar{s}$ and a commitment c within time limit δ, such that it can later complete the seed and produce an output g and a witness that will comprise a "valid" instance of unicorn and such that $t(g) = 1$. The security of unicorn relies on the assumption that computing square roots modulo a prime p is about $\log(p)$ times slower than computing squares, without the possibility of parallelization. This is formalized in Definition 11. Iterative computation of modular square roots then yields a special "hash function" which is slow to evaluate but fast to invert.

Protocol $\mathfrak{P}$		
P_0		$P_1, \ldots, P_n$
$\bar{s} \leftarrow \varepsilon$		
	.... Collection phase (t_{-1} to t_0)	
		$\bar{s}_i \leftarrow\$ \{0,1\}^{\geq h}$
	$\xleftarrow{\bar{s}_i}$	
$\bar{s} \leftarrow \bar{s} \Vert \bar{s}_i$		
	.... Commitment phase (t_0 to t_1)	
broadcast $\bar{s}$		
$s_0 \leftarrow\$ \{0,1\}^{\geq h}$		
$s \leftarrow \bar{s} \Vert s_0$		
$c \leftarrow\$ \mathfrak{P}.\mathsf{commit}(s)$		
broadcast c		
	.... Generation phase (t_1 to t_2)	
$g, w \leftarrow \mathfrak{P}.\mathsf{SH}(s)$		
broadcast s_0, g, w		
		check if $\mathfrak{P}.\mathsf{ver}(\bar{s} \Vert s_0, c, g, w) = 1$

Fig. 16. An execution of the protocol $\mathfrak{P} = \mathsf{unicorn}$.

Game $\mathrm{INCORR}^{\mathscr{B}}_{\mathfrak{P}^{h,p,\ell,\delta,t}}$
$\theta \leftarrow\$ \mathrm{Perm}(\mathbb{Z}_p^*)$
$\sigma \leftarrow\$ \mathscr{A}^{\mathrm{RO},\theta,\theta^{-1}}(\perp)$; $x \leftarrow\$ \{0,1\}^h$
$\sigma, \bar{s}, c \xleftarrow{T(\mathscr{A}) \leq \delta}\$ \mathscr{A}^{\mathrm{RO},\theta,\theta^{-1}}(x, \sigma)$; $s_0, g, w \leftarrow\$ \mathscr{A}^{\mathrm{RO},\theta,\theta^{-1}}(\sigma)$
if $(f_x(s) \neq 1)$ **then return** 0
if $(\mathfrak{P}.\mathsf{ver}^{\mathrm{RO},p,\ell,\theta}(\bar{s} \Vert s_0, c, g, w) \neq 1)$ **then return** 0
return $(t(g) = 1)$

Fig. 17. Game used to define incorruptibility of $\mathfrak{P} = \mathsf{unicorn}$ protocol. INCORR is parametrized by a positive time limit δ and a target function $t : \{0,1\}^h \to \{0,1\}$. Here $s \xleftarrow{T(\mathscr{A}) \leq \delta}\$ \mathscr{A}^{\mathrm{RO},\theta,\theta^{-1}}(x)$ denotes running the adversary $\mathscr{A}$ with oracles RO, θ and θ^{-1} and input x for time at most δ to obtain the outputs $\sigma, \bar{s}, c$; if $\mathscr{A}$ does not terminate within the time limit, $\sigma, \bar{s}, c$ all become the empty string ε. The function $f_x : \{0,1\}^* \to \{0,1\}$ checks if the seed s contains x and is a valid seed string for $\mathfrak{P}$. It returns $f_x(s) = 1$ if and only if $s = s_0 \Vert x \Vert s_1$ with $|s_i| = 0$ or $|s_i| \geq h$ for $i = 1, 2$.

Definition 11 ([36]). *Given a length $\Delta > 0$ of a time interval, a probability ϵ, and a bound on computational resources c, the (Δ, ϵ, c)-$\mathtt{sqrt}(p)$ assumption is the following: any party with computational resources bounded by c that gets a uniformly sampled $x \in QR_p$ at time t, succeeds to compute a $y \in \mathbb{Z}_p^*$ s.t. $y^2 \equiv x \pmod{p}$ before time $t + \Delta$ with probability at most ϵ.*

The intuition behind unicorn's security is that allowing the participants to contribute to the input seed during an interval that is shorter than the time necessary to evaluate the slow hash ensures that no one can predict the output of the hash fast enough to influence it. We extend the result on the security of the unicorn protocol by LW in Lemma 4. With a slight abuse of notation, for a function $f : \mathcal{D} \rightarrow \mathcal{R}$ and an element $r \in \mathcal{R}$ we let $f^{-1}(r)$ denote the set $\{d \in \mathcal{D} \mid f(d) = r\}$. The high level intuition behind Lemma 4 is that unless the adversary breaks the hash-based commitment, it will not have enough time to find a suitable seed that will satisfy the target function $t(\cdot)$, because computing $\mathfrak{P}$.SH takes more time than δ with overwhelming probability.

Lemma 4. *Assume that the (Δ, ϵ, c)-$\mathtt{sqrt}(p)$ assumption holds. Then we have*

$$\Pr[\mathrm{INCORR}^{\mathscr{B}}_{\mathfrak{P}^{h,p,\ell},\delta,t} \Rightarrow 1] \leq \frac{q+1}{2^h} + \frac{2q + |t^{-1}(1)|}{2^{h-1}} + \frac{q + \epsilon\ell q(p-1)}{p-1-q}$$

for any $\delta < \ell\Delta$ and any adversary $\mathscr{A}$ who makes at most q queries to all its oracles in total and whose computational resources are limited by c.

Proof. The proof of Lemma 4 is presented in the full version [21]. □

Corollary 1. *Given the conditions from Lemma 4, we have for the random variable g in the game* $\mathrm{INCORR}^{\mathscr{B}}_{\mathfrak{P}^{p,\ell},\delta,t}$ *that* $\Pr[g = \gamma] \leq \frac{q+1}{2^h} + \frac{2q+1}{2^{h-1}} + \frac{q+\epsilon\ell q(p-1)}{p-1-q}$ *for any $\gamma \in \mathbb{Z}_p^*$.*

Proof. For every $x \in \mathbb{Z}_p^*$, we define a target function $t_x : \mathbb{Z}_p^* \rightarrow \{0,1\}$ defined as $t_x(x') = 1$ iff $x = x'$. We thus have $\Pr[g = x] = \Pr[t_x(g) = 1]$ and because $||t_x^{-1}(1)| = 1$ for all $x \in \mathbb{Z}_p^*$, the corollary follows. □

6.2 BKSS with unicorn

In the previous section we show how parties can use the unicorn protocol to produce uncontestable randomness. In this section we show that this uncontestable source of randomness implies RESIST security. To this end we first integrate the unicorn protocol into our security definitions, we then prove a concrete bound on the key encapsulation mechanism that the `unicorn`-generated randomness seeds and conclude with the theorem that states RESIST-security of our approach.

Security Notion. We adapt the RESIST notion (Definition 9, Fig. 11) into the security notion $\overline{\mathrm{RESIST}}$ (Definition 12, Fig. 18) to capture the *entire setup* by embedding the security notion of the unicorn protocol directly into $\overline{\mathrm{RESIST}}$. The $\overline{\mathrm{RESIST}}$ game closely resembles the RESIST game, but the embedding unicorn introduces several modifications. When Big Brother $\mathscr{B}$ makes a Init query, a second instance of $\mathscr{B}$ is invoked to tamper with the unicorn protocol responsible for generating the seed used in the INIT query. Accordingly, the GENERATE procedure now inputs and outputs a state $\hat{\tau}$, allowing Big Brother to interact with this second instance during seed generation. The model includes two independent random oracles, RO and RO$'$, as well as a special random permutation θ and its inverse θ^{-1}. The use of two random oracles separates the BKSS scheme from the source of randomness[3]. The permutation θ is part of the unicorn protocol. We denote the collection of all these oracles by $\boldsymbol{\mathcal{O}}$. The $\overline{\text{RESIST}}$ game is parameterized by positive integers h, ℓ, and a prime p, which are all parameters of unicorn.

Definition 12. *Let* $\boldsymbol{\Pi} = (\boldsymbol{\mathcal{K}}, \boldsymbol{\mathcal{E}}, \boldsymbol{\mathcal{D}})$ *be a BKSS scheme and* $\tilde{\boldsymbol{\Pi}} = (\tilde{\mathcal{K}}, \tilde{\boldsymbol{\mathcal{E}}}, \tilde{\mathcal{D}})$ *a corresponding subversion. Let* $\mathscr{B}$ *be an adversary playing* $\overline{\text{RESIST}}$*, shown Fig. 18.* $\mathscr{B}$*'s advantage in winning the game is defined as*

$$\mathbf{Adv}^{\overline{\text{resist}}}_{\boldsymbol{\Pi},\tilde{\boldsymbol{\Pi}}}(\mathscr{B}) = \Pr\left[\overline{\text{RESIST}}^{\mathscr{B}}_{\boldsymbol{\Pi},\tilde{\boldsymbol{\Pi}},h,p,\ell} \Rightarrow 1\right] - \Pr\left[\overline{\text{RESIST}}^{\mathscr{B}}_{\boldsymbol{\Pi},\tilde{\boldsymbol{\Pi}},h,p,\ell} \Rightarrow 0\right].$$

We say that a BKSS scheme $\boldsymbol{\Pi}$ paired with $\mathsf{unicorn}_{h,p.\ell}$ resists simultaneous ASAs and KE if $\mathbf{Adv}^{\overline{\text{resist}}}_{\boldsymbol{\Pi},\tilde{\boldsymbol{\Pi}},h,p,\ell}(\mathscr{B})$ is small for all adversaries with reasonable resources and any subversion $\tilde{\boldsymbol{\Pi}}$ that is decryptable with respect to $\boldsymbol{\Pi}$.

DISCUSSION. The game $\overline{\text{RESIST}}$ encompasses both BKSS security and randomness generation via unicorn, so the adversarial advantage accounts for all attack vectors available to Big Brother. Moreover, $\overline{\text{RESIST}}$ demonstrates how to instantiate the general RESIST notion with a concrete protocol for generating incorruptible randomness, illustrating the generality of our approach and enabling future work to adapt our notions to alternative sources of randomness. If the $\overline{\text{RESIST}}$ advantage is provably low for a scheme Π, then Π combined with unicorn resists any leakage function and subversion, provided the following assumptions hold. First, as with RESIST and as in BKR, we assume that an APT exfiltrates leakage *before* any communication occurs. Second, we adopt the (Δ, ϵ, c)-$\mathtt{sqrt}(p)$ assumption, which appears realistic for practical parameters and remains unchallenged since LW's 2015 paper [36]. Third, we assume that the user successfully contributes their seed to the unicorn protocol. This assumption is not trivial: relying on uncompromised software to upload the seed begs the question. However, the seed can be submitted in a human-verifiable way, making timely manipulation by Big Brother difficult [36]. Furthermore, it suffices for either the encrypting or decrypting party to upload their seed for security to hold. At the end of this section, we discuss other possible sources of randomness, whose formal treatment is left as future work.

RESIST SECURITY OF SES WITH unicorn. Theorem 2 shows that SES teamed-up with unicorn is provably resistant to simultaneous ASA and KE. The only missing piece from Theorem 2 is to bound the advantage of the key encapsulation mechanism which is now seeded by unicorn. We first state the theorem and then prove the concrete bound on the key encapsulation mechanism.

[3] This is equivalent to using a single RO with prefix domain separation.

Game $\overline{\mathrm{RESIST}}^{\mathscr{B}}_{\boldsymbol{\Pi},\tilde{\boldsymbol{\Pi}},h,p,\ell}$	Oracle $\mathrm{ENC}(M, A, i)$
$\overrightarrow{\boldsymbol{K}}_i, \sigma_i \leftarrow \bot$ everywhere	**if** $(\sigma_i = \bot)$ **then return** $\bot$
$\tilde{K} \leftarrow\$ \tilde{\mathcal{K}}$	$C_0, \sigma_i \leftarrow\$ \tilde{\boldsymbol{\mathcal{E}}}.\mathsf{Enc}^{\boldsymbol{\mathcal{O}}}(\tilde{K}, \boldsymbol{K}_i, M, A, \sigma_i, i)$
$\theta \leftarrow\$ \mathrm{Perm}(\mathbb{Z}_p^*)$	$C_1 \leftarrow\$ \{0,1\}^{\lvert C_0 \rvert}$
$(\mathsf{Lk}, \tau) \leftarrow\$ \mathscr{B}^{\boldsymbol{\mathcal{O}}}(\tilde{K})$	**return** C_b
$b \leftarrow\$ \{0,1\}$	Oracle $\mathrm{INIT}(i, \hat{\tau})$
$b' \leftarrow\$ \mathscr{B}^{\mathrm{LEAK},\mathrm{INIT},\mathrm{ENC},\boldsymbol{\mathcal{O}}}(\tilde{K}, \tau)$	**if** $(\boldsymbol{K}_i = \bot)$ **then return** $\bot$
return $(b = b')$	$\hat{\tau}, R \leftarrow\$ \mathrm{GENERATE}(\hat{\tau})$
Oracle $\mathrm{LEAK}(i)$	**if** $R = \bot$ **then abort**
if $(\boldsymbol{K}_i \neq \bot)$ **then return** $\bot$	$\sigma_i \leftarrow\$ \tilde{\boldsymbol{\mathcal{E}}}.\mathsf{Init}^{\boldsymbol{\mathcal{O}}}(\tilde{K}, \boldsymbol{K}_i, R, \sigma_i, i)$
$\boldsymbol{K}_i \leftarrow\$ \boldsymbol{\mathcal{K}}$	**return** $\hat{\tau}, R$
$L \leftarrow\$ \mathsf{Lk}^{\boldsymbol{\mathcal{O}}}(\boldsymbol{K}_i)$	Procedure $\mathrm{GENERATE}(\hat{\tau})$
return L	$x \leftarrow\$ \mathcal{R};\ \hat{\tau}, \bar{s}, c \xleftarrow{T(\mathscr{B}) \leq \delta}\$ \mathscr{B}^{\boldsymbol{\mathcal{O}}}(x, \hat{\tau})$
	$\hat{\tau}, s_0, R, w \leftarrow\$ \mathscr{B}^{\boldsymbol{\mathcal{O}}}(\hat{\tau})$
	if $(f_x(s) \neq 1)$ **then** $R \leftarrow \bot$
	if $(\mathfrak{P}.\mathsf{ver}^{\boldsymbol{\mathcal{O}}',h,p,\ell}(\bar{s} \Vert s_0, c, R, w) \neq 1)$ **then** $R \leftarrow \bot$
	return $\hat{\tau}, R$

Fig. 18. The game $\overline{\mathrm{RESIST}}$. We let $\mathfrak{P}$ = unicorn. Because of the inclusion of the unicorn security notion, we fix $\mathcal{R} = \{0,1\}^h$ for a positive h. We use $\boldsymbol{\mathcal{O}}$ as a shorthand for $\mathrm{RO}, \mathrm{RO}', \theta, \theta^{-1}$ and $\boldsymbol{\mathcal{O}}'$ as a shorthand for $\mathrm{RO}', \theta, \theta^{-1}$.

Theorem 2. *Let $\Pi = (\mathcal{K}, \mathcal{E}, \mathcal{D})$ be an encryption scheme with unique ciphertexts with $\mathcal{K} = \{0,1\}^\kappa$. Let k, P, h and ℓ be positive integers. Let p be a prime number with $p \equiv 3 \pmod 4$ and $p \geq 2^h$. Let $\boldsymbol{\Pi} = \mathsf{SES}[\Pi, k, P, h]$. Let $\tilde{\boldsymbol{\Pi}} = (\tilde{\mathcal{K}}, \tilde{\boldsymbol{\mathcal{E}}}, \tilde{\mathcal{D}})$ be a subversion of $\boldsymbol{\Pi}$ that meets the decryptability condition. Let $\mathscr{B}$ be an adversary and $\overline{\mathrm{RESIST}}$ the game in Fig. 18. Assume that the (Δ, ϵ, c)-$\mathtt{sqrt}(p)$ assumption holds. Then*

$$\mathbf{Adv}^{\overline{\mathrm{resist}}}_{\boldsymbol{\Pi},\tilde{\boldsymbol{\Pi}},h,p,\ell}(\mathscr{B}) \leq \Delta_2 + \Delta_3,$$

where

$$\Delta_2 = 2 \cdot q_k \cdot \left(q_2 \cdot q_I \cdot G_{k,p}(2^{k-l}) + (q_I(2q_1 + q_I - 1)) \cdot \left(\tfrac{q+1}{2^h} + \tfrac{2q+1}{2^{h-1}} + \tfrac{q+\epsilon\ell q(p-1)}{p-1-q} \right) \right),$$

$$\Delta_3 = 2 \cdot q_I \cdot \mathbf{Adv}^{\mathrm{ind\$}}_{\Pi}(\mathscr{A}),$$

if $\mathscr{B}$ leaks at most l bits, makes at most q_K LEAK queries, at most q_I INIT queries, makes no more than q_E ENC queries which process no more than d bits of data in a session, makes at most q_1 and q_2 queries to the oracles in $\boldsymbol{\mathcal{O}}$ in the first and the second stage respectively, such that $q = q_1 + q_2$, has computational resources limited by c and runs in time t. The IND\$ − CPA *adversary $\mathscr{A}$ makes* *at most q_E encryption queries with total data bounded by d bits and runs in time $t + \gamma \cdot (q_1 + q_2 + q_K + q_I + q_E + d)$ for a positive constant γ.*

The function $G_{k,P}$ is defined by BKR [12, Theorem 2] and it is tightly approximated by $G_{k,P}\left(2^{k-l}\right) \approx 2^{-P \cdot w(\frac{l}{k})}$, for $w(\lambda) = -\lg(1 - H_2^{-1}(1-\lambda))$, where H_2 is the binary entropy function and $H_2^{-1}(1-\lambda)$ is the smaller of the two possible inverses of $1-\lambda$ under H_2.

Proof. The high level overview of the proof is depicted in Fig. 13. The proof builds on Theorem 1 with the concrete bound for Δ_3 that Lemma 5 yields. □

Lemma 5. *Let k, κ, P, h and ℓ be positive integers, and δ, Δ be lengths of time intervals such that $\ell \cdot \Delta > \delta$. Let p be a prime number with $p \equiv 3 \pmod 4$ and $p \geq 2^h$. Assume that the (Δ, ϵ, c)-$\mathtt{sqrt}(p)$ assumption holds. Let $\mathscr{A}$ be an adversary that plays the UKEY game and that leaks at most l bits, makes q_I DERIVE queries, makes at most q_1 and q_2 queries to the oracles in $\mathcal{O}$ in the first and the second stage respectively, with $q = q_1 + q_2$, and has computational resources limited by c. Then*

$$\mathbf{Adv}^{\mathrm{ukey}}_{\mathsf{XKEY}_{k,\kappa,P,h},h,p,\ell}(\mathscr{A}) \leq$$
$$\left(q_2 \cdot q_I \cdot G_{k,p}(2^{k-l}) + (q_I(2q_1 + q_I - 1)) \cdot \left(\frac{q+1}{2^h} + \frac{2q+1}{2^{h-1}} + \frac{q + \epsilon \ell q(p-1)}{p-1-q}\right)\right).$$

Proof. The proof proceeds in two steps. We first bound the probability that an adversary tampers with the unicorn protocol and we then upper bound $\mathbf{Adv}^{\mathrm{key}}_{\mathsf{XKEY}_{k,\kappa,p,r}}(\mathscr{B})$ using techniques from BKR [12, Proof of Theorem 12]. The complete proof is in the full version [21]. □

PRACTICAL INSTANTIATION. Communication secured with SES and unicorn is both practical and deployable. A secure unicorn instance (as proposed by LW) runs every 15 min, with a two-minute seed contribution window followed by a 10-minute generation phase. To start a session, both parties contribute to the next seed collection and use the resulting randomness. Contributions are posted in a publicly observable way (e.g., on Mastodon). Multiple staggered unicorn instances (e.g., one per minute) or ad-hoc instances are also possible.

As shown by BPR, any efficient nonce-based scheme that is *tidy* [40] produces unique ciphertexts [13], making it suitable for SES. Most standard schemes such as OCB [35] and GCM [37] are tidy. For GCM, if (K, N, A, C) decrypts to some $M \neq \bot$, then $C = \mathcal{E}(K, N, A, M)$: the core ciphertext is computed as XOR of M and a keys stream that is a deterministic function of K, N, A, which will cancel out with the same key stream that has been XORed to C in the decryption yielding M. If K, N, A and the core ciphertext are equal, the tag, computed as a masked keyed has dependent on the key, the nonce, the associated data and the core ciphertext will be the same as well.

Modern encryption schemes with 128-bit keys can securely process at least 280 TB[4] of data before rekeying. AES-GCM achieves this by using only 96-bit nonces, which implies birthday security without a quantitative degradation [33]. Over a 1 Gbps connection, transmitting this much data takes $\approx$ 85 h $\gg$ 15 min, well above the unicorn refresh interval.

7 Conclusion and Future Work

In this paper we show that coordinated ASAs and KE attacks render standalone symmetric encryption defenseless, but coupling encryption with verifiable external randomness restores security, thereby charting a concrete path toward cryptography resistant to mass-surveillance.

There are several avenues for further improvements. Like BKR, our model lets the adversary leak information only *before* communication; a more realistic model would allow the APT to leak very small amounts of data between queries. Future work could also relax the decryptability condition [23], allowing stronger subversions [46] or adopt a faster source of verifiable randomness. A natural avenue is to reinterpret our current unicorn primitive as a verifiable delay function (VDF) [15]; substituting a faster VDF—or the distributed randomness beacons surveyed by Choi et al. [20]—could supply the same incorruptible randomness with lower latency. Finally, our quantitative bound degrades quickly; tightening it remains an important goal for future work.

Acknowledgments. Damian Vizár's research was partly supported by the EU H2020 TREDISEC project, funded by the European Commission under grant agreement no. 644412. Simone Colombo's research was partly supported by UKRI grant EP/X017524/1. We would like to thank the EUROCRYPT and LATINCRYPT reviewers for their constructive comments. We thank Phillip Rogaway, Guy Barwell and Varun Maram for insightful comments and discussion.

References

1. Alwen, J., Dodis, Y., Naor, M., Segev, G., Walfish, S., Wichs, D.: Public-key encryption in the bounded-retrieval model. In: Gilbert, H. (ed.) EUROCRYPT 2010. LNCS, vol. 6110, pp. 113–134. Springer, Heidelberg (2010). https://doi.org/10.1007/978-3-642-13190-5_6
2. Alwen, J., Dodis, Y., Wichs, D.: Leakage-resilient public-key cryptography in the bounded-retrieval model. In: Halevi, S. (ed.) CRYPTO 2009. LNCS, vol. 5677, pp. 36–54. Springer, Heidelberg (2009). https://doi.org/10.1007/978-3-642-03356-8_3
3. Alwen, J., Dodis, Y., Wichs, D.: Survey: leakage resilience and the bounded retrieval model. In: Kurosawa, K. (ed.) ICITS 2009. LNCS, vol. 5973, pp. 1–18. Springer, Heidelberg (2010). https://doi.org/10.1007/978-3-642-14496-7_1

[4] An AES mode of operation with birthday-bounded security can process about 2^{44} blocks of 128 bits each while still having $\approx 2^{-20}$ provable bound on the adversarial advantage. This is about 280 TB.

4. Armour, M., Poettering, B.: Algorithm substitution attacks against receivers. Int. J. Inf. Sec. **21**(5), 1027–1050 (2022)
5. Ateniese, G., Magri, B., Venturi, D.: Subversion-resilient signature schemes. In: Proceedings of the 22nd ACM SIGSAC Conference on Computer and Communications Security, Denver, CO, USA, 12–16 October 2015, pp. 364–375. ACM (2015)
6. Austrin, P., Chung, K.-M., Mahmoody, M., Pass, R., Seth, K.: On the impossibility of cryptography with tamperable randomness. In: Garay, J.A., Gennaro, R. (eds.) CRYPTO 2014. LNCS, vol. 8616, pp. 462–479. Springer, Heidelberg (2014). https://doi.org/10.1007/978-3-662-44371-2_26
7. Ball, J., Borger, J., Greenwald, G.: Revealed: how US and UK spy agencies defeat internet privacy and security. The Guardian (2013). https://www.theguardian.com/world/2013/sep/05/nsa-gchq-encryption-codes-security. Accessed 10 May 2017
8. Banfi, F., Maurer, U.: Anonymous symmetric-key communication. In: Galdi, C., Kolesnikov, V. (eds.) SCN 2020. LNCS, vol. 12238, pp. 471–491. Springer, Cham (2020). https://doi.org/10.1007/978-3-030-57990-6_23
9. Bellare, M., Desai, A., Jokipii, E., Rogaway, P.: A concrete security treatment of symmetric encryption. In: 38th Annual Symposium on Foundations of Computer Science, FOCS 1997, Miami Beach, Florida, USA, 19–22 October 1997, pp. 394–403. IEEE Computer Society (1997)
10. Bellare, M., Hoang, V.T.: Resisting randomness subversion: fast deterministic and hedged public-key encryption in the standard model. In: Oswald, E., Fischlin, M. (eds.) EUROCRYPT 2015. LNCS, vol. 9057, pp. 627–656. Springer, Heidelberg (2015). https://doi.org/10.1007/978-3-662-46803-6_21
11. Bellare, M., Jaeger, J., Kane, D.: Mass-surveillance without the state: strongly undetectable algorithm-substitution attacks. In: Proceedings of the 22nd ACM SIGSAC Conference on Computer and Communications Security, Denver, CO, USA, 12–16 October 2015, pp. 1431–1440. ACM (2015)
12. Bellare, M., Kane, D., Rogaway, P.: Big-key symmetric encryption: resisting key exfiltration. In: Robshaw, M., Katz, J. (eds.) CRYPTO 2016. LNCS, vol. 9814, pp. 373–402. Springer, Heidelberg (2016). https://doi.org/10.1007/978-3-662-53018-4_14
13. Bellare, M., Paterson, K.G., Rogaway, P.: Security of symmetric encryption against mass surveillance. In: Garay, J.A., Gennaro, R. (eds.) CRYPTO 2014. LNCS, vol. 8616, pp. 1–19. Springer, Heidelberg (2014). https://doi.org/10.1007/978-3-662-44371-2_1
14. Berndt, S., Wichelmann, J., Pott, C., Traving, T., Eisenbarth, T.: ASAP: algorithm substitution attacks on cryptographic protocols. In: AsiaCCS, pp. 712–726. ACM (2022)
15. Boneh, D., Bonneau, J., Bünz, B., Fisch, B.: Verifiable delay functions. In: Shacham, H., Boldyreva, A. (eds.) CRYPTO 2018. LNCS, vol. 10991, pp. 757–788. Springer, Cham (2018). https://doi.org/10.1007/978-3-319-96884-1_25
16. Camenisch, J., Drijvers, M., Lehmann, A.: Anonymous attestation with subverted TPMs. In: Katz, J., Shacham, H. (eds.) CRYPTO 2017. LNCS, vol. 10403, pp. 427–461. Springer, Cham (2017). https://doi.org/10.1007/978-3-319-63697-9_15
17. Cash, D., Ding, Y.Z., Dodis, Y., Lee, W., Lipton, R., Walfish, S.: Intrusion-resilient key exchange in the bounded retrieval model. In: Vadhan, S.P. (ed.) TCC 2007. LNCS, vol. 4392, pp. 479–498. Springer, Heidelberg (2007). https://doi.org/10.1007/978-3-540-70936-7_26

18. Champion, J., Waters, B., Wu, D.J.: Adaptively-secure big-key identity-based encryption. In: Jager, T., Pan, J. (eds.) Public-Key Cryptography - PKC 2025. LNCS, vol. 15674, pp. 125–157. Springer, Cham (2025). https://doi.org/10.1007/978-3-031-91820-9_5
19. Checkoway, S., et al.: On the practical exploitability of dual EC in TLS implementations. In: USENIX Security (2014)
20. Choi, K., Manoj, A., Bonneau, J.: SoK: distributed randomness beacons. In: SP, pp. 75–92. IEEE (2023)
21. Colombo, S., Vizár, D.: (Im)possibility of symmetric encryption against coordinated algorithm substitution attacks and key exfiltration. Cryptology ePrint Archive, Paper 2025/1426 (2025). https://eprint.iacr.org/2025/1426
22. Crescenzo, G., Lipton, R., Walfish, S.: Perfectly secure password protocols in the bounded retrieval model. In: Halevi, S., Rabin, T. (eds.) TCC 2006. LNCS, vol. 3876, pp. 225–244. Springer, Heidelberg (2006). https://doi.org/10.1007/11681878_12
23. Degabriele, J.P., Farshim, P., Poettering, B.: A more cautious approach to security against mass surveillance. In: Leander, G. (ed.) FSE 2015. LNCS, vol. 9054, pp. 579–598. Springer, Heidelberg (2015). https://doi.org/10.1007/978-3-662-48116-5_28
24. Dodis, Y., Mironov, I., Stephens-Davidowitz, N.: Message transmission with reverse firewalls—secure communication on corrupted machines. In: Robshaw, M., Katz, J. (eds.) CRYPTO 2016. LNCS, vol. 9814, pp. 341–372. Springer, Heidelberg (2016). https://doi.org/10.1007/978-3-662-53018-4_13
25. Döttling, N., Garg, S., Sekar, S., Wang, M.: IBE with incompressible master secret and small identity secrets. In: TCC (1). Lecture Notes in Computer Science, vol. 13747, pp. 588–617. Springer (2022)
26. Dziembowski, S.: Intrusion-resilience via the bounded-storage model. In: Halevi, S., Rabin, T. (eds.) TCC 2006. LNCS, vol. 3876, pp. 207–224. Springer, Heidelberg (2006). https://doi.org/10.1007/11681878_11
27. Farrell, S., Badii, F., Schneier, B., Bellovin, S.M.: Reflections on ten years past the snowden revelations. RFC 9446 (2023). https://www.rfc-editor.org/info/rfc9446
28. Gellman, B., Nakashima, E.: U.S. spy agencies mounted 231 offensive cyber-operations in 2011, documents show. The Washington Post (2013). https://www.washingtonpost.com/world/national-security/us-spy-agencies-mounted-231-offensive-cyber-operations-in-2011-documents-show/2013/08/30/d090a6ae-119e-11e3-b4cb-fd7ce041d814_story.html. Accessed 13 May 2017
29. Green, M.: A case against security nihilism (2021). https://blog.cryptographyengineering.com/2021/07/20/a-case-against-security-nihilism/. Accessed 24 May 2022
30. Grubbs, P., Lu, J., Ristenpart, T.: Message franking via committing authenticated encryption. In: Katz, J., Shacham, H. (eds.) CRYPTO 2017. LNCS, vol. 10403, pp. 66–97. Springer, Cham (2017). https://doi.org/10.1007/978-3-319-63697-9_3
31. Hoang, V.T., Reyhanitabar, R., Rogaway, P., Vizár, D.: Online authenticated-encryption and its nonce-reuse misuse-resistance. In: Gennaro, R., Robshaw, M. (eds.) CRYPTO 2015. LNCS, vol. 9215, pp. 493–517. Springer, Heidelberg (2015). https://doi.org/10.1007/978-3-662-47989-6_24
32. IACR: IACR Statement on Mass Surveillance ("Copenhagen Resolution") (2014). https://iacr.org/misc/statement-May2014.html. Adopted at the IACR Members meeting, Eurocrypt 2014, Copenhagen, May 14th 2014

33. Iwata, T., Ohashi, K., Minematsu, K.: Breaking and repairing GCM security proofs. In: Safavi-Naini, R., Canetti, R. (eds.) CRYPTO 2012. LNCS, vol. 7417, pp. 31–49. Springer, Heidelberg (2012). https://doi.org/10.1007/978-3-642-32009-5_3
34. Joux, A., Loss, J., Wagner, B.: Kleptographic attacks against implicit rejection. In: Jager, T., Pan, J. (eds.) Public-Key Cryptography - PKC 2025. LNCS, vol. 15677, pp. 214–245. Springer, Cham (2025). https://doi.org/10.1007/978-3-031-91829-2_7
35. Krovetz, T., Rogaway, P.: The software performance of authenticated-encryption modes. In: Joux, A. (ed.) FSE 2011. LNCS, vol. 6733, pp. 306–327. Springer, Heidelberg (2011). https://doi.org/10.1007/978-3-642-21702-9_18
36. Lenstra, A.K., Wesolowski, B.: A random zoo: sloth, unicorn, and trx. IACR Cryptology ePrint Archive **2015**, 366 (2015). http://eprint.iacr.org/2015/366
37. McGrew, D.A., Viega, J.: The security and performance of the galois/counter mode (GCM) of operation. In: INDOCRYPT 2004, pp. 343–355 (2004)
38. Mironov, I., Stephens-Davidowitz, N.: Cryptographic reverse firewalls. In: Oswald, E., Fischlin, M. (eds.) EUROCRYPT 2015. LNCS, vol. 9057, pp. 657–686. Springer, Heidelberg (2015). https://doi.org/10.1007/978-3-662-46803-6_22
39. Moran, T., Wichs, D.: Incompressible encodings. In: Micciancio, D., Ristenpart, T. (eds.) CRYPTO 2020. LNCS, vol. 12170, pp. 494–523. Springer, Cham (2020). https://doi.org/10.1007/978-3-030-56784-2_17
40. Namprempre, C., Rogaway, P., Shrimpton, T.: Reconsidering generic composition. In: Nguyen, P.Q., Oswald, E. (eds.) EUROCRYPT 2014. LNCS, vol. 8441, pp. 257–274. Springer, Heidelberg (2014). https://doi.org/10.1007/978-3-642-55220-5_15
41. NIST: NIST randomness beacon. https://beacon.nist.gov. Accessed 14 Sept 2017
42. Preneel, B.: Cryptography and information security in the post-snowden era. In: TELERISE@ ICSE, p. 1 (2015)
43. Rabin, M.O.: Transaction protection by beacons. J. Comput. Syst. Sci. **27**(2), 256–267 (1983)
44. Rogaway, P.: Nonce-based symmetric encryption. In: Roy, B., Meier, W. (eds.) FSE 2004. LNCS, vol. 3017, pp. 348–358. Springer, Heidelberg (2004). https://doi.org/10.1007/978-3-540-25937-4_22
45. Rogaway, P.: The moral character of cryptographic work. IACR Cryptology ePrint Archive **2015**, 1162 (2015). http://eprint.iacr.org/2015/1162
46. Russell, A., Tang, Q., Yung, M., Zhou, H.-S.: Cliptography: clipping the power of kleptographic attacks. In: Cheon, J.H., Takagi, T. (eds.) ASIACRYPT 2016. LNCS, vol. 10032, pp. 34–64. Springer, Heidelberg (2016). https://doi.org/10.1007/978-3-662-53890-6_2
47. Russell, A., Tang, Q., Yung, M., Zhou, H.: Destroying steganography via amalgamation: kleptographically CPA secure public key encryption. IACR Cryptology ePrint Archive **2016**, 530 (2016). http://eprint.iacr.org/2016/530
48. Russell, A., Tang, Q., Yung, M., Zhou, H.-S.: Correcting subverted random oracles. In: Shacham, H., Boldyreva, A. (eds.) CRYPTO 2018. LNCS, vol. 10992, pp. 241–271. Springer, Cham (2018). https://doi.org/10.1007/978-3-319-96881-0_9
49. Scott, A., Andersen, S.: Engineering a backdoored bitcoin wallet. In: WOOT @ USENIX Security Symposium, pp. 89–100. USENIX Association (2024)
50. Scott-Railton, J., et al.: CatalanGate: Extensive Mercenary Spyware Operation against Catalans Using Pegasus and Candiru (2022). https://citizenlab.ca/2022/04/catalangate-extensive-mercenary-spyware-operation-against-catalans-using-pegasus-candiru/. Accessed 22 May 2022

51. Vaudenay, S.: Clever arbiters versus malicious adversaries. In: Ryan, P.Y.A., Naccache, D., Quisquater, J.-J. (eds.) The New Codebreakers. LNCS, vol. 9100, pp. 497–517. Springer, Heidelberg (2016). https://doi.org/10.1007/978-3-662-49301-4_31
52. Young, A., Yung, M.: The "black-box" cryptography or: should we trust capstone? In: Koblitz, N. (ed.) CRYPTO 1996. LNCS, vol. 1109, pp. 89–103. Springer, Heidelberg (1996). https://doi.org/10.1007/3-540-68697-5_8
53. Young, A., Yung, M.: Kleptography: using cryptography against cryptography. In: Fumy, W. (ed.) EUROCRYPT 1997. LNCS, vol. 1233, pp. 62–74. Springer, Heidelberg (1997). https://doi.org/10.1007/3-540-69053-0_6

A Simple Forgery Attack on Pelican

Orr Dunkelman[1,2(✉)]

[1] Computer Science Department, University of Haifa, Haifa, Israel
orrd@cs.haifa.ac.il
[2] Security in Telecommunications (SecT), Technische Universität Berlin, Berlin, Germany

Abstract. Pelican, suggested by Daemen and Rijmen, is a Message Authentication Code (MAC) with a structure that resembles a CBC-MAC. A constant IV is first encrypted under the unknown key, and then a CBC "encryption" takes place with a fixed random permutation (of 4 keyless AES rounds). The finalization is composed of applying another full keyed AES encryption.

Previous works relied on internal collisions, and resulted in an *almost universal forgery*, in which it is easy to generate the correct tag of any given message if the attacker is allowed to change a single block in it. However, no key-recovery attacks or forgery attacks invalidating the security claims of the Pelican were published.

In this paper we show a simple forgery attack against Pelican. We show that adding a block of 0 to the message (at any location) does not change the tag with probability $18 \cdot 2^{-128}$ (i.e., 18 times higher than expected), which contradicts the security claims of Pelican. We also show that one can increase the success rate of the attack up to $3,810 \cdot 2^{-128} \approx 2^{-116.1}$ by adding 951 blocks of 0 to the message. We argue that the fixed-point based attacks contradict the security claims of Pelican.

Keywords: Pelican · MAC · Cryptanalysis · Fixed points

1 Introduction

Message Authentication Codes (MAC) are a symmetric-key primitive designed to ensure the authenticity and the integrity of a message. Given a message m and a key k, a short tag is computed and transmitted with the message. The recipient of the message recomputes the tag, and compares the newly computed value and the received value to verify the integrity and authenticity of the message. The main security requirements from MACs concern the hardness of extracting the key from (possibly many) (message, tag) pairs and the hardness of forging new (message,tag) pairs.

ALRED is a family of Message Authentication Codes [8], designed in 2005 by Daemen and Rijmen. It processes messages in a chaining mode—first an IV is encrypted under the secret key k. Then, the output is processed in a

D. Escudero and I. Damgård (Eds.): LATINCRYPT 2025, LNCS 16129, pp. 333–344, 2026.
https://doi.org/10.1007/978-3-032-06754-8_12

chaining manner: each new block is treated as a key to r rounds of the block cipher, which encrypts the internal state to produce a new internal state. After the message padding, and the introduction of the last block, the secret key is used again to encrypt the output of the chain. After the publication of the original ALRED paper, several constructions that follow the design rationale were proposed, e.g., PC-MAC-AES [14], MT-MAC-AES [14], Marvin [16,17], and ALE [3]. As a result, the designers clarified the security claims (which mainly involved removing attacks based on internal collisions from being covered by the claims).

Pelican is an instantiation of ALRED—it follows the ALRED methodology. First, the message block is XORed into the chain (like in CBC-MAC) instead of going through the key schedule. Secondly, the selected block cipher is AES, and after processing each message block, a 4-round keyless AES is applied. In addition to a 60% reduction in processing time (for each message block), the lack of AddRoundKey operation is claimed to reduce side channel concerns.

Pelican was analyzed by several works [5,12,19]. All these attacks rely on the use of internal collisions, and thus, do not invalidate the (updated) security claims of Pelican. These attacks reconstruct the internal state of Pelican using different methods (e.g., differential meet in the middle attack or impossible differential attack). Once the internal state is given to the adversary, one can apply an *almost universal forgery* attack, as the adversary just needs to make sure that the input to the last keyed encryption is equal to that found at the end of the chain from the known internal state. In [19], Wang et al. used an impossible differential attack using $2^{85.5}$ data and time to reconstruct the internal state. A differential meet in the middle attack was used in [5] to find the internal state in time and data complexities of 2^{64}. An improved impossible differential attack that could attack Pelican, even with 5-round and 6-round AES was presented in [12], with data/time complexities of 2^{80} and 2^{110}, respectively. In addition, attacks based on the symmetry of keyless AES rounds is reported in [12]. It was observed in [13] that keyless AES round operating on a 128-bit state of the form (x, y, x, y) results in a state of the form (z, w, z, w) (where x may be equal to z and/or y may be equal to w). This fact can be used to reduce the possible set of internal states to only 2^{64} possible candidates, in which internal collisions can be more efficiently found. The resulting attacks of data and time complexities of 2^{96} are reported in [12].

In contrast, in this paper we do not rely on internal collisions. We present a simple forgery attack against Pelican. The attack is based on the existence of multiple fixed points in 4-round keyless AES. When the state after the 4-round keyless is one of the (at least) 18 fixed points, inserting a zero message block does not change the state, and applying again 4-round keyless AES results in the same value. Hence, the following computation chain remains the same, i.e., the tag is the same. Therefore, injecting a zero message word, does not change the tag in the case of Pelican with probability of (at least) $18 \cdot 2^{-128}$. We later show that by inserting additional zero blocks can increase the success rate of the forgery attack to $3,810 \cdot 2^{-128}$.

Table 1. Summary of Attacks on Pelican

Attack		Number of	Keyed or	Complexity			Success
Target	Type	AES Rounds	Keyless	Data	Time	Memory	Rate
State	Imp. Diff. [19]	4	Keyed	$2^{85.5}$ CM	$2^{85.5}$	2^{65}	1
State	Diff. MITM [5]	4	Keyed	2^{64} CM	2^{64}	2^{64}	0.63
State	Imp. Diff. [12]	5	Keyed	2^{80} CM	2^{80}	2^{78}	1
State	Imp. Diff. [12]	6	Keyed	2^{110} CM	2^{110}	2^{64}	1
State	Generic [12]	any	Keyless	2^{96} CM	2^{96}	2^{32}	1
State	Generic [12]	any	Keyless	2^{96} ACM	2^{96}	1	1
Forgery	Fixed Point (Sect. 3)	4[a]	Keyless	1 KM	N/A	N/A	$18 \cdot 2^{-128}$
Forgery	Fixed Point (Sect. 3.1)	4[a]	Keyless	1 KM	N/A	N/A	$3,810 \cdot 2^{-128}$

KM—Known message, CM—Chosen message, ACM—Adaptively chosen message.
Time complexity is measured in MAC evaluation units.
State—State recovery attack (used for Almost Universal Forgery).
[a] The proposed attacks can be used against different number of rounds, with a success rate that changes depending on the number of rounds and the number of message blocks used in the attack. See Sect. 3 for more details.

We note that unlike the previous results, that relied on internal collisions, our attack relies on fixed points. Hence, while the other attacks do not contradict the security claims by the designers, it seems that our attack does succeed in producing forgeries, with probability higher than expected (and claimed). We summarize and compare the different attacks against Pelican in Table 1.

The reminder of the paper is organized as follows: Sect. 2 recalls the ALRED design methodology and describes Pelican. In Sect. 3, we describe our attacks and discuss their implications. We consider several possible mitigations in Sect. 4. Finally, we conclude the paper in Sect. 5.

2 Pelican

In this section, we describe the ALRED construction and its specific instantiation Pelican.

2.1 The ALRED Construction

ALRED is a MAC construction based on an iterated block cipher and its reduced-round version. Given a message m and a secret key k, a tag is computed in four steps:

1. **Message padding and splitting:** The message is padded with a single 1 and the minimum number of 0's so that the resulting length is a multiple of ℓ_w bits, where ℓ_w is a characteristic of the MAC. The padded message is then divided into blocks $m_1, m_2, \ldots, m_\ell$ of length ℓ_w each.

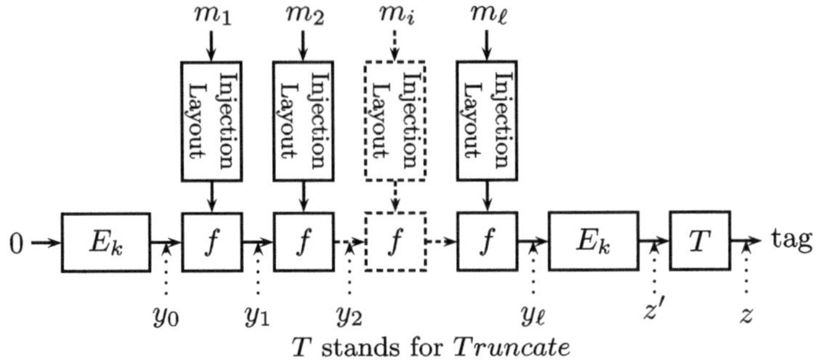

Fig. 1. The ALRED construction

2. **State initialization:** The state is initialized with the all-zero ℓ_b-bit block (where ℓ_b is the block size of E), and then the full block cipher is applied to it, to obtain $y_0 = E_k(0)$.
3. **Chaining:** The following iteration is applied to the blocks $m_1, m_2, \ldots, m_\ell$ sequentially:
   - The message block m_i is mapped to an injection input Inj_i whose length is equal to the length of r round keys of the block cipher.
   - A reduced r-round variant of the block cipher is applied to the state y_{i-1}, with Inj_i replacing the round keys. The resulting state is denoted by y_i.
4. **Finalization:** The full block cipher is applied to the state y_ℓ to obtain $z' = E_k(y_\ell)$. Then z' is truncated to the required length to obtain the tag $z = Truncate(z')$.

The construction is illustrated in Fig. 1, where f denotes a reduced r-round variant of the block cipher, and T deontes truncation.

2.2 The Pelican MAC

Pelican is the ALRED instantiation we analyze. In Pelican, the underlying block cipher is AES, the number of rounds is $r = 4$, the block length is $\ell_w = 128$ bits, and the injection input consists of using the message as the first round subkey, and zeros as the other four subkeys. An equivalent description, which is more convenient for our analysis, is that in the i'th iteration of the chaining step, the 128-bit message block m_i is XORed to the state y_{i-1}, and then *four-round keyless AES* (i.e., AES without the AddRoundKey operations) is applied to obtain the next state y_i. The equivalent description is shown in Fig. 2, where f denotes four-round keyless AES.

Pelican's Security Claims. We briefly cite Pelican's main security claims [9], for ℓ_m being the tag size (128 bits in our case), ℓ_k being the key size (128 bits in our case), and ℓ_c being the capacity of Pelican (which is 120 bits):

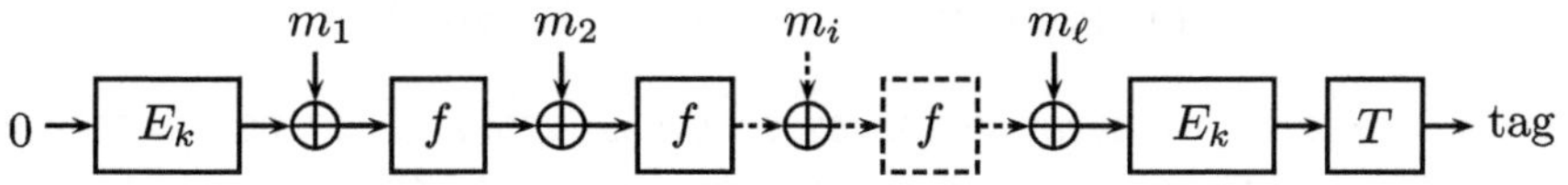

T stands for *Truncate*

Fig. 2. The structure of Pelican

Claim 1. *The probability of success of any forgery attack not involving key recovery or internal collisions is* $2^{-\ell_m}$.

Claim 2. *There are no key recovery attacks faster than exhaustive key search, i.e. with an expected complexity less than* $2^{\ell_k - 1}$ *MAC function executions.*

Claim 3. *The probability that an internal collision occurs in a set of adaptively chosen messages presented to the MAC function is not above* $1 - e^{-A^2/2^{\ell_c+1}}$, *with* A *the total number of blocks in the messages.*[1]

3 A Simple Forgery Attack

We note that in the case of Pelican, one applies 4-round keyless AES permutation to the state. The attack is based on the simple observation that 4-round keyless AES has more than one fixed point. Our search found 18 such fixed points, and we discuss how to use those to offer a simple forgery attack.

Let S_i be the internal state after adding the message block m_i. If S_i happens to be a fixed point of the permutation f, then $S_{i+1} = f(S_i) \oplus m_{i+1}$. As S_i is a fixed point:

$$S_{i+1} = f(S_i) \oplus m_{i+1} = S_i \oplus m_{i+1},$$

and $S_{i+2} = f(S_{i+1}) \oplus m_{i+2}$.

Whenever S_i is indeed a fixed point, adding a block equal to 0 between m_i and m_{i+1} leads to the following state (with a small abuse of notation we use S_{i+1} to denote the state after adding m_{i+1} which is now the $i+2$'th block):

$$S_{i+1} = f(f(S_i) \oplus 0) \oplus m_{i+1} = f(S_i \oplus 0) \oplus m_{i+1} = S_i \oplus m_{i+1}.$$

In other words, adding the 0 block just after m_i did not alter the internal state. As Pelican does not process the message length, then when S_i is indeed a fixed point the tag on $m_1 m_2 \ldots m_i m_{i+1} \ldots m_\ell$ is the same as on $m_1 m_2 \ldots m_i 0 m_{i+1} \ldots m_\ell$.

[1] We note that Claim 3 has been updated since the original publication of Pelican. Originally, it used A as the number of messages, rather than the total number of message blocks.

Table 2. Fix Points for 4-Round Keyless AES

01c88f82$_x$	01c88f82$_x$	01c88f82$_x$	01c88f82$_x$	27562faa$_x$	27562faa$_x$	27562faa$_x$	27562faa$_x$
2faa2756$_x$	2faa2756$_x$	2faa2756$_x$	2faa2756$_x$	562faa27$_x$	562faa27$_x$	562faa27$_x$	562faa27$_x$
5da35da3$_x$	5da35da3$_x$	5da35da3$_x$	5da35da3$_x$	73737373$_x$	73737373$_x$	73737373$_x$	73737373$_x$
7da3f5ad$_x$	7da3f5ad$_x$	7da3f5ad$_x$	7da3f5ad$_x$	8201c88f$_x$	8201c88f$_x$	8201c88f$_x$	8201c88f$_x$
86c086c0$_x$	86c086c0$_x$	86c086c0$_x$	86c086c0$_x$	8f8201c8$_x$	8f8201c8$_x$	8f8201c8$_x$	8f8201c8$_x$
8f8f8f8f$_x$	8f8f8f8f$_x$	8f8f8f8f$_x$	8f8f8f8f$_x$	a35da35d$_x$	a35da35d$_x$	a35da35d$_x$	a35da35d$_x$
a3f5ad7d$_x$	a3f5ad7d$_x$	a3f5ad7d$_x$	a3f5ad7d$_x$	aa27562f$_x$	aa27562f$_x$	aa27562f$_x$	aa27562f$_x$
ad7da3f5$_x$	ad7da3f5$_x$	ad7da3f5$_x$	ad7da3f5$_x$	c086c086$_x$	c086c086$_x$	c086c086$_x$	c086c086$_x$
c88f8201$_x$	c88f8201$_x$	c88f8201$_x$	c88f8201$_x$	f5ad7da3$_x$	f5ad7da3$_x$	f5ad7da3$_x$	f5ad7da3$_x$

Fixed Points in 4-Round Keyless AES. In Table 2 we list 18 fixed points for 4-round AES that we found. Hence, the probability of a random state to be a fixed point is at least $18 \cdot 2^{-128}$. This means, that adding a 0 message block does not alter the tag with probability of at least $18 \cdot 2^{-128}$.

We found those fixed points by trying all possible 2^{32} values of the form (x, x, x, x), i.e., four equal columns, and testing whether they serve as a fixed point. One advantage of this approach (besides its simplicity and efficiency) is the fact that the ShiftRows operation of AES has no impact on the state. Hence, our fixed points are actually fixed points for 4 rounds of the 32-bit cipher composed of SubBytes followed by MixColumns (as there is no AddRoundKey nor ShiftRows). Obviously, with greater computing powers, one may be able to find more such fixed points.

We note that one can easily find a lower bound for the number of fixed points in r-round keyless AES, using the fact that if all the input bytes are the same (i.e., the state is composed of the same byte value repeated 16 times), then all the operations (SubBytes, MixColumns, and ShiftRows) maintain this property. Furthermore, the MixColumns operation does not change the value (i.e., $MC(a, a, a, a) = (a, a, a, a)$ for any 8-bit value a). Hence, the question how many S-box layers are needed to return to the same value, depend on the orbit of the S-box. As the AES' S-box has orbits of lengths, 2, 27, 59, 81, 87, then one can compute a simple lower bound on the number of fixed points. There are at least 2 fixed points in 2-round keyless AES, and 256 in $lcm(2, 27, 59, 81, 87) = 277,182$ rounds of keyless AES. Obviously, there are many more fixed points (as we show in Sect. 3.1).

Almost Universal Forgery Attack. We note that once our forgery attack succeeds, we learn that indeed the state was a fixed point where the 0 input block(s) were introduced. If so, the adversary learns that internal state is one of the 18 possible fixed points. If there are many more fixed points (and thus, the knowledge which of these 18 fixed points is the correct one), then the success rate of the attack is greatly improved. Otherwise, with high probability, indeed the internal state is one of the 18 fixed points we found. One can easily test which of those is the state, by replacing the 0 block with a message block that transforms one fixed point to another[2] followed by the original message blocks. Hence, if the internal state was the first fixed point, then the new state become a different fixed point, which will be reconciled to the correct value. Once the internal state is recovered, an almost universal forgery attack can be applied.

Implications: The complexity of the attack is thus negligible—given one (message,tag) pair, just insert a zero message block any where to the message. Thus, for a tag size of 128 bits, our attack's success rate is 18 times higher than what Claim 1 suggests.

One can argue that our attack indeed uses an internal collision as we look at fixed points, which can be viewed as a *temporal internal collision* (in comparison to collision between different states during the processing of different messages). However, in such a case, Claim 3 may be nullified. We have considered the claim in [10], and it does not restrict the function. Obviously, it seems that fixing the permutation as a linear one is not going to offer any security. However, if one considers Pelican using round functions constituting of 108 AES rounds,[3] our attack finds an "internal collision" between the empty message ϵ and the 0 message with probability which is higher than $1-exp(-A^2/2^{\ell_c+1})$, as in our case $A = 1$ and $\ell_c = 120$, and probability of the collision is (at least) $129 \cdot 2^{-128} > 2^{-121}$.

We note that if one argues that the security claims need to assume that the underlying reduced-round block cipher is a random permutation, then 4-round keyless AES is not a good proposal to begin with. First, a permutation picked at random has on average a single fixed point. The probability that a random permutation (over a very large domain) has 18 fixed points is about $2^{-36.6}$. Furthermore, 4-round keyless AES can be easily distinguished[4] using a SQUARE 4-round distinguisher using 2^{32} chosen plaintexts [6] or the by the symmetry properties reported in [13].

Furthermore, reading the arguments given in [10, p5], the authors were aware of the possibility of iterating some message block $2^n!$ times to reach the same value in the internal state, which led them to count the number of message blocks, rather than the number of messages. Obviously, a simple fix to the claim (and assuming that indeed one cannot find many more fixed points in 4-round AES) is to count the number of AES rounds, rather than the number of message blocks.

Discussion. We note that other types of attacks may be used to attack Pelican based on message modification. Namely, if one finds a differential for 4-round keyless AES $\Delta_{IN} \rightarrow \Delta_{OUT}$, one could easily change two consecutive message

[2] This message block is the XOR of the two fixed points.

[3] We note that using 120, 136, 144, 180, or 188 rounds gives similar results.

[4] We use the term "distinguished", though distinguishing of a keyless primitive is trivial using a single query. One may consider this as a known-key distinguisher, but then, one can easily distinguish 4-round AES using a single pair of plaintexts, using differential arguments.

blocks, the first by Δ_{IN} and the second by Δ_{OUT}. The success probability of this attack is the probability of the differential. If we model 4-round AES as a random permutation, and following O'Connor's work on the behavior of differentials in random functions and permutations [15], we expect that there is at least one $(\Delta_{IN}, \Delta_{OUT})$ pair of differences with probability of $96 \cdot 2^{-128}$.

Again, one could argue that this sort of an attack "forces" internal collisions, and thus, Claim 1 is not relevant to it. Yet, under this interpretation of the concept of internal collisions, Claim 3 may be voided.

3.1 Improved Attack

We note that one can easily improve the success rate of the attack by adding more 0 blocks, as 8-round keyless has more fixed points than 4-round—each fixed point of 4-round AES is also a fixed point for 8-round AES, but there may be more. We found 26 fixed points for 8-round AES: 18 that appear in Table 2 and 8 additional ones. Again, due to efficiency reasons the search was done over inputs of the form (x, x, x, x). Hence, the probability that adding two blocks of zero (without changing the tag) being a successful forgery is at least $26 \cdot 2^{-128}$.

Of course, one can test other number of rounds (which is a multiple of 4). In Table 3 we list the number of fixed points found for multiple-of-4 number of keyless AES rounds (greater than 4) up to 200. As we show, one can increase the chances of successful forgery, e.g., by adding 45 message blocks of 0, resulting in a successful forgery with probability $312 \cdot 2^{-128}$.

We tested all number of rounds starting at 2 (which has 6 fixed points) until 2,000. Besides the results reported in Table 3, we list the number of rounds with more than 122 fixed points in Table 4 in Appendix A. We note that the maximal number is obtained for 1902-round keyless AES, for which 3,810 (!) fixed points exist. While 1,902 is not divisible by 4, $2 \cdot 1902 = 3,804$ is divisible by 4 (and has at least the same number of fixed points). Hence, inserting a sequence of $\frac{3804}{4} = 951$ blocks of 0, does not change the tag with probability of at least $3810 \cdot 2^{-128} \approx 2^{-116.1}$.

4 Possible Mitigations

One can think of several mitigations to our attacks. In this section we briefly analyze the implications of each such mitigation, and consider the impact they may have on the Pelican construction and our attack.

The simplest mitigation is to prohibit the all zero message block. This mitigation will immediately prevent the above mentioned attack. At the same time, it would cause problems in applying Pelican, as messages may have blocks which are zero. Of course, one could design a mechanism to support such blocks (e.g., the block 0 will be encoded as two blocks of some given values—$x, y \neq x$, and the block x will be encoded as two blocks of the form x, x). We note that this approach would cause both performance penalty and may allow for side channel attacks.

Table 3. Number of Fixed Points in r-Round Keyless AES

Rounds	Fix Points	Rounds	Fix Points	Rounds	Fix Points	Rounds	Fix Points
8	26	12	30	16	26	20	18
24	62	28	18	32	26	36	102
40	66	44	18	48	62	52	18
56	26	60	60	64	26	68	18
72	134	76	18	80	66	84	72
88	26	92	18	96	62	100	18
104	26	108	129	112	26	116	18
120	132	124	18	128	26	132	30
136	162	140	18	144	134	148	18
152	26	156	30	160	66	164	18
168	104	172	18	176	26	180	312
184	26	188	206	192	62	196	18

Another option is to reduce the block size from 128 bits to 120 bits, and fixing 8 bits to some predetermined constant. Obviously, this option would succeed in mitigating our basic fix-point based attack at the cost of reduced performance. On the other hand, the differential-based attack could still be applied (possibly with slightly lower success probability of $94 \cdot 2^{-128}$). Furthermore, despite our limited search, we found 32 fixed points for 1902-round keyless AES whose 8 least significant bits were zero. Hence, not only that a more powerful search may succeed to find a "pseudo fix point" that is preserved even with the 8 constant bits, even as it is, we can offer a forgery attack with a success rate of (at least) $32 \cdot 2^{-128}$ in this scenario.

A different approach is to replace the 4-round keyless AES with a keyed version. This would ensure that the adversary has no knowledge of the possible fix points (as those depend on the actual key). It seems that the performance impact in software and in hardware will be quite minimal. At the same time, this change may admit side channel attacks on the processing of the message.

Another option is to change the padding rule, such that one block containing the message length is also processed. For long messages, this change may not incur a high performance penalty (though it may increase the latency of producing the tag). At the same time, short messages may be greatly impacted by this change.

Finally, we note that adding unkeyed rounds may not necessarily improve the situation. As noted before (and in [10]), increasing the number of rounds may increase the number of fixed points. Hence, in addition to the performance penalty, picking any non-prime number of rounds is expected to reduce the security of the scheme.

5 Summary

In this paper we proposed a simple forgery attack against the Pelican MAC construction. The attack, while not harming any concrete uses of Pelican due to its low success rate, does seem to invalidate at least one of the security claims made by the Pelican designers.

We studied multiple mitigation possibilities, showing that the more secure ones either come with a performance penalty or reduced resistance to side channel attacks. Hence, it seems that one would need to revisit the security proofs of Pelican.

Acknowledgements. The author would like to thank Adi Shamir, Nathan Keller, and Eyal Ronen for the fruitful discussions.

A Keyless AES Rounds with a Large Number of Fix Points

Table 4. r-Round Keyless AES with a Large Number of Fixed Points

Rounds	Fix Points	Rounds	Fix Points	Rounds	Fix Points	Rounds	Fix Points
1902	3,810	1644	1,126	1096	1,122	548	1,114
1620	419	1080	411	360	384	720	384
1440	384	1800	384	1260	354	540	339
810	323	180	312	900	312	1980	312
1692	290	1890	285	1224	270	630	258
1880	254	1128	250	270	243	1350	243
648	241	1296	241	1944	241	1974	236
987	230	1410	224	564	218	705	218
90	216	450	216	990	216	1170	216
1530	216	1710	216	1269	215	376	214
752	214	1504	214	324	209	972	209
188	206	940	206	1316	206	1512	203
680	202	1360	202	1833	199	408	198
816	198	1632	198	94	194	282	194
470	194	658	194	846	194	1034	194
1222	194	1598	194	1786	194	1044	189
47	188	141	188	235	188	329	188

(*continued*)

Table 4. (*continued*)

Rounds	Fix Points	Rounds	Fix Points	Rounds	Fix Points	Rounds	Fix Points
423	188	517	188	611	188	799	188
893	188	1081	188	1175	188	1363	188
1457	188	1551	188	1645	188	1739	188
1927	188	504	176	1008	176	840	174
1680	174	756	171	136	162	272	162
544	162	952	162	1099	162	1496	162
1768	162	1904	162	216	161	432	161
684	161	1728	161	1134	155	567	149
696	149	1392	149	1701	149	1740	147
252	144	1764	144	405	137	1215	137
1218	135	72	134	144	134	288	134
576	134	792	134	936	134	1152	134
1368	134	1584	134	1656	134	1872	134
120	132	240	132	480	132	600	132
960	132	1200	132	1320	132	1560	132
1920	132	108	129	609	129	1188	129
1404	129	1827	129	1836	129	870	123

References

1. Bahrak, B., Aref, M.R.: A novel impossible differential cryptanalysis of AES. In: Proceedings of the Western European Workshop on Research in Cryptology 2007, Bochum, Germany (2007)
2. Biham, E., Keller, N.: Cryptanalysis of Reduced Variants of Rijndael (1999, unpublished manuscript)
3. Bogdanov, A., Mendel, F., Regazzoni, F., Rijmen, V., Tischhauser, E.: ALE: AES-based lightweight authenticated encryption. In: Moriai, S. (ed.) FSE 2013. LNCS, vol. 8424, pp. 447–466. Springer, Heidelberg (2014). https://doi.org/10.1007/978-3-662-43933-3_23
4. Bouillaguet, C., Dunkelman, O., Leurent, G., Fouque, P.-A.: Another look at complementation properties. In: Hong, S., Iwata, T. (eds.) FSE 2010. LNCS, vol. 6147, pp. 347–364. Springer, Heidelberg (2010). https://doi.org/10.1007/978-3-642-13858-4_20
5. Bouillaguet, C., Derbez, P., Fouque, P.-A.: Automatic search of attacks on round-reduced AES and applications. In: Rogaway, P. (ed.) CRYPTO 2011. LNCS, vol. 6841, pp. 169–187. Springer, Heidelberg (2011). https://doi.org/10.1007/978-3-642-22792-9_10
6. Daemen, J., Knudsen, L.R., Rijmen, V.: The block cipher square. In: Proceedings of Fast Software Encryption 1997. Lecture Notes in Computer Science, vol. 1267, pp. 149–165. Springer (1997)
7. Daemen, J., Rijmen, V.: The design of Rijndael: AES — the advanced encryption standard. Springer (2002)

8. Daemen, J., Rijmen, V.: A new MAC construction ALRED and a specific instance ALPHA-MAC. In: Gilbert, H., Handschuh, H. (eds.) FSE 2005. LNCS, vol. 3557, pp. 1–17. Springer, Heidelberg (2005). https://doi.org/10.1007/11502760_1
9. Daemen, J., Rijmen, V.: The Pelican MAC Function. IACR ePrint report 2005/088
10. Daemen, J., Rijmen, V.: Refinements of the ALRED construction and MAC security claims. IET Inf. Secur. **4**(3), 149–157 (2010)
11. Dunkelman, O., Keller, N., Shamir, A.: ALRED Blues: New Attacks on AES-Based MAC's. IACR ePrint report 2011/095
12. Dunkelman, O., Keller, N., Shamir, A.: Almost universal forgery attacks on AES-based MAC's. Des. Codes Crypt. **76**(2–3), 633–651 (2015)
13. Le, T., Sparr, R., Wernsdorf, R., Desmedt, Y.: Complementation-like and cyclic properties of AES round functions. In: Dobbertin, H., Rijmen, V., Sowa, A. (eds.) AES 2004. LNCS, vol. 3373, pp. 128–141. Springer, Heidelberg (2005). https://doi.org/10.1007/11506447_11
14. Minematsu, K., Tsunoo, Y.: Provably secure MACs from differentially-uniform permutations and AES-based implementations. In: Robshaw, M. (ed.) FSE 2006. LNCS, vol. 4047, pp. 226–241. Springer, Heidelberg (2006). https://doi.org/10.1007/11799313_15
15. O'Connor, L.: On the distribution of characteristics in bijective mappings. In: Helleseth, T. (ed.) EUROCRYPT 1993. LNCS, vol. 765, pp. 360–370. Springer, Heidelberg (1994). https://doi.org/10.1007/3-540-48285-7_31
16. Simplicio Jr, M.A., Barbuda, P.D.A.F., Barreto, P.S., Carvalho, T.C., Margi, C.B.: The MARVIN message authentication code and the LETTERSOUP authenticated encryption scheme. Secur. Commun. Netw. **2**(2), 165–180 (2009)
17. Simplício, M.A., Barreto, P.S.L.M., Carvalho, T.C.M.B.: Revisiting the security of the ALRED design. In: Burmester, M., Tsudik, G., Magliveras, S., Ilić, I. (eds.) ISC 2010. LNCS, vol. 6531, pp. 69–83. Springer, Heidelberg (2011). https://doi.org/10.1007/978-3-642-18178-8_7
18. Wang, L., Sakiyama, K., Nishikado, I., Ohta, K.: Security Evaluation of PC-MAC-AES. CRYPTREC report (2011). http://www.cryptrec.go.jp/estimation/techrep_id2005.pdf
19. Yuan, Z., Wang, W., Jia, K., Xu, G., Wang, X.: New birthday attacks on some MACs based on block ciphers. In: Halevi, S. (ed.) CRYPTO 2009. LNCS, vol. 5677, pp. 209–230. Springer, Heidelberg (2009). https://doi.org/10.1007/978-3-642-03356-8_13

From at Least $n/3$ to at Most $3\sqrt{n}$: Correcting the Algebraic Immunity of the Hidden Weight Bit Function

Algebraic Immunity Upper Bounds on Weightwise Degree-d Functions and Their Implications

Pierrick Méaux(✉)

Luxembourg University, Esch-sur-Alzette, Luxembourg
pierrick.meaux@uni.lu

Abstract. Weightwise degree-d (WWdd) functions are Boolean functions that, on each set of fixed Hamming weight, coincide with a function of degree at most d. They generalize both symmetric functions and the Hidden Weight Bit Function (HWBF), which has been studied in cryptography for its favorable properties. In this work, we establish a general upper bound on the algebraic immunity of such functions, a key security parameter against algebraic attacks on stream ciphers like filtered Linear Feedback Shift Registers (LFSRs). We construct explicit low-degree annihilators for WWdd functions with small d, and show how to generalize these constructions. As an application, we prove that the algebraic immunity of the HWBF is upper bounded by $3\sqrt{n}$ disproving a result from 2011 that claimed a lower bound of $n/3$. We then apply our technique to several generalizations of the HWBF proposed since 2021 for homomorphically friendly constructions and LFSR-based ciphers, refining or refuting results from six prior works.

Keywords: Boolean functions · Algebraic immunity · Symmetric functions · HWBF

1 Introduction

1.1 Weightwise Degree-d Functions, a Unifying Perspective

Weightwise degree-d (WWdd) functions are Boolean functions that, when restricted to each set of inputs of fixed Hamming weight—called a slice—coincide with a function of algebraic degree at most d. This notion, introduced in [26], was originally used to study the relationship between weightwise affine functions (the case $d = 1$) and weightwise perfectly balanced functions, *i.e.* , functions that are balanced on every slice [12]. Although the definition is recent, weightwise constant and affine functions—corresponding to the cases $d = 0$ and $d = 1$—have appeared in many earlier works, often under different names. For instance, symmetric Boolean functions (WWd0), which depend only on the Hamming weight

D. Escudero and I. Damgård (Eds.): LATINCRYPT 2025, LNCS 16129, pp. 345–369, 2026.
https://doi.org/10.1007/978-3-032-06754-8_13

of their input, have been extensively studied for their cryptographic relevance *e.g.* [3,6,7,41]. The most known example of a weightwise affine function is the Hidden Weight Bit Function (HWBF) [4], which outputs the k-th bit of the input when the Hamming weight is k, and 0 on the all-zero vector. It has drawn attention both for its exponential binary decision diagram size [2] and for its main cryptographic parameters, studied in [43]. While efficiently computable, the HWBF lacks sufficient nonlinearity to be used directly as a cryptographic filter in stream ciphers, leading to generalizations that aim to preserve its efficiency while improving its cryptographic strength [9,44].

In recent years, weightwise degree-d functions—particularly for small values of d—have gained renewed attention, both through their emergence in modern applications and their revival in classical cipher design. One primary motivation comes from the field of Hybrid Homomorphic Encryption (HHE) [40], where components of symmetric ciphers must be efficiently evaluable under homomorphic encryption. Multiple symmetric ciphers have been developed with this constraint in mind, including LowMC [1], Kreyvium [5], FLIP [34], Rasta [23], and FiLIP [33]. In this context, weightwise low-degree functions offer a good trade-off between structural simplicity and algebraic complexity, making them attractive for homomorphically friendly design. This direction is supported by ongoing advances in the homomorphic evaluation of Boolean functions. Notably, the efficient homomorphic computation of Hamming weight [27] and the use of fast multiplexer circuits in schemes such as FHEW [24] and TFHE [17] have enabled the practical evaluation of symmetric and WWdd functions on encrypted inputs. Recent implementations demonstrate HHE evaluation with latency under 10ms per bit [18,36], further underscoring the practicality of these function classes. A second motivation stems from the renewed interest in stream cipher constructions based on filtered Linear Feedback Shift Registers (LFSRs), a classical paradigm originally explored in the late 1990s and early 2000s. In this setting, WWdd functions—especially those related to the HWBF—have been proposed as filtering functions due to their low implementation cost and presumed resistance to algebraic attacks. This line of work has reemerged in recent designs such as [13,15,35], where the structured nature of WWdd functions is leveraged to combine simplicity with cryptographic strength.

1.2 Algebraic Immunity and Annihilators

Algebraic attacks are among the most powerful techniques for cryptanalyzing stream ciphers. These attacks consist in deriving, from the observed keystream, a system of algebraic equations in the secret key bits, and then solving this system of multivariate equations over $\mathbb{F}_2$. In the case of a filtered LFSR, the adversary obtains equations of degree equal to that of the Boolean filtering function. However, the algebraic attack introduced by Courtois and Meier [20] showed that one can exploit annihilators of the filtering function to obtain an even lower-degree system. Specifically, instead of using the function f directly, the attacker considers a nonzero Boolean function g of low degree such that $f \cdot g = 0$. To quantify a function's resistance to such attacks, the notion of

Algebraic Immunity (AI) was formalized in [38]. It is defined as the minimal degree of a nonzero annihilator of a Boolean function f or its complement $f+1$. A high AI is generally considered a key requirement for any Boolean function used as a filtering component in a stream cipher.

While the concept is well defined, computing or bounding the AI of a function is notoriously difficult. In most cases, known results focus on specific functions or restricted classes, and rely on ad hoc techniques. Only a few Boolean functions families are known to achieve optimal algebraic immunity (*i.e.* , ceiling of $n/2$ for n variables), such as the majority function [21] and the Carlet–Feng functions [10]. However, these functions suffer from drawbacks: the majority function has low nonlinearity, and Carlet–Feng functions are difficult to implement efficiently, as they are defined via their support over $\mathbb{F}_{2^n}$. As a result, functions with suboptimal but sufficiently high AI are often preferred in practice.

In this article, we adopt a different strategy for analyzing the algebraic immunity of the HWBF and its generalizations. Rather than relying on case-specific constructions, we leverage the structure of weightwise degree-d functions to build low-degree annihilators in a more systematic way. The key idea is that when a function has low algebraic degree on each Hamming weight slice, one can combine this slice-wise structure with symmetric functions that vanish on most slices to derive global annihilators of remarkably low degree. This approach allows us to obtain new upper bounds on the AI of a broad class of functions—including many recently proposed for cryptographic use. In particular, we show that viewing a function through the lens of weightwise degree-d structure can reveal weaknesses not captured before. In the next part, we present our main contributions, which include both theoretical results on annihilator construction and concrete applications to functions recently introduced in symmetric cryptography and homomorphic-friendly designs.

1.3 Contributions

The first part of this work is devoted to developing a general method for constructing low-degree annihilators for Boolean functions based on their representation as weightwise degree-d functions. Our starting point is the observation that certain low-degree symmetric functions vanish on most slices. This property makes them ideal candidates to multiply with functions annihilating the functions taken by the target function on the remaining slices.

We formalize this idea in our main theorem: if a Boolean function is weightwise degree-d and has no constant term on any slice, then it admits an annihilator of degree at most $\sqrt{nd}(\sqrt{2}+1)$. This yields a nontrivial upper bound on the algebraic immunity of a broad class of functions, including symmetric, weightwise linear, and many HWBF-like constructions. In some cases, refining our approach allows the construction of even lower-degree annihilators, by targeting multiple remaining slices simultaneously.

Beyond the class of WWdd functions, we also show how this methodology can be generalized to other settings. The key idea is to replace the weight slices with any partition of $\mathbb{F}_2^n$ satisfying two conditions:

i. there exists a low-degree function that vanishes on most parts of the partition, and
ii. the target function coincides with low-degree functions on the remaining parts.

Under these conditions, similar upper bounds on the degree of annihilators can be obtained, extending the scope of our approach beyond the WWdd framework.

In the second part of this work, we demonstrate the effectiveness of our method by applying it to several Boolean functions that have been proposed in the cryptographic literature. Our first result concerns the hidden weight bit function. While [43] claimed that the HWBF has algebraic immunity of at least $n/3$, we show that it actually admits an annihilator of degree at most $\sqrt{n}(\sqrt{2}+1)$ for sufficiently large n, thereby disproving the previously accepted bound. This gap between the expected and actual algebraic immunity has important consequences. Over the past decade, a number of works have used the HWBF or closely related functions under the assumption that they offer strong resistance to algebraic attacks. Our results challenge this assumption and provide new upper bounds that refine or invalidate claims in these works.

In particular, we revisit six works in which HWBF-like functions play a central role:

- We address the original result of [43] by disproving its claim on the algebraic immunity of the HWBF. We show that the first value where our technique gives an explicit annihilator that contradicts the claimed bound from [43] is $n = 27$ and we provide such an example.
- In [35], cyclic weightwise quadratic functions are introduced for efficient homomorphic evaluation. We prove that the algebraic immunity of these functions also scales proportionally to $\sqrt{n}$, and we provide explicit annihilators for the two main functions highlighted in the article.
- In [13], Boolean functions based on the HWBF and the Maiorana–McFarland construction are studied as potential filtering functions. Although these functions are not strictly weightwise quadratic, they can be analyzed in a similar manner by considering the Hamming weight of one half of the input. We establish upper bounds on the algebraic immunity for two families introduced in the paper and determine for which values of n these bounds contradict the conjectured AI.
- In [37], a generalization of the HWBF with higher nonlinearity is proposed. We apply our method to this function and derive an upper bound on its algebraic immunity.
- In [15], filtered LFSRs are revisited with large parameters, using weightwise quadratic functions as filters. We show that these functions also fall within the scope of our general bound, without contradicting the conjectured AI stated in that work.
- In [14], the authors continue this line of research with new functions based on Maiorana-McFarland construction. Unlike the functions in [13], the main

function studied here has algebraic immunity of at least $n/4$. We explain why our method does not yield annihilators of degree proportional to $\sqrt{n}$ in this case, and we establish an upper bound on the AI of this family.

In each case, we either disprove a conjecture, correct a previously stated bound, or offer new insight into the function's actual algebraic immunity.

2 Preliminaries

We denote by $[1, n]$ the set of all integers from 1 to n, *i.e.* $\{1, \dots, n\}$. For readability, we use the notation $+$ instead of $\oplus$ for addition in $\mathbb{F}_2$. For a vector $v \in \mathbb{F}_2^n$, we denote its Hamming weight by $\mathsf{w_H}(v)$, defined as $\mathsf{w_H}(v) = |\{i \in [n] \mid v_i = 1\}|$. Throughout this article, log denotes the base-2 logarithm.

2.1 Generalities on Boolean Functions and Cryptographic Criteria

In this section, we review fundamental concepts of Boolean functions and define their key cryptographic properties. For a more in-depth discussion on Boolean functions and their cryptographic properties, we refer to the book [8].

Definition 1 (Boolean Function). *A Boolean function f in n variables (an n-variable Boolean function) is a function from $\mathbb{F}_2^n$ to $\mathbb{F}_2$. The set of all Boolean functions in n variables is denoted by $\mathcal{B}_n$.*

Definition 2 (Algebraic Normal Form (ANF) and degree). *We call Algebraic Normal Form of a Boolean function f its n-variable polynomial representation over $\mathbb{F}_2$ (i.e. belonging to $\mathbb{F}_2[x_1, \dots, x_n]/(x_1^2 + x_1, \dots, x_n^2 + x_n)$):*

$$f(x) = \sum_{I \subseteq [n]} a_I \left(\prod_{i \in I} x_i \right) = \sum_{I \subseteq [n]} a_I x^I,$$

where $a_I \in \mathbb{F}_2$.

- *The algebraic degree of f is:* $\mathsf{deg}(f) = \max_{\{I \mid a_I = 1\}} |I|$ *(with the convention that* $\mathsf{deg}(0) = 0$*).*
- *Any term $\prod_{i \in I} x_i$ in such an ANF is called a monomial and its degree equals $|I|$.*

In this article, we study the algebraic immunity of various functions. Below, we provide its definition. Algebraic immunity is, among other things, the main parameter used to estimate the complexity of the algebraic attack [20] on filtered linear feedback shift registers. We then recall the concepts of balancedness and nonlinearity, which are the other key cryptographic criteria to consider for Boolean functions used in stream ciphers.

Definition 3 (Algebraic Immunity [38]). *The algebraic immunity of a Boolean function $f \in \mathcal{B}_n$, denoted as $\mathsf{AI}(f)$, is defined as:*

$$\mathsf{AI}(f) = \min_{g \neq 0}\{\mathsf{deg}(g) \mid fg = 0 \text{ or } (f+1)g = 0\},$$

The function g is called an annihilator of f (or $f+1$).

Definition 4 (Balancedness). *A Boolean function $f \in \mathcal{B}_n$ is said to be balanced if and only if $|\mathsf{supp}(f)| = |\mathsf{supp}(f+1)| = 2^{n-1}$, where the support of f denotes the set $\{x \in \mathbb{F}_2^n,$ such that $f(x) = 1\}$.*

Definition 5 (Nonlinearity). *The nonlinearity $\mathsf{NL}(f)$ of a Boolean function $f \in \mathcal{B}_n$, where n is a positive integer, is the minimum Hamming distance between f and all the affine functions in $\mathcal{B}_n$:*

$$\mathsf{NL}(f) = \min_{g,\, \mathsf{deg}(g) \leq 1}\{d_H(f, g)\},$$

with $d_H(f,g) = \#\{x \in \mathbb{F}_2^n \mid f(x) \neq g(x)\}$ the Hamming distance between f and g, and $g(x) = a \cdot x + \varepsilon$; $a \in \mathbb{F}_2^n, \varepsilon \in \mathbb{F}_2$ (where $\cdot$ is an inner product in $\mathbb{F}_2^n$).

2.2 Slices, Symmetric Functions and Weightwise Degree-d Functions

Definition 6 (Slices of the Boolean hypercube). *For $k \in [0, n]$, we define the k-th slice of the n-dimensional Boolean hypercube as the set $\mathsf{E}_{k,n} = \{x \in \mathbb{F}_2^n \mid \mathsf{w_H}(x) = k\}$.*

According to Definition 6, the Boolean hypercube is partitioned into $n+1$ slices, where each slice consists of vectors sharing the same Hamming weight. We refer to properties that hold slice-wise as weightwise properties. The n-variable symmetric Boolean functions are precisely those that are constant on each slice.

Definition 7 (Symmetric Functions). *Let $n \in \mathbb{N}^*$. A Boolean function in n variables is said to be symmetric if it is constant on each slice $\mathsf{E}_{k,n}$ for $k \in [0, n]$. The set of symmetric functions in n variables is denoted by $\mathcal{SYM}_n$, and we have $|\mathcal{SYM}_n| = 2^{n+1}$.*

We distinguish the following notable families of symmetric functions:

- ***Elementary symmetric functions.*** *For $i \in [0, n]$, the elementary symmetric function of degree i, denoted $\sigma_{i,n}$, is the Boolean function whose ANF contains all monomials of degree i, and none of other degrees.*
- ***Slice indicator functions.*** *For $k \in [0, n]$, the indicator function of the k-th slice is defined as*

$$\forall x \in \mathbb{F}_2^n, \quad \varphi_{k,n}(x) = \begin{cases} 1 \text{ if } \mathsf{w_H}(x) = k, \\ 0 \text{ otherwise.} \end{cases}$$

– ***Threshold functions.*** *For $d \in [0, n]$, the threshold function of threshold d is defined as*

$$\forall x \in \mathbb{F}_2^n, \quad \mathsf{T}_{d,n}(x) = \begin{cases} 0 \text{ if } \mathsf{w_H}(x) < d, \\ 1 \text{ otherwise.} \end{cases}$$

In particular, the majority function MAJ_n is the threshold function with $d = \lceil n/2 \rceil$.

The $n + 1$ functions in each of the three families above form a basis for $\mathcal{SYM}_n$—that is, every symmetric Boolean function can be written as a linear combination of these $n + 1$ functions.

We recall a property of elementary symmetric functions that will be useful in the sequel.

Property 1. *Let $n \in \mathbb{N}^*$ and $d \in [0, n]$. The elementary symmetric function $\sigma_{d,n}$ satisfies:*

$$\sigma_{d,n}(x) = \binom{k}{d} \bmod 2 \quad \text{for all } x \in \mathsf{E}_{k,n}.$$

We now recall the definition of weightwise degree-d functions:

Definition 8 Weightwise degree-d functions ([26]). *Let $n \in \mathbb{N}^*$. For $k \in [0, n]$, let $\varphi_{k,n}$ denote the indicator function of the slice $\mathsf{E}_{k,n}$.*

A Boolean function $f : \mathbb{F}_2^n \to \mathbb{F}_2$, written as $f = \sum_{k=0}^{n} f_k \varphi_{k,n}$, is called weightwise degree-d *(WWdd) if and only if, for each $k \in [0, n]$, the restriction f_k coincides with a function of degree at most d over $\mathsf{E}_{k,n}$.*

The set of weightwise degree-d functions in n variables is denoted by $\mathcal{WD}_n^d$.

The notion was introduced in [26], where the authors studied the relationship between weightwise perfectly balanced functions (*i.e.* functions that are balanced on every slice—see, for example [12,22,28–31,39,42]) and weightwise affine functions—that is, functions of weightwise degree-1.

Weightwise degree-0 and degree-1 functions have been studied for their cryptographic properties in many works, although not under the formalism introduced in [26]. Weightwise constant functions (*i.e.* $\mathcal{WD}_n^0$) correspond to symmetric Boolean functions (Definition 7), which have been extensively studied (see, [3,6,7,11,16,32,41]). The hidden weight bit function, introduced in [4], is a notable example of a weightwise degree-1 function. It is defined by setting $f_0 = 0$ and $f_k = x_k$ for $k \in [1, n]$. Its cryptographic properties were analyzed in [43]. In [12], the bent functions presented in Propositions 1 and 2 are shown to be weightwise affine.

Weightwise quadratic functions have also been studied more recently, starting in [35] and continuing in [13,15,37]. In this article, we rely on the formalism of weightwise degree-d functions to derive bounds on their algebraic immunity.

2.3 Properties on Binomial Coefficients

We recall some results on binomial coefficients used in a few proofs in the article.

Property 2 (Lucas' Theorem, *e.g.* [25]). *Let $a, b, p \in \mathbb{N}$ be integers such that $a > b$ and p is a prime. Consider their p-adic expansions $a = \sum_{j=0}^{q} a_j p^j$ and $b = \sum_{j=0}^{q} b_j p^j$ such that $0 \le a_j < p$ and $0 \le b_j < p$ for each $j \in [0, q]$ and $a_q \neq 0$. Then*

$$\binom{a}{b} \equiv \prod_{j=0}^{q} \binom{a_j}{b_j} \mod p.$$

Property 3 (Properties on binomial coefficients). *Let $n \in \mathbb{N}$, the following hold on the binomial coefficients:*

- $\sum_{k=0}^{n} \binom{n}{k} = 2^n$.
- $\sum_{i=k}^{n} \binom{i}{k} = \binom{n+1}{k+1}$.

3 Algebraic Immunity Upper Bound

In this section, we construct low-degree symmetric functions and show how they can be used to build annihilators for weightwise degree-d functions.

In Sect. 3.1, we present low-degree symmetric functions that vanish on most slices of the Boolean hypercube. These functions are then used in our main result, Theorem 1, to derive an upper bound on the algebraic immunity of weightwise degree-d functions whose components f_k have no constant term.

In Sect. 3.2, we explore generalizations of this result. First, we show that other symmetric functions can also be used to construct low-degree annihilators for WWdd functions. We then discuss how even lower-degree annihilators can be obtained. Finally, we explain how these techniques can be extended to partitions beyond the slice decomposition and provide an illustrative example.

3.1 Low-Degree Symmetric Functions with Low Weight

First, in this part we introduce a family of symmetric functions and show they take the value 1 only on a fraction of the slices.

Proposition 1. *Let $n \in \mathbb{N}^*$, and $r \in [0, \lfloor \log(n) \rfloor]$, we define the Boolean symmetric function $\psi_{r,n}$ as:*

$$\psi_{r,n} = \sum_{i=0}^{2^r-1} \sigma_{i,n}.$$

$\psi_{r,n}$ has the following properties:

- $\mathsf{deg}(\psi_{r,n}) = 2^r - 1$,
- $\psi_{r,n}(x) = 1 \Leftrightarrow x \in \mathsf{E}_{k,n}$ *with* $k \equiv 0 \mod 2^r$.

Proof. The degree of $\psi_{r,n}$ is $2^r - 1$ since it is the sum of homogeneous functions of different degrees, with maximum degree $2^r - 1$.

Then, we focus on the value of $\psi_{r,n}$ on a slice $\mathsf{E}_{k,n}$ (since $\psi_{r,n}$ is symmetric, it takes the same value on all elements of a slice). We denote e_k this value, using Property 1 we obtain:

$$e_k \equiv \sum_{d=0}^{2^r-1} \binom{k}{d} \mod 2.$$

From Lucas' theorem (Property 2), for all $k \in [0, n]$ we have that $\binom{k}{d} \equiv \binom{u}{d} \mod 2$ where $u \in [0, 2^r - 1]$ denotes the remainder of the Euclidean division of k by 2^r. Accordingly, using Property 3:

$$e_k = \sum_{d=0}^{2^r-1} \binom{u}{d} \equiv \sum_{d=0}^{u} \binom{u}{d} \equiv 2^u \mod 2 \equiv \begin{cases} 1 & \text{if } u = 0, \\ 0 & \text{otherwise.} \end{cases}$$

□

In other words, $\psi_{r,n}$ is the indicator function of the set $\{x \in \mathbb{F}_2^n \mid \mathsf{w_H}(x) \equiv 0 \mod 2^r\}$. These functions can be used to build annihilators of weightwise degree-d functions. We focus on the case where each restriction on the slice, f_k, has no constant component (*i.e.* $a_\emptyset = 0$ in its ANF).

Theorem 1. *Let $n \in \mathbb{N}^*$, and $f \in \mathcal{WD}_n^d$, where all restriction on the slices, f_k, are degree-d functions with no constant term, then the following holds on f:*

$$\mathsf{AI}(f) \leq \min_{0 \leq r \leq \lfloor \log(n) \rfloor} \left(2^r - 1 + d \cdot \left\lfloor \frac{n}{2^r} \right\rfloor \right).$$

Proof. We prove the upper bound on the algebraic immunity by exhibiting non trivial annihilators of f of degree $2^r - 1 + d \cdot \lfloor \frac{n}{2^r} \rfloor$ for each $r \in \lfloor \log(n) \rfloor$.

We consider the function g_r defined as:

$$g_r = \psi_{r,n} \cdot \prod_{i=1}^{\lfloor n/2^r \rfloor} (1 + f_{2^r \cdot i}).$$

Then, for all $x \in \mathbb{F}_2^n$ we get $f \cdot g_r = 0$. From Proposition 1, $\psi_{r,n}$ takes the value 0 on all slices where $k \not\equiv 0 \mod 2^r$, hence g_r and $f \cdot g_r = 0$ on these slices. On the remaining slices, we have on $\mathsf{E}_{k,n}$ $f \cdot g_r = f_k \cdot \prod_{i=1}^{\lfloor n/2^r \rfloor} (1 + f_{2^r \cdot i})$ which is null since there is a product $f_k \cdot (1 + f_k) = 0$. Accordingly, g_r is an annihilator of f.

Since g_r is the product of functions taking the value 1 in 0_n (by definition of $\psi_{r,n}$ and the restrictions of f on the slices), we get $g_r(0_n) = 1$, hence g_r is not the null function. Furthermore, since $\mathsf{deg}(\psi_{r,n}) = 2^r - 1$ and the $\lfloor n/2^r \rfloor$ functions $1 + f_i$ have degree d, g_r has degree at most $2^r - 1 + d \cdot \lfloor \frac{n}{2^r} \rfloor$. We conclude that the algebraic immunity is the minimum degree aver all non trivial annihilators of f and $f + 1$. □

Remark 1. The restriction in Theorem 1 that the functions f_k do not contain a constant term arises from the construction of the annihilator of f (see g_r in the proof). If two slices, f_k and $f_{k'}$, satisfy $f_k = 1 + f_{k'}$, then the annihilator constructed in the proof could be a multiple of $f_k \cdot (1 + f_{k'}) = 0$, resulting in the trivial annihilator. Consequently, the restriction in the theorem is sufficient to ensure that the constructed annihilator is nontrivial for all such functions.

Furthermore, we note that Theorem 1 does not apply to majority or (non-constant) threshold functions, as these functions necessarily have at least one slice f_k that corresponds to the constant function 1.

3.2 Towards Generalizations

The proof of Theorem 1 relies on the functions $\psi_{r,n}$, which are nonzero only on slices where k is congruent to 0 modulo 2^r. This choice is motivated by its simplicity and the applications studied in Sect. 4. Nevertheless, the same proof techniques can be applied using other low-degree symmetric functions that take the value 1 on exactly one slice out of every 2^r. In the following theorem, we establish the existence and degree of such functions.

Theorem 2. *Let $n \in \mathbb{N}^*$, $r \in [0, \lfloor \log(n) \rfloor]$ and $k \in [0, 2^r - 1]$, the n-variable Boolean symmetric function:*

$$f = \sum_{\substack{i=0 \\ i \equiv k \mod 2^r}}^{n} \varphi_{i,n},$$

is such that $\mathsf{deg}(f) = 2^r - 1$.

Proof. First, since the family of n-variable elementary symmetric functions forms a basis for the space of n-variable symmetric functions, it follows that f can be expressed as a linear combination of the σ_i. Using Property 1, for all $d \geq 2^r$, the function σ_d evaluates to 0 on all slices $\mathsf{E}_{k,n}$ where $k \in [0, 2^r - 1]$. Consequently, the linear combination of σ_i representing f must involve elementary symmetric functions of degree strictly less than 2^r. Next, by applying Property 1 and Property 2, since for any $d < 2^r$, the function σ_d takes the same value on all slices $\mathsf{E}_{k,n}$ that share the same congruence modulo 2^r, the linear combination of σ_i that matches f on slices of weight in the range $[0, 2^r - 1]$ also maintains the same values as f across all slices. This allows us to conclude that f has degree at most $2^r - 1$.

To show that f has exactly degree $2^r - 1$, we argue by contradiction. Since f takes the value 1 an odd number of times in the range $[0, 2^r - 1]$, the function σ_{2^r-1} must be present in the linear combination defining f. Suppose, for contradiction, that $\mathsf{deg}(f) < 2^r - 1$. Then, f would be a sum of symmetric functions that take the value 1 on an even number of slices in the range $[0, 2^r - 1]$. Indeed, for $d \in [0, 2^r - 2]$, the function σ_d takes the value $\binom{k}{d} \mod 2$ on the slice $\mathsf{E}_{k,n}$ (by Property 1). Moreover, using Property 3, Item 2, we obtain:

$$\sum_{k=0}^{2^r-1} \binom{k}{d} = \sum_{k=d}^{2^r-1} \binom{k}{d} = \binom{2^r}{d+1} \equiv 0 \mod 2,$$

where the congruence modulo 2 follows from Property 2, since $d+1 \in [1, 2^r - 1]$. Since all such σ_i functions take the value 1 an even number of times on the slices in the range $[0, 2^r - 1]$, the same must hold for any linear combination of these functions. Consequently, if $\mathsf{deg}(f) < 2^r - 1$, then f would take the value 1 on an even number of slices in the range $[0, 2^r - 1]$, contradicting the definition of f. This contradiction confirms that $\deg(f) = 2^r - 1$. □

Using Theorem 2, there exist cases where nonzero annihilators of degree lower than the bound given in Theorem 1 can be constructed. Let us call r' the value of r leading to the minimum in Theorem 1. If there exists $i \in [0, 2^{r'} - 1]$ such that a function g annihilates all the f_k with $k \equiv i \mod 2^{r'}$ and has degree lower than $d \cdot \lfloor n/2^{r'} \rfloor$, then g is a candidate for constructing an annihilator of lower degree than the upper bound. If g is nonzero on one of the slices $\mathsf{E}_{k,n}$ where $k \equiv i \mod 2^{r'}$, then it is sufficient to obtain a non-null annihilator of f with degree lower than the upper bound of Theorem 1.

It provides a more general perspective on the underlying mechanism behind the results of Sect. 3.1 for bounding the algebraic immunity. To establish an upper bound on the AI of a function f, we rely on the following facts:

1. There exists a partition $\mathcal{P}$ of $\mathbb{F}_2^n$, $\mathcal{P} = \{P_1, \ldots, P_t\}$ that allows f to be expressed as:
$$f = \sum_{i=1}^{t} f_i \cdot \mathbb{1}_{P_i},$$
where each f_i has low degree.
2. There exists a low degree function g such that g is null on most of the P_i, specifically on all P_i such that $i \in I \subsetneq [1, t]$.
3. There exists a low degree function h such that $h \cdot f_i = 0$ (at least over P_i) for all $i \in [1, t] \setminus I$.
4. The product $g \cdot h$ is nonzero.

We emphasize that the low-degree condition in item 1 is not strictly necessary. In the case of weightwise degree-d functions, it was precisely this property that allowed us to construct a low-degree function h. Generalizing these techniques to upper bound the algebraic immunity of other families of functions ultimately reduces to identifying partitions where: a low-degree function evaluates to zero on most of the parts, another low-degree function annihilates all remaining terms on the parts where they are defined, and the product of these two functions is nonzero.

For illustration we provide the following example.

Example 1. Let $\mathcal{P}$ be the partition of $\mathbb{F}_2^n$ defined by:

- $P_1 = \{x \in \mathbb{F}_2^n \mid x_1 = 1\}$,
- for $i \in [2, n]$, $P_i = \{x \in \mathbb{F}_2^n \mid x_i = 1, x_1 = \cdots = x_{i-1} = 0\}$,
- $P_{n+1} = \{0_n\}$.

Any function $f \in \mathcal{B}_n$ can be expressed as:

$$f = \sum_{i=1}^{n+1} f_i \cdot \mathbb{1}_{P_i} = f_{n+1} \cdot \mathbb{1}_{0_n} + \sum_{i=1}^{n} f_i \cdot x_i \prod_{j=1}^{i-1} (1 + x_j).$$

We observe that for $j \in [1, n]$ the linear function x_j is null over P_i for $i \in [j+1, n+1]$. Thus it can serve as the function g. Then, an annihilator h of f_i for all $i \in [1, j]$ not null on the set $\{x \in \mathbb{F}_2^n \mid x_j = 1\}$ allows us to build the non-null annihilator $x_j \cdot h$ of f, with degree $1 + \mathsf{deg}(h)$ which can be as low as $1 + \sum_{i=1}^{j} \mathsf{deg}(f_i)$.

4 AI Bound on Already Studied Functions

In this section, we apply the methodology developed in Sect. 3 to derive upper bounds on the algebraic immunity of various Boolean functions proposed in the cryptographic literature. We present six cases where our approach is applicable. In each instance, we either disprove a conjecture, revise a previously stated bound, or provide new insight into the true algebraic immunity of the function under study.

4.1 Hidden Weight Bit Function

The hidden weight bit function was introduced in [4] and is considered the simplest example of a function whose binary decision diagram has exponential size [2,4]. Its cryptographic properties, such as balancedness, nonlinearity, algebraic degree, and algebraic immunity, have been analyzed in [43]. The function's relatively strong parameters have contributed to recent interest in its generalization, particularly towards achieving higher nonlinearity. Another reason for this interest is its computational efficiency.

We begin by recalling the definition of the HWBF, both as presented in [43] and as a WWdd function.

Definition 9 (Hidden weight bit function). *The hidden weight bit function in n variables, $h \in \mathcal{B}_n$ is defined as follows:*

$$h(x) = \begin{cases} 0 & \textit{if } x = 0_n, \\ x_{\mathsf{w_H}(x)} & \textit{otherwise.} \end{cases}$$

It is a weightwise linear function, that can be written as $h = \sum_{k=0}^{n} h_k \varphi_{k,n}$ where:

$$h_0 = 0, \qquad \textit{and } \forall k \in [1, n] \quad h_k = x_k.$$

In [43], Theorem 4 states that the HWBF has an algebraic immunity of at least $\lfloor \frac{n}{3} \rfloor + 1$, based on a lengthy proof involving case disjunctions and induction. In the following, we demonstrate that this result is incorrect and show that the algebraic immunity of the HWBF does not exceed $3\sqrt{n}$.

Theorem 3 (Upper bound on the algebraic immunity of the HWBF).

Let $n \in \mathbb{N}^*$, the algebraic immunity of the n-variable HWBF h satisfies the relation:

$$\begin{aligned}\mathsf{AI}(h) &\leq \min(2^{\lfloor \frac{\log n}{2} \rfloor} + \lfloor 2^{\log(n) - \lfloor \frac{\log n}{2} \rfloor} \rfloor, 2^{\lceil \frac{\log n}{2} \rceil} + \lfloor 2^{\log(n) - \lceil \frac{\log n}{2} \rceil} \rfloor) - 1 \\ &\leq \sqrt{n}(\sqrt{2}+1) - 1.\end{aligned}$$

Proof. Since h is weightwise linear, we can apply Theorem 1 to obtain an upper bound on its algebraic immunity. The minimum is attained for $r = \lfloor (\log n)/2 \rfloor$ or $r = \lceil (\log n)/2 \rceil$, yielding the first bound. We then proceed by case disjunction. First, we assume that $(\log n)/2 - \lfloor (\log n)/2 \rfloor \leq 0.5$ and denote this quantity by ε. In this case, the bound obtained by taking $r = \lfloor (\log n)/2 \rfloor$ gives:

$$\begin{aligned}\mathsf{AI}(h) &\leq 2^{\lfloor \frac{\log n}{2} \rfloor} + \lfloor 2^{\log(n) - \lfloor \frac{\log n}{2} \rfloor} \rfloor - 1 \\ &\leq 2^{\frac{\log n}{2}} + 2^{\frac{\log n}{2} + \varepsilon} - 1 \leq \sqrt{n} + \sqrt{n} \cdot 2^{\varepsilon} - 1 \\ &\leq (1+\sqrt{2})\sqrt{n} - 1.\end{aligned}$$

Otherwise, if $0.5 < (\log n)/2 - \lfloor (\log n)/2 \rfloor < 1$, we define $\varepsilon' = \lceil (\log n)/2 \rceil - (\log n)/2$, which satisfies $\varepsilon' \leq 0.5$. In this case, the bound obtained by taking $r = \lceil (\log n)/2 \rceil$ gives:

$$\mathsf{AI}(h) \leq 2^{\lceil \frac{\log n}{2} \rceil} + \lfloor 2^{\log(n) - \lceil \frac{\log n}{2} \rceil} \rfloor - 1 \leq 2^{\frac{\log n}{2} + \varepsilon'} + 2^{\frac{\log n}{2}} - 1 \leq (\sqrt{2}+1)\sqrt{n} - 1.$$

We can conclude from the two cases: $\mathsf{AI}(h) \leq \sqrt{n}(\sqrt{2}+1) - 1$. □

We note that the inconsistency between the statement in [43] and Theorem 3 cannot be observed for small values of n, as computing the algebraic immunity of a function with 20 variables is already computationally demanding in terms of time and resources. In Table 1, we compare the two bounds for several values of n. We observe that the first value of n for which the two bounds become incompatible is $n = 27$. In this case, h admits the following degree-9 annihilator (which can be verified using a computer algebra system such as Sage):

$$(1 + \sigma_{1,n} + \sigma_{2,n} + \sigma_{3,n})(1 + x_4)(1 + x_8)(1 + x_{12})(1 + x_{16})(1 + x_{20})(1 + x_{24}).$$

Table 1. Comparison of the AI bounds of the HWBF.

Value of n	5	10	15	20	25	26	27	28	29	30	35	40	50	60
Lower bound from [43], Theorem 4	2	4	6	7	9	9	10	10	10	11	12	14	17	21
Upper bound from our result, Theorem 3	3	5	6	8	9	9	9	10	10	10	11	12	13	14

The algebraic immunity of the HWBF is significantly lower than previously thought; its value, being less than $3\sqrt{n}$ rather than greater than $n/3$, may undermine its suitability for stream ciphers susceptible to algebraic attacks [19,20].

4.2 Weightwise Quadratic Functions from [35]

The WeightWise Quadratic (WWQ) functions introduced in [35] are cyclic WWdd functions designed for efficient computation using input-oblivious algorithms, a key requirement for homomorphic evaluation. One of the primary motivations for the functions proposed in [35] is their potential application in stream ciphers for hybrid homomorphic encryption [40].

We begin by recalling the notion of cyclic WWdd function introduced in [35].

Definition 10 (Cyclic weightwise degree-$d$function [35] **Definition** 16). *Let $n \in \mathbb{N}^*$, and $g \in \mathcal{B}_n$, we call cyclic weightwise degree-d function associated to g the weightwise degree-$\mathsf{deg}(g)$ function defined by:*

- $f_1 = g$,
- *for $i \in [0, n] \setminus \{1\}$, $f_i(x) = g(\mathsf{O}^{i-1}(x))$, where O^i denotes the cyclic shift by i positions: $\mathsf{O}^i(x_1, \ldots, x_n) = (x_{1+i \mod n}, \cdots, x_{n+i \mod n})$, the representative modulo n being taken as the integer between 1 and n.*

  We denote by $\mathcal{CWD}_n^d$ the set of cyclic weightwise degree-d functions.

In particular, [35] investigates the properties of two cyclic WWQ functions, specifically those defined by $g = x_1 + x_2x_3$ and $g = x_1 + \sum_{i=1}^{\lfloor \frac{n-1}{2} \rfloor} x_{2i}x_{2i+1}$, which we denote by t and u, respectively. The following proposition provides an upper bound on the algebraic immunity of cyclic WWQ functions. We omit the proof, as it follows directly from applying Theorem 1 with $d = 2$.

Proposition 2. *Let $n \in \mathbb{N}^*$, and $f \in \mathcal{CWD}_n^2$, associated to g of degree 2 and with no constant term (i.e. $g(0_n) = 0$), then the following holds on f:*

$$\mathsf{AI}(f) \leq \min(2^{\lfloor \frac{(\log n)+1}{2} \rfloor} + 2\lfloor 2^{\log(n) - \lfloor \frac{\log n+1}{2} \rfloor} \rfloor, 2^{\lceil \frac{(\log n)+1}{2} \rceil} + 2\lfloor 2^{\log(n) - \lceil \frac{(\log n)+1}{2} \rceil} \rfloor) - 1.$$

We provide examples of annihilators for t and u when $n = 2^{2k+1}$.

Example 2. Let $k \in \mathbb{N}^*$ and $n = 2^{2k+1}$. In Table 2, we present the values of the bound obtained from Proposition 2 for the first few values of k and provide examples of annihilators for t and u of degree $2^{r+1} - 1 = 2^{\frac{(\log n)+3}{2}} - 1$.

Table 2. Algebraic immunity upper bound from Proposition 2 on cyclic WWQ functions in 2^{2k+1} variables.

k	n	r	AI bound
1	8	2	≤ 7
2	32	3	≤ 15
3	128	4	≤ 31
4	512	5	≤ 63

In particular for t we have the annihilators of degree $2\sqrt{2n}-1$:

$$\left(\sum_{i=0}^{2^r-1}\sigma_{i,n}\right)\cdot\prod_{j=1}^{2^k}\mathsf{O}^{j\cdot 2^r-1}(1+x_1+x_2x_3),\ \text{and}\ \left(\sum_{i=0}^{2^r-1}\sigma_{i,n}\right)\cdot\prod_{j=1}^{2^k}\mathsf{O}^{j\cdot 2^r-1}((1+x_1)(1+x_2)).$$

The function u admits the following annihilator:

$$\left(\sum_{i=0}^{2^r-1}\sigma_{i,n}\right)\cdot\prod_{j=1}^{2^k}\mathsf{O}^{j\cdot 2^r-1}(1+x_1+\sum_{\ell=1}^{\lfloor\frac{n-1}{2}\rfloor}x_{2\ell}x_{2\ell+1}).$$

Remark 2. We observe that the annihilators derived using the technique behind the proof of Theorem 1 have a higher degree for the functions studied in [35] compared to those for the HWBF. This difference arises from the fact that, in this case, we rely solely on the parameter d of the WWdd function, which leads to annihilators of degree close to $2\sqrt{nd}$. Formally, adapting the arguments from the proof of Theorem 3, we obtain the bound $\mathsf{AI}\leq\sqrt{nd}(\sqrt{2}+1)-1$.

4.3 Maiorana McFarland Subclass from [13]

In [13], the authors investigate various constructions of Boolean functions aimed at achieving better cryptographic properties than the state of the art and/or facilitating easier implementation. They begin by examining a specific instance of the Maiorana–McFarland construction, which we will first recall, followed by a modification to ensure balancedness. Their instantiation of the Maiorana–McFarland construction involves WWdd functions, an n-to-n permutation where each coordinate function is affine-equivalent to the HWBF, and the majority function.

Definition 11 (Maiorana-McFarland class). *Let $n\in\mathbb{N}^*$, let $\pi:\mathbb{F}_2^n\mapsto\mathbb{F}_2^n$ be a bijection, $\pi_1,\dots,\pi_n$ be the coordinate functions of π, and $h\in\mathcal{B}_n$, let $x\in\mathbb{F}_2^n$, $x=(x_1,\dots,x_n)$ and $y\in\mathbb{F}_2^n$, $y=(y_1,\dots,y_n)$. The $2n$-variable Boolean function MM_{2n} is defined as:*

$$\mathsf{MM}_{2n}(x,y)=\pi(x)\cdot y+h(x)=h(x)+\sum_{i=1}^{n}\pi_i(x)y_i,$$

where $\pi(x)\cdot y$ denotes the inner product between $\pi(x)$ and y.

To instantiate π, the work [13] first focuses on certain cyclic weightwise degree-d functions for small values of d. Then, π is instantiated by defining each coordinate function as a cyclic shift of the HWBF. We now recall the definitions of the two main constructions considered in $2n$ variables:

Definition 12 (MM and Bal instances from [13]). *Let $n\in\mathbb{N}^*$. We define the following two families of functions:*

–
$$\textit{MM-CS}_{2n}(x, y) = \textit{Rot-HWBF}(x) \cdot y + \textit{MAJ}_n(x),$$
where Rot-HWBF denotes the bijection over $\mathbb{F}_2^n$ in which the i-th coordinate is the HWBF applied to $\mathsf{O}^{i-1}(x)$.

–
$$\textit{Bal-CS}_{2n}(x, y) = \textit{MM-CS}_{2n}(x, y) + f(y) \cdot \prod_{i=1}^{n}(1 + x_i),$$
where $f \in \mathcal{B}_n$.

In [13], Conjecture 1 states the following for even $n \geq 6$:

$$\lfloor \frac{n}{3} \rfloor \leq \mathsf{AI}(\mathsf{MM\text{-}CS}_n) \leq \mathsf{AI}(\mathsf{Bal\text{-}CS}_n) \leq 1 + \lfloor \frac{n}{3} \rfloor.$$

We disprove the conjecture with the following theorem:

Theorem 4. *Let $n \in \mathbb{N}^*$. The functions MM-CS$_{2n}$ and Bal-CS$_{2n}$, as defined in Definition 12, satisfy:*

$$\mathsf{AI}(\textit{MM-CS}_{2n}) \leq \sqrt{2n}(\sqrt{2} + 1) - 1, \quad \textit{and} \quad \mathsf{AI}(\textit{Bal-CS}_{2n}) \leq \sqrt{2n}(\sqrt{2} + 1).$$

Proof. First, we rewrite MM-CS$_{2n}$ in a way the Hamming weight of x appears:

$$\begin{aligned}\mathsf{MM\text{-}CS}_{2n}(x, y) &= \mathsf{Rot\text{-}HWBF}(x) \cdot y + \mathsf{MAJ}_n(x) = \mathsf{MAJ}_n(x) + y \cdot \mathsf{O}^{\mathsf{w_H}(x)-1}(x) \\ &= \sum_{i=1}^{n} \varphi_{i,n}(x) f_i(x, y),\end{aligned}$$

where:

$$f_i(x, y) = \begin{cases} y \cdot \mathsf{O}^{i-1}(x) = \sum_{j=1}^{n} y_j (\mathsf{O}^{i-1}(x))_j & \text{if } i < n/2, \\ 1 + y \cdot \mathsf{O}^{i-1}(x) = 1 + \sum_{j=1}^{n} y_j (\mathsf{O}^{i-1}(x))_j & \text{otherwise.} \end{cases}$$

The functions $f_i(x, y)$ are quadratic. However, since their expression in terms of $\varphi_{i,n}(x)$ depends only on the weight of the first part of the input, this does not allow us to conclude that MM-CS$_{2n}(x, y)$ is WWQ. However, this expression is sufficient to determine low-degree annihilators using Proposition 1 and ideas from the proof of Theorem 1. For $r \in [1, \dots, \lceil \log n \rceil]$ we consider the function g_r defined as:

$$g_r(x, y) = \left(\sum_{i=1}^{2^r - 1} \sigma_{i,n}(x) \right) \prod_{j=1}^{\lfloor n/(2^r) \rfloor} (1 + f_{j2^r}(x, y)).$$

The function g_r has degree at most $2^r - 1 + 2\lfloor \frac{n}{2^r} \rfloor$ by construction and serves as an annihilator of MM-CS$_{2n}(x, y)$. This follows from the fact that $\sum_{i=1}^{2^r-1} \sigma_{i,n}(x)$ evaluates to 0 for all (x, y) such that $\mathsf{w_H}(x) \not\equiv 0 \mod 2^r$. Additionally, for all values of $\mathsf{w_H}(x)$ congruent to $0 \mod 2^r$ within the range $[2^r, n]$, the term $(1 + f_{j2^r}(x, y))$ in the product ensures that the overall expression evaluates to 0.

To use g_r to bound the algebraic immunity, we need to show that it is not the null function. To do so, we demonstrate the existence of an element $(u, v) \in \mathbb{F}_2^{2n}$ such that $g_r(u, v) = 1$. First, for the component $u \in \mathbb{F}_2^n$, we define $u_i = 1 \Leftrightarrow i \in [2^r, 2 \cdot 2^r - 1]$. Since u has Hamming weight $\mathsf{w_H}(u) = 2^r$, Proposition 1 ensures that $\sum_{i=1}^{2^r-1} \sigma_{i,n}(u) = 1$. Next, we observe that for each $j \in [1, \lfloor n/2^r \rfloor]$, the equation $1 + f_{j2^r}(u, y) = 1$ depends only on 2^r variables y_i:

$$1 + f_{j2^r}(u, y) = 1 \Leftrightarrow \varepsilon_j + y \cdot \mathsf{O}^{j2^r-1}(u) = 1$$
$$\Leftrightarrow \varepsilon_j + \sum_{i=1}^{2^r} y_{i+n-(j-1)2^r} = 1,$$

where $\varepsilon_j \in \mathbb{F}_2$. In the $m = \lfloor n/2^r \rfloor$ equations, each variable y_i appears at most once and in an affine equation. Hence, we can find an assignment $v \in \mathbb{F}_2^n$ that satisfies all m equations. Therefore, (u, v) is such that $g_r(u, v) \neq 0$, proving that g_r is a non-null annihilator of $\mathsf{MM\text{-}CS}_{2n}$.

By choosing $r = \lfloor \frac{\log(n)+1}{2} \rfloor$ or $r = \lceil \frac{\log(n)+1}{2} \rceil$ and applying the same arguments as in Theorem 3, we obtain: $\mathsf{AI}(\mathsf{MM\text{-}CS}_{2n}) \leq \sqrt{2n}(\sqrt{2} + 1) - 1$. For $\mathsf{Bal\text{-}CS}_{2n}$, we note that for all $i \in [1, n]$, the following holds:

$$x_i \prod_{j=1}^{n} (1 + x_j) = 0.$$

By selecting any $i \in [2^r, 2 \cdot 2^r - 1]$, we obtain $\mathsf{deg}(x_i \cdot g_r) \leq \mathsf{deg}(g_r) + 1$, ensuring that $u_i \cdot g_r(u, v) = 1$, and:

$$(x_i \cdot g_r) \cdot \mathsf{Bal\text{-}CS}_{2n}(x, y) = (x_i \cdot g_r) \cdot \left(\mathsf{MM\text{-}CS}_{2n}(x, y) + f(y) \cdot \prod_{j=1}^{n} (1 + x_j) \right)$$
$$= x_i \cdot (g_r \cdot \mathsf{MM\text{-}CS}_{2n}(x, y)) + g_r \cdot x_i \left(\prod_{j=1}^{n} (1 + x_j) \right) \cdot f(y)$$
$$= x_i \cdot 0 + g_r \cdot 0 \cdot f(y) = 0.$$

Accordingly, $x_i \cdot g_r$ is a non-null annihilator of $\mathsf{Bal\text{-}CS}_{2n}$, regardless of the choice of $f(y)$, allowing us to conclude. □

In Fig. 1, we illustrate the difference between the algebraic immunity expected from the conjecture in [13], the proven bound from Theorem 4, and the more precise bound derived from the constructed annihilators (the functions g_r in the proof of Theorem 4). We observe that for $n \geq 72$, the conjecture does not hold. Consequently, $\mathsf{MM\text{-}CS}_n$ and $\mathsf{Bal\text{-}CS}_n$ should not be used for this number of variables in contexts where the algebraic immunity needs to be as high as $n/3$.

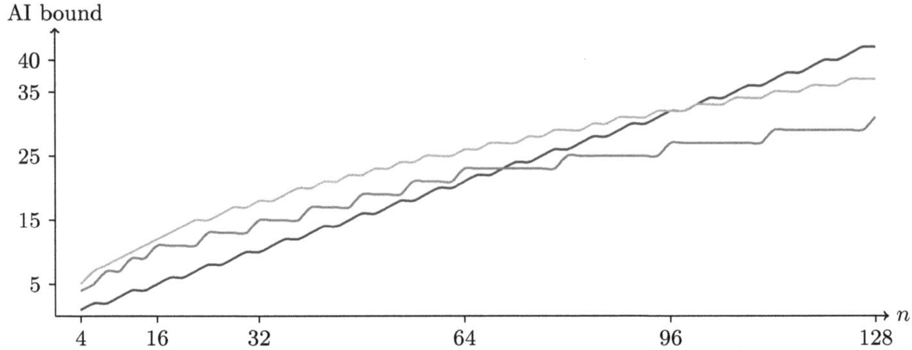

Fig. 1. Comparison of the conjecture of [13] and the AI upper bound of MM-CSn for n even. In blue the bound from Conjecture 1, in orange the tighter upper bound from the built annihilators, and in green the upper bound from Theorem 4. (Color figure online)

4.4 Revisited HWBF [37]

The revisited HWBF, introduced in [37], is a variant of the HWBF with significantly higher nonlinearity. We recall its definition:

Definition 13 (Revisited HWBF [37], Definition 14). *For an even integer $n \geq 0$, we call revisited HWBF the Boolean function $f \in \mathcal{B}_n$ defined as:*

$$f(x) = \sum_{k=1}^{n} x_k \varphi_{k,n}(x) + \sum_{i=1}^{n/2} (x_i + 1) x_{i+n/2}.$$

Rewriting this function as a WWdd function, we have $f_0 = 0$, and for $k \in [1, n]$,

$$f_k = x_k + \sum_{i=1}^{n/2} (x_i + 1) x_{i+n/2},$$

which classifies it as a WWQ function. Consequently, we can apply Theorem 1 with $d = 2$, obtaining the same upper bound as in Proposition 2.

In [37], it is proven that the AI of the revisited HWBF is at least that of the HWBF minus two. However, this does not result in an AI close to $n/3$, as initially expected based on claims about the HWBF ([43]). Instead, it leads to an AI of at most $\sqrt{n}(\sqrt{2}+1)+1$, as shown in the following proposition. This upper bound is more restrictive than the general bound for WWQ functions.

Proposition 3. *Let $n \in \mathbb{N}^*$ be even, and let f be the n-variable revisited HWBF. Then, we have:*

$$\mathsf{AI}(f) \leq \sqrt{n}(\sqrt{2}+1)+1.$$

Proof. Using Theorem 3, the n-variable HWBF function h has an algebraic immunity of at most $\sqrt{n}(\sqrt{2}+1)+1$. From the proof of Theorem 1, the annihilators used to establish this bound are annihilators of h (rather than $h+1$), where each subfunction involved takes the value 1 in 0_n. Explicitly, these annihilators of h have the form:

$$g_r = (1+\sigma_1+\cdots+\sigma_{2^r-1}) \prod_{i=1}^{\lfloor n/2^r \rfloor} (1+x_{2^r \cdot i}).$$

Moreover, the quadratic function $q = 1 + \sum_{i=1}^{n/2}(x_i+1)x_{i+n/2}$ also takes the value 1 in 0_n. Let g be the function corresponding to an index r such that $\mathsf{deg}(g_r) \leq \sqrt{n}(\sqrt{2}+1)-1$. Then, the product $g \cdot q$ in not the null function and has degree at most $\sqrt{n}(\sqrt{2}+1)+1$. Denoting by f the n-variable revisited HWBF we obtain:

$$g \cdot q \cdot f = g \cdot q \cdot h + g \cdot q \cdot \sum_{i=1}^{n/2}(x_i+1)x_{i+n/2} = q \cdot 0 + g \cdot 0 = 0,$$

which allows us to conclude. □

4.5 Weightwise Quadratic Functions from [15]

In [15], the authors propose revisiting the design of filtered linear feedback shift registers, using larger parameters than those typically employed in the 2000s, with a design tailored towards the use case of hybrid homomorphic encryption. The proposed cipher uses, as a filter, a WWQ function f in 128 variables, defined as:

$$f_k = x_k + \sum_{i=1}^{\lfloor \frac{n}{3} \rfloor} x_{k-i}x_{k+2i-1}.$$

Applying Theorem 1 with $n = 128$ and $d = 2$, we obtain the bound $\mathsf{AI}(f) \leq 31$. In [15], the family of functions f (indexed by n) is conjectured to have algebraic immunity at least $\min(\lfloor n/3 \rfloor, 2\sqrt{n})$, which is not contradicted by our results.

Since the function used is WWQ, we also obtain the same general bound as in Proposition 2 (Sect. 4.2). In particular, Remark 2 gives:

$$\mathsf{AI}(f) \leq \sqrt{2n}(\sqrt{2}+1)+1.$$

4.6 Maiorana McFarland Subclass from [14]

As a continuation of [13], the authors focus on a specific instantiation of the Maiorana–McFarland construction and its balanced variant, and propose filtered LFSRs that use this function as the filtering function. In contrast to MM-CS (Definition 12), the permutation π is replaced with the reverse-order permutation, defined by $\pi_i(x) = x_{n+1-i}$. We denote this variant by MM-CSrev.

In [14], Theorem 2 guarantees that when π is a bit permutation, the algebraic immunity of MM_{2n} is at least that of h. In particular, for MM-CSrev, Proposition 4 in [14] states that for even $n \geq 4$, we have $\mathsf{AI}(\text{MM-CSrev}) \geq \lceil n/4 \rceil$. For small values of n, the authors observed that $\mathsf{AI}(\text{MM-CSrev})$ takes the value $1 + \lfloor n/4 \rfloor$. In the following, we explain why the algebraic immunity of MM-CSrev is significantly better than that of MM-CS, which grows proportionally to $\sqrt{n}$ as shown in Theorem 4, and we establish an upper bound on its algebraic immunity.

Similarly to the approach used in the proof of Theorem 4, we can rewrite MM-CSrev in terms of the Hamming weight of the first n bits, as follows:

$$\text{MM-CSrev}_{2n}(x, y) = \pi(x) \cdot y + \mathsf{MAJ}_n(x) = \sum_{i=1}^{n} \varphi_{i,n}(x) f_i(x, y),$$

$$\text{where:} \quad f_i(x, y) = \begin{cases} y \cdot \pi(x) = \sum_{j=1}^{n} y_j x_{n+1-j} & \text{if } i < n/2, \\ 1 + y \cdot \pi(x) = 1 + \sum_{j=1}^{n} y_j x_{n+1-j} & \text{otherwise.} \end{cases}$$

We observe that the function f_i is the same for all $i < n/2$, which we denote by g, and likewise, the function f_i is the same for all $i \geq n/2$, which we denote by h. The functions g and h are complementary (*i.e.* $g = 1 + h$), meaning that their product is identically zero. Consequently, any annihilator constructed using the methodology from the proof of Theorem 4 with two f_i functions results in the null annihilator. This explains why this construction does not yield an annihilator of degree proportional to $\sqrt{n}$, nor does it for any π that is a bit permutation.

The following proposition gives an upper bound on $\mathsf{AI}(\text{MM-CSrev})$:

Proposition 4. *Let $n \in \mathbb{N}$, $n \geq 4$ be even, the following holds on MM-CSrev$_n$:*

$$\mathsf{AI}(\textit{MM-CSrev}_n) \leq 2^{\lceil \log(n/4) \rceil} + 1.$$

Proof. The MM-CSrev$_n$ function can be rewritten as $\sum_{i=1}^{n/2} \varphi_{i,n/2}(x)(\varepsilon_i + \sum_{j=1}^{n/2} y_j x_{n/2+1-j})$ where $\varepsilon_i = 0$ for $i < n/4$ and 1 otherwise. We take $r = \lceil \log(n/4) \rceil$, the function:

$$g(x, y) = \left(\sum_{i=0}^{2^r - 1} \sigma_{i,n/2}(x) \right) \cdot \left(\sum_{j=1}^{n/2} y_j x_{n/2+1-j} \right)$$

is an annihilator of MM-CSrev$_n$ of degree at most $2^{\lceil \log(n/4) \rceil} + 1$. Indeed, by Proposition 1, the first part vanishes on all inputs where x has Hamming weight different from $0 \mod 2^{\lceil \log(n/4) \rceil}$. The second part serves as an annihilator of the function $1 + \sum_{j=1}^{n/2} y_j x_{n/2+1-j}$, which is the value taken by MM-CSrev$_n$ when $\mathsf{w_H}(x) \geq n/4$. By construction, $g(x, y)$ is not the zero function: take $u \in \mathbb{F}_2^{n/2}$ to be the vector consisting of $2^{\lceil \log(n/4) \rceil}$ consecutive ones followed by zeros, and let $v \in \mathbb{F}_2^{n/2}$ be the vector with $n/2 - 1$ consecutive zeros and a single one. Then we have $g(u, v) = 1$. □

In Fig. 2, we illustrate the bounds on the algebraic immunity of MM-CSrev for even values of n, showing the proven lower bound from [14], the extrapolated values based on small n from the same work, and our proven upper bound from Proposition 4.

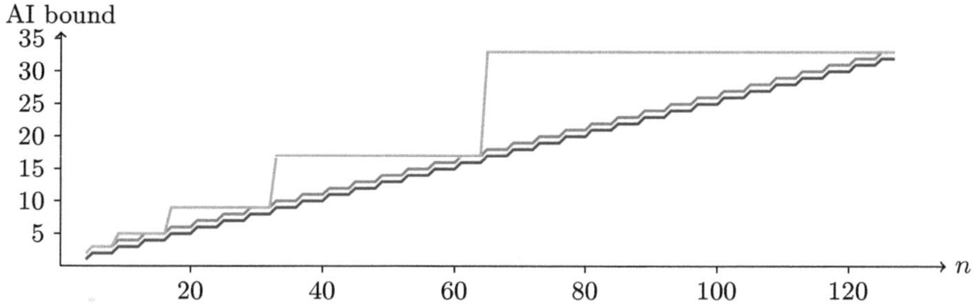

Fig. 2. Bound on the algebraic immunity of MM-CSrev for n even. In blue the proven lower bound from [14] in orange the extrapolated value from the experimental results for $n \in [4, 20]$ and in green the upper bound proven in Proposition 4. (Color figure online)

In [14], the functions MM-CS and Bal-CS are proposed in the appendix as alternative filters, as their algebraic immunity appears to be better—estimated around $n/3$ based on extrapolated values—but they are more costly to implement in the model considered. However, as shown in Sect. 4.3, this extrapolation is not valid, and for functions in more than 75 variables (as suggested for the filtered LFSR instances), the actual AI is lower.

5 Conclusions and Open Questions

In this article, we studied the algebraic immunity of weightwise degree-d functions and presented methods to construct low-degree annihilators for Boolean functions expressed in this form.

We began by showing that certain low-degree symmetric functions vanish on most slices of the Boolean hypercube. We then demonstrated how such functions can be used to construct low-degree annihilators for Boolean functions that coincide with low-degree functions on each slice. This approach was further generalized by combining annihilators across different slices to produce annihilators of even lower degree. More importantly, we showed that the same methodology can be extended to partitions beyond those defined by the slices.

In the second part of the article, we examined the impact of this method on various constructions proposed for cryptographic applications. We first showed that the previously assumed lower bound on the algebraic immunity of the HWBF was incorrect, and our result corrects the misleading belief in the high AI of HWBF and its generalizations. The upper bound we established—proportional to $\sqrt{dn}$ for a WWdd function—enabled us to correct or refine results concerning functions studied in six prior works.

These results open several directions for future work. First, while we demonstrated how the technique can be extended beyond slices, it remains an open question whether it can be generalized to other natural partitions of the Boolean hypercube—such as those arising from rotation symmetric or dihedral symmetric Boolean functions. Second, it would be interesting to investigate whether this framework could be further extended to characterize all annihilators of a given Boolean function. Such a characterization could potentially lead to new lower bounds on the algebraic immunity, complementing the upper bounds established in this work.

Acknowledgments. The author was funded by the European Research Council (ERC) under the Advanced Grant program (reference number: 787390).

References

1. Albrecht, M.R., Rechberger, C., Schneider, T., Tiessen, T., Zohner, M.: Ciphers for MPC and FHE. In: Oswald, E., Fischlin, M. (eds.) EUROCRYPT 2015, Part I. LNCS, vol. 9056, pp. 430–454. Springer, Heidelberg (2015). https://doi.org/10.1007/978-3-662-46800-5_17
2. Bollig, B., Löbbing, M., Sauerhoff, M., Wegener, I.: On the complexity of the hidden weighted bit function for various BDD models. RAIRO Theor. Inform. Appl. **33**(2), 103–116 (1999)
3. Braeken, A., Preneel, B.: On the algebraic immunity of symmetric Boolean functions. In: Maitra, S., Veni Madhavan, C.E., Venkatesan, R. (eds.) INDOCRYPT 2005. LNCS, vol. 3797, pp. 35–48. Springer, Heidelberg (2005). https://doi.org/10.1007/11596219_4
4. Bryant, R.E.: On the complexity of VLSI implementations and graph representations of Boolean functions with application to integer multiplication. IEEE Trans. Comput. **40**(2), 205–213 (1991)
5. Canteaut, A., et al.: Stream ciphers: a practical solution for efficient homomorphic-ciphertext compression. In: Peyrin, T. (ed.) FSE 2016. LNCS, vol. 9783, pp. 313–333. Springer, Heidelberg (2016). https://doi.org/10.1007/978-3-662-52993-5_16
6. Canteaut, A., Videau, M.: Symmetric Boolean functions. IEEE Trans. Inf. Theory 2791–2811 (2005)
7. Carlet, C.: On the degree, nonlinearity, algebraic thickness, and nonnormality of Boolean functions, with developments on symmetric functions. IEEE Trans. Inf. Theory 2178–2185 (2004)
8. Carlet, C.: Boolean Functions for Cryptography and Coding Theory. Cambridge University Press (2021). https://doi.org/10.1017/9781108606806
9. Carlet, C.: A wide class of Boolean functions generalizing the hidden weight bit function. IEEE Trans. Inf. Theory **68**(2), 1355–1368 (2022)
10. Carlet, C., Feng, K.: An infinite class of balanced functions with optimal algebraic immunity, good immunity to fast algebraic attacks and good nonlinearity. In: Pieprzyk, J. (ed.) ASIACRYPT 2008. LNCS, vol. 5350, pp. 425–440. Springer, Heidelberg (2008). https://doi.org/10.1007/978-3-540-89255-7_26

11. Carlet, C., Méaux, P.: A complete study of two classes of Boolean functions: direct sums of monomials and threshold functions. IEEE Trans. Inf. Theory 1 (2021)
12. Carlet, C., Méaux, P., Rotella, Y.: Boolean functions with restricted input and their robustness; application to the FLIP cipher. IACR Trans. Symmetric Cryptol. **2017**(3) (2017)
13. Carlet, C., Sarkar, P.: Constructions of efficiently implementable Boolean functions possessing high nonlinearity and good resistance to algebraic attacks. IACR Cryptol. ePrint Arch. 1305 (2024). https://eprint.iacr.org/archive/2024/1305/20240821:123900.5
14. Carlet, C., Sarkar, P.: The nonlinear filter model of stream cipher Redivivus. Cryptology ePrint Archive, Paper 2025/160 (2025). https://eprint.iacr.org/2025/160
15. Chacal, N., Méaux, P., AnonymousBeforeAcceptance: nostalgia cipher: can filtered lfsrs be secure again? ORBilu Archive (2025). https://hdl.handle.net/10993/64454
16. Chen, Y., Lu, P.: Two classes of symmetric Boolean functions with optimum algebraic immunity: construction and analysis. IEEE Trans. Inf. Theory **57**(4), 2522–2538 (2011). https://doi.org/10.1109/TIT.2011.2111810
17. Chillotti, I., Gama, N., Georgieva, M., Izabachène, M.: Faster fully homomorphic encryption: bootstrapping in less than 0.1 seconds. In: Cheon, J.H., Takagi, T. (eds.) ASIACRYPT 2016, Part I. LNCS, vol. 10031, pp. 3–33. Springer, Heidelberg (2016). https://doi.org/10.1007/978-3-662-53887-6_1
18. Cong, K., Das, D., Park, J., Pereira, H.V.: SortingHat: efficient private decision tree evaluation via homomorphic encryption and transciphering. In: Proceedings of the 2022 ACM SIGSAC Conference on Computer and Communications Security, pp. 563–577. Association for Computing Machinery (2022).https://doi.org/10.1145/3548606.3560702
19. Courtois, N.T.: Fast algebraic attacks on stream ciphers with linear feedback. In: Boneh, D. (ed.) CRYPTO 2003. LNCS, vol. 2729, pp. 176–194. Springer, Heidelberg (2003). https://doi.org/10.1007/978-3-540-45146-4_11
20. Courtois, N.T., Meier, W.: Algebraic attacks on stream ciphers with linear feedback. In: Biham, E. (ed.) EUROCRYPT 2003. LNCS, vol. 2656, pp. 345–359. Springer, Heidelberg (2003). https://doi.org/10.1007/3-540-39200-9_21
21. Dalai, D.K., Gupta, K.C., Maitra, S.: Cryptographically significant Boolean functions: construction and analysis in terms of algebraic immunity. In: Gilbert, H., Handschuh, H. (eds.) FSE 2005. LNCS, vol. 3557, pp. 98–111. Springer, Heidelberg (2005). https://doi.org/10.1007/11502760_7
22. Dalai, D.K., Mallick, K.: A class of weightwise almost perfectly balanced Boolean functions. Adv. Math. Commun. **18**(2), 480–504 (2024)
23. Dobraunig, C., et al.: Rasta: a cipher with low ANDdepth and few ANDs per bit. In: Shacham, H., Boldyreva, A. (eds.) CRYPTO 2018. LNCS, vol. 10991, pp. 662–692. Springer, Cham (2018). https://doi.org/10.1007/978-3-319-96884-1_22
24. Ducas, L., Micciancio, D.: FHEW: bootstrapping homomorphic encryption in less than a second. In: Oswald, E., Fischlin, M. (eds.) EUROCRYPT 2015, Part I. LNCS, vol. 9056, pp. 617–640. Springer, Heidelberg (2015). https://doi.org/10.1007/978-3-662-46800-5_24
25. Fine, N.J.: Binomial coefficients modulo a prime. Am. Math. Monthly **54**(10), 589–592 (1947). http://www.jstor.org/stable/2304500
26. Gini, A., Méaux, P.: On the weightwise nonlinearity of weightwise perfectly balanced functions. Discrete Appl. Math. **322**, 320–341 (2022). https://doi.org/10.1016/j.dam.2022.08.017

27. Hoffmann, C., Méaux, P., Ricosset, T.: Transciphering, using FiLIP and TFHE for an efficient delegation of computation. In: Bhargavan, K., Oswald, E., Prabhakaran, M. (eds.) INDOCRYPT 2020. LNCS, vol. 12578, pp. 39–61. Springer, Cham (2020). https://doi.org/10.1007/978-3-030-65277-7_3
28. Li, J., Su, S.: Construction of weightwise perfectly balanced Boolean functions with high weightwise nonlinearity. Discret. Appl. Math. **279**, 218–227 (2020)
29. Liu, J., Mesnager, S.: Weightwise perfectly balanced functions with high weightwise nonlinearity profile. Des. Codes Cryptogr. **87**(8), 1797–1813 (2019)
30. Mandujano, S., Ku Cauich, J.C., Lara, A.: Studying special operators for the application of evolutionary algorithms in the seek of optimal Boolean functions for cryptography. In: Pichardo Lagunas, O., Martínez-Miranda, J., Martínez Seis, B. (eds.) MICAI 2022. LNCS, vol. 13612, pp. 383–396. Springer, Cham (2022). https://doi.org/10.1007/978-3-031-19493-1_30
31. Mariot, L., Picek, S., Jakobovic, D., Djurasevic, M., Leporati, A.: Evolutionary construction of perfectly balanced Boolean functions. In: 2022 IEEE Congress on Evolutionary Computation (CEC), pp. 1–8. IEEE Press (2022)
32. Méaux, P.: On the fast algebraic immunity of majority functions. In: Schwabe, P., Thériault, N. (eds.) LATINCRYPT 2019. LNCS, vol. 11774, pp. 86–105. Springer, Cham (2019). https://doi.org/10.1007/978-3-030-30530-7_5
33. Méaux, P., Carlet, C., Journault, A., Standaert, F.-X.: Improved filter permutators for efficient FHE: better instances and implementations. In: Hao, F., Ruj, S., Sen Gupta, S. (eds.) INDOCRYPT 2019. LNCS, vol. 11898, pp. 68–91. Springer, Cham (2019). https://doi.org/10.1007/978-3-030-35423-7_4
34. Méaux, P., Journault, A., Standaert, F.-X., Carlet, C.: Towards stream ciphers for efficient FHE with low-noise ciphertexts. In: Fischlin, M., Coron, J.-S. (eds.) EUROCRYPT 2016, Part I. LNCS, vol. 9665, pp. 311–343. Springer, Heidelberg (2016). https://doi.org/10.1007/978-3-662-49890-3_13
35. Méaux, P., Ozaim, Y.: On the cryptographic properties of weightwise affine and weightwise quadratic functions. Discret. Appl. Math. **355**, 13–29 (2024)
36. Méaux, P., Park, J., Pereira, H.V.L.: Towards practical transciphering for FHE with setup independent of the plaintext space. IACR Commun. Cryptol. **1**(1), 20 (2024). https://doi.org/10.62056/ANXRXRXQI
37. Méaux, P., Seuré, T., Tang, D.: The revisited hidden weight bit function. IACR Cryptol. ePrint Arch. 2022 (2024). https://eprint.iacr.org/2024/2022. To appear at Selected Areas in Cryptography – SAC 2025
38. Meier, W., Pasalic, E., Carlet, C.: Algebraic attacks and decomposition of Boolean functions. In: Cachin, C., Camenisch, J.L. (eds.) EUROCRYPT 2004. LNCS, vol. 3027, pp. 474–491. Springer, Heidelberg (2004). https://doi.org/10.1007/978-3-540-24676-3_28
39. Mesnager, S., Su, S.: On constructions of weightwise perfectly balanced Boolean functions. Cryptogr. Commun. (2021)
40. Naehrig, M., Lauter, K., Vaikuntanathan, V.: Can homomorphic encryption be practical? In: Proceedings of the 3rd ACM Workshop on Cloud Computing Security Workshop, CCSW 2011, pp. 113–124. Association for Computing Machinery, New York (2011)
41. Sarkar, P., Maitra, S.: Balancedness and correlation immunity of symmetric Boolean functions. Discrete Math. 2351 – 2358 (2007)
42. Tang, D., Liu, J.: A family of weightwise (almost) perfectly balanced Boolean functions with optimal algebraic immunity. Cryptogr. Commun. **11**(6), 1185–1197 (2019). https://doi.org/10.1007/s12095-019-00374-6

43. Wang, Q., Carlet, C., Stanica, P., Tan, C.H.: Cryptographic properties of the hidden weighted bit function. Discret. Appl. Math. **174**, 1–10 (2014)
44. Wang, Q., Tan, C.H., Stanica, P.: Concatenations of the hidden weighted bit function and their cryptographic properties. Adv. Math. Commun. **8**(2), 153–165 (2014)

Machine Learning and Cryptanalysis

Generic Partial Decryption as Feature Engineering for Neural Distinguishers

Emanuele Bellini[1(✉)], Rocco Brunelli[2(✉)], David Gerault[1(✉)], Anna Hambitzer[1(✉)], and Marco Pedicini[2(✉)]

[1] Technology Innovation Institute, Abu Dhabi, UAE
{emanuele.bellini,david.gerault,anna.hambitzer}@tii.ae
[2] Roma Tre University, Rome, Italy
{rocco.brunelli,marco.pedicini}@uniroma3.it

Abstract. In Neural Cryptanalysis, a deep neural network is trained as a cryptographic distinguisher between pairs of ciphertexts $(F(X), F(X \oplus \delta))$, where F is either a random permutation or a block cipher, δ is a fixed difference. The AutoND framework aims to use neural distinguishers that are treated as a generic tool and discourages cipher-specific optimizations. On the other hand, works such as [LLS+24] obtain superior distinguishers by adding dedicated features, such as selected parts of the difference in the previous rounds, to the input of the neural distinguishers. In this paper, we study **Generic Partial Decryption** as a feature engineering technique and integrate it within a fully automated pipeline, where we evaluate its effect independently of the number of pairs per sample, with which feature engineering is often combined. We show that this technique matches state-of-the-art dedicated approaches on Simon and Simeck. Additionally, we apply it to Aradi, and present a practical neural-assisted key recovery for 5 rounds, as well as a 7-rounds key recovery with 2^{70} time complexity. Additionally, we derive useful information from the neural distinguishers and propose a non-neural version of our 5-round key recovery.

Keywords: Neural Cryptanalysis · Differential Cryptanalysis · Block Cipher · Partial Decryption · Simon · Simeck · Aradi

1 Introduction

Block ciphers are a cornerstone of modern cryptography, and secure block ciphers can be used as a building block for many symmetric key primitives, making their analysis one of the most fundamental problems in symmetric cryptanalysis.

Differential Cryptanalysis. Differential cryptanalysis, the study of how modifications of the inputs propagate to the output, is one of the most important techniques for establishing bounds on the resistance of block ciphers. While it was first publicly presented by Biham and Shamir in 1990 [BS91], it is believed to have been known and used as early as 1974 [Cop94]. Despite 50 years of research,

D. Escudero and I. Damgård (Eds.): LATINCRYPT 2025, LNCS 16129, pp. 373–398, 2026.
https://doi.org/10.1007/978-3-032-06754-8_14

new insights on differential cryptanalysis are still presented regularly at major security conferences. For instance, a new generic differential key recovery algorithm was presented at Eurocrypt 2024 [BDD+24]. These advances often go hand in hand with the improvement of tools. In particular, the search for differential characteristics has been made significantly easier in recent years through automatic search tools based on SAT, SMT, MILP, or CP. The ability to easily obtain, analyze, or count differential characteristics with given properties lets the cryptographer focus on novel analysis techniques rather than the tedious implementation of dedicated search algorithms. However, difficult instances keep challenging these modern tools despite the constant evolution of techniques [SWW21]; as a result, finding accurate differential bounds is still an open problem for many primitives.

These challenges become even more acute when investigating variants of differential cryptanalysis, such as multiple differential cryptanalysis [BG11], where the cryptographer considers not one but many of the possible output differences. To this day, it is extremely difficult to evaluate the resistance of a block cipher to such attacks.

Neural Distinguishers. At CRYPTO 2019, A. Gohr proposed to use deep learning in the context of differential cryptanalysis [Goh19]. In this work, *neural distinguishers* are trained to distinguish the Speck 32 [BSS+13] encryption of two plaintexts related by a fixed input difference from random pairs. The author shows that a differential distinguisher using the entire (under the Markov assumption) Differential Distribution Table (DDT) of the cipher obtains very close performance, hinting that neural distinguishers rely on multiple-differential properties. However, computing the entire DDT is usually not tractable when analyzing primitives with states larger than 32 bits. To that extent, neural distinguishers can be seen as a very potent tool to assess the resistance of a cipher to multiple differential cryptanalysis, filling a gap in automatic tools. For instance, for Speck 32, the best 7-rounds differential characteristics have at best probability 2^{-19} [LLJW21], but neural distinguishers can distinguish a single pair from random with 60% accuracy, indicating stronger multiple-differential properties than expected.

Unfortunately, neural distinguishers, like most deep-learning techniques, suffer from explainability issues. We can empirically observe that a neural distinguisher seems to be able to learn some form of the compressed representation of the DDT, but building such a compressed representation without deep learning is an open problem. Nevertheless, in the absence of a better tool, neural distinguishers can be used to improve our understanding of multiple differential properties and develop new attacks.

Automation. In that spirit, at FSE 2024, the AutoND [BGH+23] framework was introduced. This framework aims at automatically building a neural distinguisher from the implementation of a cipher, providing a bound on the number of rounds for which strong multiple differential properties exist. The authors present the tool as akin to libraries such as Tagada [LDLS21], CASCADA [RR22] or CLAASP [BGG+24], that, given a cipher implementation, build distinguishers. Such tools allow cryptographers to focus on developing new techniques rather than re-implementing already existing methodologies to find distinguishers. Similarly, training a neural distinguisher from scratch is tedious, and many recent works focused on optimizing the accuracy as much as possible through lengthy hyper-parameters tuning, custom feature engineering, or dedicated curriculum learning procedures, when the existence of a neural distinguisher for a given number of rounds is, on its own, valuable information.

The initial version of AutoND matches most of the current literature despite being completely generic and requiring no input from the cryptographer other than the cipher implementation. On the other hand, dedicated approaches using primitive-specific features can result in better distinguishers. For example, in SIMON, given two ciphertexts, their full difference at the previous round can be inferred, along with probabilistic information on the difference two rounds before. Adding this information to the input of the neural distinguisher can significantly improve its accuracy [LLS+24].

It is natural that such dedicated feature engineering provides better distinguishers in comparison to the typical black-box approach to neural cryptanalysis. For instance, [Dom12] emphasizes that the selection and engineering of features often have a greater impact on model performance than the choice of algorithm: "feature engineering is more difficult because it is domain-specific while learners can be largely general purpose" (*Communications of the ACM*, 2012).

Our goal in this research is to fill this gap in a generic way. More specifically, we add decryption with arbitrary keys to the features used in the AutoND framework and show that this is sufficient to match the state of the art. Using this approach, we preserve deterministic structural properties of the cipher without needing to specifically isolate the relevant ones. Concretely, this partial decryption naturally contains some amount of irrelevant information (the non-deterministic propagations), but it appears to be easy for the neural distinguisher to filter out useless information. We test this hypothesis on the SIMON, and SIMECK ciphers.

ARADI *as a Case Study.* The block cipher ARADI [GMW24] was published by NSA researchers without a security analysis, and very few public independent analyses have been performed (e.g. [BRRT24, BFG+24a, ADG24]). We apply our framework to ARADI and present the first practical neural key recovery attack on 5 rounds, as well its classical equivalent.

1.1 Our Contributions

1. We introduce the automated Generic Partial Decryption pipeline (Sect. 4), and obtain competitive neural distinguishers for SIMON, ARADI, and SIMECK. Our multi-pair neural distinguishers cover 12 rounds for both SIMON and SIMECK with an accuracy of 0.5156, slightly surpassing the state-of-the-art results reported in [LLS+24]. Generic Partial Decryption significantly improves the 5-round accuracy for ARADI, increasing it from approximately 60% to 77% in the single-pair setting, and 100% when in the multi-pair setting.

2. We enhance the explainability of previous results using partial decryption by comparing the outcomes across four configurations: *i)* using a simple ciphertext pair as a sample, *ii)* incorporating multiple ciphertext pairs per sample, *iii)* increasing the amount of training data, and *iv)* applying partial decryption. This approach enables a clear differentiation of the individual contributions to the overall accuracy of the neural distinguisher. The results are reported in Sect. 5.
   For SIMON and SIMECK, the primary accuracy improvements stem from employing multi-pair neural distinguishers *(ii)* and using more training data *(iii)*, while the contribution of partial decryption *(iv)* is comparatively smaller. In contrast, for ARADI, the accuracy improvement due to partial decryption *(iv)* is of a similar magnitude to the gains achieved through multi-pair usage *(ii)*.
3. Using our 4-rounds neural distinguishers, we present the first practical neural key recovery attack on 5 rounds of Aradi, with data complexity 2^9 (for 75% success rate), and time complexity dominated by 2^{40} neural distinguisher evaluations. We extend this attack to 7 rounds, albeit with non-practical time complexity. More importantly, for the first time, we leverage information learned from the neural distinguisher to build a classical key recovery attack. For 5 rounds, this attack has data complexity comparable to the neural one, and time complexity 2^{42}. These attacks are discussed in Sect. 6.

2 Preliminaries

In this paper, we use the standard symbols for the boolean operations: $\oplus$ XOR, $\lll$ (resp. $\ggg$) α for left (resp. right) rotation by α bits, $\odot$ for bitwise AND, $||$ for concatenation, and $\boxplus$ and $\boxminus$ for modular addition and subtraction.

2.1 Analyzed Ciphers

SIMON and SIMECK

SIMON [BSS+13] and SIMECK [YZS+15] are families of lightweight block ciphers, where the state $l||r$ is updated using the round key k_i as follows:

$$l_{i+1}||r_{i+1} \leftarrow ((l_{i-1} \lll \alpha) \odot (l_{i-1} \lll \beta)) \oplus (l_{i-1} \lll \gamma) \oplus r_{i-1} \oplus k_i||l_{i-1}$$

We focus on the variants using a 32-bit state and a 64-bit key, SIMON 32/64 and SIMECK 32/64, using rotational constants $\alpha = 1$, $\beta = 8$ and $\gamma = 2$ for SIMON 32/64, $\alpha = 0$, $\beta = 5$ and $\gamma = 1$ for SIMECK 32/64.

ARADI

ARADI [GMW24] is a substitution-permutation network (SPN), taking as input a 128-bit block and a 256-bit key designed for low-latency applications. The round function updates the state $(w||x||y||z)$ represented as four 32-bit words through a column-wise 4-bit S-box π followed by a row-wise linear layer Λ_i:

$$\Lambda_i(w||x||y||z) := (L_i(w)||L_i(x)||L_i(y)||L_i(z)),$$

$$L_i(s) = L_i(s_l; s_r) := (s_l \oplus (s_l \lll \alpha_i) \oplus (s_r \lll \gamma_i)||s_r \oplus (s_r \lll \alpha_i) \oplus (s_l \lll \beta_i))$$

If we denote by $\tau_v(s)$, the bitwise XOR of s with v, then the ARADI encryption function has the form:

$$\tau_{k^{16}} \circ (\Lambda_{15} \circ \pi \circ \tau_{k^{15}}) \circ \cdots \circ (\Lambda_1 \circ \pi \circ \tau_{k^1}) \circ (\Lambda_0 \circ \pi \circ \tau_{k^0})$$

where k^i denotes the round key, we consider it composed of four words of 32-bits $k^i = k^i_w||k^i_x||k^i_y||k^i_z$ corresponding to the four words of the block.

2.2 (Neural) Differential Cryptanalysis

Differential cryptanalysis [BS91] is a chosen plaintext attack in which an attacker analyzes how an injected difference δ in a plaintext pair $(P, P' = P \oplus \delta)$ propagates into the resulting ciphertext pair (C, C'). In differential cryptanalysis, the cryptanalyst is interested in finding differentials δ, γ such that the equation $F(P) \oplus F(P \oplus \delta) = \gamma$ holds for many plaintexts P for a primitive F.

Neural Differential Cryptanalysis. Neural differential cryptanalysis was introduced at CRYPTO 2019 by Gohr [Goh19]. In this seminal work, a *neural distinguisher* is trained to classify pairs of ciphertexts as *real* or *random*. The real pairs correspond to the SPECK 32/64 encryption of plaintexts P and $P \oplus \delta$, where $\delta = 0 \times 400000$ is chosen for its favorable diffusion properties, whereas the random pairs are sampled uniformly at random.

A neural distinguisher is a neural network whose architecture is tuned for cipher analysis. Concretely, it is a parametrized function f_θ composed of affine layers followed by non-linear activations, mapping the concatenated pair $(C_0 \parallel (C_0 + \delta))$ to a single score. During *supervised training* the network receives labelled examples (x, y) with $y \in \{0, 1\}$ indicating the correct class and iteratively updates θ via stochastic-gradient optimization to minimize a differentiable loss. Regularization techniques mitigate *overfitting* – memorizing the training set – thereby promoting generalization to previously unseen data. The resulting *accuracy* is evaluated on a separate test set and measures how reliably the trained model distinguishes truly random data from encrypted pairs for the chosen input difference δ. Gohr reports test accuracies exceeding 92% for 5 rounds of SPECK, falling to roughly 52% for 8 rounds, illustrating both the potential and the current limitations of neural distinguishers.

Among the almost 200 papers citing this seminal work, many investigate how to generalize it to other primitives, often using *feature engineering*, where the cryptographer uses his knowledge of the cipher's structure to craft features that may be difficult for the $\mathcal{ND}$ to learn on its own.

2.3 Feature Engineering

Feature engineering is a fundamental technique in machine learning, focusing transforming raw data into a more suitable set of features, for instance, through normalization, encoding, or aggregation, to improve the interpretability and accuracy of the model. In *"Feature Engineering for Machine Learning"* [ZC18], a *feature* is loosely described as "a numeric representation of raw data".

3 Related Work

Neural Distinguisher Works with Focus on Feature Aggregation. It is commonplace that distinguishers having access to more data tend to perform better; therefore, multi-pair distinguishers, which are trained on samples containing more than two ciphertexts ($m > 1$), have been used in works such as [BGPT21a] ($m = 20,\ 100$), [CSYY22] ($m = 8$), [HRCF21] ($m = 64, 128$), and [LLS+24] ($m = 8, 16$).

However, the use of multi-pair samples has been criticized in [GLN23], where a *combined response score* is defined to aggregate the scores produced by a single-pair distinguisher on multiple samples sharing the same label. Using this technique, the authors compare the accuracies of multi-pair ($m > 2$) distinguishers with the combination of m single-pair distinguisher scores, and conclude that "the claimed improvement [of multipair-distinguishers] is at best non-existent in most cases". This conclusion relies on a *combined response score*, which aggregates the scores produced by a single-pair distinguisher on multiple samples sharing the same label.

Depending on the strictness of the feature engineering definition, one may argue that combining multiple samples with the same label into a single sample does not constitute "feature engineering". This process does not involve modifying or generating new features but rather aggregates existing data points.

Neural Distinguisher Works with Focus on $\oplus$-Feature Engineering. In differential cryptanalysis, the ciphertext difference $C_0 \oplus C_1$ is the main feature. Many studies replace concatenated ciphertext pairs ($C_0 || C_1$) by their XOR difference ($C_0 \oplus C_1$), such as [BBCD21], Hou *et al.* [HRCF21], and Yadav *et al.* [YK21].

Using features based on $C_0 \oplus C_1$ can accelerate training due to the reduced input length, which simplifies parts of the training process. However, this approach may sacrifice some information, often resulting in distinguishers with lower accuracy compared to those trained on $C_0 || C_1$. This trade-off underscores that feature engineering is closely linked to explainability; deriving optimal input features is most effective when the learned properties of the neural network are well understood. Benamira *et al.* [BGPT21a] examined the properties of pairs that were correctly classified, suggesting that Gohr's neural distinguishers learn differential-linear features.

Neural Distinguisher Works with Focus on Feature Engineering by Partial Decryption. It is often possible to derive truncated information on the difference in the previous rounds of a cipher. This additional information, treated as an additional feature, is trivial given the algorithm of the primitive, but can be arbitrarily hard in the black-box scenario (e.g., for unkeyed cryptographic permutations). In [BGPT21a], the authors use such partial information in an explainability study. In [BGL+22] and [LLS+24], the authors improve the accuracy of neural distinguishers on SIMON through similar techniques, using inferred information from one and two rounds ahead.

The authors of [BGPT21a] propose the hypothesis that the $\mathcal{ND}$ is able to infer information on the difference from 2 rounds ahead; such feature engineering connects naturally with that hypothesis. Based on this observation, Liu et al. [LRCL23] aim to use partial decryption to improve neural distinguishers: they use randomly generated subkeys to decrypt one round and develop new data formats MRMSP (Multiple Rounds Multiple Splicing Pairs) and MSMSD (Multiple Rounds Multiple Splicing Differences).

Works with Focus on Generic Tools and Automation. Recent advancements have focused on developing generic tools and automation for cryptanalysis. Open-source cryptographic libraries, such as TAGADA [LDLS21], Cascada [RR22], and CLAASP [BGG+24], aim to enable fully automated cipher analysis, providing frameworks for analyzing a variety of cryptographic primitives.

Gohr, Leander, and Neumann [GLN23] advocate for the use of neural distinguishers as a generic tool comparable to well-established methods like SAT and MILP solvers. Their work emphasizes the potential of neural distinguishers to provide automated, flexible, and efficient solutions to cryptanalytic problems.

At FSE 2024, Bellini *et al.* [BGH+23] introduced AutoND, a cipher-agnostic neural distinguisher pipeline. AutoND achieves state-of-the-art results across various cryptographic primitives without requiring human intervention, demonstrating the feasibility of automated pipelines for neural-based cryptanalysis.

4 Design of the Generic Partial Decryption Pipeline

To design our Generic Partial Decryption pipeline, we begin by outlining our strategy for generic partial decryption in Sect. 4.1. This strategy enables the derivation of various potential data formats for the neural distinguisher. From these, we select four data formats for detailed investigation, as described in Sect. 4.2.

After determining the input data format, the next critical decisions involve selecting the input difference (Sect. 4.3) and choosing the appropriate neural network architecture (Sect. 4.4). Furthermore, we aim to simplify the complex training pipelines commonly employed in prior works by reducing the amount of training data required, leading to our streamlined training pipeline design (Sect. 4.5).

To address concerns regarding the use of multiple pairs, we choose to train single-pair distinguishers, which can also be evaluated on multiple pairs for comparison with existing literature, as detailed in Sect. 4.6.

4.1 Our Strategy for Generic Partial Decryption

The specific features utilized by the $\mathcal{ND}$ to make predictions remain largely unknown. It has been established that these features are mostly differential in nature, but a small non-differential component is shown in [Goh19], and the presence of differential-linear features has been suggested in [BGPT21a]. Various improvements, such as designing new $\mathcal{ND}$ architectures or altering the input data format, have been proposed to enhance $\mathcal{ND}$ performance. However, these enhancements are typically tailored to specific ciphers or those sharing particular characteristics, complicating the understanding of how and why the $\mathcal{ND}$ models the cipher characteristics effectively.

In [Goh19], the key recovery strategy uses the response profile of the $\mathcal{ND}$ when the last round is decrypted with an incorrect key. In [BGPT21a], the authors use a similar technique to build equivalent classical distinguishers. In addition, they observe that the right part of the Speck 32 state at the previous round can be computed without knowing the key and propose to use it as an additional feature for the neural distinguisher. In [BGL+22], the authors extend that notion to the Simon 32/64 cipher family and compare different types of related feature engineering. In [LLS+24], the authors consider not only such deterministic features but also probabilistic ones. Notably, for the Simon-like ciphers, they build features based on the (deterministically obtained) difference at round $i-1$ and an approximation of the difference at round $i-2$, obtained by decrypting the last 2 rounds with subkey 0.

According to [LLS+24], this approach significantly improves accuracy and opens avenues for further extensions. They also design $\mathcal{ND}$ architectures specifically suited for targeted tasks.

Our primary goal is to develop a general understanding of the features captured by the $\mathcal{ND}$ to enhance interpretability. Building on the work in [LLS+24], analyzing the differentials in earlier rounds could yield better input features for training $\mathcal{ND}$ models. However, if partial decryption is limited to the specific cipher under analysis, it demands significant manual effort from the cryptanalyst, thereby reducing the suitability of the $\mathcal{ND}$ as a generic cryptanalytic tool.

The propagation of a differential through a cipher typically gains more entropy at each round until full diffusion is achieved. Therefore, the difference at round $i-1$ normally holds more useful information than the difference at round i for a distinguisher. Given knowledge of the round function of a cipher, it is often possible to derive partial information about the difference in the previous rounds. For Feistel-like ciphers such as Simon and Speck, part of the previous round state can be directly obtained. For SPNs, such as Aradi, truncated differential information on the previous round can be recovered (in particular, the activity pattern of the S-Boxes). In addition, high probability differential transitions, by definition, hold for a large portion of the key space so that partial decryption with an incorrect key has a high chance of preserving them.

While such information is trivial for the cryptographer to obtain, it would be unreasonable to expect the neural distinguisher to learn it on its own. For instance, in the case of Simon, learning the round function to retrieve the previous round difference appears difficult for a neural distinguisher. By construction of Feistel-like ciphers, it is trivial for a cryptographer to retrieve information on the previous round difference; on the other hand, if the round function is sufficiently complex, it becomes arbitrarily hard for a neural network with black-box access to do so.

A cryptographer's natural approach would be to observe which parts of the previous rounds' differences can be recovered with a high probability and use them only. This is also the approach taken by [LLS+24]. On the other hand, following the goal to limit human input to the mere specification of the cipher, we would like to derive such information automatically in a generic fashion. More specifically, we provide partial decryption with a random key as a feature and let the neural distinguisher find the relevant parts and discard the less relevant ones. Without loss of generality, we use the subkey 0 in our experiments rather than a random one; intuitively, the exact choice has no impact as long as the expected Hamming distance with the actual key is $\frac{n}{2}$.

The number of rounds for which such partial decryption holds information varies depending on the cipher under consideration; for instance, in [GLN22a], the authors use information from many previous rounds in their analysis of KATAN. In this paper, for the sake of confirming the benefit of partial decryption as a feature, we restrict ourselves to 2 rounds of partial decryption. This captures the relevant information for most block ciphers while keeping the size of the dataset and experimental time reasonable. We expect our conclusions to hold when including the partially decrypted difference in all rounds, but it may scale poorly for specific examples such as KATAN, where dozens of rounds would make the sample size unpractical.

We extend the concept of *Partial Decryption*, originally tailored to a specific cryptographic primitive, to the broader framework of *Generic Partial Decryption.* This approach is formalized as follows:

Definition 1. *Let $\mathcal{P}$ the plaintext set, $\mathcal{C}$ the ciphertext set, $\mathcal{K}$ the key space, f the encryption round function and g the decryption round function such that:*

$$f : \mathcal{P} \times \mathcal{K} \to \mathcal{C}, \quad f_k^i(C^{i-1}) := f(k_i, C^{i-1}) = C^i$$
$$g : \mathcal{C} \times \mathcal{K} \to \mathcal{P}, \quad g_k^i(C^i) := g(k_i, C^i) = C^{i-1}.$$

where k_i is the i-th round key, derived from the master key $k \in \mathcal{K}$.
Then, we can define the encryption function *and the* decryption function *as:*

$$E_k^n(C^0) = f_k^{n-1} \circ \cdots \circ f_k^0(C^0) = C^n, \quad D_k^n(C^n) = g_k^0 \circ \cdots \circ g_k^{n-1}(C^n) = C^0,$$

such that:

$$f_k^i \circ g_k^i(C) = C \quad \text{and} \quad g_k^i \circ f_k^i(P) = P \quad \text{with } i = 1, \ldots, n.$$

Definition 2. *Let $(C^i, (C')^i) = (E_k^i(P), E_k^i(P'))$ be a pair of the encryption function outputs after i rounds. Then, the* differential *at the i-th round is:*

$$\Delta^i = E_k^i(P) \oplus E_k^i(P') = C^i \oplus (C')^i.$$

We call the ***1-Partial Differential*** *at round* $i-1$ *and the* ***2-Partial Differential*** *at round* $i-2$*:*

$$\tilde{\Delta}^{i-1} = g(0, C^i) \oplus g(0, (C')^i), \quad \tilde{\Delta}^{i-2} = g\left(0, g(0, C^i)\right) \oplus g\left(0, g(0, (C')^i)\right) \quad (1)$$

where 0 is the round key (i.e. $k_i = 0$*). More in general, the* k***-Partial Differential*** *is:*

$$\tilde{\Delta}^{i-k} = \underbrace{g(0, g(0, \ldots, g(0, C^i))}_{k-times} \oplus \underbrace{g(0, g(0, \ldots, g(0, (C')^i))}_{k-times}.$$

In the Generic Partial Decryption technique, the ciphertexts are decrypted with round key 0. In contrast to the approach in [LLS+24], we do not select which parts of the resulting words are kept. For the remainder of this paper, we focus exclusively on the application of $\tilde{\Delta}^{i-1}$ and $\tilde{\Delta}^{i-2}$.

4.2 Choice of the Data Format

Based on our Generic Partial Decryption strategy, several choices of data formats are possible. We focus on three specific formats:

Given an input difference δ and a pair of plaintexts $(P,\ P \oplus \delta)$, we denote ciphertext pairs encrypted with the same key as $(C, C') = (E_k^r(P), E_k^r(P \oplus \delta))$ for some $k \in \mathcal{K}$.

Simple Pair (SP). The first data format, SP, is the most commonly used in the literature; It provides a baseline to evaluate whether adding additional features can improve training:

$$(C^r, (C')^r).$$

Last Differential, Simple Pair, 1-Partial Differential and 2-Partial Differential (LD, SP, 1PD, 2PD). The second format, (LD, SP, 1PD, 2PD), is closely related to options recently investigated in [LLS+24] and incorporates both ciphertext pairs and partial differentials:

$$(\Delta^r, C^r, (C')^r, \tilde{\Delta}^{r-1}, \tilde{\Delta}^{r-2}).$$

Last Differential, 1-Partial Differential and 2-Partial Differential (LD, 1PD, 2PD). The third format (LD, 1PD, 2PD) is unique in that it does not utilize ciphertext pairs, relying solely on differential values. This format serves to evaluate the influence of non-differential features on the accuracy of the $\mathcal{ND}$:

$$(\Delta^r, \tilde{\Delta}^{r-1}, \tilde{\Delta}^{r-2}).$$

It is commonly assumed, following the conclusions of [Goh19], that the ciphertexts themselves are needed to reach optimal accuracy; our last format (LD, 1PD, 2PD) aims at testing this hypothesis.

4.3 Choice of Input Differences

The choice of the input difference used in a neural distinguisher has been shown to have a significant impact on the number of distinguished rounds and the accuracy [BGPT21a]. A good input difference for a neural distinguisher is not necessarily the input difference for the best classical differential trail. It suffices to observe that differential trails for a few rounds have relatively low probability (*e.g.,* 2^{-9} for 5 rounds of SPECK), whereas neural distinguishers distinguish based on a single pair. Therefore, the property that they identify has to occur with significantly higher probability than a classical trail, and properties such as multiple differentials and differential-linear play an important role.

It is commonplace in neural distinguishers research to pick an input difference with a low Hamming Weight, as it is expected to propagate slowly and enable longer neural distinguishers. These input differences are often chosen from intermediate rounds of known trails for the cipher under study, as is the case in [LLS+24].

At FSE 2024, the authors of [BGH+23] introduced an evolutionary optimizer for identifying suitable input differences for neural distinguishers in a generic manner. This optimizer operates on the premise that neural distinguishers detect truncated differentials from earlier rounds [BGPT21a]. Given this approach, the existing evolutionary optimizer appears well-suited for application to partially decrypted input data formats.

4.4 Choice of the Neural Network Architecture

For a comprehensive overview of the neural network architectures for cryptanalysis, we refer readers to the recent systematization of knowledge [GHHP24]. To motivate our choice of neural network architecture, we provide the following summary: Multi-layer perceptrons (MLPs) have been widely explored as a basic yet lightweight architecture, for example in [BR21,ZZY+21,ERP22]. While MLPs are efficient and easy to implement, their performance is often surpassed by more advanced architectures. The majority of subsequent works build upon Gohr's original neural network design, which has been adapted and refined in various studies, among others [SZM21,BBCD22,WTZ+22]. Although Gohr's network can be adapted to new ciphers, this process necessitates careful tuning of numerous hyper-parameters [GLN23]. Advanced components, such as attention mechanisms [DCC23], LSTMs [BBCD22,SSL+22], GoogLeNet-inspired Inception modules [ZWC23,ZLWL23,BLYZ23], and DenseNets [SM23], have also been explored. While these approaches demonstrate strong results for specific ciphers, they are often highly cipher-specific and are accompanied by significantly increased training times.

At FSE 2024, DBITNET was introduced as a "cipher-agnostic" architecture [BGH+23]. This architecture avoids cipher-specific components, employs a simplistic design, and achieves state-of-the-art results across various primitives without requiring any modifications or hyper-parameter adjustments. Given our goal of developing generic applicability, we focus on two specific architectures:

DBitNet, which emphasizes generalization across ciphers, and GohrAMS, a variant of Gohr's network that incorporates AMSGrad learning rate adaptation also introduced in [BGH+23].

The Neural Networks we consider are Gohr's original depth-1 network [Goh19] with AMSGrad learning rate GohrAMS and DBitNet [BGH+23]. We will briefly describe them and refer to their respective publications for more details.

GohrAMS. The Neural Network proposed in [Goh19] is composed of a preprocessing layer in which the input dimension is reshaped, followed by three main blocks: one slicing Convolutional Layer, n iterations of a Residual Block, and a Prediction layer. We use the AMSGRAD optimizer [RKK19] instead of the original learning rate scheduler, as it was shown in [BGH+23] to achieve equivalent performance without the need for manual fine-tuning of the original cyclic learning rate schedule.

DBitNet. DBitNet employs dilated convolutional layers to effectively combine long-range and short-range dependencies across consecutive convolutional layers. The architecture begins with a dilated convolutional layer that adapts to the input size, with an initial dilation rate of $dr_0 = \lfloor \frac{\text{input size}}{2} - 1 \rfloor$. This is followed by a layer targeting local interactions with a fixed dilation rate of 2. Each dilated convolutional layer reduces the neuronal width by approximately half. The alternation between dilated convolution and standard convolution of neighboring bits continues for $dr_i = \left\lfloor \frac{r_{i-1}+1}{2} - 1 \right\rfloor, \quad \text{with } i = 1, \ldots, \lfloor \log_2(\text{input size}) - 3 \rfloor$.

As the neuronal width decreases with each dilated step, the number of filters increases incrementally to compensate for the reduced spatial dimensions. This design ensures a balance between dimensionality reduction and feature extraction, enabling the network to achieve effective representation and generalization across a variety of ciphers.

4.5 Choice of the Training Pipeline

The training pipeline is known to be determinant when targeting higher rounds, for which the signal of the distinguisher becomes weaker. In [Goh19], the 8-round distinguisher was obtained by retraining the best distinguishers starting from likely differences in the middle rounds and increasing the amount of training data by a factor of 100. Similarly, in [LLS+24], the 12-round Simon 32/64 distinguisher is built by iteratively retraining the best distinguishers on curated data, with a dedicated cyclic learning rate. The authors adopt a similar pipeline for Simeck 32/64.

We aim to achieve similar accuracies without using such dedicated techniques. In particular, we improve the (already competitive) results we obtain with a simple training pipeline by applying the simple polishing pipeline defined in [BGH+23].

4.6 Choice of Single- or Multi-pair Distinguisher

The [LLS+24]'s $\mathcal{ND}$s are multi-pair Distinguishers trained with samples composed of 8 pairs, increasing the amount of data required for training and testing. On the other hand, [GLN22a] proposes a method to create a multi-pair distinguisher from a single-pair distinguisher. The algorithm, described below Eq. 2, takes as input m ciphertext pairs, either all real or all random, but otherwise assumed to be independent. The $\mathcal{ND}$ is assumed to be perfectly calibrated so that the pairwise scores $ND(c_i) = p_i$ can be interpreted as probabilities. Under these assumptions, the Multi-Pair distinguisher derives the probabilities $P_{real} = \mathbb{P}[\text{all real} \mid \text{observed scores}]$ and $P_{rand} = \mathbb{P}[\text{all random} \mid \text{observed scores}]$, aggregates them as the combined response score:

$$\frac{P_{real}}{P_{real} + P_{rand}} = \frac{1}{1 + \frac{P_{rand}}{P_{real}}} = \frac{1}{1 + \prod_{i=1}^{m} \frac{1-p_i}{p_i}}. \tag{2}$$

We use Eq. 2 following [GLN22a]: (i) We validate our $\mathcal{ND}$ for each format on 10^6 pairs; these datasets are denoted $(X_j)_j$. (ii) We split the dataset according the labels; (X_j^1) are the real samples and (X_j^0) the random ones. Let $N^t = \#(X_j^t)$, be the cardinality of the set for $t \in \{0, 1\}$. (iii) We obtain the respective scores of the samples as $p_j^t = ND(X_j^t)$ with $t \in \{0, 1\}$. (iv) We divide the corresponding (p_j^t) into m subgroups and apply Eq. 2. We obtain in total $M^t = \lfloor N^t/m \rfloor$ prediction for $t \in \{0, 1\}$. (v) Each M^t subsample is classified based on its combined response score. (vi) The accuracy is given from the ratio of the right-labeled subsamples over the total subsamples we have.

4.7 Final Pipeline for Generic Partial Decryption

Based on the previously presented considerations, we arrive at the following pipeline for generic partial decryption: The main algorithm trains a neural distinguisher $\mathcal{ND}$ to identify the highest non-random round of a block cipher implementation $E_k(\cdot)$. It adopts a curriculum learning approach, beginning from an initial round r_0 and progressively training the $\mathcal{ND}$ on datasets generated for increasing rounds. The training process continues until the validation accuracy drops below a predefined threshold (ten standard deviations (10σ) above the random accuracy of fifty percent).[1] Datasets for each round are created using the chosen data format in the GeneratePDDataset algorithm.

The GeneratePDDataset sub-algorithm constructs a labeled dataset $\mathcal{D}$ for a given round r. It generates N samples through the following steps: (i) Randomly select plaintexts $P \in \mathcal{P}$ and keys $k \in \mathcal{K}$. (ii) Assign a random label $y \in \{0, 1\}$. (iii) Compute ciphertext pairs (C, C') using the r-round encryption function $E_k^r(\cdot)$ on $(P, P \oplus \delta_0)$. (iv) C, C' becomes a random pair of bit string if $y = 0$. The dataset $\mathcal{D}$ consists of labeled feature vectors according to the

[1] The expected standard deviation for the accuracy depends on the samples n in the dataset as $\sigma = 1/(2\sqrt{n})$ (see, for example [BGH+23]); resulting in $\sigma = 0.0005$ for $N_{\text{val}} = 10^6$.

Algorithm 1. GENERICPARTIALDECRYPTION($E_k(\cdot)$)

Input: Oracle access to an r-round block cipher $E_k(\cdot)$, where $P \in \mathcal{P}$, $k \in \mathcal{K}$, and $C \in \mathcal{C}$ such that $C = E_k(P)$.
Output: Neural distinguisher $\mathcal{ND}$ for the highest non-random round.

$\mathcal{ND} \leftarrow$ randomly initialize the neural network (cf. Section 4.4)
$(r_0, \delta_0) \leftarrow$ Evolutionary Optimizer (select starting round r_0 and input difference δ_0, cf. Section 4.3)
▷ Execute curriculum learning starting from round r_0 (cf. Section 4.5)
$A_{\text{val}} \leftarrow 1.0$
$r \leftarrow r_0$
while $A_{\text{val}} > 0.50 + 10\sigma$ **do**
  $\mathcal{D}_{\text{train}} \leftarrow$ GENERATEPDDATASET($r, N_{\text{train}}, \delta_0,$ *dataformat*)
  $\mathcal{D}_{\text{val}} \leftarrow$ GENERATEPDDATASET($r, N_{\text{val}}, \delta_0,$ *dataformat*)
  Train $\mathcal{ND}$ on $\mathcal{D}_{\text{train}}$
  $A_{\text{val}} \leftarrow$ accuracy of $\mathcal{ND}$ on $\mathcal{D}_{\text{val}}$ ▷ Evaluate neural distinguisher
  $r \leftarrow r + 1$ ▷ Progress to next round r
end while
return $\mathcal{ND}$

Algorithm 2. GENERATEPDDATASET(r, N, δ_0, *dataformat*)

Input: Round r, number of samples N, and input difference δ_0.
Output: Dataset $\mathcal{D}$ with N labeled samples for round r.

$\mathcal{D} \leftarrow \emptyset$
for $j = 1, \ldots, N$ **do**
  $P, k \leftarrow$ random choice of $P \in \mathcal{P}$, $k \in \mathcal{K}$
  $y \leftarrow$ random choice from $\{0, 1\}$ ▷ Randomly choose a label
  $(C, C') \leftarrow (E_k^r(P), E_k^r(P \oplus \delta_0))$ ▷ Generate ciphertext pair
  $(C, C') \leftarrow$ random pair of bit strings if $y = 0$
  $\mathcal{D} \leftarrow \mathcal{D} \cup \{$bit vector according to *dataformat*$\}$ ▷ cf. Section 4.1
end for
return $\mathcal{D}$

chosen data format, which is subsequently used to train and validate the neural distinguisher in the main algorithm.

Our parameter choices follow the ones of [BGH+23]: All our $\mathcal{ND}$s are trained over 40 epochs per round using $N_{\text{train}} = 10^7$ samples, with a batch size of 5000, and validated on $N_{\text{val}} = 10^6$ samples. Therefore, each of the five fresh test sets contains 10^6 samples drawn with equal class priors; the expected imbalance per set is $\leq 0.05\%$. Averaging accuracy over the five sets reduces any residual bias to $\leq 0.02\%$, making the reported mean robust. Our reporting is consistent with prior works such as [BGH+23] and statistically robust. Additionally, we apply the simple polishing step of [BGH+23], where the final network undergoes retraining for three iterations. Each iteration involves repeating the training for one epoch 100 times on 10^7 fresh training samples, resulting in a total training dataset of $100 \times 10^7 = 10^9$ samples per iteration. Since the additional data we are using, we decide to apply the polish step just for the round attacked and not for every step of the staged training. With a batch size of 10,000, we use the ADAM optimizer, gradually decreasing the constant learning rate at each iteration from 10^{-4} to 10^{-5} and finally to 10^{-6}. Validation is performed on 10^7 samples at each iteration.

Our single-pair classifiers, with $m = 1$, are extrapolated to multi-pair distinguishers ($m = 8$), using the combined response computed as in Sect. 4.6, to enable fair comparison with the related work. In both cases, the reported accuracies are the average on five fresh testing datasets of size 10^6.

5 Neural Distinguishers via Generic Partial Decryption

In the following, we apply our GENERICPARTIALDECRYPTION (cf. Sect. 4.7) to SIMON, SIMECK, and ARADI. Summarizing the results discussed in detail below, we find that for SIMON and SIMECK, our generic pipeline achieves competitive accuracies compared to the highly specialized approach of [LLS+24]. Moreover, we can explain the accuracies obtained by [LLS+24] by their distinct contributions: the use of multiple pairs, additional data, and the actual partial decryption.

5.1 SIMON and SIMECK

We perform the training starting from round 8 to round 12 with input difference: 0×400 and 0×80 respectively for SIMON 32/64 and SIMECK 32/64 (Table 1) (for the choice of the input differences cf. Sect. 4.3). In each table, we present our results for GENERICPARTIALDECRYPTION applied to SIMON in the DBITNET-columns alongside the results of [LLS+24], which exploit specific features of the SIMON and SIMECK ciphers.

SIMON. For SIMON (Table 1), in the simple data format (C, C'), DBITNET distinguishes better than random up to 11 rounds; in the multi-pair setting ($m = 8$), the 11 rounds accuracy increases by 4 points, and the 12 rounds accuracy remains borderline, at 2.6σ above randomness. Applying the simple polishing step (cf. Sect. 4.7) brings the accuracy to 0.5097 (19σ above random). These results indicate that a 12-round distinguisher for SIMON can be achieved with the simple data format by combining *i)* multi-pair evaluation and *ii)* a simple polishing step with additional training data.

The remaining gap with the 12-rounds accuracy 0.5152 from [LLS+24] is filled by feature engineering: DBITNET, combined with the GENERICPARTIALDECRYPTION, achieves slightly higher accuracy (0.5153) using the same feature engineering technique, and up to 0.5156 under the (LD, 1PD, 2PD) format.

SIMECK. For SIMECK (Table 1), we observe similar results, unsurprisingly, due to the similarities of the two primitives. However, the key schedule difference between the two primitives does not seem to impact the accuracy of the $\mathcal{ND}$. More importantly, these results show that, contrary to the common-held belief, the presence of the ciphertexts is not always mandatory to reach optimal accuracy; indeed, our best performing format for Simon and Speck, (LD, 1PD, 2PD), only uses differences.

Table 1. Results for SIMON 32/64, SIMECK 32/64, and ARADI. SIMON: (†) See Sect. 4.5; (a) Refer to [LLS+24]; (b) The $\mathcal{ND}$ is the same of the case $m = 1$ but we change the evaluation step according Sect. 4.6. SIMECK: (†) See Sect. 4.5; (a) Refer to [LLS+24]; (b) The $\mathcal{ND}$ is the same as the case $m = 1$ but we change the evaluation step according Sect. 4.6. ARADI: (a) The $\mathcal{ND}$ is the same of the case $m = 1$ but we change the evaluation step according Sect. 4.6.

	[LLS+24]	DBitNet			DBitNet			DBitNet		
	$(\Delta^r, C, C', \Delta_R^{r-1}, \tilde{\Delta}_R^{r-2})$	(C, C')			$(\Delta^r, C, C', \tilde{\Delta}^{r-1}, \tilde{\Delta}^{r-2})$			$(\Delta^r, \tilde{\Delta}^{r-1}, \tilde{\Delta}^{r-2})$		
SIMON32/64	$m = 8$	$m = 1$	$m = 8$	$m = 8$	$m = 1$	$m = 8$	$m = 8$	$m = 1$	$m = 8$	$m = 8$
Round	adv.	Simple	Simple	Pol.	Simple	Simple	Pol.	Simple	Simple	Pol.
8	-	0.8367	0.9991	-	0.8417	0.9993	-	0.8408	0.9993	-
9	0.9176	0.6556	0.8892	-	0.6584	0.8938	-	0.6580	0.8933	-
10	0.6975	0.5626	0.6761	-	0.5655	0.6859	-	0.5646	0.6827	-
11	0.5609	0.5150	0.5479	-	0.5177	0.5567	-	0.5173	0.5561	-
12	**0.5152**	0.5004	0.5013	0.5097	0.5022	0.5077	**0.5153**	0.5023	0.5064	**0.5156**

	[LLS+24]	DBitNet			DBitNet			DBitNet		
	$(\Delta^r, C, C', \Delta_R^{r-1}, \tilde{\Delta}_R^{r-2})$	(C, C')			$(\Delta^r, C, C', \tilde{\Delta}^{r-1}, \tilde{\Delta}^{r-2})$			$(\Delta^r, \tilde{\Delta}^{r-1}, \tilde{\Delta}^{r-2})$		
SIMECK32/64	$m = 8$	$m = 1$	$m = 8$	$m = 8$	$m = 1$	$m = 8$	$m = 8$	$m = 1$	$m = 8$	$m = 8$
Round	adv.	Simple	Simple	Pol.	Simple	Simple	Pol.	Simple	Simple	Pol.
8	-	0.8470	0.9998	-	0.9022	1.0000	-	0.9025	1.0000	-
9	0.9952	0.6819	0.9276	-	0.7075	0.9562	-	0.7074	0.9564	-
10	0.7354	0.5601	0.6832	-	0.5700	0.7127	-	0.5702	0.7133	-
11	0.5646	0.5133	0.5472	-	0.5168	0.5595	-	0.5170	0.5612	-
12	**0.5146**	0.5007	0.5028	0.5109	0.5026	0.5100	**0.5155**	0.5028	0.5090	**0.5156**

	DBitNet			DBitNet			GohrAMS			DBitNet		
	(C, C')			$(\Delta^r, C, C', \tilde{\Delta}^{r-1}, \tilde{\Delta}^{r-2})$			$(\Delta^r, C, C', \tilde{\Delta}^{r-1}, \tilde{\Delta}^{r-2})$			$(\Delta^r, \tilde{\Delta}^{r-1}, \tilde{\Delta}^{r-2})$		
ARADI	$m = 1$	$m = 8$	$m = 8$	$m = 1$	$m = 8$	$m = 8$	$m = 1$	$m = 8$	$m = 8$	$m = 1$	$m = 8$	$m = 8$
Round	Simple	Simple	Pol.	Simple	Simple	Pol.	Simple	Simple	Pol.	Simple	Simple	Pol.
3	1.0000	1.0000	-	1.0000	1.0000	-	1.0000	1.0000	-	1.0000	1.0000	-
4	1.0000	1.0000	-	1.0000	1.0000	-	1.0000	1.0000	-	1.0000	1.0000	-
5	0.5974	0.7533	0.7634	**0.7732**	**0.9984**	**0.9988**	**0.7733**	**0.9988**	**0.9988**	**0.7721**	**0.9988**	**0.9988**

5.2 ARADI

We train the neural distinguisher ($\mathcal{ND}$) for ARADI from round 3 to round 5 using the input difference 0x1000000000000000000000. The distinguishers (Table 1) reach 100% accuracy on 3 and 4 rounds, while the best differential trail over 4 rounds has probability 2^{-32}. Furthermore, with the input difference we used, the best differential trail has probability 2^{-60} (found using CLAASP [BGG+24]). Another previous work [BFG+24b, Table 10] achieves 5-round accuracy of 0.5954. This accuracy is close to our results in the (C, C') scenario. In the multi-sample and partially decrypted scenario, we significantly surpass these results, reaching accuracies of up to almost perfect accuracy in round 5.

On 5 rounds, the addition of features derived from partial decryption has a considerable positive impact on the accuracy, with DBitNet going from just under 60% accuracy in the (C, C') format to around 77% with the composite format $(\Delta^r, C, C', \tilde{\Delta}^{r-1}, \tilde{\Delta}^{r-2})$. GOHRAMS reaches a similar performance. In contrast, the best 5-round differential trail has probability 2^{-50}; if the input difference is restricted to the one used by our distinguisher, the best trail has probability 2^{-94}.

On the other hand, we can observe deterministic truncated differential properties when the input difference is in a single S-Box position. Namely, by construction of the linear layer, such an input difference propagates to 3 non-zero differences after one round with probability 1. At round 2, the truncated propagation is still deterministic, and 9 S-Box positions are active. At round 3, the activity pattern of 22 S-Boxes is non-deterministic, while 10 S-Boxes have a 0 difference with probability 1. This 40-bit property is sufficient to build a strong distinguisher and can be directly checked from the round 4 difference. Indeed, when inverting the last round, the round 4 key addition does not change the difference, and the linear layer propagates it in a deterministic way. The input difference before and after the inversion of S-boxes depends on the round 4 key, but we are only interested in whether they have a zero difference. For bijective S-Boxes, a zero input difference always goes to a 0 output difference and vice versa so that we can observe which S-Box positions are 0 at round 3. Therefore, giving the partial decryption to the neural distinguisher directly gives it a strong property to observe, which it otherwise would have to learn.

6 Key Recovery Attack via Generic Partial Decryption

6.1 Neural Key Recovery in the Literature

In [Goh19], neural distinguishers are used to mount a key recovery attack. The attack divides the cipher into three parts: the Prepended n_{PP} rounds, the Neural Distinguisher on n_{ND} rounds, and the Key Recovery part on n_{KR} rounds.

The Basic Attack. In its most basic form, Gohr's neural key recovery [Goh19] targets $n_{\text{ND}} + n_{\text{KR}}$ rounds. The attacker queries the encryption of plaintext pairs with difference δ. For each candidate subkey in the last n_{KR} rounds, the pairs are decrypted and submitted to the neural distinguisher. Based on the wrong key randomization hypothesis, the distribution induced by incorrect key decryption is assumed to differ from the distribution learned by the neural distinguisher.

Wrong Key Response Profile. Decryption with an incorrect key does not, in practice, induce a random distribution of the pairs for SPECK 32. The author of [Goh19] observes that the XOR difference between a wrong key and the actual key influences the scoring output by the neural distinguisher. A *wrong key response profile* quantifies, for each key difference value, the expected distribution of the output of the neural distinguisher. This information helps greatly reduce the number of examined candidate keys, as it selects which direction to walk to get closer to the correct key.

Reaching More Rounds. If there exists an input difference γ, which has probability p to propagate to the $\mathcal{ND}$ input difference δ after n_{PP} rounds, then a pair with input difference γ encrypted for $n_{\text{PP}} + n_{\text{ND}}$ rounds should be classified as real by the n_{ND} rounds neural distinguisher with probability $p \cdot \texttt{TPR} + (1-p) \cdot \texttt{FPR}$, where TPR and FPR denote respectively the true positive and false positive rates of the neural distinguisher. For a random permutation, this probability simply becomes FPR. The number of positive predictions can, therefore, be used as a distinguisher for $n_{\text{PP}} + n_{\text{ND}}$ rounds. However, the number of pairs required to reach over 50% confidence with the above distinguisher grows with the square of the inverse of p; to counter that effect, the author of [Goh19] proposes to use *Probabilistic Neutral Bits* (PNBs) to build structures within which all the pairs are expected to behave similarly in the first n_{PP} rounds.

Definition 3. *(Probabilistic Neutral Bit) Let π_k be a keyed permutation, and $\gamma \rightarrow \delta$ be a differential for π_k. A bit i is a* Neutral Bit *for γ, δ if it does not influence the differential. Let x_i^* denote plaintext x with bit position i flipped; if prob$\pi_k(x_i^*) \oplus \pi_k(x_i^* \oplus \gamma) = \delta | \pi_k(x) \oplus \pi_k(x \oplus \gamma) = \delta = 1$, then bit i is neutral. More generally, i is a* Probabilistic Neutral Bit *with probability p if*

$$\mathbb{P}[\pi_k(x_i^*) \oplus \pi_k(x_i^* \oplus \gamma) = \delta | \pi_k(x) \oplus \pi_k(x \oplus \gamma) = \delta] = p.$$

Attacking Large Round Keys. The above attack requires iterating over all possible key error bit vectors. Therefore, little attention has been given to neural key recovery on block ciphers with larger round keys. The main result for that setting [CBSY22] proposes to use different neural distinguishers for different subsets of the key bits. These subsets are identified through the *bit sensitivity test* [CSY23], which identifies *informative bits* of the ciphertext w.r.t the classification by the neural distinguisher. A key recovery using this technique focuses on key bits in the last round key that have a high impact on the corresponding ciphertext bits after partial decryption.

6.2 Neural Key Recovery on Aradi

Aradi uses large (128-bit) round keys. Therefore, we build an alternative key recovery strategy using probabilistic neutral bits in the *decryption direction.* This technique was introduced by Aumasson for differential-linear cryptanalysis against ChaCha [AFK+08]. To distinguish these bits from the neutral bits used in the encryption direction, we call them Probabilistic Neutral Key Bits (PNKBs).

PNKBs and How to Find Them. A bit of the last round key is said to be a PKNB when, if it is incorrectly guessed, it does not change the prediction of the neural distinguisher for the corresponding partially decrypted ciphertext pair. In [AFK+08], probabilistic neutral bits are defined as follows for a function $f(k, W)$ of an unknown partial key k and known information W:

Definition 4. *Probabilistic Neutral Key Bit (PNKB) The neutrality measure of the key bit k_i with respect to the function $f(k, W)$ is defined as γ_i, where*

$$\mathbb{P}[f(k, W) = f(k_i^*, W)] = \frac{1}{2} \cdot (1 + \gamma_i)$$

is the probability (over all k and W) that complementing the key bit k_i does not change the output of $f(k, W)$.

In our analysis, given an $r+1$-round ciphertext pair, we decrypt the last round using a candidate key k and build the candidate decryptions $C_0^* = g_{r+1}^k(C_0)$ and $C_1^* = g_{r+1}^k(C_1)$, adapting the notations introduced in Definition 1; from these, we set $W = (\Delta^{r*}, \tilde{\Delta}^{r-1*}, \tilde{\Delta}^{r-2*})$, and set $f(k, W) = \mathcal{ND}(W)$. A PNKB is a key bit that does not change the output of the neural distinguisher when guessed incorrectly. To test whether a key bit b is a PNKB, we build a dataset $\mathcal{D}_{\text{PNKB}}$, in which the random samples are defined as usual, and the real samples are built from $C_0^* = g_{r+1}^{k^b}(C_0)$ and $C_1^* = g_{r+1}^{k^b}(C_1)$, where k^b is the correct round key k with bit b randomized. If the bit is indeed a PNKB, then the accuracy of the neural distinguisher on this modified dataset is equivalent to its accuracy on a normal r round dataset. Preliminary experiments show that some key bits are naturally almost neutral in our trained $\mathcal{ND}$ for ARADI. However, building a practical attack requires a sufficient number of PNKBs, with neutrality measure as high as possible. We, therefore, retrain our neural distinguishers to reduce their sensitivity to changes in the PNKBs. More specifically, starting from an empty set of PNKBs, and for each last round key bit position i, we retrain our $\mathcal{ND}$ on the corresponding $\mathcal{D}_{\text{PNKB}}$ dataset. If the accuracy remains sufficiently close to the basic $\mathcal{ND}$, we keep bit i as neutral and proceed to the next. If not, bit i is re-set to its correct value, and the next bit is investigated. At the end of this procedure, we have a set of PNKBs, as well as the dual set of important key bits.

A Simple 5-rounds Key Recovery. The simplest version of our attack targets 5 rounds of ARADI and uses a 4-round neural distinguisher, trained on input difference 0× 10000000000000000000000. This neural distinguisher has over 99% accuracy, which enables low data complexity key recoveries. Furthermore, it exhibits a set of 88 PNKBs, for last round key indices 0, 3, 4, 7, 8, 9, 10, 11, 12, 14, 15, 17, 18, 19, 21, 22, 23, 26, 27, 28, 30, 31, 32, 35, 36, 39, 40, 41, 42, 43, 44, 46, 47, 49, 50, 51, 53, 54, 55, 58, 59, 60, 62, 63, 64, 67, 68, 71, 72, 73, 74, 75, 76, 78, 79, 81, 82, 83, 85, 86, 87, 90, 91, 92, 94, 95, 96, 99, 100, 103, 104, 105, 106, 107, 108, 110, 111, 113, 114, 115, 117, 118, 119, 122, 123, 124, 126, 127. In addition, we use a set of 16 rotationally equivalent neural distinguishers for rotations in the weight 1 input difference in the leftmost 16 bits of word x of the state. The distinguishers have all equivalent accuracies and map to equivalent rotated PKNBs. When viewing the cipher state as 4 rows of 32 bits, considered as a left and right part, each composed of 4 rows of 16 bits, a rotation of r positions in the input difference results in a rotation of r positions in the left and right parts independently. The basic key recovery strategy is to fix the

88 PNKBs to a random value and attack the remaining 40 non-neutral key bits. Using 16 neural distinguishers for the corresponding 16 rotated input differences and PNKB sets, we iteratively recover the round 5 subkey.

In our attack, we start by recovering the 40 key bits associated with one of our neural distinguishers. Some of these key bits have a very strong signal in that the scoring output by the neural distinguisher for the corresponding key guesses is consistently high; on the other hand, some key bits do not exhibit such a clear behavior. We, therefore, assign a confidence score to each of the guessed key bits and only consider a bit *valid* when this score is high enough. We then iteratively select a new input difference and its set of key bits to attack. The choice of the next input difference is guided by the amount of corresponding *leftover bits*, bits which are part of the input difference's PNKBs and not part of the valid bits set. To keep the attack practical, we need the set of attacked bits to be as small as possible, so we aim for 20 or fewer leftover bits. The attack continues until the set of valid bits has size 128 (*i.e.,* the entire last round key is recovered), or no new bit is recovered for a threshold number of iterations. The remaining 128 bits of the key can be recovered using a similar strategy with a 3-round neural distinguisher. In order to experimentally validate this practical key recovery, the neural network evaluation for 2^{40} potential key candidates was an obstacle. However, the PNKB sets for different distinguishers overlap so that once a small number of key bits have been recovered, it is usually possible to find an overlapping set with less than 20 key bits to enumerate. We, therefore, assume preliminary knowledge of 30 key bits in the first explored set for practical validation and successfully recover the remaining 98 bits of the round 5 key. This attack was performed 25 times, each time with a fresh random key and a random selection of 30 known key bits, and successfully recovered the entire last round key 21 times, with a maximum data complexity of 520 pairs, slightly over 2^9 chosen plaintexts. More specifically, each enumeration of a non-neutral key bits set is tested against 10 pairs, and the maximum number of iterations of the enumeration algorithm was 52 (with some PNKB sets attacked several times until a high enough confidence is achieved). It is likely that the data complexity and success rate of the attack can be further improved, for instance by using more pairs at each iteration (therefore increasing the confidence in the corresponding guesses and reducing the number of iterations), or with a smarter exploration of the connections between overlapping PNKB sets.

Extending the Attack. Our attack can be extended to 7 rounds, at the cost of non-practical time complexity, by having the distinguisher start from round 2 instead of round 0. This requires retraining a neural distinguisher, as the rotational constants of rounds 2 to 6 are not the same as the ones from rounds 0 to 4. Nonetheless, equivalent distinguishers can be built from round 2, which is consistent with observations on the deterministic propagation of input differences through the cipher. In addition, we observe that due to the SPN structure of Aradi, the accuracy of neural distinguishers and differential propagation are similar regardless of the row of the Hamming weight 1 input difference (when we consider the Aradi state as 4 rows). Furthermore, truncated differences within a single row share similar properties, meaning that when prepending rounds, we do not need to target a specific bit but a column and benefit from a differential effect. For Aradi, the best 2-round differential trails that end with a single-column output difference have probability 2^{-24}. We focus, without loss of generality, on the differential transition from $(0 \times \texttt{ca10314}, 0 \times \texttt{ca10314}, 0, 0)$ to an output difference where a single active S-Box is present in column 15. This truncated differential transition holds with approximate probability 2^{20} (as experimentally verified). We experimentally find a set of 76 neutral bits for this differential transition, which may enable longer key recoveries. For a 7-round attack, however, we can use significantly less. Remember that our 4-round distinguishers have over 99% accuracy, so the response profile for pairs that do not follow the differential is very distinct. Therefore, in the attack, we can build small structures of 2^8 pairs; we need on average 2^{20} structures to find one that follows the 2-round differential. Within each structure, we test one pair at a time by testing the corresponding 40 key-bit candidates; the response profile of the correct structure is expected to be the highest. From there, the attack proceeds as in the previous section, using different neural distinguishers for different key-bit subsets. We expect that with 2^8 pairs per structure, the key recovery procedure will require a single pass for each of the input differences, resulting in a worse-case data complexity of $2^{20} \cdot 2^8 \cdot 16 = 2^{32}$. The time complexity is on average 2^{20} neural distinguisher evaluations per pair, but dominated by the initial 2^{40} neural evaluations for the first PKNB set, yielding a total time complexity of 2^{72} $\mathcal{ND}$ evaluations.

From Neural to Classical Key Recovery. The neural distinguisher findings are helpful in identifying that there is a relevant property for 4 and 5 rounds. However, for cryptographers, knowing there is an attack is not sufficient, and understanding it is crucial. We therefore propose to use the $\mathcal{ND}$ results to mount a classical key recovery. For the 4-round distinguishers, the key property is that a set of 40 bits (10 columns) in round 3 is always 0 due to the slow diffusion of the single active nibble in the input difference. The activity pattern of the S-Boxes is preserved by one round of partial decryption so that decrypting the 4-round pair with a random key is sufficient to observe the 40 zeros pattern for a real pair. On the other hand, for random pairs, it occurs with probability 2^{-40}, so that the corresponding distinguisher is highly accurate: its true positive rate is 1 (as all real pairs follow this pattern), and its false positive rate is 1-2^{-40}.

Transforming this distinguisher into a 5-round key recovery requires identifying the key bits involved in the computation of the 40 fixed positions in round 3. Each of these columns depends, by the construction of the linear layer, on 3 columns of the round 4 difference. Since we are only interested in the activity pattern and not the actual value of the S-Box inputs, we do not need the corresponding round 4 key. On the other hand, each of these round 4 columns depends on 3 columns of round 5, for which we do need to obtain the key to get the correct values for the columns of round 3. More specifically, there are 10 sets of 36 key bits, each corresponding to one column, to be recovered.

The probability for an incorrect key guess to result in the expected 4-zeros column pattern is 2^{-4}; after analyzing N pairs, the probability for a wrong key guess to appear for all N pairs is $2^{-4 \cdot N}$. This figure matches the neural key recovery experiments, where 10 pairs were sufficient for each key guessing phase. The data complexity of the corresponding key recovery is 10 pairs, and the time complexity, $2^{36} \cdot 4 \cdot 10$, rounded up to 2^{42}. In comparison, the first step of the neural key recovery of the previous section requires $10 \cdot 2^{40}$ $\mathcal{ND}$ evaluations, with each $\mathcal{ND}$ evaluation accounting for significantly more than a simple operation, resulting in higher time complexity. On the other hand, the neural key recovery may perform similarly, or better, if retrained for the subsets of 36 non-neutral key bits used in the classical attack; however, we did not perform such experiments, as we find the classical attack more satisfying.

7 Conclusion

In this paper, we recognize neural distinguishers as a useful tool for identifying differential properties that do not immediately appear from classical differential characteristics. We, therefore, aim to make their application to new primitives easier, building on the generic AutoND framework and making it more competitive with dedicated approaches. In particular, we notice that recent works, such as [LLS+24], break the classical black-box model (where the neural distinguisher is only given ciphertext pairs) to include information on the structure of the cipher, by including features derived from the deterministic (and sometimes probabilistic) propagation of the difference to the previous rounds. We propose Generic Partial Decryption as a way to include such features automatically, and evaluate the resulting framework on Simon, Simeck, and Aradi. By separating feature engineering from other techniques, such as multiple-pair distinguishers, we observe that the addition of these features is not determinant to the advantage of [LLS+24] over the AutoND framework, but that the multi-pair aspect plays the most important role (even though feature engineering helps fill a small gap between the two techniques). In addition, we propose the first neural key recovery on 5 rounds of Aradi, with practical complexity, and propose an equivalent classical attack, informed by the biases exhibited by the neural distinguisher, with better complexity. In future work, it would be interesting to observe how much similar insight can be leveraged to improve classical attacks. On the neural distinguisher side, it appears that the addition of features sometimes lowers the accuracy, possibly due to larger inputs. Addressing this limitation would help further improve automated neural cryptanalysis, in turn improving our understanding of multiple differential properties.

A Useful Diagrams of the Analyzed Ciphers

In this section, we report some useful diagrams that can help visualize the design of the analyzed cipher (Figs. 1, 2 and Table 2).

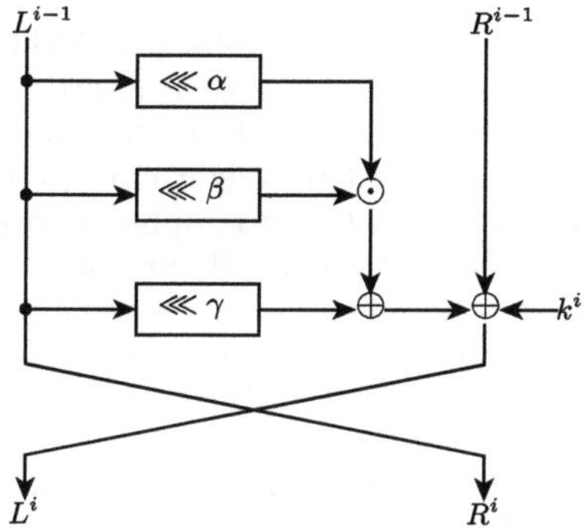

Fig. 1. Round function of SIMON and SIMECK.

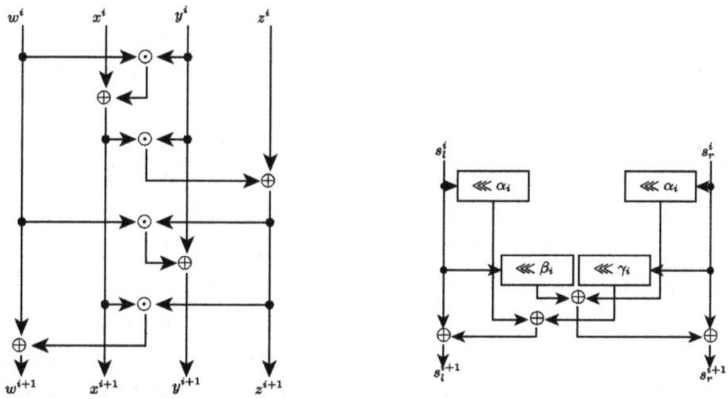

Fig. 2. On the left the S-box π and on the right the component function L_i of the linear layer Λ_i in ARADI.

Table 2. Constants used in ARADI.

$i \mod 4$	α_i	β_i	γ_i
0	11	8	14
1	10	9	11
2	9	4	14
3	8	9	7

References

[ADG24] Avanzi, R., Dunkelman, O., Ghosh, S.: A note on ARADI and LLAMA. IACR Cryptology ePrint Archive, p. 1328 (2024)

[AFK+08] Aumasson, J.-P., Fischer, S., Khazaei, S., Meier, W., Rechberger, C.: New features of Latin dances: analysis of Salsa, ChaCha, and Rumba. In: Nyberg, K. (ed.) FSE 2008. LNCS, vol. 5086, pp. 470–488. Springer, Heidelberg (2008). https://doi.org/10.1007/978-3-540-71039-4_30

[BBCD21] Baksi, A., Breier, J., Chen, Y., Dong, X.: Machine learning assisted differential distinguishers for lightweight ciphers. In: Design, Automation &

Test in Europe Conference & Exhibition, DATE 2021, Grenoble, France, 1–5 February 2021, pp. 176–181. IEEE (2021)

[BBCD22] Baksi, A., Breier, J., Chen, Y., Dong, X.: Machine learning-assisted differential distinguishers for lightweight ciphers. In: Classical and Physical Security of Symmetric Key Cryptographic Algorithms, pp. 141–162 (2022)

[BDD+24] Boura, C., David, N., Derbez, P., Heim Boissier, R., Naya-Plasencia, M.: A generic algorithm for efficient key recovery in differential attacks – and its associated tool. In: Joye, M., Leander, G. (eds.) EUROCRYPT 2024. LNCS, vol. 14651, pp. 217–248. Springer, Cham (2024). https://doi.org/10.1007/978-3-031-58716-0_8

[BFG+24a] Bellini, E., et al.: Claasping ARADI: automated analysis of the ARADI block cipher. IACR Cryptology ePrint Archive, p. 1324 (2024)

[BFG+24b] Bellini, E., et al.: CLAASPing ARADI: automated analysis of the ARADI block cipher. Cryptology ePrint Archive, Paper 2024/1324 (2024)

[BG11] Blondeau, C., Gérard, B.: Multiple differential cryptanalysis: theory and practice. In: Joux, A. (ed.) FSE 2011. LNCS, vol. 6733, pp. 35–54. Springer, Heidelberg (2011). https://doi.org/10.1007/978-3-642-21702-9_3

[BGG+24] Bellini, E., et al.: CLAASP: a cryptographic library for the automated analysis of symmetric primitives. In: Carlet, C., Mandal, K., Rijmen, V. (eds.) SAC 2023. LNCS, vol. 14201, pp. 387–408. Springer, Cham (2024). https://doi.org/10.1007/978-3-031-53368-6_19

[BGH+23] Bellini, E., Gerault, D., Hambitzer, A., Rossi, M., et al.: A cipher-agnostic neural training pipeline with automated finding of good input differences. IACR Trans. Symmetric Cryptol. **2023**(3), 184–212 (2023)

[BGL+22] Bao, Z., Guo, J., Liu, M., Ma, L., Tu, Y.: Enhancing differential-neural cryptanalysis. In: Agrawal, S., Lin, D. (eds.) ASIACRYPT 2022. LNCS, vol. 13791, pp. 318–347. Springer, Cham (2022). https://doi.org/10.1007/978-3-031-22963-3_11

[BGPT21a] Benamira, A., Gerault, D., Peyrin, T., Tan, Q.Q.: A deeper look at machine learning-based cryptanalysis. In: Canteaut, A., Standaert, F.-X. (eds.) EUROCRYPT 2021. LNCS, vol. 12696, pp. 805–835. Springer, Cham (2021). https://doi.org/10.1007/978-3-030-77870-5_28

[BLYZ23] Bao, Z., Lu, J., Yao, Y., Zhang, L.: More insight on deep learning-aided cryptanalysis. In: Guo, J., Steinfeld, R. (eds.) ASIACRYPT 2023. LNCS, vol. 14440, pp. 436–467. Springer, Singapore (2023). https://doi.org/10.1007/978-981-99-8727-6_15

[BR21] Bellini, E., Rossi, M.: Performance comparison between deep learning-based and conventional cryptographic distinguishers. In: Arai, K. (ed.) Intelligent Computing. LNNS, vol. 285, pp. 681–701. Springer, Cham (2021). https://doi.org/10.1007/978-3-030-80129-8_48

[BRRT24] Bellini, E., Rachidi, M., Rohit, R., Tiwari, S.K.: Mind the composition of Toffoli gates: structural algebraic distinguishers of ARADI. IACR Cryptology ePrint Archive, p. 1559 (2024)

[BS91] Biham, E., Shamir, A.: Differential cryptanalysis of DES-like cryptosystems. J. Cryptol. **4**(1), 3–72 (1991). https://doi.org/10.1007/BF00630563

[BSS+13] Beaulieu, R., Shors, D., Smith, J., Treatman-Clark, S., Weeks, B., Wingers, L.: The SIMON and SPECK families of lightweight block ciphers. Cryptology ePrint Archive, Paper 2013/404 (2013)

[CBSY22] Chen, Y., Bao, Z., Shen, Y., Yu, H.: A deep learning aided key recovery framework for large-state block ciphers. Cryptology ePrint Archive (2022)

[Cop94] Coppersmith, D.: The Data Encryption Standard (DES) and its strength against attacks. IBM J. Res. Dev. **38**(3), 243–250 (1994)

[CSY23] Chen, Y., Shen, Y., Hongbo, Yu.: Neural-aided statistical attack for cryptanalysis. Comput. J. **66**, 2480–2498 (2023)

[CSYY22] Chen, Y., Shen, Y., Yu, H., Yuan, S.: A new neural distinguisher considering features derived from multiple ciphertext Pairs. Comput. J. (2022)

[DCC23] Deng, H., Cao, X., Cheng, Y.: Attention in differential cryptanalysis on lightweight block cipher SPECK. In: 2023 20th Annual International Conference on Privacy, Security and Trust (PST), pp. 1–9. IEEE (2023)

[Dom12] Domingos, P.: A few useful things to know about machine learning. Commun. ACM **55**(10), 78–87 (2012). https://dl.acm.org/doi/pdf/10.1145/2347736.2347755

[ERP22] Ebrahimi, A., Regazzoni, F., Palmieri, P.: Reducing the cost of machine learning differential attacks using bit selection and a partial ML-distinguisher. In: Jourdan, G.V., Mounier, L., Adams, C., Sèdes, F., Garcia-Alfaro, J. (eds.) FPS 2022. LNCS, vol. 13877, pp. 123–141. Springer, Cham (2022). https://doi.org/10.1007/978-3-031-30122-3_8

[GHHP24] Gerault, D., Hambitzer, A., Huppert, M., Picek, S.: SoK: 5 years of neural differential cryptanalysis. Cryptology ePrint Archive (2024)

[GLN22a] Gohr, A., Leander, G., Neumann, P.: An assessment of differential-neural distinguishers. Cryptology ePrint Archive, Paper 2022/1521 (2022). https://eprint.iacr.org/2022/1521

[GLN23] Gohr, A., Leander, G., Neumann, P.: An assessment of differential-neural distinguishers. In: AICrypt 2023 - 3RD Workshop on Artificial Intelligence and Cryptography (2023)

[GMW24] Greene, P., Motley, M., Weeks, B.: ARADI and LLAMA: low-latency cryptography for memory encryption. Cryptology ePrint Archive, Paper 2024/1240 (2024)

[Goh19] Gohr, A.: Improving attacks on round-reduced speck32/64 using deep learning. In: Boldyreva, A., Micciancio, D. (eds.) CRYPTO 2019. LNCS, vol. 11693, pp. 150–179. Springer, Cham (2019). https://doi.org/10.1007/978-3-030-26951-7_6

[HRCF21] Hou, Z., Ren, J., Chen, S., Fu, A.: Improve neural distinguishers of SIMON and SPECK. Sec. Commun. Netw. **2021** (2021)

[LDLS21] Libralesso, L., Delobel, F., Lafourcade, P., Solnon, C.: Automatic generation of declarative models for differential cryptanalysis. In: Michel, L.D. (ed.) 27th International Conference on Principles and Practice of Constraint Programming, CP 2021, Montpellier, France (Virtual Conference), 25–29 October 2021. LIPIcs, vol. 210, pp. 40:1–40:18. Schloss Dagstuhl - Leibniz-Zentrum für Informatik (2021)

[LLJW21] Liu, Z., Li, Y., Jiao, L., Wang, M.: A new method for searching optimal differential and linear trails in ARX ciphers. IEEE Trans. Inf. Theory **67**(2), 1054–1068 (2021)

[LLS+24] Jinyu, L., Liu, G., Sun, B., Li, C., Liu, L.: Improved (related-key) differential-based neural distinguishers for SIMON and SIMECK block ciphers. Comput. J. **67**(2), 537–547 (2024)

[LRCL23] Liu, J.S., Ren, J.J., Chen, S.Z., Li, M.M.: Improved neural distinguishers with multi-round and multi-splicing construction. J. Inf. Secur. Appl. **74**, 103461 (2023)

[RKK19] Reddi, S.J., Kale, S., Kumar, S.: On the convergence of adam and beyond (2019)

[RR22] Ranea, A., Rijmen, V.: Characteristic automated search of cryptographic algorithms for distinguishing attacks (CASCADA). IET Inf. Secur. **16**(6), 470–481 (2022)

[SM23] Sajwan, A., Mishra, G.: Comparative analysis of ResNet and DenseNet for differential cryptanalysis of SPECK 32/64 lightweight block cipher. In: Chaturvedi, A., Hasan, S.U., Roy, B.K., Tsaban, B. (eds.) ICCNSML 2023. LNNS, vol. 918, pp. 495–504. Springer, Singapore (2024). https://doi.org/10.1007/978-981-97-0641-9_34

[SSL+22] Sun, T., Shen, D., Long, S., Deng, Q., Wang, S.: Neural distinguishers on TinyJAMBU-128 and GIFT-64. In: Tanveer, M., Agarwal, S., Ozawa, S., Ekbal, A., Jatowt, A. (eds.) ICONIP 2022. CCIS, vol. 1792, pp. 419–431. Springer, Singapore (2023). https://doi.org/10.1007/978-981-99-1642-9_36

[SWW21] Sun, L., Wang, W., Wang, M.: Accelerating the search of differential and linear characteristics with the SAT method. IACR Trans. Symmetric Cryptol. **2021**(1), 269–315 (2021)

[SZM21] Su, H.-C., Zhu, X.-Y., Ming, D.: Polytopic attack on round-reduced simon32/64 using deep learning. In: Wu, Y., Yung, M. (eds.) Inscrypt 2020. LNCS, vol. 12612, pp. 3–20. Springer, Cham (2021). https://doi.org/10.1007/978-3-030-71852-7_1

[WTZ+22] Wang, H., Tian, J., Zhang, X., Wei, Y., Jiang, H.: Multiple differential distinguisher of SIMECK32/64 based on deep learning. Secur. Commun. Netw. (2022)

[YK21] Yadav, T., Kumar, M.: Differential-ML distinguisher: machine learning based generic extension for differential cryptanalysis. In: Longa, P., Ràfols, C. (eds.) LATINCRYPT 2021. LNCS, vol. 12912, pp. 191–212. Springer, Cham (2021). https://doi.org/10.1007/978-3-030-88238-9_10

[YZS+15] Yang, G., Zhu, B., Suder, V., Aagaard, M.D., Gong, G.: The SIMECK family of lightweight block ciphers. Cryptology ePrint Archive, Paper 2015/612 (2015)

[ZC18] Zheng, A., Casari, A.: Feature Engineering for Machine Learning: Principles and Techniques for Data Scientists. O'Reilly Media Inc. (2018)

[ZLWL23] Zhang, L., Jinyu, L., Wang, Z., Li, C.: Improved differential-neural cryptanalysis for round-reduced Simeck32/64. Front. Comput. Sci. **17**(6), 176817 (2023)

[ZWC23] Zhang, L., Wang, Z., Chen, Y.: Improving the accuracy of differential-neural distinguisher for des, chaskey, and present. IEICE Trans. Inf. Syst. **106**, 1240–1243 (2023)

[ZZY+21] Zhang, R., Zhang, M., Yan, J., Li, Y., Wu, X., Li, L.: Differential cryptanalysis of TweGIFT-128 based on neural network. In: 2021 IEEE Sixth International Conference on Data Science in Cyberspace (DSC), pp. 529–534. IEEE (2021)

Extracting Some Layers of Deep Neural Networks in the Hard-Label Setting

Isaac A. Canales-Martínez[1] and David Santos[2(✉)]

[1] Cryptography Research Center, Technology Innovation Institute, Abu Dhabi, United Arab Emirates
isaac.canales@tii.ae
[2] Instituto de Computação, Universidade Estadual de Campinas, Campinas, Brazil
d261032@dac.unicamp.br

Abstract. Although studied for several years now, parameter extraction of Deep Neural Networks (DNNs) has seen the major advances only in recent years. Carlini et al. (Crypto 2020) and Canales-Martínez et al. (Eurocrypt 2024) showed how to extract the parameters of ReLU-based DNNs efficiently (polynomial time and polynomial number of queries, as a function on the number of neurons) in the *raw-output* setting, i.e., when the attacker has access to the raw output of the DNN. On the other hand, the more realistic *hard-label* setting gives the attacker access only to the most likely label after the DNN's raw output has been processed. Recently, Carlini et al. (Eurocrypt 2025) presented an efficient parameter extraction attack in the hard-label setting applicable to DNNs having a large number of parameters.

The work in Eurocrypt 2025 recovers the parameters of all layers except the output layer. The techniques presented there are not applicable to this layer due to its lack of ReLUs. In this work, we fill this gap and present a technique that allows recovery of the output layer. Additionally, we show parameter extraction methods that are more efficient when the DNN has contractive layers, i.e., when the number of neurons decreases in those layers. We successfully apply our methods to some networks trained on the CIFAR-10 dataset. Asymptotically, our methods have polynomial complexity in time and number of queries. Thus, a complete extraction attack combining the techniques by Carlini et al. and ours remains with polynomial complexity. Moreover, real execution time is decreased when attacking DNNs with the required contractive architecture.

Keywords: ReLU-Based Deep Neural Networks · Neural Network Extraction · Hard-label Attack

1 Introduction

Artificial Intelligence (AI) has become a major topic of interest and discussion due to its increasing presence and impact in our technological environment. In

This work was conducted while doing an internship at Technology Innovation Institute, UAE.

D. Escudero and I. Damgård (Eds.): LATINCRYPT 2025, LNCS 16129, pp. 399–421, 2026.
https://doi.org/10.1007/978-3-032-06754-8_15

very simple terms, the goal of AI is to provide computational systems with processing capabilities generally linked with human intelligence. Machine Learning is the field of AI focused on making computational systems learn from large amounts of data to later perform computations on new data. Deep Neural Networks (DNNs) are prominent computing models within Deep Learning, a subfield of Machine Learning. DNNs have found several real-world applications and are typically used for classification, computer vision, language processing and medical diagnosis.

A Deep Neural Network is an artificial neural network consisting of multiple fully connected layers containing *neurons*. The input to a DNN is a vector of real numbers which is propagated through the layers of the network to produce the output vector. Each neuron performs a linear operation on its inputs followed by a non-linear operation called the *activation function*. An example of such function is the Rectified Linear Unit (ReLU). Before DNNs can perform meaningful computations, they must be trained. Training is the process in which the *parameters* of the network are initialised and iteratively adjusted in order to minimise the loss function on training data. The parameters are the *weights* and *bias* of each neuron in the network.

The parameters of a trained neural network may be a highly valuable asset. For instance, training a network can translate to great monetary costs if this process requires high computational time. Even when training is not as resource demanding (e.g., it can be done in polynomial time), the amount of available training data affects the quality of the resulting network. Thus, we may be interested in learning the parameters of a network if we do not have sufficient training data or computational resources to produce a comparable network.

Assume we have oracle access to a deep neural network, that is, we can query the network on an input of our choice and we receive the network's output as the response. Whether the parameters of this network can be extracted having exclusively oracle access is a long standing question. The effort to find an answer can be traced back to the 1990s. If we restrict our attention to DNNs using the ReLU as the activation function, recent results [5–7] show that it is indeed possible to extract the parameters. In the process, it was noted that extracting the parameters of ReLU-based DNNs resembles differential cryptanalysis on block ciphers. DNNs and block ciphers are comprised of layers and each layer consists of a linear operation followed by a non-linear one. In both cases, the linear operation computes on secret data (round keys in block ciphers and neuron parameters in DNNs) and the non-linear operation is publicly known (S-boxes and ReLUs, respectively). Indeed, the extraction attacks in [5–7] can be regarded as differential attacks.

Depending on the information provided by the oracle, an extraction attack has different levels of difficulty for the attacker. In [12], five different scenarios are identified. The least challenging one is when the attacker receives the raw output of the DNN (i.e., the vector of real numbers produced by the network); on the other hand, the most challenging scenario is the so-called *hard-label*, where the attacker only receives the label of the most likely class. The complexity of extraction attacks is typically measured as a function of the total number of neurons in the network. Almost all attacks are framed in the easier raw-output scenario, and the work by Carlini et al. [7] and Canales-Martínez et al. [5] showed that parameter extraction in this setting can be done efficiently: the attack has polynomial complexity in both number of queries to the oracle and execution time. The most challenging hard-label setting is first addressed in [8] by Chen et al. Their attack is limited to DNNs with a low number of neurons and layers; although it requires polynomial number of queries, it has exponential time complexity. However, the recent work by Carlini et al. [6] introduces novel ideas yielding an attack in the hard-label scenario that enjoys polynomial time complexity while preserving polynomial query complexity.

1.1 State-of-the-Art Parameter Extraction Attacks on DNNs

The problem of DNN parameter extraction can be traced back to the initial work by Baum [1,2], Fefferman [10] and Blum and Rivest [3] over thirty years ago. This problem has received more attention in recent years and has motivated a great amount of research that considers different attack scenarios and security models. In [14], Oliynyk et al. present a comprehensive survey which shows the vast amount of work in the field. One of the main type of attacks against machine learning models are side-channel attacks. They exploit side-effects caused by the model during its execution; these side-effects could be arising from software or hardware. These attacks can allow recovery of the architecture and the parameters of the model. Another type of attacks are those where the attacker can obtain information from querying the model, but has no access to side-channel information.

In this work, we are interested in the security model where the attacker exclusively has oracle access to a ReLU-based DNN. Although there exists a great amount of literature on DNN parameter extraction, here we give a high-level overview of state-of-the-art attacks in the raw-output and hard-label settings. In Sects. 2.2 and 2.3, we give a more detailed explanation which introduces only the ideas and notation required later in the manuscript.

The idea of the raw-output attack [5,7] is to recover the parameters of the first layer, "peel off" that layer, then recover the parameters of the second layer, peel off that layer and repeat until the last layer. Recovering the parameters comprises two steps: recover a multiple of the weights and biases, and recover the *sign* of each neuron in the layer, i.e., the sign of the multiplicative constant. To recover the parameters we employ *critical points*, which are inputs to the DNN where the slope of the output changes abruptly. These points provide highly valuable information: a neuron in the network takes value exactly zero before applying the activation function. If we collect enough critical points, we can recover, in polynomial time, (a multiple of) the parameters of the target layer by computing derivatives and solving a system of linear equations. Sign recovery as proposed by Carlini et al. [7] has exponential time complexity. Canales-Martínez et al. provide in [5] three sign-recovery techniques with polynomial time complexity. In [11], Foerster et al. present an implementation combining the parameter recovery in

[7] and sign recovery in [5]; the authors also propose improvements to reduce the real execution time of the attack.

Any ReLU-based DNN is a piecewise linear map. Critical points are exactly the points where the slope of the function changes. The set of critical points of a neuron form a *critical hyperplane.* These hyperplanes partition the input space into regions and the linear map is different in each region; Fig. 1a shows an example of this. Crossing critical hyperplanes is the reason we observe the abrupt changes in the slope of the raw output of the network.

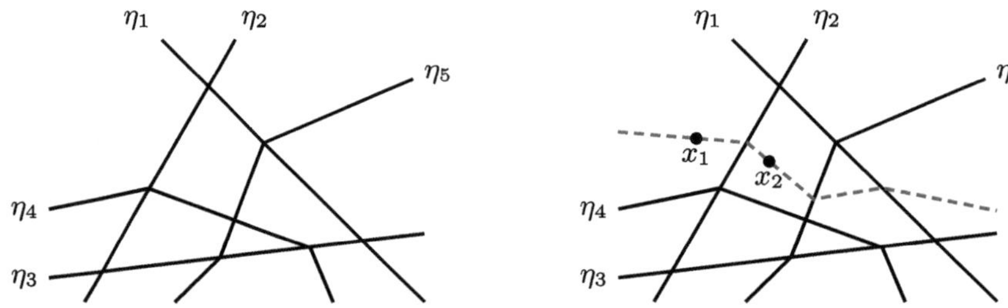

(a) Partition of the input space into linear regions.

(b) A bent decision boundary (dotted line).

Fig. 1. Partition of the input space by critical hyperplanes. Hyperplanes of neurons in the second layer (η_4, η_5) are bent by hyperplanes of neurons in the first layer (η_1, η_2, η_3). Decision boundaries are bent by all critical hyperplanes. (Figure inspired from Fig. 3 in [7] and Fig. 2 in [6].

In the hard-label setting, we lose access to the raw output, thus, we lose the ability to compute derivatives and detect critical points. The only noticeable event is the change in the output of the network from one class to another. An input where the network's decision changes between classes is called a *transition point.* The set of transition points between two classes forms a hyperplane called *decision boundary.* Since the linear map changes between regions, a decision boundary "bends" when it crosses a critical hyperplane. Figure 1b depicts the partition of the input space together with a transition point x_1 and its decision boundary. Looking the figure, if walk from x_1 in a fixed direction along the decision boundary, we will eventually cross a critical hyperplane and we can find another point x_2 in the same decision boundary on the other side. The intersection of the bent decision boundaries is a subspace of the critical hyperplane, thus, we find critical points when we find this intersection. Repeating this procedure, we can recover the full description of the critical hyperplane.

The hard-label attack by Carlini et al. [6] follows the same strategy as the raw-output attack: recover the parameters of a layer, peel it off and repeat. Recovering the signature is equivalent to recovering the critical hyperplane using transition points with the procedure above. The sign is recovered using a metric relating the *state* of the target neuron with the speed of change in the value of neurons in subsequent layers. This speed of change is captured by measuring distances in contiguous linear regions on both sides of the target neuron's critical plane. The signature and sign recovery techniques in [6] require a polynomial number of queries and have polynomial time complexity. The attack recovers the parameters of all layers, except the output layer.

1.2 Our Contributions

The output layer generates the raw output of the DNN and it typically does not have ReLUs. Due to this, the signature recovery technique in [6] is not applicable. Our main contribution is a method to extract the output layer in the hard-label setting. We exploit the fact that, in a transition point between two classes, the raw-output value of these classes is the same. This allows us to construct a linear equation where the variables are the parameters of the output layer. We can gather several linearly independent such equations and solve the system to recover the parameters. One caveat is that we cannot obtain a full-rank system. This is because there are several choices of values for the parameters in the output layer that yield an *equivalent* network. In particular, if the number of neurons in the last layer is r and the number of outputs in the DNN is n, the system has $n(r+1)$ variables and the maximum number of linearly independent equations we can get is $n(r+1)-r-2$. Thus, to recover the last layer, we fix the value for $r+2$ variables and solve the reduced full-rank system. The unique solution gives the value of the remaining parameters yielding an equivalent network.

Additionally, we show a hard-label version of two sign-recovery techniques from the raw-output attack. Namely, a hard-label version of the *freeze* method in [7] and the *SOE* method in [5]. We present a brief discussion on the conditions required for these methods to be applicable. As in the raw-output setting, SOE is preferable over freeze since it requires less calls to the oracle. Although these new hard-label techniques have limited applicability, the real time execution to recover some layers can be reduced.

We applied our new techniques to the CIFAR10 network used in [6]. We successfully recovered the output layer of that network. Execution time was over 6 h in a non-parallelised execution and, in practice, all the time was spent finding transition points yielding the required number of linearly independent equations. The hard-label freeze and SOE methods are applicable to the first layer only and we successfully recovered the signs for that layer; in particular, SOE exclusively requires linear algebra operations and our experiments finished in under a second. To showcase the correctness of the sign-recovery techniques in deeper layers, we trained a new CIFAR10 network containing 1 480 neurons spread across four layers. Our experiments with this network were also successful and we observed the same behaviour: SOE is practically instantaneous and the high execution time to recover the last layer (13 h in this case) is due to the hardness of finding transition points generating the system of equations.

1.3 Organisation

In Sect. 2, we first present necessary definitions and introduce notation used in the rest of the manuscript; then, we give a more detailed explanation of the raw-output and hard-label parameter extraction attacks in [5,7] and [6], respectively. Section 3 discusses the new hard-label parameter extraction technique for the last layer, while the hard-label version of freeze and SOE are presented in Sect. 4. Our experimental results and conclusions are shown in Sect. 5.

2 Preliminaries

In this section, we first present necessary definitions and results used throughout the manuscript. These are standard in the literature (e.g., [5–8]) and we replicate them here keeping a consistent notation. Then, we give a description of the state of the art in parameter extraction attacks on deep neural networks.

2.1 Basic Definitions

Definition 1 (r-Deep Neural Network [7]). *An* r-deep neural network f *is a function that takes inputs from an input space* $\mathcal{X}$ *and returns values in an output space* $\mathcal{Y}$. *This function is composed as a sequence of functions alternating between affine layers* f_i *and a non-linear function* σ*:*

$$f = f_{r+1} \circ \sigma \circ f_r \circ \ldots \circ \sigma \circ f_2 \circ \sigma \circ f_1. \tag{1}$$

We will only consider deep neural networks (DNNs) operating with real numbers, i.e., where $\mathcal{X} = \mathbb{R}^{d_0}$, $\mathcal{Y} = \mathbb{R}^{d_{r+1}}$ and d_0, d_{r+1} are positive integers.

Definition 2 (Fully Connected Layer [7]). *The* i-th fully connected layer *of a neural network is a function* $f_i : \mathbb{R}^{d_{i-1}} \to \mathbb{R}^{d_i}$ *given by the affine transformation*

$$f_i(x) = A^{(i)}x + b^{(i)}, \tag{2}$$

where $A^{(i)} \in \mathbb{R}^{d_i \times d_{i-1}}$ *is the* weight matrix, $b^{(i)} \in \mathbb{R}^{d_i}$ *is the* bias vector *and* d_{i-1}, d_i *are positive integers.*

Definition 3 (Neuron [5,7]). *A* neuron *is a function determined by the corresponding weight matrix, bias vector and* activation function. *Particularly, the* j*-th neuron of layer* i *is the function* η *given by*

$$\eta(x) = \sigma\left(A_j^{(i)}x + b_j^{(i)}\right),$$

where σ, $A_j^{(i)}$ *and* $b_j^{(i)}$ *denote, respectively, the activation function, the* j*-th row of* $A^{(i)}$ *and the* j*-th coordinate of* $b^{(i)}$. *An* r*-deep neural network has* $N = \sum_{k=1}^{r} d_k$ *neurons.*

We will restrict the activation function σ to be the ReLU function, which is defined as $\sigma : x \mapsto \max(x, 0)$.

Definition 4 (Neural Network Architecture [5,7]). *The* architecture *of a fully connected neural network captures its structure: (a) the number of layers, (b) the dimension d_i of each layer $i = 1, \cdots, r+1$ and (c) any additional constraints imposed on the weights and biases. We say that d_0 is the dimension of the input to the neural network and d_{r+1} denotes the number of outputs of the network.*

Definition 5 (Neural Network Parameters [7]). *The* parameters *θ of an r-deep neural network are the concrete assignments to the weights $A^{(i)}$ and biases $b^{(i)}$ for $i \in \{1, 2, \ldots, r+1\}$.*

Definition 6 (Neuron State [5]). *Let $\mathcal{V}(\eta; x)$ denote the value that neuron η takes with $x \in \mathcal{X}$ before applying σ. If $\mathcal{V}(\eta; x) > 0$ then the* state *of η is* active*. Otherwise, the state of η is* inactive[1]*. The state of η on input x is denoted by $\mathcal{S}(\eta; x)$.*

Definition 7 (Linear Neighbourhood [5]). *The* linear neighbourhood *of $x \in \mathcal{X}$ is the set*

$$\{u \in \mathcal{X} \mid \mathcal{S}(\eta; x) = \mathcal{S}(\eta; u) \textit{for all neurons } \eta \textit{ in the network}\}.$$

A deep neural network behaves as an affine transformation when its inputs are restricted to a linear neighbourhood. This is because no neuron toggles its state and the action of the ReLU can be seen as a constant. Let $F_{i,j} = \sigma \circ f_j \circ \cdots \circ \sigma \circ f_i$, $1 \leq i \leq j \leq r$. Then, for all x in the same linear neighbourhood,

$$\begin{aligned} F_{i,j}(x) &= I^{(j)}(A^{(j)} \cdots (I^{(i+1)}(A^{(i+1)}(I^{(i)}(A^{(i)}x + b^{(i)})) + b^{(i+1)}) \cdots + b^{(j)}) \\ &= \Gamma x + \beta, \end{aligned}$$

where $I^{(\ell)}$ are diagonal matrices such that the k-th entry in the diagonal is 1 when neuron k in layer ℓ is active and 0 otherwise. That is, within a linear neighbourhood we can "collapse" contiguous layers into an affine transformation. Consequently, we can observe the change in the value of the layer-j neurons when we apply a change Δ to the input of the network, such that $x + \Delta$ is in the linear neighbourhood of x:

$$F_{i,j}(x + \Delta) - F_{i,j}(x) = \Gamma(x + \Delta) + \beta - (\Gamma(x) + \beta) = \Gamma\Delta. \tag{3}$$

Definition 8 (Critical point [5,7]). *A* critical point *for a neuron η is $x \in \mathcal{X}$ such that $\mathcal{V}(\eta; x) = 0$.*

---

[1] The authors in [5,7] consider an additional *critical* state when $\mathcal{V}(\eta; x)$ is exactly 0; we follow [6,8] and consider the critical state as a special case of the inactive state.

When the DNN is evaluated at a critical point x for a neuron η, that neuron is at the boundary of toggling between the active and inactive states. Critical points define the boundaries of the different linear neighbourhoods the input space $\mathcal{X}$ is partitioned into. These boundaries are called *critical hyperplanes* and each hyperplane is defined by one neuron in the network; see Fig. 1a. Since one affine transformation corresponds to one linear neighbourhood, ReLU-based DNNs are piecewise linear functions.

Definition 9 (Hard-Label [8]). *Let $f : \mathcal{X} \to \mathcal{Y}$ be an r-deep neural network, where $\mathcal{Y} = \mathbb{R}^{d_{r+1}}$. The* hard-label *on the output $f(x)$ is a label indicating the class with the largest probability when $f(x)$ is transformed into a probability vector. When $d_{r+1} = 1$, it is computed as*

$$z(f(x)) = \begin{cases} 1, & \text{if } f(x) > 0, \\ 0, & \text{otherwise.} \end{cases}$$

When $d_{r+1} > 1$, $z(f(x))$ is the coordinate of $f(x)$ with the maximum value.

Definition 10 (Transition point [6]). *A* transition point *is a point $x \in \mathcal{X}$ where the network's decision changes from one class to a different class, i.e., for all $\varepsilon > 0$ there exists $y \in \mathcal{X}$ with $d(y, x) < \varepsilon$ so that $z(f(y)) \neq z(f(x))$. Here, d denotes a distance in $\mathcal{X}$, for example $d(x, y) = \|y - x\|_2$ if $\mathcal{X} = \mathbb{R}^{d_0}$.*

Definition 11 (Dual point [6]). *A* dual point *is a point $x \in \mathcal{X}$ that is both a transition point and a critical point for some neuron η.*

Transition points define hyperplanes, called *decision boundaries*, where the decision of the network changes between classes. Figure 1b depicts a decision boundary crossing critical hyperplanes. Since the affine transformation on each side of the critical hyperplane is different, the decision boundary is bent when crossing from one side to the other.

Definition 12 (Model parameter extraction attack [7]). *Let f_θ denote a DNN with specific parameters θ, i.e., the values of its weights and biases. In a* model parameter extraction attack, *the attacker is given access to an oracle which, on query x, responds with $f_\theta(x)$. The objective of the attacker is to obtain a set of parameters $\hat{\theta}$ such that $f_{\hat{\theta}}(x)$ is as similar as possible to $f_\theta(x)$.*

We will use the symbol ˆ to denote the recovered parameters. For example, $\hat{A}^{(i)}$ denotes the recovered weight matrix of layer i, whereas $A^{(i)}$ denotes the matrix of the original network.

2.2 Parameter Extraction Attack on DNNs-Raw-Output Setting

Carlini et al. introduced in [7] a model parameter extraction attack targeting ReLU-based DNNs. The idea is to recover the parameters of the first layer, "peel off" that layer and then repeat this process for the subsequent layers. Recovering the parameters of a layer consists of two steps: (1) recover the weights and biases, and (2) recover the *sign* of the neurons.

In the context of the attack, the DNN can be regarded as a composition of an *input function* F_{i-1}, the current target layer i and an *output function* G_{i+1}:

$$f = \underbrace{f_{r+1} \circ \sigma \circ \cdots \circ \sigma \circ f_{i+1}}_{G_{i+1}} \circ \underbrace{\sigma \circ f_i}_{\text{layer } i} \circ \underbrace{\sigma \circ f_{i-1} \circ \cdots \circ \sigma \circ f_1}_{F_{i-1}},$$

where F_0 is the identity map on the input when $i = 1$ and G_{r+2} is the identity map on the output when $i = r + 1$. The input function comprises the recovered layers while the output function comprises the non-recovered layers. The layers in those functions can be collapsed when the inputs x' to the network are restricted to be in the same linear neighbourhood of a point x:

$$F_{i-1}(x') = F_x^{(i-1)} x' + b_x^{(i-1)} \quad \text{and} \quad G_{i+1}(x') = G_x^{(i+1)} x' + b_x^{(i+1)}. \tag{4}$$

In order to perform the first step of the attack, we need to find critical points. Since any ReLU-based DNN f is a piecewise linear function, we have that $\frac{\partial^2 f}{\partial x^2}$ is 0 almost everywhere, except at those points. One method to find critical points, is to identify the discontinuities in the output of f when an input $x_1 \in \mathbb{R}^{d_0}$ is linearly transformed into another point $x_2 \in \mathbb{R}^{d_0}$. A detailed algorithm is given in [4]. By the coupon collector's argument and assuming uniformity, we expect to find multiple critical points for every neuron in the network by sampling enough pairs x_1, x_2 [7]. With critical points available, we can recover the parameters of the target layer. In particular, we recover a multiple of the weights of each neuron, called *signature*, and a multiple of the bias.

Definition 13 (Signature [6]**).** *A* signature *of the j-th neuron in layer i is $\alpha A_j^{(i)}$, for some $\alpha \in \mathbb{R}$.*

The signature $A_j^{(i)}/A_{j,1}^{(i)}$ of the j-th neuron in layer i, where $A_{j,1}^{(i)}$ is the first coordinate of $A_j^{(i)}$, can be recovered via partial second derivatives [7]. Obtaining signatures for first-layer neurons is a straightforward process, however, in deeper layers, we must account for the effect of neurons in other layers and process partial signatures; we refer to [7] for details on signature recovery. Using Equations (1) and (2) with the recovered signature $\hat{A}_j^{(i)}$ and the recovered previous layers, we obtain the bias $\hat{b}_j^{(i)} = b_j^{(i)}/A_{j,1}^{(i)}$ for the target neuron. Even though we do not recover the exact parameters from the target DNN, but a multiple of them, we can recover a network that is *equivalent* to the original network. Equivalent networks exist due to symmetries in them. For example, permuting the order of neurons or multiplying the weights and bias of a neuron by a positive constant are symmetries, whereas multiplying by a negative constant is not due to the nonlinearity of the ReLU. In our case, we recover $\hat{A}_j^{(i)} = \alpha A_j^{(i)}$ and $\hat{b}_j^{(i)} = \alpha b_j^{(i)}$, where $\alpha = 1/A_{j,1}^{(i)}$. Thus, before peeling-off a layer, we must determine the *sign* of each neuron, i.e., the sign of the multiplicative constant α.

Carlini et al. present in [7] a sign recovery method specific to the first layer of the network. We refer to this method as *freeze* and it is discussed in detail in Sect. 4.1. In [5], Canales-Martínez et al. show three improved sign extraction methods with polynomial time complexity and requiring polynomial number of queries. The first technique, called *SOE*, recovers simultaneously the sign of all neurons in a layer by solving a system of linear equations. This method is typically restricted to the first few layers in the network and is discussed in Sect. 4.3. The *neuron wiggle* technique is a general method that in principle is applicable to any layer in the DNN. The main idea is to maximise the change in the target neuron and observe the output of the DNN to decide whether the large change was blocked or not by the ReLU. The third technique is applicable only to the last layer of the network; this method also solves a system of linear equations and leverages the fact that, due to the lack of ReLUs in that layer, there is always a fixed output function. We refer to [5] for the details.

2.3 Parameter Extraction Attack on DNNs-Hard-Label Setting

In the raw-output setting, the attacker has access to the raw output of the network. This information is required to find critical points, where the behaviour of the DNN changes from one linear map to another. Critical points provide highly useful information regarding the value of the neurons, namely, they reveal that the input to the neuron's ReLU is exactly zero at those points. In the hard-label setting, the attacker no longer receives the raw output of the DNN, only the label of the class with the highest probability. Therefore, it is not possible to detect critical points as before. The only event that can be exploited is passing through a transition point, i.e., observing that the hard-label output of the network changes from one label to another. This event, however, is not necessarily associated to a change in the internal state of the network (such as a ReLU toggle in the case of critical points).

The novel attack by Carlini et al. [6] finds dual points from transition points. Thus, the attacker regains access to critical points even though they are not readily accessible. The attack has polynomial complexity in both, number of queries and execution time, and follows the same strategy as in the raw-output setting: recover the parameters of the target layer, recover the sign of the neurons and repeat for the subsequent layers. In the remainder of this section, we briefly describe the main ideas behind the attack and refer to [6] for details.

The first step is to find the signature of neurons. The idea is depicted in Fig. 2. We find a transition point x_1 between two classes and move along its $d-1$ dimensional decision boundary in direction δ until we encounter a critical hyperplane. When we move in the same direction and cross the critical hyperplane, we end up in a point outside the decision boundary (because it was bent by the critical hyperplane). We project this point onto the decision boundary on the other side of the critical hyperplane to get another transition point x_2. By carefully choosing inputs in the vicinity of x_1 and x_2, we can obtain the normal vectors m_{off} and m_{on} of the decision boundary on each side of the critical hyperplane. The normal vectors give a complete definition of the decision boundaries and allow us to compute the $d-2$ dimensional subspace D of dual points where they intersect. This subspace also gives us a partial definition of the $d-1$ dimensional critical hyperplane, since the former is a subspace of the latter. To recover the missing dimension, we repeat the same procedure in a different location of the input space and, with very high probability, we find a different subspace of dual points D' for the same neuron (i.e., critical hyperplane). Then, we obtain the full description of the critical hyperplane with D and D' which in turn yields the signature of the neuron.

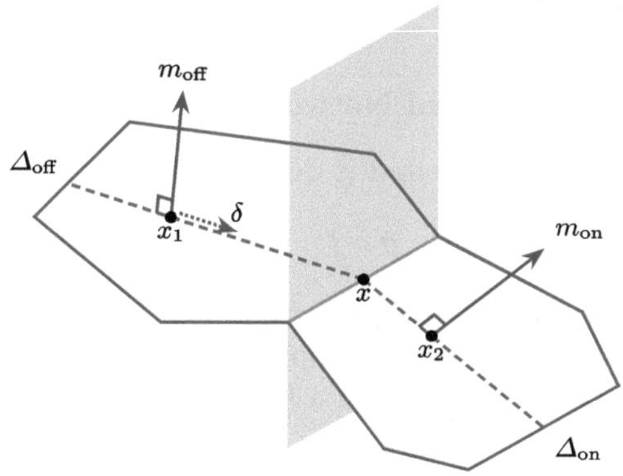

Fig. 2. Graphical representation of the procedure to find a space of dual points D. The distances Δ_{off} and Δ_{on} are used to recover the sign of the target neuron. (Figure inspired from Fig. 4 in [6].)

To recover the sign, Carlini et al. employ a measurement strongly correlated to the speed of change in the value of neurons. The main idea is also depicted in Fig. 2. Starting from a dual point x, we move along the decision boundary in a direction that is perpendicular to the subspace of dual points D until we find the hyperplane of another neuron. We do this traversal on both sides of the target neuron's critical hyperplane and measure the distances Δ_{on} and Δ_{off}. The speed of change in inputs for neurons in future layers is affected by the status of the current target neuron. Then, in most cases, we expect linear neighbourhoods on the positive side of the ReLU to be narrower compared to those on the negative side, in other words, $\Delta_{\text{on}} < \Delta_{\text{off}}$. This property is used to make a decision on the sign of the neuron. However, to overcome making wrong decisions, we decide the sign of the neuron after testing a sufficiently large number of dual points.

The one piece missing in the attack by Carlini et al. is the extraction of the output layer. This layer computes the output of the neural network before the hard-label function is applied. It is not possible to recover this layer with the techniques in [6] due to the lack of ReLUs (see Definition 1). In Sect. 3 we present a method to recover the output layer in the hard-label setting. Additionally, in Sect. 4, we show how to recover the sign of neurons in layers that are *sufficiently contractive* more efficiently. Our methods require finding transition points which can be done with the algorithm in [6].

3 Extracting the Output Layer

In this section, we show how to recover the output layer. Section 3.1 first discusses how equivalent networks can be generated by varying the parameters in that layer. Then, in Sect. 3.2, we describe a technique applicable for networks with one output, also called binary classifiers, while networks with multiple outputs are addressed in Sect. 3.3.

3.1 Equivalent Deep Neural Networks

The output layer has no ReLUs and is defined by $A^{(r+1)}$ and $b^{(r+1)}$. Let

$$f_{1..i}(x) = \sigma \circ f_i \circ \cdots \circ \sigma \circ f_1(x)$$

be the function computing the output of the i-th layer, where $1 \leq i \leq r$, and recall that a hard-label function z is applied to the output of the DNN. Then, with input x, the hard-label output of a DNN is

$$z(A^{(r+1)}y^{(r)} + b^{(r+1)}),$$

where $y^{(r)} = f_{1..r}(x)$ is the output of layer r. In the rest of this section, we will simple write A, b and y instead of $A^{(r+1)}$, $b^{(r+1)}$ and $y^{(r)}$, respectively.

The hard-label function first transforms the raw output of the DNN into a probability vector and then returns the label with the highest probability. We will assume that the function computing the probability vector (i) is invariant under translation by a vector with the same value in all its coordinates and (ii) assigns larger probability values to larger coordinates in the input vector. An example of such a function is *softmax*. This function is very frequently used in neural networks and we will use it as the default choice. On input $u \in \mathbb{R}^n$, softmax produces a vector $\mathsf{s}(u) \in (0,1)^n$ as follows:

$$\mathsf{s}(u)_i = \frac{e^{u_i}}{\sum_{j=1}^{n} e^{u_j}}.$$

Let $\bar{c} \in \mathbb{R}^n$ be a vector with all coordinates having the same value c. Softmax is invariant under translation by $\bar{c}$:

$$\mathsf{s}(u+\bar{c})_i = \frac{e^{u_i+c}}{\sum_{j=1}^{n} e^{u_j+c}} = \frac{e^{u_i}e^{c}}{e^{c}\sum_{j=1}^{n} e^{u_j}} = \mathsf{s}(u)_i.$$

Even though softmax is not invariant under scaling (i.e., $\mathsf{s}(u) \neq \mathsf{s}(c{\cdot}u)$ for $c \in \mathbb{R}$), larger coordinates in u will remain larger when scaled by a positive constant c, and therefore, the larger probability values will still be assigned to them. Thus, even though the probability value is not the same after scaling by $c > 0$, the label corresponding to the largest probability value will remain the same. These properties are required to obtain equivalent networks as discussed below.

Let $\bar{c} \in \mathbb{R}^{d_{r+1}}$ have all its coordinates equal to a real number c. Define

$$\tilde{A} := \begin{pmatrix} A_{*,1} & \cdots & A_{*,j} + \bar{c} & \cdots & A_{*,d_r} \end{pmatrix} \quad \text{and} \quad \tilde{b} := b + \bar{c},$$

where $A_{*,k}$ denotes the k-th column of A, i.e., $\tilde{A}$ is the matrix A with $\bar{c}$ added to its j-th column. Then,

$$z(Ay + \tilde{b}) = z(Ay + b + \bar{c}) = z(Ay + b),$$

where the second equality holds since $\bar{c}$ translates the output of the DNN. Also,

$$z(\tilde{A}y + b) = z(Ay + b + y_j\bar{c}) = z(Ay + b),$$

where the first equality holds because $(\tilde{A}y)_i = \sum_k A_{i,k}y_k + y_j c$, and the second because $y_j\bar{c}$ translates the output of the DNN. Finally, when $c > 0$,

$$z((cA)y + cb) = z(c\,(Ay + b)) = z(Ay + b),$$

where the second equality holds because $c > 0$.

Any of the transformations above to the parameters of the output layer yield an equivalent network. Namely, we can translate any of the d_r columns in the matrix A, translate the bias vector b or scale A and b by a positive constant c. Moreover, any combination of these transformations also yields an equivalent network. To see this, let c be a positive real number and define

$$\tilde{A} := \begin{pmatrix} A_{*,1} + \bar{c}_1 & \cdots & A_{*,k} + \bar{c}_k & \cdots & A_{*,d_r} + \bar{c}_{d_r} \end{pmatrix} \quad \text{and} \quad \tilde{b} := b + \bar{c}_b,$$

where each vector $\bar{c}_j$, $j = 1, \ldots, d_r$, and $\bar{c}_b$ has the same value in all its coordinates. Then

$$\begin{aligned} z((c\tilde{A})y + c\tilde{b}) &= z\left(c\left(Ay + \sum_{j=1}^{d_r} y_j\bar{c}_j\right) + c\,(b + \bar{c}_b)\right) \\ &= z\left(c\,(Ay + b) + c\left(\sum_{j=1}^{d_r} y_j\bar{c}_j + \bar{c}_b\right)\right) \\ &= z(c(Ay + b)) = z(Ay + b). \end{aligned}$$

That is, we have $d_r + 2$ *degrees of freedom* to generate equivalent networks while recovering the output layer.

3.2 Single-Output Deep Neural Networks

In this case, the DNN makes a decision between two classes: C0 and C1. If the input x belongs to C0, $f(x) < 0$, whereas $f(x) > 0$ when x belongs to C1. With a transition point x, we have $Ay + b = 0$, where $y = f_{1..r}(x)$. Notice that, when the DNN has one output, A is a vector of length d_r and b is a scalar. Therefore, $Ay + b = 0$ can be regarded as an equation where the coordinates of A and b are the unknown values. With d_r transition points x_k such that $y_k = f_{1..r}(x_k)$ are linearly independent, the system of linear equations

$$Ay_k = -b, \quad k = 1, \ldots, d_r,$$

has a unique solution. We do not know the value of b, however, the system above is equivalent to

$$b^{-1}Ay_k = -1, \quad k = 1, \ldots, d_r.$$

Thus, by solving this new system we recover $\hat{A}^{(r+1)} = b^{-1}A$ and $\hat{b}^{(r+1)} = 1$.

As discussed in Sect. 3.1, an equivalent network is recovered if we multiply A and b by a positive constant. In this case, we multiply by b^{-1}. If $b > 0$, we recover an equivalent network. When $b < 0$, the network is not equivalent and it will classify the inputs incorrectly. In order to verify the correctness of the recovered parameters, we simply compare the output of the original DNN with the output of the recovered network; if the outputs are different, we flip the signs of $\hat{A}^{(r+1)}$ and $\hat{b}^{(r+1)}$.

This method requires finding transition points and solving a system of linear equations. We find transition points with the algorithm in [6], which requires polynomial number of queries and has polynomial time complexity. Solving the system is done in polynomial time and requires no additional queries.

3.3 Multiple-Output Deep Neural Networks

The idea to recover the parameters of the output layer is again to solve a system of linear equations. We will construct the system such that all the weights and biases in that layer are the unknown variables.

Let x be a transition point between classes i and j, where $1 \leq i, j \leq d_{r+1}$, and let $y = f_{1..r}(x)$. Then, $A_i y + b_i = A_j y + b_j$, which is equivalent to

$$A_i y + b_i - A_j y - b_j = 0.$$

We can extend the equation above to include all parameters in the output layer:

$$A_1\mathbf{0} + 0b_1 + \cdots + A_i y + b_i + \cdots - A_j y - b_j + \cdots + A_{d_{r+1}}\mathbf{0} + 0b_{d_{r+1}} = 0, \quad (5)$$

where $\mathbf{0}$ is the zero vector in $\mathbb{R}^{d_{r+1}}$. If we collect the corresponding expression (5) from various transition points, we create a system of equations with $d_{r+1}(d_r + 1)$ variables which can be written as

$$C\underbrace{(A_1, b_1, A_2, b_2, \ldots, A_{d_{r+1}}, b_{d_{r+1}})^T}_{\boldsymbol{A}} = (0, \ldots, 0)^T, \quad (6)$$

where C is a matrix whose rows are defined by the coefficients from Eq. 5. If we obtained $d_{r+1}(d_r + 1)$ linearly independent equations, we would find a unique solution, however, that is not possible. Let $\tilde{A}_i$ denote (A_i, b_i), thus $\boldsymbol{A} = (\tilde{A}_1, \ldots, \tilde{A}_{d_{r+1}})$. By Eq. (5), each row in C can be written as

$$(y,1)\underbrace{(\mathbf{0} \cdots \tilde{I} \cdots -\tilde{I} \cdots \mathbf{0})}_{\tilde{I}_{i,j}},$$

where $\tilde{I}_{i,j}$ is a block matrix of size $(d_r+1) \times d_{r+1}(d_r+1)$ whose i-th and j-th blocks are the only non-zero blocks and $\tilde{I}$ is the identity matrix of size (d_r+1). Then, the rows of C are in the span of

$$\begin{array}{c} \\ 1 \\ 2 \\ \vdots \\ d_{r+1}-1 \end{array} \begin{array}{c} \begin{array}{ccccc} 1 & 2 & 3 & \cdots & d_{r+1} \end{array} \\ \begin{pmatrix} \tilde{I} & -\tilde{I} & \mathbf{0} & \cdots & \mathbf{0} \\ \tilde{I} & \mathbf{0} & -\tilde{I} & \cdots & \mathbf{0} \\ \vdots & \vdots & \vdots & \ddots & \vdots \\ \tilde{I} & \mathbf{0} & \mathbf{0} & \cdots & -\tilde{I} \end{pmatrix} \end{array}.$$

This matrix has $d_{r+1}(d_r+1)-(d_r+1)$ rows, $d_{r+1}(d_r+1)$ columns and has full rank $d_{r+1}(d_r+1)-(d_r+1)$. Moreover, by (6), C is in the kernel of $\boldsymbol{A}$ and since $\dim(\mathrm{Im}(\boldsymbol{A})) = 1$, the maximal rank that C can have is $d_{r+1}(d_r+1)-(d_r+2)$.

To recover the parameters of the output layer, we gather $d_{r+1}(d_r+1)-(d_r+2)$ linearly independent equations (5) and solve the system (6). Notice that C not having full rank implies that there are multiple solutions; they represent the parameter values that yield different equivalent networks. Alternatively, we can fix a value for d_r+2 variables and solve the system to obtain a unique solution. By fixing the value of the variables, we are choosing one among the many networks that are equivalent to the original one.

Similarly to the single-output case, this method entails finding transition points and solving a system of linear equations, therefore, its complexity is also polynomial in both, number of queries and time complexity.

4 Efficient Sign-Recovery in Contractive-Enough Layers

A layer is *contractive* when the number of inputs to that layer is larger than the number of neurons it contains; in other words, layer i is contractive when $d_{i-1} > d_i$. Carlini et al. show in [7, §4.2] a technique to determine the correct sign of the neurons in the first layer when it is contractive; as in [5], we will refer to this technique as *freeze*. Also in [5], the authors introduce the *SOE* sign recovery technique, which is applicable when consecutive layers are "contractive-enough". In Sect. 4.1 we first discuss the applicability of freeze for deeper layers in the raw-output setting. Then, we present a version of freeze and SOE for the hard-label setting in Sect. 4.2 and Sect. 4.3, respectively.

4.1 Freezing Deeper Layers in the Raw-Output Setting

Assume the first layer to be contractive and that we already recovered $\hat{A}^{(1)}$ and $\hat{b}^{(1)}$. We want to determine the correct sign of the j-th neuron in that layer, denoted by η. The freeze technique in [7] works as follows. Let

$$\hat{f}_1(x) = \hat{A}^{(1)}x + \hat{b}^{(1)}$$

and x^* be a critical point for η; then the j-th coordinate of $\hat{h} = \hat{f}_1(x^*)$ is exactly 0. We compute $x_+, x_- \in \mathbb{R}^{d_0}$ such that $\hat{f}_1(x_+) = \hat{h} + \varepsilon e_j$ and $\hat{f}_1(x_-) = \hat{h} - \varepsilon e_j$, where ε is a small positive real number and e_j is the j-th standard basis vector in $\mathbb{R}^{d_1}$. Notice that, regardless of the correctness of the recovered signs, we have the same behaviour with the original DNN: the j-th coordinate of $h = f_1(x^*)$ is 0 and f_1 evaluated at x_+ and x_- will only change the j-th coordinate of h (i.e., x_+ and x_- freeze the value before the ReLU of all neurons in the layer except η). Thus, the correct sign of η can be determined by observing whether $f(x_+) = f(x^*)$ or $f(x_-) = f_1(x^*)$. If $f(x_-) = f(x^*)$ holds, the recovered sign of η is correct, because $\sigma(h - \varepsilon e_j) = \sigma(h)$. However, if $f(x_+) = f(x^*)$ holds, we invert the sign of the j-th row of $\hat{A}^{(1)}$ and $\hat{b}_j^{(1)}$.

The freeze technique entails finding pre-images x_+ of $h + \varepsilon e_j$ and x_- of $h - \varepsilon e_j$ under $\hat{f}_1$, for all $j \in \{1, \ldots, d_1\}$. Since no ReLUs are involved in $\hat{f}_1$, we can compute pre-images when the $d_1 \times d_0$ matrix $A^{(1)}$ has rank d_1. This holds with very high probability when $d_0 > d_1$, i.e., the first layer is contractive. Freeze may be applicable in deeper layers as well. Daniely and Granot [9] employ freeze when recovering the second layer of a three-layer network. We discuss below the conditions to apply freeze in deeper layers.

We want to recover the signs for layer $i > 1$. Assume we have recovered $\hat{A}^{(i)}$ and $\hat{b}^{(i)}$. Let $F_{i-1}(x') = F_x^{(i-1)}x' + b_x^{(i-1)}$ be the map representing all $i-1$ previously recovered layers when the inputs $x' \in \mathbb{R}^{d_0}$ are restricted to the linear neighbourhood of $x \in \mathbb{R}^{d_0}$ (see Eq. (4)). Also, let

$$\hat{f}_i(x') = \hat{A}^{(i)}F_{i-1}(x') + \hat{b}^{(i)} = \hat{A}^{(i)}F_x^{(i-1)}x' + (\hat{A}^{(i)}b_x^{(i-1)} + \hat{b}^{(i)}). \quad (7)$$

Then, we can apply freeze using $\hat{f}_i$ instead of $\hat{f}_1$. In this case, however, each critical point x^* for a neuron in layer i will induce a different map F_{i-1}. Thus, for each neuron, we first obtain $F_{x^*}^{(i-1)}, b_{x^*}^{(i-1)}$ and then compute x_+ and x_- to determine the sign. The pre-images can be computed if the matrix $\hat{A}^{(i)}F_x^{(i-1)}$ has rank d_i. This holds when the $d_i \times d_{i-1}$ matrix $A^{(i)}$ has rank d_i (implying $d_{i-1} \geq d_i$) and $\operatorname{rank}(F_x^{(i-1)}) \geq d_i$. Almost always, the $d_{i-1} \times d_0$ matrix $F_x^{(i-1)}$ does not have full rank due to the ReLUs in layers 1 to $i-1$. Therefore, we require $d_{i-1} > d_i$ in practice. Additionally, ε must be small enough so that x_+ and x_- do not toggle any neuron in layers 1 to i except the target neuron.

4.2 Freeze in the Hard-Label Setting

Freeze requires access to the raw output of the DNN to check whether $f(x_+) = f(x^*)$ or $f(x_-) = f_1(x^*)$. However, we cannot access that information in the hard-label setting, we only receive the most likely class label as the response to our queries. Here we present a version of freeze for the hard-label setting.

Let us focus on the first layer. Again, assume we already recovered $\hat{A}^{(1)}, \hat{b}^{(1)}$ and we want to determine the correct sign of η, the j-th neuron in that layer. Let $x \in \mathbb{R}^{d_0}$ be a transition point (between any two classes) that is not a dual point. If the first layer is contractive, we can compute $x' \in \mathbb{R}^{d_0}$ such that $\hat{f}_1(x') = \hat{h} + \varepsilon e_j$, where $\hat{h} = \hat{f}_1(x)$ and ε is a small real number. Unlike the raw-output case, the j-th coordinate of $\hat{h}$ is not 0. Let us consider the state of η in the original DNN when we choose ε such that η has the same state with x and x':

- When η is inactive, the output of the first layer is the same with x and x'. Therefore, $f(x') = f(x)$ and x' is another transition point in the same decision boundary as x; see Fig. 3a.
- When η is active, the output of the first layer is different with x and x'. With very high probability, x' is not in the decision boundary; see Fig. 3b. x' remains in the decision boundary when the vector $x' - x$ is parallel to that hyperplane.

We do not know the state of η with input x, but we can determine it as follows. Take a random direction Δ and compute $f(x' + \Delta)$ and $f(x' - \Delta)$. Consider Fig. 3a again when the neuron is inactive; $f(x')$ is in the decision boundary, therefore, evaluating at $x' + \Delta$ and $x' - \Delta$ will result in different labels. On the other hand, when η is active, $f(x')$ is outside the decision boundary and $x' + \Delta$ and $x' - \Delta$ will result in the same labels; see Fig. 3b. For the latter to hold, the magnitude of Δ should be sufficiently small not to cross the decision boundary and incorrectly determine the state of the neuron.

(a) Neuron inactive. (b) Neuron active.

Fig. 3. Idea behind determining the state of the target neuron.

Knowing the state of η in the original DNN allows us to directly check whether the recovered sign is correct or not. We can also employ freeze in the hard-label case for deeper layers $i > 1$ using $\hat{f}_i$, as defined in Eq. (7), instead of $\hat{f}_1$. The requirements to apply freeze in the hard-label setting are almost the same as in the raw-output case. For the first layer, we can use freeze if $\text{rank}(A^{(1)}) = d_1$. For layers $i > 1$, we can apply it when (i) $\text{rank}(F_x^{(i-1)}) \geq d_i$, where x is a transition point between any two classes and (ii) ε is small enough so that x' does not toggle any neuron in layers 1 to i. Notice that condition (ii) is slightly different compared to the raw-output case.

Let t_T and q_T denote, respectively, the polynomial time and polynomial query complexity to find a transition point with the algorithm in [6]. To apply this method, we find a transition point x, then we find x' in polynomial time t_1 using linear algebra operations and we query the oracle on inputs $x + \Delta$ and $x - \Delta$. These steps are performed per neuron. In total, this method has polynomial time complexity $d_i(t_T + t_1)$ and query complexity $d_i(q_T + 2)$.

4.3 SOE in the Hard-Label Setting

Unlike the freeze technique, with SOE we can simultaneously recover the sign of all neurons in the target layer. Once more, assume that we have already recovered $\hat{A}^{(i)}$ and $\hat{b}^{(i)}$. Recall that when we restrict DNN inputs to be in the linear neighbourhood of a point x, we can collapse contiguous layers and we can observe the effect of a small change at the input of the network (see Eq. 3). Assume the DNN has one output only; if it has multiple outputs, we can simply ignore all but one. Then, the effect of a change Δ_k can be written as

$$\underbrace{G_x^{(i+1)} I_x^{(i)}}_{c} \underbrace{A^{(i)} F_x^{(i-1)} \Delta_k^T}_{y_k} = \underbrace{f(x + \Delta_k) - f(x)}_{z_k}.$$

With the recovered weights, we can obtain the value of y_k, however, we do not know the value of c. Additionally, in the raw-output setting we have access to the raw output the network and therefore the value z_k is known. Thus, the equation above can be rewritten as

$$c \cdot y_k = z_k,$$

which is an equation on the variables c. If we collect d_i linearly independent equations, we can solve for c and learn the state of each neuron: the j-th neuron is inactive if $c_j = 0$ and active otherwise. Knowing the state of the neurons allows us to recover the correct sign.

In the hard-label setting, we no longer have access to the value of z_k. However, the SOE method can still be applied. Let x be a transition point between classes α and β. Also, let $G_{x,\alpha}^{(i+1)}$ and $G_{x,\beta}^{(i+1)}$ be the rows of the matrix $G_x^{(i+1)}$ corresponding to the outputs of classes α and β, respectively. We choose Δ_k such that $x+\Delta_k$ is also a transition point between classes α and β and is in the linear neighbourhood of x. Then,

$$\begin{aligned} G_{x,\alpha}^{(i+1)} I_x^{(i)} A^{(i)} F_x^{(i-1)} \Delta_k^T &= f_\alpha(x + \Delta_k) - f_\alpha(x), \\ G_{x,\beta}^{(i+1)} I_x^{(i)} A^{(i)} F_x^{(i-1)} \Delta_k^T &= f_\beta(x + \Delta_k) - f_\beta(x), \end{aligned}$$

where f_α and f_β denote the DNN output corresponding to classes α and β, respectively. Subtracting the first equation above from the second, we get

$$\left(G_{x,\beta}^{(i+1)} - G_{x,\alpha}^{(i+1)}\right) I_x^{(i)} A^{(i)} F_x^{(i-1)} \Delta_k^T = f_\beta(x + \Delta_k) - f_\alpha(x + \Delta_k) - (f_\beta(x) - f_\alpha(x)).$$

Since x and $x + \Delta_k$ are transition points for the same classes, $f_\beta(x) - f_\alpha(x) = 0$ and $f_\beta(x + \Delta_k) - f_\alpha(x + \Delta_k) = 0$, therefore

$$\underbrace{\left(G_{x,\beta}^{(i+1)} - G_{x,\alpha}^{(i+1)}\right) I_x^{(i)}}_{c} \underbrace{\left(G_{x,\beta}^{(i+1)}\right) A^{(i)} F_x^{(i-1)} \Delta_k^T}_{y_k} = 0.$$

Thus, we can collect d_i linearly independent equations and solve that system to recover the sign of the neurons.

When we recover $\hat{A}^{(i)}$ using the technique in [6], we also obtain the normal vector m to the decision boundary between classes α and β (see Fig. 2). Since x and $x + \Delta_k$ are transition points in that decision boundary, both are orthogonal to m, therefore, $\langle m, \Delta_k \rangle = 0$, where $\langle \cdot, \cdot \rangle$ denotes the dot product. Notice that we want to find a vector c such that $cA^{(i)} F_x^{(i-1)} \Delta_k^T = 0$. Let $(A^{(i)} F_x^{(i-1)})^{-1}$ denote the pseudo-inverse of $A^{(i)} F_x^{(i-1)}$. If we set $c = m(A^{(i)} F_x^{(i-1)})^{-1}$,

$$cA^{(i)} F_x^{(i-1)} \Delta_k^T = m\Delta_k^T = 0$$

and we obtain a solution to the system of equations.

To construct the system of equations, we must find $d_i + 1$ transition points (namely, x and $x + \Delta_k$, for $k = 1, \ldots, d_i$) and then solve a system of equations in polynomial time t_1. Again, let t_T and q_T denote, respectively, the polynomial time and query complexity for finding a transition point. Then, hard-label SOE has polynomial time complexity $(d_i + 1)t_T + t_1$ and polynomial query complexity $(d_i + 1)q_T$. When we use the normal vector m, we require no oracle calls and the polynomial time complexity t is given by the linear algebra operations required to compute the pseudo-inverse of $A^{(i)} F_x^{(i-1)}$ and a vector-matrix multiplication.

5 Experiments and Conclusions

In this section, we present our experiments to evaluate the parameter recovery technique for the output layer and the sign-recovery methods. We first explain our choices for target networks in Sect. 5.1. Then, in Sects. 5.2 and 5.3, respectively, we show our experimental results for the CIFAR10 network in [6] and our own network. Finally, conclusions from this work are in Sect. 5.4.

The experiments are executed using our non-optimised Python implementation. This implementation mainly uses the `numpy` and `scipy` libraries, and takes as a base the code from [5,6]. Our software implementation is available in https://github.com/deividafonso281/hard-label-contract-output.

5.1 Choice of Target Architectures

Here, we will denote the architecture of a network as $d_0 - d_1 - \cdots - d_{r+1}$, where d_0 and d_{r+1} are, respectively, the length of the inputs and outputs of the DNN, and d_i, $1 \leq i \leq r$, is the number of neurons in layer i. If k successive layers have the same number of neurons d, we will group them together as $d \times k$, e.g., $30 - 20 \times 3 - 10$ denotes $30 - 20 - 20 - 20 - 10$.

Given that our output-layer technique together with the methods in [6] would enable a full hard-label attack, we decided to use the same CIFAR10 network[2] in [6]. This network has the following architecture: $3072 - 256 \times 3 - 64 - 10$. All neurons use ReLU as activation function and the output layer uses softmax.

Recall that our new sign-recovery methods are applicable when the number of neurons in the target layer i is lower than the rank of the transformation $F_x^{(i-1)}$ given by a transition point x and the previously recovered layers (see Sect. 4). Thus, our methods should be applicable to the first and fourth layers of the network above. However, we could apply them to the first layer only since the rank condition was not met when recovering signs in the fourth layer; we did not investigate why that network presented this behaviour. Instead, we trained a new network whose layers always contract, specifically, its architecture is $3072 - 1000 - 350 - 100 - 30 - 10$. This new network allowed us to successfully apply our sign recovery techniques. We trained this network on the CIFAR10 dataset and used the same training strategy as in [5,6,13]. More precisely, we used stochastic gradient descent with momentum equal to 0.9 for the training method, sparse categorical cross entropy for the loss function, batch size equal to 64 and learning rate 0.001.

5.2 Experimental Results - Network From [6]

The main goal was to test the recovery of the output layer. For this, we assume that we have already extracted the parameters of all layers. The first step is to find transition points to create the matrix C with the largest possible rank. In this case, $d_r = 64$ and $d_{r+1} = 10$, therefore, the maximum rank of C is $10(64+1) - (64+2) = 584$ (see Sect. 3.3). The experiments required about 6 h and 30 min to build the system of equations. Next, as discussed in Sect. 3.3, we fixed the value of 66 parameters in the output layer. Particularly, we heuristically chose to set the 64 weights and bias of the first output to 0, and the first weight of the second output to 1, i.e., $\hat{A}_1^{(5)} = (0, \ldots, 0)$, $\hat{b}_1^{(5)} = 0$ and $\hat{A}_{2,1}^{(5)} = 1$. Finally, solving the system of equations took a fraction of a second. To validate the accuracy of the recovered parameters, we sampled 5 000 input vectors whose coordinates were taken uniformly at random from $(-1, 1)$. Then, we counted the number of inputs for which the output of the original and recovered networks matched. This was the case for all inputs.

We also applied our sign-recovery techniques. Freeze requires computing the pre-image x' of $\hat{h} + \varepsilon e_j$ and the evaluation of $x' + \Delta$ and $x' - \Delta$ (see Sect. 4.2). Using $\varepsilon = 10^{-5}$ and $\|\Delta\| = 10^{-9}$ in the experiments, we successfully recovered the sign for all 256 neurons in the first layer. The total execution time was 33.41 s, which is 6.5× faster than the 220 s reported in [6] to recover a single batch of 64 signs with a parallel implementation (in total $220 \times 4 = 880$ seconds for the whole layer).

Recall that to get the parameters of the current target layer, the technique by Carlini et al. computes the normal vector m of the decision boundary. To

[2] Available in https://github.com/jchavezsaab/hard-label-dnn-extraction.

test hard-label SOE, we executed first an experiment that does not use m and then a second experiment using this vector. In the first SOE experiment, the execution time was 358.27 s, which is slower than freeze, but still faster than the result in [6]. The whole time is practically spent finding transition points that yield a full-rank system. Due to some signs recovered wrongly, we executed the experiment multiple times to correctly recover the sign of all neurons. We attribute the wrong signs to precision errors when finding the critical points $x + \Delta_k$. Our experiments are performed with 64-bit floating point arithmetic, therefore, not exact. Also, as in [6], we know that in practice we cannot obtain transition points exactly in the decision boundary, but ϵ away from it. In our experiments, we estimated this distance to be 10^{-13}. On the other hand, we observed that re-executing the experiment still produced a few wrong signs, but different from those in previous executions. This is different from the *difficult neuron* behaviour [5], where the recovered sign for some neurons is consistently wrong. Therefore, we executed the experiment multiple times, 10 in our case, and decided the sign as the one with the highest frequency. This allowed correct sign recovery in the less realistic SOE experiment.

Since we obtain the signatures with the technique by Carlini et al., we already know the normal vector m. We can think that the work required in our first SOE experiment is already done by the signature-recovery procedure. This procedure also requires searching for transition points to get a basis of the decision boundary and in turn, the critical hyperplanes; as reported in [6], signature recovery is the most time-consuming step. Thus, the second SOE experiment is the more realistic attack scenario. In this case, we simply compute the pseudo-inverse of a matrix and perform a matrix-vector multiplication (see Sect. 4.3). The execution time is under a second and, therefore, the best option available.

5.3 Experimental Results - Our Network

The main goal of the experiments with our network was to test the sign recovery techniques for deeper layers. We obtained successful results with freeze for all layers 1 to 4 using the same values $\varepsilon = 10^{-5}$ and $\|\Delta\| = 10^{-9}$ as in Sect. 5.2. The execution times are in Table 1. We also executed two experiments with SOE, the first one solving the system of linear equations and the second one using the normal vector m. The results are also in Table 1. Again, the less realistic scenario requires sensibly more time to find the transition points and construct the system of equations. The more realistic scenario is practically instantaneous.

Finally, we recovered the parameters of the output layer. In this case, $d_r = 30$ and $d_{r+1} = 10$, therefore, the maximum rank of C is $10(30+1) - (30+2) = 278$ and it took about 13 h to build the system of equations. As in the experiment with the other network, we fixed $\hat{A}_1^{(5)} = (0, \ldots, 0)$, $\hat{b}_1^{(5)} = 0$, $\hat{A}_{2,1}^{(5)} = 1$ and solving the system of equations took a fraction of a second. The time to build the system of equations was higher due to some neurons being rarely active, therefore, we required to test a large amount of points; this situation is not rare and is also reported in [6].

Table 1. Time to recover all neuron signs in layers 1 to 4 of our network.

Method	Time (in seconds)			
	Layer 1	Layer 2	Layer 3	Layer 4
Freeze	131.79	50.87	18.78	9.15
SOE (no m)	1457.88	516.65	150.59	47.35
SOE (using m)	0.50	0.30	0.23	0.22

5.4 Conclusions

We continued the study of parameter extraction of ReLU-based DNNs in the hard-label setting when the attacker exclusively has oracle access to the network. The recent novel attack by Carlini et al. demonstrated how to efficiently recover the parameters for all layers except the output layer. Here, we introduced a new method to extract this missing layer. Thus, a full hard-label recovery attack is now possible. Additionally, we presented new sign-recovery techniques applicable on contractive-enough layers. We showed experimentally that these techniques can have a big impact in real execution time.

One natural future direction is to develop an end-to-end implementation of the full hard-label attack. Also, to reduce the real time complexity, we need more efficient algorithms to obtain the signature from transition points. Other possible lines of research are to study extraction attacks for networks using activation functions that are not piece-wise linear and to address the seemingly more challenging problem of extraction attacks on other machine learning architectures (e.g., transformers).

Acknowledgments. We would like to express our sincere gratitude to Adi Shamir for valuable ideas and discussions which helped shape this work and Francisco Rodríguez-Henríquez for insightful feedback. Finally, we thank the reviewers for their helpful comments and suggestions.

Disclosure of Interests. The authors have no competing interests to declare that are relevant to the content of this article.

References

1. Baum, E.B.: A polynomial time algorithm that learns two hidden unit nets. Neural Comput. **2**(4), 510–522 (1990). https://doi.org/10.1162/neco.1990.2.4.510
2. Baum, E.B.: Neural net algorithms that learn in polynomial time from examples and queries. IEEE Trans. Neural Networks **2**(1), 5–19 (1991). https://doi.org/10.1109/72.80287
3. Blum, A.L., Rivest, R.L.: Training a 3-node neural network is NP-complete. Neural Netw. **5**(1), 117–127 (1992). https://doi.org/10.1016/S0893-6080(05)80010-3
4. Canales-Martínez, I.A., Chávez-Saab, J., Hambitzer, A., Rodríguez-Henríquez, F., Satpute, N., Shamir, A.: Polynomial Time Cryptanalytic Extraction of Neural

Network Models. Cryptology ePrint Archive, Paper 2023/1526 (2023). https://eprint.iacr.org/2023/1526
5. Canales-Martínez, I.A., Chávez-Saab, J., Hambitzer, A., Rodríguez-Henríquez, F., Satpute, N., Shamir, A.: Polynomial time cryptanalytic extraction of neural network models. In: Joye, M., Leander, G. (eds.) Advances in Cryptology – EUROCRYPT 2024. Lecture Notes in Computer Science, vol. 14653, pp. 3–33. Springer, Cham (2024). https://doi.org/10.1007/978-3-031-58734-4_1
6. Carlini, N., Chávez-Saab, J., Hambitzer, A., Rodríguez-Henríquez, F., Shamir, A.: Polynomial time cryptanalytic extraction of deep neural networks in the hard-label setting. In: Fehr, S., Fouque, P.A. (eds.) Advances in Cryptology – EUROCRYPT 2025. Lecture Notes in Computer Science, vol. 15601, pp. 364–396. Springer, Cham (2025). https://doi.org/10.1007/978-3-031-91107-1_13
7. Carlini, N., Jagielski, M., Mironov, I.: Cryptanalytic extraction of neural network models. In: Micciancio, D., Ristenpart, T. (eds.) Advances in Cryptology – CRYPTO 2020. Lecture Notes in Computer Science, vol. 12172, pp. 189–218. Springer, Cham (2020). https://doi.org/10.1007/978-3-030-56877-1_7
8. Chen, Y., Dong, X., Guo, J., Shen, Y., Wang, A., Wang, X.: Hard-label cryptanalytic extraction of neural network models. In: Chung, K.M., Sasaki, Y. (eds.) Advances in Cryptology – ASIACRYPT 2024. Lecture Notes in Computer Science, vol. 15491, pp. 207–236. Springer, Singapore (2025). https://doi.org/10.1007/978-981-96-0944-4_7
9. Daniely, A., Granot, E.: An exact poly-time membership-queries algorithm for extracting a three-layer ReLU network. In: The Eleventh International Conference on Learning Representations, ICLR 2023. OpenReview.net (2023). https://openreview.net/forum?id=-CoNloheTs
10. Fefferman, C.: Reconstructing a neural net from its output. Revista Matemática Iberoamericana **10**(3), 507–555 (1994). http://eudml.org/doc/39464
11. Foerster, H., Mullins, R., Shumailov, I., Hayes, J.: Beyond slow signs in high-fidelity model extraction. In: Globerson, A., et al. (eds.) Advances in Neural Information Processing Systems, vol. 37, pp. 19496–19522. Curran Associates, Inc. (2024). https://proceedings.neurips.cc/paper_files/paper/2024/file/22ae669a35bb9e70eb93ab77c1eff5b4-Paper-Conference.pdf
12. Jagielski, M., Carlini, N., Berthelot, D., Kurakin, A., Papernot, N.: High accuracy and high fidelity extraction of neural networks. In: Capkun, S., Roesner, F. (eds.) Proceedings of the 29th USENIX Conference on Security Symposium, SEC 2020, pp. 1345–1362. USENIX Association, USA (2020)
13. Lin, Z., Memisevic, R., Konda, K.R.: How far can we go without convolution: improving fully-connected networks (2015). https://arxiv.org/abs/1511.02580
14. Oliynyk, D., Mayer, R., Rauber, A.: I know what you trained last summer: a survey on stealing machine learning models and defences. ACM Comput. Surv. **55**(14s), 1–41 (2023). https://doi.org/10.1145/3595292

Implementation and Efficiency

Rhizomes and the Roots of Efficiency—Improving Prio

Armando Faz-Hernandez(✉)

Cloudflare, Inc., 101 Townsend St., San Francisco, CA 94107, USA
armfazh@cloudflare.com

Abstract. Prio, tailored under privacy-by-design principles, is a protocol for aggregating client-provided measurements between non-colluding entities. The validity of measurements is determined by using a fully linear probabilistically-checkable proof (FLPCP). The Prover distributes secret shares of the measurement and the proof to multiple Verifiers. These Verifiers can only use linear queries on the input statement for validation without accessing the actual measurement. Efficiency is key for the practical application of Prio. The FLPCP operates with polynomials represented in the Lagrange basis using roots of unity as the nodes. However, we observe opportunities to improve its performance by embracing the Lagrange basis more extensively. For instance, we show an inversion-free $O(n)$ time-complexity algorithm for polynomial evaluation in the Lagrange basis (an alternative to the classic rational barycentric formula). By applying our methods to libprio-rs, a cutting-edge Rust implementation, the Sharding phase (proof generation) runs a 36% faster and the Prep-Init phase (proof verification) is twice as fast, showing a substantial acceleration of the most time-consuming phases of Prio.

Keywords: Polynomial Basis · Lagrange Basis · Fully Linear Proofs · Distributed Aggregation Functions · Pólya Basis

1 Introduction

Calculating statistical functions on data generated by multiple users comes with the problem of leaking user's data points to collectors. Privacy-preserving techniques address this problem by allowing only the calculation of aggregated functions without revealing the individual contributions of each user. A recurrent use case is enabling service providers to run statistical measurements on its clients (e.g., to inspect the quality of the service) without learning any information about individual client measurements. Thus, protecting the privacy of users while still getting the aggregated values. Privacy-preserving measurements are a category of protocols that provide this functionality.

Under this category, Prio [16], introduced by Corrigan-Gibs and Boneh, is a cryptographic protocol that allows aggregation of some statistical functions. Other private aggregation algorithms exists, such as Prio+ [3], based

D. Escudero and I. Damgård (Eds.): LATINCRYPT 2025, LNCS 16129, pp. 425–449, 2026.
https://doi.org/10.1007/978-3-032-06754-8_16

on Boolean secret sharing, and Precio [4] based on oblivious shuffling. However, these protocols have not seen the same widespread use of Prio. In 2018, Mozilla [19,27] announced privacy-preserving telemetry collection for the Firefox browser. In 2020, ISRG [1] introduced a system infrastructure for private collection of metrics as well as continued support of libprio-rs, an open-sourced Prio's implementation. After 2020's global pandemic, the ENPA system [2,25], developed in conjunction by ISRG, Apple, Google, MITRE, and NIC, uses Prio for enabling health authorities to obtain epidemiology metrics from an exposure notification system. Cloudflare [24,35] has invested efforts in Prio's development. Davis et al. [17] showed that (with minor changes to) Prio meets formal security goals. Moreover, Prio is a candidate for standardization. The Privacy Preserving Measurement [29] working group at the Internet Engineering Task Force (IETF) has the goal of specifying protocols for the aggregation of statistics, and Prio is currently under consideration by the Crypto Forum Research Group [6].

Overview of Prio. At a high level, Prio allows multiple non-colluding servers to aggregate measurements of multiple clients. The protocol, shown in Fig. 1, starts with a client sending secret shares of its measurement to multiple servers. Each server, in possession of input shares from clients, is limited to compute some functions (e.g., sum) on them to produce aggregate shares of the result. After that, the collector (or one of the servers) takes the aggregate shares from the participating servers and computes the final aggregate result. The protocol must be *private*, so the attacker learns nothing about the measurements, and *robust*, to prevent corruption of the aggregated result.

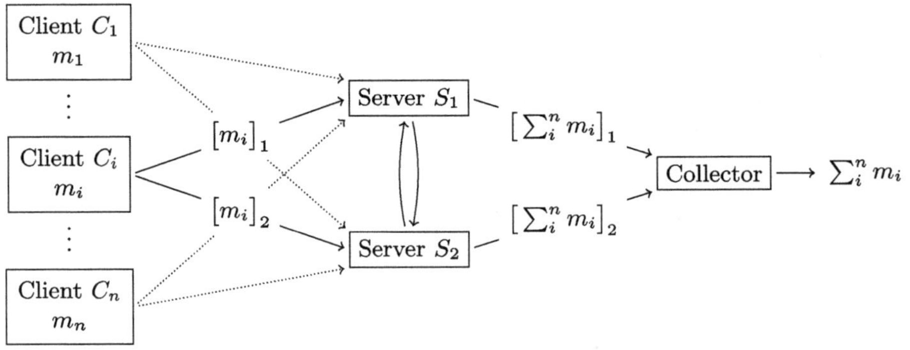

Fig. 1. Overview of the Prio protocol.

The protocol must prevent clients from entering invalid values that corrupt the aggregated value. To do so, clients produce a zero-knowledge proof that asserts the validity of the measurement. Thus, servers only aggregate measurements that have valid proofs. If the validity function is simple, e.g. checking a value is binary, specialized proof systems can be used instead of general-purpose proof systems. However in most proof systems, the input statement must be known for proof verification. For example, in a digital signature scheme, the message and the signature must be known during verification. In Prio, the server only has access to secret shares of the input measurement and the proof. For this reason, the proof system must make it possible to validate statements using only secret shares of the input *and* secret shares of the proof.

For validation of measurements, the validation function must be expressed as an arithmetic circuit over $\mathbb{F}$ with M multiplication gates. First, the client evaluates the circuit on its measurement x, such that u_t and v_t are the inputs of the multiplication gate number t, for $1 \leq t \leq M$. Then, the client defines three polynomials f, g, h, such that $h = fg$, $f(t) = u_t$, and $g(t) = v_t$. Given x and h, the client uses an additive secret sharing function to produce secret shares of $x = \sum_{i=1}^{k}[x]_i$ and $h = \sum_{i=1}^{k}[h]_i$, where k is the number of servers. Finally, the client sends $([x]_i, [h]_i)$ to the ith server.

Upon receiving $([x]_i, [h]_i)$, the server recovers secret shares of $[f]_i$ and $[g]_i$, and performs the Schwartz-Zippel randomized polynomial identity test [39,43] to check whether $h = fg$; if so, the measurement is declared as valid. To do so, the server evaluates the secret-shared polynomials at $r \leftarrow_{\$} \mathbb{F}^*$ chosen at random to obtain $[f(r)]_i$, $[g(r)]_i$, and $[h(r)]_i$. Using these values, each server calculates $\sigma_i = [f(r) \times g(r) - h(r)]_i$, where $\times$ is a protocol for multiplication of secret shares. Finally, every server publishes its σ_i value and checks whether $\sum_{i=0}^{k} \sigma_i = 0$, if this check passes the measurement is valid for aggregation.

A Seed of Motivation. The authors of Prio [16] proposed an optimization for performing verification without using interpolation. Their observation is that a polynomial P in the Lagrange basis can be evaluated at r in linear time whenever r is fixed and known in advance, instead of sampling it at random each time.

To see why this works, it is known that any polynomial P of degree n can be written as $P(x) = \sum_{i=0}^{n} y_i \ell_i(x)$, where y_i are the values and $\ell_i(x)$ are the Lagrange polynomials. Calculating the set of $\ell_i(x)$ requires $O(n^2)$ operations. However if they are precomputed, evaluating $P(r)$ takes $O(n)$ operations accounting for the dot product between $\ell_i(r)$ and the values y_i sent by the client.

In Prio, the value r must be a chosen at random, otherwise it affects the soundness of the protocol. If the server fixes the value r, then it must be guaranteed that the client never learns r, and that the server samples r frequently. The substantial overhead in computation and, more critically, in the security of the protocol presents a significant barrier for applying this optimization. This paper addresses these limitations and details a successful approach for implementing this (and other) optimizations.

Contributions. Motivated by the traction gained in the past few years, its use on practical applications, and its path towards standardization, our focus centered on ways to reduce the computational cost of Prio.

- We show an inversion-free $O(n)$ time-complexity algorithm for polynomial evaluation in the Lagrange basis. Our algorithm is not derived from the well-known barycentric formula. It relies on the use of *Pólya polynomials* [8], whose

origin traces back to a probabilistic model known as the Pólya urn. These polynomials are in close connection with B-splines and have been proven useful in computer-aided geometric design [9].
- A direct consequence of the above is showing a new application of the Pólya polynomials in the field of cryptography. Our algorithm enables that Prio's verification runs in linear time, without calculating inverses, and without making extra security assumptions on the server's sampled values.
- We study the basis extension operation for compactly storing polynomials and for polynomial multiplication. In both cases, we present explicit formulas and optimizations that are of general interest when working with polynomials in the Lagrange basis.
- We implement the proposed algorithms in (a fork of) libprio-rs, a state-of-the-art open-sourced Rust implementation of Prio. We plan to contribute the changes proposed in this investigation to the library maintainers as well as to the authors of the IETF specification document [6].
- At the Prio protocol level, we observe significant savings in the execution time of the Sharding phase (when the client generates a FLPCP proof) and during the Prep-Init phase (when the server verifies the proof).

To process polynomial arithmetic efficiently, we make an effort to update Prio to use the Lagrange representation for all polynomial arithmetic. In doing so, we faced several challenges including the change of representations, the basis extension, and the polynomial multiplication. We remark that while some standard techniques for Lagrange basis are already in place, we show more opportunities for improving the execution time of the protocol.

We discovered significant performance improvements by a careful analysis of Prio's operations. We found it fruitful to explore methods and solutions developed in other fields. For instance, we found abundant polynomial representations from numerical analysis, particularly those used in computer-aided geometric design, proved invaluable to our approach. However, these representations are less popular in the cryptographic community. This cross-disciplinary inspiration was a key factor in achieving our results.

The diversity of optimizations goals is a limitation for connecting fields of research. In numerical analysis, a primary goal is to reduce errors caused by ill-conditioned functions or the loss of precision during computation. These errors often arise when working with infinite domains like real and complex numbers. Consequently, algorithms in this field are designed to minimize errors first, with the reduction of computational operations being a secondary concern. In cryptography, most algorithms operate within finite domains, ensuring all calculations are exact and free of rounding errors or loss of precision. After guaranteeing security, common optimization goals in cryptography include improving the efficiency and security of implementations, as well as protecting against side-channel attacks. Despite their optimization goals differ, combining knowledge from both areas has yielded useful benefits. This work introduces new ideas from numerical analysis methods and shows how to apply them effectively to reduce the number of operations of a cryptographic protocol.

2 Background

2.1 The Roots of Unity

Let $\mathbb{K}$ be a field, for any $x \in \mathbb{K}$ is said to be an *Nth-root of unity* if $x^N = 1$ over $\mathbb{K}$ for $N > 0$. The Nth-roots of unity in $\mathbb{K}$ forms a cyclic group of order N under multiplication and is generated by a primitive Nth-root of unity ω_N.

From now on, N denotes a positive power of two, and $\mathbb{K}$ is restricted to be a finite field $\mathbb{F}$. The Nth-roots of unity have really useful properties:

$$\begin{aligned}
&\text{Sum:} && \sum_{i=0}^{N-1} {\omega_N}^i = 0\,. \\
&\text{Inverse:} && {\omega_N}^{-j} = {\omega_N}^{N-j}\,. \\
&\text{Negative:} && -{\omega_N}^j = {\omega_N}^{j+\frac{N}{2}}\,,\ \text{for } j > 0\,. \\
&\text{Exponent:} && (\omega_{jN})^{jk} = (\omega_N)^k\,,\ \text{for } j, k > 0\,.
\end{aligned} \tag{2.1.1}$$

Figure 2 shows the relation of the Nth-roots of unity for the first powers of two.

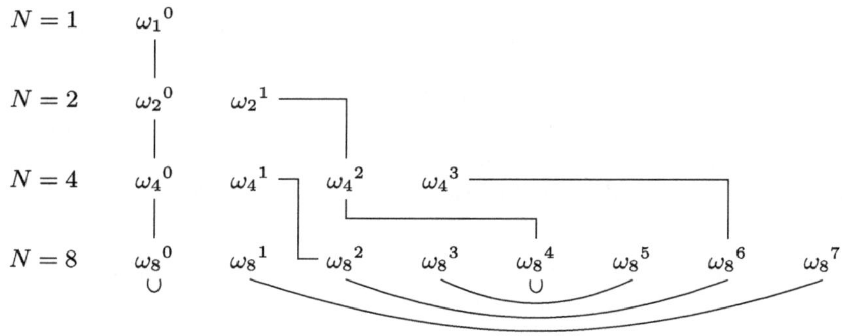

Fig. 2. Each row shows the Nth-roots of unity. Straight lines connecting the roots show that ${\omega_N}^j = {\omega_{2N}}^{2j}$, and curved lines show that ${\omega_N}^{-j} = {\omega_N}^{N-j}$ for $j \geq 0$.

It is possible to ensure the presence of the Nth-roots of unity in $\mathbb{F}$ [36]. Let p be the characteristic of $\mathbb{F}$, then any p of the form[1] $p = f2^k + 1$, such that f is odd and $0 < f < 2^k$, guarantees the existence of subgroups of order 2^i in $\mathbb{F}^*$, for all $0 \leq i \leq k$. Each subgroup corresponds to the 2^ith-roots of unity and is generated by $\omega_{2^i} = g^{f2^{(k-i)}}$ for all $0 \leq i \leq k$, where g is a generator of $\mathbb{F}^*$.

2.2 Polynomials as a Vector Space

We describe well-known forms of representing polynomials: the monomial basis and the Lagrange basis. To facilitate the explanation of our methods, we opted to use vector spaces. This comes in handy, for example, when describing a change of polynomial representations (as a change of basis) rather than recurring to polynomial interpolation.

[1] This family of primes is also known as Proth primes [34].

Vector Space. A vector space V over a field $\mathbb{F}$ is a set of elements where vector addition and scalar multiplication operations are defined. A set $B \subset V$ is a basis of V if every element $v \in V$ can be expressed as a linear combination of the elements in B. The coefficients of this linear combination are known as the coordinates of v with respect to the base B and are denoted as $[v]_B$. Every basis of V has the same number of elements, which is the dimension of V. We denote by $V_{[d]}$ the vector space of dimension d and by B_d its basis. It holds that $V_{[i]} \subsetneq V_{[d]}$, for all $0 < i < d$.

Let $k \in \mathbb{F}$, and $u, v \in V_{[d]}$ be two vectors of with coordinates $(u_0, \dots, u_{d-1})$ and $(v_0, \dots, v_{d-1})$, respectively; then vector addition and scalar multiplication is defined as

$$\begin{aligned} +\colon\ V \times V &\to V \\ \big((u_0, \dots, u_{d-1}), (v_0, \dots, v_{d-1})\big) &\mapsto (u_0 + v_0, \dots, u_{d-1} + v_{d-1}), \\ \cdot\colon\ \mathbb{F} \times V &\to V \\ \big(k, (u_0, \dots, u_{d-1})\big) &\mapsto (ku_0, \dots, ku_{d-1}). \end{aligned} \tag{2.2.1}$$

Polynomials. Let $\mathbb{F}[x]$ denotes the univariate polynomial ring over a field $\mathbb{F}$. Elements of this ring are called *polynomials*. The set of polynomials also behaves as a vector space over $\mathbb{F}$ of countable-infinite dimension. The basis elements of $\mathbb{F}[x]$ are also polynomials. For finite dimension, $\mathbb{F}[x]_{[d]}$ is a d-dimensional vector space of polynomials, and they are compactly stored as a tuple of its coordinates. Evaluating a polynomial $P \in \mathbb{F}[x]$ at a given value z, denoted as $P(z)$, is the value calculated from the resulting expression after replacing x with z.

Monomial Basis. The set $\mathcal{M} = \{x^0, \dots, x^{n-1}\}$ is the *monomial basis* of $\mathbb{F}[x]_{[n]}$. So any $P \in \mathbb{F}[x]_{[n]}$ is represented as

$$P(x) = \sum_{i=0}^{n-1} c_i x^i, \text{ where } c_i \in \mathbb{F}. \tag{2.2.2}$$

The c_i values are the coordinates of P simply known as its coefficients. The degree of P is the largest exponent of the basis element with a non-zero coefficient. $\mathbb{F}[x]_{[n]}$ contains all polynomials of degree lesser than n.

Lagrange Basis. Given a set of $n+1$ distinct values $x_0, \dots, x_n \in \mathbb{F}$, called *nodes*, the Lagrange polynomials are defined as

$$\ell_i(x) = \prod_{\substack{j=0 \\ j \neq i}}^{n} \frac{x - x_j}{x_i - x_j}, \text{ for } 0 \leq i \leq n. \tag{2.2.3}$$

Each of them has degree n, and it holds that $\ell_i(x_i) = 1$, and $\ell_i(x_j) = 0$ if $i \neq j$, for $0 \leq i, j \leq n$.

The set $\mathcal{L} = \{\ell_0(x), \ldots, \ell_n(x)\}$ is the *Lagrange basis* of $\mathbb{F}[x]_{[n+1]}$, and any $P \in \mathbb{F}[x]_{[n+1]}$ is represented as

$$P(x) = \sum_{i=0}^{n} y_i \ell_i(x)\,, \text{ where } y_i \in \mathbb{F}\,. \tag{2.2.4}$$

The y_i values are the coordinates of P called the *values* (or ordinates) of P. The evaluation of P at the nodes corresponds to the values, i.e., $y_i = P(x_i)$ for $0 \leq i \leq n$. For storing P use a tuple containing the pairs (x_i, y_i) for $0 \leq i \leq n$, or one can store only the values when the nodes are well-known.

Change of Basis. Switching between polynomial basis can be expressed with matrix operations. Gander [22] showed explicit vector-matrix products to change between several polynomial basis. In particular, the monomial and Lagrange basis are related as $V^T\mathcal{M} = \mathcal{L}$, and the coefficient and values as $V[P]_{\mathcal{M}} = [P]_{\mathcal{L}}$, where V is a Vandermonde matrix with entries $V_{i,j} = {x_i}^j$ for $0 \leq i, j \leq n$. The inverse transformation is possible since V is invertible whenever the nodes are distinct. In the general case, changing between basis of dimension n takes $O(n^2)$ field operations, which is the computational cost of a vector-matrix product.

Basis Extension. Let $\mathbb{F}[x]_{[n]}$ and $\mathbb{F}[x]_{[m]}$ of dimension $n < m$, and let B_n and B_m be its basis, respectively. For any $P \in \mathbb{F}[x]_{[n]}$, the *basis extension*[2] of P is a function that given $[P]_{B_n}$, it finds $[P]_{B_m}$. That is, it produces an equivalent set of coordinates that represents the same polynomial in a basis of larger dimension; this is always possible since $\mathbb{F}[x]_{[n]} \subsetneq \mathbb{F}[x]_{[m]}$.

In the monomial basis, basis extension is easy by setting the higher-degree coefficients to zero, i.e., $c_i = 0$ for $n < i \leq m$. In the Lagrange basis, extending a polynomial in basis $\mathcal{L}_n$ to $\mathcal{L}_{n+1}$ takes $O(n)$ field operations [38]. Hence, in the general case, it takes $O(nm)$ field operations to arbitrarily extend polynomials in the Lagrange basis. In Sect. 3.3, we show faster algorithms for basis extension for certain special cases of interest.

Polynomial Multiplication. There is a substantial gap in the computational complexity of polynomial multiplication [42]. For an n-dimensional basis, the standard algorithm in the monomial basis takes $O(n^2)$ field operations[3], in contrast to the $O(n)$ field operations performed while working in the Lagrange basis. This complexity requires input polynomials of the correct dimension. If dimensions are wrong, a basis extension is needed and must be factored in.

[2] This extension is sometimes denominated as degree extension. However, this term may not be the best since the degree of the polynomial must remain unchanged.

[3] Asymptotically faster algorithms for polynomial multiplication exist: Karatsuba [31] algorithm takes $O(n^{\log(3)/\log(2)})$ operations, and Toom-Cook [13,40] algorithm takes $O(n^{\log(5)/\log(3)})$ operations.

For any $P \in \mathbb{F}[x]_{[n]}$ and $Q \in \mathbb{F}[x]_{[m]}$, we have that $P \times Q \in \mathbb{F}[x]_{[n+m-1]}$. Let $(p_0, \dots, p_{n-1})$ and $(q_0, \dots, q_{m-1})$ be the coordinates of P and Q. In the monomial basis, the coefficients of $P \times Q$ are calculated as

$$\left((p_0, \dots, p_{n-1}), (q_0, \dots, q_{m-1})\right) \mapsto (r_0, \dots, r_{n+m-2}), \tag{2.2.5}$$

where $r_{i+j} = \sum_{i=0}^{n-1} \sum_{j=0}^{m-1} p_i q_j$ for $0 \le i < n$ and $0 \le j < m$. In the Lagrange basis, the values of $P \times Q$ are calculated as

$$\left((p_0, \dots, p_{n+m-2}), (q_0, \dots, q_{n+m-2})\right) \mapsto (p_0 q_0, \dots, p_{n+m-2} q_{n+m-2}). \tag{2.2.6}$$

This algorithm holds under the assumption that P and Q were previously extended to a basis of dimension $n + m - 1$. If this is the case, polynomial multiplication takes $O(n)$ operations. Otherwise, input polynomials must initially be extended to a higher dimension, an operation requiring $O(n^2)$ operations in the general case, yielding the same complexity as the monomial basis algorithm. Fortunately when restricting the nodes to some special values enables faster $O(n \log n)$ methods for polynomial multiplication. In Sect. 3.3, we present these methods and demonstrate how to optimize execution speed by reducing the constant factors behind the asymptotic notation.

Polynomial Evaluation. There exist efficient algorithms for polynomial evaluation. Horner's method [28] is an $O(n)$ time-complexity algorithm for evaluating polynomials represented in the monomial basis and is shown in Algorithm 1. For the Lagrange basis, directly calculating Eq. (2.2.4) takes $O(n^2)$ field operations. That is, evaluating a dot product between the values and the Lagrange polynomials. However, one can derive an asymptotically faster algorithm from the *barycentric*[4] formula [38]. In Sect. 3.1, we show an alternative $O(n)$ time-complexity algorithm for polynomial evaluation in the Lagrange basis.

Barycentric Algorithm. Given a polynomial $P \in \mathbb{F}[x]_{[n]}$ represented by its set of nodes and values, (x_i, y_i) for $0 \le i \le n$, we can evaluate $P(x)$ using the second form of the barycentric formula as

$$P(x) = \frac{\sum_{i=0}^{n} \frac{w_i}{x - x_i} y_i}{\sum_{i=0}^{n} \frac{w_i}{x - x_i}}, \quad \text{where } w_i = 1 / \prod_{\substack{j=0 \\ j \ne i}}^{n} (x_i - x_j) \in \mathbb{F}. \tag{2.2.7}$$

If all the w_i scalars are computed in advance (a task taking $O(n^2)$ field operations), then evaluating the barycentric formula takes $O(n)$ field operations, as shown in Algorithm 2.

[4] A barycentric combination is a weighted sum of points where weights sum to one. See [20, Ch. 2] for a description on the origin of the barycentric term.

Algorithm 1. Horner's Algorithm for Polynomial Evaluation in $\mathcal{M}$ Basis

Input: $[P]_{\mathcal{M}} = (c_0, \dots, c_n)$, and x.
Output: $P(x)$.
$y = c_n$
for $i = n - 1$ **to** 0 **do**
  $y = yx + c_i$
end for
return y

Algorithm 2. Barycentric Algorithm for Polynomial Evaluation in $\mathcal{L}$ Basis

Input: $[P]_{\mathcal{L}} = (y_0, \dots, y_n)$, and x.
Constant: $x_0, \dots, x_n$.
Precompute: $w_0, \dots, w_n$.
Output: $P(x)$.
$u = 0$, and $v = 0$
for $i = 0$ **to** n **do**
  $t = w_i(x - x_i)^{-1}$
  $u = u + ty_i$
  $v = v + t$
end for
return u/v

Let **A**, **M**, **S**, and **I** represent the cost of calculating, respectively, additions (or subtractions), multiplications, squares, and multiplicative inverses over $\mathbb{F}$. The number of field operations for evaluating a polynomial $P \in \mathbb{F}[x]_{[n]}$ is:

$$\begin{aligned} \text{Horner Algorithm: } & n\mathbf{M} + n\mathbf{A} \\ \text{Barycentric Algorithm: } & 2(n+1)\mathbf{M} + 3(n+1)\mathbf{A} + (n+2)\mathbf{I} \end{aligned} \tag{2.2.8}$$

Despite both algorithms having $O(n)$ time-complexity, the practical efficiency is heavily influenced by the cost of field operations. Inverses, for example, are generally more computationally expensive than multiplications and additions, which significantly impacts the overall execution time. Consequently, developing an inversion-free algorithm is a crucial goal for improving efficiency.

2.3 The Roots of Unity as the Nodes of the Lagrange Basis

A number of simplifications and faster algorithms result from choosing the Nth-roots of unity as the nodes in the Lagrange basis representation. We use $\mathcal{L}\mu$ to denote this choice and distinguish it from the general case $\mathcal{L}$.

Polynomial Evaluation. A classic result, often found in some textbooks [30, 37], is that any $P \in \mathbb{F}[x]_{[N]}$ represented in $\mathcal{L}\mu$ can be expressed as

$$P(x) = \frac{x^N - 1}{N} \sum_{i=0}^{N-1} \frac{{\omega_N}^i y_i}{x - {\omega_N}^i}\,. \tag{2.3.1}$$

This holds, in part, because the following calculations are simplified:

$$w_i = \prod_{\substack{j=0 \\ j \neq i}}^{N-1} \frac{1}{({\omega_N}^i - {\omega_N}^j)} = \frac{{\omega_N}^i}{N}, \text{ and } \prod_{i=0}^{N-1} (x - {\omega_N}^i) = x^N - 1\,. \tag{2.3.2}$$

Based on the above, Algorithm 3 evaluates a polynomial taking $(2N+2)\mathbf{M} + \log_2(N)\mathbf{S} + (2N+1)\mathbf{A} + (N+1)\mathbf{I}$. This requires a similar number of operations as the general case, but without precomputation.

Algorithm 3. Barycentric Algorithm for Polynomial Evaluation in $\mathcal{L}\mu$ Basis

Input: $[P]_{\mathcal{L}\mu} = (y_0, \dots, y_{N-1})$, and x.
Constant: ${\omega_N}^0, \dots, {\omega_N}^{N-1}$.
Output: $P(x)$.

$u = 0$
for $i = 0$ **to** $N-1$ **do**
  $t = {\omega_N}^i (x - {\omega_N}^i)^{-1}$
  $u = u + t y_i$
end for
$r = x$
for $i = 0$ **to** $\log_2(N) - 1$ **do**
  $r = r^2$
end for
return $(r-1) u N^{-1}$

Algorithm 4. NTT Algorithm

Input: ω_N, and $U = (u_0, \dots, u_{N-1})$.
Output: $\mathtt{NTT}(\omega_N, U)$.

$V_i = U_{\mathtt{bitrev}(i, \log_2(N))}$ for $0 \le i < N$.
for $l = 1$ **to** $\log_2(N)$ **do**
  $w = 1$ {★}
  $y = 2^{l-1}$
  $r = \omega_{2^l}$
  for $i = 0$ **to** $y - 1$ **do**
    for $j = 0$ **to** $N/2y - 1$ **do**
      $x = 2^l j + i$
      $u = V_x$
      $v = w V_{x+y}$
      $V_x = u + v$
      $V_{x+y} = u - v$
    end for
    $w = wr$
  end for
end for
return V

Faster Change of Basis (i.e., Fast Fourier Transform). The Faster Fourier Transform (FFT) is an $O(N \log N)$ time-complexity algorithm, independently proposed by Cooley-Tukey [14] and Gentleman-Sandle [23], for the Discrete Fourier Transform over $\mathbb{K}$. When it is specialized to $\mathbb{F}$, it is known as the Number Theoretic Transform (NTT).

Changing between the monomial and Lagrange basis is asymptotically faster by using NTT. Let $(c_0, \dots, c_{N-1})$ be the coefficients of $P \in \mathbb{F}[x]_{[N]}$, the NTT algorithm is defined as

$$\mathtt{NTT}\colon \big(\omega_N, (c_0, \dots, c_{N-1})\big) \mapsto \big(P({\omega_N}^0), \dots, P({\omega_N}^{N-1})\big). \tag{2.3.3}$$

Thus, it holds that $[P]_{\mathcal{L}\mu} = \mathtt{NTT}(\omega_N, [P]_{\mathcal{M}})$. NTT also makes it possible to obtain the coefficients from the values. The inverse NTT takes the values $(y_0, \dots, y_{N-1})$ and calculates the coefficients as

$$\mathtt{iNTT}\colon \big(\omega_N, (y_0, \dots, y_{N-1})\big) \mapsto \tfrac{1}{N}\mathtt{NTT}\big({\omega_N}^{-1}, (y_0, \dots, y_{N-1})\big). \tag{2.3.4}$$

Algorithm 4 implements NTT taking $N \log_2(N)(\mathbf{M} + \mathbf{A})$. Since NTT takes $O(N \log N)$ operations, switching between the $\mathcal{M}$ and $\mathcal{L}\mu$ basis is asymptotically faster than the $O(N^2)$ algorithm for switching between the $\mathcal{M}$ and $\mathcal{L}$ basis.

3 Improvements for Lagrange Polynomial Basis $\mathcal{L}\mu$

We propose algorithms that use the Nth-roots of unity as Lagrange basis nodes to reduce the operations needed for polynomial evaluation and basis extension. These algorithms have utility beyond the specific optimization problem addressed in this work.

3.1 Inversion-Free Linear-Time Polynomial Evaluation in Lagrange Basis $\mathcal{L}\mu$

We show an $O(n)$ time-complexity algorithm for polynomial evaluation, an inversion-free alternative to the barycentric formula. We first discuss limitations of the barycentric formula's implementation that motivated our algorithm.

Motivation. In Sect. 2.3, we show that polynomials in the Lagrange basis can be evaluated with a linear number of operations using either Algorithm 2 in the general case, or Algorithm 3 over a field where the Nth-roots of unity exist. Both algorithms calculate $(N+1)\mathbf{I}$. For finite fields[5], inverses are more expensive to compute and are often avoided. Given $a \in \mathbb{F}^*$, its inverse is often calculated in constant-time as $a^{-1} = a^{q-2}$, where q is the number of elements of $\mathbb{F}$. Thus, the ratio $\mathbf{I}/\mathbf{M}$ grows with the size of the field, which potentially dominates the execution time of polynomial evaluation for large fields.

Two well-known methods for reducing inversions in the barycentric formula calculation are immediately apparent. The Montgomery's trick [32] is a classic technique for calculating $n\mathbf{I}$ inverses at the expense of $3(n-1)\mathbf{M}+\mathbf{I}$ operations. A different approach is to express the barycentric formula as an algebraic fraction, i.e., as the ratio of two values in $\mathbb{F}$. So all the calculations use fraction arithmetic, with a single inversion at the end for the final fraction value.

Problem. Unfortunately, neither approach completely eliminates the calculation of inverses. The cost of polynomial evaluation in large fields can be dominated by even one inverse calculation. Is it possible to develop an inversion-free algorithm for polynomial evaluation in the Lagrange basis $\mathcal{L}\mu$?

Solution. Our response is affirmative. We observe that Horner's algorithm evaluates a polynomial without inverses. In numerical analysis [12,26], Horner's algorithm is described as a nested multiplication algorithm, and some textbooks use ladder diagrams to visualize its flow of operations. Inspired by this structure, we looked for an algorithm with a similar approach and found Warren's algorithm [41] that evaluates polynomials represented in the *Pólya basis*. Consequently, the Pólya polynomial basis, introduced by Barry and Goldman [8,10] as a way to generalize the Bézier and Lagrange polynomials, served us as a starting point. We then analyze the operations of Warren's algorithm and explore potential improvements.

[5] For applications in which $\mathbb{K} = \mathbb{R}$, programs use floating-point arithmetic. Multiplications and inverses are calculated with the FMUL and FDIV instructions, where the ratio $\mathbf{I}/\mathbf{M} = \frac{16}{4} = 4$ clock cycles according to Fog's report [21].

Pólya Basis. Let $t_1, \dots, t_{2n} \in \mathbb{F}$ be arbitrary scalars, the Pólya basis functions $d_i(x)$ are polynomials of degree n defined as

$$d_i(x) = \prod_{j=1}^{n} (t_{i+j} - x). \tag{3.1.1}$$

The set $\mathcal{P} = \{d_0(x), \dots, d_n(x)\}$ is the *Pólya basis* of $\mathbb{F}[x]_{[n+1]}$, so any $P \in \mathbb{F}[x]_{[n+1]}$ is represented as

$$P(x) = \sum_{i=0}^{n} p_i d_i(x), \text{ where } p_i \in \mathbb{F}\,. \tag{3.1.2}$$

The p_i values are its coordinates. More details about the properties of Pólya polynomials can be found in [9, Ch 2, pp. 28] and [8,10]. For our purposes, the most relevant property is that both the monomial and the Lagrange basis are special cases of the Pólya basis.

Change of Basis: Lagrange ↔ Pólya. To instantiate the Pólya basis as the Lagrange basis, assign $(t_1, \dots, t_n, t_{n+1}, \dots, t_{2n}) = (x_1, \dots, x_n, x_0, \dots, x_{n-1})$, so the elements in the basis are related as

$$d_i(x) = \alpha_i \ell_i(x), \text{ where } \alpha_i = \prod_{\substack{j=0 \\ j \neq i}}^{n} (x_j - x_i) \text{ for } 0 \leq i \leq n\,, \tag{3.1.3}$$

and the coordinates are related as $(p_0, \dots, p_n) = (y_0/\alpha_0, \dots, y_n/\alpha_n)$.

Polynomial Evaluation. As Warren's algorithm [41] generalizes Horner's algorithm means no inverses are required. Given $(t_1, \dots, t_{2n})$, Warren's algorithm evaluates a polynomial $P \in \mathbb{F}[x]_{[n+1]}$ with coordinates $(p_0, \dots, p_n)$ in Pólya basis. It requires $3n\mathbf{M} + 3n\mathbf{A}$, as shown in Algorithm 5.

Algorithm 5. Warren's Algorithm for Polynomial Evaluation in $\mathcal{P}$ Basis

Input: $[P]_{\mathcal{P}} = (p_0, \dots, p_n)$, and x.
Constant: $t_1, \dots, t_{2n}$.
Output: $P(x)$.

1: $l = 1$
2: $u = p_0$
3: **for** $i = 0$ **to** $n - 1$ **do**
4: $\quad l = l(t_{i+n+1} - x)$
5: $\quad u = u(t_{i+1} - x) + l p_{i+1}$
6: **end for**
7: **return** u

Proposed Algorithm. We describe the last step that takes us to the promised $O(n)$ time-complexity algorithm for polynomial evaluation: namely, to instantiate Warren's algorithm leveraging the presence of the Nth-roots of unity, plus some additional tricks. We denote this choice as $\mathcal{P}\mu$ to distinguish it from the general case $\mathcal{P}$.

Here we describe some simplifications we observed, which could potentially be helpful in other contexts. First, Warren's algorithm uses $2n$ auxiliary scalars (t_i) that correspond directly to the nodes, so no additional storage is required. Moreover, at the ith iteration the algorithm calculates $(t_{i+n+1}-x)$ and $(t_{i+1}-x)$, and after instantiating with the roots of unity the values are $({\omega_N}^i - x)$ and $({\omega_N}^{i+1} - x)$, respectively. So in the next iteration we can reuse the second value effectively removing one subtraction per iteration.

Let us describe the change of basis. Each value y_i is converted to a Pólya coordinate as $p_i = y_i/\alpha_i$ for $0 \le i < N$. A direct implementation of this conversion takes $N(\mathbf{M}+\mathbf{I})$, or $(4N-3)\mathbf{M}+\mathbf{I}$ by applying the Montgomery's trick [32]. However, one (undesired) inverse remains.

We present an inversion-free method for the change of basis. Observe that α_i is related to w_i (defined in Sect. 2.3) as follows

$$\begin{aligned}\alpha_i &= \prod_{\substack{j=0\\ j\neq i}}^{N-1} ({\omega_N}^j - {\omega_N}^i) = \prod_{\substack{j=0\\ j\neq i}}^{N-1} (-1)({\omega_N}^i - {\omega_N}^j) = (-1)^{N-1} \prod_{\substack{j=0\\ j\neq i}}^{N-1} ({\omega_N}^i - {\omega_N}^j)\\ &= -1/w_i = -{\omega_N}^i/N, \quad \text{for } 0 \le i < N\,.\end{aligned} \tag{3.1.4}$$

This equivalence replaces inversions of α_i with multiplications by ${\omega_N}^i$. Since the scalar $1/N$ appears in every coordinate, we can evaluate the scaled polynomial, and perform a scalar multiplication after evaluating the polynomial.

For implementation purposes, N can be either a fixed constant (hard-coded in the program), or a dynamic value. In the latter case, $1/N$ can be calculated faster with $O(\log N)$ operations and no inverses. First, store the fixed constant $H = 2^{-1} \in \mathbb{F}$, for $N > 1$. Then, set $h = H$ and repeat $\log_2(N) - 1$ squares on $h = h^2$. Finally $1/N = h$ because N is always a power of two.

Finally, we present the proposed inversion-free $O(N)$ time-complexity algorithm for evaluating polynomials in the Lagrange basis with the Nth-roots of unity as nodes. We present two cases depending whether one or multiple polynomials are evaluated.

Single Evaluation. Given a polynomial $P \in \mathbb{F}[x]_{[N]}$ with values $(y_0, \dots, y_{N-1})$ in the Lagrange basis $\mathcal{L}\mu$, Algorithm 6 evaluates $P(x)$ taking $(4N-3)\mathbf{M}+2N\mathbf{A}$, plus $(\log_2(N)-1)\mathbf{S}$ when $1/N$ is not precomputed.

Batched Evaluation. Evaluating multiple polynomials at the same value of x is faster when processed as a batch. Given k polynomials $P_j \in \mathbb{F}[x]_{[N]}$ with values $\big((y_0)_j, \dots, (y_{N-1})_j\big)$ in Lagrange basis $\mathcal{L}\mu$, for $0 < j \le k$, Algorithm 7 evaluates $P_j(x)$ taking $\big((2N-1)(k+1)-1\big)\mathbf{M}+N(k+1)\mathbf{A}$. This eliminates the need to compute $2(N-1)(k-1)\mathbf{M}+N(k-1)\mathbf{A}$ when invoking Algorithm 6 k times. As expected, $k=1$ covers the single evaluation case.

Algorithm 6. Our Algorithm for Polynomial Evaluation in $\mathcal{L}\mu$ Basis

Input: $[P]_{\mathcal{L}\mu} = (y_0, \dots, y_{N-1})$ and $x \in \mathbb{F}$.
Constant: ${\omega_N}^0, \dots, {\omega_N}^{N-1}$.
Output: $P(x)$.

$N' = 1/N$ {Using $(\log_2(N) - 1)\mathbf{S}$.}
$l = 1$
$u = y_0$
$d = {\omega_N}^0 - x$
for $i = 1$ **to** $N - 1$ **do**
  $l = ld$
  $d = {\omega_N}^i - x$
  $u = ud + l{\omega_N}^i y_i$
end for
return $-uN'$

Algorithm 7. Batched Algorithm for Polynomial Evaluation in $\mathcal{L}\mu$ Basis

Input: $[P_j]_{\mathcal{L}\mu} = \big((y_0)_j, \dots, (y_{N-1})_j\big)$, for $0 < j \leq k$, and $x \in \mathbb{F}$.
Constant: ${\omega_N}^0, \dots, {\omega_N}^{N-1}$.
Output: $P_j(x)$ for $0 < j \leq k$.

$N' = 1/N$ {Using $(\log_2(N) - 1)\mathbf{S}$.}
$l = 1$
$u_j = (y_0)_j$ for $0 < j \leq k$.
$d = {\omega_N}^0 - x$
for $i = 1$ **to** $N - 1$ **do**
  $l = ld$
  $d = {\omega_N}^i - x$
  $t = l{\omega_N}^i$
  for $j = 1$ **to** k **do**
    $u_j = u_j d + t(y_i)_j$
  end for
end for
return $-u_j N'$ for $0 < j \leq k$.

3.2 Compactly Storing Polynomials

Motivation. Suppose we want to compactly store a polynomial of degree k represented in an N-dimensional basis such that $0 < k < N$. Storing the N coordinates is suboptimal since it is know that $k + 1$ coordinates are enough to determine a polynomial of degree k uniquely. In the monomial basis, we store only the first $k + 1$ coefficients because the others are zero. To recover the polynomial from storage, we take the $k+1$ coefficients and pad them with zeros until obtaining N coefficients.

Problem. In the Lagrange basis, it is likely that the N values of the polynomial be non-zero. So, is it safe to store the first $k + 1$ values and discard the others (even if they are non-zero)? If this is possible, how to recover the N original values (without switching to the monomial basis, nor re-evaluating the polynomial)?

Solution. As mentioned in Sect. 2.2, extending a polynomial in a Lagrange basis of dimension n to dimension $n + 1$ takes $O(n)$ operations in the general case. To solve the problem described above, we give explicit formulas for basis extension for the special case of the Lagrange basis $\mathcal{L}\mu$.

Let $(y_0, \dots, y_{N-1})$ be the values of a polynomial of degree k, where $0 < k < N$, given the first $k + 1$ values, $(y_0, \dots, y_k)$, the term y_{k+1} is calculated as

$$y_{k+1} = -\frac{1}{W_{(k+1,N-1)}} \sum_{i=0}^{k} y_i W_{(k+1,i)}, \quad \text{where } W_{(m,i)} = 1/\prod_{\substack{j=0 \\ j \neq i}}^{m} ({\omega_N}^i - {\omega_N}^j). \tag{3.2.1}$$

This process takes $O(N)$ field operations, and can be iterated until the N original values are recovered taking $O(N^2)$ field operations in total.

Special Case. We describe the case when $k = N - 2$, i.e., the degree of the polynomial is one below the maximum degree allowed in an N-dimensional basis. In the monomial basis, padding one zero coefficient is enough. In the Lagrange basis $\mathcal{L}\mu$, the value y_{N-1} is calculated with $(N-1)\mathbf{M} + (N-2)\mathbf{A}$ as

$$\begin{aligned} y_{N-1} &= -\frac{1}{W_{(N-1,N-1)}} \sum_{i=0}^{N-2} y_i W_{(N-1,i)} = -\frac{1}{w_{N-1}} \sum_{i=0}^{N-2} y_i w_i \\ &= \sum_{i=0}^{N-2} -\frac{w_i}{w_{N-1}} y_i = \sum_{i=0}^{N-2} -\frac{{\omega_N}^i}{{\omega_N}^{N-1}} y_i \\ &= \sum_{i=0}^{N-2} {\omega_N}^j y_i \,, \text{ where } j = (i + 1 + N/2) \bmod N \,. \end{aligned} \tag{3.2.2}$$

The formulas presented in this section are helpful when extending polynomials just by a few number of dimensions. Increasing the dimension by one requires a linear number of operations, whereas extending to an arbitrarily larger dimension takes $O(N^2)$ operations. Despite this, particular instances of this basis extension are amenable to optimizations, as discussed in the next section.

3.3 Polynomial Multiplication in the Lagrange Basis $\mathcal{L}\mu$

Motivation. Many high-level applications involve polynomial arithmetic, but are often implemented using the monomial basis. For efficiency, switching to alternative polynomial basis results in faster computations. For instance, polynomial multiplication takes, in general, $O(N^2)$ operations (see Fig. 3a), but only $O(N \log N)$ operations over a field where the Nth-roots of unity exist.

NTT is key for achieving such a complexity. Let $\mathbf{NTT}_k$ denote the cost of calculating an NTT over a vector of size $k > 0$, and $\mathbf{iNTT}_k = \mathbf{NTT}_k + k\mathbf{M}$ (recall calculating $1/N$ is cheap). Also, $\mathbf{NTT}_{2k} = 2\,\mathbf{NTT}_k + k\mathbf{M}$ due to the two-way recursive structure of the algorithm.

We describe the classic $O(N \log N)$ algorithm for polynomial multiplication in monomial basis, as shown in Fig. 3b. Starting with $P, Q \in \mathbb{F}[x]_{[N]}$ in basis $\mathcal{M}$, we want to calculate $R = P \times Q \in \mathbb{F}[x]_{[2N-1]}$ also in basis $\mathcal{M}$. First, P and Q must be extended to a basis of dimension $2N$. This step is trivial in $\mathcal{M}$, a reason why basis extension does not receive too much attention. After that, P and Q are changed to basis $\mathcal{L}\mu$ by means of two $\mathbf{NTT}_{2N}$. Then, the values are multiplied taking $2N\mathbf{M}$, and the result is converted back to basis $\mathcal{M}$ taking one $\mathbf{iNTT}_{2N}$. In total, this method takes

$$\begin{aligned} \mathrm{Cost}_{\mathrm{PolyMul}}(\mathcal{M}) &= 2\,\mathbf{NTT}_{2N} + \mathbf{iNTT}_{2N} + 2N\mathbf{M} \\ &= 6\,\mathbf{NTT}_N + 7N\mathbf{M} \,. \end{aligned} \tag{3.3.1}$$

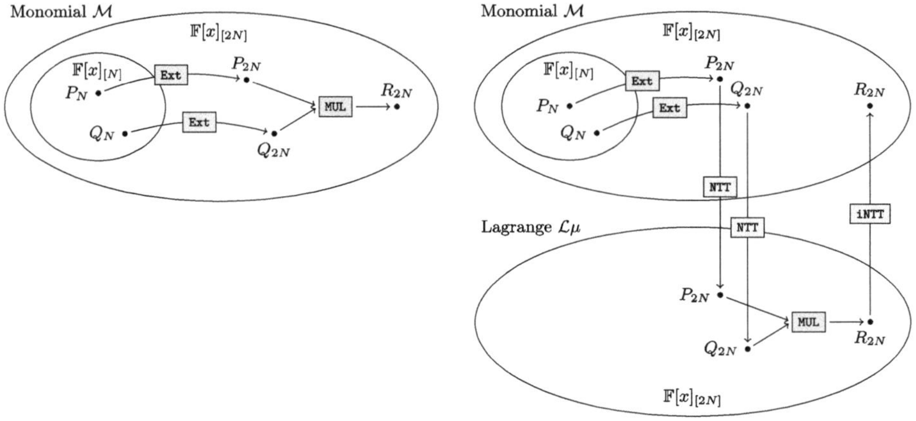

(a) $O(N^2)$ conventional algorithm. (b) $O(N \log N)$ NTT-based algorithm.

Fig. 3. Algorithms for Polynomial Multiplication in the Monomial Basis $\mathcal{M}$.

Because this method is asymptotically faster than the conventional algorithm, it has seen widely adopted in practice.

Problem. Now we turn to the case of the Lagrange basis $\mathcal{L}\mu$. Starting with $P, Q \in \mathbb{F}[x]_{[N]}$ in basis $\mathcal{L}\mu$, we want to calculate $R = P \times Q \in \mathbb{F}[x]_{[2N-1]}$ also in basis $\mathcal{L}\mu$. The first step is to extend the basis of the input polynomials from a basis of dimension N to a basis of dimension $2N$. Unlike in the monomial basis, this basis extension is not trivial since it takes $O(N^2)$ operations in the general case. Once the polynomials are extended, it takes $2N\mathbf{M}$ to multiply their values for obtaining R. The challenge now is to determine efficient methods for this specific basis extension.

Faster Basis Extension from $\mathcal{L}\mu_N$ to $\mathcal{L}\mu_{2N}$. We describe two methods for polynomial multiplication based on two efficient algorithms for basis extension in Lagrange basis $\mathcal{L}\mu_N$.

Strategy 1 (Stolon). As shown in Fig. 4a, convert each polynomial to basis $\mathcal{M}$ of dimension N (taking $2\,\mathbf{iNTT}_N$), and pad with zeros the resultant polynomials to get $2N$ coefficients (basis extension in basis $\mathcal{M}$). Then, convert the extended polynomials back to the Lagrange basis $\mathcal{L}\mu$ (taking $2\,\mathbf{NTT}_{2N}$), and multiply them in $\mathcal{L}\mu_{2N}$ basis (taking $2N\mathbf{M}$). In total, Strategy 1 requires

$$\begin{aligned} \mathrm{Cost}_{\mathrm{PolyMul}}(\mathcal{L}\mu) &= 2\,\mathbf{iNTT}_N + 2\,\mathbf{NTT}_{2N} + 2N\mathbf{M} \\ &= 6\,\mathbf{NTT}_N + 6N\mathbf{M}\,. \end{aligned} \tag{3.3.2}$$

Strategy 2 (Rhizome). We introduce a more efficient polynomial multiplication algorithm based on a faster basis extension. Note that Strategy 1 uses NTTs of size $2N$. In contrast, our method uses only NTTs of size N to generate N new values, capitalizing on the existing N input values.

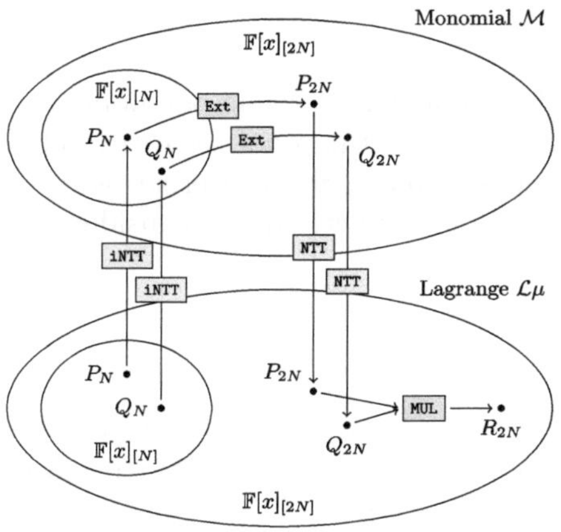

(a) Strategy 1 – Stolon.

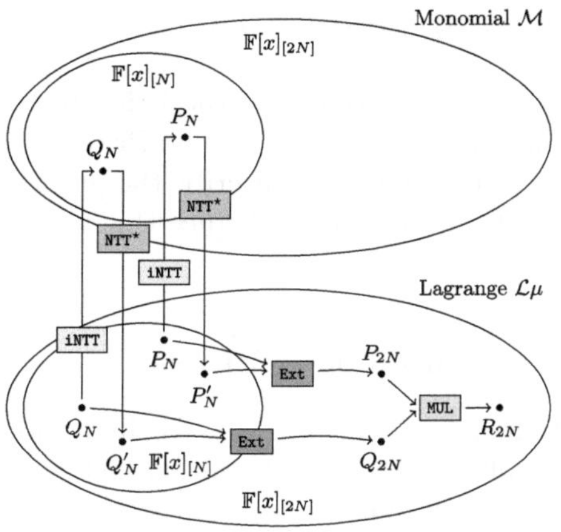

(b) Strategy 2 – Rhizome.

Fig. 4. Strategies for polynomial multiplication in the Lagrange basis $\mathcal{L}\mu$.

We define the NTT* function, a slightly modified version of the NTT, as

$$\texttt{NTT}^{\star}\colon \big(\omega_N, s, (c_0, \dots, c_{N-1})\big) \mapsto \big(P(s{\omega_N}^0), \dots, P(s{\omega_N}^{N-1})\big), \text{ where } s \in \mathbb{F}\,. \tag{3.3.3}$$

The implementation of this function is identically to the NTT in Algorithm 4, except that the Step 3 (marked with ★) is replaced with $w = s$. NTT* runs as fast as NTT. It can be seen that $\texttt{NTT}(\omega_N, \cdot) = \texttt{NTT}^{\star}(\omega_N, 1, \cdot)$.

Given the values $[P]_{\mathcal{L}\mu_N} = (y_0, \dots, y_{N-1})$ on dimension N, we calculate the values $[P]_{\mathcal{L}\mu_{2N}} = (y'_0, \dots, y'_{2N-1})$ on dimension $2N$ as

$$\begin{aligned}(v_0, \dots, v_{N-1}) &= \texttt{NTT}^{\star}(\omega_N, \omega_{2N}, \texttt{iNTT}(\omega_N, (y_0, \dots, y_{N-1})))\\ [P]_{\mathcal{L}\mu_{2N}} &= (y'_0, \dots, y'_{2N-1}) = (y_0, v_0, \dots, y_{N-1}, v_{N-1})\end{aligned} \tag{3.3.4}$$

This basis extension takes $\mathbf{NTT}_N + \mathbf{iNTT}_N$, i.e., it evaluates NTTs of size N.

Polynomial multiplication using Strategy 2, shown in Fig. 4b, is as follows. Extend each input polynomial with the basis extension describe above, and multiply the extended polynomials taking $2N\mathbf{M}$. In total, Strategy 2 requires

$$\begin{aligned}\mathrm{Cost}_{\mathrm{PolyMul}}(\mathcal{L}\mu) &= 2\,(\mathbf{NTT}_N + \mathbf{iNTT}_N) + 2N\mathbf{M}\\ &= 4\,\mathbf{NTT}_N + 4N\mathbf{M}\,.\end{aligned} \tag{3.3.5}$$

In summary, Strategy 2 avoids the calculation of two NTTs of size N in comparison to Strategy 1. This results in polynomial multiplications in Lagrange basis $\mathcal{L}\mu$ being one third faster.

Although the polynomial multiplication algorithms described above share the same $O(N \log N)$ time-complexity, we have demonstrated that their actual efficiency is significantly affected by the choice of basis and the specific inner operations used.

4 Improving Prio

We show key points of the Prio protocol that benefit from using polynomials in the Lagrange basis $\mathcal{L}\mu$. The Prio's core component is the proof used to validate measurements. We describe the proof system used in the (work-in-progress) specification document [6] since this version of Prio is currently under consideration for standardization.

4.1 Fully Linear Proofs

Boneh et al. [11] introduced the notion of fully linear probabilistically-checkable proofs (FLPCP) that allows the verifier to make linear queries to the input statement. This is useful in settings where the input statement (and the proof) is not available to the verifier. Davis et al. [17] showed a provable security treatment of verifiable distributed aggregation functions (VDAF). They showed that with minor changes to a version of Prio (the one described in the draft-v03 [7]), Prio is private and robust if the fully linear proof is sound and honest-verifier zero-knowledge. This FLPCP construction corresponds to the 1.5-round, public coin, fully linear, interactive oracle proof system by Boneh et al. [11].

A FLPCP is proof system for the relation $R_C = \{(x, w) \mid C(x, w) = 0\}$, where x is the input, w is the witness, and C is an arithmetic circuit over $\mathbb{F}$ composed of M instances of a G-gate and any number of affine gates. A G-gate is an L-arity circuit composed of multiplication gates and affine gates.

`FLPCP.Prove` The Prover evaluates C on input (x, w). While doing so, it defines polynomials $f_1, \dots, f_L \in \mathbb{F}[x]$ as follows: $f_i(0)$ is chosen at random, and $f_i(j)$ is the value on the ith input wire to the jth G-gate, for all $1 \le i \le L$, and $1 \le j \le M$. Then, it constructs a polynomial $p = G(f_1, \dots, f_L) \in \mathbb{F}[x]$ such that $p(j)$ is the value on the output wire of the jth G-gate, for all $1 \le j \le M$. By construction, $p(M) = C(x, w)$. Finally, the Prover outputs the proof $\pi = (w, f_1(0), \dots, f_L(0), p)$.

`FLPCP.Query` The Verifier receives $\pi' = (w', z'_1, \dots, z'_L, p')$, such that $z'_i = f'_i(0)$, and uses these values to recover the polynomials $f'_1, \dots, f'_L \in \mathbb{F}[x]$. The goal is to check whether $p' = G(f'_1, \dots, f'_L)$ and $p'(M) = 0$. To do so, the Verifier samples $r \leftarrow_\$ \mathbb{F} \setminus \{1, \dots, M\}$ at random and outputs the verifier message $V = \{p'(r), f'_1(r), \dots, f'_L(r), p'(M)\}$.

`FLPCP.Decision` The decision algorithm takes $V = (a, a_1, \dots, a_L, b)$, such that $a = p'(r)$, $a_1 = f'_1(r), \dots, a_L = f'_L(r)$, and $b = p'(M)$. The Verifier accepts if $a = G(a_1, \dots, a_L)$ and $b = 0$.

The FLPCP construction is useful scenarios where exist k verifiers. The Prover obtains a proof π by running `FLPCP.Prove`, produces secret shares $\pi = \sum_{i=1}^{k} [\pi]_i$, and sends $[\pi]_i$ to the ith verifier. Each verifier runs `FLPCP.Query` on $[\pi]_i$ to get secret shares of the verifier message $[V]_i$. After that, all verifiers publish $[V]_i$ for recovering $V = \sum_{i=1}^{k} [V]_i$, and then invoking the `FLPCP.Decision` algorithm.

4.2 Efficient Proof Generation

To benefit from the asymptotically faster algorithms derived from the Lagrange basis $\mathcal{L}\mu$, the first observation is to evaluate on the polynomials on powers of a root of unity. That is, $f_i(\omega^j)$ for all $1 \leq j \leq M$, where ω is a root of unity in $\mathbb{F}$.

In FLPCP.Prove, the polynomials $f_1, \ldots, f_L$ are represented in the Lagrange basis $\mathcal{L}\mu$ by construction and must remain in this representation. We note that libprio-rs converts every f_i to the monomial basis invoking an iNTT of size $2N$ per polynomial. All these iNTT can be eliminated if the polynomials f_i remain in the Lagrange basis $\mathcal{L}\mu$.

To construct the polynomial p, the Prover requires to calculate a product of polynomials $f_1 \times f_2$ for each multiplication gate. We observe that it is faster to perform polynomial multiplications entirely in the Lagrange basis $\mathcal{L}\mu$ employing Strategy 2, presented in Sect. 3.3. As p is a product of polynomials f_1 and f_2 of degree $N-1$, the degree of p is $2N-2$ and the coefficient of the highest-degree term is always zero.

Once p was generated, the Prover encodes p as part of the proof. Storing a polynomial takes the same amount of space in any basis as long as the dimension remains invariant. We note that the polynomial can be compactly stored in monomial basis: the Prover encodes only the first $2N-1$ coefficients (because the last one is zero), and the Verifier pads with one zero to get p in monomial basis of dimension N. We have shown in Sect. 3.2 that this trick is also applicable when p is in the Lagrange basis $\mathcal{L}\mu$ representation.

4.3 Verification in Linear-Time

Once the changes in FLPCP.Prove have been adopted, now the Verifier receives $\pi' = (w', z'_1, \ldots, z'_L, p')$, where p' is a polynomial in the Lagrange basis $\mathcal{L}\mu$. If the Prover sent only $2N-1$ values of p', the Verifier is able to recover the last value by performing basis extension taking $O(N)$ operations, as we have shown in the special case of Sect. 3.2.

The Verifier recovers the polynomials $f'_1, \ldots, f'_L \in \mathbb{F}[x]$ from $z'_1, \ldots, z'_L$. Along with p these polynomials are, by construction, in the Lagrange basis $\mathcal{L}\mu$. The Verifier samples $r \leftarrow_\$ \mathbb{F}\backslash\{\omega^0, \ldots, \omega^M\}$ at random and evaluates these polynomials at r. Note that no extra security assumptions are necessary on r.

In libprio-rs, the polynomials f_i are changed to the monomial basis and then evaluated. So for each polynomial, it performs one iNTT of size N and one invocation of Horner's algorithm, which takes $O(N \log N)$ operations. This procedure can be improved.

It is faster to evaluate the polynomials directly in the Lagrange basis $\mathcal{L}\mu$ using our proposed Algorithm 6, described in Sect. 3.1. Moreover, note that all the f_i polynomials must be evaluated at the same value r, this enables the use of a batched evaluation by employing Algorithm 7 for greater efficiency. Since both algorithms have $O(N)$ time-complexity, this demonstrates that proof verification runs in linear time and without performing inverses.

5 Performance Benchmarks

We show our algorithms in practice. Looking for existing implementations, the authors of Prio [15] made available a prototype written in Go. Mozilla's implementation [33] is a C language library used for experimentation purposes only, but is not maintained anymore. On the other hand, the libprio-rs [18] is a Rust library actively maintained and is compliant with the VDAF specification document [6]. We forked libprio-rs in https://github.com/armfazh/rhizomes/ applying the recommendations given in Sect. 4. We plan to contribute the changes to the upstream library.

For performance measurements, the library includes a test suite and a set of benchmarks for different aggregation functions. It also supports field arithmetic for 64-bit and 128-bit NTT-friendly prime fields. We use the bigger field, specifically, $\mathbb{F} = \mathrm{GF}(p)$, where $p = 2^{66} \cdot 4611686018427387897 + 1$ is a 128-bit prime. We use the Rust compiler v1.71 and run benchmarks on a Core i7-13800H processor. The measurements reported are obtained using the Criterion.rs library [5], which is a tool for performing statistical measurements of code's execution time.

Several benchmarks for the high-level phases of the Prio protocol are supported in the libprio-rs library. We focus on the most time-consuming phases of the Prio protocol that benefit from our recommendations:

- Sharding. In this phase, a client takes its measurement and creates a proof to be sent to the Verifier. Internally, this phase invokes to `FLPCP.Prove` for generating the proof.
- Prepare-Init. After a server received a secret share of the proof from the client, the server validates the measurement for aggregation. Internally, here is when the `FLPCP.Query` algorithm is executed.

We report execution times of two aggregation functions used in practice, where the time required scales with the input size n (which internally determines the degree of polynomials):

- SumVec sums n-length vectors of integers in the range 0 to 2^b, for some b.
- Histogram estimates the distribution of some measurements. Let n be the number of buckets, each measurement increments the counter of one bucket. The aggregate result is the counter of each bucket.

Table 1 and Table 2 show, respectively, the execution time of the Sharding and Prepare-Init phases as the input size grows. These measurements are plotted in logarithmic scale and are shown in Fig. 5 and Fig. 6.

For the Sharding phase, larger speedup factors are obtained as the input size n grows. From Fig. 5, we can see that the inflection point appears as n approaches to $n = 1000$ in both aggregation functions. The optimizations described in Sect. 4.2 resulted in a 19% to 36% reduction in execution time for both the SumVec and Histogram aggregation functions.

For the Prepare-Init phase, we replaced the interpolate-and-evaluate method in `FLPPC.Query` with a direct polynomial evaluation in the Lagrange basis, as

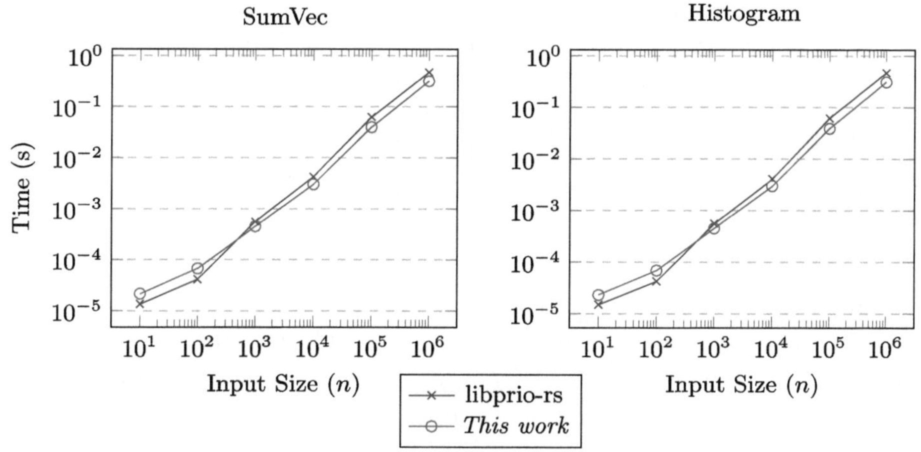

Fig. 5. Execution time (plotted in logarithmic scale) of Prio's Sharding phase.

Table 1. Execution time of Prio's Sharding phase.

Aggregation Function	Code	Input Size (n)					
		10^1	10^2	10^3	10^4	10^5	10^6
SumVec	libprio-rs	13.5 µs	41.0 µs	556.7 µs	4.2 ms	62.3 ms	471.7 ms
	This work	21.5 µs	67.1 µs	449.5 µs	3.0 ms	39.6 ms	316.0 ms
	Speedup	0.62x	0.61x	1.24x	1.37x	1.58x	1.49x
Histogram	libprio-rs	14.9 µs	42.3 µs	554.5 µs	4.1 ms	61.2 ms	465.8 ms
	This work	23.0 µs	68.5 µs	449.9 µs	3.0 ms	38.9 ms	308.1 ms
	Speedup	0.64x	0.61x	1.23x	1.39x	1.57x	1.51x

described in Sect. 4.3. As Table 2 shows, the latency of the Prepare-Init phase achieves significant speedup factors. For $n \geq 1000$, its execution time is now twice as fast. Moreover, the fact that no inverses are calculated brings savings even for small values of n.

These results confirm that Prio clearly benefits from the use of efficient representations for polynomial arithmetic. The speedups achieved are result of removing redundant operations. We show that switching to the monomial basis is unnecessary, it is better to keep polynomials in the Lagrange basis because this enables faster operations. These modifications to Prio positively influence the design of the protocol currently proposed for standardization.

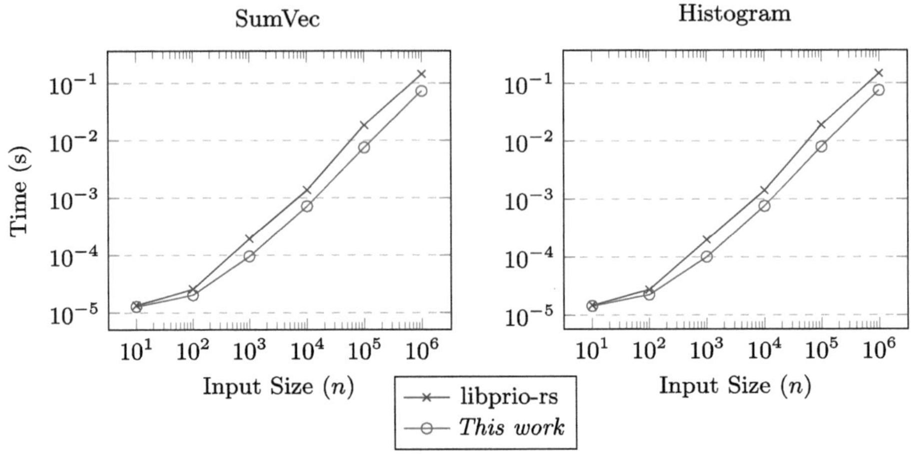

Fig. 6. Execution time (plotted in logarithmic scale) of Prio's Prepare-Init phase.

Table 2. Execution time of Prio's Prepare-Init phase.

Aggregation Function	Code	Input Size (n)					
		10^1	10^2	10^3	10^4	10^5	10^6
SumVec	libprio-rs	13.4 μs	25.6 μs	192.5 μs	1360.8 μs	18.3 ms	143.1 ms
	This work	12.8 μs	20.3 μs	95.5 μs	715.6 μs	7.5 ms	72.3 ms
	Speedup	1.04x	1.26x	2.02x	1.90x	2.44x	1.98x
Histogram	libprio-rs	14.7 μs	27.4 μs	196.2 μs	1395.2 μs	18.7 ms	145.8 ms
	This work	14.4 μs	22.5 μs	100.0 μs	753.4 μs	7.9 ms	74.8 ms
	Speedup	1.02x	1.22x	1.96x	1.85x	2.38x	1.95x

6 Conclusions

Polynomials are useful in many research areas. In cryptographic protocols like Prio, polynomials help to detect invalid client inputs. When dealing with polynomial arithmetic operations, there is a need for methods that are not only asymptotically efficient, but also faster in practice.

Our focus centered on finding optimizations for polynomial arithmetic in the Lagrange basis. Relying on the Pólya basis, we show an $O(n)$ time-complexity algorithm for polynomial evaluation in the Lagrange basis. The proposed algorithm is an inversion-free alternative to the barycentric formula. In addition, we study the case of basis extension showing explicit formulas with applications on compact storage of polynomials and polynomial multiplication.

Prio achieved significant savings in its execution time. This is in part because we make extensive use of the Lagrange basis across the time-consuming operations. With our algorithm for polynomial evaluation, verification runs in linear time without extra security assumptions. Evaluation of our changes demonstrated that Sharding is 36% faster, and Prepare-Init runs in half the time.

A key takeaway for protocol designers is the critical importance of selecting efficient data representations as part of the protocol development. As we demonstrated in this optimization work, effective parametrization is fundamental for achieving high efficiency, which directly impacts on the performance and scalability of the deployed systems.

Acknowledgments. The author appreciates the anonymous reviewers for their feedback. My sincere thanks to Cefan Rubin for reading and providing thoughtful comments on an early draft, and to Christopher Patton for his encouragement to pursue work on fully linear proof systems.

Disclosure of Interests. The author has no conflicts of interests to declare that are relevant to the content of this article.

References

1. Aas, J., Geoghegan, T.: Introducing ISRG Prio services for privacy respecting metrics. Technical report, Internet Security Research Group (2020). https://www.abetterinternet.org/post/introducing-prio-services/
2. Aas, J., Gran, S.: ISRG prio services for preserving privacy in COVID 19 EN apps. Technical report, Internet Security Research Group (2021). https://www.abetterinternet.org/post/prio-services-for-covid-en/
3. Addanki, S., Garbe, K., Jaffe, E., Ostrovsky, R., Polychroniadou, A.: Prio+: privacy preserving aggregate statistics via Boolean shares. In: Galdi, C., Jarecki, S. (eds.) SCN 2022. LNCS, vol. 13409, pp. 516–539. Springer, Cham (2022). https://doi.org/10.1007/978-3-031-14791-3_23
4. Anderson, E., Chase, M., Durak, F.B., Laine, K., Weng, C.: Precio: private aggregate measurement via oblivious shuffling. In: Proceedings of the 2024 on ACM SIGSAC Conference on Computer and Communications Security, CCS 2024, pp. 1819–1833. Association for Computing Machinery, New York (2024). https://doi.org/10.1145/3658644.3670280
5. Aparicio, J., Heisler, B.: Criterion.rs: statistics-driven microbenchmarking in rust (2025). https://github.com/bheisler/criterion.rs. Version 0.7.0
6. Barnes, R., Cook, D., Patton, C., Schoppmann, P.: Verifiable distributed aggregation functions. Internet-Draft draft-irtf-cfrg-vdaf-15, Internet Engineering Task Force (2025). https://datatracker.ietf.org/doc/draft-irtf-cfrg-vdaf/15. Work in Progress
7. Barnes, R., Patton, C., Schoppmann, P.: Verifiable distributed aggregation functions. Internet-Draft draft-irtf-cfrg-vdaf-03, Internet Engineering Task Force (2022). https://datatracker.ietf.org/doc/draft-irtf-cfrg-vdaf/03/. Work in Progress
8. Barry, P.J., Goldman, R.N.: Interpolation and approximation of curves and surfaces using Pólya polynomials. CVGIP: Graph. Models Image Process. **53**(2), 137–148 (1991). https://doi.org/10.1016/1049-9652(91)90057-Q
9. Barry, P.J., Goldman, R.N.: Chapter 2: algorithms for progressive curves: extending B-spline and blossoming techniques to the monomial, power, and newton dual bases. In: Goldman, R.N., Lyche, T. (eds.) Knot Insertion and Deletion Algorithms

for B-Spline Curves and Surfaces, chap. 2, p. 11–63. Other Titles in Applied Mathematics (1992). https://doi.org/10.1137/1.9781611971583.ch2
10. Barry, P.J., Goldman, R.N., DeRose, T.D.: B-splines, Pólya curves, and duality. J. Approx. Theory **65**(1), 3–21 (1991). https://doi.org/10.1016/0021-9045(91)90109-N
11. Boneh, D., Boyle, E., Corrigan-Gibbs, H., Gilboa, N., Ishai, Y.: Zero-knowledge proofs on secret-shared data via fully linear PCPs. In: Boldyreva, A., Micciancio, D. (eds.) CRYPTO 2019. LNCS, vol. 11694, pp. 67–97. Springer, Cham (2019). https://doi.org/10.1007/978-3-030-26954-8_3
12. Burden, R.L., Faires, .D.: Numerical Analysis, 9th edn. Brooks/Cole, Cengage Learning (2010). https://faculty.cengage.com/works/9781305253667
13. Cook, S.A., Aanderaa, S.O.: On the minimum computation time of functions. Trans. Am. Math. Soc. **142**, 291–314 (1969). https://doi.org/10.2307/1995359
14. Cooley, J.W., Tukey, J.W.: An algorithm for the machine calculation of complex Fourier series. Math. Comput. **19**(90), 297–301 (1965). https://doi.org/10.2307/2003354
15. Corrigan-Gibbs, H., Boneh, D.: Prototype implementation of Prio, a system for the private computation of aggregate statistics. https://github.com/henrycg/prio
16. Corrigan-Gibbs, H., Boneh, D.: Prio: private, robust, and scalable computation of aggregate statistics. In: 14th USENIX Symposium on Networked Systems Design and Implementation (NSDI 17), pp. 259–282. USENIX Association, Boston (2017). https://www.usenix.org/conference/nsdi17/technical-sessions/presentation/corrigan-gibbs
17. Davis, H., Patton, C., Rosulek, M., Schoppmann, P.: Verifiable distributed aggregation functions. Proc. Priv. Enhanc. Technol. (PoPETs) **2023**(4), 578–592 (2023). https://doi.org/10.56553/popets-2023-0126
18. Divvi Up: libprio-rs: Implementation of Prio in Rust (2025). https://github.com/divviup/libprio-rs. Version 0.17.0-alpha.0
19. Englehardt, S.: Next steps in privacy-preserving telemetry with Prio. Technical report, Mozilla Security Blog (2019). https://blog.mozilla.org/security/2019/06/06/next-steps-in-privacy-preserving-telemetry-with-prio/
20. Farin, G.: Chapter 2 - Introductory material. In: Farin, G. (ed.) Curves and Surfaces for Computer-Aided Geometric Design, 3rd edn., p. 13–28. Academic Press, Boston (1993). https://doi.org/10.1016/B978-0-12-249052-1.50007-6
21. Fog, A.: Instruction tables: lists of instruction latencies, throughputs and micro-operation breakdowns for Intel, AMD, and VIA CPUs (2025). https://www.agner.org/optimize/instruction_tables.pdf
22. Gander, W.: Change of basis in polynomial interpolation. Numer. Linear Algebra Appl. **12**(8), 769–778 (2005). https://doi.org/10.1002/nla.450
23. Gentleman, W.M., Sande, G.: Fast Fourier transforms: for fun and profit. In: Fall Joint Computer Conference, AFIPS 1966 (Fall), vol. 29, pp. 563–578. Association for Computing Machinery, New York (1966). https://doi.org/10.1145/1464291.1464352
24. Geoghegan, T., Patton, C., Rescorla, E., Wood, C.A.: Standardizing MPC for privacy preserving measurement. In: Real World Crypto Symposium 2022 (2022). https://rwc.iacr.org/2022/
25. Geoghegan, T., Raykova, M., Jacobs, F.: Exposure notifications private analytics. In: Real World Crypto Symposium 2022 (2022). https://rwc.iacr.org/2022/
26. Goldman, R.: Lecture 24: blending functions: an alternative approach to freeform curves and surfaces. Technical report, Rice University (2004). https://www.clear.rice.edu/comp360/lectures/old/BasisFText.pdf

27. Helmer, R., Miyaguchi, A., Rescorla, E.: Testing privacy-preserving telemetry with Prio. Technical report, Mozilla Hacks (2018). https://hacks.mozilla.org/2018/10/testing-privacy-preserving-telemetry-with-prio/
28. Horner, W.G.: A new method of solving numerical equations of all orders, by continuous approximation. Philos. Trans. Roy. Soc. London **109**, 308–335 (1819). https://doi.org/10.1098/rstl.1819.0023
29. IETF Security Area: Privacy Preserving Measurement (Working Group) (2022). https://datatracker.ietf.org/wg/ppm/
30. Ivanov, K.G., Saff, E.B.: Behavior of the lagrange interpolants in the roots of unity. In: Ruscheweyh, S., Saff, E.B., Salinas, L.C., Varga, R.S. (eds.) Computational Methods and Function Theory. LNM, vol. 1435, pp. 81–87. Springer, Heidelberg (1990). https://doi.org/10.1007/BFb0087899
31. Karatsuba, A., Ofman, Y.: Multiplication of multidigit numbers on automata. Sov. Phys. Dokl. **7**(7), 595–596 (1963)
32. Montgomery, P.L.: Speeding the Pollard and elliptic curve methods of factorization. Math. Comput. **48**(177), 243–264 (1987). https://doi.org/10.1090/s0025-5718-1987-0866113-7
33. Mozilla: libprio - A Prio library in C using NSS (2020). https://github.com/mozilla/libprio. Version 1.6
34. OEIS Foundation Inc.: Proth primes, Entry A080076. In: The on-line encyclopedia of integer sequences (2025). https://oeis.org/A080076
35. Patton, C., Galicer, M.: Privacy-preserving measurement and machine learning. Technical report, The Cloudflare Blog (2023). https://blog.cloudflare.com/deep-dive-privacy-preserving-measurement
36. Pollard, J.M.: The fast Fourier transform in a finite field. Math. Comput. **25**(114), 365–374 (1971). https://doi.org/10.1090/S0025-5718-1971-0301966-0
37. Pólya, G., Szegö, G.: Problems and Theorems in Analysis II, Classics in Mathematics, vol. 2, 1st edn. Springer, Heidelberg (1976). https://doi.org/10.1007/978-3-642-61905-2
38. Rutishauser, H.: Lectures on Numerical Mathematics, 1st edn. Birkhäuser, Boston (1990). https://doi.org/10.1007/978-1-4612-3468-5
39. Schwartz, J.T.: Fast probabilistic algorithms for verification of polynomial identities. J. ACM **27**(4), 701–717 (1980). https://doi.org/10.1145/322217.322225
40. Toom, A.L.: The complexity of a scheme of functional elements realizing the multiplication of integers. Dokl. Akad. Nauk SSSR **150**, 496–498 (1963)
41. Warren, J.: An efficient algorithm for evaluating polynomials in the Pólya basis. In: Hagen, H., Farin, G., Noltemeier, H. (eds.) Geometric Modelling. Computing Supplement, vol. 10, pp. 357–361. Springer, Vienna (1995). https://doi.org/10.1007/978-3-7091-7584-2_24
42. Winograd, S.: On the time required to perform multiplication. J. ACM **14**(4), 793–802 (1967). https://doi.org/10.1145/321420.321438
43. Zippel, R.: Probabilistic algorithms for sparse polynomials. In: Ng, E.W. (ed.) Symbolic and Algebraic Computation. LNCS, vol. 72, pp. 216–226. Springer, Heidelberg (1979). https://doi.org/10.1007/3-540-09519-5_73

Runtime Code Generation for Constant-Time Secret-Indexed Array Accesses: Applications to PERK and NTRU

Décio Luiz Gazzoni Filho[1(✉)], Rafael G. Flores e Silva[1], Alessandro Budroni[2], Marco Palumbi[2], and Gora Adj[2]

[1] Department of Electrical Engineering, State University of Londrina, Londrina, Brazil
{dgazzoni,rafael.guilhermefs}@uel.br
[2] Technology Innovation Institute, Abu Dhabi, UAE
{alessandro.budroni,marco.palumbi,gora.adj}@tii.ae

Abstract. One of the main guidelines to prevent timing side-channel attacks against cryptographic implementations is to avoid array accesses indexed by secret data. However, alternatives and countermeasures often incur significant performance losses. We propose a novel methodology for secure, constant-time implementation of algorithms that read and write to small arrays with secret-dependent indices, with a constant-factor performance impact compared to timing-unprotected accesses. It is specifically suitable for simple in-order CPUs like those in embedded systems, e.g., the ARM Cortex-M4 core. Although our methodology is general, we illustrate it with secure implementation of permutation operations, such as composition, inversion, and sampling, the latter using the Fisher-Yates shuffle. We apply this methodology to the post-quantum cryptosystems PERK and NTRU, bridging most of the performance gap to unprotected implementations that employ secret-dependent array accesses.

Keywords: Shuffling · Constant-time implementation · PERK · NTRU · Post-quantum Cryptography

1 Introduction

Side-channel attacks are a class of implementation-level attacks that exploit physical information unintentionally leaked by a computing device during cryptographic operations. Such information includes timing variations, power consumption traces, electromagnetic emissions, or cache access patterns. These leakages can be measured and analyzed to extract secret keys or data, without directly solving the underlying hardness assumption of the scheme implemented.

To prevent such attacks, secure cryptographic implementations must follow strict development guidelines. For example, algorithms should always run in

D. Escudero and I. Damgård (Eds.): LATINCRYPT 2025, LNCS 16129, pp. 450–487, 2026.
https://doi.org/10.1007/978-3-032-06754-8_17

constant time with respect to secret inputs, and when accessing arrays, indices must be independent of secret data. Unfortunately, adhering to these principles often comes at a significant performance cost increase. For instance, some of the fastest implementations of the Advanced Encryption Standard (AES) use pre-computed lookup tables to speed up substitution and mixing operations. However, such implementations typically involve memory accesses indexed by secret key or plaintext bytes, which can leak sensitive information through cache-based side-channel attacks [16]. To mitigate this, constant-time variants replace table lookups with arithmetic or bit-sliced operations that eliminate secret-dependent memory access [4,48]. While these approaches improve security, they come at a notable performance cost, especially on general-purpose CPUs where table lookups are efficient and cache access is fast. This trade-off illustrates the broader challenge of balancing side-channel resistance with computational efficiency in cryptographic implementations. Another relevant example is the Fisher–Yates shuffle [28], a standard algorithm for sampling permutations and fixed Hamming-weight vectors uniformly at random. Its time complexity is $O(n)$ in its basic form. However, when modified to avoid secret-dependent memory accesses for side-channel resistance, its complexity increases to $O(n^2)$ [21,49]. Other alternatives to perform such operations involve constant-time sorting algorithms based on sorting networks [17,18], which exhibit a time complexity of $O(n \log^2 n)$, and an $O(n)$ constant-time algorithm specific to fixed weight sampling [27].

Our Contribution. This work presents a novel approach specifically designed to eliminate secret-dependent memory accesses. The core idea is to leverage the CPU's register file as temporary storage for arrays. Unlike memory, registers are not subject to caching effects[1] and thus do not leak information through access patterns based on secret indices. While registers cannot be indexed dynamically in machine code—since register operands are hardcoded in instruction encodings—we overcome this limitation by generating code at runtime that encodes the desired register accesses directly into the instruction stream. This enables the secure implementation of algorithms such as the Fisher-Yates shuffle without secret-dependent memory operations. We demonstrate that our approach outperforms constant-time algorithms for permutation and fixed-Hamming weight vector sampling based on sorting, already accounting for the cost of both code generation and execution of the generated code. For instance, our method achieves a 5× speed-up for permuting vectors and an 8× speed-up for inverting permutations, compared to constant-time sorting-based techniques. Furthermore, we evaluate the overall impact of our technique within the post-quantum schemes PERK [1] and NTRU [22] on an embedded platform based on the ARM Cortex-M4 core, observing overall consistent performance improvements.

[1] While registers may be written back to memory during e.g. context switches or interrupts – and thus pass through the cache memory subsystem – such accesses are performed in a data-independent fashion and, to the best of our knowledge, do not introduce new avenues for timing side-channel attacks.

Related Work. The problem of protecting cryptographic implementations on cache-enabled architectures from timing attacks has been extensively studied in the context of AES. One early and influential mitigation is the use of vector permute instructions, introduced by Hamburg [29]. Another widely adopted technique is *bitslicing*, originally proposed by Biham for DES [20], and later adapted to AES in several implementations [33,37,40,41,48]. More recently, Adomnicai and Peyrin presented an efficient bitsliced AES implementation tailored for embedded platforms [4].

In the context of sampling fixed-Hamming weight vectors and permutations, Bernstein et al. [18] proposed the use of constant-time sorting networks as a general countermeasure. Alternative algorithms for sampling fixed-Hamming weight vectors were proposed by Sendrier [49] and by Gazzoni Filho et al. [27]; the former, while asymptotically slower, achieves acceptable performance in the sparse vector setting, whereas the latter exploits the fact that the vector has a small, fixed set of entries to obtain a constant-time $O(n)$ variant of the Fisher-Yates shuffle. A comprehensive systematization of algorithms for sampling random permutations was recently made by Budroni et al. [21].

Artifacts. The source code used to run the experiments in this paper is published under an open-source license.[2,3]

Organization. We give in Sect. 2 the necessary notation and background notions. In Sect. 3 we introduce our approach for runtime code generation for constant time array accesses indexed by secret data. We display secure algorithms for permutation operations, and how they apply to the PERK and NTRU schemes, in Sect. 4. We collect and analyze performance results for these schemes in Sect. 5. Finally, we give our conclusions and future directions in Sect. 6.

2 Preliminaries

Notation. We denote the set of natural, integer and real numbers as $\mathbb{N}, \mathbb{Z}$ and $\mathbb{R}$, respectively. We use calligraphic capital letters (e.g., $\mathcal{A}$) to denote sets. The notation $U(\mathcal{A})$ denotes the uniform distribution over a finite set $\mathcal{A}$. The notation $r \leftarrow U(\mathcal{A})$ indicates that the element r has been sampled uniformly at random from the set $\mathcal{A}$. The notation $|\cdot|$ is used to indicate either the cardinality of a set (e.g., $|\mathcal{A}|$) or the absolute value of a real number (e.g., $|a|$, for $a \in \mathbb{R}$). We denote with $[m, n]$ the set $\{m, m+1, \ldots, n-1\}$, for integers $m \leq n$, and $[n] = [0, n] = \{0, 1, \ldots, n-1\}$.

2.1 Timing Side-Channel Attacks

Timing side-channel attacks leverage variations in execution time that depend on secret data to recover sensitive information. This concept was introduced in

[2] https://github.com/Crypto-TII/arm-shuffling-codegen.
[3] https://github.com/Crypto-TII/arm-shuffling-codegen-pqm4.

the seminal work of Kocher [36] in 1996, demonstrating that cryptosystems like Diffie-Hellman and RSA could leak secrets through variations in the execution time of certain modular exponentiation algorithms; it was first demonstrated in practice by Dhem et al. [25] by successfully extracting the private key from a smart card implementation of the RSA cryptosystem.

Tsunoo et al. [50,51] observed that cache memory, present in many modern CPUs, could give rise to variable timings for table lookups. This was published soon after the standardization of the AES block cipher [5], which heavily relied on table lookups, with indices correlated with the plaintext or secret key, for efficient software implementation in CPUs of the time. Bernstein [16] demonstrated how to mount a cache timing attack on AES, assuming that a remote attacker is able to trigger AES operations and precisely measure their execution timings. The attacker can recover key-dependent information by correlating timing variations with known plaintext inputs. This cemented the understanding that secret-dependent array accesses are potentially a devastating vulnerability in cryptographic implementations.

Cache attacks were only the beginning, as many other attacks targeted michoarchitectural leaks in modern, large (PC- or mobile-class) CPUs; a few examples are Spectre [35], Meltdown [39] and Hertzbleed [52]. It is now widely recognized that cryptosystems must be carefully implemented on such CPUs to avoid these attacks. However, CPU cores found in embedded systems, e.g. those based on the ARM M-profile architecture, employ much simpler microarchitectures, and the literature on timing side-channel attacks targeting embedded systems is not as rich. However, as embedded microarchitectures evolve, it seems inevitable that they may be subject to microarchitectural leakage attacks, whether previously-known types or new attacks that exploit particularities of embedded systems.

For instance, cache memories were historically less prevalent in embedded systems. However, the increasing clock speed of embedded cores, coupled with physical limitations on the access times of Flash memory (currently the most prominent memory technology for non-volatile storage), led to the introduction of Flash memory caches, e.g., the ART Accelerator found in ST Microelectronics parts [42, Section 3.3.4]. Thus, tables stored in more plentiful non-volatile storage become vulnerable to cache timing attacks. On the other hand, static RAM (SRAM), used for volatile memory, can keep up with core clock speed increases and is usually uncached[4]. Even so, other mechanisms are conjectured to induce timing variabilities in SRAM accesses (see [15, p. 14] and [45, p. 8]); recently, side-channel attacks have been demonstrated on ARM M-profile CPUs by exploiting a vulnerability of this kind, i.e., timing differences in the memory bus arbitration logic [46]. In response to this attack, ARM issued guidance [13] reinforcing the need to ensure that "control flow and memory access patterns created by the program do not depend on a secret state".

[4] However, Matthias Kannwischer (personal communication) reports that, on a Cortex-M85 part (Renesas RA8M1), enabling RAM data cache results in noticeable performance improvements.

Threat model. The goal of our proposed technique is to protect implementations against timing side-channel attacks. To that end, we seek to eliminate any execution time variations that are correlated with secret data; this is usually referred to, somewhat imprecisely, in the implementation literature as *constant-time execution*, a terminology which we employ regardless, given its prevalence. In particular, our technique is concerned with avoiding timing variations due to array accesses indexed by secret data, which can be eliminated from implementations (through our proposed technique or other countermeasures) by replacing such accesses with other kinds of operations that are widely assumed to be constant-time. For instance, Pornin [44, Section "Generic Tools/Execution Model"] claims that "(m)ost elementary operations (opcodes in the machine language) are constant-time", and proceeds to list potentially non-constant-time operations: memory accesses (indexed by secret data), conditional jumps, integer divisions, shifts and rotations (with secret shift/rotation amounts) and multiplications. This mirrors the prevailing view of the cryptographic implementation community. When arguing that some of our implementations are constant-time, we only discuss issues related to such potentially non-constant-time operations.

2.2 Permutations

Let n be a positive integer. The set of all bijections $[n] \rightarrow [n]$ is denoted by $\mathcal{S}_n$ and is referred to as the *symmetric group of order* n. We call a permutation an element π of $\mathcal{S}_n$ and represent it as

$$\pi = \begin{pmatrix} 0 & 1 & \dots & n-1 \\ \pi(0) & \pi(1) & \dots & \pi(n-1) \end{pmatrix} =: (\pi(0), \pi(1), \dots, \pi(n-1)),$$

meaning that π acts on the elements of $[n]$ by sending i to $\pi(i) = j \in [n]$, for some $0 \le j < n$. $\mathcal{S}_n$, paired with the composition operation $\circ$, forms a group. The identity element is the identity permutation $id = (0, 1, \dots, n-1) \in \mathcal{S}_n$ and $|\mathcal{S}_n| = n!$. Also, we denote with π^{-1} the inverse π, i.e., $\pi \circ \pi^{-1} = id$. As in PERK [1], we adopt the convention that the resulting vector o of applying π to a size-n vector v is computed as $o[i] = v[\pi^{-1}(i)]$ for $i \in [n]$.

In cryptography, it is often required to sample random permutations from the set $\mathcal{S}_n$. Generally, there are two main strategies used in practice: *Fisher-Yates shuffle* and *sorting*. We give below a brief review of these two approaches. For more details, we refer the reader to [21].

Fisher-Yates Shuffle. To sample a permutation uniformly at random from the symmetric group $\mathcal{S}_n$, one can sequentially select elements from the set $[n]$ without replacement and record them in the order selected. Sampling without replacement is computationally non-trivial, but can be efficiently achieved using the Fisher–Yates shuffle algorithm [28], which we report in its modern version due to Durstenfeld [26] in Algorithm 1.

Assuming that the *swap* operation has complexity $O(1)$, the Fisher–Yates shuffle has both time and memory complexity $O(n)$, making it the most efficient known algorithm for uniform random sampling of permutations. However,

Algorithm 1. Fisher-Yates shuffle.

Input: A positive integer n
Output: A random permutation $\pi \in \mathcal{S}_n$
Initialize $\pi = (0, 1, \ldots, n-1)$
for $i = n$ **down to** 1 **do**
  $j \leftarrow U([i])$
  $swap(\pi(i), \pi(j))$
return π

when used in a cryptographic context, it presents a critical flaw: if the permutation must remain secret, the sampling routine must be resistant to side-channel attacks. The *swap* operation performs memory accesses that depend on secret indices of the permutation, which, as exposed in Sect. 2.1, is a practice generally discouraged in secure cryptographic implementations. To mitigate this issue, side-channel-resistant variants of the Fisher–Yates shuffle have been proposed [21,49], albeit with increased time complexity of $O(n^2)$ when sampling a full size-n permutation.

Sorting. Another approach used in cryptography to sample permutations is based on sorting algorithms. Consider the following list of pairs

$$((x_0, 0)\ (x_1, 1) \cdots (x_{n-1}, n-1)), \qquad \text{for} \quad x_0, \ldots, x_{n-1} \leftarrow U([M]),$$

for an integer $M \geq n$. If we sort this list with respect to the x_i values on the left-hand side of each entry, the values on the right-hand side would get *permuted.* This routine allows to sample a random permutation, reported in Algorithm 2, whose time complexity depends on the sorting subroutine. One important consideration to make here is that there must not be any repetition in the list of integers x_i to sort in order to avoid the introduction of any bias.

In cryptography, the main sorting algorithm used [17,18] is based on sorting networks, with a time complexity of $O(n \log^2 n)$ [34, Sec. 5.3.4]; it is employed in post-quantum schemes such as McEliece [6], NTRU [22], and PERK [1].

Permutation Composition and Inversion. Besides sampling, it is often required to implement additional operations on permutations, such as inversion, composition and application to a vector. The naïve algorithms for these operations are as follows.

- **Composition.** Let $\pi_1, \pi_2 \in \mathcal{S}_n$. One computes the composition $\tau := \pi_1 \circ \pi_2$ by setting $\tau(i) = \pi_1(\pi_2(i))$, for $i \in [n]$.
- **Inversion.** Let $\pi \in \mathcal{S}_n$. One computes its inverse π^{-1} by setting $\pi^{-1}(\pi(i)) = i$, for $i \in [n]$.
- **Application to a vector.** Let $\boldsymbol{v} \in \mathbb{F}^n$ be a vector with coefficients in a field $\mathbb{F}$, and $\pi \in \mathcal{S}_n$ be a permutation. One computes $\boldsymbol{w} \in \mathbb{F}^n$, the permutation of $\boldsymbol{v}$ by π, by setting $\boldsymbol{w}(i) = \boldsymbol{v}(\pi^{-1}(i))$.

Algorithm 2. Sorting-based random permutation sampling.

Input: Positive integers n, M such that $n \leq M$, a sorting algorithm $sort(\cdot)$
Output: A random permutation $\pi \in \mathcal{S}_n$

Initialize a list ℓ of length n
repeat
  for $i = 0$ to $n - 1$ **do**
    $x \leftarrow U([M])$
    $\ell(i) = (x, i)$
  $\ell' = sort(\ell)$ `# according to the left-hand side entries`
  Extract the lists τ, π from ℓ' such that $\ell'(i) = (\tau(i), \pi(i))$, $0 \leq i \leq n - 1$
until There are no repetitions in τ
return π

Similar to Fisher–Yates, the above algorithms have a time complexity of $O(n)$ but present the same problem of secret-dependent memory accesses when the permutations are private. Constant-time alternatives for these algorithms, either using sorting or a similar approach as Sendrier's variant of the Fisher–Yates shuffle, have been studied and compared in [21, Appendix A] and present an increase in the time complexity.

2.3 Runtime Code Generation

The first digital computers, arising during or shortly after World War II, used mechanisms such as plugboards for programming; thus, reprogramming them is laborious and time-consuming. Shortly afterwards, computers almost universally adopted the *stored program* concept, in which the computer's instructions are stored in memory, just as its data. This implies that a computer program itself may manipulate instructions, a fact widely exploited by development tools such as compilers, assemblers, linkers, etc. Originally, such tools performed code generation *ahead of time*, at compilation or link time, but as processing power increased, *interpreted code* became popular for non-performance-critical applications. In programming environments such as Sun Microsystems' Java and Microsoft's .NET runtimes, source code is compiled to bytecode which runs in a virtual machine, allowing for portable binaries across different architectures. To bridge the performance gap between interpreted and compiled code, the Just-In-Time (JIT) paradigm was adopted; rather than executing code in an interpreter loop, with recurring performance penalties, JIT environments pay a one-time cost to translate bytecode into machine code[5], achieving performance characteristics that are closer to compiled code, and can benefit from optimizations specific to the CPU running the code. Currently, JIT compilers are also widely employed for the Javascript programming language that powers the client side and, increasingly, the server side as well of the World Wide Web. This shows that the core idea behind this paper, of *runtime code generation*, has a rich history.

[5] Some environments perform another translation pass if a given block is identified as a hotspot, meriting extra optimization; this can still be viewed as a bounded cost.

Decades ago, when computers were much less powerful, but there was interest in computationally intensive applications such as graphical interfaces and video games, code generation and the related concept of *self-modifying code* (essentially, meshing the code generation and the execution of the generated function in a single pass) were fairly popular. Examples of its use in computer graphics were the runtime generation of specific operations in the fundamental *bit block transfer* or bit-blit operation, which applies bitwise operations to the frame buffer, loosely analogous to using bitslicing in cryptography. Graphics libraries for Microsoft Windows[6] and the Blit experimental bitmap terminal [43] achieved the required performance through on-the-fly code generation: given the desired bitwise operation to apply, they synthesized and then ran code to apply the specific operation to the selected area of the display.

A final example, which is quite close in spirit to our proposed technique, was the `int86` function provided by libraries of Intel PC development tools in the DOS era[7]. This function executes the Intel software interrupt instruction `INT`, which has an 8-bit parameter, the interrupt number. However, `int86` receives the interrupt number as an argument to the function call, i.e., it is a runtime, not compile-time, value. This would be easily implemented if the instruction could read the interrupt number from a register, but this is not the case [47, p. 281]: it is encoded as an 8-bit immediate field of the instruction[8]. To implement `int86`, a jump table (i.e., a `switch/case` statement) with all possible 256 interrupt numbers could be used, but this would take up a fairly large amount of memory for PCs of that period. An alternative that reduces code size is the use of self-modifying code [47, p 281], by patching into the encoding of the `INT` instruction to use the desired interrupt number, and then running the instruction.

2.4 The ARMv7-M Architecture

In this section, we recall some details of the ARMv7-M architecture used by our target platform (the ARM Cortex-M4 core) and describe the main instructions used by our implementation.

The original ARM architecture is a 32-bit RISC load-store architecture. Its integer register file is 16 entries long, numbered from `R0` through `R15`. Of these, `R13` (`SP`, the stack pointer) and `R15` (`PC`, the program counter) are special-purpose and must not be directly used. Although `R14` is also reserved for use as the link register (`LR`), in practice, it can be repurposed by the programmer, so long as a copy is stored in the stack. ARM's original instruction encoding uses 32-bit words only, although an option was later introduced for a 16-bit encoding called Thumb, with a limited choice of instructions and accessible registers.

The seventh version of the architecture, released in 2003, was branched into three *profiles*: A (Application), R (Real-Time), and M (Microcontroller). The

[6] https://devblogs.microsoft.com/oldnewthing/20180209-00/?p=97995.

[7] See e.g., the Borland Turbo C manual: https://www.itlnet.net/programming/program/Reference/tc/ng2fc48.html.

[8] https://www.felixcloutier.com/x86/intn:into:int3:int1.

former is found in mobile phones, tablets, and laptops (and was extended to 64 bits with the release of the eighth version in 2011), but our focus in this work is on the M-profile, as implemented by various ARM Cortex-M cores. This architecture is known as ARMv7-M.

In particular, we are interested in the Cortex-M4 core [10], which conforms to ARMv7-EM, the 'E' indicating support for additional instructions referred to by ARM as "DSP extensions". The Cortex-M4 optionally supports single-precision floating-point (FP) acceleration in hardware, in the form of additional instructions, and crucially, a dedicated FP register file with 32 entries, numbered from `S0` through `S31`; the core may be denoted Cortex-M4F in this case. Although our technique does not perform any FP arithmetic, we do use the FP registers as additional storage for arrays[9], and as such employ instructions to move data among memory, FP and integer registers. In practice, most commercially available Cortex-M4 parts include floating-point hardware.

Due to its application in the cost-sensitive embedded space and thus limited available memory, ARMv7-M employs the Thumb-2 instruction set, with a very similar programming model and choice of instructions; its main differentiating factor is the availability of both 16- and 32-bit instruction encodings, to improve code density. However, it is not a variable-length instruction set in the general sense, such as Intel's x86, since only 16- and 32-bit encodings exist. Most instructions used in our technique, as demonstrated in this paper, only admit of 32-bit encodings, so for simplicity we declare arrays for generated code to have only 32-bit elements[10].

Our implementations generate code for complete function calls rather than inserting instruction snippets in the middle of existing code. As such, the generated code must adhere to the ARM Architecture Procedure Call Standard (AAPCS32)[11]. We highlight the main points of interest for our implementations:

- If a function has at most 4 arguments, all of which are integers of width 32 bits or less or pointers, then such arguments are passed in the same order as found in the function prototype, through registers `R0`, `R1`, `R2` and `R3`;
- Integer or pointer return values are stored in `R0`;
- The callee-saved integer registers are `R4` through `R12`, and similarly for floating-point registers `S16` through `S31`.

Review of ARMv7-M Instructions. In Sects. 3 and 4, we give many examples of algorithms employing our proposed technique (Algorithms 3 to 10). We thus review the operations performed by the instructions that we use in these

[9] This technique has been previously used, e.g., in [2,3,7–9,23,24,30] and others.

[10] Most instructions that can be encoded in 16 bits also have alternate 32-bit encodings, an important exception being the `BX` (branch and exchange) instruction, which is generally the last instruction in a code sequence; we pair it with a 16-bit `NOP` instruction, which does not actually execute as it follows the `BX` instruction.

[11] https://github.com/ARM-software/abi-aa/blob/main/aapcs32/aapcs32.rst.

algorithms, so that the reader unfamiliar with the ARMv7-M architecture may follow them. They are briefly described in Table 1; the relevant section in [12] is indicated, if a full description of a given instruction is sought.

Table 1. ARMv7-M instructions used in Algorithms 3 to 10.

Instruction	Section of [12]	Description
`BFI Rd, Rn, #l, #w`	A.7.7.14	`Rd`$[l+w-1:l] \leftarrow$ `Rn`$[w-1:0]$
`BX Rm`	A7.7.20	Unconditional branch to address in `Rm`; to return from a function call, usually `Rm` = `LR`.
`LDMIA Rn, {regs}`	A7.7.41	Load 32-bit words from memory, starting at address `Rn`, to integer registers in `{regs}`
`MOV Rd, Rm`	A7.7.77	`Rd` $\leftarrow$ `Rn`
`MOVW Rd, #i16`	A7.7.76	`Rd` $\leftarrow$ `i16`
`NOP`	A7.7.88	No-operation
`POP {regs}`	A7.7.99	Pop integer registers in `{regs}` from the stack
`PUSH {regs}`	A7.7.101	Push integer registers in `{regs}` to the stack
`STMIA Rn, {regs}`	A7.7.159	Store integer registers in `{regs}` to 32-bit words in memory, starting at address `Rn`
`STRB Rt, [Rn, Rm]`	A7.7.164	Stores the least significant byte of `Rt` to a byte at the memory address `Rn` + `Rm`
`UBFX Rd, Rn, #l, #w`	A7.7.193	`Rd`$[w-1:0] \leftarrow$ `Rn`$[l+w-1:l]$
`VLDMIA Rn, {regs}`	A7.7.235	Load 32-bit words from memory, starting at address `Rn`, to FP registers in `{regs}`
`VMOV Sn, Rt`	A7.7.243	`Sn` $\leftarrow$ `Rt` (bit-by-bit copy)
`VMOV Rt, Sn`	A7.7.243	`Rt` $\leftarrow$ `Sn` (bit-by-bit copy)
`VPOP {regs}`	A7.7.251	Pop the list of FP registers from the stack
`VPUSH {regs}`	A7.7.252	Push the list of FP registers to the stack
`VSTMIA Rn, {regs}`	A7.7.258	Store FP registers in `{regs}` to 32-bit words in memory, starting at address `Rn`

We briefly review the syntax of instructions displayed in the table. The first field corresponds to the instruction mnemonic. Fields starting with the letter `R` are integer registers, and the first such field after the instruction mnemonic is usually the destination register (most of the time, denoted by `Rd`), if there is one. Other (usually source) integer registers are referred to as `Rm`, `Rn`, and `Rt`. Floating-point registers start with the letter `S`, rather than `R`. Immediate fields, directly encoded into instructions, are preceded by the `#` character.

Some instructions (load/store multiple, push and pop) take a list of registers as an argument between braces, denoted in Table 1 as `{regs}`; usually, integer registers are encoded as bitfields in the instruction and thus may include an arbitrary set of such registers, whereas corresponding floating-point instructions encode only the first and last register indices of the range, and thus must be consecutive. In our algorithms, only consecutive ranges were used, which we compactly represent using the same notation as ARM assembly language, e.g., `{R0-R12}` represents the list of integer registers `R0`, `R1`, ..., `R12`.

We adopt a pseudocode notation to simplify the description of some instructions in Table 1. Additionally, "slices" of bit registers are represented by $[b_h : b_l]$, to indicate that only bits $b_h, b_{h-1}, \ldots, b_{l+1}, b_l$ (numbered from most to least significant) are to be read or written.

Lastly, note that floating-point data movement instructions (between registers, either integer or floating-point, and/or memory) are done in a bit-by-bit fashion, oblivious to issues of representation as IEEE-754 floating-point numbers; therefore, no operations such as floating-point normalization are performed which might change the bit representation of operands.

3 Runtime Code Generation for Secure Array Accesses

As discussed in Sect. 2.1, array accesses indexed by secret data are vulnerable to cache timing attacks, which have been demonstrated in practice on larger out-of-order CPUs such as those found in PCs, laptops, servers, mobile phones, and tablets. Embedded systems are equally vulnerable in some cases, such as lookups from constant tables stored in cached Flash memory, and possibly even for RAM accesses.

One level of the memory hierarchy in computer systems that has been overlooked in previous works is the CPU register file(s). Registers almost always have zero-latency access times (i.e., their access time is included in instruction execution). As a corollary, access time is independent of which exact register is accessed by a given instruction. Our work investigates whether this property can be exploited to obtain constant-time array accesses indexed by secret data.

This idea may not have been considered previously due to the roadblocks of accessing CPU registers in an indexed manner. Recall from Sect. 2.4 that register indices are hardcoded into the instruction encoding in the ARMv7-M architecture, which is typical of most CPU architectures. A notable exception is SIMD extensions found in larger CPUs, some of which provide vector permutation instructions such as Intel x86-64's `PSHUFB` and ARM A-profile `TBL`, which may be repurposed to perform array lookups, a fact which Hamburg exploited to accelerate the AES block cipher [29]. However, such instructions are not available in embedded CPUs, even in ARM's recently introduced Helium M-profile Vector Extensions (MVE) found in cores such as the Cortex-M55 and Cortex-M85; moreover, while Hamburg's technique addresses the issue of *reading* from arrays, to the best of our knowledge no corresponding techniques for *writing* to arrays have been proposed, which is required in many algorithms such as those for permutation operations, displayed in Sect. 2.2.

Our Proposed Approach. We propose a new approach to utilize the CPU register file(s) to perform constant-time reads and writes to arrays with secret indices. Since indices are hardcoded in the instruction encoding, we overcome the apparent impossibility of indexing the register file by *generating code at runtime* to perform such array accesses; i.e., secret data is directly encoded into instructions as register indices. We split the implementation of algorithms requiring protected array accesses into two passes: in the first, we run a code generator which writes executable (machine) code to RAM implementing the desired algorithm, and in the second, we execute the generated code. The key observation is that, as the first pass executes at runtime, it has access to secret indices used for arrays and can encode them directly into the generated instructions.

To ensure that the implementation is not vulnerable to timing attacks, both the code generator and the generated code must avoid any timing variations correlated with secret data; to this end, many standard techniques to write constant-time code can be employed. Indeed, we show various algorithms, in the remainder of this section and in Sect. 4, that perform meaningful operations while eschewing any secret-dependent timing variations.

Limitations. Our technique comes with certain limitations and potential issues; we encourage further research to assess their severity and develop possible workarounds.

The available storage space in the CPU register file(s) is fairly limited, on the order of hundreds to few thousands of bits, which restricts the applications of this technique; nevertheless, we demonstrate its applicability to relevant post-quantum cryptosystems in the resource-constrained ARMv7-M architecture, such as all variants of PERK with NIST security levels I and III, as well as NTRU HPS2048509 (NIST security level I).

Larger out-of-order CPUs may struggle with the JIT paradigm, mainly due to the need to shuffle data between level 1 data and instruction caches for code generation and execution, respectively, since these caches are rarely coherent; executing generated code requires a cache invalidation procedure, which may be costly. For other uses of JIT such as in Java, Javascript and .NET runtimes, this is usually not an issue, as code is often generated once and run multiple times, amortizing the cost of cache invalidation. However, our technique is very specific to the array values and indices used, and as such the generated code is run only once. Although we have not investigated this issue in depth for larger CPUs, we theorize that such an issue may be overcome when batch code generation is applicable: first generate code for multiple applications of an algorithm, and later run them. This is the case for the PERK digital signature scheme, which applies many permutation operations in parallel.

Other issues arise from the software side, as out-of-order CPUs usually run full-fledged OSes such as Windows, Linux, macOS, Android, iOS, etc. Due to evolving security threats, recent OS versions restrict code execution outside of "sanctioned" use cases; however, the popularity of JIT runtimes dictates that this should still be possible, and without incurring excessive overhead[12].

---

[12] For instance, Apple discusses a workflow to enable JIT compilation in macOS at https://developer.apple.com/documentation/apple-silicon/porting-just-in-time-compilers-to-apple-silicon.

A potential issue with out-of-order CPUs, and possibly in-order but superscalar ones, is that of microarchitectural side-channels that are specific to the code generation paradigm. In such CPUs, there is control logic to recognize dependencies between instructions, in order to determine whether a pair of instructions can be scheduled to execute in parallel. This control logic looks at the destination and source registers of instructions[13], to detect so-called *data hazards* that prevent parallel execution: Read-After-Write (RAW) or *true dependencies*; Write-After-Read (WAR) or *anti-dependencies*; and Write-After-Write (WAW) or *output dependencies.* These refer to the temporal ordering of register reads and writes between earlier and later instructions in the instruction stream.

As our proposed approach recasts secret-indexed array accesses as instructions operating on secret-indexed registers, varying dependency graphs (and hence potential data hazards) are induced by secret data, which may in turn induce timing variations. WAR and WAW hazards may be resolved by the out-of-order machinery through register renaming, although conceptually timing differences may arise in case the virtual register file is oversubscribed; in our opinion, this is a mostly theoretical concern that should be impossible or nearly impossible to exploit in practice. A more serious concern arises from RAW hazards: two copies of the same instruction sequence, but using different register operands, may execute in a different number of cycles. If there is no dependency between these registers, the instruction may execute at the fastest possible rate, whereas dependencies introduce pipeline stalls. Note that such timing variations are not a concern in conventional code (i.e., not generated at runtime): register operands are fixed at compile- or assembly-time, independently of secret data, which results in an equally fixed pattern of pipeline stalls (or lack of them). We note that we have not implemented our technique in out-of-order CPUs, and thus do not have experimental confirmation of this issue; even if confirmed, it is unclear whether it can be exploited to mount a successful side-channel attack.

We stress that the above discussion only applies to more complex CPUs. We have performed extensive experiments in the Cortex-M4, and have been unable to reproduce any instances of timing variations in generated code based on our approach. We credit this to the in-order, single-issue nature of the Cortex-M4, with all instructions of interest (i.e., those which we use to operate on secret data) executing in a single cycle; as such, hazards between them cannot possibly occur, as we have confirmed in practice.

Building Blocks. In the remainder of this section, we illustrate how to employ our proposed methodology to perform constant-time array accesses (reads and writes) with secret indices. We denote the array length by n, and while we display algorithms for fixed n for simplicity, the algorithms are easily adapted to handle differently-sized arrays; indeed, our implementations of Sect. 4 take n as a runtime parameter of the code generation functions.

[13] For instructions that interact with the memory subsystem, addresses may also be inspected, but this case is not relevant for the present discussion.

3.1 Accessing 32-Bit Arrays

The simplest possible case consists of an array of elements matching the word size of the target CPU (in the case of the Cortex-M4, 32 bits), and small enough to fit in the integer register file of the CPU. We consider the case of an array of $n = 8$ elements for simplicity of the code, although in practice, slightly larger arrays still fit on integer registers.

For this scenario, after loading the array into the register file, the core instruction to be synthesized is a `MOV`, where its source register depends on the desired index. We use the 32-bit T3 encoding of the integer register-to-register `MOV` instruction [12, Section A7.7.77], which is displayed in Fig. 1. For this initial example, we display in Listing 1.1 C implementations that generate code for a function that performs the desired operation, and call it afterwards.

15	14	13	12	11	10	9	8	7	6	5	4	3	2	1	0	15	14	13	12	11	10	9	8	7	6	5	4	3	2	1	0
1	1	1	0	1	0	1	0	0	1	0	S	1	1	1	1	0	0	0	0	Rd				0	0	0	0	Rm			

Fig. 1. `MOV` instruction between integer registers. Adapted from [12, Section A7.7.77, encoding T3].

A first note is that writing code as in Listing 1.1, using "magic constants", is laborious, error-prone and very hard to read and maintain. As such, we provide in our source code package a set of macros that simplify the task of writing code generators, and make them much more readable. For instance, the core of the `array32x8_read` function would look like the following using our macros:

```
APPEND_INSN(PUSH(PUSH_REGRANGE(R(4), R(8))));
APPEND_INSN(LDMIA(R(0), LDM_REGRANGE(R(1), R(8))));
APPEND_INSN(MOV_REG(R(0), R(i + 1)));
APPEND_INSN(POP(POP_REGRANGE(R(4), R(8))));
APPEND_INSN(BX_NOP(LR));
```

In the remainder of the paper, we adopt a higher-level notation which emphasizes the generated assembly code, eschewing the auxiliary setup code, instruction encoding, and the call to the generated function. We illustrate this notation for the same example of 32-bit array reads and writes as Algorithms 3 and 4, respectively. However, this notation may include auxiliary variables computed in the generator (with variables in mathematical italic font, in contrast to the monospaced font used for assembly instructions). Such variables are usually referenced as fields encoded in the generated instructions, e.g., in immediate values and register indices, in which case the notation `R[`i`]` is used to indicate the register of index i; i.e., if $i = 10$, then `R10` is accessed.

The general strategy of the functions in Listing 1.1 is to generate code for a function that loads the array into the register file, performs the desired operation, and then if necessary writes the register file contents back to the array; the function is then immediately called to perform the desired operation.

Listing 1.1. C implementations of constant-time 32-bit array accesses

```c
uint32_t array32x8_read(uint32_t* v, int i) { // Returns v[i]
  // Generated code array; volatile prevents strict aliasing bugs
  volatile uint32_t code[5];

  // Cast to function pointer, adding 1 to address since it is a
  // call to a Thumb-encoded function
  uint32_t (*f)(uint32_t *) =
    (uint32_t (*)(uint32_t *))((uint8_t *)code + 1);

  code[0] = 0x01f0e92d;                          // PUSH  {R4-R8}
  code[1] = 0x01fee890;                          // LDMIA R0, {R1-R8}
  code[2] = 0x0000ea4f | ((i + 1) << 16); // MOV   R0, R[i + 1]
  code[3] = 0x01f0e8bd;                          // POP   {R4-R8}
  code[4] = 0xbf004770;                          // BX    LR + NOP

  return f(v);
}

void array32x8_write(uint32_t* v, int i, uint32_t x) { // v[i] = x;
  volatile uint32_t code[6];
  void (*f)(uint32_t *, int) =
    (void (*)(uint32_t *, int))((uint8_t *)code + 1);

  code[0] = 0x03f0e92d;                          // PUSH  {R4-R9}
  code[1] = 0x03fce890;                          // LDMIA R0, {R2-R9}
  code[2] = 0x0001ea4f | ((i + 2) << 24); // MOV   R[i + 2], R1
  code[3] = 0x03fce880;                          // STMIA R0, {R2-R9}
  code[4] = 0x03f0e8bd;                          // POP   {R4-R9}
  code[5] = 0xbf004770;                          // BX    LR + NOP

  f(v, x);
}
```

Of course, as written, there is no advantage to this approach, due to the cost of loading (and, in the case of writes, storing) the full array from/to the register file; it could instead be implemented by a full scan of the array along with constant-time conditional operations, similar to e.g., [49, Algorithm 4, lines 3–4]. However, in the context of an algorithm that performs such accesses in a loop (assuming $O(n)$ iterations), the cost of loading and storing the array is amortized across all loop iterations. Therefore, the amortized cost of each array read or write is also $O(1)$, just as with a regular timing-unprotected access, although the involved constants are larger; this is the case for Algorithms 7 to 10, described in Sect. 4.

Algorithm 3. Constant-time read from 32-bit array.

Input: Generator: 32-bit array $v[0, \ldots, 7]$, index i. Generated code: `R0`: address of v.
Output: $v[i]$, returned via `R0`.

```
PUSH  {R4-R8}          ▷ Save R4-R8 per AAPCS32
LDMIA R0, {R1-R8}      ▷ Load v to registers R1-R8
MOV   R0, R[i + 1]     ▷ Copy v[i] to R0 (return register per AAPCS32)
POP   {R4-R8}          ▷ Restore R4-R8 per AAPCS32
BX    LR               ▷ Return from function
```

Algorithm 4. Constant-time write to 32-bit array: set $v[i]$ to x.

Input: Generator: 32-bit array $v[0, \ldots, 7]$, index i, value to be written x. Generated code: `R0`: address of v, `R1`: x.

```
PUSH  {R4-R9}          ▷ Save R4-R9 per AAPCS32
LDMIA R0, {R2-R9}      ▷ Load v to registers R2-R9
MOV   R[i + 2], R1     ▷ Write x to R[i + 2], i.e., the copy of v[i] in the register file
STMIA R0, {R2-R9}      ▷ Write registers R2-R9 back to v
POP   {R4-R9}          ▷ Restore R4-R9 per AAPCS32
BX    LR               ▷ Return from function
```

Constant Time Considerations. Recall that the goal of our technique is to avoid array accesses indexed by a secret value, denoted `i` in both functions above. More generally, any operation whose execution time varies with this secret index must be avoided to ensure constant-time behavior. We now analyze how the code above depends on `i`:

- In the generator, full sequential loads (and stores, in `array32x8_write`) of the array are performed in lines 11, 25 and 27 of Listing 1.1. These are independent of the secret index `i`, thus nothing can possibly be leaked. Indeed, the only use of `i` is in the generation of `MOV` instructions (lines 12 and 26), where its encoding is obtained by combining with a constant (fixed fields in the instruction encoding) using constant-time operations: additions, shifts by a fixed amount and bitwise OR.
- In the generated code, only the `MOV` instruction depends on `i`, for which we assume (per the discussion in Sect. 2.1) that execution time is independent of the registers being accessed. Thus, although the choice of one of the registers is correlated with `i`, no information can be leaked due to the constant-time nature of `MOV`.

Also, note that the generator outputs executable code sequentially to memory, also avoiding any leakage by monitoring the order in which instructions are written to the generated code array. A similar reasoning can be made for the remaining algorithms of this section, and those of Sect. 4.

3.2 Accessing Arrays with Smaller Elements

The arrays to be accessed may have elements smaller than the CPU word size, which is 32 bits for the Cortex-M4. Given the fairly small amount of storage space in the register file, it is crucial to pack arrays as compactly as possible, using $k < 32$ bits. For the applications considered in this paper, we mostly use $k = 8$ bits/element (PERK), except for the permutation application algorithm, or $k = 2$ bits/element (NTRU). Thus, each register contains multiple array elements. In the following, we refer to each element as a k-bit *slice* of the corresponding register, and assume that k is a power of two.

Generating a single `MOV` instruction is no longer suitable, as it operates over the full 32-bit contents of the target register. For array reads, the full register could be returned from the generated function, and the slice of interest later isolated using shifts and bitwise masks; however, for writes, it is imperative to ensure that the generated code only modifies the target slice and leaves the remaining bits of the register unchanged. The extraction and placement of slices in a register can be performed using only shifts and bitwise masks, which are available in virtually all architectures, but in the particular case of ARMv7-M, a more efficient solution uses the `UBFX` instruction to extract the desired slice (for reads), and `BFI` to place it in the desired slice (for writes). Algorithm 5 illustrates how one might implement a constant-time copy of $v[j]$ to $v[i]$, assuming that i and j are secret, for an array of k-bit elements of length $8 \times 32/k$.

Algorithm 5. Constant-time copy of one element to another of a k-bit array: set $v[i]$ to $v[j]$.

Input: Generator: k-bit array $v[0, \ldots, 256/k]$, indices i and j, slice width k in bits.
Generated code: `R0`: address of v.

1: `PUSH {R4-R9}` ▷ Save `R4-R9` per AAPCS32
2: `LDMIA R0, {R2-R9}` ▷ Load v to registers `R2-R9`
▷ Aux. variables below computed in generator in CT, using right shifts or ANDs
3: $r_i, r_j \leftarrow \lfloor i/(32/k) \rfloor, \lfloor j/(32/k) \rfloor$
4: $p_i, p_j \leftarrow i \bmod (32/k), j \bmod (32/k)$
5: `UBFX R1, R[`$2 + r_j$`], #`p_j`, #`k ▷ Extract p_j-th slice of `R[`$2 + r_j$`]` to `R1`
6: `BFI R[`$2 + r_i$`], R1, #`p_i`, #`k ▷ Place `R1` in p_i-th slice of `R[`$2 + r_i$`]`
7: `STMIA R0, {R2-R9}` ▷ Write registers `R2-R9` back to v
8: `POP {R4-R9}` ▷ Restore `R4-R9` per AAPCS32
9: `BX LR` ▷ Return from function

3.3 Use of Floating-Point Registers for Storage

Unfortunately, the integer register file in ARMv7-M is fairly small, with only 14 registers available for use by the generated code, some of which must be used as temporaries for execution of the actual algorithm of interest (e.g., the Fisher-Yates shuffle). Although it is possible to perform such algorithms in a sliced fashion to different bit groups of the array, a fact which we exploit for one of the algorithms needed for PERK, the cost quickly grows as the slice size decreases.

However, as stated in Sect. 2.4, most commercial parts based on the Cortex-M4 core include hardware support for single-precision floating-point arithmetic, and in particular, an additional 32-entry register file for a total of 1024 bits of storage. As most cryptographic code eschews the use of floating-point arithmetic, particularly if only single-precision support is available, these registers are available for storage in our approach. Thus, the algorithm can be applied to arrays that are over twice as large, and the integer register file can be freed up for exclusive use of the algorithm of interest.

Algorithms 3 and 4 can be straightforwardly modified to use floating-point instructions such as `VLDMIA`, `VSTMIA` and `VMOV` in place of `LDMIA`, `STMIA` and `MOV`. However, when packing is used as in the case of Algorithm 5, a complication arises, in that floating-point instructions equivalent to `UBFX` and `BFI` (or, in general, bitwise operations which could replace them) are not available. Our strategy is to use the `VMOV` instruction to move data between floating-point and integer register files, so that integer-only operations can be performed on them. The main downside of this strategy is the additional cost to generate and execute such `VMOV` instructions. This approach is illustrated in Algorithm 6, which is a variant of Algorithm 5 using the floating-point register file, and thus capable of handling arrays with up to $1024/k$ elements. For example, this is sufficient for storing the 508-element ternary array used in fixed-weight sampling for NTRU HPS2048509, or PERK permutations for NIST security levels I and III.

Algorithm 6. Constant-time copy of one element to another of a k-bit array using floating-point registers: set $v[i]$ to $v[j]$.

Input: Generator: k-bit array $v[0, \ldots, 1024/k]$, indices i and j, slice width k in bits.
Generated code: `R0`: address of v.

`VPUSH {S16-S31}` ▷ Save `S16-S31` per AAPCS32
`VLDMIA R0, {S0-S31}` ▷ Load v to registers `S0-S31`
▷ Aux. variables below computed in generator in CT, using right shifts or ANDs
$r_i,\ r_j \leftarrow \lfloor i/(32/k) \rfloor,\ \lfloor j/(32/k) \rfloor$
$p_i,\ p_j \leftarrow i \bmod (32/k),\ j \bmod (32/k)$
`VMOV R1, S[`r_j`]` ▷ Copy FP register containing $v[j]$ to `R1`
`VMOV R2, S[`r_i`]` ▷ Copy FP register containing $v[i]$ to `R2`
`UBFX R1, R1, #`p_j`, #`k ▷ Extract p_j-th slice of `R1` to least signif. bits of itself
`BFI R2, R1, #`p_i`, #`k ▷ Place least significant bits of `R1` in p_i-th slice of `R2`
`VMOV S[`r_i`], R2` ▷ Copy `R2` to FP register containing $v[i]$
`VSTMIA R0, {S0-S31}` ▷ Write registers `S0-S31` back to v
`VPOP {S16-S31}` ▷ Restore `S16-S31` per AAPCS32
`BX LR` ▷ Return from function

One might consider a variant that stores part of the array in floating-point registers (say, the first 1024 bits) and the rest in integer registers to maximize the available storage space. Under a very reasonable assumption of having six integer registers available for array storage, it would be possible to implement PERK security level V. Under a more generous assumption of 11 available integer registers, NTRU HPS2048677 fixed-weight sampling could also be implemented.

The main tradeoff with such a variant is additional complexity. The generator code must decide, in constant time, whether the data should be sourced from (and possibly later written to) a floating-point or integer register, using either a `VMOV` or `MOV` instruction, respectively. Both are single-cycle instructions in the Cortex-M4, but their performance may vary in future cores; if one of these instructions performed differently from the other, this would give rise to a timing distinguisher[14]. We have envisioned a workaround, by using a "decoy register" so that, for every iteration, exactly one floating-point and one integer register are read and/or written; the correct one is selected in constant time. As this increases implementation complexity, we leave investigations into the simultaneous use of floating-point and integer registers as future work.

4 Secure Permutations Applied to PERK and NTRU

In this section, we present algorithms that perform operations on permutations and fixed-weight sampling, required by the PERK digital signature scheme and the NTRU key encapsulation mechanism. We implement these algorithms using the code generation approach described in Sect. 3, allowing them to be efficiently carried out in constant time. As we change one of the underlying sampling algorithms in these schemes, we remark that our changes are not compatible with the official KATs. We first recall the relevant background on PERK and NTRU, and then describe the algorithms for the required operations.

4.1 Brief Overview of PERK and NTRU

PERK. The MPCitH signature scheme PERK [1] is built assuming the hardness of the relaxed inhomogeneous Permuted Kernel Problem (r-IPKP). Informally, the r-IPKP is: given a matrix $\mathbf{H} \in \mathbb{F}_q^{m\times n}$ and pairs of vectors $(\mathbf{x}_i, \mathbf{y}_i)_{i\in\{t\}} \in \mathbb{F}_q^n \times \mathbb{F}_q^m$, find a permutation $\pi \in \mathcal{S}_n$ such that $\mathbf{H}\pi(\mathbf{x}) = \mathbf{y}$, where $\mathbf{x} = \sum_{i\in[t]} \kappa_i \mathbf{x_i}$, $\mathbf{y} = \sum_{i\in[t]} \kappa_i \mathbf{y_i}$, for some vector $(\kappa_1, \ldots, \kappa_t) \in \mathbb{F}_q^t \backslash \{0, \ldots, 0\}$. For the different NIST security levels PERK-I, PERK-II and PERK-III, we have respectively $n \in \{79, 83\}$, $n \in \{112, 116\}$, $n \in \{146, 150\}$, and q is fixed as the prime 1021. In the commitment phase of the signing algorithm, one has to sample many random permutations (e.g., up to 5120 for PERK-I) and perform several types of operations on them, consisting essentially of inversions, compositions and application to vectors. Sampling permutations and applying them to vectors are performed similarly in the verification algorithm. The submitted reference and optimized implementations of PERK to the NIST standardization process use djbsort sorting software [17] to sample random permutations in constant time, as described in Algorithm 2. Sorting is also used in these implementations to compose and invert permutations.

[14] As more general advice, synthesizing different instructions conditional on secret data should be performed with care when using our proposed approach.

NTRU. The NTRU key encapsulation mechanism (KEM) [22] is a post-quantum cryptosystem build on top of the NTRU deterministic public key encryption scheme. Its security relies on the difficulty of finding short vectors in lattices of high dimension. Most of the computations take place in polynomial rings $\mathbb{Z}[x]/(p, \Phi)$, where $p \in \{2, 3, q\}$, with q a positive power of two, and Φ is one of the polynomials $(x^n - 1)/(x - 1)$ or $x^n - 1$ for some prime number n.

In its NTRUHPS variant, the NTRU KEM specification proposes three sets of parameters: $(n = 509, q = 2048)$, $(n = 677, q = 2048)$ and $(n = 821, q = 4096)$, whose corresponding instances are respectively denoted NTRU HPS2048509, NTRU HPS2048677 and NTRU HPS4096821. During the key generation and encapsulation, the scheme requires sampling from the set $\mathcal{T}(d) \subset \mathbb{Z}[x]/(3, (x^n - 1)/(x-1))$ of polynomials having $d/2$ coefficients equal to 1, $d/2$ coefficients equal to -1 and the rest equal to 0, with $d = q/4 - 2$. The natural way to sample from $\mathcal{T}(d)$ is to start from a fixed polynomial in $\mathcal{T}(d)$ and then apply a random permutation to its coefficients. Hence, any significant speedup in secure shuffling routines will directly impact the performance of the NTRU key generation and encapsulation processes.

4.2 Secure Permutation Operations via Runtime Code Generation

All of PERK's permutation operations, i.e., sampling, application, inversion, and composition, are built on the fundamental operations of reading and writing from arrays in constant time described in Sect. 3. As PERK permutation sizes exceed the available storage space in integer registers, all algorithms are written to use floating-point registers as array storage.

Since the permutation application in PERK and fixed-weight sampling in NTRU constitute simple variants of the fully-described inversion and sampling algorithms, respectively, we just indicate required modifications to implement them. Nonetheless, implementations of all the algorithms are included in our source code package and thus available for inspection by the interested reader.

As every operation described in this section is performed inside loops, the general strategy for all of them is to load a permutation into the register file, loop over it in the generator (while generating unrolled code to be later run), and if necessary, write it back to memory only at the end. Thus, as discussed in Sect. 3, the cost of loading (and possibly storing) the array is amortized over all loop iterations to a cost of $O(1)$. As such, the following algorithms retain their original $O(n)$ asymptotic performance.

Permutation Inversion. One of the simplest operations is permutation inversion: given $\pi \in \mathcal{S}_n$, represented as a byte array, it computes $o = \pi^{-1}$ as $o[\pi[i]] = i$ for $i = 0, 1, \ldots, n-1$. Our implementation of this operation is displayed in Algorithm 7. As written, it may seem that both π and o must be held in registers, in which case the available storage space would be insufficient. However, note that only o is accessed with secret indices; π is accessed sequentially, and thus it would be possible to generate load instructions to π while keeping the code constant time. We opt to apply a different strategy: it can be seen that the generated code only receives the output permutation o as a parameter – π is not passed at all. This may appear counterintuitive initially, but note that each element of π is read by the generator and encoded as part of the instructions that populate o when the generated code is run. This explains why π is not directly used by the generated code, and thus only the storage space for a single array o is required. Moreover, as o is uninitialized when passed to the algorithm, and is completely populated during its execution, it is not necessary to load o into the register file at the beginning of the algorithm.

Algorithm 7. Permutation inversion.

Input: Generator: a permutations $\pi \in \mathcal{S}_n$. Generated code: `R0`: address of a byte array o of length n.
Output: The inverse permutation $o = \pi^{-1}$.

1: `VPUSH {S16-S[`$\lfloor (n-1)/4 \rfloor$`]}` ▷ Save FP registers `S16` onwards per AAPCS32
2: **for** $i = 0$ **to** $n - 1$ **do** ▷ Loop in generator; generated code must be unrolled
3: $i_\pi,\ b_\pi \leftarrow \lfloor \pi[i]/4 \rfloor,\ \pi[i] \bmod 4$ ▷ Auxiliary variables computed in generator
4: `VMOV R1, S[`i_π`]` ▷ Copy FP register containing $o[\pi[i]]$
5: `MOVW R2, #`i ▷ Load constant i
6: `BFI R1, R2, #`b_π`, #8` ▷ Set b_π-th byte of `R1` to i
7: `VMOV S[`i_π`], R1` ▷ Save to FP register containing $o[\pi[i]]$
8: `VSTMIA R0, {S0-S[`$\lfloor (n-1)/4 \rfloor$`]}` ▷ Store FP registers back to o
9: `VPOP {S16-S[`$\lfloor (n-1)/4 \rfloor$`]}` ▷ Restore FP registers `S16` onwards per AAPCS32
10: `BX LR` ▷ Return from function

Otherwise, the main loop of the implementation is simple: the floating-point register containing $o[\pi[i]]$ and neighboring elements is copied to a temporary integer register (`R1`) in line 4; i is loaded, as an immediate, into another temporary (`R2`) in line 5 using the `MOVW` instruction; `BFI` places i into the appropriate byte of `R1` in line 6; and finally, `R1` is stored back to the floating-point register containing $o[\pi[i]]$. Note that all accesses to p in the generator are performed sequentially, and thus do not leak any information about the secret indices. In the generated code, the full array is loaded sequentially at the beginning and written back also sequentially at the end, again not leaking any information about the secret indices; out-of-order accesses to $o[\pi[i]]$ are made using `VMOV` instructions, and thus are constant-time.

Permutation Composition with Inverse. The next operation we consider is permutation composition with inverse: given $\pi_1, \pi_2 \in \mathcal{S}_n$, we compute $\pi = \pi_1 \circ \pi_2^{-1}$. It is implemented as $\pi[\pi_2[i]] = \pi_1[i]$, which implementation-wise is almost identical to the permutation inversion; the only difference is that the value stored is $\pi_1[i]$ rather than i. Other than renaming variables, we make a single change in line 5 of Algorithm 7 to obtain Algorithm 8: we load $\pi_1[i]$ rather than i. Secret data leakage is not a concern as π_1 is accessed sequentially.

Algorithm 8. Permutation composition with inverse.

Input: Generator: permutations $\pi_1, \pi_2 \in \mathcal{S}_n$. Generated code: `R0`: address of a byte array π of length n.
Output: $\pi = \pi_1 \circ \pi_2^{-1}$.

1: `VPUSH {S16-S[`$\lfloor (n-1)/4 \rfloor$`]}` ▷ Save FP registers `S16` onwards per AAPCS32
2: **for** $i = 0$ **to** $n-1$ **do** ▷ Loop in generator; generated code must be unrolled
3: $i_{\pi_2}, b_{\pi_2} \leftarrow \lfloor \pi_2[i]/4 \rfloor,\ \pi_2[i] \bmod 4$ ▷ Auxiliary variables computed in generator
4: `VMOV R1, S[`i_{π_2}`]` ▷ Copy FP register containing $\pi_2[i]$
5: `MOVW R2, #`$\pi_1[i]$ ▷ Load constant $\pi_1[i]$
6: `BFI R1, R2, #`b_{π_2}`, #8` ▷ Set b_{π_2}-th byte of `R1` to $\pi_1[i]$
7: `VMOV S[`i_{π_2}`], R1` ▷ Save to FP register containing $\pi_2[i]$
8: `VSTMIA R0, {S0-S[`$\lfloor (n-1)/4 \rfloor$`]}` ▷ Store FP registers back to π
9: `VPOP {S16-S[`$\lfloor (n-1)/4 \rfloor$`]}` ▷ Restore FP registers `S16` onwards per AAPCS32
10: `BX LR` ▷ Return from function

Permutation Application. Another operation required by PERK is permutation application: an input 16-bit array v of length n must be permuted according to $\pi \in \mathcal{S}_n$, writing the output to a second 16-bit array o. The operation can be described as $o[\pi[i]] = v[i]$ for $i = 0, 1, \ldots, n-1$. It is essentially identical to permutation composition with inverse, and so if o and v were 8-bit arrays, Algorithm 8 could be used directly.

However, since the arrays have 16-bit elements, a problem arises: there is insufficient storage space in the floating-point register file. Indeed, even including all 14 integer registers would prove insufficient for NIST level III. We resolve this conundrum by noting that permutations can be independently applied, in two passes, to the least significant and most significant bytes of the 16-bit arrays. Also, we depart from the strategy of Algorithm 8 of loading $\pi_1[i]$ (denoted by $v[i]$ in this case) as an immediate in line 5; instead, we also pass v as an argument to the generated function, and load $v[i]$ directly from it[15]. Thus, we can generate the function only once, but call it twice (for each array containing the lower and upper half of the 16-bit array elements), halving the cost of code generation.

For this to work, however, only the least or most significant byte of each element must be stored in each pass, precluding the generation of a single instruction (`VSTMIA`) for storing the array in line 8. A naive solution is to generate instructions to copy each floating-point register to a temporary integer register using `VMOV`, extract each byte (either the least or most significant one of each element) using `UBFX`, and store that byte using `STRB`. The overhead of such byte-by-byte processing would be very significant, and thus we opt to change the representation of the array. Before calling the generated code, we apply a byte-wise perfect unshuffle operation to deinterleave the least significant and most significant bytes of each element into two separate arrays. Next, we run the generated code twice to apply the permutation to each of these arrays, and finally interleave the least significant and most significant bytes using a byte-

[15] Note that such a direct load from memory does not leak any secret information, since v is loaded sequentially from memory.

wise perfect shuffle operation. Interleaving and deinterleaving are implemented very efficiently using instructions from the Cortex-M4 DSP extensions, although shifts and bitwise instructions could be used instead, with a small performance impact, to support ARM cores without this extension or other architectures.

Permutation Composition. The next operation required for PERK is permutation composition: Given $\pi_1, \pi_2 \in \mathcal{S}_n$, compute $\pi = \pi_1 \circ \pi_2$, which can be implemented as $\pi[i] = \pi_1[\pi_2[i]]$ for $i = 0, 1, \ldots, n-1$. Note that π and π_2 are accessed sequentially, and thus only π_1 needs to be stored in registers to avoid leakage. This operation is implemented by Algorithm 9. The main novelty with regard to the previous algorithms is that we synthesize a store instruction (`STRB`) in line 7 to write to the output array π directly; this eschews the need to write the floating-point registers back to memory.

Algorithm 9. Permutation composition.

Input: Generator: permutations $\pi_1, \pi_2 \in \mathcal{S}_n$. Generated code: `R0`: address of a byte array π of length n, `R1`: address of π_1, represented as a byte array of length n.

Output: $\pi = \pi_1 \circ \pi_2$.

1: `VPUSH {S16-S[`$\lfloor (n-1)/4 \rfloor$`]}` ▷ Save FP registers `S16` onwards per AAPCS32
2: `VLDMIA R0, {S0-S[`$\lfloor (n-1)/4 \rfloor$`]}` ▷ Load π_1 to FP registers
3: **for** $i = 0$ **to** $n-1$ **do** ▷ Loop in generator; generated code must be unrolled
4: $\quad i_{\pi_2}, b_{\pi_2} \leftarrow \lfloor \pi_2[i]/4 \rfloor,\ \pi_2[i] \bmod 4$ ▷ Auxiliary variables computed in generator
5: $\quad$ `VMOV R2, S[`i_{π_2}`]` ▷ Copy FP register containing $\pi_2[i]$
6: $\quad$ `UBFX R2, R2, #`b_{π_2}`, #8` ▷ Shift b_{π_2}-th byte of `R2` to its least significant byte
7: $\quad$ `STRB R2, [R0, #`i`]` ▷ Store `R2` to $\pi[i]$
8: `VPOP {S16-S[`$\lfloor (n-1)/4 \rfloor$`]}` ▷ Restore FP registers `S16` onwards per AAPCS32
9: `BX LR` ▷ Return from function

Permutation Sampling. Now we turn to the issue of sampling a permutation, which can be performed using a variant of the Fisher-Yates shuffle. Listing 1.2 displays the C code for the function that performs permutation sampling in a timing-unprotected implementation of PERK, where `PARAM_N1` corresponds to the array length n. It is seen to be similar to Algorithm 1, but slightly rewritten so as to eschew the need to initialize the permutation array `p` (and therefore the initial load to the register file in our implementation). The `rnd_buff` array is sampled according to line 3 of Algorithm 1, using a fast and constant-time technique due to Lemire [38], which does not require division instructions.

Algorithm 10 displays our implementation of Listing 1.2 using the code generation approach. Although it is, at a high level, a straightforward translation of the unprotected implementation, care must be taken in the case that $i_i = i_r$, i.e., when the same floating-point register contains $\pi[i]$ and i (which is true in particular if $\pi[i] = i$). If the code were to keep copies of both `S[`i_i`]` and `S[`i_r`]` in different integer registers and update them separately, then, when writing back

Listing 1.2. Timing-unprotected C implementation of permutation sampling

```
int sig_perk_perm_gen_given_random_input(
  perm_t p, const uint16_t rnd_buff[PARAM_N1]) {
  for (int i = 0; i < PARAM_N1; i++) {
    p[i] = p[rnd_buff[i]];
    p[rnd_buff[i]] = i;
  }
  return EXIT_SUCCESS;
}
```

both copies to floating-point registers, one of the updates would be shadowed by the other. This introduces a correctness error analogous to a race condition in a parallel program.

To address this issue, we compute a variable t in the code generator, which is set to 0 if $i_i = i_r$ and 1 otherwise; this computation is easily performed in constant time. We copy `S[`i_i`]` to `R1` in line 6 and `S[`i_r`]` to `R[`$1+t$`]` in line 7; thus, if $t = 0$ (i.e., $i_i = i_r$), they are copied to the same register (`R1`), but otherwise they are copied to different registers (`R1` and `R2`). The same idea is used when copying the updated version to `S[`i_i`]` in line 12 and `S[`i_r`]` in line 13, thus ensuring that the generated code is both correct and constant time.

Algorithm 10. Permutation sampling using Fisher-Yates, baseline version.

Input: Generator: an array of random integers r of length n, such that $r[i] \leftarrow \mathcal{U}([i])$.
Generated code: `R0`: address of a byte array π of length n.
Output: A random permutation $\pi \in \mathcal{S}_n$.

1: `VPUSH {S16-S[`$\lfloor (n-1)/4 \rfloor$`]}` ▷ Save FP registers `S16` onwards per AAPCS32
2: **for** $i = 0$ **to** $n - 1$ **do** ▷ Loop in generator; generated code must be unrolled
3: $i_i,\ b_i \leftarrow \lfloor i/4 \rfloor,\ i \bmod 4$ ▷ Auxiliary variables computed in generator
4: $i_r,\ b_r \leftarrow \lfloor r[i]/4 \rfloor,\ r[i] \bmod 4$ ▷ Auxiliary variables computed in generator
5: $t \leftarrow 0$ if $i_i = i_r$, else 1 ▷ Auxiliary variable computed in CT in generator
6: `VMOV R1, S[`i_i`]` ▷ Copy FP register containing $\pi[i]$ to `R1`
7: `VMOV R[`$1+t$`], S[`i_r`]` ▷ Copy FP register containing $r[i]$ to `R1` or `R2`
8: `UBFX R3, R[`$1+t$`], #`b_r`, #8` ▷ Copy b_r-th byte of `R1` or `R2` to `R3`
9: `BFI R1, R3, #`b_i`, #8` ▷ Set b_i-th byte of `R1` to the value of `R3`
10: `MOVW R3, #`i ▷ Load constant i
11: `BFI R[`$1+t$`], R3, #`b_r`, #8` ▷ Set b_r-th byte of `R[`$1+t$`]` to i
12: `VMOV S[`i_i`], R1` ▷ Save to FP register containing $\pi[i]$
13: `VMOV S[`i_r`], R[`$1+t$`]` ▷ Save to FP register containing $r[i]$
14: `VSTMIA R0, {S0-S[`$\lfloor (n-1)/4 \rfloor$`]}` ▷ Store FP registers back to π
15: `VPOP {S16-S[`$\lfloor (n-1)/4 \rfloor$`]}` ▷ Restore FP registers `S16` onwards per AAPCS32
16: `BX LR` ▷ Return from function

Algorithm 10 is labeled as a "baseline version", since our actual implementation includes some performance improvements which we omit from this description, although they are available for perusal in our source code package. The two main improvements are:

1. The initial 48 iterations of the loop use only integer, rather than floating-point, registers. Note that 12 integer registers can be dedicated to array storage, and that the i-th iteration is limited to accessing the first i entries of the permutation array. Fewer instructions are required as no `VMOV` instructions must be synthesized. At the end of the 48th iteration, these 12 integer registers are saved to memory and then reloaded to floating-point registers.
2. The loop body handles four iterations at a time, rather than one. Note that, in a sequence of four iterations starting with $i \equiv 0 \pmod 4$, the value of i_i in line 3 of Algorithm 10 is identical for all four iterations. Therefore, it is only necessary to generate the `VMOV` instructions of lines 6 and 12 once for each block of four iterations. Therefore, only $2 + 6 \times 4 = 26$ instead of $8 \times 4 = 32$ instructions need to be generated for each block of four iterations.

Fixed-Weight Sampling for NTRU. The final operation we consider is fixed-weight sampling for NTRU. It can be implemented by initializing a vector with the prescribed number of 0, 1, and −1 elements and randomly permuting it, using the Fisher-Yates shuffle. Our implementation closely follows Algorithm 1, while implementing the improvements just discussed for permutation sampling: avoiding a correctness issue when $i_i = i_r$; use of integer registers when possible; handling four iterations of the loop body at a time to reduce the number of generated instructions.

5 Performance Results

Benchmarking Methodology. To study the impact of Algorithms 7 to 10, we integrate them into the implementations of PERK and NTRU from the `pqm4` framework [31,32], and conduct experiments on an STMicroelectronics NUCLEO-L4R5ZI development board. The compiler is `gcc 13.2`. All schemes' variants are tested using their `test.py` and `testvectors.py` scripts to verify correctness. In particular, the reference implementation used to generate test vectors using the `testvectors.py` script is based on unprotected Fisher-Yates and permutation operations (using array accesses indexed by secret data), therefore ensuring that our code generation implementation produces identical results to these unprotected implementations. Benchmarks are compiled with speed optimizations, and we report average cycle counts for 10 runs of each combination of scheme, variant, and security level.

We perform some configurations of the target system to eliminate slowdowns during the execution of generated code from SRAM, which we detail in Appendix A, where we also quantify the effect of foregoing such configurations. All performance figures listed next, for implementations based on our approach, employ such configurations to attain maximum generated code performance.

In all tables in this section, the implementations employing the techniques introduced in Sects. 3 and 4 are referred to as **codegen**, and their benchmarks include the cost of both code generation and execution of the generated code. Additionally, to compare them with the presumably best achievable performance, we report in gray the benchmarks corresponding to non-constant-time instantiations of the same algorithms. The speed-up and percentages improvement are given with respect to the reference implementation.

5.1 Microbenchmarks

We display microbenchmarks for the permutation operations discussed in Sect. 4, using the same parameters (array lengths) as the PERK submission for NIST security levels I and III, in Table 2. We also report fixed-weight sampling performance for $n = 508$, as used in NTRU HPS2048509, in Table 3. Each benchmark is run only once with fixed inputs; due to the simple, deterministic nature of the Cortex-M4 core, cycle counts are essentially identical across multiple runs.

We consider the following implementation strategies: constant-time sorting, secret-indexed array accesses, and our code generation approach, and additionally the algorithm of [27] for NTRU. Figures include the cost of setting up and extracting data from arrays for the sorting approach, and Lemire sampling for permutation and fixed-weight sampling. However, we exclude the cost of sampling pseudorandom bits, which varies widely depending on the symmetric primitive chosen for such sampling, which is additionally scheme- and/or platform-dependent. We estimate that, for PERK, the amount of randomness required by the different approaches for permutation sampling is similar: both consume a minimum of 16 bits per element, and rejection probabilities for Lemire sampling (per the analysis of [27, p. 10]) or the sorting approach (in case of collisions in the sorting keys, which can be analyzed using a birthday paradox argument) are in the range of 5–10%. An additional issue is that collisions in the sorting approach require rerunning the algorithm, but we have disabled this behavior in our microbenchmarks; if this were taken into account, a birthday paradox argument suggests that the cycle counts of the sorting approach in Table 2 would increase by approximately 4.8–10.7%, depending on security level, on average.

As for NTRU, the sorting approach consumes approximately 78% more random bits for the considered parameter set, but the sorting approach does not check for collisions. Thus, the figures in Table 3 also underestimate the performance advantage of non-sorting approaches, but only due to the cost of pseudorandomness sampling.

5.2 Performance for PERK

To evaluate the impact of our contribution, we integrate our work into the dedicated implementation of PERK for resource-constrained devices [19]. We replace all permutation-related routines with our code generation variants, Algorithms 7 to 10, and measure the resulting performance improvements. Comparative results are presented in Tables 4 and 5, corresponding to the parameter sets for

Table 2. Microbenchmarks for Algorithms 7 to 9, the optimized version of Algorithm 10, and vector permutation against their variants based on either non-constant-time secret-indexed array accesses (which we denote as "Table lookup") or constant-time sorting. The parameter n is the length of the permutations/vectors. For `sampling`, we exclude from these benchmarks the cost of the pseudorandomness sampling. Performance figures are in clock cycles, and speedup is calculated as the ratio of reference to codegen cycle counts.

n	Method	`compose`	`comp_inv`	`sampling`	`inverse`	`vec_permute`
79	Table lookup	481	798	2345	719	613
	Codegen	**1702**	**2279**	**4909**	**2185**	**3409**
	Reference [19]	32462	16071	17690	16275	16163
	Speedup	19×	7.1×	3.6×	7.4×	4.7×
83	Table lookup	500	792	2468	723	622
	Codegen	**1812**	**2393**	**5225**	**2238**	**3586**
	Reference [19]	34500	17222	18832	17291	17243
	Speedup	19×	7.2×	3.6×	7.7×	4.8×
112	Table lookup	810	974	3376	903	826
	Codegen	**2367**	**3319**	**7565**	**2818**	**4940**
	Reference [19]	49460	24793	26765	24785	24739
	Speedup	21×	7.5×	3.5×	8.8×	5.0×
116	Table lookup	834	1010	3440	991	807
	Codegen	**2450**	**3434**	**7885**	**2916**	**5105**
	Reference [19]	51636	25786	27936	25765	25705
	Speedup	21×	7.5×	3.5×	8.8×	5.0×

Table 3. Microbenchmarks for NTRU's fixed-weight sampling routine, exclusive of the cost for pseudorandomness sampling. The parameter n is the length of the vectors. Performance figures are in clock cycles, and speedup is calculated as the ratio of CT sort to codegen cycle counts.

n	Method	`sample_fixed_weight`
508	CT shuffle [27]	13354
	Fisher-Yates	13703
	Codegen	**43261**
	CT sort	163388
	Speedup	3.8×

security levels I and III. Additionally, we provide benchmark results using only the naïve Fisher–Yates shuffle and standard permutation algorithms, in order to have a plausible baseline for optimal performance without side-channel protection. It can be observed that our code generation approach is significantly faster than the sorting-based method used in [19], and achieves performance close to that of the naïve Fisher–Yates implementation. This improvement is particularly notable in the signing operation, where it yields speedups in the range of 33–35%. The trade-off, as expected, is an increase in RAM usage and code size.

Table 4. PERK-128 (NIST security level I) key generation, signing and verification performance and RAM usage on the NUCLEO-L4R5ZI board, using different methods for implementing permutations. Performance figures are in millions of clock cycles, averaged over 10 runs, and sizes are in KB. Speedup is calculated as the ratio of reference to codegen cycle counts, and size impact as the ratio of codegen to reference.

Variant	Method	Keygen Perf.	Keygen RAM	Sign Perf.	Sign RAM	Verify Perf.	Verify RAM	.1Code size
fast-3	Table lookup	0.579	7.62	138	24.0	66.5	20.7	12.7
	Codegen	**0.594**	**9.25**	**153**	**25.7**	**68.8**	**22.3**	**14.6**
	Ref. [19]	0.644	7.71	245	24.0	81.1	20.7	11.6
	Speedup / size impact	1.08×	20.0%	1.60×	7.08%	1.18×	7.73%	26%
fast-5	Table lookup	0.715	9.03	132	25.2	63.4	21.8	12.7
	Codegen	**0.732**	**10.8**	**145**	**26.9**	**65.7**	**23.5**	**14.6**
	Ref. [19]	0.823	9.03	240	25.2	78.1	21.8	11.6
	Speedup / size impact	1.12×	19.6%	1.66×	6.75%	1.19×	7.80%	25.9%
short-3	Table lookup	0.579	7.62	747	27.8	378	25.2	25.6
	Codegen	**0.589**	**9.25**	**830**	**29.4**	**392**	**26.9**	**27.5**
	Ref. [19]	0.641	7.71	1321	27.8	461	25.2	24.5
	Speedup / size impact	1.09×	20.0%	1.59×	5.76%	1.18×	6.75%	12.2%
short-5	Table lookup	0.716	9.03	694	28.6	348	26.1	25.7
	Codegen	**0.732**	**10.8**	**763**	**30.4**	**361**	**27.8**	**27.5**
	Ref. [19]	0.823	9.03	1245	28.6	428	26.1	24.6
	Speedup / size impact	1.12×	19.6%	1.63×	6.29%	1.19×	6.51%	11.8%

5.3 Performance for NTRU

Table 6 showcases the efficiency of our code generation approach in the context of NTRU. Analogously to PERK, we report benchmarks obtained by using naïve

Table 5. PERK-192 (NIST security level III) key generation, signing and verification performance and RAM usage on the NUCLEO-L4R5ZI board, using different methods for implementing permutations. Performance figures are in millions of clock cycles, averaged over 10 runs, and sizes are in KB. Speedup is calculated as the ratio of reference to codegen cycle counts, and size impact as the ratio of codegen to reference.

		Keygen		Sign		Verify		.1Code size
Variant	Method	Perf.	RAM	Perf.	RAM	Perf.	RAM	
fast-3	Table lookup	1.39	14.8	322	47.7	157	41.4	12.3
	Codegen	**1.41**	**17.3**	**357**	**50.2**	**163**	**43.8**	**14.6**
	Ref. [19]	1.49	15.0	582	47.8	195	41.4	12.0
	Speedup / size impact	1.06×	15.3%	1.63×	5.02%	1.20×	5.80%	21.7%
fast-5	Table lookup	1.65	16.9	306	48.8	150	42.4	12.3
	Codegen	**1.68**	**19.4**	**337**	**51.3**	**156**	**45.0**	**14.6**
	Ref. [19]	1.80	16.9	560	48.8	187	42.4	11.9
	Speedup / size impact	1.07×	14.8%	1.66×	5.12%	1.20×	6.13%	22.7%
short-3	Table lookup	1.39	14.8	1829	51.3	964	46.7	24.3
	Codegen	**1.41**	**17.3**	**2030**	**53.8**	**998**	**49.1**	**26.6**
	Ref. [19]	1.51	15.0	3281	51.5	1179	46.7	23.9
	Speedup / size impact	1.07×	15.3%	1.62×	4.47%	1.18×	5.14%	11.3%
short-5	Table lookup	1.65	16.9	1687	51.9	894	47.3	24.9
	Codegen	**1.68**	**19.4**	**1868**	**54.5**	**926**	**49.8**	**27.2**
	Ref. [19]	1.81	16.9	3045	51.9	1101	47.3	24.6
	Speedup / size impact	1.08×	14.8%	1.63×	5.01%	1.19×	5.29%	10.6%

Fisher-Yates for comparison. We also include the performance of the constant-time sorting-based method (implemented using the djbsort library), which is the default in the NTRU implementation, and the specific-purpose shuffle method from [27]. The results show that our method provides a significant speedup over the similarly non-specific sorting approach, maintaining a reasonable code size. It is worth noting that our method also applies to other variants of NTRU, such as those of NTRU Prime [22], which have similar requirements for sampling fixed-weight polynomials.

Table 6. NTRU HPS2048509 (NIST security level I) performance and RAM usage for key generation and encapsulation on the NUCLEO-L4R5ZI board, for different fixed-weight sampling methods. Decapsulation performance is not reported, as it does not employ fixed-weight sampling. Performance figures are in thousands of clock cycles, averaged over 10 runs, and sizes are in KB. Speedup is calculated as the ratio of CT sort to codegen cycle counts, and size impact as the ratio of codegen to reference.

	Key generation		Encapsulation		.1Code size
Sampling method	Perf.	RAM	Perf.	RAM	
CT shuffle [27]	2665	20.5	240	13.2	192
Fisher-Yates	2670	20.5	245	13.2	192
Codegen	**2701**	**31.3**	**276**	**24.0**	**198**
CT sort	2834	21.3	409	14.0	192
Speedup / size impact	1.05×	46.9%	1.48×	71.4%	3.12%

6 Conclusion

This work introduces a novel approach for implementing, in constant time, algorithms that inherently require array accesses indexed by secret data, without altering their asymptotic time complexity. We apply our method to permutation-related operations commonly used in cryptography, including sampling, composition, and inversion. Our experiments show that this technique outperforms existing constant-time alternatives, significantly narrowing the performance gap with the most efficient, but non-constant-time, implementations. When integrated into the post-quantum schemes PERK and NTRU, our method yields notable performance improvements over the alternative based on constant-time sorting; it is only incapable of overcoming a constant-time algorithm that efficiently exploits the specific structure of fixed-weight sampling for NTRU [27].

6.1 Future Work

We envision many opportunities to extend the applicability of our technique.

Application to Larger Arrays. At the end of Sect. 3, we have alluded to the possibility of simultaneously using integer and floating-point registers for array storage, but cautioned about additional complexity. Nevertheless, this extends the applicability of our techniques to higher security levels such as PERK-V and NTRU HPS2048677, and given that alternatives may have higher asymptotic complexity (e.g., $O(n \log^2 n)$ for constant-time sorting), our technique may still outperform alternatives despite increased constant factors.

Another strategy to work around storage limits was discussed in Sect. 4, in the context of permutation application: one may apply permutation operations in multiple passes, to different "slices" of each element of the permutation array (in that particular case, 16-bit elements were split into their least and most significant bytes). For instance, by separately shuffling each of the two bits in packed NTRU fixed-weight sampling arrays, our approach can be extended to NTRU HPS4096821. When both strategies are applicable, it is unclear which of the two would perform better; we encourage investigations into the relative performance of both.

Application to More Schemes. While we have demonstrated the validity of our technique for PERK and NTRU, other applications could benefit from it. For instance, the LESS post-quantum signature scheme [14] employs an unprotected version of the Fisher-Yates shuffle; our technique would increase its side-channel resistance. Going beyond post-quantum cryptosystems, symmetric schemes could benefit from constant-time table lookups, a prime example being AES. Given the limited storage space in registers, the use of full T-tables is impractical, and even the S-boxes are too large to be directly used; however, this can be overcome, using floating-point registers only, by applying the strategy of the previous paragraph, i.e., splitting each element of the cipher state into 4-bit halves and performing lookups in two passes.

Extending to Other Architectures. A natural extension of our work is applying it to other architectures. RISC-V has been gaining traction in the embedded space, and appears well-suited to the use of our technique, due to its RISC philosophy, with simple, regular instruction encodings and a large integer register file. Larger out-of-order CPUs might be investigated as well, although the caveats discussed in Sect. 3 should be kept in mind; in particular, a robust benchmarking methodology should be employed to account for the costs of cache invalidation, and its constant-time properties should be thoroughly validated prior to recommending its use.

Optimization of the Code. Lastly, we envision further optimizations to our technique, which may reduce constant factors in its application. While many instructions depend on values that are only known at runtime (and indeed, that is the main point of our technique), others do not; for instance, lines 6, 10, 9 and 12 of Algorithm 10 depend only on the loop variable i. Thus, the generated code array can be initialized with the (fixed) instruction encodings corresponding to these lines for all iterations of the loop, reducing the amount of work that must be performed during code generation. Yet another possibility to investigate is moving away from the two-pass process (code generation and generated code execution) to a self-modifying code paradigm; that is, an instruction may directly modify the following one in the instruction stream, which is then immediately executed. This presents challenges (register pressure; foregoing the possibility of writing the generator code in a high-level language; unfriendliness to caches and prefetch queues) but also potential benefits, mainly in terms of eliminating overhead, such as generating code for function prologue and epilogue, loading and storing arrays to/from the register files and other instructions that are independent of runtime values.

A Speeding up Code Execution from SRAM

The default (power-on reset) configuration of the NUCLEO-L4R5ZI development board, used for benchmarking in Sect. 5, unnecessarily slows down code execution from SRAM. This is usually not a concern, as embedded applications almost always executes from Flash memory, but it is critical for our code generation approach. We outline some steps to be taken to ensure that code executes from SRAM with minimal slowdowns.

In the STM32L4R5ZI microcontroller unit (MCU) at the core of the NUCLEO-L4R5ZI development board, the connection among the Cortex-M4 core, memory-mapped peripherals and different types of memory (Flash, SRAM, external, and memory-mapped peripherals) is realized by means of a bus matrix, a typical organization for MCUs from ST and other vendors. The particular layout of the bus matrix for the STM32L4R5ZI is displayed in Fig. 2, which also highlights a characteristic of this particular ST part: the use of a banked memory organization, splitting SRAM into three banks (SRAM1, SRAM2 and SRAM3).

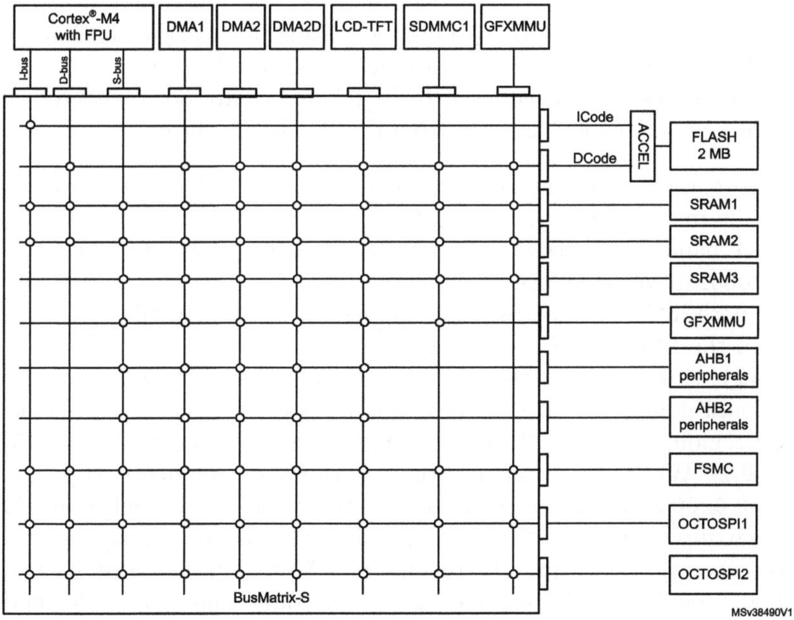

Fig. 2. STM32L4R5ZI memory bus architecture. Reproduced from [42, Figure 1].

Additionally, the memory map of the Cortex-M4 core is subdivided in 8 regions of 512 MB each (see [11, Figure 3-1 and Table 3-3] and [42, Figure 3]). We are mostly concerned with the Code and SRAM regions, spanning the memory address ranges of `0x0000 0000`–`0x1FFF FFFF` and `0x2000 0000`–`0x3FFF FFFF`, respectively.

It is noted that the Cortex-M4 core is connected to the bus matrix through three different bus interfaces (see [42, Sections 2.1.1–2.1.3] and [11, Section 2.2.1]):

- I-bus/ICode memory interface: used for instruction fetches from the Code region.
- D-bus/DCode memory interface: used for data (literal loads) and debug access from the Code region.
- S-bus/System interface: used for instruction fetches, data and debug access from other regions, in particular the SRAM region.

Regarding the System interface, ARM's Cortex-M4 Technical Reference Manual [11, p. 2-25] states that:

> **Pipelined instruction fetches**
> To provide a clean timing interface on the system bus, instruction and vector fetch requests to this bus are registered.
> This results in an extra cycle of latency because instructions fetched from the system bus take two cycles. This also means that back-to-back instruction fetches from the system bus are not possible.
> **Note**: Instruction fetch requests to the ICode bus are not registered. Performance critical code must run from the ICode interface.

Therefore, it is important to ensure that generated code is run from the ICode bus to attain maximum performance. However, one runs into the roadblock that the SRAM banks are accessible from the SRAM region, starting at address `0x2000 0000`, rather than the Code region that starts at address `0x0000 0000`. However, note in Fig. 2 that SRAM1 and SRAM2 (but not SRAM3) have connections to the I-bus and D-bus, in addition to the S-bus.

Although this indicates that access via the I-bus and D-bus are possible, an additional configuration step is required to remap the SRAM region into the Code region, using the `SYSCFG_MEMRMP` register of the STM32L4R5ZI [42, Section 9.2.1]. When this configuration is performed, any accesses to addresses starting at `0x0000 0000` are remapped to the same address with the 29th bit set, i.e. starting from `0x2000 0000`; note that this remapping is more precisely an alias, since accesses directly to the SRAM region, to addresses starting at `0x2000 0000`, are still possible. This procedure must be performed carefully, due to the interrupt vector table that is normally stored in Flash memory at `0x0800 0000` and remapped (per the default configuration) to address `0x0000 0000`. When the remap is performed, the vector table must be available at address `0x2000 0000`, which must be reserved by editing the linker script, and a copy made from Flash to this address in SRAM1, prior to performing the remap. It is also necessary to enable the clock for the SYSCFG peripheral, and interrupts must be disabled during the remapping to avoid race conditions; the exact procedure can be reviewed in our source code package, in the remap_setup function found in either hw/hal.c file of the microbenchmarking project or common/hal-opencm3.c file of the pqm4 project.

Recall from Fig. 2 that only SRAM1 and SRAM2 banks are connected to the I-bus. Therefore, another important point is to ensure that arrays storing generated code must be declared in either one of these banks, rather than SRAM3. The exact placement of variables is determined by the linker script; we will refrain from discussing all intrincacies of linker script writing, and instead point out that for a typical linker script organization, global variables are placed starting at the beginning of SRAM (i.e. SRAM1 in our case), whereas the stack pointer is set to the end of SRAM (i.e. SRAM3) and grows down. Therefore, code arrays should be declared as global variables to place them in SRAM1, and this is the strategy followed in our implementations.

Unfortunately, this is still not sufficient to ensure the code runs from the Code region. Linker scripts place references to any SRAM object at addresses starting at 0x2000 0000; this must not be changed directly in the linker script, as the MCU boots up with the default remapping configuration, aliasing Flash addresses starting at 0x0800 0000 to 0x0000 0000. Therefore, prior to the remapping, SRAM addresses must remain in their original range starting at 0x2000 0000. Also, accesses to the code array during code generation can use the default address in the SRAM region; the issue raised above pertains only to execution of the code. Thus, only the function pointer, used to call the generated code, actually needs to point to an address in the Code range, i.e. with the 29th bit cleared. We solve this conundrum by casting the code array to a function pointer while clearing the 29th bit. Concretely, we illustrate the required change for lines 7 and 8 of the function array32x8_read in Listing 1.1; similar changes can be performed for any implementations using the code generation approach:

```
uint32_t (*f)(uint32_t *) =
  (uint32_t (*)(uint32_t *))((uint32_t)code - 0x20000000 + 1);
```

In order to quantify the effect of such configuration changes, we display in Table 7 microbenchmarks for permutation ($n \in \{79, 83, 112, 116\}$) and fixed-weight ($n = 508$) sampling, using the code generation approach, for both the default configuration and an optimized one. The same methodology as Sect. 5.1 is followed, and therefore cycle counts for the optimized configuration are identical to those of Tables 2 and 3. It is seen that the speedups from using an optimized configuration range from 3.3–5.7%.

Table 7. Microbenchmarks for permutation and fixed-weight sampling, using either a default or optimized configuration. The parameter n is the length of the permutations/vectors. Speedup is reported as the ratio between cycle counts of the default and optimized configuration. All cycle counts are exclusive of pseudorandomness sampling.

Configuration	$n = 79$	$n = 83$	$n = 112$	$n = 116$	$n = 508$
Optimized	**4909**	**5225**	**7565**	**7885**	**43261**
Default	5184	5519	7990	8328	44717
Speedup	1.06×	1.06×	1.06×	1.06×	1.03×

References

1. Aaraj, N., et al.: PERK. Technical report, National Institute of Standards and Technology (2024). available at https://csrc.nist.gov/Projects/pqc-dig-sig/round-2-additional-signatures
2. Abdulrahman, A., Chen, J.P., Chen, Y.J., Hwang, V., Kannwischer, M.J., Yang, B.Y.: Multi-moduli NTTs for saber on Cortex-M3 and Cortex-M4. IACR Trans. Cryptogr. Hardw. Embed. Syst. **2022**(1), 127–151 (2022). https://doi.org/10.46586/tches.v2022.i1.127-151
3. Abdulrahman, A., Hwang, V., Kannwischer, M.J., Sprenkels, A.: Faster kyber and dilithium on the Cortex-M4. In: Ateniese, G., Venturi, D. (eds.) ACNS 22: 20th International Conference on Applied Cryptography and Network Security. LNCS, vol. 13269, pp. 853–871. Springer, Cham (2022). https://doi.org/10.1007/978-3-031-09234-3_42
4. Adomnicai, A., Peyrin, T.: Fixslicing AES-like ciphers. IACR Trans. Cryptogr. Hardw. Embed. Syst. **2021**(1), 402–425 (2021). https://doi.org/10.46586/tches.v2021.i1.402-425, https://tches.iacr.org/index.php/TCHES/article/view/8739
5. Advanced Encryption Standard (AES). National Institute of Standards and Technology, NIST FIPS PUB 197, U.S. Department of Commerce (2001)
6. Albrecht, M.R., et al.: Classic McEliece. Technical report, National Institute of Standards and Technology (2022). available at https://csrc.nist.gov/projects/post-quantum-cryptography/round-4-submissions
7. Alkim, E., et al.: Polynomial multiplication in NTRU prime. IACR Trans. Cryptogr. Hardw. Embed. Syst. **2021**(1), 217–238 (2021). https://doi.org/10.46586/tches.v2021.i1.217-238, https://tches.iacr.org/index.php/TCHES/article/view/8733
8. Anastasova, M., Azarderakhsh, R., Kermani, M.M., Beshaj, L.: Time-efficient finite field microarchitecture design for Curve448 and Ed448 on cortex-M4. In: Seo, S.H., Seo, H. (eds.) ICISC 22: 25th International Conference on Information Security and Cryptology. LNCS, vol. 13849, pp. 292–314. Springer, Cham (2022). https://doi.org/10.1007/978-3-031-29371-9_15
9. Anastasova, M., Bisheh-Niasar, M., Azarderakhsh, R., Kermani, M.M.: Compressed SIKE round 3 on ARM Cortex-M4. Cryptology ePrint Archive, Report 2021/1511 (2021). https://eprint.iacr.org/2021/1511
10. Arm Limited: Arm Cortex-M4 datasheet (2020). https://developer.arm.com/documentation/102832/latest/

11. Arm Limited: Arm® Cortex® -M4 processor technical reference manual revision r0p1 (2020). https://developer.arm.com/documentation/100166/0001/
12. Arm Limited: Arm® v7-M architecture reference manual (2021). https://developer.arm.com/documentation/ddi0403/ee/
13. Arm Limited: Arm CPU security update: Timing side channel attacks on TrustZone enabled Cortex-M based systems (2025). https://developer.arm.com/documentation/110390/1-1/
14. Baldi, M., et al.: LESS — Linear Equivalence Signature Scheme. Technical report, National Institute of Standards and Technology (2024). available at https://csrc.nist.gov/Projects/pqc-dig-sig/round-2-additional-signatures
15. Becker, H., Hwang, V., Kannwischer, M.J., Panny, L., Yang, B.Y.: Efficient multiplication of somewhat small integers using number-theoretic transforms. In: Cheng, C.M., Akiyama, M. (eds.) IWSEC 22: 17th International Workshop on Security, Advances in Information and Computer Security. LNCS, vol. 13504, pp. 3–23. Springer, Cham (2022). https://doi.org/10.1007/978-3-031-15255-9_1
16. Bernstein, D.J.: Cache-timing attacks on AES (2005). https://cr.yp.to/antiforgery/cachetiming-20050414.pdf
17. Bernstein, D.J.: Djbsort software library (2019). https://sorting.cr.yp.to/
18. Bernstein, D.J., Chuengsatiansup, C., Lange, T., van Vredendaal, C.: NTRU prime: reducing attack surface at low cost. In: Adams, C., Camenisch, J. (eds.) SAC 2017: 24th Annual International Workshop on Selected Areas in Cryptography. LNCS, vol. 10719, pp. 235–260. Springer, Cham (2017). https://doi.org/10.1007/978-3-319-72565-9_12
19. Bettaieb, S., Bidoux, L., Budroni, A., Palumbi, M., Perin, L.P.: Enabling PERK and other MPC-in-the-head signatures on resource-constrained devices. IACR Trans. Cryptogr. Hardw. Embed. Syst. **2024**(4), 84–109 (2024). https://doi.org/10.46586/tches.v2024.i4.84-109
20. Biham, E.: A fast new DES implementation in software. In: Biham, E. (eds.) Fast Software Encryption. FSE 1997. LNCS, vol. 1267, pp. 260–272. Springer, Berlin, Heidelberg (1997). https://doi.org/10.1007/BFb0052352
21. Budroni, A., Canales-Martínez, I.A., Perin, L.P.: SoK: methods for sampling random permutations in post-quantum cryptography. Cryptology ePrint Archive, Report 2024/008 (2024). https://eprint.iacr.org/2024/008
22. Chen, C., et al.: NTRU. Technical report, National Institute of Standards and Technology (2020). available at https://csrc.nist.gov/projects/post-quantum-cryptography/post-quantum-cryptography-standardization/round-3-submissions
23. Chen, M.S., Chou, T.: Classic McEliece on the ARM Cortex-M4. IACR Trans. Cryptogr. Hardw. Embed. Syst. **2021**(3), 125–148 (2021). https://doi.org/10.46586/tches.v2021.i3.125-148, https://tches.iacr.org/index.php/TCHES/article/view/8970
24. Chung, C.M.M., Hwang, V., Kannwischer, M.J., Seiler, G., Shih, C.J., Yang, B.Y.: NTT multiplication for NTT-unfriendly rings. IACR Trans. Cryptogr. Hardw. Embed. Syst. **2021**(2), 159–188 (2021). https://doi.org/10.46586/tches.v2021.i2.159-188, https://tches.iacr.org/index.php/TCHES/article/view/8791
25. Dhem, J.F., Koeune, F., Leroux, P.A., Mestré, P., Quisquater, J.J., Willems, J.L.: A practical implementation of the timing attack. In: Quisquater, J.J., Schneier, B. (eds.) Smart Card Research and Applications. CARDIS 1998. LNCS, vol. 1820, pp. 167–182. Springer, Berlin, Heidelberg (2000). https://doi.org/10.1007/10721064_15
26. Durstenfeld, R.: Algorithm 235: random permutation. Commun. ACM **7**(7), 420 (1964). https://doi.org/10.1145/364520.364540

27. Filho, D.L.G., Silva, T.S.R., López-Hernández, J.C.: Efficient isochronous fixed-weight sampling with applications to NTRU. IACR Commun. Cryptol. (CiC) **1**(2), 14 (2024). https://doi.org/10.62056/a6n59qgxq
28. Fisher, R.A., Yates, F.: Statistical Tables for Biological, 6th edn. Agricultural and Medical Research. Oliver & Boyd, London (1938)
29. Hamburg, M.: Accelerating AES with vector permute instructions. In: Clavier, C., Gaj, K. (eds.) Cryptographic Hardware and Embedded Systems – CHES 2009. LNCS, vol. 5747, pp. 18–32. Springer, Berlin, Heidelberg (2009). https://doi.org/10.1007/978-3-642-04138-9_2
30. Huang, J., Zhang, J., Zhao, H., Liu, Z., Cheung, R.C.C., Koç, Ç.K., Chen, D.: Improved plantard arithmetic for lattice-based cryptography. IACR Trans. Cryptogr. Hardw. Embed. Syst. **2022**(4), 614–636 (2022). https://doi.org/10.46586/tches.v2022.i4.614-636
31. Kannwischer, M.J., Krausz, M., Petri, R., Yang, S.Y.: PQM4: benchmarking NIST additional post-quantum signature schemes on microcontrollers. Cryptology ePrint Archive, Report 2024/112 (2024). https://eprint.iacr.org/2024/112
32. Kannwischer, M.J., Rijneveld, J., Schwabe, P., Stoffelen, K.: PQM4: testing and benchmarking NIST PQC on ARM Cortex-M4. Cryptology ePrint Archive, Report 2019/844 (2019). https://eprint.iacr.org/2019/844
33. Käsper, E., Schwabe, P.: Faster and timing-attack resistant AES-GCM. In: Clavier, C., Gaj, K. (eds.) Cryptographic Hardware and Embedded Systems – CHES 2009. LNCS, vol. 5747, pp. 1–17. Springer, Berlin, Heidelberg (2009). https://doi.org/10.1007/978-3-642-04138-9_1
34. Knuth, D.E.: The Art of Computer Programming, Volume 3: Sorting and Searching, 2nd edn. Addison-Wesley, Boston (1997)
35. Kocher, P., et al.: Spectre attacks: exploiting speculative execution. In: 2019 IEEE Symposium on Security and Privacy, pp. 1–19. IEEE Computer Society Press (May 2019). https://doi.org/10.1109/SP.2019.00002
36. Kocher, P.C.: Timing attacks on implementations of Diffie-Hellman, RSA, DSS, and other systems. In: Koblitz, N. (ed.) Advances in Cryptology – CRYPTO'96. LNCS, vol. 1109, pp. 104–113. Springer, Berlin, Heidelberg (1996). https://doi.org/10.1007/3-540-68697-5_9
37. Könighofer, R.: A fast and cache-timing resistant implementation of the AES. In: Malkin, T. (ed.) Topics in Cryptology – CT-RSA 2008. LNCS, vol. 4964, pp. 187–202. Springer, Berlin, Heidelberg (2008). https://doi.org/10.1007/978-3-540-79263-5_12
38. Lemire, D.: Fast random integer generation in an interval. ACM Trans. Model. Comput. Simul. **29**(1) (2019). https://doi.org/10.1145/3230636
39. Lipp, M., et al.: Meltdown: reading kernel memory from user space. In: Enck, W., Felt, A.P. (eds.) USENIX Security 2018: 27th USENIX Security Symposium, pp. 973–990. USENIX Association (2018)
40. Matsui, M.: How far can we go on the x64 processors? In: Robshaw, M.J.B. (ed.) Fast Software Encryption – FSE 2006. LNCS, vol. 4047, pp. 341–358. Springer, Berlin, Heidelberg (2006). https://doi.org/10.1007/11799313_22
41. Matsui, M., Nakajima, J.: On the power of bitslice implementation on intel core2 processor. In: Paillier, P., Verbauwhede, I. (eds.) Cryptographic Hardware and Embedded Systems – CHES 2007. LNCS, vol. 4727, pp. 121–134. Springer, Berlin, Heidelberg (2007). https://doi.org/10.1007/978-3-540-74735-2_9
42. Microelectronics, S.: RM0432 reference manual: STM32L4+ series advanced Arm®-based 32-bit MCUs (2021). https://www.st.com/resource/en/

reference_manual/rm0432-stm32l4-series-advanced-armbased-32bit-mcus-stmicroelectronics.pdf
43. Pike, R., Locanthi, B., Reiser, J.: Hardware/software trade-offs for bitmap graphics on the blit. Softw. Pract. Exp. **15**(2), 131–151 (1985). https://doi.org/10.1002/spe.4380150203, https://onlinelibrary.wiley.com/doi/abs/10.1002/spe.4380150203
44. Pornin, T.: Why constant-time crypto? (2018). https://bearssl.org/constanttime.html
45. Pornin, T.: Falcon on ARM cortex-M4: an update. Cryptology ePrint Archive, Report 2025/123 (2025). https://eprint.iacr.org/2025/123
46. Rodrigues, C., Oliveira, D., Pinto, S.: BUSted!!! Microarchitectural side-channel attacks on the MCU bus interconnect. In: 2024 IEEE Symposium on Security and Privacy, pp. 3679–3696. IEEE Computer Society Press (May 2024). https://doi.org/10.1109/SP54263.2024.00062
47. Schulman, A.: Unauthorized Windows 95: A Developer's Guide to Exploring the Foundations of Windows "Chicago". International Data Group Company (1994)
48. Schwabe, P., Stoffelen, K.: All the AES you need on Cortex-M3 and M4. In: Avanzi, R., Heys, H.M. (eds.) SAC 2016: 23rd Annual International Workshop on Selected Areas in Cryptography. NCS, vol. 10532, pp. 180–194. Springer, Cham (2016). https://doi.org/10.1007/978-3-319-69453-5_10
49. Sendrier, N.: Secure sampling of constant-weight words – application to BIKE. Cryptology ePrint Archive, Report 2021/1631 (2021). https://eprint.iacr.org/2021/1631
50. Tsunoo, Y., Saito, T., Suzaki, T., Shigeri, M., Miyauchi, H.: Cryptanalysis of DES implemented on computers with cache. In: Walter, C.D., Koç, Çetin Kaya., Paar, C. (eds.) Cryptographic Hardware and Embedded Systems – CHES 2003. LNCS, vol. 2779, pp. 62–76. Springer, Berlin, Heidelberg (2003). https://doi.org/10.1007/978-3-540-45238-6_6
51. Tsunoo, Y., Tsujihara, E., Minematsu, K., Miyauchi, H.: Cryptanalysis of block ciphers implemented on computers with cache. In: Proceedings of the International Symposium on Information Theory and Its Applications, ISITA 2002, pp. 803–806 (2002)
52. Wang, Y., Paccagnella, R., He, E.T., Shacham, H., Fletcher, C.W., Kohlbrenner, D.: Hertzbleed: turning power side-channel attacks into remote timing attacks on x86. In: Butler, K.R.B., Thomas, K. (eds.) USENIX Security 2022: 31st USENIX Security Symposium, pp. 679–697. USENIX Association (2022)

Author Index

D. Escudero and I. Damgård (Eds.): LATINCRYPT 2025, LNCS 16129, p. 489, 2026.
https://doi.org/10.1007/978-3-032-06754-8

MIX
Papier aus verantwortungsvollen Quellen
Paper from responsible sources
FSC® C105338

If you have any concerns about our products,
you can contact us on
ProductSafety@springernature.com

In case Publisher is established outside the EU,
the EU authorized representative is:
Springer Nature Customer Service Center GmbH
Europaplatz 3, 69115 Heidelberg, Germany

Printed by Libri Plureos GmbH
in Hamburg, Germany